THEORETICAL ISSUES
IN READING
COMPREHENSION

Perspectives from
Cognitive Psychology,
Linguistics,
Artificial Intelligence,
and Education

THE PSYCHOLOGY OF READING

A series of volumes under the general editorship of
Rand J. Spiro

THEORETICAL ISSUES IN READING COMPREHENSION

Perspectives from
Cognitive Psychology,
Linguistics,
Artificial Intelligence,
and Education

Edited by
RAND J. SPIRO
Center for the Study of Reading,
University of Illinois, Urbana–Champaign

BERTRAM C. BRUCE
Center for the Study of Reading,
Bolt Beranek and Newman Inc.

WILLIAM F. BREWER
Center for the Study of Reading,
University of Illinois, Urbana–Champaign

 LAWRENCE ERLBAUM ASSOCIATES, PUBLISHERS
1980   Hillsdale, New Jersey

Lawrence Erlbaum Associates, Inc., Publishers
365 Broadway
Hillsdale, New Jersey 07642

Library of Congress Cataloging in Publication Data

Main entry under title:

Theoretical issues in reading comprehension.

(The Psychology of reading)
Bibliography: p.
Includes index.
1. Reading, comprehension—Addresses, essays,
lectures. 2. Reading, Psychology of—Addresses,
essays, lectures. I. Spiro, Rand J. II. Bruce,
Bertram, C. III. Brewer, William F. IV. Series:
Psychology of reading.
LB1050.45.T48   428.4'3   80-20716
ISBN 0-89859-036-1

Printed in the United States of America

Contents

Preface

For many years, the study of reading was taken to apply almost exclusively to the process of learning the written code. It was often assumed that once a child could recognize words in their written form, the understanding system already available from the child's oral language experience would permit comprehension to proceed smoothly. We now know that reading comprehension is not nearly so simple a matter. First, there is reason to doubt the logic that equates reading comprehension with word recognition plus oral language comprehension. Second, researchers have become increasingly aware of the complexities of comprehension itself, written or oral.

One problem faced by anyone seeking to understand current beliefs about reading comprehension is the interdisciplinary nature of research in the area. There are no readily available syntheses of the relevant work in the diverse disciplines of cognitive psychology, artificial intelligence, linguistics, and reading education. This book is one step towards such a synthesis. Our approach is outlined in the introduction, where an overview is also presented. Here, let us just offer a few general words about the planning and execution of the volume.

We have tried to put together a fairly complete interdisciplinary survey while avoiding frequent repetition and overlap in the topics addressed. In line with this goal, we drafted chapter summaries that anticipated (in a general fashion) the final form of the book. We then selected experts in each area to address each of the subjects along the lines of the charges we provided for them. Our goal was for the volume to have the cohesion and completeness of the work of a single individual. To the extent that this ideal was not achieved, the responsibility must rest with the editors. Whatever success was attained in meeting this goal we owe to the splendid cooperation of the contributors.

The National Institute of Education provided support to most of the authors through Contract No. US-NIE-C-400-76-0116 to the Center for the Study of Reading. We are all especially grateful to the Institute for providing so favorable a climate for the kind of basic research from interdisciplinary perspectives that this volume exemplifies. Naturally, the views expressed in this volume are those of the individual authors and do not represent National Institute of Education policy.

RAND J. SPIRO
BERTRAM C. BRUCE
WILLIAM BREWER

THEORETICAL ISSUES
IN READING
COMPREHENSION

Perspectives from
Cognitive Psychology,
Linguistics,
Artificial Intelligence,
and Education

Introduction

The ability to read with understanding is an essential skill in modern society. Yet it is a skill that a substantial number of people never completely master. They go unprotected into the struggle with job application forms, insurance policies, lease agreements, newspapers, recipes, and advertisements; and, they also miss much of the joy of reading for pleasure. Why hasn't the massive research literature on the reading process given us answers to the problems encountered in learning to read? One reason, perhaps, is that the problem area has been too narrowly conceived. By far, the largest share of basic research in reading has been concerned with the process of going from symbols to sounds and from written words to spoken words. We take a different approach. Underlying most of the contributions of this volume are the assumptions that skilled reading is the process of comprehending the meaning of connected discourse and that it involves far more than simply chaining together the meanings of a string of decoded words.

The goal of this book is to bring recent developments in several disciplines to the study of reading comprehension. The major focus is on understanding the processes involved in the comprehension of written text. However, we are aware that this is simply one part of a much larger and more complex problem. Clearly, a complete understanding of the overall problems of reading will consider such issues as motivation, physical health, parental attitudes, socio-economic status, teacher personality, and classroom organization. However, within this global set of issues, we have chosen to tackle the problem of the cognitive processes involved in reading comprehension.

Some of the ideas in this book should seem familiar to those experienced in teaching reading comprehension. The field of reading education has many insightful practitioners whose intuitions about comprehension have been very valuable. However, most of these ideas are based on practitioners' wisdom and instructional lore. One of the goals of this book is to provide a systematic and scientific basis for the understanding of reading comprehension problems. Without such a basis, it is not possible to resolve those aspects of the conventional wisdom that are in conflict, and it will not be possible to put reading instruction on a firm scientific foundation.

Given the need for a scientific understanding of the cognitive processes in reading comprehension, where does one turn? There is no single discipline that has concerned itself exclusively with this issue. Rather, developments with important implications for reading comprehension have been scattered across a number of fields. Clearly, we need to bring together the relevant information as a first step toward building a comprehensive theory of reading comprehension. This book attempts just that, incorporating research in the three disciplines that have the most direct application to an understanding of the mental processes in reading: cognitive psychology, linguistics, and artificial intelligence. This interdisciplinary approach has the advantage of representing a broad base of methodology and data. Ideally, the outcome should be deeper insights, of greater generalizability, than those possible when restricted by the paradigm constraints of a single discipline.

This book could not have been written 10 or 20 years ago because, in an interesting sense, the practical educators at that time were far ahead of the relevant theoretical and empirical work in psychology, linguistics, and artificial intelligence. An examination of textbooks on the teaching of reading or teacher's guides (cf. Rosenshine, Chapter 23, this volume: Jenkins & Pany, Chapter 24, this volume) shows that experienced educators consider that the process of reading comprehension involves such things as abstracting the main idea, understanding the sequence of events, recognizing the author's purpose, and drawing inferences. Until recent times such concerns were simply not among the issues addressed by these three disciplines. In a book on reading written 20 years ago, psychology might have offered some help with the problem of decoding and syntax. In a book written 10 years ago, psychology could have added some work on decoding and syntax, and artificial intelligence was just beginning to become organized as a discipline. However, in the last few years there has been a rapidly accelerating trend in these areas toward dealing with more and more complex problems, so that it is now possible to deal with the issues deemed most important by the practical workers in the area.

Although many of the chapters in this book are only statements of orienting positions or sketches of possible directions for research, taken together they give promise that a comprehensive theory of the reading process can be developed. The following conclusions about the nature of reading are shared by most of the contributors. Reading is a multilevel interactive process; that is, text must be analyzed at various levels, with units of analysis going from the letter to the text as a whole. In addition to processing the explicit features of text, the reader must bring considerable preexisting knowledge to the reading comprehension process. The interaction of text-based and knowledge-based processes and of levels within each is essential to reading comprehension. Because the meaning of text is only partially determined by the text itself, reading must be an inferential, constructive process, characterized by the formation and testing of hypotheses or models about what the text is "about," a process similar in many ways to problem solving. Finally, reading is strategic. It is a flexible process that is adapted to the purposes of reading at a given time and is monitored to determine whether the purposes are being met.

Can the theoretical insights in this book be applied to education? Educational practitioners have too often been frustrated on this score in the past. The shift of attention in the three disciplines toward issues of greater relevance to reading certainly encourages optimism that a successful transfer from research to practice will occur. Unfortunately, in the short term we must be less sanguine. This book offers few immediate solutions to the practical problems of teaching reading. In fact, the strongest conclusion one can draw is that the comprehension process is far more complex than it seems at first. In the same way that recent studies in linguistics lead one to marvel at the process of language acquisition, one cannot help but be impressed by the complexity of the task the child faces in learning to comprehend ordinary textual material. The surprise may be not that some children have difficulty in learning to read, but that any learn to read at all!

Nevertheless, there may be some obvious practical implications of the work described in this book. Some of the ideas can be taken as suggesting particular approaches to teaching reading. However, putting reading instruction on a scientific basis will be a long-term proposition. Even if we had a complete understanding of the reading process (and we certainly do not), we would not automatically know how reading instruction should be carried out. Going from a model of the reading process to instruction requires another complete program of research to answer questions such as: What types of texts and what sequences of exposure will produce optimum development of reading skill? Are the optimum scientific solutions practical in the classroom setting?

This book was written primarily for those concerned with the reading process. However, we think basic science researchers in psychology, linguistics, artificial intelligence, and surrounding disciplines will also find this book of considerable interest. Chapters on the common topic of reading illuminate connections among the disciplines, common areas of concern, and potentials for interdisciplinary work. They also occasionally reveal sharp contrasts in approach or analysis.

OVERVIEW

In inviting the authors and presenting them with specific charges for their chapters, we have tried to give this book a coherence beyond that usually found in collections of papers. Some of the authors in this book originally carried out their research with little thought of its impact on the problem of teaching reading comprehension. We have tried very hard to get each author to place his or her work in the context of reading comprehension and to draw the relevant implications. In some cases we may have pushed them beyond their own inclinations along this line, but we hope it was for a good cause. Additionally, we have urged the contributors not to restrict their discussions to their own research. Rather, in order to draw as comprehensive and unfragmented a picture as possible, we have asked them to sample widely from the related work of others in their area.

The topics that are discussed in the chapters that follow are divided into five general areas. The first areas concerns what we call *Global Issues*, including such things as a discussion of the levels of analysis, a discussion of aspects of hypothesis generation, and a discussion of a framework within which to conceptualize the representation of knowledge and the processes that bring it into play. These issues are global in the sense that they are relevant to many areas of intellectual endeavor. They represent conceptions about some of the fundamental operations and structures of cognition.

The second area that is covered concerns various properties of texts and some of their psychological consequences. This section, labeled *Text Structure*, deals specifically with sentence syntax, anaphora, the interaction of text structure with pragmatic considerations, and structural and stylistic characteristics of text as a whole.

The third main division we call *Language, Knowledge of the World, and Inference*. The emphasis here is on various aspects of language comprehension that need to be considered in any account of reading comprehension. The chapters in this section deal with the way in which the meaning of a discourse is constructed by the reader and the contribution that knowledge of the world makes to that construction. There are discussions of the organization of concepts and categories in memory and the processes by which words receive meaning in context. The role of inference and knowledge about plans and social actions in building a model for a given text are explored. Metaphor and other figurative uses of language are discussed.

The comprehension of written language inevitably shares some of the processes involved in the comprehension of oral language. In fact, some theorists think that the comprehension of written language is little more than a transformation of the written words to speech, followed, essentially, by oral language comprehension. However, there are good reasons for believing that comprehending written language is not so simple. The relation between comprehension in the two modes is discussed in the section on *Effects of Prior Language Experience*. Additionally, there is a discussion of the effects of oral language experiences in nonstandard dialects on the understanding of standard English.

In the final section, there are several chapters dealing with *Comprehension Strategies and Facilitators*. Issues discussed include metacognitive development, study strategies, the role of illustrations, effects of topic interest, the independence of reading skills, and the nature and effectiveness of reading comprehension instruction.

I GLOBAL ISSUES

The chapters in this book cover a wide range of topics from diverse perspectives. Nevertheless, several themes run throughout, indicating some consensus about the major questions. This section contains three chapters that each focus on different aspects of the broad themes. Later chapters will return to these themes as they pertain to specific areas of inquiry.

The authors in this section argue that any adequate model of reading comprehension will possess three essential characteristics. It will be *multilevel, interactive,* and *hypothesis-based. Multilevel* implies that knowledge structures at several different levels are actively used in the reading process. Traditionally proposed levels include orthographic, phonological, lexical, syntactic, and semantic. Clearly, however, higher level knowledge sources such as inference rules and expectations about story structure are also crucial components of the skilled reading process.

To say that the model needs to be *interactive* means that, although the knowledge sources or levels seem to form a "natural" hierarchy running from orthographic knowledge to expectations about discourse structure, communication between these levels is not limited to adjacent members of the hierarchy. Thus, the knowledge sources interact in a heterarchical fashion. The general model proposed by some psychologists (e.g., Gough, 1972; LaBerge & Samuels, 1974), which involves a visual input progressing linearly through the various knowledge levels to arrive finally at a "meaning," is not supported here. Instead, it appears that each knowledge source can contribute input at various points in the complex process of comprehending text. Comprehension proceeds from the top down as well as from the bottom up. Comprehension is "driven" by preexisting concepts as well as by the "data" from the text (Bobrow & Norman, 1975).

The coordination of these multiple contributions requires a mechanism for collecting evidence for various interpretations of the text. This is the *hypothesis-based* aspect of reading. Three characteristics of these hypotheses are relevant here. First, these hypotheses may be tacit. Second, a hypothesis represents a *possible* interpretation that may later either be continued or rejected. Third, part of the structure of a hypothesis is the specification of those pieces of evidence that would support or contradict it.

Several existing reading theories share significant properties with the general form described here. For example, Goodman (1973) describes receptive language processes in general as hypothesis-based, defining them as "cycles of sampling, predicting, testing, and confirming." Productive reading is seen as requiring strategies that facilitate the selection of the most useful cues. Smith (1971) also emphasizes the contribution of what he terms "nonvisual" information to reading. This nonvisual knowledge includes what people already know about reading, language, and the world in general. He argues particularly that reading is not decoding to sound, but rather that semantic and other nonvisual processes intercede between visual processes and reading aloud. Perfetti (1975) proposes at least three levels of sentence processing that obviously require corresponding levels of knowledge. He also focuses more explicitly on how the various component processes might interact, basing his overall conclusions on the fact that all the processes that occur during reading comprehension must share a "limited capacity processor."

Though the approach here shares much with that of these and other investigators, there are also some differences in emphasis. The authors are more explicit in the designation of different levels of knowledge sources, particularly in the areas Goodman terms "semantic." Examples of types of knowledge recognized are word semantics, logical inference rules, social action patterns, story schemata, and strategic knowledge about how to use the various knowledge sources. In addition, the explicit definition of the interaction between knowledge components is considered to be of the utmost importance. This approach suggests the possibility that some unskilled reading may be the result of not knowing how to use and interweave knowledge, rather than of a lack of knowledge itself.

Another emphasis in these chapters is on the dynamic nature of the reading process. These authors propose that a reader's working hypothesis may be wrong and that at various points during the reading process it may be in a state of limbo, only partially specified, needing more evidence. They consider as well the possibility that as a consequence of some of the intermediate stages, the reader must "back up" and rehypothesize about the meaning of a text.

A final theme in these chapters is the emphasis on *structure-building*. These structures or *schemata* are important for both the final representation of the meaning of the text and the intermediate hypotheses that are so crucial to attaining the final goal. Three classes of knowledge are necessary for building such structures. First of all, a reader must have sufficient information about the types of schemata that are possible at each level, how to recognize them, and what implications they have for further processing. Second, the reader must have strategic knowledge—information on how to *use* the structural knowledge, what priorities to use in evaluating hypotheses, and what form the final "understood" structure should take. Third, there is knowledge about the way the purpose of reading a particular text relates to the structural and strategic knowledge used.

The global features we have outlined are addressed with differing emphasis in each of the three chapters in this section. Adams focuses on the levels of analysis involved in reading comprehension and their interaction. Rumelhart discusses characteristics of schemata and their role in hypothesis formation and testing. Woods also concerns himself with hypothesis-related processes, as well as drawing implications for reading comprehension from research on computer simulation of natural language processing.

ACKNOWLEDGMENT

Andee Rubin contributed to the writing of this section's introduction.

REFERENCES

Bobrow, D. G., & Norman, D. A. Some principles of memory schemata. In D. G. Bobrow & A. M. Collins (Eds.), *Representation and understanding: Studies in cognitive science.* New York: Academic Press, 1975.

Goodman, K. S. Psycholinguistic universals in the reading process. In F. Smith (Ed.), *Psycholinguistics and reading.* New York: Holt, Rinehart & Winston, 1973.

Gough, P. B. One second of reading. In J. F. Kavanagh & I. G. Mattingly (Eds.), *Language by ear and by eye.* Cambridge, Mass.: MIT Press, 1972.

LaBerge, D., & Samuels, S. J. Toward a theory of automatic information processing in reading. *Cognitive Psychology,* 1974, *6,* 293-323.

Perfetti, C. A. *Language comprehension and fast decoding: Some psycholinguistic prerequisites for skilled reading comprehension.* Paper presented to The Development of Reading Comprehension Seminar of the International Reading Association. Newark, Del., July 1975.

Smith, F. *Understanding reading.* New York: Holt, Rinehart & Winston, 1971.

1 Failures to Comprehend and Levels of Processing in Reading

Marilyn Jager Adams
*Center for the Study of Reading,
Bolt Beranek and Newman Inc.*

Reading deficiency is one of the most significant problems facing educators today. By recent estimates, as many as 40% of the school-age children in the U.S. may be handicapped by reading difficulties (Goldberg & Schiffman, 1972). The significance of the problem, however, is only partially reflected by such statistics, as reading difficulties may result in poor performance in other educational activities. Reading is one of the basic ways of acquiring information in our society and in academic settings in particular. The individual who cannot read well is at a serious disadvantage with respect to educational and, consequently, vocational opportunities.

Why so many children have trouble learning to read is not well understood. In some cases, mental or physical disabilities can be cited as the underlying cause. But more often, reading problems have not been clearly associated with diagnosable mental or physical deficits. This has led to the definition of clinical syndromes such as dyslexia and minimal brain dysfunction that acknowledge and label the problem but do not explain it.

A basic assumption of this chapter is that skilled reading depends on a multiplicity of perceptual, linguistic, and cognitive processes and that, for many children, reading difficulties reflect the inadequate development of one or more of these processes. The purpose of this chapter is to consider some of the processes that may be especially problematic for the young reader. The chapter begins with an overview in which skilled reading is described as the product of both analytic and synthetic, or bottom-up and top-down activities. Following this overview, potential sources of difficulties are discussed under three general topics: word recognition, syntactic processing, and semantic processing.

OVERVIEW

For the skilled reader, the processes involved in reading are so well learned and integrated that written information can flow almost automatically from sensation to meaning. As the letters of the text are identified, they simultaneously prime or set up expectations about the identities of the words to which they belong. As the words are identified, they prime the most probable syntactic and semantic structures. More generally, since the end products of each level of analysis are the elements for some other level, the information is naturally propagated upward through the system, through increasingly comprehensive levels of analysis. This is known as bottom-up processing. While all of this is happening, the partially activated candidates at each level are competing for completion; as they do so, they reciprocally prime or facilitate the processing of their missing elements. This is known as top-down processing. For the skilled reader, top-down and bottom-up processing are occurring at all levels of analysis simultaneously as she or he proceeds through the text. The reader is therefore able to make optimal use of the information on the page, the redundancy of the language, and the contextual environment with minimal effort. The top-down processes ensure that lower order information that is consistent with the reader's expectations will be easily assimilated, as it will already have been partially processed. Meanwhile, the bottom-up processes ensure that the reader will be alerted to any information that is novel or that does not fit her or his ongoing hypotheses about the content of the text. (For a more thorough description of these processes, see Rumelhart's Chapter 2 in this book, or Adams & Collins, 1979.)

The efficient operation of such a system depends as much on the information in the reader's mind as on the information in the written text. If the reader is lacking any critical skill or piece of knowledge, the flow of information through the system will be obstructed. In these cases, the reader must find a way to compensate. One option is to direct extra processing energy to the difficulty until it is resolved; for example, the reader may pause and articulate a difficult word. Alternatively, she or he may rely on top-down processes to evade the problem; for example, she or he may use contextual information to infer the meaning of an unfamiliar word. Both of these solutions are normal and adaptive and are regularly used by skilled readers. Thus, one kind of difficulty that we might expect of beginning readers is they might fail to adopt either of these strategies. However, equally serious problems might arise if they adopt either of these strategies to the extreme.

The danger of relying too heavily on top-down processing is obvious. The proper balance between the information that the reader should bring to the text and that which the text should bring to the reader will be lost. To the extent that guesses are based on prior guesses, the individual is not really reading in any useful way. Yet, as is discussed in the sections to follow, some of the most basic aspects of reading may also be the most foreign for the beginner. By contrast, the beginning reader already has a wealth of real-world knowledge, and in terms of content, her or his required reading materials are probably quite simple. Thus, she or he may find, for example, that the identity of an unfamiliar word can often be guessed as accurately and more easily than it can be sounded out or that the conceptual relationships implied by a sentence can be inferred without attending to its syntactic structure. It should not be surprising to find young readers who have learned to depend on such top-down strategies.

In the long run, the alternative strategy of focusing attention on the difficulty may be more adaptive. At least it provides an opportunity for learning. The danger in using this strategy is that comprehension may consequently suffer. The problem is that the human mind is a limited-capacity processor. As LaBerge and Samuels (1974) have pointed out, the reader can selectively direct attention to any particular subprocess but only by taking it away from deeper levels of analysis. In G. Stanley Hall's words (1911), true reading only occurs "when the art has become so secondarily automatic that it can be forgotten and attention be given solely to the subject matter. Its assimilation is true reading and all else is only the whir of the machinery and not the work it does [p. 134]."

The problem of limited processing capacity is especially critical for the young reader. First, many of the necessary subskills are not well learned and, therefore, demand considerable attention. Second, the functional memory capacity of the young child tends to be less than that of the adult. It is not entirely clear why this is so: Some have argued that the span itself increases with age (e.g., Farnham-Diggory, 1972); some have attributed it to young children's failure to "chunk" or organize the material for efficient storage (e.g., Flavell, 1970; Olson, 1973; Simon, 1974); still others have argued that it only reflects the differential effort that children must invest in the encoding of to-be-remembered items (e.g., Huttenlocher & Burke, 1976). Regardless of which explanation is correct, the important implication for the present discussion is that processing capacity is least yielding at the point when task demands are highest.

Craik and Lockhart (1972) have cited two other factors that may divert attention from meaningful levels of analysis. The first of these is the nature of the material to be encoded; unless it is potentially meaningful, processing will naturally stop at structural levels of analysis. Although Craik and Lockhart were specifically concerned with the appropriateness of digit lists and the like as stimuli in memory tasks, the point is easily extended to the reading situation. Materials intended to support comprehension in beginning tests must be chosen with careful consideration of the knowledge and interests of their young readers. The second factor cited by Craik and Lockhart is the nature of the ostensible task demands. If the encoders are instructed to focus on nonmeaningful aspects of a stimulus, they will do so. A major criticism of the instructional programs that emphasize the mechanics of reading is that they may effectively teach readers to ignore semantic dimensions of the text.

Again, true reading is only possible if the whole complex of subprocesses are functioning easily and in proper coordination. None of the processes can be absent or require undue attention, or comprehension will suffer. For the skilled reader, difficulties will be few and far between; when they do arise, she or he will probably find an effective way to overcome them. By contrast, beginning readers will frequently encounter difficulties. Their first challenge is to discover ways to overcome them; their second is to learn how to do so without forfeiting the meaning of the text. The remainder of this chapter focuses on specific problems that might beset beginning readers and the ways in which these might affect their reading comprehension.

WORD RECOGNITION

Many of the components of the reading process are not new to the beginning reader. Through oral language experience, the child has already acquired a substantial vocabulary and basic syntactic competence. She or he is used to making sense out of language and has a wealth of real-world knowledge to draw on in this effort. The child may even have some appreciation of what reading is all about. What is most flagrantly lacking is the ability to decipher the written word.

It is not surprising, therefore, that early reading instruction is concentrated on word recognition skills, Despite this, reading difficulties are often traceable to deficits at the level of word recognition. For example, Perfetti and Hogaboam (1975) have shown that more skilled comprehenders can name a printed word faster than less skilled comprehenders and that this advantage is especially marked with less frequent or unfamiliar words. Further, poor readers have been found to rely heavily on the initial letters of words, ignoring or failing to synthesize the cues from medial or final portions (Rayner & Hagelberg, 1975; Shankweiler & Liberman, 1972), to be less sensitive than good readers to the spatial redundancy of English orthography (Mason, 1975), and to be less facile with the spelling-to-sound correspondences of English (Jorm, 1977; Venezky, 1976).

The ability to recognize single written words is, in itself, a very complicated skill. That we do not fully understand it is evidenced by the hundreds of theoretical and experimental papers on the topic; that we do not know how best to teach it is evidenced by the hundreds of early reading programs that purport to do so. Inasmuch as letters were not designed for maximal discriminability, letter recognition presupposes a fair amount of perceptual learning (Gibson & Levin, 1975). Moreover, the ability to recognize single letters is many steps removed from the ability to recognize printed words, and there are many conflicting ideas about how these skill levels should be introduced and integrated.

A long-standing controversy in this vein is whether instruction should be focused on letter-to-sound correspondences or whole words. The major advantage of whole word approaches is that they provide a more direct path from symbol to meaning. Thus, whole word approaches may make the task of learning to recognize words more interesting for the beginner, and they may also make it easier: whereas young children have little difficulty in learning to associate arbitrary visual patterns with meaningful, familiar responses, they have great difficulty in learning to associate such patterns with individual speech sounds or nonsense syllables (Venezky, 1976). Further, many children have trouble relating individual speech sounds to syllables or whole words (Savin, 1972; Wallach, Wallach, Dozier, & Kaplan, 1977).

But even if whole words are initially easier to learn, children who have been taught to read without due emphasis on the mechanics of decoding are found to be at a disadvantage in the long run (Barr, 1975; Chall, 1967). Venezky and Massaro (1976) have argued that the most important component of letter-to-sound instruction is that it directs the child's attention to frequent spelling patterns. Orthographic regularity has a strong influence on the ease with which skilled readers can encode a string of letters (Baron & Thurston, 1973; Gibson, Pick, Osser, & Hammond, 1962; McClelland, 1976; Mewhort, 1974. However, such sensitivity to orthographic regularity develops only gradually through years of reading experience. For the less skilled reader, a more immediate benefit of instruction in letter-to-sound correspondences is that they provide a means toward identifying words that are in her or his listening vocabulary but are visually unfamiliar.

Because the beginning reader is bound to encounter many visually unfamiliar words, we should consider what is involved in sounding them out. First, the reader must parse the letter string into sets of one or more letters that correspond to phonemic units. Notably, there may be more than one apparent way to do this (e.g., no*whe*re vs. no*w*here). In addition, she or he must look for graphemic markers, such as final *e*'s, that might modify the phonemic significance of any of these sets. Next, the sounds corresponding to each graphemic set must be generated. Even if the graphemic string has been correctly segmented, this process may depend on trial and error as a graphemic set may signify more than one pronunciation (e.g., throu*gh* vs. rou*gh*. Moreover, to do the job right, the reader cannot focus exclusively on one graphemic set at a time; the pronunciation of a graphemic unit may vary with both its position in the word (e.g., *gh*ost vs. rou*gh*) and its graphemic environment (e.g.,*ci*ty vs. *ca*ll). Next, these sounds must be blended together, and this, in itself, may be hard for some children (Savin, 1972). Having thus translated the printed word into a spoken correspondent, the reader must check to see that the result makes sense in the larger context of the sentence. If not, the process must be reiterated.

In short, the process of sounding out a word can be very complicated. As mere vocalization of a word may absorb a substantial proportion of the young child's processing capacity (Conrad, 1972), the additional load imposed by decoding must push the capacity to its limits. Evidence for this conjecture occurs repeatedly in MacKinnon's (1959) observational study of beginning readers. Although many of the children in his study could successfully sound out new words, they tended, as a consequence, to block on previously familiar words in the sentence.

Further, if the child must focus attention on the structural properties of words, she or he may lose the meaningful dimensions of the passage (Craik & Lockhart, 1972; LaBerge & Samuels, 1974). Jenkins and his colleagues (see Jenkins, 1974, for a review) have demonstrated this effect with adults through free recall studies. If, during list presentation, subjects are asked to perform semantic orienting tasks on the items (such as rating them for pleasantness or activity, estimating their frequency, or generating semantically appropriate syntagmatic responses), their associative clustering and total recall scores are at least as good as those of subjects who are simply and explicitly instructed to memorize the lists. By contrast, subjects who are instructed to focus on orthographic, phonetic, or syntactic aspects of the items during presentation show little clustering and poor recall. Apparently, high levels of recall in this task depend on the subject's having interrelated semantic attributes of the items. When attention is focused on nonmeaningful dimensions of the stimuli, retention suffers as semantic organization is preempted. In keeping with this, nonsemantic orienting tasks have been shown to exert similarly deleterious effects on the retention and comprehension of meaningful sentences (Rosenberg & Schiller, 1971; Till, Cormak, & Prince, 1977).

Perfetti (1975) has provided more direct evidence that reading comprehension may suffer as the result of devoting too much attention to decoding activities. The children in his study were periodically interrupted by a memory probe as they read a passage to themselves. When reading silently, the poor decoders tended to have *better* memory than the good decoders for words that immediately preceded the probe. This would be expected if the poor decoders were paying more attention to individual words. As would also be expected in this case, the poor decoders' memory for words that were only slightly more distant from the probe was substantially *worse* than the good decoders'.

Strong attention to decoding should pay off in the long run as the reader becomes familiar with more and more words. In the meantime, however, it will detract from more meaningful levels of analysis. Further, the reading difficulty of laborious decoders may well be misdiagnosed. If their efforts are successful, *they may appear to be having little difficulty with individual words. The only symptoms may be that they are not remembering or comprehending and perhaps that they are reading in a word-by-word manner. The diagnostic problem is that these same symptoms may alternatively reflect syntactic or semantic difficulties.

The other means of coping with visually unfamiliar words is that of using the syntactic and semantic constraints of the text to guess their identity. In this way, processing at higher levels may compensate for decoding difficulties. As was argued in the introduction, this is a normal aspect of skilled reading (see also Goodman, 1970; Smith, 1973), and recent studies suggest that, even for young children, reading is, in part, a generative, top-down process. For example, Perfetti (1975) has demonstrated that children's ability to read a word is facilitated almost as much by their having heard the word before as by their having heard *and* seen it before. Weber (1970) has shown that the substitution errors of first graders during oral reading are more strongly controlled by the syntactic and semantic constraints of the text than by the graphemic cues of the mistaken words. And Wittrock, Marks, and Doctorow (1975) have shown that children are better able to process unfamiliar words if they are embedded in a familiar as opposed to an unfamiliar story.

Biemiller (1970) tracked oral reading errors longitudinally through the first grade. Like Weber, he found that the majority of his subjects' reading errors consisted in a substitution of the correct word with an alternative that was semantically and syntactically acceptable within the sentence. However, he further found that the proportion of substitutions that were graphemically similar to the correct word *increased* toward the end of the year. This study provides a strong rationale for the initial emphasis on decoding skills. Apparently, beginning readers find it easier to guess at the identity of an unfamiliar word than to decode it. Inasmuch as this strategy seems to work quite well for simple beginning texts, there may be little incentive for the development of decoding skills. However, when the child is advanced to more complex and less constrained reading material, decoding skills must be well developed because guessing will not suffice. Top-down processing clearly changes from a help to a hindrance when it is used to avoid decoding altogether.

Kolers (1975) has recently presented evidence that such use of top-down processing to avoid decoding may be a fairly common source of reading difficulty among older children. In his experiment, good and poor readers between the ages of 10 and 14 years were presented with sentences in normal and reversed type. When the sentences were read aloud, the substitution errors of both good and poor readers were, in general, grammatically appropriate. But the poor readers made almost 10 times as many substitution errors as the good readers. In addition, the poor readers were relatively insensitive to graphemic or typographic aspects of the stimuli. Whereas the number of letters in the substitution responses of the good readers was highly correlated with the number in the printed word, the number of letters in the substitution responses of the poor readers was not. Although the poor readers read the normally typed sentences more slowly than the good readers, their reading speeds were less affected by the reversed typography than were those of the good readers. Finally, recognition scores indicated that the poor readers remembered the typography of the stimuli less well than did the good readers. In short, among Koler's subjects, poor reading was coupled with frequent guessing and relatively little attention to the typographic and graphemic aspects of the stimuli; taken together, these symptoms clearly indicate an overreliance on top-down processing.

In summary, the reader can cope with visually unfamiliar words through either top-down or bottom-up processes. Although both types of processes are important, neither is satisfactory by itself. For the skilled reader, top-down and bottom-up processes operate as complements rather than substitutes for one another. But this can only happen when the processes involved in word recognition have become sufficiently overlearned that they require minimal effort.

SYNTACTIC PROCESSING

Although word recognition is a necessary component of language comprehension, it is not sufficient. The meanings of individual words are diffuse and ambiguous. In discourse, they become defined only as they are interrelated to one another. In large part, the intended meaning of a word may be defined by its semantic intersection with other concepts in the context (Quillian, 1969). Just as "a good play" will be interpreted differently in a theater than a ballpark, "ball" will be interpreted differently if it is preceded by "soccer" rather than "inaugural" (see Anderson & Shifrin, Chapter 13, this volume). But the intersections between meanings are not always enough, as shown by the difference between "play the horses" and "the horses play" or "John was kicked by Mary" and "John kicked Mary." Syntax is the primary means by which we can specify the intended relation among words. Thus, syntax subserves communication not only by disambiguating the referents of the words but also by defining new relations among them. It is clear that syntactic competence is an important dimension of linguistic competence in general. The question to be addressed in this section is whether there are aspects of syntactic processing that are peculiar to the domain of reading.

The traditional emphasis on decoding skills in reading instruction derives from the view that written language is no more than ciphered speech. According to this view, if the child can learn to break the code—to translate the letters into their corresponding sounds—then the problem of reading is solved. The remainder of the task simply requires the application of previously acquired aural/oral language skills to the deciphered text. Given the prevalence of this argument, the paucity of studies on the role of syntactic processes in reading probably should not be surprising.

But the validity of this argument rests on two highly suspect assumptions. The first of these is that beginning readers are only lacking in decoding skills—that if they could recognize the words, they have the linguistic competence to realize the meaning of the text. The second is that the processes that they use in the interpretation of spoken strings of words are adequate and appropriate for the interpretation of written strings of words.

The assumption that the beginning reader lacks only decoding skills has been bolstered by the common assertion that children are linguistically mature by the time they get to elementary school. However, as Palermo and Molfese (1972) have pointed out, this is an overstatement: Children continue to demonstrate substantial gains in their ability to understand syntactic structures until they are at least 13 years old. Apparently, the more popular view evolved from the observation by developmental psycholinguists that all of the basic syntactic transformations that, according to Chomsky's (1965) theory of generative grammar, underlie adult sentence structures can be found in the utterances of many children by the time they are 4 or 5 years old (Brown, 1965; Menyuk, 1963). This is very different from saying that young children can produce sentences of the same syntactic complexity as an adult can. Even so, those who believed in transformational grammar argued that a working knowledge of all of the basic transformations is formally equivalent to basic syntactic *competence;* if young children cannot produce sentences of arbitrary complexity, it must be primarily due to factors constraining *performance,* like memory limitations (McNeill, 1966). The data and the argument were inevitably condensed into such statements as "[children] acquire syntax almost completely at 48 to 60 months" (McNeill, 1970, p. 1062) or that by 4 of 5 years of age, children have succeeded "in mastering the exceedingly complex structure of [their] native language" (Slobin, 1971, p. 1). These statements were meant to provoke interest in the remarkable language accomplishments of very young children; as an unfortunate side effect, they may have discouraged interest in syntactic development in older children.

Whatever the status of a child's syntactic competence, decoding difficulties aside, shouldn't she or he be able to understand any written sentence that she or he would be able to understand if it were spoken? Not necessarily. Children probably need relatively little syntactic sophistication to understand most of what is said to them. The interpretation of any utterance may be strongly guided by its real-world context and the tone and stress patterns of the speaker. Typically none of these cues is present in written language. To the extent that children have only the words and their interrelationships to work with, syntactic competence is critical for reading.

Suppose that a child does have the syntactic competence to interpret a given sentence structure in spoken discourse. Can we then assume that the child could understand it if she or he read it? Again, the answer is no. In speech, syntactic boundaries are marked by prosodic cues. When speaking fluently, people tend to restrict pauses and breaths to syntactic boundaries (Henderson, Goldman-Eisler, & Skarbek, 1965, 1966). In addition, the durations of the spoken elements themselves vary reliably with the phrase structure of the utterance (Huggins, 1974; Klatt, 1975). Apparently, the listener depends on these temporal cues; when they are distorted, comprehension falls precipitously (Huggins, 1978). Except for punctuation marks, written discourse provides no such cues. The segregation of phrasal and clausal units is left largely to the reader. The implication is again that reading presumes a level of syntactic proficiency that is not required for listening. (For further discussion of differences between comprehension of oral and written language, see Rubin, Chapter 17, this volume.)

In view of these considerations, we may conclude that the processing differences between reading and listening do indeed extend beyond the level of word recognition. First, reading demands more syntactic sophistication than does listening. Second, whereas the syntactic structure of a spoken sentence is largely given to the listener through prosodic cues, the syntactic structure of a written sentence must, in large part, be discovered by the reader. Unless the reader can recover or construct the syntactic structure of the printed sentence, it doesn't matter whether she or he has the syntactic competence to understand it.

For skilled readers, the recognition of syntactic units is so automatic that it has become an integral part of the input process itself. Cattell (1886) found that when whole phrases or short sentences are tachistoscopically presented, skilled readers tend to recognize them completely or not at all. Similarly, skilled readers tend to encode connected discourse in phrasal units; if the text is abruptly removed, their "reading" typically does not stop until a phrasal boundary has been reached (Levin & Kaplan, 1970; Schlesinger, 1969). Thus, not only can skilled readers take in whole phrases at a glance, but their glances are apparently programmed to do so.

How are readers able to coordinate their visual fixations with the phrase structure of the text? Somehow they must be able to anticipate the upcoming syntactic units when they plan their fixations. One possible explanation for this phenomenon is that the readers' fixations are determined by graphical information gleaned from the peripheral visual field. Yet, peripheral acuity is quite poor. Only the one or two words within one or two degrees of visual angle from the fixation point are fully legible. A little further into the periphery, only the initial and final letters and the gross shape of the words can be discerned (Rayner, 1975). A little further still, only word length cues are available (McConkie, 1976). Because short words are often functors (e.g., in, on, of, to) which introduce phrases, word length cues may exert an important influence on eye movements (Hochberg, 1970). Given the impoverished nature of the peripheral visual cues, an equally plausible explanation is that the readers' fixations are primarily controlled by their hypotheses about what they are about to read. In keeping with this, the amount of information a person can recite after the text is taken away increases with the syntactic and semantic predictability of the passage (Lawson, 1961; Morton, 1964a, 1964b).

Marcel (1974) has recently provided evidence that both of these explanations are correct. In Marcel's experiments, subjects were presented with two successive strings of words. They were allowed to study the first string for as long as they wanted; its purpose was to provide a context for the second string. The second string was presented for only 200 milliseconds and therefore could be fixated only once. The subjects' task was to report as much information as they could from the second sequence of words. Marcel found that the amount of reported information increased with the semantic and syntactic constraints of the sequences. In order to discover the reason for this increase, Marcel analyzed the errors. In support of both of the hypotheses just described, almost all of the subjects' erroneous reponses were either visually or grammatically comparable to the presented word. With increasing contextual constraint, the balance tipped slightly toward grammatically acceptable substitutes, as might be expected. But Marcel's most exciting finding was that increased contextual constraint led to a disproportionate increase in the number of errors that were simultaneously grammatically *and* visually acceptable; thus, it apparently increased the visual angle at which the subjects could discern graphical details of the printed information. This is a compelling demonstration of interfacilitation between top-down and bottom-up processes.

The importance of parsing the sentence on input relates back to the fact that the human mind is a limited-capacity processor. If an unstructured string of words were presented to an individual at the rate of normal reading, she or he would lose track after four or five words: her or his active memory capacity would be exceeded (Miller, 1956). When we are reading or listening to connected discourse, we get around this problem by recoding the information at syntactic boundaries (Fodor, Bever, & Garrett, 1974; Jarvella, 1971; Kleiman, 1975).

For the reading situation, Kleiman (1975) has specified the process most completely. According to his model, as the reader proceeds through the text, each word is entered into a short-term memory buffer. After each word is entered, the reader checks to see whether or not it completes a constituent structure. If not, she or he proceeds to the next word. As soon as the reader thinks a phrase has been completed, the contents of the buffer are recoded or collapsed into a composite meaning complex. At this point a check is made to see whether the sentence has been completed. If it has not, the reader starts working on the words of the next syntactic unit. If it has, the contents of the short-term buffer are transferred to long-term memory, and the reader is ready for a clean start on the next sentence. (A parallel model for aurally presented text has been proposed by Jarvella, 1971).

If Kleiman's (1975) model is correct, then it underscores the importance of correctly isolating syntactic constituents during input. If the reader recodes after each individual word, then she or he will miss their interrelationships and, consequently, the meaning of the sentence as a whole. If the reader does not segment the sentence at all, then she or he is liable to overload the short-term, buffer; as a result, some of the words will be lost, and comprehension will suffer. If the reader incorrectly analyzes the sentence, then the recoded meaning-complexes will misrepresent the text and may even be anomalous.

To the extent that the processes and even the necessity of actively identifying the syntactic units of a sentence are unique to reading, we might expect them to be troublesome for the beginner. Indeed, beginning readers do not sample written material in phrasal units (Levin & Kaplan, 1970). They indulge in many more fixations per line of text than do mature readers (Kolers, 1976). In part, this is probably because they must devote more attention to the reading of individual words. In part, it is probably because such cues as word length, word shape, and terminal letters become useful only with considerable reading experience. But some children may fail to recognize the surface structure of a sentence during encoding only because they do not know how to or because they have not figured out that they are supposed to.

In keeping with this, several studies have shown that good readers are more sensitive to syntactic structure per se than are poor readers. For example, Cohen and Freeman (1978) found that, when reading fourth order approximations to English aloud, "good readers struggled to impose an intonation pattern on the material, segmenting it into phrase-like units. Poor readers read in a monotone as if it were a word list [p. 8]." Weinstein and Rabinovitch (1971) investigated the effect of syntactic structure on good and poor readers' memory for sentences such as *Zalfly they when, veg the hanashed, sivoled they* versus *When they sivoled the veg, they hanashed zalfly.* Differences in decoding abilities were controlled by presenting the sentences aurally. Whereas the good readers performed better with the well structured materials, the poor readers did not, and the two groups performed equally poorly with the unstructured strings.

One might question the pertinence of studies using nonsense materials. As Huggins and Adams point out (Chapter 4, this volume), semantic variables normally contribute heavily to syntactic processing. But semantic cues are not always sufficient. Using meaningful materials, Cromer (1970) has shown that the reading comprehension of some poor readers can be improved by superficially demarcating phrasal boundaries. Even skilled readers may benefit from superficial syntactic cues given a complex structure; Fodor and Garrett (1967) have shown that embedded sentences, such as *The girl (that) the boy (that) the man knew saw left,* are easier to understand if the "that's" are included. Conversely, if the structure of a sentence is obscured or distorted, good readers are less able to understand or remember it (Anglin & Miller, 1968; Oakan, Wiener, & Cromer, 1971).

Weaver (1977) has recently completed a very encouraging study on the trainability of syntactic sensitivity. In her study, third grade readers were given series of individual tutorials on solving sentence anagrams. The tutorials were designed to induce the children, first, to pick out phrases and clauses from the scrambled words and then to arrange the phrases and clauses into meaningful, complete sentences. More specifically, the children were taught to look for an "action" word first and then to ask a series of "why" questions so as to group the remaining words into phrases and clauses and determine how they were related to the verb. Thus, the procedure implicitly required the children to attend both to word order and to different parts of speech (cases) and the syntactic devices by which they are signaled. The training procedures resulted not only in an improvement in the children's unassisted ability to solve sentence anagrams, but also in an improvement in their performance on several other tests of reading comprehension and memory.

To summarize this section, reading requires a syntactic awareness that is generally not required for listening. If the reader does not have the necessary competence to organize written material into syntactic constituents, both comprehension and memory for the material will suffer. Syntactic difficulties may be peculiarly treacherous. In children's first textbooks, the sentences are simple and may even be presented on separate lines of print. Thus, at this stage, when teachers are concentrating on reading skills, the children may experience no difficulties. Yet, later, when they must manage more complex texts—when they are supposed to be reading to learn rather than learning to read—their problems may be overwhelming. Moreover, such problems may be difficult to either detect or correct. If readers cannot recognize a word, they generally *know* they cannot. If they cannot correctly recognize a syntactic structure, they may not even realize it. Further, at the lexical level, it is easy to distinguish between whether readers do not know a word or just cannot read it. The parallel distinction at the. syntactic level may be unclear.

SEMANTIC PROCESSING

The meaning of a text is in the mind of the reader. The text itself consists only of instructions for the reader as to how to retrieve or construct that meaning. The words of a text evoke in the reader concepts, their past interrelationships, and their potential interrelationships as defined by their semantic properties. The syntactic structures of a text help the reader to select among these conceptual conglomerates. In order to understand a written text, the reader must therefore be able to recognize the words and to analyze the syntax. But she or he must also be able to access and organize the appropriate conceptual knowledge, and this depends on a variety of semantic knowledge and processes.

At a gross level of analysis, there are two classes of difficulties that might beset the reader at the semantic level. The first class of difficulties has to do with the fidelity or completeness with which the reader can map the intended meaning of the textual elements onto her or his own conceptual structures. The second class of difficulties has to do with the reader's ability to organize the meaning of the passage. Many of the specific issues subsumed by these categories are discussed in detail elsewhere in this volume. The purpose of the present section is to illustrate, at a categorical level, the particular relevance of each to the young reader.

Beyond general naivety, there are many kinds of problems that may impede the mapping process for the young reader. Among those discussed in the chapters to follow are: a lack of appreciation of pragmatic dimensions of discourse (Bruce; Morgan & Green); differences between the dialects of the child's reading materials and her or his oral language environment (Hall); difficulties in coordinating references (Webber); difficulties with polysemy, metaphor, and figurative language (Ortony); and difficulties in appropriately altering her or his point of view (Rubin). The point to be made here is that any of these difficulties could arise from either of two sources. On one hand, the child may have the conceptual knowledge to understand the meaning of the text but be unfamiliar with the words or linguistic devices by which it is expressed. Alternatively, she or he may lack the concepts signified by the text. Furthermore, these two sources are not independent, as the child's linguistic sophistication is bounded by her or his conceptual sophistication.

This point is illustrated with the problem of insufficient vocabulary. This is a common problem for young readers and one that may reflect nothing more than a lack of linguistic experience. As an example, Bradshaw and Anderson (1968) traced the development of nine adverbial modifiers from first grade through adulthood. The modifiers were: *slightly, somewhat, rather, pretty, quite, decidedly, unusually, very,* and *extremely,* and they were used to modify the word large. The children's differentiation of the meanings of these modifiers was tested through a paired-comparison procedure. Bradshaw and Anderson found that for the youngest children the meanings of *slightly* and *somewhat* were neutral or perhaps empty; not until fourth grade in the case of the former and eighth grade in the case of the latter, was the minimizing impact of these modifiers realized. Similarly, *extremely* was not regularly interpreted as signifying more than *very* until fifth grade. It seems unlikely that children's ability to conceptualize relative differences in quantity would develop so unevenly. Rather, the most plausible interpretation of these results is that the differences in the meanings of these words are subtle and the semantic elaboration that is necessary to distinguish between them is only picked up through considerable experience. Meanwhile, the child's understanding of sentences using these words will be impoverished.

Indeed, vocabulary is the single best predictor of a child's ability to comprehend written material (see Rosenshine, Chapter 23, this volume). But this is only partly because a bigger vocabulary means fewer word comprehension failures. There are at least two, more important reasons for this correlation. First, both vocabulary and reading comprehension skills must depend on the quantity and quality of the child's general linguistic experience. Second, some vocabulary difficulties may be rooted in conceptual deficiencies inasmuch as the meaningful acquisition of a word presumes an understanding of the concepts to which it refers (Nelson, 1974).

The order in which words come to be understood by a child reflects the relative complexity of their underlying meanings. To demonstrate this, Gentner (1975) asked children between the ages of 3 and 8 to make dolls act out the verbs: *give, take, buy, sell, trade, pay,* and *spend (money).* According to Gentner's analysis, the meanings of *give* and *take* were the simplest: something is transferred from one person to another. The meanings of *buy* and *sell* were supposed to be the most complex: something is transferred from one person to another and some money is transferred in exchange. Consistent with this, only *give* and *take* were reliably understood by the youngest subjects. The full meanings of the others were mastered in the expected order. For the 8-year-olds, only *sell* presented difficulties. Moreover, the children's performance indicated that before the more complex words were mastered, their interpretations were not wrong but incomplete. For example, *buy* was most frequently misinterpreted as *take, sell* as *give,* and *trade* as a one-way transfer in either direction. The suggestion is that the meanings of the simpler words are fundamental to the whole set; the meanings of the more complex words develop from them through layers of semantic elaboration. Thus, the meanings of complex words effectively contain the meanings of simpler ones within their family. It is interesting from this perspective that age of acquisition rivals frequency as a predictor of a word's accessibility (Carroll & White, 1973; Loftus & Suppes, 1973). More to the point of the present discussion, a child's understanding of a rare word implies her or his undertanding of a host of related but simpler concepts. The utility of vocabulary tests is, therefore, not just that they provide an estimate of the number of words that a child can recognize and understand; in addition, they provide a rough index of her or his conceptual sophistication (see also Anderson & Shifrin, Chapter 13, this volume).

Sinclair-de-Zwart (1969) has shown that the acquisition of syntactic structures may also depend on the child's level of cognitive development. In her experiment, children were first tested for the understanding of conservation of quantity, or, in other words, for their appreciation of the fact that excess on one dimension may compensate for shortages on another. They were then asked to verbally compare objects that differed on two quantitative dimensions—for example, to describe the difference between a short, fat pencil and a long, thin pencil. All of the children who had clearly demonstrated conservation used different terms to describe the different dimensions (e.g., "short" vs. "thin" and "long" vs. "fat"), and 80% of them described the objects contrastively (e.g., "this pencil is longer but thinner; the other is shorter but fatter"). Of the children who had not demonstrated conservation, 75% did not differentially describe the two dimensions (e.g., they used "big" in reference to both length and diameter). Further, 90% of the nonconservers did not use the contrastive structure: They either compared the dimensions sequentially or ignored one of them altogether. To dispel the argument that the children's language was controlling their ability to conserve rather than vice-versa, Sinclair-de-Zwart tried to teach the nonconservers how to describe the difference between the objects with the contrastive construction. She found that very few of them could learn to do so and that those who did generally failed the conservation posttest anyhow.

Moreover, a remarkably close temporal correlation between the development of related logical and linguistic skills is often observed (e.g., Olson, 1970; Palermo & Molfese, 1972; Taplin, Staudenmeyer, & Taddonio, 1974). Almost certainly, this is not mere coincidence. It would seem more likely that the emergence of both kinds of skills presupposes the acquisition of some common conceptual structures. If this is true, then the trick for the educator is to figure out, at each point in time, which semantic distinctions can be usefully taught and which should be postponed until the child is conceptually more mature.

The second class of semantic problems has to do with the reader's ability to organize the concepts of the text into a coherent structure. Many of the issues within this category are discussed in detail elsewhere in this volume (e.g., Chapter 19 by Brown). The importance of this kind of organization has been experimentally demonstrated: When the thematic structure of a passage is obscured or confused, both comprehension of and memory for the passage plummet (Bransford & Johnson, 1973; Bransford & McCarrell, 1974; Frase, 1972).

In order to comprehend a passage as a whole, readers must be sensitive to the relative importance of its various concepts. The central ideas of the text will then be placed at the foundation of their own reconstruction of the meaning of the discourse. Less important ideas will be successively added in proper relation to the central theme, irrelevant or superfluous information may be discarded, and extralinguistic information will be added as necessary to complete the structure. Adults' recall of connected discourse shows strong evidence of this sort of ideational scaffolding (Bransford & McCarrell, 1974;

Dooling & Lachman, 1971; Johnson, 1970; Spiro, 1977), and Brown & Smiley (1977) have found that the same organizational tendency exists among young readers. However, Smiley, Oakley, Worthen, Campione, and Brown (1978) have recently demonstrated that sensitivity to gradations in the importance of ideational units is quite poor among beginning readers and increases only gradually with reading experience. Further, they found the same sort of insensitivity among older children who were poor readers. The results of Smiley et al. cannot be attributed to the confounding of lower order reading processes for they obtained in listening conditions as well.

If we could teach these children to recognize the relative importance of the ideas in a discourse, their ability to comprehend would necessarily be improved. To this end, several investigators have tried highlighting the important units by means extrinsic to the text itself. As one example, Hershberger and Terry (1965) tried to guide reader's attention by printing the essential concepts of the text in red; in the same vein, Rothkopf (1972) has studied the utility of adjunct questioning. These techniques work in the sense that readers do tend to remember the highlighted information better. However, there is some question as to how effectively such experiences will transfer to new texts and tasks. An alternative tack is suggested by Meyer's (1975) discovery of certain structural and stylistic features that correlate with the thematic significance of the units in a text; perhaps it would be fruitful to point these out to the young reader—but again, there is some question as to how well such clues will generalize across reading situations.

The real problem in this effort is that there are few general rules by which we can identify important units of meaning across all reading situations. As T. Anderson discusses in Chapter 20 of this volume, the ability of the skilled reader to focus on important units must pivot on her or his expectations about the message and structure of the passage. The optimal reading strategy will depend partly on the general nature of the passage—that is, on whether it is a political essay, an algebra problem, an allegory, a contract, or a game instruction (see Brewer, Chapter 9, this volume); partly on aspects of the particular passage, regardless of its rhetorical category; and partly on the reader's reasons for reading it (Frederiksen, 1975). Thus, the most important ingredient of teaching children to read at this level may be that of exposing them to a variety of different kinds of texts and a variety of reading goals so that they can develop a useful variety of analytic strategies. But this must be coupled with an effort to teach them to select and implement these strategies on their own. Somehow they must acquire the notion that reading is a thinking game—that they should always try to figure out what they are looking for as they read a passage.

The problems discussed in this section will affect not only reading but language comprehension in general. However, if such problems exist, they will be magnified in the reading situation, especially when the texts become

more complex and informative. In listening situations, the child's comprehension will be guided by the real-world context (see Rubin, Chapter 17, this
volume). In reading, there is only the text itself. The presence of pictures may
help, but there is some controversy as to how much (Gibson & Levin, 1975;
see also Chapter 5 by Morgan & Green and Chapter 21 by Schallert). The
reading material in primers is typically based on simple, stereotyped schemata
so that semantic difficulties will be minimized. However, the content of more
advanced texts will shift away from information that children can retrieve and
toward information that they must construct. Thus, semantic processing
demands will increase and, at the same time, children will be less able to check
their interpretations against things they already know.

Difficulties in comprehending spoken discourse are also much easier to
overcome. First, perceptive speakers will often be able to tell when their
listeners do not understand; speakers can, therefore, try to clarify the message
as they go along. Second, if listeners do not understand something that is said
to them, they can usually ask questions of the speaker. Because written texts
are not nearly so accommodating, readers must develop strategies for
recognizing and overcoming semantic difficulties on their own. There is, after
all, little point in reading without comprehending.

SUMMARY

Skilled reading depends on a host of perceptual, linguistic, and cognitive
processes. The importance of each of these processes must be defined not only
in terms of the work for which it is directly responsible, but also in terms of the
support it must lend to other, higher and lower level processes in the system.
Thus, deficiencies in any of the requisite processes or in their coordination
may result in profound difficulties for the reader. Although beginning readers
come equipped with many of these skills as the result of their oral language
experience, there are also, at each level of analysis, certain interpretive
processes that are unique to reading. The purpose of this chapter was to
describe some of these processes and the ways in which deficiencies in them
affect reading comprehension.

ACKNOWLEDGMENTS

The author extends special thanks to Bill Huggins and Ray Nickerson who have been
wonderfully helpful. This research was supported by the National Institute of
Education under Contract No. US-NIE-C-400-76-0116.

REFERENCES

Adams, M. J., & Collins, A. M. A schema-theoretic view of reading. In R. O. Freedle (Ed.), *Discourse processing: Multidisciplinary perspectives.* Norwood, N.J.: Ablex Publishing Co., 1979.

Anglin, J. M., & Miller, G. A. The role of phrase structure in the recall of meaningful verbal material. *Psychonomic Science,* 1968, *10,* 343–344.

Baron, J., & Thurston, I. An analysis of the word-superiority effect. *Cognitive Psychology,* 1973, *4,* 207–228.

Barr, R. The effect of instruction on pupil reading strategies. *Reading Research Quarterly,* 1975, *10,* 555–582.

Biemiller, A. The development of the use of graphic and contextual information as children learn to read. *Reading Research Quarterly,* 1970, *6,* 75–96.

Bradshaw, W. L., & Anderson, H. E., Jr. Developmental study of the meaning of adverbial modifiers. *Journal of Educational Psychology,* 1968, *59,* 111–118.

Bransford, J. D., & Johnson, M. K. Considerations of some problems of comprehension. In W. G. Chase (Ed.), *Visual information processing.* New York: Academic Press, 1973.

Bransford, J. D., & McCarrell, N. S. A sketch of a cognitive approach to comprehension. In W. B. Weimer & D. S. Palermo (Eds.), *Cognition and the symbolic processes.* Hillsdale, N.J.: Lawrence Erlbaum Associates, 1974.

Brown, A. L., & Smiley, S. S. Rating the importance of structural units of prose passages: A problem of metacognitive development. *Child Development,* 1977, *48,* 1–8.

Brown, R. *Social psychology,* New York: The Free Press, 1965.

Carroll, J. B., & White, M. N. Word frequency and age of acquisition as determiners of picture-naming latency. *Quarterly Journal of Experimental Psychology,* 1973, *25,* 85–95.

Cattell, J. McK. The time taken up by cerebral operations. *Mind,* 1886, *11,* 220–242.

Chall, J. *Learning to read: The great debate.* New York: McGraw-Hill, 1967.

Chomsky, N. *Aspects of the theory of syntax.* Cambridge, Mass.: MIT Press, 1965.

Cohen, G., & Freeman, R. Individual differences in reading strategies in relation to handedness and cerebral asymmetry. In J. Requin (Ed.), *Attention and performance VII.* Hillsdale, N.J.: Lawrence Erlbaum Associates, 1978.

Conrad, R. The developmental role of vocalizing in short-term memory. *Journal of Verbal Learning and Verbal Behavior,* 1972, *11,* 521–533.

Craik, F., & Lockhart, R. Levels of processing: A framework for memory research. *Journal of Verbal Learning and Verbal Behavior,* 1972, *11,* 671–684.

Cromer, W. The difference model: A new explanation for some reading difficulties. *Journal of Education Psychology,* 1970, *61,* 471–483.

Dooling, D. J., & Lachman, R. Effects of comprehension on retention of prose. *Journal of Experimental Psychology,* 1971, *88,* 216–222.

Farnham-Diggory, S. The development of equivalence systems. In S. Farnham-Diggory (Ed.), *Information processing in children.* New York: Academic Press, 1972.

Flavell, J. H. Developmental studies of mediated memory. In H. V. Reese & L. P. Lipsitt (Eds.), *Advances in child developmental and behavior* (Vol. 5). New York: Academic Press, 1970.

Fodor, J. A., Bever, T. G., & Garrett, M. F. *The psychology of language: An introduction to psycholinguistics and generative grammar.* New York: McGraw-Hill, 1974.

Fodor, J. A., & Garrett, M. F. Some syntactic determinants of sentential complexity. *Perception and Psychophysics,* 1967, *2,* 289–296.

Frase, L. T. Maintenance and control in the acquisition of knowledge from written materials. In J. B. Carroll & R. O. Freedle (Eds.), *Language comprehension and the acquisition of knowledge.* Washington, D.C.: V. H. Winston, 1972.

Frederiksen, C. H. Effects of context-induced processing operations on semantic information acquired from discourse. *Cognitive Psychology,* 1975, *7,* 139–166.

Gentner, D. Evidence for the psychological reality of semantic components: The verbs of possession. In D. A. Norman & D. E. Rumelhart (Eds.), *Explorations in cognition.* San Francisco: Freeman, 1975.

Gibson, E. J., & Levin, H. *The psychology of reading.* Cambridge, Mass.: MIT Press, 1975.

Gibson, E. J., Pick, A., Osser, H., & Hammond, M. The role of grapheme-phoneme correspondence in the perception of words. *American Journal of Psychology,* 1962, *75,* 554–570.

Goldberg, H. K., & Schiffman, G. B. *Dyslexia: Problems of reading disabilities.* New York: Grune & Stratton, 1972.

Goodman, K. S. Psycholinguistic universals in the reading process. *Journal of Typographic Research,* 1970, *4,* 103–110.

Hall, G. S. *Educational problems.* New York: Appleton, 1911. Cited by P.A. Koler in Huey, 1968, p. xxii.

Henderson, A., Goldman-Eisler, F., & Skarbek, A. Temporal patterns of cognitive activity and breath control in speech. *Language and Speech,* 1965, *8,* 236–242.

Henderson, A., Goldman-Eisler, F., & Skarbek, A. Sequential temporal patterns in spontaneous speech. *Language and Speech,* 1966, *9,* 207.

Hershberger, W. A., & Terry, D. F. Typographical cueing in conventional and programmed texts. *Journal of Applied Psychology,* 1965, *19,* 42–46.

Hochberg, J. Components of literacy: Speculations and exploratory research. In H. Levin & J. P. Williams (Eds.), *Basic studies on reading.* New York: Basic Books, 1970.

Huggins, A. W. F. *An effect of syntax on syllable timing* (QPR No. 114 for National Institutes of Health). Cambridge, Mass.: MIT Research Lab., 1974.

Huggins, A. W. F. Timing and speech intelligibility. In J. Requin (Ed.), *Attention and performance, VII.* Hillsdale, N.J.: Lawrence Erlbaum Associates, 1978.

Huttenlocher, J., & Burke, D. Why does memory span increase with age? *Cognitive Psychology,* 1976, *8,* 1–31.

Jarvella, R. Syntactic processing of connected speech. *Journal of Verbal Learning and Verbal Behavior,* 1971, *10,* 409–416.

Jenkins, J. J. Can we have a meaningful theory of memory? In R. L. Solso (Ed.), *Theories in cognitive psychology: The Loyola symposium.* Potomac, Md.: Lawrence Erlbaum Associates, 1974.

Johnson, R. E. Recall of prose as a function of the structural importance of the linguistic units. *Journal of Verbal Learning and Verbal Behavior,* 1970, *9,* 12–20.

Jorm, A. F. Effect of word imagery on reading performance as a function of reader ability. *Journal of Educational Psychology,* 1977, *69,* 46–54.

Klatt, D. H. Vowel lengthening is syntactically determined in a connected discourse. *Journal of Phonetics,* 1975, *3,* 129–140.

Kleiman, G. M. Speech recoding in reading. *Journal of Verbal Learning and Verbal Behavior,* 1975, *14,* 323–339.

Kolers, P. A. Pattern analyzing disability in poor readers. *Developmental Psychology,* 1975, *11,* 282–290.

Kolers, P. A. Buswell's discoveries. In R. A. Monty & J. W. Senders (Eds.), *Eye movements and psychological processes.* Hillsdale, N.J.: Lawrence Erlbaum Associates, 1976.

LaBerge, D., & Samuels, S. J. Toward a theory of automatic information processing in reading. *Cognitive Psychology,* 1974, *6,* 292–323.

Lawson, E. A note on the influence of difference orders of approximation to the English language upon eye-voice span. *Quarterly Journal of Experimental Psychology,* 1961, *13,* 53–55.

Levin, H., & Kaplan, E. L. Grammatical structure and reading. In H. Levin & J. P. Williams (Eds.), *Basic studies on reading.* New York: Basic Books, 1970.

Loftus, E. E., & Suppes, P. Structural variables that determine the speed of retrieving words from long-term memory. *Journal of Verbal Learning and Verbal Behavior,* 1973, *11,* 770-777.

MacKinnon, A. R. *How do chldren learn to read?* Vancouver, Canada: Copp Clark, 1959.

Marcel, T. The effective visual field and the use of context in fast and slow readers of two ages. *British Journal of Psychology,* 1974, *65,* 479-492.

Mason, M. Reading ability and letter search time: Effects of orthographic structure defined by single letter positional frequency. *Journal of Experimental Psychology: General,* 1975, *104,* 146-166.

McClelland, J. L. Preliminary letter identification in perception of words and nonwords. *Journal of Experimental Psychology: Human Perception and Performance,* 1976, *2,* 80-91.

McConkie, G. W. The use of eye-movement data in determining the perceptual span in reading. In R. A. Monty & J. W. Senders (Eds.), *Eye movements and psychological processes.* Hillsdale, N.J.: Lawrence Erlbaum Associates, 1976.

McNeill, D. Developmental psycholinguistics. In F. Smith & G. A. Miller (Eds.), *The genesis of language: A psycholinguistic approach.* Cambridge, Mass.: MIT Press, 1966.

McNeill, D. The development of language. In P. H. Mussen (Ed.), *Carmichael's manual of child psychology.* New York: Wiley, 1970.

Menyuk, P. Syntactic structures in the language of children. *Child Development,* 1963, *34,* 407-422.

Mewhort, D. J. K. Accuracy and order of report in tachistoscopic identification. *Canadian Journal of Psychology,* 1974, *28,* 383-398.

Meyer, B. J. F. *The organization of prose and its effects on memory.* Amsterdam: North-Holland, 1975.

Miller, G. A. The magical number seven, plus or minus two. *Psychological Review,* 1956, *63,* 81-97.

Morton, J. The effects of context upon speed of reading, eye-movements and eye-voice span. *Quarterly Journal of Experimental Psychology,* 1964, *16,* 340-351. (a)

Morton, J. A model for continuous language behavior. *Language and Speech,* 1964, *7,* 40-70. (b)

Nelson, K. Concept, word, and sentence: Interrelations in acquisition and development. *Psychological Review,* 1974, *81,* 267-285.

Oakan, R., Wiener, M., & Cromer, W. Identification, organization and reading comprehension for good and poor readers. *Journal of Educational Psychology,* 1971, *62,* 71-78.

Olson, D. R. Language and thought: Aspects of a cognitive theory of semantics. *Psychological Review,* 1970, *77,* 257-273.

Olson, G. M. Developmental changes in memory and the acquisition of language. In T. Moore (Ed.), *Cognitive development and the acquisition of language.* New York: Academic Press, 1973.

Palermo, D. S., & Molfese, D. L. Language acquisition from age five onward. *Psychological Bulletin,* 1972, *78,* 409-427.

Perfetti, C. A. *Language comprehension and fast decoding: Some psycholinguistic prerequisites for skilled reading comprehension.* Paper presented to the Development of Reading Comprehension Seminar of the International Reading Association, Newark, Delaware, July 1975.

Perfetti, C. A., & Hogaboam, T. The relationship between single word decoding and reading comprehension skill. *Journal of Educational Psychology,* 1975, *67,* 461-469.

Quillian, M. R. The teachable language comprehender. *Communications of the Association for Computing Machinery,* 1969, *12,* 459-476.

Rayner, K. The perceptual span and peripheral cues in reading. *Cognitive Psychology*, 1975, *7*, 65–81.

Rayner, K., & Hagelberg, E. M. Word recognition cues for beginning and skilled readers. *Journal of Experimental Child Psychology*, 1975, *20*, 444–455.

Rosenberg, S., & Schiller, W. Semantic coding and incidental sentence recall. *Journal of Experimental Psychology*, 1971, *90*, 345–346.

Rothkopf, E. Z. Structural text features and the control of processes in learning from written materials. In J. B. Carroll & R. O. Freedle (Eds.), *Language comprehension and the acquisition of knowledge*. Washington, D.C.: V.H. Winston, 1972.

Savin, H. B. What the child knows about speech when he starts to learn to read. In J. G. Kavanaugh & I. G. Mattingly (Eds.), *Language by ear and by eye*. Cambridge, Mass.: MIT Press, 1972.

Schlesinger, I. M. *Sentence structure and the reading process*. New York: Humanities Press, 1969.

Shankweiler, D. E., & Liberman, I. Y. Misreading: A search for causes. In J. F. Kavanagh & I. G. Mattingly (Eds.), *Language by ear and by eye*. Cambridge, Mass.: MIT Press, 1972.

Simon, H. A. How big is a chunk? *Science*, 1974, *183*, 482–488.

Sinclair-de-Zwart, H. Developmental psycholinguistics. In D. Elkind & J. H. Flavell (Eds.), *Studies in cognitive development: Essays in honor of Jean Piaget*. Oxford: Oxford University Press, 1969.

Slobin, D. I. *The ontogenesis of grammar: Facts and theories*. New York: Academic Press, 1971.

Smiley, S. S., Oakley, D. D., Worthen, D., Campione, J. C., & Brown, A. L. Recall of thematically relevant material by adolescent good and poor readers as a function of written versus oral presentation. *Journal of Educational Psychology*, 1978, *69*, 381–387.

Smith, F. *Psycholinguistics and reading*. New York: Holt, Rinehart & Winston, 1973.

Spiro, R. J. Remembering information from text: Theoretical and empirical issues concerning the 'State of Schema' reconstruction hypothesis. In R. C. Anderson, R. J. Spiro, & W. E. Montague (Eds.), *Schooling and the acquisition of knowledge*. Hillsdale, N.J.: Lawrence Erlbaum Associates, 1977.

Taplin, J. E., Staudenmayer, H., & Taddonio, J. L. Developmental changes in conditional reasoning: Linguistic or logical? *Journal of Experimental Child Psychology*, 1974, *17*, 360–373.

Till, R. E., Cormak, D. R., & Prince, P. L. Effects of orienting tasks on sentence comprehension and cued recall. *Memory and Cognition*, 1977, *5*, 59–66.

Venezky, R. L. *Theoretical and experimental base for teaching reading*. The Hague, Netherlands: Mouton, 1976.

Venezky, R. L., & Massaro, D. W. *The role of orthographic regularity in word recognition*. Madison: Wisconsin Research and Development Center for Cognitive Learning, 1976.

Wallach, L., Wallach, M. A., Dozier, M. G., & Kaplan, N. E. Poor children learning to read do not have trouble with auditory discrimination but do have trouble with phoneme recognition. *Journal of Educational Psychology*, 1977, *69*, 36–39.

Weaver, P. A. *Improving reading comprehension: Effects of sentence organization instruction*. Unpublished manuscript, Harvard University, 1977.

Weber, R. First-graders' use of grammatical context in reading. In H. Levin & J. Williams (Eds.), *Basic Studies in Reading*, New York: Basic Books, 1970.

Weinstein, R., & Rabinovitch, M. Sentence structure and retention in good and poor readers. *Journal of Educational Psychology*, 1971, *62*, 25–30.

Wittrock, M. C., Marks, C., & Doctorow, M. Reading as a generative process. *Journal of Educational Psychology*, 1975, *67*, 484–489.

2 Schemata: The Building Blocks of Cognition

David E. Rumelhart
*University of California, San Diego
and
Center for the Study of Reading*

The notion of a schema and the related notions of beta structures, frames, scripts, plans, and so on have formed the focus of research in Cognitive Science over the past 3 or 4 years. (cf. Bobrow & Norman, 1975; Chafe, 1976; Minsky 1975; Moore & Newell, 1973; Rumelhart, 1975; Schank & Abelson, 1975; Winograd, 1975). In this paper, I introduce these concepts to those unfamiliar with them and show why so much attention has been paid to them. These various terms have been used by different authors to refer to any of a set of interrelated concepts. These terms are *not all synonymous*. Different authors have different things in mind when they use these different terms. Nevertheless, the various concepts are closely enough related that a discussion of any one of them will serve as an introduction to the others. I thus focus my discussion on the one I know best, *schemata* (the singular is *schema*), as developed in Rumelhart and Ortony (1977).

The term *schema* comes into psychology most directly from Bartlett (1932). Bartlett himself attributes his use of the term to Head (1920). However, it would appear that Kant's (1787/1963) use of the term already anticipated its major conceptual content. The *OED* gives the following definition of the term: "In Kant: Anyone of certain forms of rules of the 'productive imagination' through which the understanding is able to apply its 'categories' to the manifold of sense-perception in the process of realizing knowledge or experience." Some further discussion of Kant's view is given in Rumelhart and Ortony (1977). It is because of this historical precedence that I have chosen to retain the term *schema*.

For all of the aforementioned authors, schemata truly are *the building blocks of cognition*. They are the fundamental elements upon which all information processing depends. Schemata are employed in the process of interpreting sensory data (both linguistic and nonlinguistic), in retrieving information from memory, in organizing actions, in determining goals and subgoals, in allocating resources, and, generally, in guiding the flow of processing in the system. Clearly, any device capable of all these wondrous things must be powerful indeed. Moreover, because our understanding of none of these tasks that schemata are supposed to carry out has reached maturity, it is little wonder that a definitive explication of schemata does not yet exist and that skeptics view theories based on them with some suspicion. In this chapter, I spell out, as clearly as possible, the nature of schemata and the kinds of problems they were devised to solve. In addition, I present a convincing case that the framework provided by schemata and allied concepts does, in fact, form the basis for a reasonable theory of human information processing.

My discussion through the next several sections of the paper is abstract. Although I do not make direct application of these concepts to a theory of reading until near the end of the chapter, many of the chapters in this volume illustrate the ways in which schemata can lead to insightful analyses of the reading process.

WHAT IS A SCHEMA?

A schema theory is basically a theory about knowledge. It is a theory about how knowledge is represented and about how that representation facilitates the *use* of the knowledge in particular ways. According to schema theories, all knowledge is packaged into units. These units are the schemata. Embedded in these packets of knowledge is, in addition to the knowledge itself, information about how this knowledge is to be used.

A schema, then, is a data structure for representing the generic concepts stored in memory. There are schemata representing our knowledge about all concepts: those underlying objects, situations, events, sequences of events, actions and sequences of actions. A schema contains, as part of its specification, the network of interrelations that is believed to normally hold among the constituents of the concept in question. A schema theory embodies a *prototype* theory of meaning. That is, inasmuch as a schema underlying a concept stored in memory corresponds to the *meaning* of that concept, meanings are encoded in terms of the typical or normal situations or events that instantiate that concept.

Rather than attempting a formal description of schemata and their characteristics at this point, I turn instead to some useful analogies to give the reader a more concrete notion of the nature of schemata as I understand them. I turn first to one of the more fruitful analogies, that of a play.

Schemata Are Like Plays

The internal structure of a schema corresponds, in many ways, to the script of a play. Just as a play has characters that can be played by different actors at different times without changing the essential nature of the play, so a schema has *variables* that can be associated with (bound to) different aspects of the environment on different instantiations of the schema. As an example, consider the schema for the concept *buy*. One can imagine a playwright having written a most mundane play in which the entire play consisted of one person purchasing some object from another person. At minimum, such a play must have two people, some merchandise, and some medium of exchange. Whatever else happens, at the outset of the play one character (call him or her the PURCHASER) must possess the medium of exchange (call it the MONEY). The second person, the SELLER must possess the object in question, the MERCHANDISE. Then, by some interaction (BARGAIN-ING) a bargain is struck and the SELLER agrees to give the MER-CHANDISE to the PURCHASER in exchange for a quantity of the MONEY. There would, of course, be many ways of playing this little play. The MERCHANDISE could vary from a trinket of little value to an object of incalculable worth. The SELLER and the PURCHASER could vary in status, occupation, sex, nationality, age, and so on; the MONEY could vary in amount and whether it was actually money or clam shells; and the BARGAINING could vary in form. Still, through all of this variation, as long as the fundamental plot remained the same, we could say that the BUY play was being performed.

Now, this little play is very much like the schema that I believe underlies our understanding of the concept *buy* or that for *sell*. There are variables, corresponding to the characters in the play. We have the PURCHASER, the SELLER, the MONEY, the MERCHANDISE, and the BARGAINING. When we understand a situation to be a case of BUYING, we come to associate persons, objects, and subevents with the various variables of our schema. Having made these associations, we can determine to what degree the situation we are observing corresponds to this *prototype* case of BUYING.

Just as a playwright often specifies characteristics of the characters in his play (age, sex, disposition, etc.), so, too, as part of the specification of a schema, we have associated knowledge about the variables of the schema. We know, for example, that the PURCHASER and SELLER are normally people and that the MONEY is normally money. Moreover, we know that the value of the MONEY in question will covary with the value of the MERCHANDISE, and so on. Such knowledge about the typical values of the variables and their interrelationships is called the *variable constraints*.

These constraints serve two important functions in a schema theory. In the first place, variable constraints help in the identification of the various aspects of the situation with the variables of the schema. If we know that we are observing a case of BUYING, we are not going to map the PURCHASER variable into the object in the world that should serve as the MONEY. We know this, in part, because we know that the PURCHASER is normally an animate being, whereas the MONEY is normally money or some other inanimate object. In the second place, variable constraints can help by serving as *default values* (cf. Minsky, 1975) or initial "guesses" for variables whose values we have not yet observed. Thus, for example, if we take a certain transaction to be one of BUYING but do not notice the MONEY, we can *infer* that there was MONEY and that, in fact, the MONEY probably *was money* amounting in value to about the value of the MERCHANDISE. In this way, the schema can help us make inferences about unobserved aspects of a situation.

It is perhaps useful to note here that variable constraints offer default values for unobserved variables *conditional on the values of the observed variables.* Moreover, the constraints are not *all-or-none* constraints that *require* that certain variables have a fixed range of values. Rather, they are merely specifications of the *normal* range of values for each variable and how this normal range varies with the specification of various combinations of other values on the other variables. Thus, as Rumelhart and Ortony (1977) suggest, it is perhaps most useful to think of variable constraints as forming a kind of *multivariate distribution* with correlations among the several variables.

There is also the notion of an *instantiation of a schema* that corresponds to an *enactment of a play.* A play is enacted whenever particular actors, speaking particular lines, perform at a particular time and place. Similarly, a schema is *instantiated* whenever a particular configuration of values is bound to a particular configuration of variables at a particular moment in time. Interpreting a situation to be an instance of some concept, such as an instance of buying, involves, according to the present view, the instantiation of an appropriate schema, say the BUY schema, by associating the various variables of the schema with the various aspects of the situation. Such a schema, along with its variable bindings, is called an instantiated schema. Just as we could, say, take a movie of an enactment of a play and thereby save for posterity a trace of the enactment, likewise it is the traces of our instantiated schemata that serve as the basis of our recollections.

Before leaving the analogy between the script of a play and a schema, it is useful to note that neither is a complete specification of every detail—both allow room for irrelevant variation and creative interpretation. The script of a play, no matter how meticulous the playwright, allows for an infinity of variations, each of which can properly be considered an enactment of the play. Certain lines composed by the playwright are sometimes changed to suit the interpretation of the director. Nevertheless, within limits, it is the same play. So it is with schemata. A schema is not so rigidly applied that no variation is allowed. The schema only provides the skeleton around which the situation is interpreted. Variations orthogonal to the specifications of the schema have no bearing on the quality with which the schema is said to account for the situation. Moreover, even minor aspects of the situation that might be considered central to the schema can undergo some variation before we completely reject the interpretation provided by the schema.

Finally, despite all of the ways in which a schema is like a play, there are also numerous ways in which a schema is unlike a play. Perhaps most important of these is degree of abstraction. In our example of the BUY schema, we imagined a play that was more abstract than one any playwright, would ever compose. Normally, the playwright would determine the *kind* of buying involved, as well as more detail about the characters and more constraints on the dialogue. The BUY schema, on the other hand, must be applicable to *any* case of buying and, thus, must necessarily be more abstract that any actual play would ever be. Moreover, whereas a play is normally about people and their actions, a schema may be about events and objects of any sort. Indeed, a schema may merely be about the nature of a wholly inactive object such as a chair. In this case, the schema specifies not action or event sequences but spatial and functional relationships characteristic of chairs. Finally, although a play may contain acts, each with their own structure, a script for a play exists really only on one level. A script does not consist of a configuration of subscripts. A schema, on the other hand, should be viewed as consisting of a configuration of subschemata corresponding to the constituents of the concept being represented. These points are made clearer in the following sections, where I draw analogies between schemata and other familiar concepts.

Schemata Are Like Theories

Perhaps the central function of schemata is in the construction of an interpretation of an event, object, or situation—that is, in the process of comprehension. In all of this, it is useful to think of a schema as a kind of informal, private, unarticulated theory about the nature of the events, objects, or situations that we face. The total set of schemata we have available for interpreting our world in a sense constitutes our private theory of the nature of reality. The total set of schemata instantiated at a particular moment in time constitutes our internal model of the situation we face at that moment in time, or, in the case of reading a text, a model of the situation depicted by the text.

Thus, just as the activity surrounding a theory is often focused on the evaluation of the theory and the comparison of the theory with observations we have made so it is that the primary activity associated with a schema is the determination of whether it gives an adequate account for some aspect of our current situation. Just as the determination that a particular theory accounts for some observed results involves the determinations of the *parameters of the theory,* so the determination that a particular configuration of schemata accounts for the data presently available at our senses requires the determination of the values of the *variables of the schemata.* If a promising schema fails to account for some aspect of a situation, one has the options of accepting the schema as adequate in spite of its flawed account or of rejecting the schema as inadequate and looking for another possibility. Therefore, the fundamental processes of comprehension are taken to be analogous to hypothesis testing, evaluation of goodness to fit, and parameter estimation. Thus, a reader of a text is presumably constantly evaluating hypotheses about the most plausible interpretation of the text. Readers are said to have understood the text when they are able to find a configuration of hypotheses (schemata) that offers a coherent account for the various aspects of the text. To the degree to which a particular reader fails to find such a configuration, the text will appear disjointed and incomprehensible.

Schemata are like theories in another important respect. Theories, once they are moderately successful, become a source of predictions about unobserved events. Not all experiments are carried out. Not all possible observations are made. Instead, we use our theories to make inferences with some confidence about these unobserved events. So it is with schemata. We need not observe all aspects of a situation before we are willing to assume that some particular configuration of schemata offers a satisfactory account for that situation. Once we have accepted a configuration of schemata, the schemata themselves provide a richness that goes far beyond our observations. On deciding that we have seen an automobile, we assume that it has an engine, headlights, and all of the standard characteristics of an automobile. We do this without the slightest hesitation. We have complete confidence in our little theory. This allows our interpretations to far outstrip our sensory observations. In fact, once we have determined that a particular schema accounts for some event, we may not be able to determine which aspects of our beliefs are based on direct sensory information and which are merely consequences of our interpretation.

Schemata Are Like Procedures

There are at least two inadequacies of the analogies presented earlier. In the first place, plays and theories are passive. Schemata are active processes. In the second place, the relationship between a theory and its constitutent subtheories or between a play and its constitutent subplays are not always evident. Schemata, on the other hand, have a very well-defined constitutent structure.

In both of these ways, schemata resemble procedures or computer programs. Schemata are active computational devices capable of evaluating the quality of their own fit to the available data. That is, a schema should be viewed as a procedure whose function it is to determine whether, and to what degree, it accounts for the pattern of observations. This includes, among other things, associating its variables to the appropriate aspects of its environment—that is, binding its own variables. Thus, to the degree that schemata underlying concepts are identified with *meaning of those concepts,* a schema theory is *both* a *prototype theory* and a *procedural theory* of meaning. Obviously, the degree to which a schema theory of human information processing can work depends on the degree to which procedures can actually be constructed to carry out the tasks I have just assigned to them. I believe they can, and I address this issue in the following sections.

The second characteristic that schemata share with procedures is a structural one. Procedures normally consist of a network (or a tree) of subprocedures. A particular procedure normally carries out its task by invoking a pattern of subprocedures, each of which in turn operates by invoking its subprocedures. Each procedure or subprocedure can return values that can serve as conditions determining which other subprocedures, if any, are to be invoked. So it is with schemata. A schema is a network (or possibly a tree) of subschemata, each of which carries out its assigned task of evaluating its goodness of fit whenever activated. These subschemata represent the conceptual constituents of the concept being represented.

Thus, for example, suppose we had a schema for a FACE. This would consist of a certain configuration of subschemata, each representing a different constituent of a face. For example, there would presumably be a subschema representing the MOUTH, one for the NOSE, and one for each EAR and each EYE. These subschemata would, in turn, consist of a configuration of constituents. The EYE schema, for example, would consist of a configuration of subschemata including, perhaps, an IRIS, EYE-LASHES, and EYEBROW, and so on.

Just as a procedure uses results produced by its subprocedures to carry out its task, so too a schema uses results produced by its subschemata to carry out its tasks. As I indicated previously, the primary activity of a schema is the evaluation of its goodness of fit. An important mechanism of this evaluation involves the evaluation of the goodness of fit of each of its constituent parts. Thus, if a good EYE is found and a good MOUTH is found, the FACE schema can use this information along with its own evaluation of whether the entire *configuration* is right for a face to generate an overall evaluation of its goodness of fit.

To summarize, then, just as a procedure consists of subprocedures and those subprocedures, in turn, consist of more subprocedures, and so on, so a schema consists of subschemata each of which, in turn, is specified as a configuration of its subschemata, and so on. One may be struck by the fact that this process must stop somewhere. If each and every schema were merely a configuration of subschemata, the process would never end. The solution to this dilemma for schemata is identical to the solution for procedures. When a computer program is written, this embedding process does not continue indefinitely. Eventually, some subprocedure consists entirely of a configuration of *elementary instructions* for the machine in question. Likewise, with schemata, there must be a set of schemata that are elementary in the sense that they do not consist of a further breakdown in terms of subschemata. Such elementary schemata correspond to what Norman and Rumelhart (1975) call *primitives.*

Schemata Are Like Parsers

A parser is a device that, given a sequence of symbols, determines whether that sequence forms a legal sentence (according to the rule of some grammar) and, if it does, determines the *constituent structure* of the sentence. That is, it determines which symbols in the sequence correspond to which constituents of the sentence. The process of finding and verifying appropriate schemata is thus a kind of parsing process that works with conceptual elements—finding constituents and subconstitutents among the data currently impinging on the system in much the same way that a sentence parser must find the proper parse for the input string of words.

One particularly useful aspect of this analogy is the substantial body of work carried out in computational linguistics on various parsing procedures. I believe that the processing strategies developed for some of the most sophisticated of these carry over nicely in their application to schemata in general. As I discuss later, I have in mind here especially the work of Kaplan (1973) and his development of the general syntactic processor (GSP).

Summary of the Major Features of Schemata

Rumelhart and Ortony (1977) listed four major characteristics of schemata. These were:

1. Schemata have variables.
2. Schemata can embed, one within another.
3. Schemata represent knowledge at all levels of abstraction.
4. Schemata represent knowledge rather than definitions.

The analogies just presented illustrate all of these features. Whereas schemata have variables, so plays have roles, theories have parameters, and procedures have arguments. The embedding characteristic of schemata is best illustrated by the analogy between schemata and procedures. Schemata consist of subschemata as procedures consist of subprocedures. Just as theories can be about the grand and the small, so schemata can represent knowledge at all levels—from ideologies and cultural truths to knowledge about what constitutes an appropriate sentence in our language, to knowledge about the meaning of a particular word, to knowledge about what patterns of excitations are associated with what letters of the alphabet. We have schemata to represent all levels of our experience, at all levels of abstraction. Finally, our schemata *are* our knowledge. All of our generic knowledge is embedded in schemata.

In addition to these four features, the analogies presented here indicate at least two more general features of schemata:

5. Schemata are active processes.
6. Schemata are recognition devices whose processing is aimed at the evaluation of their goodness of fit to the data being processed.

THE CONTROL STRUCTURE OF SCHEMATA

Perhaps the central questions in the development of a schema-based model of perception and comprehension are: First, how is an adequate configuration of schemata discovered? Second, how is the goodness of fit evaluated? These are largely problems of *control structures*. There are many schemata. Not all of them can be evaluated at once. Somehow, there must be a scheme for activating just those schemata that are most promising. There are two basic sources of activation for schemata. These are usually referred to as *top-down* and *bottom-up* activation. These two directions correspond to what Bobrow and Norman (1975) have called *conceptually driven* and *data-driven* processing. I turn now to a discussion of these two modes of activation.

Conceptually Driven and Data-Driven Processing

A schema may activate a subschema in the way a procedure invokes its subprocedures. This is called *conceptual-driven* processing. In a sense, conceptually driven processing is expectation-driven processing. That is, when a schema is activated and it, in turn, activates its subschemata, the activation of these subschemata derive from a sort of expectation that they will be able to account for some portion of the input data. For example, suppose that, through some mechanism, the FACE schema is considered a promising account for the input and thereby activated and set about evaluating its goodness of fit. The *promise* of the FACE schema is, in a sense, transferred to its MOUTH, NOSE, EYE, EAR, and so on, subschemata.

A second mechanism for schema activation is bottom-up or *data-driven* activation. A schema is said to be activated from the bottom-up whenever a subschema that has been somehow activated causes the various schemata of which it is a part to be activated. If the activation of the FACE schema led to the activation of the PERSON schema, we would say that the activation of the PERSON schema was data driven. Thus, where *conceptually driven* activation goes from *whole to part, data-driven* activation goes from *part to whole*. In schema-directed processing, activation goes in *both* directions.

Schema-directed processing is assumed to proceed in roughtly the following way: Some event occurs at the sensory system. The occurrence of this event "automatically" activates certain "low-level" schemata (such schemata might be called *feature detectors*). These low-level schemata would, in turn, activate (in a data-driven fashion) certain of the "higher level" schemata (the most probable ones) of which they are constituents. These "higher level" schemata would then initiate conceptually driven processing by activating the subschemata not already activated in an attempt to evaluate its goodness of fit.

At some point, when one of these higher level schemata has begun to get further positive results about its goodness of fit (i.e., it has found evidence for other of its constituents), it would activate still higher level schemata, that would look for still larger constituents.

This higher, more abstract schema would then activate, from the top down, still other of its constituent schemata, and this activation would flow through its subschemata back down to lower level schemata. Lower level schemata would eventually either make contact with other schemata that have been activated from the bottom up or would initiate a search for the "predicted" sensory inputs.

Whenever a schema initiates a search for sensory data that are not present, that counts as evidence against that schema and also as evidence against all of those schemata that require the presence of that schema as a constituent subschema. When sufficient evidence is accumulated against a schema, processing of that schema is suspended and processing resources are allocated to other currently more promising schemata. Whenever enough evidence is gained in favor of a schema, that schema is taken as an adequate account for the relevant aspect of the input, and the interpretation offered by that schema is taken as the "correct" interpretation of the relevant event. Later processing on other, higher level schemata may eventually disconfirm a temporarily accepted schema, and we will have the phenomenon of the "double-take."

My discussion of the processing system to this point has been rather abstract. In the following section I examine, in some detail, an example of this mixed initiative processing system. In addition, Woods (Chapter 3, this volume) gives a more complete discussion of these issues.

An Example

Consider the following brief passage:

> Business had been slow since the oil crisis. Nobody seemed to want anything really elegant anymore. Suddenly the door opened and a well-dressed man entered the showroom floor. John put on his friendliest and most sincere expression and walked toward the man.

Although merely a fragment, most people generate a rather clear interpretation of this story. Apparently, John is a car salesman fallen on hard times. He probably sells rather large elegant cars—most likely, Cadillacs. Suddenly a good prospect enters the showroom where John works. John wants to make a sale. To do that he must make a good impression on the man. Therefore, he tries to appear friendly and sincere. He also wants to talk to the man to deliver his sales pitch. Thus, he makes his way over to the man. Presumably, had the story continued John would have made the sales pitch and, if all went well, sold the man a car.

How do people arrive at such an interpretation? Clearly, people do not arrive at it all at once. As the sentences are read, schemata are activated, evaluated, and refined or discarded. When people are asked to describe their various hypotheses as they read through the story, a remarkably consistent pattern of hypothesis generation and evaluation emerges. The first sentence is usually interpreted to mean that business is slow *because* of the oil crisis. Thus, people are inclined to believe that the story is about a business that is suffering as a result of the oil crisis. Frequent hypotheses involve either the selling of cars or of gasoline. A few interpret the sentence as being about the economy in general. The second sentence, about people not wanting elegant things anymore, leads people with the gas-station hypothesis into a quandary. Elegance just does not fit with gas stations. The gas station hypothesis is weakened, but not always rejected. On the other hand, people with hypotheses about the general economy or about cars have no trouble incorporating this sentence into their emerging interpretation. In the former case they conclude that people don't buy luxury items and in the latter they assume that people do not buy large elegant cars—Cadillacs—much anymore. The third sentence clinches the car interpretation for nearly all readers. They are already looking for a business interpretation—that most probably means a SELLING interpretation—and when a *well-dressed man* enters the door he is immediately labeled as someone with MONEY—a prospective BUYER. The phrase *showroom floor* clearly invalidates the gas-station interpretation and strongly implicates automobiles, which are often sold from a showroom. Moreover, the occurrence of a specific event does not fit at all well with the view that the passage is a general discussion of the state of the economy. Finally, with the introduction of John, we have an ideal candidate for the SELLER. John's actions are clearly those stereotypic of a salesman. John wants to make a sale and his "putting on" is clearly an attempt on his part to "make a good impression." His movement toward the man fits nicely into this interpretation. If he is a salesman, he must make contact with the man and deliver the stereotypic "pitch."

Qualitatively, this little account (which was derived from an analysis of a number of readers describing their current interpretation of the story after each sentence) fits well with the general approach I have been outlining. The process of comprehension is very much like the process of constructing a theory, testing it against the data currently available, and as more data become available, specifying the theory further—that is, refining the default values (as perhaps was the case when those holding the "car hypothesis" from the beginning encountered the sentence about nobody wanting anything elegant anymore). If the account becomes sufficiently strained, it is given up and a new one constructed, or, alternatively, if a new theory presents itself that obviously gives a more cogent account, the old one can be dropped and the new one accepted.

But where do these theories come from? The theories are, of course, schemata. Presumably, through experience, we have built up a vast repertoire of such schemata. We have schemata for salesmen, the kinds of motives they have, and the kinds of techniques they employ. We have schemata for automobiles, including how and where they are sold. We have built up schemata for the "oil crisis"—what kinds of effects it has on what kinds of businesses. We have schemata about business people, the kinds of motives they have, and the kinds of responses they make to these motives. The knowledge embedded in these schemata form the framework for our theories. It is some configuration of these schemata that ultimately forms the basis for our understanding.

But how does a relevant schema suggest itself? It is here that the control structures discussed earlier play an essential role. Presumably, it is the "bottom-up" observation that a certain concept has been referenced that leads to the suggestion of the initial hypotheses. The notion that business was slow suggests schemata about business and the economy. Because the slowness was dated from the occurrence of the oil crisis, it is a natural inference that the oil crisis was the *cause* of the slowness. Thus, a BUSINESS schema is activated. The particular TYPE of business is presumably a variable that must be filled. The information about the oil crisis suggests that it may be an oil-related business. Thus, readers are led to restrict the TYPE variable of the BUSINESS schema to oil-related businesses.

At this point, after the bottom-up activation of the high-level BUSINESS schema has occurred, this schema would generate a top-down activation of the various possible oil-related businesses. Prime candidates for these are, of course, automobile-related businesses. Of these, selling gasoline and automobiles are the two most salient possibilities.

When the second sentence is encountered, an attempt is made to fit it into the schemata currently considered most promising. As I discussed previously, this information could serve to further restrict the TYPE variable in the automobile BUSINESS schema but does not fit well with the gasoline business schema.

The BUSINESS schema presumably has, as part of its specification, a reference to the BUY or SELL schema discussed previously. Once activated, these schemata search for potential variable bindings. In the case of the automobile business, the MERCHANDISE variable is bound to an automobile. The second sentence suggests an elegant automobile. When the third sentence is encountered, the reader has not yet found a candidate for BUYER or SELLER. The sentence about a well-dressed man immediately suggests a potential BUYER. The phrase "showroom floor" offers additional bottom-up support for the automobile hypothesis. In fact, it is a strong enough clue itself that it can suggest automobile sales to a reader who currently considers an alternative schema more likely. We thus have a BUYER and some MERCHANDISE. The well-dressed quality of the BUYER is consistent with our view that the MERCHANDISE is elegant and therefore expensive—being well-dressed suggests MONEY. We need only a SELLER—that is, an automobile salesman. Readers probably already bring a relatively complete characterization of the "default value" for car salesmen. We need but little additional information to generate a rather detailed description of his goals and motives.

In spite of the length of this example, it should be noted that I have provided only a sketch of the elaborate processing that must occur in the comprehension of even so simple and direct a story as this. The problem is indeed a complex one, and no one yet has been able to construct a model capable of actually carrying out the tasks involved. It is the conviction that the concept of the *schema* is the most promising route to the solution to these problems that has led to its current popularity.

THE MAJOR FUNCTIONS OF SCHEMATA

My intent to this point has been primarily definitional. I have tried to show what schemata were in general and how they generally are supposed to work. In this section I give a few examples, mostly taken from the psychological literature, of phenomena for which schemata appear to offer promising accounts. I first turn to a discussion of *perception,* especially as it relates to reading.

Schemata and Perceiving

There are numerous examples in the psychological literature that suggest a schema-like theory to account for them. I mention just a few examples here. Perception, like language comprehension, is an interactive process. Information comes in from our sense organs, which suggest but do not determine appropriate schemata for the interpretation of the sense data. It is often only in the context of the whole that the individual parts of an object can be identified. Similarly, the whole itself cannot be identified apart from its parts. The interpretation of parts and wholes must proceed jointly. Our final interpretation is determined both by the local clues and by consistency among the various levels of analysis. Consider, as an example, Fig. 2.1 taken from Palmer (1975). The object on the left is clearly recognizable as a face, but its parts (series A) are not recognizable out of context. Thus, it cannot be that we first perceive the parts and then construct an interpretation of the whole. Rather, the various shapes of the lines *suggest,* but do not determine, possible interpretations (the wiggly line suggests a possible nose, the acute angle suggests a possible eye, etc.). Lower level NOSE and EYE schemata may be activated, which in turn may activate higher level schemata such as the FACE schema. The FACE schema then activates schemata for all of the parts of the FACE not receiving bottom-up activation. (For example, the lips may not be close enough to LIPS to activate this schema at all out of context. In this case, the LIPS schema would be activated by the FACE schema and find sufficient evidence to serve—in context—to count as LIPS.)

As can be noted from series *B* of Fig. 2.1, it is not that parts of a face cannot *ever* be recognized without the face as a context. But, in order to be

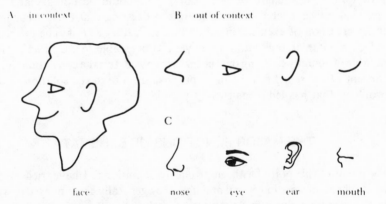

FIG. 2.1.   An illustration of part-whole context. Facial features recognizable in the context of a profile (A) are not recongizable out of context (B). When the internal part structure of the facial features is differentiated (C), however, the features become recognizable out of context (Palmer, 1975).

recognized out of context, they, too, must have an internal structure. If enough data are available about its internal structure, a schema, such as the NOSE schema, can serve the function of an organizing whole perfectly well.

There is ample evidence of similar processes in reading. It is well known, for example, that the strings of characters that form words are more easily apprehended than strings that do not form words. The reason for this presumably stems from the fact that we have schemata corresponding to words and none for random letter strings. Just as evidence for a NOSE indirectly constitutes evidence for LIPS through the FACE schema, so too evidence for one letter can constitute evidence for other letters through the schema for the word in question. Thus, for example, evidence favoring a *T* in the first position and an *E* in the third position of a three-letter word indirectly constitutes evidence for an *H* in the second position through activation of the THE schema. The use of such information is presumably the mechanism whereby words are easier to see than random letter strings. Moreover, one of the characteristics that may separate skilled readers from those with less skill is the availability of a greater number of more completely developed word schemata.

It is interesting that schemata not only *contribute* toward the development of an accurate percept, but, by the same token, they can sometimes cause a distortion. An experiment by Bruner and Potter (1964) illustrates the debilitating effect of premature commitment to a particular schema. In their study, subjects were presented with defocused slides of familiar objects. The slides were slowly brought into focus. At each step along the way, as the slides were brought into focus, subjects were to report their best guess of what the slide was. Under these conditions, subjects continued to misidentify the object long after naive subjects (those started with less severe amounts of de-focusing) were able to readily identify the object in question.

This result is presumably due to the fact that subjects became committed to their early interpretations of the slide and then required more information to disconfirm their original hypothesis than is normally required.

Schemata and Understanding Discourse

As discussed previously, the process of understanding discourse is the process of finding a configuration of schemata that offers an adequate account of the passage in question. The analysis of the "oil crisis story" given earlier illustrates generally how such a process is supposed to operate. Clues from the story suggest possible interpretations (instantiations of schemata) that are then evaluated against the successive sentences of the story until finally a consistent interpretation is discovered. Sometimes, a reader fails to correctly understand a passage. There are at least three reasons implicit in schema theory as to why this might occur:

1. The reader may not have the appropriate schemata. In this case he or she simply cannot understand the concept being communicated.
2. The reader may have the appropriate schemata, but the clues provided by the author may be insufficient to suggest them. Here again the reader will not understand the text but, with appropriate additional clues, may come to understand it.
3. The reader may find a consistent interpretation of the text but may not find the one intended by the author. In this case, the reader will "understand" the text but will misunderstand the author.

There are numerous examples of these three phenomena in the literature. Perhaps the most interesting set of studies along these lines were carried out by Bransford and Johnson (1973). They studied the comprehension of texts for which subjects could not provide the appropriate schemata, texts in which the schemata were potentially available but there were not sufficient clues to suggest the correct ones as well as texts in which subjects were led to choose a "wrong" interpretation. Consider, as an example, the following paragraph used in one of Bransford and Johnson's (1973) studies:

> The procedure is actually quite simple. First you arrange things into different groups. Of course, one pile may be sufficient depending on how much there is to do. If you have to go somewhere else due to lack of facilities, that is the next step, otherwise you are pretty well set. It is important not to overdo things. That is, it is better to do too few things at once than too many. In the short run this may not seem important but complications can easily arise. A mistake can be expensive as well. At first the whole procedure will seem complicated. Soon, however, it will become just another facet of life. It is difficult to forsee any end to the necessity for this task in the immediate future, but then one can never tell. After the procedure is completed, one arranges the materials into different groups again. Then they can be put into their appropriate places. Eventually they will be used once more and the whole cycle will then have to be repeated. However, that is part of life [p. 400].

Most readers find this passage extremely difficult to understand. However, once they are told that it is about washing clothes, they are able to bring their clothes-washing schema to the fore and make sense out of the story. The difficulty with this passage is, thus, not that readers do not have the appropriate schemata; rather, it stems from the fact that the clues in the story never seem to *suggest* the appropriate schemata in the first place. The "bottom-up" information is inadequate to initiate the comprehension process appropriately. Once the appropriate schemata are suggested, most people have no trouble understanding the text.

Although most readers simply find the passage incomprehensible, some find alternative schemata to account for it and thus render it comprehensible.

Perhaps the most interesting interpretation I have collected was from a Washington bureaucrat who has no difficulty with the passage. He was able to interpret the passage as a clear description of his job. He was, in fact, surprised to find that it was supposed to be about "washing clothes" and not about "pushing papers." Here then, we have an example of the third kind of comprehension failure, "understanding the story" but "misunderstanding the author."

Obviously, a detailed account of the comprehension process requires a detailed description of the schemata readers have available as well as an account of the conditions under which certain of these schemata are activated. A number of researchers have been developing such specific models of specific schemata (cf. Rumelhart, 1975, 1977; Schank & Abelson, 1977).

Schemata and Remembering

In addition to the important role assigned to schemata in comprehension and perception, schemata are assumed to be the guiding forces behind remembering as well. Perhaps the clearest way to see this is to consider some of the commonalities between remembering and apprehension. Rumelhart and Ortony (1977) suggest that the process of remembering is essentially similar to the process of perceiving, except that, in remembering, the data source is no longer sensorial but memorial. To quote:

> There is thus a kind of continuum between understanding and remembering where in the former we have the imposition of an interpretation primarily on incoming "sensory fragments," and in the latter we have the imposition of an interpretation primarily on "memorial fragments." In both cases schemata are employed. It should be emphasized that although remembering can be thought of as perceiving with memory as the modality, the episodic memories on which it is usually based are not merely fragments of the initial sensory input, but a fragmentary representation of our interpretation of that input [p. 27].

Thus, important aspects of the memory process can be seen as identical to the process of comprehension. I have thus, implicitly alluded to two ways in which schemata affect recollection. First, they are the mechanisms whereby initial interpretations are formed and, as such, they determine the *form* of the memorial fragments. Second, schemata are used to *reinterpret* the stored data in order to *reconstruct* the original interpretation. There is ample evidence for both of these roles. The first point suggests that we remember our *interpretations* of an event or text rather than the text or event itself. Bartlett's (1932) original finding that we remember the *gist* of a story rather than the details suggests this conclusion. Tulving and Thomson's (1973) arguments about encoding specificity would seem to require the same conclusion.

Perhaps the most convincing results, however, come from some recent experiments by Bransford and his associates (cf. Bransford, Barclay, & Franks, 1972; or Barclay, Bransford, Franks, McCarrell, & Nitsch, 1974). In one of their experiments (Bransford, Barclay, & Franks, 1972), they presented subjects with sentences drawn from pairs such as: (1a) The woman stood *on* the stool and the mouse sat on the floor beneath *it*. (1b) The woman stood *on* the stool and the mouse sat on the floor beneath *her*. Or sentences were drawn from pairs such as (2a) The woman stood *beside* the stool and the mouse sat on the floor beneath *it*. (2b) The woman stood *beside* the stool and the mouse sat on the floor beneath *her*. They found that on subsequent recognition tests, subjects could not tell which of the first pair of sentences had been presented to them, but those given sentences drawn from the second pair had no difficulty recognizing which had been presented. Because the two pairs differ by exactly the same number of words, it cannot be a difference in memory for the sentences per se that accounts for the difference in recognizability but rather differences in *interpretation* that account for the differential distinguishability between the two pairs.

The second role of schemata in remembering involves their use in reconstructing the original interpretation. Here, perhaps the best evidence comes from a recent experiment reported by Spiro (1977). Spiro designed his experiment to carefully discriminate between those inferences drawn at the time of comprehension and those drawn at the time of recall. In his experiment, subjects read stories that they were led to believe were true. Then, after reading the stories, subjects were given an additional piece of information that was either *consistent with the implications* of the story or *inconsistent with the implications* of the story. On later recall of the story, there was a general tendency for those with information inconsistent with the thrust of the story to *distort* their recall of the story so as to make it consistent with the later information. Moreover, this cannot entirely be due to a reinterpretation of the story at the time they received the additional information, because the longer the delay between the addition of the information and the recall test, the greater the degree of distortion. In terms of the framework under discussion in this paper, this fact suggests that the longer the amount of time between presentation and recall, the fewer memorial fragments are available and the more the subject must rely on generic knowledge of similar situations—that is, the subject's schemata. The less consistent the original information is from the typical, the more room (and need) there is for distortion.

Thus, just as comprehension is presumed to be identical to the process of selecting and verifying conceptual schemata to account for the situation to be understood, so the process of remembering involves, as a major component, the process of selecting and verifying an appropriate configuration of schemata to account for the memorial fragments found in memory. Such an account constitutes a recollection.

There is an important omission in this account of remembering. It has been tacitly assumed in our account of perception (and therefore in that for remembering) that data present themselves passively to the sensory system, directly exciting certain low-level "features" and that comprehension (or perception) involves the discovery of an adequate account of the spatio-temporal pattern of excitation of these low-level feature detectors. Similarly, in this account of remembering, it appears as if there is, somehow, a set of memorial fragments that are presenting themselves to the memory system for interpretation and that the process of interpretation (selecting potential configurations of schemata and verifying that they are consistent with the stored data—memory fragments) is simply all there is to remembering. *This is quite obviously false for both understanding and remembering.* First, consider the case of perception; then I will show how this extends to remembering.

Perception is goal directed. We do not passively wait for some stimuli to arrive and then at that late date attempt an interpretation. Instead, we actively seek information relevant to our current needs and goals. When we want a phone number, we do not merely interpret our current sensory input as if it were a phone number but we actively *seek* information to be so interpreted. This information-seeking process must go hand in hand with the information interpretation process. Just as expectations (embodied by certain activated schemata) can serve an important function in guiding our process of interpreting input that happens to reach our sensory organs, so these same schemata guide our *information seeking.* Not only do schemata tell us *what to see,* but they also tell us *where to see it.* I have not emphasized this aspect of the comprehension process.

If perception is goal directed, then remembering is even more so. In remembering, we are not merely perusing around our memories, making sense about what "happens to come to mind." The ordinary case of memory is probably more akin to the process of looking for a phone number than watching a TV program or reading a text. Here the "search" problem is severe. Whatever memory probe or question we have available will bring some fragments of memory to mind (activate some of the appropriate memory structures). Perhaps sometimes this is enough—the interpretation of this fragment of memory is enough to respond to the question at hand. More often, however, this is probably not the case. The appropriate fragments are just not "in front of us," impinging on our memory interpretation system. In these cases we must instigate a *search.* Just as in the case of looking for a telephone number, the search is not random. Rather, it must be guided by schemata that represent the layout of our memories in the same way as schemata encode the layout of our homes or our telephone books. When we want a phone number, we realize we might be able to use a phone book. Thus, we might search our house for the phone book. Knowing the layout of our house, we know the typical location of the phone book and will immediately go there to find it. Note the location of the phone book is a subgoal in the search for the phone number in much the same way that a "retrieval context" is a subgoal in a memory search. When we find the phone book, we use our knowledge of the structure of the phone book to guide us to the appropriate region of the book. Finally, once there, we use our expectations about the structure and meaning of phone numbers to construct an appropriate interpretation of the symbols on the page. Not much work has been done on mapping out the search paths through memory while trying to recollect events after a long delay. Recent work by Williams (1977) would seem to be a promising approach toward the study of these scan paths through memory.

Schemata and Learning

One of the central problems of a schema theory is a specification of the process (or processes) whereby new schemata are developed. Even if it is granted that a set of "hand-crafted" procedures *could* carry out the tasks assigned to them by schema theories, it remains to be shown that there are plausible learning procedures that could result in such a set of schemata. There is currently very little known about what kinds of learning principles would be necessary for such a development. From a logical point of view, there are three basically different modes of learning that are possible in a schema-based system.

1. Traces of comprehension processes form a sort of learning inasmuch as upon having understood some text or perceived some event, we can retrieve stored information about that text or event. Such learning corresponds roughly to "fact learning." Rumelhart and Norman (1977) have called this learning *accretion*.

2. Existing schemata may *evolve* or undergo change to make them more in tune with experience. Our concepts presumably undergo continual change as we gain more experience with new exemplars. This corresponds to the elaboration and refinement of concepts through continued experience. Rumelhart and Norman (1978) have called this sort of learning *tuning*.

3. The third sort of learning involves the *creation* of new schemata. This involves the actual development of new concepts. There are, in a schema theory, at least two ways in which new concepts can be generated: They can be patterned on existing schemata or they can (in principle) be induced from experience. Rumelhart and Norman call learning of new schemata *restructuring*.

I now turn to a discussion of these three modes of learning and the conditions under which they occur.

Accretion. Learning by accretion is probably the most common sort of learning. It is also the sort of learning that has least effect on the operation of the system. Whenever new information is encountered, there is assumed to be some trace of the comprehension process laid down in memory. This memory trace is the basis for recollections. Generally, these traces are assumed to be partial copies of the original instantiated schemata. Thus, memory traces are assumed to be very much like schemata themselves. They differ only inasmuch as they are fragmentary and they have representations for particular aspects of the original situation in place of the variables of the original schemata. Thus, as we experience the world, we store, as a natural side effect of comprehension, traces that can serve as the basis of future recall. Later, during retrieval, we can use this information to reconstruct an interpretation of the original experience—thereby remembering the experience.

Such an accumulation of knowledge is the normal sort of learning. Although the accumulation of a substantial body of knowledge may be necessary for more fundamental kinds of learning, it causes no new schemata to be formed. Such learning occurs whenever our schemata available at the time of the original experience are deemed adequate for the interpretation of the experience. When we encounter a situation in which currently available schemata do not prove adequate, there is the possibility of schema change and thus a modification of the very devices through which we experience the world.

Tuning.   Tuning involves the actual modification or evolution of existing schemata. There are essentially three ways in which schemata can evolve. First, our knowledge of the variable constraints and default values can be upgraded continuously as we continue to use the schemata. Whenver we find a case in which we determine that a certain schema offers an adequate account of a particular situation, we can modify the variable constraints and default values in the direction of the current experience. This will make the schema sensitive to slow changes in the population of cases to which the schema is applied. As this process continues, it will continue to sharpen the variables and default values to make the schema better represent the population of situations to which it is applied. Note, however, that this sort of tuning will only occur when the schema is deemed to offer an adequate account of the situation at hand. Thus, because cases that deviate widely from the appropriate variable constraints and default values will not be accommodated by the schema in question, change must be slow.

The second sort of tuning involves replacing a constant portion of a schema with a variable one—that is, adding a new variable to a schema. This sort of schema modification amounts to *concept generalization*—making a schema more generally applicable. Presumably, the occasion for such learning is the discovery, at some point in time, that a particular schema would offer a good account for a particular situation if only some presumably constant feature of the schema were allowed to vary. To the degree that a constant is merely a variable with very tight constraints, this can be seen as a special case of the previous kind of tuning, namely, a case in which the change is from a variable with highly constrained constraints that becomes one with somewhat more relaxed constraints.

The third sort of tuning is, in a sense, the opposite of the last one, namely, the process of making a variable into a constant or specializing the use of the concept. One occasion for such learning would be the discovery that certain "outlier" situations are better accounted for by other schemata and that the apparent variable is better thought of as a constant. As before, this can also be thought of as a special case of changing variable constraints—in this case tightening them.

Restructuring. If accretion and tuning were the only learning mechanisms, no new schemata could be created. The third learning mode discussed previously involves the creation of new schemata. There are basically two ways in which new schemata can be formed. Rumelhart and Norman (1978) called these *patterned generation* and *schema induction.*

Patterned generation involves the creation of a new schema by copying an old one with a few modifications. Such learning is, in essence, learning by analogy. We learn that a new concept is like an old one except for a few differences. A new schema can differ from an old one by having variables where the old one had constants (a generalization of the old schema), by having constants where an old schema had variables (a further specification of the old schema), or by substituting a new variable or constant for an old variable or constant of the original schema. Once a new schema is created by such processes, the process of tuning will continue to modify the newly created schema to bring it more into line with experience.

The second way in which new schemata can be formed is through the process of schema induction. The notion here is that if a certain spatio-temporal configuration of schemata is repeated, there is reason to assume that the particular configuration forms a meaningful concept and a schema can be formed that consists of just that configuration. This, of course, is the classical contiguity learning. It is interesting that, in spite of the ubiquity of the notion of contiguity learning in learning theories of the past, there is no real *need* for it in a schema-based system. Provided we begin with a sufficiently general set of schemata, the processes of tuning, accretion, and patterned generation can carry us a long way. Schema induction does cause some difficulty for the notion of schemata as I have outlined them. In order for schema induction to work properly, we must posit some aspect of the system sensitive to the recurrence of configurations of schemata that do not, at the time they occur, match any existing schemata. Such a system is not a natural part of a schema-based system.

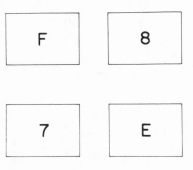

FIG. 2.2. Stimuli presented to the "Label Factory" subjects (from D'Andrade—see footnote 1).

Schemata and Solving Problems

Schemata play a central role in all of our reasoning processes. Most of the reasoning we do apparently *does not* involve the application of general-purpose reasoning skills. Rather, it seems that most of our reasoning ability is tied to particular schemata related to particular bodies of knowledge.

One of my favorite demonstrations of the critical role of schemata in reasoning comes from the work of Wason and Johnson-Laird (1972) and some more recent replications and extensions of their work carried out by Roy D'Andrade.[1] Subjects in D'Andrade's experiments were given one of two formally equivalent problems to solve. Half of the subjects were given the task illustrated in Fig. 2.2.

Subjects were shown the four cards illustrated in the figure and told that they were to imagine themselves as quality control experts in a label-making factory whose task it is to determine whether any labels are incorrectly constructed. A label is properly constructed if, when there is a vowel on one side of the label, there is an odd number on the other side. Then, they were asked to indicate which of the cards must be turned over to assure that the rule is being appropriately followed. Only 13% of the subjects correctly indicated that cards 2 and 4 must be checked. Card 4 must, of course, be checked because it may have an even number on the back. Card 2 must also be checked because it might have a vowel on the back and thus violate the rule. No other cards must be checked. However, about 70% of the subjects felt that card 3 should also be checked.

Here we have a classical failure of human reasoning. It has been argued that this is a case of our interpreting the simple conditional as a biconditional. In any case, results like these are often used to illustrate the weakness of the

---

[1]Roy D'Andrade has kindly given me access to the data from his as yet unpublished experiment.

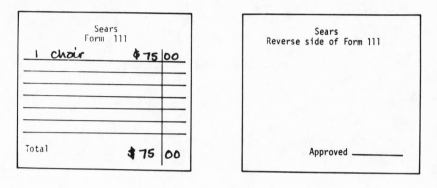

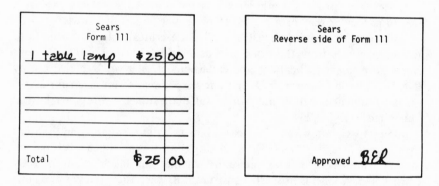

FIG. 2.3.   Stimuli for the "Sears" subjects (from D'Andrade—see footnote 1).

human reasoning system. However, the results of the second part of D'Andrade's experiment point out the fallacy in this conclusion. Figure 2.3 illustrates the stimuli for these subjects. Subjects were told that they were to imagine themselves as store managers for Sears and that they were to inspect receipts at the end of the day to be certain that they were properly filled out. The rule is that, if any purchase exceeded $30, the receipt must have the signature of the department manager on the back. Again, subjects were asked which of the cards were supposed to be turned over; in this case nearly 70% indicated cards 1 and 2. Formally, these two problems are identical. Yet, when phrased in terms of the familiar setting of the Sears store, over five times as many subjects were able to correctly solve the problem. What is the difference here? Why do people appear not to understand the meaning of "if" in the first case and understand it nearly perfectly in the second? In terms of schema theory, the answer is rather straightforward. The first case is unfamiliar and subjects have no schemata in which to incorporate the problem and, therefore, can bring only very general problem-solving strategies to bear on the problem. The second case more nearly approximates our "real life" problem-solving situations. Once we can "understand" the situation by encoding it in terms of a relatively rich set of schemata, the conceptual constraints of the schemata can be brought into play and the problem readily solved. It is as if the schema already contains all of the reasoning mechanism ordinarily required in the use of the schemata. Thus, understanding the problem and solving it is nearly the same thing.

CONCLUSION

It was my intent in this chapter to give the reader who is unfamiliar with schemata an intuition through which he or she could interpret the rest of this volume and the increasing number of studies employing these conceptualizations. I have aimed for generality rather than specificity in my account. I have tried to show the many domains to which the concept of a schema has been applied and the heuristic value of thinking about psychological and educational problems in terms of schemata. Many of the remaining chapters in this volume as well as some of the papers cited previously provide a more detailed account of schemata and more definite examples of their applicability. Although the development of schema-based theories such as the ones I mentioned previously is yet in its infancy and these ideas have not yet proved their usefulness, I believe that they offer the most promising leads for those of us interested in the difficult problems posed when we try to apply psychological theories directly to domains relevant to education.

ACKNOWLEDGMENT

This paper was written through the support of the National Institute for Education to the Center for the Study of Reading under Contract No. US-NIE-C-400-76-0116.

REFERENCES

Bartlett, F. C. *Remembering*. Cambridge: The Cambridge University Press, 1932.
Barclay, J. R., Bransford, J. D., Franks, J. J., McCarrell, N. S., & Nitsch, K. Comprehension and semantic flexibility. *Journal of Verbal Learning and Verbal Behavior*, 1974, *13*, 471–481.
Bobrow, D. G., & Norman, D. A. Some principles of memory schemata. In D. G. Bobrow & A. M. Collins (Eds.), *Representation and understanding: Studies in cognitive science*. New York: Academic Press, 1975.
Bransford, J. D., Barclay, J. R., & Franks, J. J. Sentence memory: A constructive versus interpretive approach. *Cognitive Psychology*, 1972, *3*, 193–209.

Bransford, J. D., & Johnson, M. K. Consideration of some problems of comprehension. In W. Chase (Ed.), *Visual information processing*. New York: Academic Press, 1973.

Bruner, J. S., & Potter, M. C. Interference in visual rcognition. *Science,* 1964, *144,* 424–425.

Chafe, W. L. Givenness, contrastiveness, definiteness, subjects, topics, and point of view. In C. N. Li (Ed.), *Subject and topic.* New York: Academic Press, 1976.

Head, H. *Studies in neurology* (2 vols.). London: Frowde, 1920.

Kant, E. *Critique of pure reason* (2nd ed.; N. Kemp Smith, trans.). London: Macmillan, 1963 (originally published, 1787).

Kaplan, R. M. A general syntactic processor. In R. Rustin (Ed.), *Natural language processing.* New York: Algorithmics Press, 1973.

Minsky, M. A framework for representing knowledge. In P. H. Winston (Ed.), *The psychology of computer vision.* New York: McGraw-Hill, 1975.

Moore, J., & Newell, A. How can Merlin understand? In L. W. Gregg (Ed.), *Knowledge and cognition.* Potomac, Md.: Lawrence Erlbaum Associates, 1973.

Norman, D. A., Rumelhart, D. E., & The LNR Research Group. *Explorations in cognition.* San Francisco: Freeman, 1975.

Palmer, S. E. Visual perception and world knowledge: Notes on a model of sensory–cognitive interaction. In D. A. Norman, D. E. Rumelhart, & The LNR Research Group, *Explorations in cognition.* San Francisco: Freeman, 1975.

Rumelhart, D. E. Notes on a schema for stories. In D. G. Bobrow & A. M. Collins (Eds.), *Representation and understanding: Studies in cognitive science.* New York: Academic Press, 1975.

Rumelhart, D. E. Understanding and summarizing brief stories. In D. LaBerge & S. J. Samuels (Eds.), *Basic processes in reading: Perception and comprehension.* Hillsdale, N.J.: Lawrence Erlbaum Associates, 1977.

Rumelhart, D. E., & Norman, D. A. Accretion, tuning and restructuring: Three modes of learning. In J. W. Cotton & R. L. Klatzky (Eds.), *Semantic factors in cognition.* Hillsdale, N.J.: Lawrence Erlbaum Associates 1978.

Rumelhart, D. E., & Ortony, A. The representation of knowledge in memory. In R. C. Anderson, R. J. Spiro, & W. E. Montague (Eds.), *Schooling and the acquisition of knowledge.* Hillsdale, N.J.: Lawrence Erlbaum Associates, 1977.

Schank, R. C., & Abelson, R. P. Scripts, plans, and knowledge. *Advance Papers of the Fourth International Joint Conference on Artificial Intelligence.* Tbilisi, Georgia, USSR, 1975.

Schank, R. C., & Abelson, R. P. *Scripts, plans, goals, and understanding.* Hillsdale, N.J.: Lawrence Erlbaum Associates, 1977.

Spiro, R. J. Remembering information from text: The "state of schema" approach. In R. C. Anderson, R. J. Spiro, & W. E. Montague (Eds.), *Schooling and the acquisition of knowledge.* Hillsdale, N.J.: Lawrence Erlbaum Associates, 1977.

Tulving, E., & Thomson, D. M. Encoding specificity and retrieval processes in episodic memory. *Psychological Review,* 1973, *80,* 352–373.

Wason, P. C., & Johnson-Laird, P. N. *Psychology of reasoning.* Cambridge, Mass.: Harvard University Press, 1972.

Williams, M. D. *The process of retrieval from very long term memory.* Unpublished doctoral dissertation, University of California, San Diego, 1977.

Winograd, T. Frame representations and the declarative–procedural controversy. In D. G. Bobrow & A. M. Collins (Eds.), *Representation and understanding: Studies in cognitive science.* New York: Academic Press, 1975.

3 Multiple Theory Formation in Speech and Reading

William A. Woods
Center for the Study of Reading,
Bolt Beranek and Newman Inc.

OVERVIEW

High-level perceptual tasks such as reading, speech understanding, and visual scene interpretation are characterized by the need to dicover a structured interpretation that accounts for the stimuli present. This process is prerequisite to deciding what has been perceived and thus precedes whatever process decides what to do with the resulting perception—what significance to attach to it, whether to remember it, how to incorporate it into the knowledge base of the perceiver, and so on. In this chapter, I attempt to make the case that the process of arriving at an interpretation of the input involves the formation and evaluation of many alternative partial hypotheses about the input and that this process goes on largely below the level of introspective awareness of the perceiver. Even though skilled reading involves a variety of "metacognitive" strategies (Brown, Chapter 19, this volume), in normal reading these processes are themselves invoked without conscious attention to the process of doing so.

I focus on the problem of reading and draw on insights and analogies from work in Natural Language Parsing and Continuous Speech Understanding. Because I do not have space here to give an adequate introduction to all of the background material that I would like to use, I will instead refer the reader to three previous papers: Woods, 1973a; Woods, 1975a; and Woods, 1975b. The most recent material on speech understanding is unfortunately only contained in technical reports. I recommend in particular the BBN final report (Woods, Bates, Brown, Bruce, Cook, Klovstad, Makhoul, Nash-Webber, Schwartz, Wolf, & Zue, 1976), vols. I, III, IV, and V. For a brief overview of the BBN speech understanding system, see Wolf and Woods (1977).

MULTIPLE HYPOTHESES, BACKTRACKING, AND NONDETERMINISM

Many of our intuitions about techniques for dealing with multiple hypotheses come from work in parsing algorithms for formal grammars. This is an area in which both theoretical results in automata theory and empirical results from programmed parsers are available. Other areas in which such insights can be gained are formal theorem proving, machine vision, and continuous speech understanding. Perhaps the earliest and most widely known mechanism for handling multiple hypotheses is the predictive analyzer or pushdown store parser (Kuno & Oettinger, 1963), using backtracking to handle the possibility of multiple alternatives.

A pushdown store parser is essentially an algorithm for analyzing a sentence in terms of rules such as "a sentence consists of a noun phrase followed by a verb phrase." It operates by using a stack or "pushdown store" of words and phrases that are expected to occur in the sentence and at each step compares the next input word against the top item on the stack, either finding a match between the current word and the predicted category, finding that the current word is incompatible with the predicted category, or expanding a predicted phrase type to a sequence of words and phrases that would realize it (in which case the new predicted categories replace the one from which they are derived on the stack). The stack operates very much like the spring-loaded stacks of dishes and trays that one finds in some cafeterias (from which it derives its name). Backtracking refers to the process of saving enough information before making a choice among alternatives (in this case before choosing a particular rule to expand a phrase type) so that, at a later time, the situation prior to the choice can be reconstructed and a different choice selected.

For example, if a backtracking parser encounters a word that can be either a noun or a verb in a context in which both nouns and verbs would be acceptable (albeit with different interpretations), then enough information is saved to remember the current position in the sentence and all of the decisions made so far before making one of the choices—i.e., treating the word as a noun. Subsequently, if this choice does not lead to an acceptable complete parsing (or if all possible parsings are required), the saved information is restored and the other choice is tried.

Backtracking is not the only way of implementing an algorithm for exploring multiple alternatives, however. Other methods involve the creation of separate virtual processes for each of the alternative choices. These processes can then be run in parallel or in some prioritized order. (A virtual process behaves conceptually as if it were an ongoing process but may in fact be competing for time and resources with other such processes so that the

3. MULTIPLE THEORY FORMATION 61

number of processes actually receiving resources at any given moment may be fewer than the number of "virtual" processes that are conceptually active.")

A general method for specifying and discussing algorithms for this kind of processing of multiple alternatives is to treat the algorithms as procedures, one of whose basic instruction types has the meaning "choose one of the following alternatives:...." Such procedures are "executed" by an interpreter that systematically considers all possible combinations of such choices, either by backtracking or by the method of separate virtual processes. Such algorithms are referred to as *nondeterministic* algorithms, not because their eventual behavior is not determined but because the specification of the exact order in which the various alternatives will be considered and the mechanism by which the combinations of choices will be enumerated are not overtly specified as part of the algorithm.

Parsing natural language is fundamentally a nondeterministic process. That is, it is not possible to make all of the correct decisions based solely on local information. Rather tentative decisions must be made and explored to see if their consequences are plausible. For example, the decision as to whether a given word is being used as a noun or a verb depends on whether a complete parsing can be found under one or the other of the two assumptions. Thus, *Fly* in Fly fishing is fun" is a noun (used as a modifier), whereas in "Fly fishing equipment to Lakeview Lodge as soon as possible," it is a verb. (If you required a few seconds to find the correct interpretation of this sentence due to an initial incorrect interpretation of "Fly fishing," then you have experienced what is known as the "garden-path" phenomenon.) Occasionally, several choices will lead to a complete parsing, in which case the sentence is ambiguous (as in "The girl guides fish," which could either be a statement about what girl guides do in their spare time or a description of a shepherdess for fish).

Predictive parsing is an intuitively satisfying analogy for thinking about human sentence processing because it seems to correspond well to our introspective awareness of stages of the parsing process. Notably, if the sentence is stopped at some point, we can generate a completion; in general, we know what kinds of words to expect next at each point and, occasionally, we are aware of having made a false early decision and having to back up to look for another alternative (in garden-path sentences like the one mentioned earlier). One soon gets into difficulty with this analogy, however, because systematic predictive analysis for a natural language grammar makes many more extraneous, tentative excursions down false parsing paths than people seem to. Also, the time required by people to recover from a garden path seems to be much shorter than that required by a backtracking parser (Collins & Quillian, 1971). In the Artificial Intelligence field, this has given rise to a search for techniques to make the enumeration of parse paths more selective (e.g., by using "semantic" information) in order to correspond more closely to the level of backtracking that we are aware of when we read. In other quarters, it has given rise to the labeling of such processes as "Gestalt," treating the process as a black box whose internal workings one does not attempt to understand.

In this chapter I attempt to make the case for another account, namely, that the amount of partial hypothesis formation that a person actually performs in such tasks is far more than it seems and that the bulk of it occurs below the level of introspective awareness. I draw largely on experience in constructing speech understanding systems. In the speech understanding task, it is relatively easy to make the case that there is a great deal of hypothesis formation and testing required even to know what words have been heard, much less how they are to be parsed and interpreted. However, most of this processing takes place exceedingly fast and without conscious effort. Once it is realized that the human perceptual processes are capable of making large numbers of alternative hypotheses and choosing among them on the basis of relatively high-level plausibility judgments—all without conscious effort or awareness—it is not difficult to imagine such capabilities being used in reading and other high-level perceptual tasks.

CHARACTERISTICS OF THE
SPEECH UNDERSTANDING PROCESS

A naive view of speech understanding might consider it as a process of successively recognizing speech sounds (called phonemes), grouping phonemes into words, parsing word sequences into sentences, and finally interpreting the meanings of those sentences. However, considerable experience now indicates that the acoustic evidence present in the original speech signal is not sufficient to support such a process (Woods & Makhoul, 1974). For sentences recorded from continuous speech, it is not generally possible to reliably determine the phonetic identity of the individual phonemes (or even to be sure how many phonemes are present) using the acoustic evidence alone. Experiments in spectrogram reading (Klatt & Stevens, 1971) indicate that the reliability of such determinations can be increased by use of the redundancy provided by knoweldge of the vocabulary, the syntax of the language, and semantic and pragmatic considerations.

Tape-splicing experiments (Wanner, 1973) seem to indicate that this low-level acoustic ambiguity is an inherent characteristic of speech and not just a limitation of human spectrogram reading. Specifically, intelligibility of inividual words excised from continuous speech is very low, but the intelligibility increases when sequences of two or three words are used. It appears that the additional constraint of having to make sense in a larger context begins to resolve the ambiguities that were present when only the local acoustic evidence was considered. This processing, however, happens below the level of introspection and has all of the subjective characteristics of a wholistic or Gestalt phenomenon. That is, if a sufficiently long sequence of continuous speech is heard, its correct interpretation usually appears immediately and effortlessly, without conscious awareness of the details of the process. The vast majority of our spoken communications are understood in this manner, and it is markedly contrasted with those cases in which an utterance is garbled sufficiently to invoke conscious effort to decide what was said.

THEORIES, MONITORS, NOTICES, AND EVENTS—A COMPUTATIONAL FRAMEWORK FOR PERCEPTION

The BBN speech understanding system (Woods et al., 1976; Wolf & Woods, 1977) has evolved within a general framework for viewing perceptual processes. Central to this framework is an entity called a *theory*. A theory presents a particular hypothesis about some or all of the sensory stimuli that are present. Perception is viewed as the process of forming a believable, coherent theory that can account for all the stimuli. This is arrived at by successive refinement and extension of partial theories until a best complete theory is found.

In general, a high-level perception process requires the ability to recognize any member of a potentially infinite class of perceptible objects that are constructed out of elementary constituents according to known rules. That is, the object perceived is generally a compound object, constructed from members of a finite set of elementary constituents according to some kind of well-formedness rules. These elementary constituents, as well as the relationships among them that are invoked in the well-formedness rules, must be directly perceptible. Thus, a perceptual system must incorprate some basic epistemological assumptions about the kinds of things that it can perceive and the rules governing their assembly. The well-formedness rules can be used to reject impossible interpretations of the input stimuli and may also be usable to predict other constituents that could be present if a given partial theory is correct.

This perception framework assumes mechanisms for using subsets of the input stimuli to form initial "seed" hypotheses for certain elementary constituents (stimulus-driven hypothesization) and mechanisms for deriving hypotheses for additional compatible constituents from a partial theory

(theory-driven, or predicted, hypothesization)[1]. It also assumes mechanisms for verifying a hypothesis against the input stimuli and evaluating the well-formedness of a compound hypothesis to assign it some measure of quality and/or likelihood. A theory may therefore be thought of as a hypothesis that has been evaluated in this way and assigned a measure of confidence.

In the case of speech understanding, a theory, can range from an elementary hypothesis that a particular word is present at a particular point in the input (a *word match*) to a complete hypothesis of a covering sequence of words with a complete syntactic and semantic interpretation. (In general, a theory can be a set of compatible word hypotheses with gaps between them and with partial syntactic and semantic interpretations.) A partial theory may be able to generate predictions for appropriate words or classes of words either adjacent to the words already hypothesized or possibly elsewhere in the utterance.

Predictions are dealt with in our computational framework by two kinds of devices: *monitors,* which are passively waiting for expected constituents, and *proposals,* which are elemntary hypotheses that are to be evaluated against the input. Proposals result in actively seeking stimuli that would verify them, whereas monitors passively wait for such hypotheses to be formed. The functioning of monitors assumes that there is an organizing structure into which all derived partial hypotheses are placed as they are discovered and that the monitors can essentially set "traps" in this structure for the kinds of events for which they are watching. This is to be contrasted with continuous parallel evaluation of special processes (frequently called *demons*) to watch for expected patterns in the input stream. Monitors perform no computation until and unless some other process makes an entry of the kind they are waiting for in some data structure.

The functioning of monitors is illustrated by an early speech understanding system dealing with concentrations of chemical elements in lunar rocks. There, for example, a word match for *concentration* would set monitors on the concept nodes for SAMPLE and CHEMICAL ELEMENT in the semantic network. If a word such as *Helium* was subsequently found anywhere else in the utterance, a check in the semantic network starting with helium would lead to the superset category CHEMICAL ELEMENT where it would wake up the monitor from *concentration,* thus detecting the coincidence of a detected hypothesis and a predicted hypothesis (Nash-Webber, 1975).

---

[1]Our notion of stimulus-driven hypothesization is essentially the same as that of bottom-up processing referred to in many discussion of such processes. However, our notion of theory-driven hypothesization is slightly different from the sense usually given to top-down processing in that it does not necessarily imply any global (*topmost*) hypothesis but only predictability by some other hypothesis, which may itself have been derived bottom-up. The terms *top-down* and *bottom-up* in this sense come from the literature on formal parsing algorithms.

When a monitor is triggered, an *event* is created calling for the evaluation of a new hypothesis and the creation of a new theory if the hypothesis is not rejected. In general, a number of events are competing for service by the processor at any moment. In human perception, there may be full parallel processing of such events, but in a serial machine, these events must be queued and given processing resources on the basis of some priority ordering. (Even in human perception, there is probably some sort of priority allocation of resources, because various kinds of interference can occur.) In our computational framework, events are maintained on a queue in order of priority, the top event being processed at each step.

The processing of an event can result in new proposals being made, new monitors being set, and existing monitors being triggered to produce new events. Because so much hinges on the event chosen for processing, a major issue is that of assigning priorities to events in order to find the most likely interpretation of the input. In the BBN system, priority scores are assigned on the basis of Bayesian estimates of the probabilities of the competing theories, and certain control strategies and priority scoring metrics can be guaranteed to discover the most probable interpretation of the input.

CONTROL STRATEGIES

The previous discussion leaves open issues such as when seeds should be formed, how many should be considered, should all seeds be worked on in parallel, and so on. We refer to these issues as control issues. They have been critically important in computerized speech understanding systems. In the BBN system, for example, there are a variety of different control strategies that all fit within the paradigm mentioned earlier. Table 3.1 illustrates one class of strategies in which seeds are formed anywhere in the utterance that sufficiently salient word matches are found. The table shows the seed events formed as a result of an initial scan of an utterance for high-likelihood word matches anywhere in the utterance. Each theory is assigned a score expressing its likelihood of being correct (actually a logarithm of the ratio of the likelihood of the acoustic evidence given the theory over the a priori likelihood of that evidence occurring independently). The region of the utterance covered by the theory is indicated by specifying its left and right boundary positions in a list of potential boundary positions (the left end of the utterance is numbered 0 and in this case the right end is numbered 18). The exclamation marks indicate the theories that are actually part of the correct interpretation.

For this general class of control strategies, referred to as *middle-out*, theories are grown by starting with a seed word, asking a higher-level linguistic component to predict categories of words that can occur on either

TABLE 3.1
Seed Events for Middle-Out Strategy

NO.	SCORE	REGION	THEORY
1	0	11–14	ADD
2	0	4–7	NEED
3	–.455	0–3	SHOW!
4	–.605	12–17	TRIP
5	–.727	1–5	ROME
6	–.769	8–11	THERE
7	–1.25	12–18	TRIP-S!
8	–1.47	0–5	SHELLY
9	–1.65	15–17	END
10	–1.72	11–14	AND
11	–1.73	1–5	ANN
12	–1.74	0–5	CHEYENNE
13	–2.19	8–14	BERT
14	–2.26	2–6	ANY
15	–2.82	0–5	SOME

+15 ADDITIONAL EVENTS

side of it, asking a lexical retrieval component to find the best matching words in those categories on the appropriate sides, and generating events for each such word found to extend the theory by adding that word. Thus, events will be placed on the event queue to add words both on the left and on the right ends of given theories. These "new word" events will compete with each other and with the remaining seed events on the basis of scores to determine which event will be processed next, causing the processor to sometimes continue adding words to a given theory and at other times to shift its processing to a different competing theory.

Table 3.2 shows the sequence of theories that are formed as a result of this process, starting with the event queue of Table 3.1. Notice that the final theory is developed in this case by working independently on two different portions of the utterance starting from the seeds *show* and *trips*. The final theory in Table 3.2 is in fact derived from a kind of event called a *collision* event that combines the theories *show me* (9) and *trips* (13) when they both notice the word *her* filling the gap between them. This event is formed during the processing of Theory 13, although its score is such that it does not reach the top of the queue until Theory 23.

Woods et al. (1976), Vols. I and III, discuss control strategy issues in more detail and describe several other control strategies, including a "hybrid" strategy that performs middle-out recognition on a bounded initial portion of an utterance and processes the rest left to right. The hybrid strategy is also discussed in Woods (1977). Among the various possible control strategies for speech understanding, the middle-out strategies are probably the most

TABLE 3.2
Theories Formed for Middle-Out Strategies

Theory Number[a]	Theory[b]
1	ADD
2	NEED
3	SHOW!
4 (3)	[SHOW!
5 (4)	[SHOW ALL
6 (3)	SHOW ALL
7	TRIP
8	ROME
9 (4)	[SHOW ME!
10 (3)	SHOW ME!
11 (7)	HER TRIP
12	TRIP-S!
13 (12)	TRIP-S]!
14 (13)	HER TRIP-S]!
15 (12)	HER TRIP-S!
16	SHELLY
17 (16)	[SHELLY
18 (9,7)	[SHOW ME HER TRIP
19 (10,7)	SHOW ME HER TRIP
20 (11)	HER TRIP IS
21 (20)	HER TRIP IS]
22 (20)	OF HER TRIP IS
23 (9,13)	[SHOW ME HER TRIP-S]!

[a]Numbers in parentheses after a theory number are the numbers of preceding theories from which the indicated theory was formed by adding a new word. Brackets in the Theory column indicate theories that include the hypothesis that the left or right ends of the utterance have been reached.

[b]Indenting of items under Theory heading corresponds to the position of the theory in the input utterance.

relevant as analogs for the reading process, which can involve considerable jumping around in a text. None of the speech strategies, however, are likely to model the details of the reading process exactly without some adaptation.

SUBCONSCIOUS PROCESSING OF ALTERNATIVES IN SPEECH AND READING

Essential in all of the various control strategies is that, at any given time, there are a number of incomplete, competing possible interpretations requiring a strategy to determine when processing resources should shift from one partial theory to another. One might initially suspect that a listener would be consciously aware of such competing possible theories and that shifting from one to another would correspond to the noticeable phenomena experienced with garden-path sentences. However, our, experience with speech under-standing systems indicates that the construction and evaluation of competing partial hypotheses is far more prevalent than our introspective awareness makes apparent. It seems, then, that there must be some process for handling multiple alternative hypotheses that is subconscious and highly efficient (for perhaps a limited class of phenomena), and there is some other process that makes alternatives visible to our perception (perhaps for a more difficult class of phenomena or for those that have not been frequent enough to have been "compiled" into our subconscious process).

This distinction between conscious and subconscious processing is, of course, not an original observation. For example, Becker (1972) has referred to the former, subconscious processes as intermediate level cognition. It is likely that the bulk of our intelligent processing consists of this kind of subconscious intermediate-level processing and that the "thinking" of which we are aware at the conscious level is merely the tip of the iceberg. Conscious processing seems to be largely sequential and relatively slow, whereas the subconscious processes must (by virtue of the information-processing tasks that they accomplish) be either highly parallel or exceptionally fast (or both). Other examples of the kinds of subconscious processes to which I refer are the retrieval of an association given a stimulus and the recognition of a face.

I argue that the reading process contains large components of this kind of subconscious processing. In general, a reader is aware only of the final interpretation that he places on a sentence in a text; he is not aware of all of the intermediate states of the derivation of that interpretation, all of the local ambiguities that were resolved by later context, and the accessing of factual memory to evaluate plausibility of competing partial interpretations. Never-theless, a close examination of the information processing required to arrive at the final interpretation indicates that large amounts of such processing must be going on. By way of example, consider the resolution of the antecedent of the pronoun *they* in the following pair of sentences adapted from Winograd (1971):

1. The city council refused to grant the women a parade permit because they feared violence.
2. The city council refused to grant the women a parade permit because they advocated violence.

This resolution appears to happen effortlessly, but the criteria that are needed to make the selection indicate that a very sophisticated inferential process is acting here below the level of awareness. It is not sufficient to choose the preferred interpretations ("council feared violence" in the first case and "women advocated violence" in the second) on the basis of some simple strength of association, between *council* and *fear* or between *women* and *advocate*. If anything, one's a priori expectations for such associations would go the other way. It would appear that on a priori grounds, women fearing violence would be at least as plausible as city councils fearing violence. It is only at the level at which one begins to evaluate what would be plausible grounds for a city council to make a refusal that the preference emerges. This implies a process in which very high-level evaluations of alternative interpretations of the sentence are required before fairly low-level ambiguities are resolved. It does not seem possible even to formulate the necessary question to resolve the ambiguity until both possible interpretations have been formulated and elaborated at least to the level of justification of grounds for refusal. It is clearly not the case that a process must be simple and easy just because it happens in the head very rapidly and without apparent effort. In subsequent sections we will consider many more examples of this kind of interference in reading.

IMPLICATIONS FOR
PSYCHOLOGICAL MODELS OF READING

This picture of the perception process as involving many competing partial hypotheses that are formed and evaluated below the level of introspection has significant implications for the design of experiments to investigate the reading process. For example, it is possible that a large percentage of the reaction time for understanding sentences is due to the evaluation of competing alternatives and not due at all to aspects of the correct interpretation. Thus, two different sentences or texts having some identified difference in the structure of their correct interpretation(s) that one would like to investigate may also have differences in reaction time due to extraneous differences in the number or complexity of competing partial hypotheses that are not part of the final interpretation.

To make matters worse, the effect of such competition depends critically on whether the process for handling alternatives is a serial or parallel process. As a simple example, consider a parallel processing control strategy that at each step extends the n most likely theories in the event queue for some number n (perhaps large). Then, up to n different theories may be pursued as alternatives without introducing reaction-time delay, but alternatives in excess of n would introduce delays.

The speech understanding models also predict that a favored competitor may be found much sooner than an unfavored competitor and that the reaction time for a given interpretation may be longer if the correct interpretation is delayed by a partial theory that looks better locally but does not extend as well.

In the human brain, the implementation of such capabilities may not correspond to that of a queue sorted by priority. Other "implementations" could involve a large number of active memory elements that interact among themselves in such a way that the highest priority member is selected for processing, or resources could be allocated to all pending events in proportion to their priorities, and so on. Thus, timing predictions cannot be made directly from the performance of computerized systems running on serial machines but have to be made from an extrapolation of such behavior to hypothesized mechanisms in the brain. Unfortunately, the number of degrees of freedom in such extrapolation is large, so working out a psychologically verifiable model of the process is likely to be lengthy with many intermediate models that have to be formulated and then rejected.

A CLOSE LOOK AT SOME READING MATERIAL

Having now given, I hope, sufficient reason to believe that both in speech understanding and in reading there are significant inferential processes that occur below the level of introspection and that the characteristics of these processes are quite different from those of conscious inferential processes (especially with respect to apparent degree of perceived difficulty vs. the amount of information processing actually done), I now look in some detail at the reading process.

I present fragments from two passages with significantly different levels of reading difficulty, accompanied by an analysis of some of the inferential problems that must be solved for their full understanding. Each fragment comes from a passage of four to six paragraphs that is relatively self contained but has apparently been extracted from some larger work. The passages are from the Riverside Research Institute Reading Competency Test (Riverside Research Institute, 1974).

Passage 1

Taffy

Taffy is a puppy. She is small. She is soft. She is sweet. What if Taffy belonged to you? Would you know what to do? Read this story. You will find out how to take care of Taffy.

Taffy sleeps a lot. She needs a place to rest. Take a large box and cut out one side. Put in something soft to lie on. This will be Taffy's bed. Put it in a warm place. Keep it dry and clean.

The apparent purpose of this story is to let a child know what having a puppy is like. This includes preparing the child to empathize with the puppy and take care of it. The story assumes knoweldge of what a puppy is. It adds to the concept, if not already present, the attributes of smallness, softness, and sweetness, (Notice that the child must conclude that sweet is not a taste but a personality attribute.) Prominent in the story are rhetorical questions, designed to make the child think, to extrapolate from the given attributes. The story sets up the impression of holding a small, soft puppy. Then it asks rhetorically whether the child would know what to do with a puppy. The intention apparently is to set the child up in the imaginary situation of having a puppy and not knowing what to do with it. The story then suggests a resolution of the dilemma—namely, read the story. The result will be that the child will know how to take care of a puppy.

Although the entire story is written in terms of a particular puppy, Taffy, it is clear that what the reader is to get from it is to apply to all puppies. How is this distinguished from, say, a story about Lassie, in which the story is intended to give attributes of a particular dog rather than dogs in general?

The rest of the story, of which the foregoing is only a brief excerpt, is a conditional program for taking care of a puppy. It involves following directions. The story might be read for general information, in which case the goal of the story is for the child to remember at some later time something about taking care of puppies. It could also be read with an immediate need at hand and followed like a cookbook. Woods (1977) gives a more detailed, sentence-by-sentence account of some of the characteristics of this passage.

Passage 2

Growth

Growth is characterized by organization. Group growth charts show many age level uniformities and predictable age level changes. Differences between individuals in growth certainly exist. However, most individuals tend to be only slightly variable in their rate of growth from one age level to another.

This story is much more abstract and sophisticated than the Taffy story. It is apparently intended to impart to readers some general information about the growth process for some indefinite future use. The passage could possibly be an excerpt from a biological text book. It is characterized by a much greater necessity for readers to suspend judgment on possible interpretations of portions of the passage until they have read further. Among other things, it is characterized by a large number of noun–noun modification constructions (*group growth charts, age level uniformities,* etc.), in which a noun is used to modify another noun. The intended meaning of such constructions is critically dependent on world knowledge of the habitual relationships between the two nouns. An account of some of the difficulties in just the first two sentences of this passage follows:

1. *Growth is characterized by organization.*
    This sentence introduces the topic "growth" and focuses on its organizational aspect. It doesn't say much as a factual assertion. If the reader asks himself a great deal about this question out of context, he may try to instantiate examples of kinds of growth and try to find instances of organization associated with them. In all likelihood, however, he will do little with this sentence but go on to see what's coming next.

2. *Group growth charts show many age level uniformities and predictable age level changes.*
    This is a difficult sentence syntactically. It has three noun–noun modifier constructions that require inference to determine their meaning. If the phrase *group growth charts* means something to the reader as a technical term in some field, then the sentence is considerably easier, but otherwise, he is left wondering "groups of what?" (possibly people, but the story doesn't say). The most general possible assumption is growth of organisms (or perhaps even more general still—including institutions, cultures, empires, and so on—all of this is consistent with the very abstract first statement, and it is possible that the vagueness and abstractness of the first sentence is intended to make such general interpretations of the second possible).

    The phrases *age level uniformities* and *age level changes* are again considerably more easy to understand if they are previously known technical phrases than if they have to be figured out from scratch. In the latter case, the reader needs to decide whether the phrases use the word *age* to modify the phrases *level uniformities* and *level changes* or whether the phrase *age level* modifies *uniformities* and *changes*. In this case, we assume that the reader is familiar with the concept of *age level* and would for that reason choose the latter interpretation, because he is not likely to find a plausible reference for the phrase *level uniformities*. (Note that *level changes* is a perfectly good phrase but would require a sub-question—"what kinds of levels?") The sentences would be more properly punctuated as "age-level uniformities" and "age-level changes", but such punctuation is frequently missing and a good reader is expected to be able to understand the phrases anyway. The difficulty is greater without the hyphens, because it opens up the possibility of different interpretations and requires the reader to resolve the ambiguity using semantic and pragmatic considerations.

The remaining sentences of the "Growth" passage are discussed at a similar level of detail in Woods (1977). Interesting observations include the way that Sentence 3 sets up expectations for what is to come (and possibly constrains the possible interpretations of previous sentences), the interaction between *certainly* in Sentence 3 and *however* in Sentence 4, and the varying degrees of difficulty posed by this passage to readers of different levels of skill—especially the fact that certain readers of intermediate skill may have more trouble than less skilled readers who effectively ignore some of the cues and jump to conclusions.

Notice that the purpose of this story seems to be to build up a fairly abstract model of how growth occurs. Readers are not asked to do anything immediately except somehow to assimilate the story. The purpose of the readers in reading the story thus becomes of paramount importance, and if their purpose is to prepare themselves to perform in some way in the future using a model of how growth occurs, then they are likely to do different things in reading the story than if their purpose is, let us say, to be prepared to answer questions at the end of the passage or to fill in missing blanks in the story. Of course, if this passage is read by elementary school readers, it is likely that they do not have the goal to prepare for some specific future performance, because it is likely that they cannot even imagine a specific use for the information. However, the author may have such a use in mind in writing it. In particular, the author might be writing for adolescents who may be concerned that their own rate of growth is too slow or too fast and may want to convey such a growth model so that such readers can understand what is happening to them. It seems likely that two students, one of whom is concerned about a slow rate of growth and another who is determined to become a biologist, will get completely different things out of this story.

SOME DETAILS OF THE READING PROCESS

The previous discussion has outlined some of the inferences that need to be made in the course of understanding these two passages. However, it sheds little light on how those inferences might be organized and carried out. Experience with computerized language-understanding programs and speech understanding systems can give us some insight into how these processes might happen, although the picture at the moment is far from complete. In the remainder of this chapter, I discuss in more detail some of the low-level decisions that have to be made and alternative hypotheses that have to be generated and considered, pointing out examples in which existing techniques in natural language processing by computers have been developed to handle similar problems. I consider in particular the first two sentences of the "Growth" passage.

The first sentence "Growth is characterized by organization," is not difficult syntactically. It is a straightforward, passive sentence with little potential for syntactic ambiguity. The first word can only be a noun, the second is unambiguously a verb (although it is not clear after only two words whether it is the main verb of a copular sentence or an auxiliary verb of a passive). The fact that the third word is a past participle resolves the sense of *is* to that of an auxiliary in a passive sentence. Woods (1970) gives a detailed account of how ATN grammars can be used to recognize and disambiguate this main-verb/auxiliary distinction. After this, *by* is unambiguously a preposition (although whether it is indicating the agent of the action or introducing something beside which an action takes place is not unambiguous). *Organization* is unambiguously a noun. Hence, the discovery of the syntactic structure of this sentence is straightforward and involves little nondeterminism. Every local syntactic ambiguity is resolved by the immediately following word.

What the sentence means, however, is something else again. Both noun phrases in this sentence are mass nouns (nouns that can be used without determiners in the singular form as if they denoted a substance, as opposed to count nouns, which can be counted). When used in the singular with no determiner, they are to be interpreted as referring to the general concepts that they name. (*A growth, growths,* or *an organization* would get completely different interpretations; the difference is flagged by the way the words are used syntactically.)

Growth, as was pointed out previously, can name several different concepts that the reader might have in his head. If he has only one such concept, then the reading task is easier (although it may get difficult later on if the concept he has is not the one the author intended). If he has several, then the interpretation of the sentence is semantically ambiguous with respect to the reference of this phrase. This can be represented temporarily by associating with the noun phrase a list of alternative possible interpretations (such as is done in the semantic interpretation procedure of the LUNAR system [Woods, 1973b]).

The interpretation of *organization* appears to be somewhat different, largely because of its absence from surface subject position in the sentence. (Notice that "Organization characterizes growth" would not have the same effect as the initial sentence of this passage.) The correct interpretation of the sentence is an assertion about growth, and what is being asserted is that it has many of the properties associated with organization. That is, *organization* names a concept in which certain characteristics are to be found that are to be associated now with growth.

The differences in interpretation of the two noun phrases are due to their position in context as different arguments of the verb *characterize* and as different role fillers in the surface structure of the sentence. The LUNAR system handles such differences in interpretation as a function of context by providing context-dependent parameters to the routine that computes possible interpretations of constituents. These parameters are used to determine the interpretation rules to be used for interpreting a constituent. (It is possible, in general, for different possible higher interpretations to call for the interpretation of a constituent in different ways, so provisions are required to keep alternative interpretations of different constituents coordinated with each other.)

For interpreting the clause as a whole, a semantic pattern for *characterize* (or perhaps for *is characterized by*) is required. This is a fairly abstract and somewhat vague semantic relation. My edition of Webster's gives two senses of "characterize": (1) to describe the character or quality of—DELINEATE; and (2) to be a characteristic of—DISTINGUISH. Leaving aside the problems of the adequacy of such dictionary definitions, I interpret these definitions to focus on two senses of "characterize"—one in which sufficient conditions are given, as in "four equal length sides and right angles characterize a square," and the other in which merely prominent characteristics or only some characteristics are given. Which of these two senses is chosen would make a big difference in what the reader believed the passage to say. In the first case, it would say that anything that was organized would be growth—obviously false if one knows anything about growth and organization. The second interpretation is that organization is a prominent characteristic of growth. Readers must decide whether this sentence is trying to inform them of an astounding new fact or is merely asserting organization as a property of growth. Presumably the second choice is more plausible than the former.

In the LUNAR system, such ambiguity of word sense was indicated by having several semantic interpretation rules associated with a given head word, both of which might match a given constituent being interpreted. Thus, a procedure for generating both possible interpretations is straightforward. The problem of evaluating which of two interpretations is more plausible is more difficult, and no computer system at the moment makes such plausibility evaluations. Almost all current computer models of such processes make all-or-nothing decisions that an interpretation is either possible or impossible, with no shades in between.

One is tempted to say that the earlier choice is obvious (and implicitly, therefore, easy), but it is not clear exactly how far each of the two alternative interpretations has to be elaborated before the choice can be made. It seems to be necessary to actually formulate the erroneous interpretation and pose it as a question against one's knowledge in order to determine that it is false, and therefore, that the other interpretation is to be preferred.

Consider here the understanding task imposed on a reader who was not aware of both senses of the verb *characterize*. If the reader had only the correct interpretation, then the task would in fact be easier than for a more advanced reader who knew them both. On the other hand, if the reader had only the wrong sense, then the first sentence would be apparently false, and he or she would have a difficult time with the passage. An additional possibility is that the reader does not really understand what "characterize" means and interprets this sentence merely as establishing some kind of association between growth and organization, which, as it turns out, is about all that the sentence is intended to accomplish anyway. The primary role of this first sentence seems to be merely to establish growth as the topic and perhaps bring certain aspects of growth into focus (the organizational aspects). Thus, the reader can get the appropriate effect without fully understanding the sentence at all.

The second sentence, "Group growth charts show many age level uniformities and predictable age level changes," is far more complex syntactically as well as semantically. English syntax permits the use of nouns to modify other nouns in almost infinite profusion, but the interpretation of the meaning depends on nonsyntactic world knowledge. Moreover, when more than one such noun modifier is used, a structural syntactic ambiguity is introduced that requires world knowledge to resolve it.

If *group growth* occurred in isolation, the structure of a noun, *group,* modifying another noun, *growth,* would be the only possible syntactic interpretation. The determination of what it means would depend on the ability of the reader to identify a plausible relation between the two words (in this case, a group of things can grow, giving rise to an interpretation growth of a group"). However, in *group growth charts* it is ambiguous whether *group* modifies *growth charts* or *group growth* modifies *charts.*

The fact that charts are devices for depicting things gives *growth charts* the possible interpretation "charts depicting growth", and *group growth charts* the possible interpretation "charts depicting the growth of groups." However, the correct intepretation is probably "charts depicting growth by group" derived from *group* modifying *growth charts,* which requires that the reader either know about or imagine a kind of growth chart that would be distinguishable by having something to do with groups. This meaning is not very distinct from one of the possible interpretations of "charts depicting growth of groups" (indicating that the meaning of that structure is far from unique), and there is certainly not enough evidence at this point in the passage to resolve which of these different syntactic structures or which of their semantic interpretations is to be taken as the author's intention. The possibility of this phrase having any of several possible interpretations needs to be held open until more of the sentence is processed.

The process of deciding that *charts* is the last word in the noun phrase and that *show* is the main verb requires some further local ambiguity, although the fact that there is no determiner on the noun phrase requires that it end either with a plural noun or a mass noun, so that *show* could only be included if it were followed by another noun. (*Show* could be a noun instead of a verb, although it would be difficult to put a plausible interpretation on "Group growth charts show" as a noun phrase in this context.)

Exactly similar problems are encountered in interpreting "age level uniformities" and "predictable age level changes." This latter has even greater potential ambiguity due to the possibilities of *predictable* modifying *age, level,* or *changes* (e.g., "predictable changes in age level," "changes in the predictable age level," or "changes in the level of predictable age"). Somehow a reader makes a choice from among these different possible interpretations, usually without much conscious effort and usually correct (or at least one of several equally acceptable interpretations). In this case, none of the previously mentioned possibilities is correct, but instead, the thing that is doing the changing is elliptical (presumably growth or some growth parameter such as height or weight) and the correct interpretation is closer to "predictable changes (in some growth parameter) (as a function of) age level." Changes in a growth parameter as a function of age are certainly to be expected and therefore "predictable," whereas it is difficult to imagine anything on a growth chart that would correspond to a predictable age level (What would be doing the predicting?). Hence, a probable role of *predictable* is to modify the concept *age level changes* as a whole, although probably as a nonrestrictive modifier.

The above interpretation is not completely correct, since if a similar evaluation of *age level uniformities* is carried out, one is led to look for something that is uniform within an age level (again, presumably some growth parameter). The fact that conjunctions require some degree of parallelism between the two things being conjoined appears to demand that the role of the phrase *age level* should be the same in the two conjuncts. This slightly contradicts the otherwise well-motivated interpretation of "predictable age level changes" discussed above. Instead, an interpretation in which something changes within an age level rather than as a function of age level is required to maintain this parallelism. This can be met by replacing the relation "as a function of age level" that was postulated with "within an age level." This, however, removes the foundation for the argument justifying *predictable*. Looking further for a different justification, one can suppose that the charts somehow show predictable changes (i.e., the charts do the prediction?), and that *predictable* is a restrictive adjective here telling something about the kinds of changes that the charts show.

Computerized parsing algorithms using formal grammars for extensive subsets of English can systematically enumerate all of the possible ways of grouping the words in such noun–noun modifiers, but the process is usually combinatorically expensive and few computer models deal with such constructions. Attempts to use semantic information to guide a parser to construct only possible interpretations have been attempted, but nothing that begins to match the complexity of this discussion has currently been implemented. In general, the techniques for efficiently coupling syntactic and semantic knowledge in such situations are still being explored and the results are not in.

The discovery of the preferred interpretation in this example requires the judgment that all of the various ways of grouping the individual words in this noun–noun modifier sequence have implausible interpretations in this context (what a group growth chart would show) without the addition of an additional elliptical participation in the underlying representation (namely, what changes). The chain of reasoning justifying the correct choice is something like:

> I know that a growth chart should show changes in some growth parameter (that's what growth is) and not changes in growth (at least not directly—that's the derivative of what a growth chart would depict), so that must fill the "changee" role of the change being discussed. I recognize *age level* as a concept, so that is probably the role that *age* is filling and not a modifier of *level changes*. (*Level changes* is such a concept also, but I can find a plausible connection between *age level* and *changes* and cannot find one, or at least not a different one, between *age* and *level changes*). To relate *age level* to *changes* (in a growth parameter), I can take advantage of further knowledge (or imagination) about growth charts and speculate that the charts might be broken down by *age level*. That could be the role that *age level* is filling here, but that would violate parallelism of conjunction with the previous phrase. I could either try to reinterpret the previous phrase to establish parallelism or I could try the same relation between *age level* and *changes* that I used with *uniformities* before. The latter works, so I'll try that. Finally, *predictable* must modify *changes* rather than *age* or *age level,* because I can imagine charts somehow predicting changes more easily than their predicting ages.

Making this justification, as complicated as it seems, is relatively easy compared to the steps that were required to find it among all the other possibilities—formulating alternatives, making negative evaluations of some of them and differential choices among others, and finally settling on a chosen interpretation or several likely ones. Clearly, some readers may boggle in the face of such a passage and give up. Others may have the processing capacity to carry through the kind of analysis outlined here, either entirely or partially below the level of introspection. Still others may adopt some control strategy that does not consider all of the alternatives. Some of them may do so with strategies that are still likely to obtain the correct interpretation most of the time (assuming that there is one), whereas others may adopt erroneous strategies that doom them to misunderstanding. Even these latter may find interpretations that are intellectually satisfying to themselves, causing them to assert that they understood the passage, although what they have understood may be almost totally unrelated to what the passage says.

To close our discussion of the interpretation of this second sentence, let me point out that much of the reasoning that was used for selecting an intended interpretation for *predictable age level changes* depends on the fact that the intended interpretation must fit the context *Group growth charts show...* in the passage whose topic is known to be growth (of something). Effectively, many different possible interpretations had to be hypothesized and tried in this context for a possible fit. It appears that below the level of conscious awareness, a great deal more hypothesis enumeration and evaluation is going on than one would first suspect. Current computer models tend to be based on the assumption that the amount of such hypothesis formation can be controlled by having the right dominating "frame" or "script", because the cost of considering many alternative hypotheses on a serial computer is prohibitive. I suspect, however, that this is one of the differences between the serial computer and the human brain that is significant and that in this respect the characteristics of computers as models of human processing are misleading. Much of AI work will continue to be focused in this direction because of the desirability of getting computers to do such tasks, but I suspect that valid models of human performance will include parallel evaluation of alternative hypotheses.

CONCLUSION

The previous discussion does not go into detail at the level of recognition of individual words and letters, but one can model them with similar processes so that the overall reading process is a cascade of levels, each of which is making only tentative decisions. Each level will be formulating many alternative hypotheses that are to be partially selected by virtue of the degree to which they are compatible with hypotheses at other levels. For example, the syntactic component in the BBN speech understanding system makes many alternative hypotheses about possible syntactic paths through each of the theories that it is given to consider by the control component. Rumelhart (1977) gives a sketch of such a multilevel model based on the hypothesis structure of the Hearsay II speech understanding system (Lesser, Fennel, Erman, & Reddy, 1975).

I have tried to give, at a fairly concrete level, some picture of the hypothesis formation and evaluation processes that must go on during reading, although we are not normally aware of them. Many of these processes include inferences involving the kinds of metaknowledge discussed by A. Brown (Chapter 19, this volume), although the presentation here puts those processes in a somewhat different light. Here, I would stress that, although we have some knowledge about what we know and how we know it, this knowledge is based on introspective observation in much the same way that our knowledge of any aspect of the world is based on observation. We do not, in general, have any privileged access to some "internal truth" in this respect. We do have an awareness of certain internal mental events that are perceivable in much the same way that our external sense organs perceive the world, but they do not give us a complete awareness of our internal mental processing, and we have to learn the significance of what awareness they do give us. This is presumably why the metacognitive abilities come rather late in the stage of mental development.

Experiments repeatedly show that what appears to be memory is in fact reconstruction and that many "memories" about which we are absolutely certain turn out to be mistaken. Thus, our metaknowledge of what we know and how we know it is only as good as the model we have built up, based on our observations of our own performance, and cannot generally be relied on as absolute truth. Conversely, a correct understanding at the metalevel of how we should go about some mental process does not automatically translate into an ability to carry out that process. The attempt to consciously follow a set of instructions is not the same as fully incorporating those instructions into one's internal procedures. Examples of this phenomenon abound in such processes as learning to drive, to sail, to play chess, to solve mathematical problems, and so on. The process whereby repeated attempts to follow such instructions eventually "compiles" an internal procedure for doing the task and the means whereby conscious resolution to "do it different next time" actually modifies such procedures are almost totally mysterious. It is the attempt at modeling such (nonintrospectable) procedures by computer programs and abstract automata that I believe holds the key to understanding them, and it is this understanding that is the key to effective educational strategies.

I will not pretend that the results of Artificial Intelligence and Natural Language Processing research to date can give a complete account of the processes outlined in this chapter. However, they do provide a very rich inventory of analogies out of which one can construct hypothetical "brain computer architectures" and reasoning strategies that might model the information-processing operations that go on while reading. The major contribution that the AI approach has to offer, I think, is that it reveals and makes concrete information-processing steps that one might not otherwise have suspected. It can thus serve a very valuable function in the investigation of the reading process. On the other hand, one has to be careful in extrapolating results from computer models to human processes, because certain characteristics of any computer implementation will be determined by the nature of the computer on which they are implemented and may not be true of the "computer" in our heads.

In certain theoretical senses, investigations of abstract automata, such as Turing machines and abstract neural networks, can tell us what kinds of functions various subparts of the brain might perform and what their limitations might be. However, we do not yet have a complete enough account of human intelligence in such terms to derive practical results. Humans are presumably heir to the same limitations that Turing machines are known to have in that they cannot possess algorithms to solve formally unsolvable problems, but, beyond that, we cannot begin to derive predictions such as how much new information per minute can humans learn, how many facts can they store and remember, or any of the myriad practical questions that one would like to know to design effective educational pedagogies.

What AI can do is serve a role very much like that which theoretical physics or chemistry serve for their respective fields. It can suggest models that have theoretical characteristics that fit the known data and predict unknown data. As such models converge and begin to be supported by empirical study, they can be put to a wide range of practical uses, such as designing pedagogical strategies and training material. However, the path between where we are and the ability to make such predictions will require a great deal of work.

Computer models up to and including the sentence level are now relatively well articulated and can be used quite well for analogies with human processing. Above the sentence level, however, current capabilities of computer systems are limited, and recognition of the intended interpretation of stories has a number of characteristics that make it fundamentally more difficult than individual sentence parsing. Most current attempts at this level rely on preselected scripts that constrain the possible interpretations of the sentences that they will encounter to a microscopic fraction of what could otherwise occur. Because human beings have encyclopedic amounts of knowledge that are drawn on and used in understanding what they read, something much more than the current script-based theories will be required to deal with general human behavior. However, increasing interest in this problem by linguists, computational linguists, philosophers, psychologists, and researchers in artificial intelligence gives promise for the development of increasingly more adequate models of the overall reading process.

ACKNOWLEDGMENT

This research was supported by the National Institute of Education under Contract No. MS-NIE-C-400-76-0116.

REFERENCES

Becker, J. D. *An information-processing model of intermediate-level cognititon* (BBN Rep. No. 2335, Doctoral dissertation, Cambridge, Mass.: Bolt Beranek and Newman Inc., 1972.

Collins, A. M., & Quillian, M. R. *Tripping down the garden path* (BBN Rep. No. 2008). Cambridge, Mass.: Bolt Bernaek and Newman Inc., 1971.

Klatt, D. H., & Stevens, K. N. *Strategies for recognition of spoken sentences from visual examination of spectograms* (BBN Rep. No. 2154). Cambridge, Mass.: Bolt Beranek and Newman Inc., 1971.

Kuno S., & Oettinger, A. G. Multiple-path syntactic analyzer. In *Information Processing 1962*. Amsterdam: North-Holland, 1963.

Lesser, V. R., Fennel, R. D., Erman, L. D., & Reddy, D. R. Organization of hearsay II speech understanding system. *IEEE Trans. on Acoustics, Speech, and Signal Processing*, 1975, *23*(1).

Nash-Webber, B. L. The role of semantics in automatic speech understanding. In D. Bobrow & A. Collins (Eds.), *Representation and understanding: Studies in cognitive science*. New York: Academic Press, 1975.

Riverside Research Institute. *The reading competency test* (form B-1). Albany, N.Y.: The State University of New York, State Education Department, 1974.

Rumelhart, D. E. Toward an interactive model of reading. In S. Dornic (Ed.), *Attention and performance VI*. Hillsdale, N.J.: Lawrence Erlbaum Associates, 1977.

Wanner, E. Do we understand sentences from the outside-in or from the inside-out? *Daedalus,* Summer 1973, 163-183.

Winograd, T. *Procedures as a representation for data in a computer program for understanding natural language* (Project MAC Rep. No. TR-84). Cambridge, Mass.: M.I.T., 1971.

Wolf, J. J., & Woods, W. A. The HWIM speech understanding system. *IEEE International Conference on Acoustics, Speech and Signal Processing Record,* May 1977, 784-787 (Catalogue No. 77CH1197-3).

Woods, W. A. Transition network grammars for natural language analysis. *Communications of the ACM,* 1970, *13*(10), 591-602.

Woods, W. A. Meaning and machines. In A. Zampolli (Ed.), *Computational and mathematical linguistics,* Florence: Leo S. Olschki 1973. (a)

Woods, W. A. Progress in natural language understanding—An application to lunar geology. *AFIPS Proceedings,* National Computer Conference and Exposition, 1973. (b)

Woods, W. A. Syntax, semantics, and speech. In D. R. Reddy (Ed.), *Speech recognition: Invited papers of the IEEE symposium*. New York: Academic Press, 1975. (a)

Woods, W. A. What's in a link: Foundations for semantic networks. In D. Bobrow & A. Collins (Eds.), *Representation and understanding: Studies in cognitive science*. New York: Academic Press, 1975. (b)

Woods, W. A. *Multiple theory formation in high-level perception* (Tech. Rep. CSR-38). Urbana, Ill.: Center for the Study of Reading, University of Illinois, 1977; & Cambridge, Mass.: Bolt Beranek and Newman Inc., 1977.

Woods, W. A., Bates, M., Brown, G., Bruce, B., Cook, C., Klovstad, J., Makhoul, J., Nash-Webber, B., Schwartz, R., Wolf, J. J., & Zue, V. *Speech understanding systems* (BBN Final Rep. No. 3438). Cambridge, Mass.: Bolt Beranek and Newman Inc., 1976.

Woods, W. A., & Makhoul, J. I. Mechanical inference problems in continuous speech understanding. *Artificial Intelligence,* 1974, *5*(1), 73-91.

II TEXT STRUCTURE

This section clearly reflects the overall themes of the book. For those not aware of recent developments in the study of language, the chapters in this section may come as somewhat of a shock. The pure, formal constructs of transformational linguistics are replaced by an array of new ideas that invoke constructs traditionally considered to be outside the domain of linguists. Morgan and Green (Chapter 5) draw a distinction between two broad approaches to the study of language—the formalist position, which treats linguistic structures as abstract formal objects to be studied in isolation, and the intentionalist position, which treats linguistic structures as devices used by speakers or writers to convey their intentions to hearers or readers. Clearly all the authors in this section of the book are practicing intentionalists.

Even though the authors come from different disciplines (linguistics, psychology, and artificial intelligence) and are writing on different topics, there is a remarkable consistency in their approach. They show that the traditional study of the literal meaning of isolated sentences must be supplemented by analysis at many different levels: speech acts, conversational implicatures, reader's discourse model, plot, discourse force, rhetorical strategies, and so on. One of the basic modes of argument in several of the chapters is to take a syntactic structure that has been studied in isolation and show that a complete understanding of its behavior requires analysis at some other level.

The authors have rejected the apparent simplicity of studying sentences in isolation for the ecological validity gained by studying language in its linguistic and nonlinguistic context. Looking at the nonlinguistic context of utterances leads to the analysis of language in terms of indirect speech acts and conversational implicatures. Looking at text instead of single sentences leads to the use of constructs such as plot, point of view, and rhetorical structure.

An orientation that has systematic impact across these chapters is the relatively simple notion that text is a medium for communication. It appears that an adequate analysis of linguistic phenomena from syntax to literary genres requires one to consider that writers structure text in accord with their model of their intended reader. And conversely, the reader's understanding of text is based on assumptions that the reader makes about the intentions of the writer (e.g., "this writer really intends to support a certain position"; or "no, the writer couldn't possibly believe that, so the text must be taken as satire"). From the point of view of the reader, the comprehension of text results from the powerful interplay of top-down and bottom-up processes. The writer has used a variety of linguistic devices to encode his or her intentions: these linguistic forms can be understood only by bringing into operation a variety of higher order processes.

Another thread through these chapters is the contribution that knowledge of the world plays in understanding text. The authors treat text as a set of linguistic guides to underlying information. In order to understand text, the reader must make a wide variety of inferences based on schemata that represent the reader's knowledge of relevant nonlinguistic information. It turns out the text cannot be understood with a grammar and a dictionary—an encyclopedia is required too.

Thus, in this section the themes developed in the earlier section on global issues can be seen somewhat more concretely as applied to the structure of text. Understanding text requires analysis at many different levels and requires the interplay of linguistic knowledge and schema-based knowledge of the world. The study of text must take place in the context of a writer who is attempting to convey his or her intentions to a reader and of an active reader who is attempting to form a representation of the intentions of the author. The chapters in this section apply these general approaches in quite different ways.

Huggins and Adams (Chapter 4) take a revisionist approach to syntax. They review a variety of experiments that attempted to study syntax within the framework of early versions of transformational linguistics. They show the difficulties with this approach and suggest that a much more valid approach to the psychological study of syntax would ask the question—what is the function of a given syntactic form? They propose that many syntactic forms can be looked at in terms of a trade-off between efficiency for the writer versus difficulty of comprehension for the reader and suggest that the optimum syntactic forms may vary along this dimension as the age of the reader shifts.

Morgan and Green review a number of issues in the study of language that are often loosely classified together as pragmatics and point out the enormous impact these ideas have been having in linguistics in the last few years. They provide a clear guide to the issues of speech acts, indirect speech acts, and conversational implicatures and suggest some of the difficulty these phenomena cause for transformational linguistics. Finally, Morgan and Green raise the question of how these aspects of language are acquired and how they relate to the reading process.

Webber's Chapter 6 deals with the issue of anaphora. Anaphora has, for the most part, been treated as a straightforward syntactic phenomenon in which one linguistic form is used to replace another. However, in this chapter, Webber presents evidence that what we were all taught in elementary school is not true. Pronouns do not stand for nouns; they stand for entities that have been introduced into the reader's model of what the discourse is about. The chapter outlines a systematic approach to anaphora and gives a number of interesting examples of the interaction of linguistic and nonlinguistic factors in the use of anaphora. By analyzing in great detail a single language phenomenon, many of the global processes discussed in the earlier chapters can be elucidated by concrete examples. Webber also shows the implication her approach has for some of the experiments dealing with children's use of anaphora.

Morgan and Sellner (Chapter 7) point out that linguists have conducted very little research on connected discourse and argue that the work that has been carried out has attempted to mimic the conceptual framework of transformational linguistics. They suggest that an adequate analysis of text will require a radical shift in orientation. They conclude that a treatment of narrative text will have to include a representation of plot and that this requires the introduction of a whole range of constructs unlike those dealt with in current linguistics.

Chapter 8 by Goetz and Armbruster reviews recent experimental work by psychologists on the understanding and memory of text. They find that very little experimental effort has been directed at text, but the work that has been carried out has so far has produced three basic findings: (1) Text material behaves very differently from lists of sentences; (2) Thematically important elements in a text tend to be recalled best; and (3) The understanding and memory of text is strongly influenced by context and the knowledge brought to the text by the reader.

Brewer's Chapter 9 argues that psychologists do not yet have the conceptual tools to deal with discourse and suggests that theoretical and experimental work might be aided by examining the long tradition of work on text in the humanities. He reviews work from the areas of literary theory, rhetoric, and stylistics and draws several implications for psychology. He suggests the need for a much more sophisticated approach to textual material; for example, he suggests a classification of types of text along dimensions of underlying cognitive structure and discourse force. He outlines a wide variety of topics that are open for exerimental investigation: point of view, plot, rhetorical strategies, literary style, and so on. Brewer points out that rhetoric books and proscriptive books on how to write describe how a given structural option will affect reading comprehension and suggests that these opinions can be used as the starting point for the development of an experimental rhetoric. He concludes by suggesting that an experimental understanding of these issues would have strong implications for the construction of children's texts.

Taken as a whole, this section appears to capture a field in a state of ferment. Many of the ideas discussed here are just beginning to be worked out, and it will be some time before the full implications are realized. Even less well understood are some of the issues that must be resolved before they can be directly applied to the problems of reading comprehension. Most of the work has dealt with adults, and the impact on our understanding of children's reading comprehension is yet to come. However, the chapters suggest that we are on the way to developing a theoretical and experimental understanding of some of the dimensions of text difficulty and that this information will be a necessary component of a scientifically based theory of reading instruction.

4 Syntactic Aspects of Reading Comprehension

A. W. F. Huggins
Marilyn Jager Adams
Center for the Study of Reading,
Bolt Beranek and Newman Inc.

INTRODUCTION

Psycholinguists have been trying for years to account for the differences in psychological complexity associated with different syntactic constructions. It is probably impossible to measure the psychological complexity of a sentence without involving the *meaning* that the syntax encodes into it. As a result, neither readability formulas nor surface structure measures are adequate descriptions of complexity for single sentences, because they scrupulously avoid meaning. According to current theories, comprehension depends on recovering the simple propositions that underlie each clause in the message. How easily perceivers recover this information depends critically on their processing capabilities.

In this view, syntax provides a set of tools for adjusting the complexity and compactness of messages to achieve the best balance between economy and clarity, taking into account the level of competence and processing ability of the perceiver. This position leads to an emphasis on the pragmatics of syntax and to such questions as:

1. What objectives do the various syntactic constructions allow the user to achieve?
2. Would children become syntactically competent more easily if these uses were formalized and taught explicitly?

There are several aspects of syntax that children must acquire. First, they must learn how single words are combined to form larger syntactic units, such as a noun and a verb to make a sentence, or later, a determiner, an adjective, and a noun to make a noun phrase. Then they must learn simple syntactic rules, such as those used to generate the passive or the negative, which modify the order of the constituents or introduce auxiliary verbs or function words where necessary. Later still, they must learn how single syntactic rules are combined to generate complex sentences. In addition to learning each construction, they must learn to restrict the construction to appropriate contexts.

To demonstrate the problems that can arise: If the content of sentence Y, *The teacher has a dog,* is to be used to qualify *dog* in sentence Z, *The dog has fleas,* Y must first be recast into a different syntactic form. At least four different syntactic rules are available for performing this transformation. They yield several different complex sentences with a common (literal) meaning: *The teacher's dog has fleas* (Y transformed into a possessive); *The dog of the teacher has fleas* (Y is a prepositional phrase); *The dog that the teacher has has fleas* (Y is a relative clause); and *The dog the teacher has has fleas* (Y is a reduced relative). All of the foregoing are fairly acceptable. But when a third simple sentence, X, *My son has a teacher,* must be used to qualify *teacher* in sentence Y, the syntactic rules used for embedding X in Y and Y in Z can no longer be arbitrarily selected. The results of using the four constructions, two at a time in all 16 possible combinations, can be seen in Table 4.1. Some of these are acceptable, others are not (marked with *), and people would disagree about still others. Semiacceptable sentences like 2+A, 3+A, and 4+A, with the hyphenated possessives, can sometimes be heard in children's speech, which supports the idea that the rules themselves are acquired first and the restrictions on their use only later. Such overgeneralization of rules is very common during language acquisition.

This chapter concentrates on the syntactic aspects of competence. The various other skills required for reading comprehension and the differences between written and spoken language are addressed in detail in other chapters. But one difference between listening and reading deserves special emphasis here. In spoken language, the prosodic pattern of what is said (pitch, stress, timing, and pauses) contains many clues about how spoken words should be grouped and how the resulting groups of words are related. In written language, this information is not explicit, except minimally as punctuation. In informal coaching, several colleagues and I have noticed that poor readers, even in fifth and sixth grades, are often insensitive to even the grossest syntactic units. When reading aloud, they ignore the periods and capitalization that mark the boundaries between written sentences, although in conversation they correctly mark the ends of their sentences by lowering their voice pitch and pausing. They seem not to understand the concept of a "sentence," so obvious to the adult, in terms of what they do when they speak. But when shown explicitly what to do, they catch on very quickly. Thus, some

TABLE 4.1
Some Combinations of Constructions

Four different syntactic constructions are used to convert the content of a simple sentence into a form appropriate for it to qualify the subject of a second. Each construction is applied to X, *My son has a teacher,* to make it appropriate for qualifying "teacher" in Y, *The teacher has a dog* (left column: examples 1—4), and also to Y, *The teacher has a dog,* to make it appropriate for qualifying "dog" in Z, *The dog has fleas* (right column: examples A–D). The four constructions are the possessive (*1* and *A*), the prepositional phrase (*2* and *B*), the relative (*3* and *C*), and the reduced relative (*4* and *D*). Each of the forms in the left column (*1–4*) are then combined with each of the forms in the right column (*A–D*) to yield 16 different sentences, each of which contains the information in all three simple sentences (X, Y, and Z). Some combinations are not acceptable complex sentences and are marked with an asterisk. (Without the parentheses and hyphens, sentence *2* × *A* is acceptable but has a different meaning: The teacher has fleas, rather than the dog.) See text for more details.

1: son's teacher	A: teacher's dog (possessive)
2: teacher's of my son	B: dog of the teacher (prep. phrase)
3: teacher that my son has	C: dog that the teacher has (relative)
4: teacher my son has	D: dog the teacher has (reduced relative)

1 + A   My son's teacher's dog has fleas.   (possess + possess)
1 + B   The dog of my son's teacher has fleas.   (possess + prep. phrase)
1 + C   The dog that my son's teacher has has fleas.   (etc.)
1 + D   The dog my son's teacher has has fleas.

2 + A *   The (teacher-of-my-son)'s dog has fleas.
2 + B   The dog of the teacher of my son has fleas.
2 + C ?   The dog that the teacher of my son has has fleas.
2 + D ?   The dog the teacher of my son has has fleas.

3 + A *   The (teacher-that-my-son-has)'s dog has fleas.
3 + B   The dog of the teacher that my son has has fleas.
3 + C *   The dog that the teacher that my son has has has fleas.
3 + D *   The dog the teacher that my son has has has fleas.

4 + A *   The (teacher-my-son-has)'s dog has fleas.
4 + B   The dog of the teacher my son has has fleas.
4 + C *   The dog that the teacher my son has has has fleas.
4 + D *   The dog the teacher my son has has has fleas.

of the difficulties faced by poor readers can perhaps be ascribed to the lack of instruction (as opposed to practice) in reading after a child has mastered word decoding skills. For, in addition to recognizing the words in the text, the reader must divine their syntactic function.

The remainder of this chapter is in two parts. The first addresses what determines the difficulty of different syntactic constructions and the second presents some evidence that young children have difficulty coping with complex syntax.

SYNTACTIC COMPLEXITY

Why is complex syntax necessary? Because complex ideas and relationships cannot always be expressed in syntactically simple sentences alone (Bar-Hillel, Kasher, & Shamir, 1967): "Not everything that can be said at all, can be said, in a particular language, by the use of syntactically simple sentences only [p. 31]." In other words, decomposing complex sentences into simple sentences may *change meaning*. As a concrete example, consider a conditional construction: *If John is late, Mary will marry Peter.* The conditional marks a specific relationship between two clauses, which cannot be expressed if the two clauses appear in separate simple sentences. Similar arguments apply to most sentences containing subordinate conjunctions (e.g., although, since, if, unless, while, etc.).

What is syntactic complexity? Can it be measured or described in the abstract, divorced from the meaning of the message it encodes? Can the formal models of syntax developed in linguistics and elsewhere be of help in answering these questions? The attempts by linguists to capture the enormous richness and variety of syntactic regularity in the form of sets of axiomatic rules has expanded the study and understanding of syntax by orders of magnitude. But when such a model has been used to try to account for the effects of syntactic complexity on comprehension, the magnitude of its failure has been proportional to the model's determination to exclude meaning. Although it may be possible in principle to describe syntactic complexity in the abstract, such a description is of little relevance—at least to reading—because the results become invalid as soon as meaning is reintroduced, as it must be if the effect of the syntactic complexity on *people* is of interest. Some of the most recent models, from linguistics, artificial intelligence, and cognitive psychology, are at last coming to grips with these problems.

Surface Structure and Complexity

Clearly, syntactic complexity can be defined in terms of any particular model of syntax, but the critical question is the extent to which the resulting measure of complexity is useful outside of the model. The earliest models of syntax that were used to describe syntactic complexity were also those that were most determined to exclude meaning. These models attended only to the "surface structure" of sentences, which corresponds (roughly) to the information in the hierarchical tree diagram that can be drawn above the words in a sentence, such that each group of words comprising a syntactic unit, or "immediate constituent" of the sentence, is dominated by a node of the tree. Although each constituent (node) is labeled as a noun phrase, noun, determiner, and so on, the surface structure description does not specify the syntactic *function* of the constituent in the sentence, such as whether it is the subject or object of the main verb. The axiomatic rule systems that were invented to generate the surface structures found in the language were called "phrase structure grammars."

Attempts to apply surface structure concepts to practical problems, such as predicting text readability from a variety of statistical measures on the text, were relatively unsuccessful. Some of these measures, such as average sentence length and the number of subordinate clauses or prepositional phrases per sentence, attempted to account for syntactic factors. Others, such as the proportion of concrete as opposed to abstract words, were aimed at semantic factors. Although readability measures can be found that correlate fairly well with text difficulty (Bormuth, 1966), their main weakness is that the difficulty of a passage involves its comprehension, and surface structure descriptions capture only some of the syntactic variables necessary to comprehension. As an extreme example of the inadequacy of these formulas, most of them would yield the same readability index on a passage if the word order within each phrase, and the order of the phrases within each sentence, were scrambled!

The surface structure approach to syntax has two major shortcomings. The first is one of scope: There is no elegant way to handle discontinuous constituents (e.g., "look...up" in *He looked his old aunt up while he was in Toronto*). The second is more general: The surface structure parsing does not indicate the syntactic *function* of the identified units nor how they are interrelated. The best-known example of this shortcoming (Chomsky, 1965) concerns a pair of sentences with identical surface structure: *John is eager to please,* and *John is easy to please. John* is the subject of *please* in the first of these but its object in the second. Surface structure descriptions fail to mark such differences, although they are clearly vital for comprehension.

Transformational Grammar and Derivational Complexity

Transformational grammar evolved partly in response to the foregoing shortcomings of phrase structure grammars. We will make only a few points here about transformational grammar because a description that would do it justice is well beyond the scope of this chapter, and excellent introductions are available elsewhere (e.g., Dale, 1976; Fromkin, 1976).

Transformational grammar is a *linguistic* theory, and its purpose is to describe and explain the structural constraints on allowable sequences of words. It explicitly denies any ambition to represent what people do when they speak or listen. The transformational component of a grammar takes as input one or more underlying phrase markers and applies one transformation at a time to transform them into a sequence of derived phrase markers. The underlying phrase markers (or "deep-structure sentoids," or "elementary propositions") contain all the information necessary for semantic interpretation of the sentence, whereas the final derived phrase marker is closely related to the sound pattern of the sentence as it would be spoken (or written). Some transformations perform mundane tasks such as ensuring number agreement between subject and verb; others may reorder or delete constitutents, introducing function words where appropriate; still others may conjoin two underlying phrase markers, or embed one in another, in a variety of ways, to yield complex sentences.

Two points should be made about deep structures. First, because the theory locates all information relevant to semantic interpretation in the inferred underlying deep-structure sentoids, transformations are abstract, devoid of meaning. And, because the underlying structures are never observable, their presence and properties can only be inferred. The choice between competing ways of describing them can be based only on which leads to the wider generalization or which can be more concisely and elegantly expressed. Second, by definition, deep sentoids are always active, affirmative, and declarative, although perhaps they bear appropriate tags to force later transformations into negative or passive form. Consequently, the first noun phrase in an underlying sentoid is always its subject. Since a full transformational description of a sentence specifies the underlying sentoids and their dominance relations, it also specifies the subject and object of the sentence.

Given the dramatic success of transformational grammar in describing a large subclass of English syntax, it was not long before a serious attempt was made to use transformational grammar directly as a psychological model. The model assumed, in essence, that people think in structures that can be adequately represented by deep-structure sentoids. These sentoids are converted into a form appropriate for speaking by a series of processing steps, isomorphic with the transformational derivation of each sentence. The listener then has to go through the reverse process, undoing the effect of each transformation until finally the underlying sentoids representing the speaker's intended message are recovered. From this model, it follows that the syntactic complexity of a sentence is directly determined by the number of transformations applied during its derivation from the underlying sentoids. Hence its name: the derivational theory of complexity.

Several experiments yielded strong support for the theory (Miller, 1962). For example, subjects have been timed as they verified statements about integers (McMahon, 1963; see also Gough, 1965). The statements were true or false, active or passive, affirmative or negative, and used the reciprocal verbs *precede* and *follow,* as in the following examples:

    5 precedes 7
    7 follows 5
    5 is followed by 7
    7 is not followed by 5
    7 is not preceded by 5

Redundant filler words that did not add to derivational complexity were added to some sentences to vary length independently of derivational complexity. Passive or negative sentences took longer to verify than their active or affirmative counterparts, and in each case the increment in reaction time was remarkably independent of what other transformations had been applied. In other words, the passive took the same amount longer to verify than the active, in negative as in affirmative sentences. This was taken as evidence that a special operation was required to handle the passive, regardless of the context in which it appeared.

Other studies showed that sentences took up progressively more memory space as their derivational complexity increased (Savin & Perchonock, 1965). Each sentence to be memorized was followed by a list of unconnected words to fill up the subject's memory in a mental analogue of Archimedes bath. The more derivationally complex the syntax of the stored sentence, the less room there was for extra words. The result has been replicated for the negative, passive, and question transformations (Bever, Fodor, Garrett, & Mehler, 1966), but other researchers have noted the dependence of the results on the timing of events during a trial (see Olson & Clark, 1976, for more detail).

Despite these initial successes, the derivational theory of complexity has few supporters today. First, there are convincing counterexamples to derivational complexity. Fodor and Garrett (1966), among others, pointed out that some transformations, especially those that cause deletions, *decrease* rather than increase the perceptual complexity of a sentence, which contradicts derivational complexity. For example, a sentence such as *The boy was given a book by someone* becomes simpler, rather than more complex, when an additional transformation deletes the *by someone*. But not all deletions lead to perceptually simpler sentences: Deleting the relative pronoun from a relative clause makes the sentence harder to perceive, understand, or remember (Fodor & Garrett, 1967). It appears that the only deletion transformations that simplify sentences are those that delete optional cases within a single sentoid rather than those that delete phrases that are duplicated in two sentoids being crunched together. (The different cases represent the different possible relationships between a noun, or prepositional phrase, and the verb of a sentoid; see Fillmore, 1968.) Further counterarguments to derivational complexity have been offered by Watt (1970).

Second, the foregoing counterexamples can be interpreted either as disproving the rationale of derivational complexity or as a criticism of the particular formulation of the grammar used to determine derivational complexity. This is a formidable problem in psycholinguistics: The rate at which linguistic description has developed over the past 20 years, together with the lag before new developments are taken up by psycholinguists, means that, often, the formal descriptions psychologists seize on for testing are obsolete before the testing begins—not to mention possible further delays before they reach educators.

Clauses as Psychological Units

Despite the shortcomings of derivational complexity, some of the assumptions underlying the theory have become widely accepted. A variety of studies suggest that clauses, both in the surface structure of a sentence and also in the deep structure, are treated as psychological units during comprehension.

The surface structure of a sentence has a strong influence on how subjects "chunk" materials they are asked to remember, with words being remembered or forgotten together if they fall in the same constituent (Johnson, 1965). Surface structure also affects comprehension: A set to expect one sort of surface structure (e.g., *They are buying gloves*) interfered with verification of a sentence with a structure that looked identical but was in fact different (e.g., *They are boxing gloves;* Mehler & Carey, 1967). Clausal units also seem to be processing units in sentence perception. Garrett, Bever, and Fodor (1966, and many others) asked subjects to report the location of an extraneous noise (a click) in recorded sentences. The position of a clause boundary in the sentence was controlled by preceding context, as marked by commas in the pair:

> Your constant hope of marrying Anna, is surely impractical.
> In her hope of marrying, Anna is surely impractical.

There was a strong tendency for the clicks to be mislocated into the clause break, although the clause break was not marked acoustically as a consequence of an ingenious experimental design. (In normal speech, of course, clause boundaries are marked by prosodic cues, and these are highly influential in controlling segmentation, see Wingfield & Klein, 1971). Although both the interpretation and the methodology of the "click" experiments have been criticized (e.g., Olson & Clark, 1976; Watt, 1970), enough of the criticisms have been answered by now to justify tentative acceptance of the conclusion that the clause acts as a psychological unit (Carroll & Bever, 1976; Fodor, Bever, & Garrett, 1974).

Perhaps the most interesting findings were those of Jarvella (1971), who showed that, when recording of a continuous passage was unexpectedly interrupted, verbatim memory for earlier words dropped sharply at the preceding clause boundary, whereas memory for content, or meaning, showed no such drop. Similarly, Caplan (1972) showed that reaction time to decide whether a probe word had occurred in a preceding sentence was longer if the probe had occurred in the preceding, rather than the immediate clause. These findings suggest that the clause boundary triggers semantic interpretation of the preceding clause and that the surface form is then erased from working memory. Similar conclusions follow from studies by Sachs (1967) and by Johnson-Laird (1970), and Kleiman (1975) has proposed a theory of reading along these lines.

The foregoing results are equivocal between surface and deep clauses being psychologically important, because a surface structure clause boundary always coincides with a clause boundary in the deep structure, although the reverse need not be true. Bever, Lackner, and Kirk (1969) showed that clicks were mislocated into deep structure clause boundaries even when these were not marked in surface structure. For example, clicks migrated differently in pairs of sentences like:

I defied John to leave.
I desired John to leave.

which have identical surface structure, but different deep structure clause boundaries. Bever et al. argued that much of the variability of earlier click data could be explained in this way (see Carroll & Bever, 1976, for more discussion).

Blumenthal (1967; Blumenthal & Boakes, 1967) showed that surface structure could not account for all of the psychological organization found in sentence-memory tasks but that deep structure relationships must be invoked too. They showed that a deep structure subject was a better prompt for recall than was a noun in an adverbial phrase, even though the surface structures seemed identical. Thus the word "tailors" was a better prompt for the sentence, *The gloves were made by tailors,* than the word "hand" was for the sentence, *The gloves were made by hand.* These results also suggest that it is the deep structure clause, rather than the surface structure clause, that represents a psychological meaning unit. Note that case grammar (Fillmore, 1968) might use this example to argue that the agentive case is more closely involved in the meaning of the verb than is the instrumental case. But the case grammar formulation would agree that it is the structural relations captured in the deep structure sentoid that matter.

One aspect of syntactic complexity on which all approaches agree is that the more underlying propositions a sentence contains, the more difficult it will be to understand. Evidence supporting this assertion has been provided by Forster (1970) and by Kintsch and Keenan (1973), among others. The implication of this, taken together with the studies reviewed earlier, is that sentence complexity is jointly determined by: (1) the difficulty of parsing the surface structure to extract the deep structure sentoids; and (2) the number of sentoids and the complexity of their interrelationships.

Processing Limitations in the Language User

Inevitably, increasing complexity will interact with the processing abilities of the language user. Indeed, in contrast to the linguist's concern with the abstract structure of syntax, a psychologist might argue that the function of syntax is to provide tools for optimizing the transfer of meaning from a speaker or writer to a listener or reader, allowing for the limited short-term memory and processing abilities of each. Whatever form meaning has in the heads of producer and receiver, language permits it to be transferred between them only in a message that is sequential. The speaker's capacities place an upper bound on both the conceptual and the syntactic complexity of what is said. But the speaker may choose to simplify the syntax to accommodate the listener. The message can be made very "thin" (and simultaneously very "long"), for example, by using only simple, active, declarative statements. Messages in this "long, thin" form have the advantage of requiring little syntactic processing, but they tax the temporal limitations of the receiver's memory, since comprehension may require that early and late items be related. Further, simple syntax limits the conceptual complexity that can be expressed (Bar-Hillel et al., 1967). On the other hand, if syntactic tools are applied so as to yield a very compact, rich message, the computation involved in unraveling it to recover the expressed relationships may cause a processing overload, and comprehension may fail altogether.

The idea of trying to include the processing operations required of the listener in the definition of syntactic complexity was first popularized by Yngve (1961). Constructions that embed one sentoid is another are a major source of syntatic complexity. Further, these constructions can be applied recursively: The embedded sentence can itself be a complex sentence with an embedded clause, and so on. Although such recursively applied transformations can lead to highly complicated sentences, they are not necessarily hard to understand. For example, the sentences *The dog chased the cat, The cat killed the rat,* and *The rat ate the malt* can be combined to yield the nursery rhyme fragment:

(This is) the dog, that chased the cat, that killed the rat, that ate the malt.

The right-branching structure is simple enough to be enjoyed by quite young children—it may well be their first exposure to recursively applied transformations. But when the same sentoids are combined into a center-embedded instead of a right-branching construction, the resulting sentence is virtually unintelligible, although it was produced by correctly applying the rules for relativization:

(This is) the malt that the rat that the cat that the dog chased killed ate.

Savin (quoted in Bever, 1970) showed that even single center embeddings are more complex than corresponding right-branching structures, although Sheldon (1974) has more recently reported conflicting evidence.

Several attempts have been made to explain the difficulty of such constructions. When a relative clause modifies the subject of a sentence, it intervenes between the subject and its verb. Since interpretation requires the integration of subject with verb, this forces the listener to remember the subject while processing the interrupting relative. Processing difficulty, and thus syntactic complexity, increases in proportion to the number of units awaiting completion, and it was this that Yngve's "depth" measure captured. When there are two such interruptions, it obviously becomes harder to keep track of which noun goes with which verb. Miller and Isard (1964) proposed an "interrupted subroutine" model, in which the second call on the subroutine for processing relatives caused the "return vector" for the preceding call to be lost. Schlesinger (1968) showed that the difficulty of center embeddings is largely removed if the underlying sentoids are semantically constrained such that the noun from one cannot be combined with the verb from another, and Blumenthal (1966) found that subjects who were unaware of the double-embedding construction simply treated the sentences as ungrammatical. Carroll and Bever (1976) have pointed out that such results are consistent with listeners trying to identify the deep-structure sentoids, together with their grammatical relations.

There is probably a limit to how long an embedded relative can be before it forces a restructuring of the sentence, but Sheldon (1974) has shown recently that other factors, such as similarity of syntactic function in the main and relative clauses, may be even more important. Sheldon pointed out that the experiments that led to the "interruption" hypothesis were unbalanced, in that the presence or absence of an interruption was confounded with syntactic function. Only self-embedded sentences were used as exemplars of interruption, and in these sentences the *subject* of the main clause was relativized. On the other hand, the noninterrupted control sentences had a right-branching structure, in which the *object* of the main clause was relativized. Sheldon's results (described in more detail in a later section) demonstrate that the interruption introduced by the relative clause is not an adequate explanation of the difficulty of self-embedded sentences, and that syntactic function plays an important role.

Strategies in Perception and Recoverability

The processing problems highlighted by center-embedded sentences are in fact much more pervasive than the foregoing specialized examples suggest, especially in language acquisition. Bever (1970) proposed a theory that addressed directly the problem of how a listener decodes syntax. The theory implicitly incorporates a theory of syntactic complexity. In order to extract meaning, the listener must determine how the sentence constituents were related in the deep-structure sentoids. Bever suggested a set of strategies the listener might use to recover deep structure. He called them strategies, rather than algorithms, because they are not infallible. When applied inappropriately, they may lead to misinterpretations typical of children learning language.

The first strategy is to look for a sequence of words that could correspond to the subject-verb-object (i.e., actor-action-object) of the deep structure. The second strategy is to assume that the first sequence consisting of noun-verb (-noun) must be the main clause of the sentence, unless the verb is marked by a subordinate conjunction such as *although, if, while,* or *because.* When these words appear first in a sentence, they indicate that the subordinate clause precedes the main clause, as in so-called "cleft" sentences (e.g., *Although John was a bore, we invited him to the party*). The third strategy is to use semantic constraints to guide the assignment of syntactic function whenever possible. This strategy would reliably lead young children to misinterpret *The egg ate the boy.* In extreme cases, syntactic analysis may not be necessary at all. Fourth, in the absence of semantic clues, a noun-verb-noun sequence is assumed to correspond to the subject-verb-object in the deep structure. Fifth, a determiner is assumed to mark the beginning of a noun phrase, which continues until the first word is encountered that is less "noun-like" than its predecessor. (Bever found this description was able to account for several puzzling details about adjective-order in English, such as preference for *the red plastic ball* over *the plastic red ball;* see Bever, 1970, and Ford & Olson, 1975, for more discussion.)

The five strategies have been revised slightly in the latest statement of the theory (Carroll & Bever, 1976), but the changes are not critical to the discussion here. The crucial idea underlying all the strategies is the problem of *recoverability*—that is, how the deep-structure sentoids can be recovered from the surface form of the sentence. Bever argued that the strategies are special language-related cases of a set of general perceptual principles closely related to the Gestalt rules of organization.

An appealing aspect of Bever's model is the ease with which it deals with so-called garden-path sentences, such as *The old man the boats* or *The horse raced past the barn fell.* Most people reject these sentences as ungrammatical, although a perfectly acceptable parsing exists for each. The difficulty with *The old man* is that the word *man* is gobbled up as the head of the noun phrase begun by the determiner *The,* following Bever's fifth strategy, when in fact it is the only word in the sentence that can function as the verb. *Old* then has to be the head of the noun phrase. Similarly, in the second example, Bever's first strategy leads to *The horse raced past the barn* being identified as the actor-action(-object) of the deep structure, with the result that the final *fell* is not parsable. In fact, however, *fell* is the main verb, and *The horse raced past the barn* is an elaborated noun phrase, which contrasts this horse with another that was *not* raced past the barn. These sentences are called garden paths because they trick the parser into making an error. The errors are hard to recover from because they involve a group of words being misidentified as a completed clause, with the result that they are interpreted and erased from working memory. Therefore, they are no longer available when the parser has to back up to recover from the failure later in the sentence. Thus, garden-path sentences can be seen as the result of overdeletion of syntactic markers that facilitate recovery of the intended deep structure. Similar arguments apply to some types of ambiguity. They have been developed in more detail by Limber (1976) and by Wanner (1976).

Toward a Compromise

The most recent processing models are attempting a synthesis of the good points in the theories considered previously. Recent processing models have been based on a new formalism called Augmented Transition Network (ATN) parsers (Bobrow & Fraser, 1969; Woods, 1970). Although any formal grammar can be represented by an ATN, most current ATN's are phrase-structure grammars that have been augmented to handle discontinuous constituents by allowing calls on subroutines. These parsers have grown out of efforts to make computers comprehend. It was soon realized that identifying the syntactic function of each parsed constituent was vital; otherwise, far too many parsings were possible (Thorne, Bratley, & Dewar, 1968). Even this was not enough: It has also been necessary to work within a limited semantic domain and to use the semantics to elminate alternative parsings.

Kaplan (1972) has shown that the heuristic strategies described by Bever (1970) can be directly translated into an ATN, with the exception of the semantic strategy. Extremely powerful ATN parsers are now available: One that will handle a very large subset of English was described in detail by Woods, Kaplan, and Nash-Webber (1972), and new improvements and developments appear frequently. A discussion of current models is unfortunately beyond the scope of this book.

More recently, the ATN model has been proposed and defended as a model of the psychological process in understanding sentences. Wanner and Maratsos (1977) used a modification of Savin and Perchonock's Archimedean task to measure "on-line" memory load during sentence processing and found that the more complicated, or the longer, the modifying material was, the heavier the load placed on memory. Wanner (1976) has attempted to show that an ATN grammar can provide reasonable accounts of subjects' difficulties with ambiguous and garden-path sentences, and Stevens and Rumelhart (1975) have used an ATN model to account for reading errors. A particularly appealing aspect of some ATN models is that, in performing their single left-to-right pass (parse) through the input, they develop simultaneously all the possible parsings of the sentence (Woods, Chapter 3, this volume). The models are thus *predictive* in that, at any instant, each possible parsing has only a limited range of possible continuations. Such prediction clearly occurs in human listeners, as shown by the extremely short-latency shadowing experiments of Marslen-Wilson (1973, 1975).

The Pragmatics of Syntax

An aspect of syntax that has been relatively neglected by linguists, at least recently, concerns the reasons for existence for each of the various constructions. Austin (1961) asked parallel questions about English vocabulary—in particular, why there are so many synonyms. He concluded that no two words or expressions are exactly synonymous. Instead, each captures a slightly different shade of meaning, and a context can be found in which they are not interchangeable. One of his most compelling examples is the pair *by mistake* and *by accident,* which are more or less interchangeable in common usage. But if I shoot your donkey *by mistake,* the implication is that I intended to shoot a donkey—mine, for instance—and carried out my intention only to find I had misidentified your donkey as mine. That is, my act was performed as intended, but I had misperceived the state of the world in which the act was performed. If I shoot your donkey *by accident,* on the other hand, either my act was unintended or the performance of my intended act was somehow flawed. For example, a bird flew into the rifle as I pulled the trigger, or my donkey ducked, so the bullet hit the wrong donkey.

Similar questions apply to syntax: Why is a particular syntactic construction needed? What determines that one construction is more appropriate than another in a particular context? Although everyone who has tried his hand at writing prose has intuitive answers to these questions, relatively little effort has been devoted to reducing them to explicit rules (but see Fraser, 1972, and Ross, 1975, for useful preliminary attempts).

Some of the objectives achieved by particular constructions have become apparent in earlier sections. For example: (1) Deletion transformations increase the compactness of a message, in conformity with a hypothetical Least Effort principle; and (2) the passive can be used (among other things) for restructuring a sentence to move an "interrupting" clause to a noninterrupting position. Both of these objectives concern processing limitations on language users. A further possible use of the passive, as we see later, is to change the topic of a sentence. This is an example of an objective set by the intended *meaning* of the message: False conclusions may be drawn from experiments that ignore such objectives.

To demonstrate the dangers inherent in studying a construction divorced from its objectives, consider the following paradox. The passive voice is reported to be psychologically more difficult than the active: Passives take longer to verify than actives (Gough, 1965; McMahon, 1963) and are learned later (Brown & Hanlon, 1970). The additional complexity of the passive has been blamed on the extra transformation required in its derivation. But since transformations supposedly do not alter meaning (Chomsky, 1957), the active and passive have the same meaning. Therefore, why should the passive ever be used, because it apparently adds to complexity without modifying meaning?

The paradox is resolved when the objective achieved by the passive is taken into account. One use of the passive is to modify the topic or theme of a sentence. In the absence of other constraints, the first concept presented in a new sentence is usually "given" information, because then the new information that the sentence imparts can be related to the given information as it arrives (Haviland & Clark, 1974; Perfetti & Lesgold, 1977). When the given information of the new sentence is the object rather than the subject of the verb, the object can be "topicalized" by using the passive voice (or, alternatively, a verb with a reciprocal meaning can be used). In such a context, the passive is no longer harder or more complex than the active, and children can both produce and understand passives in such contexts at a considerably younger age than had formerly been thought (Turner & Rommetveit, 1968).

The foregoing example shows that, in appropriate contexts, the passive is easier than the active and that ignoring such pragmatic factors can produce misleading results. It is presumably partly because of its usefulness in these contexts that the passive is kept in the language. A detailed description of all the constraints that operate in the choice of one syntactic construction over another would be extremely useful. The pragmatics of syntax are further discussed by Morgan and Green (Chapter 5, this volume).

SYNTAX AND CHILDREN

The problem of recoverability also affects children. Three main points are made in this section: First, children entering grade school are far from possessing the syntactic competence they will have as adults (see also Palermo & Molfese, 1972). Second, mastery of a syntactic construction is acquired in stages, with very heavy semantic support being essential in the early stages. That is, when a construction first appears in a child's repertoire, it is understood in only a very limited subset of the contexts in which an adult would understand or apply it, and the size of the subset grows by discrete steps until it corresponds to adult mastery. Third, children acquire control of a construction before they learn all the restrictions on its use, with the result that they sometimes apply it inappropriately. At any particular age, there is some level of syntactic complexity that is best suited to the child's abilities. This level of complexity will depend on how much support is available from the semantics of the context. The focus in what follows will be on language and syntax development after age 5 since the main concern here is with problems of reading comprehension, and the earlier stages of development have been extensively reviewed elsewhere (Brown, 1974; Dale, 1976; McNeill, 1970; Menyuk, 1971; Slobin, 1971).

When Bever was developing his account of the strategies people use for recovering deep-structure sentoids, he was strongly influenced by the problems children face in learning language. Therefore, it is not surprising that the strategies were so framed as to be consistent with children's performance also. However, the relative importance of the strategies is quite different in children and adults. Young children rely almost exclusively on the semantic strategy. As Macnamara (1972) has observed, "infants use meaning as a clue to language, rather than language as a clue to meaning." Strohner and Nelson (1974) have provided supporting evidence. The initial, overwhelming dependence on semantic support recedes only as the various syntactic strategies are acquired.

Children are constrained, just as adults are, by the prime conversational postulate (Grice, 1975), which asserts that people speak with the purpose of communicating something; therefore, the listener's prime obligation is to try by any means possible to interpret what is said. Consequently, children faced with a syntactic construction beyond their capacities do not discard the message as frivolous or nonsensical. Either they rely on semantics, or they try to apply known syntactic rules that work for similar constructions. This may lead to interesting misunderstandings, which can be teased out by clever experiments, thus clarifying children's syntactic development.

The best examples of such misunderstandings involve anaphoric expressions such as pro-nouns (pronouns) and their more complex relatives pro-verbs and pro-clauses. Pronouns stand for nouns (actually noun phrases), and similarly pro-verbs stand for verb phrases, and pro-clauses for clauses. Anaphoric reference is perhaps the most important mechanism for condensing messages and raising the level of complexity of the interrelationships that can be expressed. It is a particularly rich source of children's misunderstandings for two reasons. First, pronouns and other anaphora are extremely common in the oral speech of quite young children, who often seem oblivious to the comprehension difficulties that ensue when they change the antecedent of a pronoun in midsentence (e.g., "I saw John and his Dad, and he told me he said he would buy him an icecream"). Second, in written language, the clues that determine the possible antecedents for an anaphoric expression are entirely syntactic, although selection of the *correct* one may also depend on semantics. The rules for determining antecedents are exceedingly rich and complex and have not yet been completely described (see Webber, Chapter 6, this volume).

The most convincing examples of children's misunderstandings were provided by C. Chomsky (1969). Her well-known study involved children's comprehension of pairs of sentences that have the same surface structure but differ in deep structure. Sometimes, semantic coherence, or selection restrictions that apply between words in the sentence, are sufficient to eliminate one of the possible deep structures and thus determine syntactic function unambiguously. For example, children have little difficulty with sentences such as:

The customer is ready to eat.
The omelette is ready to eat.

because the semantic strategy yields a unique solution (or, the verb *eat* normally takes an animate subject and an inanimate object). But in the absence of such constraints, there may be two deep structures, with two different interpretations, as in:

The missionary is ready to eat (said the cannibal).

No genuine ambiguity, such as the foregoing, can be resolved without additional context. But equivalent ambiguities may arise whenever a missing antecedent must be supplied. A strategy that is helpful for recovering missing antecedent subjects is: Whenever two noun phrases are present, assign the second (closer) one as the missing subject; but when there is only one noun phrase, then that one must be the subject. The strategy is called the "minimal distance principle," because when a missing subject has to be supplied, the nearest noun phrase is used. Applying the principle to the sentence *John told Bill what he should do* correctly assigns "Bill" rather than "John" as the subject of "do."

Chomsky tested individual children aged 5 to 9 in a variety of tasks involving such sentences. In the first of the two tasks we consider here, the child was asked whether a blindfolded doll was easy to see. The younger children incorrectly used the minimal distance principle, as shown by the following example (Chomsky, 1969, p. 30):

Q: Is this doll easy to see or hard to see?
A: Hard to see.
Q: Why?
A: 'Cause she got a blindfold.

When asked to make the doll easy to see, the child typically made it easy for the *doll* to see, by removing the blindfold. Only 22% of Chomsky's 5-year-olds interpreted the question correctly, this proportion increasing with age until all the 9-year-olds in her sample gave the right answer.

The other task showed explicitly how overdeletion can interfere with children's comprehension. The minimal distance principle was again involved, this time with the verbs *tell* and *ask*. Consider the pair of sentences:

John told Bill what to do.
John asked Bill what to do.

The minimal distance principle yields the correct subject for the first of these, in which *Bill* is the do-er, but not for the second, in which *John* is the do-er. Initial tests showed that, in accordance with the minimal distance principle, children interpreted *ask* in such contexts as if it were *tell,* as the following exchange demonstrates (Chomsky, 1969, p. 55):

> Q: Ask Eric his last name.
> A: Handel.
> Q: Ask Eric this doll's name.
> A: I don't know.
> Q: Ask Eric what time it is.
> A: I don't know how to tell time.

Yet, the word *ask* itself was not the problem, because appropriate responses were given to requests such as: If you were going to ask your friend to dinner, what would you say? This sort of performance was the rule, rather than the exception, in 5-year-olds. The children followed a clear developmental sequence in acquiring control of *ask*. The sequence consisted of differential mastery of three different syntactic forms:

> Class 1 (wh-clause, with subject supplied):
> 1A: Ask Laura what color this book is.
> 1B: Ask Laura what you should feed the doll.
> Class 2 (Noun phrase):
> 2A: Ask Laura the color of this book.
> Class 3 (wh-clause, with subject omitted):
> 3A: Ask Laura what to feed the doll.

Children fell into one of five ordered stages, those in the first, making errors on all three classes, and those in the last, showing mastery of all three classes. The third syntactic class was mastered in two stages: First, the child would correctly produce a question but would insert the wrong subject, as if the sentence read: "Ask Laura what *she* should feed the doll."Only later, at about age 10, was the right subject chosen.

There are two particularly interesting pairs of sentences in the foregoing examples: *1A* and *2A;* and *1B* and *3A.* Sentences 1A and 2A encode exactly the same message, and both require exactly the same response of the subject. The same is true of sentences *1B* and *3A.* Yet some children responded correctly to *1A* but failed on *2A.* Others, at a slightly more advanced stage, responded correctly to *1A* and *2A,* and to *1B,* but not to *3A.* In each case, the only difference between the two sentences, only one of which was understood, was in how much deletion had occurred. The conclusion is inescapable: In the second member of each pair, too much deletion has occurred for the deep-structure clauses to be correctly recovered, and comprehension fails. The fact that performance on the easier of the two sentences is satisfactory, in each case, shows that there is nothing intrinsic to the task that is beyond the child's capacities.

The minimal distance principle seems to account adequately for how children supply missing subjects in the foregoing cases. But the picture is not always so simple and results diametrically opposed to the minimal distance principle have been reported by Sheldon (1974), although with younger children. Her study involved children's comprehension of sentences containing a main and a relative clause, each of which contained a subject and an object. There are four ways in which the syntactic functions in the main and relative clauses can be combined: the subject of the main clause can be either the subject or the object of the relative clause, and similarly for the object of the main clause. For example:

1. *S-S* The dog that bumps into the lion jumps over the pig.
2. *S-O* The dog that the lion bumps into jumps over the pig.
3. *O-S* The dog jumps over the pig that bumps into the lion.
4. *O-O* The dog jumps over the pig that the lion bumps into.

The children acted out, with toy animals, relativized sentences such as those just cited and also control sentences that consisted of the same clauses in coordinate structure (*the dog bumps into the lion AND the dog jumps over the pig*). All the control sentences were equally well understood, but the relativized sentences with parallel syntactic function (*S-S* and *O-O*) were understood much more often than those with crossed syntactic function (*S-O* and *O-S*). The result discredits the "interruption" hypothesis, mentioned earlier, which makes the unsupported prediction that interrupted sentences (*S-S* and *S-O*) should be harder than their noninterrupted counterparts (*O-S* and *O-O*).

Although the parallel function hypothesis was able to account for two thirds of the mistakes made on both object and subject relatives, the exceptions were particularly interesting. Sheldon reported that for almost one third of the children, the only kind of mistake made on object relatives was that the relative was interpreted as though it were modifying the *subject*, instead of the object, of the main clause. That is, in Sentences 3 and 4, it is the *dog*, rather than the much closer pig, that bumps into the lion (3), or is bumped into by the lion (4). This not only further disconfirms the interruption hypothesis, since it shows that children *preferred* discontinuous over continuous constituents in this context, but it is also the opposite of what the minimal distance principle would predict, because the missing antecedent subject for the relative clause was identified as the farthest, rather than the nearest, noun phrase. Sheldon's results are not necessarily fatal to the minimal distance principle, unlike the interruption hypothesis, because the children in Sheldon's study may have been too young to have learned—or even seen the need for—the minimal distance principle. Sheldon suggests the children may have been overapplying an extraposition rule, which is normally used to move an interrupting embedded clause to the outside. Note that all the rules apparently used by the children are legitimate, and children must learn them. The misunderstandings arise because the rules are overapplied.

Finally, a possible flaw in Sheldon's experiment should be pointed out. We saw previously how important it is that a construction be presented in a context in which the objective it achieves is required (Turner & Rommetveit, 1968). But Sheldon apparently failed to present her relatives in such a context: Her relative clauses *qualified* the subjects (or objects) of her sentences, although such qualification was not required in her context since only one animal of each type was presented. That is, it was not necessary to qualify *the dog* as *the one that bumped the lion,* because there was no other dog present with which it could have been confused.

A recent thesis by Richek (1976–77) further supports several of the conclusions drawn here. Her study involved three different types of sentences, as follows:

1. John saw Mary, and JOHN said hello to Mary.
2. John saw Mary, and HE said hello to her.
3. John saw Mary, and said hello to her.

Richek described the third of these as a *null* anaphor, although it would more commonly be called a conjoined verb phrase. In a carefully controlled and counterbalanced experiment, different children saw each of the three forms in an identical paragraph context. Within each context, the form with the repeated noun (1) was consistently the best understood, and the null form (3) was the worst understood, as recoverability would predict. The third-grade children showed little understanding of the null form, although it was modeled on sentences that occurred in their reading texts with high frequency. If the purpose of the texts was to give children experience in extracting meaning from texts, the syntax was probably too complex to be compatible with that aim. If, on the other hand, the purpose was to teach new syntactic forms (null anaphora) by exposing children to them in supportive contexts, the support was inadequate, so again the texts were failing in their aims. In addition, Richek found major differences in difficulty between different versions of a single anaphoric form as a function of the semantic context. Since comprehension depends heavily on inference skills and world knowledge (Bruce, Chapter 15, and Spiro, Chapter 10, this volume), which vary widely from one child to another, this illustrates the importance of controlling semantic context in any study of children's syntactic abilities.

The vital role played by semantic context was demonstrated even more convincingly in a study by Lesgold (1974). He set out to replicate the difficulty-ordering of different forms of anaphora reported by Bormuth, Manning, Carr, and Pearson (1970). For example, Bormuth et al. found that pro-verb anaphora such as *I like Sara. SO DOES Bill,* and pro-clause anaphora such as *Dan may come. If SO, we will have a party,* were understood by 83% and 87% respectively of their 420 fourth-grade subjects, whereas only 65% understood personal pronoun forms such as *Dick went to the store. HE bought an apple.* Each task item consisted of a paragraph, embedded within which was the sentence containing the antecedent of the anaphor, followed by a second sentence containing the anaphor. The subject answered a question such as *"Who bought an apple?"* Lesgold argued that three sources of variability must be controlled in such a task. First, foils must be included so that errors can occur: If a *who* question is to be asked, the test paragraph must contain more than one animate referent. Second, the choice of content words for the paragraph may have undesired influences on the difficulty of the question. Third, for the pro-clause forms, it is important to equate the complexity of the antecedent clauses for the two exemplars of anaphora that are to be compared. As an example, the following two sentence pairs use the same type of anaphora, but the second should be harder to understand because the antecedent is much more complex:

1. Dan may come.
   If SO, we will have a party.
2. Dan told us he will try to get here soon after dinner.
   If SO, we will have a party.

When Lesgold controlled these sources of variability, the difficulty-ordering he obtained was not only different, it was significantly negatively correlated with Bormuth's! Lesgold concluded that whether or not fourth-graders understand a particular form of anaphora depends critically on the semantic and other context in which it is presented, and that "there are very few syntax forms which children in the fourth grade cannot understand in at least some contexts [p. 337]." This constitutes further evidence that syntactic mastery of a construction is acquired in stages. Part of the semantic influence on whether a construction is understood in a particular context may be ascribable to the appropriateness in that context of the objective achieved by the construction. In any event, "the potential reliability and validity of syntax tests with uncontrolled semantics is low [p. 338]." Unfortunately, this indictment probably applies to a large proportion of *all* earlier work on syntactic complexity, including studies on adults.

Many of the problems encountered in more advanced syntax depend on the case properties of particular words, in conjunction with deletions. For example, the difficulties associated with sentences such as *John is easy to please* and *John is eager to please,* or with the *tell* versus *ask* example given previously, depend on the fact that one or more of the case slots of a particular word are empty, perhaps as a result of deletion. Verbs and some other words (easy, eager, ready) can be classified by the case forms with which they are associated (e.g., Fillmore, 1968), and this classification can be used as a basis for ordering the words by complexity. A developmental study of how children acquire mastery of this sequence would be most helpful. Gentner (1975) has made a valuable start in this direction, in her studies of the verbs of possession (see Anderson & Shifrin, Chapter 13, this volume, for more discussion).

All of the studies detailed here involved children's difficulties in recovering the antecedents for anaphora of various types. Unfortunately, the clever experimental paradigms that can be invented for studying anaphora cannot easily be adapted for use with other simpler syntactic constructions, which are nevertheless of interest. An alternative approach has been described by Pearson (1974-75) in a study that also addressed two of the questions asked earlier in this chapter: For what purpose is a particular construction needed? How does (or should) a language producer decide which of two alternative constructions is appropriate for expressing a particular proposition? Pearson recast simple propositions, typical of third- and fourth-grade readers, into several different syntactic forms, such as the following

1. The tall man thanked the young woman.
2. The man who was tall thanked the young woman.
3. The man thanked the young woman. He was tall.
4. The man thanked the woman. He was tall. She was young.

Besides some other tasks, the subjects (third- and fourth-graders, excluding poor readers) were asked to rank order the different versions for their appropriateness as answers to questions such as:

QA: Who thanked the young woman?
QB: Which man thanked the young woman?

The subjects preferred the most complicated form. Pearson interpreted this result as disconfirming both the readability theory of complexity and also the transformational deep-structure theory. Pearson assumed that, because extraction of a sentence's meaning requires the identification of deep-structure sentoids, subjects should therefore prefer a form of presentation in which this identification has already been done for them, by presenting each deep-structure sentoid in a single, isolated, simple sentence in the surface structure, as in Example 4 just given. This corresponds to the "long, thin message" described in an earlier section, which is unnecessarily long because it fails to make efficient use of the processing ability available to the receiver. Subjects should prefer the "long thin" message *only* if the more compact form strains their syntactic processing capacities, as might occur for the foregoing examples if the same task could be presented to very young children. A second factor that might have biased subjects against the more elaborated form of Example 4 is that the questions posed to the subjects (QA or QB) were already phrased in the more compact form, so that if the compact form challenged the child's abilities, he would not even be able to understand the questions. Finally, the qualification of the man as "tall" and the woman as "young" was superfluous unless there were a second man and woman presented with which the tall man and the young woman could be confused.

In summary, there are several causes for comprehension failures in children. First, the semantic complexity of the content being communicated may be beyond the child's abilities. The ideas and their interdependencies may simply be too complicated for the child to grasp. Second, the syntactic form in which the content is encoded may be beyond the child's competence or beyond his real-time processing abilities. If the aim is to increase the richness of content that can be handled, it is important to present the material in a form that does not simultaneously tax syntactic skills. Conversely, if the aim is to teach new syntactic skills, it is important to do so at a level of content richness that is within the child's abilities. Too many texts exceed the child's capacities in both areas at once.

CONCLUSIONS

1. An attempt should be made to formalize the pragmatics of syntax. That is, answers are needed to questions such as: What are the pragmatic reasons for using a particular construction? What is the objective that dictates the use of a particular construction?
2. Syntax can become too complex for a child to unravel for two separate reasons, either because the semantic relations expressed are too advanced for him to understand yet require complex syntax for their expression, or because the syntax overloads his processing or memory abilities.
3. Careful control of semantic and discourse factors is essential for all studies of syntax, if the results are to be meaningful.

ACKNOWLEDGMENTS

This report was prepared under Contract No. US-NIE-C-400-76-0116 from the National Institute of Education. We thank Charles Teggatz for helpful suggestions.

REFERENCES

Austin, J. L. A plea for excuses. In J. O. Urmson & G. J. Warnock (Eds.), *J. L. Austin: Philosophical papers.* London: Oxford University Press, 1961.

Bar-Hillel, Y., Kasher, A., & Shamir, E. Measures of syntactic complexity. In A. D. Booth (Ed.), *Machine translation,* New York: Wiley, 1967.

Bever, T. G. The cognitive basis for linguistic structures. In J. R. Hayes (Ed.), *Cognition and the development of language.* New York: John Wiley, 1970.

Bever, T. G., Fodor, J. A., Garrett, M. F., & Mehler, J. *Transformational operations and stimulus complexity.* Unpublished manuscript, MIT, 1966.

Bever, T. G., Lackner, J. R., & Kirk, R. The underlying structures of sentences are the primary units of immediate speech processing. *Perception and Psychophysics,* 1969, *5,* 225–231.

Blumenthal, A. L. Observations with self-embedded sentences. *Psychonomic Science,* 1966, *6,* 453–454.

Blumenthal, A. L. Prompted recall of sentences. *Journal of Verbal Learning and Verbal Behavior,* 1967, *6,* 203–206.

Blumenthal, A. L., & Boakes, R. Prompted recall of sentences, a further study. *Journal of Verbal Learning and Verbal Behavior,* 1967, *6,* 674–676.

Bobrow, D., & Fraser, B. An augmented state transition network analysis procedure. In N. Walker & L. Norton (Eds.), *Proceedings of the International Joint Conference on Artificial Intelligence,* Washington, D.C., 1969, 557–568.

Bormuth, J. R. Readability: A new approach. *Reading Research Quarterly,* 1966, *1,* 79–132.

Bormuth, J. R., Manning, J. C., Carr, J. W., & Pearson, P. D. Children's comprehension of between- and within-sentence syntactic structures. *Journal of Educational Psychology,* 1970, *61,* 349–357.

Brown, R. *A first language.* Cambridge, Mass.: Harvard University Press, 1974.

Brown, R., & Hanlon, C. Derivational complexity and order of acquisition. In J. R. Hayes (Ed.), *Cognition and the development of language.* New York: Wiley, 1970.

Caplan, D. Clause boundaries and recognition latencies for words in sentences. *Perception and Psychophysics,* 1972, *12,* 73–76.

Carroll, J. M., & Bever, T. G. Sentence comprehension: A case study in the relation of knowledge and perception. In E. C. Carterette, & M. P. Friedman, (Eds.), *Handbook of perception, Vol. VII: Language and speech.* New York: Academic Press, 1976.

Chomsky, C. *The acquisition of syntax in children from 5 to 10.* Cambridge, Mass.: MIT Press, 1969.

Chomsky, N. *Syntactic structures,* The Hague: Mouton, 1957.

Chomsky, N. *Aspects of the theory of syntax.* Cambridge, Mass.: MIT. Press, 1965.

Dale, P. S. *Language development,* (2nd ed.), Hinsdale, Ill.: Dryden Press, 1976.

Fillmore, Charles J. The case for case. In E. Bach & R. T. Harms (Eds.), *Universals in linguistic theory.* New York: Holt, Rinehart & Winston, 1968.

Fodor, J. A., Bever, T. G., & Garrett, M. F. *The psychology of language: An introduction to psycholinguistics and generative grammar.* New York: McGraw-Hill, 1974.

Fodor, J. A., & Garrett, M. F. Competence and performance. In J. Lyons & R. Wales (Eds.), *Psycholinguistic papers.* Edinburgh: University of Edinburgh Press, 1966.

Fodor, J. A., & Garrett, M. F. Some syntactic determinants of sentential complexity. *Perception and Psychophysics,* 1967, *2,* 289–296.

Ford, W., & Olson, D. The elaboration of the noun phrase in children's description of objects. *Journal of Experimental Child Psychology,* 1975, *19,* 371–382.

Forster, K. I. Visual perception of rapidly presented word sequences of varying complexity. *Perception and Psychophysics,* 1970, *8,* 215–221.

Fraser, B. Optional rules in grammar. *23rd Annual Round Table Monograph No. 25,* Georgetown University, 1972.

Fromkin, V. A. The formal nature of language and linguistic theories. In E. C. Carterette & M. P. Friedman (Eds.), *Handbook of perception, Vol. VII: Language and speech.* New York: Academic Press, 1976.

Garrett, M. F., Bever, T. G., & Fodor, J. A. The active use of grammar in speech perception. *Perception and Psychophysics,* 1966, *1,* 30–32.

Gentner, D. Evidence for the psychological reality of semantic components: The verbs of possession. In D. A Norman & D. E. Rumelhart (Eds.), *Explorations in cognition.* San Francisco: W. H. Freeman, 1975.

Gough, P. B. Grammatical transformations and speed of understanding. *Journal of Verbal Learning and Verbal Behavior,* 1965, *4,* 104–111.

Grice, H. P. Implicature. In P. Cole & J. Morgan (Eds.), *Syntax and semantics, Vol. 3: Speech acts.* New York: Academic Press, 1975.

Haviland, S. E., & Clark, H. H. What's new? Acquiring new information as a process in comprehension. *Journal of Verbal Learning and Verbal Behavior,* 1974, *13,* 512–521.

Jarvella, R. Syntactic processing of connected speech. *Journal of Verbal Learning and Verbal Behavior,* 1971, *10,* 409–416.

Johnson, N. F. The psychological reality of phrase structure rules. *Journal of Verbal Learning and Verbal Behavior,* 1965, *4,* 469–475.

Johnson-Laird, P. N. The perception and memory of sentences. In J. Lyons (Ed), *New horizons in psycholinguistics.* London: Penguin Books, 1970.

Kaplan, R. M. Augmented transition networks as psychological models of sentence comprehension. *Artificial Intelligence,* 1972, *3,* 77–100.

Kintsch, W., & Keenan, J. Reading rate and retention as a function of the number of propositions in the base structure of sentences. *Cognitive Psychology,* 1973, *5,* 257–274.

Kleiman, G. M. Speech recoding in reading. *Journal of Verbal Learning and Verbal Behavior,* 1975, *14,* 323–339.

Lesgold, A. M. Variability in children's comprehension of syntactic structures. *Journal of Educational Psychology,* 1974, *66*(3), 333–338.

Limber, J. Syntax and sentence interpretation. In E. C. T. Walker & R. J. Wales (Eds.), *New approaches to language mechanisms.* Amsterdam: North-Holland, 1976.

Macnamara, J. Cognitive basis of language learning in infants. *Psychological Review,* 1972, *79,* 1–13.

Marslen-Wilson, W. Linguistic structure and speech shadowing at very short latencies. *Nature,* 1973, *244,* 522–523.

Marslen-Wilson, W. Sentence perception as an interactive parallel process. *Science,* 1975, *189,* 226–227.

McMahon, L. *Grammatical analysis as part of understanding a sentence.* Unpublished doctoral dissertation, Harvard University, 1963.

McNeill, D. The development of language. In P. H. Mussen (Ed.), *Carmichael's manual of child psychology.* New York: Wiley, 1970.

Mehler, J., & Carey, P. Role of surface and base structure in the perception of sentences. *Journal of Verbal Learning and Verbal Behavior,* 1967, *6,* 335–338.

Menyuk, P. *The acquisition and development of language.* Englewood Cliffs, N. J.: Prentice-Hall, 1971.

Miller, G. A. Some psychological studies of grammar. *American Psychologist,* 1962, *17,* 748–762.

Miller, G. A., & Isard, S. Free recall of self embedded English sentences. *Information and Control,* 1964, *7,* 292–303.

Olson, G. M., & Clark, H. H. Research methods in psycholinguistics. In E. C. Carterette & M. P. Friedman (Eds.), *Handbook of perception. Vol. VII: Language and speech.* New York: Academic Press, 1976.

Palermo, D. S., & Molfese, D. L. Language acquisition from age five onward. *Psychological Bulletin,* 1972, *78,* 409-427.

Pearson, P. D. The effects of grammatical complexity on children's comprehension, recall, & conception of certain semantic relations. *Reading Research Quarterly,* 1974-75, *10*(2), 155-192.

Perfetti, C. A., & Lesgold, A. M. Discourse comprehension and individual differences. In P. Carpenter & M. Just, (Eds.), *Cognitive Processes in Comprehension: 12th Annual Carnegie Symposium on Cognition.* Hillsdale, N.J.: Lawrence Erlbaum Associates, 1977.

Richek, M. A. Reading comprehension of anaphoric forms in varying linguistic contexts. *Reading Research Quarterly,* 1976-77, *12,* 145-165.

Ross, J. R. Parallels in phonological and semantactic organization. In J. F. Kavanagh & J. E. Cutting (Eds.), *The role of speech in language.* Cambridge, Mass.: MIT Press, 1975.

Sachs, J. Recognition memory for syntactic and semantic aspects of connected discourse. *Perception and Psychophysics,* 1967, *2,* 437-442.

Savin, H., & Perchonock, E. Grammatical structure and the immediate recall of English sentences. *Journal of Verbal Learning and Verbal Behavior,* 1965, *4,* 348-353.

Schlesinger, I. M. *Sentence structure and the reading process.* The Hague: Mouton, 1968.

Sheldon, A. The role of parallel function in the acquisition of relative clauses in English. *Journal of Verbal Learning and Verbal Behavior,* 1974, *13,* 272-281.

Slobin, D. I. *The ontogenesis of grammar: Facts and theories.* New York: Academic Press, 1971.

Stevens, A. L., & Rumelhart, D. E. Errors in reading: Analysis using an augmented transition network model of grammar. In D. A. Norman & D. E. Rumelhart (Eds.), *Explorations in cognition.* San Francisco: W. H. Freeman, 1975.

Strohner, H., & Nelson, K. E. The young child's development of sentence comprehension: Influence of event probability, nonverbal context, syntactic form, and strategies. *Child Development,* 1974, *45,* 567-576.

Thorne, J., Bratley, P., & Dewar, H. The syntactic analysis of English by machine. In D. Michie (Ed.), *Machine intelligence 3.* New York: American Elsevier, 1968.

Turner, E. A., & Rommetveit, R. Focus of attention in recall of active and passive sentences. *Journal of Verbal Learning and Verbal Behavior,* 1968, *7,* 543-548.

Wanner, E. *Garden paths in relative clauses.* Paper given at Convocation on Communication, sponsored by AT&T and MIT in Celebration of the Centennial of the Telephone, 1976.

Wanner, E., & Maratsos, M. An ATN approach to comprehension. In J. Bresnan & M. Halle, (Eds.), *Linguistic theory and psychological reality.* Cambridge, Mass.: MIT Press, 1977.

Watt, W. C. On two hypotheses concerning psycholinguistics. In J. R. Hayes (Ed.), *Cognition and the development of language.* New York: Wiley, 1970.

Wingfield, A., & Klein, J. F. Syntactic structure and acoustic pattern in speech perception. *Perception and Psychophysics,* 1971, *9*(1A), 23-25.

Woods, W. A. Transition network grammars for natural language analysis. *Communication of the ACM,* 1970, *13,* 591-606.

Woods, W. A., Kaplan, R. M., & Nash-Webber, B. *The lunar sciences natural language information system: Final report* (Report No. 2378). Cambridge, Mass.: Bolt Beranek and Newman Inc. 1972.

Yngve, V. H. The depth hypothesis. *Proceedings of the XII Symposium in Applied Mathematics.* providence, R.I.: American Mathematical Society, 1961.

5 Pragmatics and Reading Comprehension

Jerry L. Morgan
Georgia M. Green
*Center for the Study of Reading,
University of Illinois, Urbana-Champaign*

INTRODUOTION

Are you my mother? is a popular trade book intended for beginning readers.
In it, a baby bird has lost his mother and goes in search of her. When the baby
bird encounters a cow, the following dialogue ensues: "Are you my mother?"
he said to the cow. "How could I be your mother?" said the cow. "I am a cow."
The bird asks a straightforward yes–no question and receives a curious
answer. The cow asks him for an explanation of how she could be his mother,
then informs him that she is a cow. How can the baby bird, or the reader,
make sense of the cow's queer response? Taken literally, this passage is quite
bizarre. Any adult, of course, will have no trouble making sense of it, by
recognizing that the cow's question is only rhetorical, an indirect way of
saying *no*, and that" *I am a cow*" follows as an explanation, a motivation, for
this negative statement. It is an elliptical response, of course, in that the other
premises—that the cow and the baby bird are of different species and that a
member of one species cannot be the mother of a member of another—are left
unstated and must be inferred by the reader.

It is an open question when children are able to fully comprehend passages
as demanding as this. But it is clear that children's reading materials are full of
such demands, which may or may not turn out to be a source of difficulty for
the beginning readers. In this chapter we discuss the subfield of linguistics in
which such matters are studied, *pragmatics*. Pragmatic descriptions and
explanations are currently attracting interest not only in linguistics but also in
philosophy, psychology, and related fields. The term *pragmatics* has come to
be used not only for such relatively well-defined problems as the interpreta-

tion and use of deictic expressions but also for practically every communicative aspect of language use not analyzable as literal meaning, including certain types of inference, speech acts, indirect speech acts, conversational implicature, and the relations and interactions among them. Pragmatics has even been used to refer to matters of politeness (Brown & Levinson, 1974) and turn-taking (Schegloff, 1972), but we do not discuss these two areas. Here, we survey some recent developments in pragmatics and briefly discuss their relation to reading. We begin with a brief discussion of semantics so that we can contrast semantics and pragmatics.

In philosophy, and more recently in linguistics, one can discern two opposing positions on the nature of meaning. Shortening Strawson's (1971) labels, we call them the *formalist* and *intentionalist* positions. Strawson succinctly characterizes the intentionalist position:

> According to [the intentionalist position], it is impossible to give an adequate account of the concept of meaning without reference to the possession by speakers of audience-directed intentions of a certain complex kind. The particular meanings of words and sentences are, no doubt, largely a matter of rule and convention; but the general nature of such rules and conventions can be ultimately understood only by reference to the concept of communication-intention [p. 171].

His characterization of the formalist position is this:

> Of course we may expect a certain regularity of relationship between what people intend to communicate by uttering certain sentences and what those sentences conventionally mean. But the system of semantic and syntactical rules, in the mastery of which knowledge of a language consists—the rules which determine the meanings of sentences—is not a system of rules *for* communication at all. The rules can be exploited for this purpose; but this is incidental to their essential character. It would be perfectly possible for someone to understand a language completely —to have a perfect linguistic competence—without having even the implicit thought of communication... [pp. 171–172].

The intentionalist, then, tends to look at sentences as instances of communicative acts. For the intentionalist, sentence meanings are complex intentions conveyed in these acts, and rules of language (at least rules of meaning) are conventions for conveying intentions by means of acting in conformance to the conventions. The formalist, on the other hand, looks at sentences as abstract formal objects, considered independent of speaker, hearer, or context—indeed, entirely independent of anything having to do with communication. For the formalist, meanings are relations between members of one set of objects—sentences—and members of another set of objects—

truth conditions. The formalist sees rules of language as specifying the mapping function between the two sets. For the intentionalist, to specify the meaning of a sentence is to say what intentions are communicated in uttering it. For the formalist, to specify the meaning of a sentence is to say under what conditions the sentence is true. It was from the formalist viewpoint that the need for a separate "pragmatics" became obvious. One can see this clearly in sentences containing indexicals—elements whose meaning is context-bound—the pronouns *I* and *you*, for example, and words like *this, that, here,* and *now*. It is clearly impossible to specify the truth conditions of sentences containing such elements, without reference to speaker, hearer, time and place of utterance, and other aspects of context. One cannot specify the conditions under which a sentence like *I saw you here yesterday* is true independent of use context, because without it, the referents of *I, you, here,* and *yesterday* cannot be determined. Who *I* is and when *yesterday* was depend on the facts of the utterance: who said the sentence and when. Obviously, then, the formalist account of meaning cannot succeed unless it incorporates what might be considered a concession to the intentionalist position: a system for assigning some meaning properties that is dependent on matters of context of use. For the formalist, this system, called *pragmatics,* is a separate system.

The term *pragmatics* was first used by Morris (1938) for aspects of language that involve users and contexts of use of linguistic expressions, as opposed to "syntax" (the study of linguistic form) and "semantics" (the study of the literal meanings of expressions, independent of context). But Morris' discussion was programmatic, and pragmatics received relatively little attention after Morris' work. A more specific discussion was presented by Bar-Hillel (1954). He proposed that pragmatics be concerned with indexical expressions, whose meanings can only be determined relative to user and context of use.

In spite of these discussions, the study of pragmatics received little attention from linguists until the early 1970s, when growing interest in the topics of presupposition and conversational implicature (to be discussed in more detail later) provoked strong interest in pragmatics among philosophers and linguists (especially, but not exclusively, those linguists associated with so-called "generative semantics"). Stalnaker (1972), for instance, follows Morris (1938) in characterizing pragmatics as "the study of linguistic acts and the contexts in which they are performed." In the scheme he presents, semantics is the study of propositions, not sentences; sentences are the vehicles people use to express propositions. Thus sentences are not evaluated directly for truth or falsity, although the propositions they express may be. For example, the truth or falsity of a sentence like *They are here now* can only be determined by constructing, from the situational context in which it was uttered or written, a proposition that includes particular values (references) for *they, here,* and *now* (e.g., *John and Loretta Smith are in Peoria on June 1, 1979*). The truth of this proposition can now be directly evaluated. Pragmatics, then, is the study of "the ways in which linguistic context determines the propositions expressed by a given sentence in that context" and includes the study of speech acts and illocutionary force, as discussed in Austin (1962) and Searle (1969); indexicals; knowledge, beliefs, expectations, and intentions of the speaker and hearer; and other aspects of context that bear on determination of the proposition expressed by the use of a sentence in a particular context.

In historically parallel developments, the term *pragmatics* has come to be used also for the study of meaning implied by the proposition which the sentence is used to express. The philosopher H. P. Grice, in a very influential paper (Grice, 1975) that was circulated in manuscript form for several years before publication, gives an insightful account of certain aspects of indirectly conveyed meaning, which he called "conversational implicature." These implicatures cannot be considered part of the literal meaning of sentences but, rather, are the result of inferences that hearers make (and that the speaker intends for the hearer to make) about the speaker's intentions in saying what he says. Interest in these issues has led to an increased concern on the part of linguists, philosophers, psychologists, anthropologists, and others with matters of context, communication, and intention, so that now the term *pragmatics* is applied to studies of discourse structure, politeness and deference, and social interaction in conversation, as well as to more traditional concerns. What unites all these apparently disparate areas under the same term is the crucial role played in each by inference in context about the intention of the speaker. Whether it is useful to consider such a wide range of phenomena as a unified area remains to be seen. The category is not entirely vacuous, however, in that inferences that are not about the speaker/author's communicative intentions are excluded.

HIGHLIGHTS OF RECENT WORK IN PRAGMATICS

Speech Acts

J. L. Austin's (1962) concept of the "speech act" has had a pervasive influence on the study of language over the past few years. Austin's basic observation is contrary to the view of sentences as formal objects to be treated as well-formed formulae of a logico-mathematical system, independent of speaker, hearer, and context. His observation is that many sentences of deceptively declarative form, like (1) following, are nonetheless not regardable as true or false. These are *performative* sentences, which are used to accomplish the acts they mention, and they must be described as *illocutionary acts* that may succeed or go awry in various ways, depending on matters of intention and context, that Austin calls *felicity conditions*. For example, Sentence 1 is special in that in uttering it in the right contexts, one thereby does what the sentence says, namely, by saying it one christens a certain ship *Esmerelda.* In uttering Sentence 2, on the other hand, one does not *thereby* live in Kankakee.

1. I christen this ship the USS Esmerelda.
2. I live in Kankakee.

Furthermore, one can see that Sentence 2 is the sort of thing one can argue about; it can be true or false. In the case of Sentence 1, though, there seems no point to argue; if the context is right, one does christen by saying the sentence, and there can be no argument about it. It seems not the sort of thing that can be true or false, in spite of its declarative form. It can, however, be evaluated as succeeding or failing, as (part of) an act of christening, depending on whether the speaker has authority to christen, whether the right ship is present, and so on. Austin provides a classification of types of speech acts and raises the question whether *all* sentences, including those like Sentence 2, ought not to be considered as instances of various kinds of speech acts.

Austin's (1962) work has inspired an extensive literature on theoretical and philosophical problems of the notion "speech act"; for example, Cohen (1964), Searle (1969), McCawley (1977), and Stampe (1975). The goal of most of this work is the refinement and elaboration of the theory of speech acts, and its relation to semantics.

It has also inspired an important transformational theory of performative sentences—the *performative hypothesis*—proposed by Ross (1970) and Sadock (1974). The basic claim of this theory is that *every* sentence has as its main verb in underlying structure a *performative verb*—roughly, a verb that names the speech act the sentence is used to perform. This entails abstract verbs of saying for ordinary declarative sentences, of asking for ordinary questions, and of ordering for ordinary imperatives. Thus, a declarative sentence like Sentence 3 would have an underlying structure similar to that of Sentence 4.

3. It's raining in Philo.
4. I say to you that it's raining in Philo.

And Sentence 5 would have an underlying structure of the same sort as Sentence 6.

5. Is it raining in Philo?
6. I ask you whether it is raining in Philo.

The performative analysis was originally intended to explain certain apparently syntactic phenomena (a goal it has never completely achieved). All syntactic arguments for it are of the same general form.

1. A certain lexical item, syntactic construction, or syntactic rule can be seen to be conditioned by two apparently distinct conditions.

   a. In main clauses, there is some condition relative to first or second person subject, or on the type of sentence in which the element can occur (declarative, interrogative, or imperative), or some combination of these.

   b. In subordinate clauses, there is some condition about agreement in person/number between some NP in the main clause and some NP in the subordinate clause, or on the type of verb that must occur in the main clause (a verb of saying, asking, or ordering), or some combination of these.

2. It is shown that if main clauses are taken to be underlyingly embedded under various verbs of saying (deleted in surface structure) with first person subject and second person indirect object, the *a* condition can be reduced to a subcase of the *b* condition. As a consequence, a single general condition can be given, rather than the more complex disjunctive one that is required without the hypothesis of abstract underlying performative verbs.

As an illustration of this kind of analysis, take the idiomatic expression *be damned if,* with the meaning of emphatic denial, as in Sentence 7.

7. I'll be damned if I'll go to that conference.

Be damned if can occur in a subordinate clause just in case it is in the complement of a verb of stating and its subject is coreferential to the subject of the verb of stating, as shown in Sentences 8, 9 and 10. (Following the practice usual in linguistics, sentences that are ungrammatical are marked with an asterisk.)

8. John says he'll be damned if he'll vote for that man again.
9. *John regrets that he'll be damned if he'll vote for that man again.
10. *John says you'll be damned if you'll vote for that man again.

It can occur in a main clause, just in case its subject is first person and the sentence is declarative, as shown in Sentences 11, 12, and 13.

11. I'll be damned if I'll vote for that man again.
12. *Will I be damned if I'll vote for that man again?
13. *You'll be damned if you'll vote for that man again.
14. I say to you that I'll be damned if I'll vote for that man again.

If the performative hypothesis is correct, and a sentence like Sentence 11 is in underlying structure the object complement of a clause whose subject refers to the speaker of the sentence (i.e. is first person), and whose verb is a verb of stating, as in Sentence 14, then these conditions can be reduced to a single condition, stated as condition 15.

15. The idiom *be damned if* can occur only embedded in the complement of a verb of stating, and the subject of the idiom must be identical in reference to that of the verb of stating.

Without the performative hypothesis, Sentences 12 and 16 are treated as anomalous for entirely unrelated reasons, since they violate entirely unrelated conditions; under the performative hypothesis, Sentence 12 has an underlying structure like that of Sentence 16, and thus they are anomalous for the same *syntactic* reason: both violate condition 15 in the same way.

16. *I ask you whether I'll be damned if I'll vote for that man again.

Conversational Implicature

Perhaps as influential in the development of pragmatic theories (of discourse comprehension) as Austin's (1962) concept *speech act* has been the work of Grice and others on *conversational implicature* and *indirect speech acts.*

Grice (1975) begins by demonstrating that much more is conveyed in the utterance of a sentence than merely the literal meaning of the sentence. For example, if on being asked to a party I reply with Sentence 17,

17. I have an 8 o'clock class to teach.

I will probably succeed in conveying a refusal of the invitation, even though the literal meaning of my reply is not the same as that of Sentence 18.

18. I won't come to your party.

Or, to use Grice's example, if someone asks me how a friend is doing in his new job at a bank, and I reply by saying Sentence 19,

19. Oh quite well, I think; he likes his colleagues, and hasn't been to prison yet.

I will probably succeed in conveying indirectly the opinion that the friend's honesty is open to question, although it would be entirely implausible to attribute that meaning directly as the literal meaning of any part of Sentence 19.

Grice offers an informal account of such indirectly conveyed meaning, which he terms *conversational implicature.* His account may be described as a framework for inferring what the speaker's intentions are in uttering a particular sentence, with whatever literal meaning it has. To avoid a common confusion, it should be pointed out that this kind of treatment depends directly on a sentence (or utterance of a sentence) having some kind of literal meaning assigned by the rules of the language. It is not intended as replacement for the notion "literal meaning," but is, in fact, parasitic on it.

Grice's account consists of a set of rules for conversational interactions, these rules having as their basis the *Cooperative Principle:* "Make your conversational contribution such as is required, at the stage at which it occurs, by the accepted purpose or direction of the talk exchange in which you are engaged [p. 45]." From this Grice derives conversational "maxims" of four categories: *Quantity, Quality, Relation,* and *Manner.* These include such requirements as.

> Make your contribution as informative as is required.
> Do not say what you do not believe to be true.
> Be relevant.
> Avoid ambiguity of expression [pp. 45–46].

Grice takes pains to point out that these maxims are not unique to language use but are merely the application, to the special case of langauge, of general principles of rational behavior, a point often overlooked in subsequent literature on conversational implicature.

Indeed, we spend most of our waking hours consciously or unconsciously interpreting the behavior of other people by making inferences about the intentions behind their acts. What is special about communicative acts is that the speaker intends for the hearer to make such inferences and intends for the hearer to realize that the speaker intends that the inferences be made (see Bruce's Chapter 15, this volume). And, in the case of linguistic communicative acts, conventions are exploited for this purpose. Grice's maxims thus could be considered from the hearer's viewpoint as a set of rules for making inferences about the speaker's intentions in the linguistic acts performed, and from the speaker's perspective as a set of rules for selecting linguistic acts that make her intentions as clear as she wants them to be (cf. Weiser 1974, 1975, for discussion).

Grice's maxims sometimes seem trivial to the casual reader but it is in their obvious simplicity that their beauty lies. Results very important for theories of logic, language, and communication have been derived by Grice and others from these seemingly trivial principles.

Horn (1973), for example, attacks some difficult problems of quantifiers and scalar predicates from a Gricean viewpoint and arrives at a number of significant conclusions. One of Horn's results is a demonstration that certain problems of apparent entailment relations between quantified statements can be solved by an analysis involving conversational implicature. The problem is this: At first glance, a sentence containing *some* seems to entail a corresponding sentence containing *some not;* that is, if someone said Sentence 20,

20. Some linguists can read.

one would be likely to conclude that the speaker also believed Sentence 21,

21. Some linguists can't read.

But if *some* entails *some not*, then Sentence 22 ought to be a contradiction; yet it is not contradictory.

22. Some linguists, perhaps all, can read.

Horn shows that the problem can be solved by treating the *some/some not* relation not as a matter of entailment but as a matter of conversational implicature, produced by the interaction of Grice's maxims with certain properties of scalar predicates. The essence of his analysis is this: If one has good reason to believe that Sentence 23 is true, then to say Sentence 20 violates Grice's maxim of quantity.

23. All linguists can read.

If what is at issue is the membership of the set of linguists who can read, then to say Sentence 20 in thse circumstances, even though it is true, is to be insufficiently informative. Since the hearer will ordinarily be assuming that the speaker of sentence 20 is conforming to the conversational maxims and giving as much relevant information as she has evidence for, the hearer will assume that the speaker had no reason to believe Sentence 23, for if the speaker believed it and was cooperating, Sentence 23 would have been used instead of Sentence 20. Sentence 20 is true, but its utterance in this context is misleading in that uttering it will convey by implicature that some linguists *cannot* read.

Since, under this analysis, Sentence 20 does not entail that some linguists cannot read, there is nothing contradictory about Sentence 22; in fact, it exhibits conformity with the maxim of quality in that, in hedging on the appropriate quantifier, the speaker indicates that he does not have sufficient evidence for a more precise quantifier. By hedging he indicates that he knows that Sentence 20 is true and thinks that Sentence 23 might *also* be true.

In general, interest in conversational implicature has focussed linguists' attention on the crucial distinction between sentence-meaning (the meaning the sentence has by virtue of the semantic rules of the language) and speaker-meaning (what the speaker means to convey in uttering the sentence), generally with the result of greater insight into difficult problems of meaning.

Indirect Speech Acts

One special case of conversational implicature is *indirect speech acts*. An indirect speech act is characterized as the use of a sentence with a certain speech-act nature to convey what amounts to a second speech act, perhaps of a different kind. For example, yes–no questions can be used to indirectly make assertions, offers, requests, or wh–interrogative questions, among other things. Thus the following (a) examples might, in the right circumstances, be used with the effect of the respective (b) examples.

24a. Would I lie to you?
24b. I wouldn't lie to you.
25a. Wouldn't you like a drink?
25b. Have a drink.
26a. Can you please hand me that hammer?
26b. Please hand me that hammer.
27a. Do you know where the bathroom is?
27b. Where's the bathroom?

The problem of indirect speech acts has been investigated by a number of linguists and philosophers. Grice's notion of conversational implicature was adopted by Gordon and Lakoff (1975) as a starting point for arriving at their account of indirect speech acts via a concept of *conversational postulate*. Gordon and Lakoff propose various conversational postulates to account for various indirect speech acts. For Sentence 26(a), for example, adopting Searle's (1969) notion of sincerity condition (a condition that must hold for a speech act to be sincere), they propose this conversational postulate: "One can convey a request by: (1) asserting a speaker-based sincerity condition; or (2) questioning a hearer-based sincerity condition [p. 86]." Thus they intend to explain the fact that Sentence 26(a) can be used to convey 26(b) by the fact that 26(a) questions a sincerity condition that refers to the hearer: For a request to be sincere, it must be the case that the speaker believes that the hearer is able to carry out the act requested. But the exact nature of these conversational postulates is left unclear in their paper. In particular, it is not clear whether they intend their conversational postulates to be taken as just consequences of Grice's maxims or as additional rules independent of the maxims. Sadock (1970) has discussed the same kind of data and has proposed an analysis different from Gordon and Lakoff's in that the request nature of sentences like *Can you pass the salt?* is treated not as implicature but as part of literal meaning. Sadock's analysis appeals to the fact that implicatures can become frozen as the literal meaning of expressions under the right circumstances (this point is discussed in greater detail in a later section of this chapter on semantics and pragmatics).

Green's (1975) discussion and catalogue of various kinds of conveyed requests argues for distinguishing two types: an idiomatic type like Sentence 28, whose request nature is treated as part of its literal meaning, and a type like Sentence 29, which she calls *hints* and which, she argues, are truly indirect and conveyed by implicature.

28. Can you pass the salt.
29. This broccoli needs salt.

Davison (1975) and Fraser (1975) discuss various other kinds of indirect speech acts. Searle (1975), construing Gordon and Lakoff's conversational postulates as independent of general rules of conversation, argues against the need for them, proposing instead a treatment of indirect speech acts based on inference. Morgan (1977a) criticizes some crucial flaws in Gordon and Lakoff's construal of indirect speech acts, in particular, their treatment of implicature as a kind of entailment and their use of transderivational syntactic conditions, which Sadock (1975) also criticizes on other grounds.

Pragmatics and Syntax

From the linguist's viewpoint, one of the most intriguing results of recent work in pragmatics is the strong indication of interactions between syntax and various pragmatic functions. Along with this development has come a gradual realization that the application of so-called "optional" transformations were labeled as optional in that whether or not the rules applied in the the early days of transformational grammar, many well-known transformations were labeled as optional in that, whether or not the rules applied in the derivation of a sentence did not affect grammaticality. Thus rules like Passive were regarded as optional in that the nonapplication of such rules does not yield ungrammatical sentences, as opposed to supposedly "obligatory" rules like Chomsky's (1957) Affix-Shift rule. Optional rules were often considered to be a matter of "free variation" in syntactic form. Early on, however, this view came under suspicion as analysts began to notice that sentences related by supposedly optional rules actually differed in subtle ways and were not, in fact, in free variation. A typical case is the rule of Tough-movement, which (oversimplified) transforms sentences like Sentence 30 into sentences like 31.

30. It is hard to play that sonata on this kazoo.
31. This kazoo is hard to play that sonata on.

At first glance, these sentences might seem to be identical in meaning, but close inspection reveals a subtle difference in that the latter would be more likely to be understood as about a property of the kazoo whereas the former is neutral as to whether it is a property of the sonata or of the kazoo. Similar differences, often subtle, have been found to be associated with most syntactically optional rules. It may be useful to maintain the notion *syntactically optional* within syntactic theory, but this clearly gives an incomplete picture. The factors determining the application of optional syntactic rules must be described in some part of linguistic theory.

One common assumption about such determining factors places them in the syntactic component; this assumption is that anything that determines the application of a rule in a syntactic derivation must be present in the syntactic structure of the sentence at some level. But this is not a necessary assumption. Indeed, Gordon and Lakoff (1975), in their paper on conversational postulates, propose that certain rules are conditioned by the presence of some conversational implicature. Morgan (1975, 1977) argues, however, that (insofar as Gordon and Lakoff's observations are correct) it is not conversational implicature in Gordon and Lakoff's sense but the communicative intentions of the speaker that determine the application of such rules, the rules then being seen as having the function of signaling certain kinds of communicative intentions.

At any rate, it is slowly becoming clear that there are a number of kinds of correlations between pragmatics and syntactic form, ranging from the role pragmatic considerations play in the determination of stress and intonation (Bolinger, 1972; Sag & Liberman, 1975; Schmerling, 1976) and rule application (Kuno, 1975, 1976; Schmerling, 1975) to less obvious matters like their interaction with universal constraints on the properties of syntactic rules, as in Morgan (1975).

Schmerling (1976), for instance, discusses (among other matters) the fact that the different stress patterns assigned by speakers to Sentences 32 and 33, when the content of these sentences was "news," depended on their assumptions about whether the events referred to were expected or not.

32. Trùman díed.
33. Jóhnson dìed.

A wide variety of pragmatic considerations have been shown to affect syntactic rule applications. This means that rule applications can be seen as reflecting speaker's attitudes, assumptions, and/or intentions not only about the items under discussion but also about the addressee's assumptions about these and the addressee's ability to keep track of what the speaker is saying. There are two ways that such considerations can determine the application of syntactic rules. The first, perhaps more common, is that a rule or set of rules is exploited for expressive ends that may be independent of the rule itself. Subject-creating and subject-destroying rules, such as those exemplified in Sentences 34 through 42, as well as lexical choices, as in Sentences 43 and 44, are instances of this. The second way is that a particular rule may have a certain constant function (this is not to deny that some rules have, or can be exploited to fulfill, a perceptual or processing function as well; see Bever [1970] for discussion). Other constituent reordering rules, such as those exemplified in Sentences 45 and 46, and tag-question rules (Sentences 47 and 48), seem to always have a certain communicative value.

A clear case of the first kind is that a number of rules can be exploited to emphasize some part of the sentence (usually a noun phrase) by allowing the emphasized element to occur in a prominent position—sentence final position, especially predicate position. In cases like this, it is clearly the position, not the rule, that has a constant function. Practically any rule that puts a given element in the same position will have the same effect. (There is a large amount of literature on the communicative effect on surface syntactic position, mainly associated with the Functional Sentence Perspective theory of Prague and elsewhere; see Danes [1974] for discussion). For example, the content of the extraposed clause in Sentence 35 is more effectively conveyed as new information than it is in Sentence 34, where it is not extraposed.

34. That a change of venue ought to be granted, to keep Judge Little's rape case spectator ban from becoming the cause of feminist riots, is obvious.
35. It is obvious that a change of venue ought to be granted, to keep Judge Little's rape case spectator ban from becoming the cause of feminist riots.

The same function may be served by other syntactic rules that position clausal material at the end of the sentence, as in Sentence 37 as opposed to Sentence 36 (see Ziv, 1976, for further discussion).

36. A man who has three ears came in.
37. A man came in who has three ears.

In a probably related fashion, rules that distribute clausal noun phrases in subject position (see Horn, in preparation) allow the speaker to imply that they represent propositions which are, at least in the context, accepted as true. The passive has this function in Sentence 39, as opposed to Sentence 38.

38. The government has never acknowledged that distilled water is effective in treating warts.
39. That distilled water is effective in treating warts has never been acknowledged by the government.

As another example, the agent deletion which accompanies the passive can serve either to allow identification of the agent to be omitted, because it is unknown or irrelevant, as in Sentence 40, or it can be used to very subtly suggest, for instance in academic and bureaucratic prose, that there is no identifiable agent, as in Sentence 41 (see Sinha, 1974, for further discussion), presumably to make the statement sound more scientific and less personal, or, as in Sentence 42, more offical and less alterable (see Stanley, 1971 for discussion).

40. John's dog was run over yesterday.
41. It was proposed that all grammars be considered as models of behavior.
42. Violators will be prosecuted to the full extent of the law.

The lexical choice between *some* and *any* in questions and conditionals serves to convey expectation, and can thereby function to influence responses, as illustrated in Sentences 43 and 44. Sentence 43 is more likely to provoke a positive response than 44, as it reflects the speaker's expectation that the addressee will want more soup, whereas Sentence 44 reflects the opposite (or at least neutral) expectation (see R. Lakoff, 1969a for discussion).

43. Would you like some more chicken soup?
44. Would you like any more chicken soup?

There are a number of cases that appear to be of the second type, in which a rule seems to have a constant communicative value. For example, as Dwight Bolinger has observed (reported in R. Lakoff, 1969b), the rule (or relation) of negative transportation weakens the negative assertion, or at least the speaker's responsibility for it. Thus the speaker conveys a greater sense of certainty in Sentence 45 than in Sentence 46.

45. John thinks Bill won't win.
46. John doesn't think that Bill will win.

Another example: R. Lakoff (1973) has observed that the tag-question construction, illustrated in Sentence 47, can be used for numerous pragmatic purposes, depending on intonation.

45. The boys are outside, aren't they?

A speaker may use a tag question with rising intonation to convey uncertainty, or with falling intonation to try to influence the content of his addressee's response, often in order to force a confession or coerce agreement, as in Sentence 48 as compared to 49, which is more nearly neutral.

48. You forgot to pick up your toys again, didn't you?
49. Did you forget to pick up your toys again?

The full range of the interactions of syntax and pragmatics remains to be explored.

PROBLEM AREAS

Theoretical work in pragmatics has barely begun, and there are a number of problems outstanding. These fall into three main areas: formalism, the relation between speech acts and semantics, and the problem of empirically distinguishing semantic from pragmatic properties.

Formalism

Fundamental work on pragmatics (e.g., Austin, 1962; Grice, 1975; Searle, 1969) has been purposely informal in that it is not accompanied by an interpreted formalization. Although it is possible to judge the insight and explanatory power of this work without the tools of formalism, formalizations would be a prod to the sharpening and refinement of concepts and would make relevant theories more directly vulnerable to empirical test. There have been scattered attempts at formalization in various frameworks, Montague (1972), Kasher (1974), G. Lakoff (1975), Gazdar (1976), for example. But the bulk of the job of formalization remains to be done. The most important issues in formalization are, first, what kind of system is pragmatics? Can pragmatics be formalized as merely an adjunct to standard truth-conditional semantic theories or must an adequate formalism be, in effect, a model of discourse comprehension, or perhaps based on a general theory of acts and intentions? Second, will standard logics suffice for formalization of natural inference or will it be necessary to formulate new kinds of systems, perhaps in "fuzzy logic" (see G. Lakoff, 1973, for discussion). Answers to such questions are a prerequisite to meaningful work in formalization. But there is no reason to take seriously the frequent complaint that "this kind of thing can't be formalized," and therefore cannot be the subject of serious theoretical work.

Speech Acts and Semantics

The nature of the relation between speech acts and semantics has been a difficult problem for theories of language. In linguistics, the performative hypothesis is sometimes taken, perhaps in some extended version, as a way of treating the relation by reducing the speech act properties of a sentence to a matter of the logical structure of the sentence. This approach has been criticized on various grounds by Anderson (1968), Fraser (1971), Morgan (1976), and Searle (1976), among others.

The criticisms fall into three major categories. First, a syntactic objection: There are a number of apparent counterexamples to the hypothesis that the performative verb is always the highest verb in underlying structure, as in the counterexamples 50 through 54.

50. I'm afraid I must ask you to leave.
51. May I be so bold as to congratulate you?
52. Your behavior leaves me no alternative but to sentence you to 20 years.
53. The University takes great pleasure in announcing that there will be no raises next year.
54. I regret to say that I have no money.

In these sentences, the verb that names the act that the sentence is used to perform (*ask, congratulate, sentence, announce,* and *say,* respectively) is not in the main clause but in a subordinate clause, and is thus not the "highest" verb.

This objection could, at least in principle, be countered in either of two ways. First, it could be claimed that a given case is an *indirect* speech act (see discussion following) and therefore not a genuine counterexample. This approach seems quite appropriate for cases like Sentence 51, which one might plausibly claim is a question and only indirectly a congratulation; a similar claim of indirectness is not entirely implausible for cases like Sentences 50, 52, and 53. Second, it could be argued that it is only in surface structure that the performative verb is in a subordinate clause, and that in the underlying structure, the performative verb is in the highest clause. Thus, one might propose for a sentence like 54 an underlying structure like structure 55 in which the performative verb is in the main clause.

55. I say that I have no money, and I say that I regret it.

But no entirely satisfactory account in these terms has appeared, and this class of counterexamples remains a problem.

A second, more difficult problem for the performative hypothesis is data that suggest that the arguments for a syntactic treatment of such phenomena are mistaken in the first place. Examples like Sentences 56 and 57 point to the conclusion that it is the intended effect of the sentence, not any of its syntactic properties, that determines the distribution of the elements in question.

56. I want you to know that I'll be damned if I'll ever vote for that man again.
57. I hope it's obvious to everybody that I'll be damned if I'll ever vote for that man again.

Want you to know is not the name of a speech act, nor a performative verb, nor is *hope it's obvious to everybody*. The correct condition on the occurrence of *be damned if* seems to be a use condition, not a syntactic condition. The idiom must be used as a denial of something, which may be conveyed directly, as in Sentence 11, in a report of such a denial, as in Sentence 8 (both repeated here for convenience), or in a denial that is conveyed indirectly by inference, as in 56 and 57).

  8. John says he'll be damned if he'll vote for that man again.
 11. I'll be damned if I'll vote for that man again.

It would seem that, in cases like these, one must either abandon the assumption that the distribution of phrases like *be damned if* is to be stated in terms of a syntactic environment or reduce the notion "syntactic envrionment" to vacuity. But if the conclusion is that the distribution of such elements, and application of some syntactic rules, is determined not by syntactic (or even truth-conditional semantic) properties of the sentence, but by the nature of the communicative purposes for which the sentence is used, then the result is a theory of grammar of a new and unfamiliar type, whose nature remains to be explored.

  The third serious problem for the performative hypothesis, indeed, for any analysis of performative sentences, is providing an account of the relation between semantic properties of linguistic elements and the speech-act properties of the sentences in which they occur. The relation is sometimes construed as a simple and straightforward one, in which the semantic properties assigned to a sentnece by the compositional semantic rules allow one to predict what speech acts it can be used to perform or, in fact, provide an account of them. It might be claimed, for example, that knowing the meaning of the words in Sentence 58 and the compositional semantic rules is sufficient to allow one to know that Sentence 58 can be used to apoligize.

 58. I apologize.

So a child who knows the meaning of the pronoun *I* and knows enough about the verb *apologize* to understand Sentence 59,

 59. John apologized.

would know automatically that 58 can be used to apologize. Likewise, this view implies that in knowing the regular English semantic rules of combination and the meanings of the words *I, christen, this,* and so on, and knows *thereby* that Sentence 60 can be used to christen a ship Thelma.

60. I christen this ship Thelma.

But this simple construal of the relation between semantics and speech acts is probably mistaken; at least there are some severe difficulties in making it work. For example, given this view of things, one would expect from the meaning of the verb *fire* in Sentence 61 that 62 ought to be a way of firing people. But sentence 63 is used instead.

61. John fired Bill.
62. I fire you.
63. You're fired.

Similarly, this simple semantic approach to speech-act properties seems to imply that Sentence 64 can be used to divorce; but it can't, at least not in American culture.

64. I divorce you.

And it is hard to see how a semantic approach can possibly yield a perspicuous account of the situation in a culture in which Sentence 65 is used to divorce. Is each sentence one-third performative?

65. I divorce you. I divorce you. I divorce you.

It appears from such cases that a semantic analysis provides neither necessary nor sufficient conditions for a given expression to be usable performatively. Rather, semantic criteria (of the sort discussed by McCawley, 1977, for example) characterize only a class of natural candidates for use as performative formulae. But the natural candidate may not be actually usable, because rules for successful performance of the act in question do not call for use of any performative formula at all, because some other natural candidate is used, or because (conceivably) some expression that is *not* a natural candidate is used, perhaps by some historical accident. For example, a culture could just as well establish a convention whereby boats must be christened not by saying "I christen . . . ," but by saying the boat's name twice, reciting the Lord's Prayer backwards, and spitting in a porthole. Such a christening ritual might well be considered silly but it certainly would not be a violation of English grammar. So it appears that knowledge of language must be distinguished from knowledge of other kinds of conventions that happen to include rules about ways in which expressions can be used (see Morgan, 1978, for further discussion). Knowledge of language provides only a class of expressions that *could* be used, by virtue of the meanings of their parts, as performative formulae; knowledge of culture (law, religion, games, etiquette, etc.) tells us which (if any) of the natural candidates is actually recognized as a valid performative formula for a given purpose.

That is not to say, though, that there are *no* sentences whose speech-act potential is a matter of knowledge of language. For instance, the knowledge that Sentences 67, and 68 can be used, respectively, to state, question, and order would seem to be knowledge of English, not knowledge of 20th-century Anglo-American social conventions.

66. It's 5 o'clock.
67. Is dinner ready?
68. Sit down!

Semantics and Pragmatics

Another difficult and controversial issue in pragmatics is the problem of distinguishing conversational implicature from literal meaning, of deciding between pragmatic and semantic accounts of particular phenomena, and, generally, of determing the boundary line between semantics and pragmatics. For example, by saying Sentence 69, one usually conveys that disrobing preceded getting into bed.

69. I took off my clothes and got into bed.

But is this part of the literal meaning of the sentence or the result of conversational implicature? Both approaches have a certain amount of initial plausibility, and the question is not an easy one (see Schmerling, 1975, for discussion). Semantic and pragmatic analyses compete, at least potentially, as accounts of many other phenomena as well, raising questions as to how much of the traditional domain of semantics should properly be given over to pragmatics. As another example, the question has arisen whether many problems of reference—Donnellan's (1966) attributive–referential distinction is a good example—are more appropriately dscribed in pragmatic terms than in semantic terms. In a similar vein, Nunberg and Pan (1975) propose a pragmatic solution to the problem of generic sentences, of the type illustrated in Sentences 70 and 71.

70. Movies are not any good any more.
71. Elephants never forget.

Though there is no surface quantifier in such sentences, they are nonetheless understood as general statements, in this case general statements about movies and elephants, respectively. One is therefore tempted to hypothesize an *all*-like quantifier in the underlying structure of such sentences. But one major difficulty with generic sentences such as these is that, unlike other *all*-statements, they are not disconfirmed by one or two counterexamples or even by a good handful of counterexamples. Finding one forgetful elephant wold not cause one to abandon Sentence 71, and one good movie does not disconfirm Sentence 70. Nunberg and Pan (1975) attempt a solution of these and other problems of generics by proposing an analysis in which the quantifiers involved in the understanding of such sentences are not part of the literal meaning of the expressions but are inferred via pragmatic principles; in other words, the sentence contains no quantifiers in its logical structure, but the hearer infers that it is intended as a general statement.

Horn (1975) and Halpern (1976) have discussed accounts of the semantico–syntactic rule of negative-transportation that is often proposed as an account of the fact that a sentence like 72 can be used to convey what Sentence 73 conveys.

72. I don't think it's raining.
73. I think it's not raining.

Even presupposition, traditionally taken to be a semantic problem, has recently been recast as at least partially pragmatic in nature (Karttunen, 1973, 1974; Morgan, 1973; Stalnaker, 1972).

The reason that there is so much difficulty in distinguishing semantic from pragmatic properties is that reliable empirical criteria for distinguishing them have not yet been established. Grice's (1975) discussion provides some informal tests for conversational implicature, but Sadock (1976) shows that they are not sufficient as tests. The problem is made especially difficult by the fact that various kinds of nonliteral, indirectly conveyed meaning can become frozen as literal menaing, a very common diachronic process. Breal (1964) long ago pointed out that metaphorical senses are often taken on as literal meaning, and Sadock (1974), Cole (1975), and Morgan (1978) have argued more recently that conversational implicature can become "grammaticalized" as literal meaning, no doubt a common source of semantic change. This kind of diachronic development is frequent in the fossilzation of euphemisms, to choose a common example, with the result that the very meaning that the euphemism is employed to avoid is later fossilized as the literal meaning of the expression. For instance, the phrase *go to the bathroom* was originally a circumlocution used to refer to taboo bodily functions without directly mentioning them, but for many speakers it now means literally what formerly it only hinted at. Consequently, some speakers may now say sentences like 74 and 75 without any sort of contradiction or semantic anomaly.

74. The dog went to the bathroom on the living room rug.
75. The baby went to the bathroom all over my lap.

Given the possibility of this kind of diachronic development, it follows that it may often be difficult to distinguish a genuine case of conversational implicature from a case in which implicature has been frozen as the literal meaning of some expression that wears its history on its sleeve. Sadock (1974) has argued that the use of sentences such as *Can you pass the salt?* to make requests exemplifies the latter possibility. *Can you,* according to Sadock, is, in present-day English, an idiom whose literal meaning is that of a request, but which derives historically from the conversational implicature of a request from a question about ability. As a consequence, according to Sadock, *can you* is now genuinely ambiguous, between the frozen implicature and the word-for-word literal meaning, just as most idioms are. Sadock's position is supported by two particularly interesting observations. First, *can you* requests are judged to be more direct requests than parallel expressions with very similar word-by-word literal meanings. Thus, Sentence 76 is a fairly direct request, but 77 and 78 are closer to hints (See Schweller, 1978, for experimental examination of this question).

76. Can you pass the salt?
77. Are you able to pass the salt?
78. Is it possible for you to pass the salt?

Second, *can you* requests, but not the seemingly synonymous questions in Sentences 77 and 78, have some of the syntactic properties of direct imperative-form requests—for example, preverbal *please,* as in Sentences 79 through 81.

79. Can you please pass the salt?
80. *Are you able to please pass the salt?
81. *Is it possible for you to please pass the salt?

Morgan (1978) suggests a third point of view concerning such problematic expressions—that they are conventional, but not idioms. In this approach, the hearer employs knowledge of how-things-are-done-indirectly in a fashion that makes it possible to recognize immediately that an inference is intended, and to recognize what the *inference* is, without going through the inferential process. The hearer knows that people commonly use certain expressions intending certain inferences, and this knowledge makes it possible to recognize such an instance immediately and thereby to recognize what was intended without having to infer it from literal meaning. The distinction between conventions of literal meaning and conventions of use is discussed, and a schema for the latter is presented that allows some insight into how expressions can change diachronically from conventions of use to conventions of literal meaning.

PRAGMATICS AND PROBLEMS OF READING

Questions of pragmatics and reading fall into two main areas. The first is the set of questions that relate to all language comprehension, written or oral. The primary reading questions in this area are developmental. The second area concerns questions of pragmatics that are unique to written language.

Developmental Questions

The developmental question most directly relevant for reading problems is this: To what extent has the reader acquired the ability to perform all the pragmatic tasks necessary for comprehension of connected discourse? Answers depend on determining what demands are made on the reader by particular texts, developmental research on the age at which children become competent at various pragmatic tasks, and the order in which the various skills and abilities are acquired. It appears that children can cope with at least some indirect speech acts somewhere between two and four (see Shatz, 1974; Bates, 1976); but it may be that young children do not process these indirect speech acts the same way adults do. Shatz argues that rather than understanding indirect speech acts by inference, as in Searle (1975) and Clark & Lucy (1975), young children may interpret them by a brute force heuristic that circumvents the inference-from-literal-meaning route:

> find some element (or elements), either action or object, in Mama's speech which you can act out or act upon. Then, perform some action which communicates to Mama that you have heard, are responding, are taking your turn in the interaction, and so on [p. 9].

Morgan (1977) speculates in a similar vein that children may know how to use some expressions, or at least give the appearance of knowing how to use them, before they learn how that use relates to the literal meaning of the expression. The child learns to recognize (and use) certain expressions that are frequently used by adults to perform indirect speech acts and will recognize from experience what the main intent behind the utterance is. Yet the child may not connect this use with the literal meaning of the sentence and may not even be aware that indirectness could be involved.

The question arises, then, of the stage at which children begin to interpret indirect speech acts, conversational implicature, definite determiners, and other pragmatic aspects of language, using the same system that adults use. If children can seem to understand things the same way, while actually using a different interpretation strategy, nonobvious differences between the child's interpretation and an adult's (teacher, parent) might lead to the mistaken conclusion that the child has a reading problem.

A related question in regard to particular instances is whether the child has the world knowledge necessary for making pragmatic inferences; probably every case of inference involves some knowledge without which the inference cannot be made. Although there is next to nothing in the way of clear answers to any of these questions, the problem is an important one. In reading, the child is faced with a task of interpreting adult language usage or language that the adult author judges to be right for the reader's abilities. The accuracy of the intuitions of children's authors about what children are likely to understand easily is an open question. Moreover, it is conceivable that there are "dialects" of pragmatic strategies, such that a given child's competence may lead to an interpretation different from what the author intended or from the teacher's interpretation. There has been very little linguistic research on this topic.

Pragmatics and Written Language

There are three areas of potentially important pragmatic difference between spoken conversation and reading: differences that are due to the nature of the written channel, in particular to the physical separation of reader and author; differences that are due to pragmatic rule differences between oral and written materials; and the matter of pragmatic relations between text and illustrations.

Reading differs from oral interactions not only in the medium of communication, but in other important ways as well. Use of the written mode usually entails that the reader is removed in time and space from the writer, whereas a speaker and hearer generally have immediate access to each other and generally share the same physical surroundings. This makes possible the use of various verbal (intonation, tone of voice) and nonverbal (gestures, facial expressions, head movements) devices to facilitate the hearer's task of inferring speaker's intentions. The lack of this kind of information makes the pragmatics of reading potentially more difficult and could be a factor for children who have not yet fully mastered the ins and outs of pragmatic inference. But on the other side of the coin, a few things may be made easier as well. Obviously, the writer cannot reasonably employ expressions whose purpose is to evoke responses or feedback from the interlocutor, like tag-questions. Nor will the reader have to guess, if he encounters a question such as Sentence 82, whether it is real or a rhetorical question.

82. Who can tell whether John would have married Martha if George had been killed in the war?

The reader may be able to infer immediately that a genuine question is not intended because the author is not present to receive the answer.

The fact that the reader does not share the writer's physical surroundings also means that there will be virtually no deictic uses of pronouns, adverbs, and the like; words such as *he, there,* and *this* will always refer anaphorically, that is, to something the writer has previously introduced explicitly or implicitly. The primary exception, of course, is the use of *this, here, now,* and perhaps one or two other deictics to refer to an illustration on the same page, mainly in story books that are written to be read to young children, usually in the style of an oral story-teller. A. A. Milne's *Winnie the Pooh* and the version of *Alice in Wonderland* that Lewis Carroll wrote for "children aged from nought to five" are well-known examples. But in other children's materials, the demands for inferring references for deictics based on contexts outside the text will probably be lighter.

It is not yet clear whether written materials contain deictic or other pragmatic problems for the reader that the child is not already equipped to deal with from his experience with oral language. It is quite possible that there are different pragmatic "rules" for oral and written language, or for different kinds (genres, styles, registers) of written texts (see Rubin, Chapter 17, this volume, for discussion of the oral-written question). Such differences could constitute a comprehension problem for the beginning reader who has not been read to often.

The matter of illustrations in children's books is another difference in discourse comprehension that readers (as opposed to listeners) have to deal with (see Schallert, Chapter 21, this volume, for extensive discussion). Illustrations may serve in the books written for younger children as a sort of substitute for the shared physical environment of the speaker and hearer. Accompanying the prose with appropriate illustrations may absolve a writer from describing all the details of setting and context that need to be referred to later. Adults are expected to be able to infer the implied reference (e.g., to an automobile, a road, and a tire in Sentence 83), but writers of children's books, perhaps feeling that so much cannot be demanded of children, accompany their texts with illustrations providing appropriate reference points.

83. The farmer was driving to town when he went over a bump and had a flat.

In the sort of storybook written for preschoolers and beginning readers that has illustrative material on every page or every other page, the illustrations may depict up to 40% or 50% of the content of the story—or, more strictly, may contain "information" from which up to 40% or 50% of the content of the story may be inferred (measured roughly by constructing text descriptions of relevant parts of the illustrations).

Some children's book go so far as to make the illustrations as integral and essential part of the story. If the preschooler does not attend to all the details of the illustration, the text is incoherent. Adult readers occasionally find these texts barely comprehensible, perhaps because they are not accustomed to looking at illustrations that are not directly referred to while they read. A particularly striking example of the dependence of a story on the illustrations is found in *Hi, Cat,* written and illustrated by the prize-winning children's author, Ezra Jack Keats. For instance, the following continuous passage from that text is incomprehensible without reference to the pictures that accompany the lines quoted in 84 and 85.

84. [Archie] looked at his reflection in a store window [p. 5].
85. Peter was waiting at the corner. "Make way for your 'ol gran'pa," Archie said in a shaky voice. He looked Peter up and down. "My, my, Peter, how you've grown!" [next page:] "Why gran'pa," Peter said. "It's good to see you" [pp. 7, 8].

The text of 84 is accompanied by an illustration whose content is given in 86; 85 by an illustration described in 87.

86. A small boy with a half-eaten ice cream cone is looking at his reflection in a plate-glass window. There is a pale green substance in the ice cream cone and on his face, between his nose and upper lip, and on his chin. A cat, barely noticeable, is walking in the background.
87. The small boy, still with the green substance (presumably ice cream) on his face, is hunched over like a lame old man. He is holding a closed umbrella like a cane and faces a group of six children and a dachshund. The cat, seated erect, is barely noticeable in the background.

A less striking, though no less interesting example may be seen in Jacky Jeter's *The Cat and the Fiddler,* illustrated by Lionel Kalish. Although the author nowhere describes or even implies any emotions or intentions of the cat, from various illustrations it is possible to infer the cat's pride, grief, anger, contempt, or smugness, and from these emotions one can infer certain knowledge and intentions that the cat must have had.

How significant the reading-specific aspects of pragmatic inference are in determining ease of comprehension remains to be seen. And while the other pragmatic aspects of discourse comprehension are not specific to reading, it is not obvious either that a child can reasonably be expected to control them by the age when reading instruction typically begins, nor is it obvious that all children will be equally capable of transferring to the reading task the discourse comprehension skills that they have mastered for oral communication. Empirical research can perhaps be designed that will indicate if this might be one of the paths by which being read to makes it easier to learn to read.

ACKNOWLEDGMENT

This research was supported by the National Institute of Education under Contract No. US-NIE-C-400-76-0116.

REFERENCES

Anderson, S. *On the linguistic status of the performative/constative distinction*. Bloomington: Indiana University Linguistics Club, 1968.

Austin, J. *How to do things with words*. Oxford: University Press, 1962.

Bar-Hillel, Y. Indexical expressions. *Mind*, 1954, *63*, 359–379.

Bates, E. *Language and context; The acquisition of pragmatics*. New York: Academic Press, 1976.

Bever, T. The cognitive basis for linguistic structures. In J. R. Hayes (Ed.), *Cognition and the development of language*. New York: Wiley, 1970.

Bolinger, D. Accent is predictable (if you're a mind reader). *Language*, 1972, *48*, 633–644.

Breal, M. *Semantics* (Mrs. Henry Cust, trans.). New York: Dover, 1964.

Brown, P., & Levinson, S. *Universals in language usage: Politeness phenomena*. Unpublished manuscript, 1974.

Chomsky, N. *Syntactic structures*. The Hague: Mouton, 1957.

Clark, H., & Lucy, P. Understanding what is meant and said: A study in conversationally conveyed requests. *Journal of Verbal Learning and Verbal Behavior*, 1975, *14*, 56–72.

Cohen, L. Do illocutionary forces exist? *Philosophical Quarterly*, 1964, *14*, 118–137.

Cole, P. The synchronic and diachronic status of conversational implicature. In P. Cole & J. Morgan (Eds.), *Syntax and semantics. Vol. 3: Speech acts*. New York: Academic Press, 1975.

Danes, F. *Papers on functional sentence perspective*. Prague: Publishing House of the Czech Academy of Sciences, 1974.

Davison, S. Indirect speech acts and what to do with them. In P. Cole & J. Morgan (Eds.), *Syntax and semantics. Vol. 3: Speech acts*. New York: Academic Press, 1975.

Donnellan, K. Reference and definite descriptions. *Philosophical Review*, 1966, *75*, 281–304.

Fraser, B. *An examination of the performative analysis*. Bloomington: Indiana University Linguistics Club, 1971.

Fraser, B. Hedged performatives. In P. Cole & J. Morgan (Eds.), *Syntax and semantics. Vol. 3: Speech acts*. New York: Academic Press, 1975.

Gazdar, G. *Formal pragmatics for natural language*. Unpublished doctoral dissertation. Reading, England: University of Reading, 1976.

Gordon, D., & Lakoff, G. Conversational postulates. In P. Cole & J. Morgan (Eds.), *Syntax and semantics. Vol. 3: Speech acts*. New York: Academic Press, 1975.

Green, G. How to get people to do things with words: The whimperative question. In P. Cole & J. Morgan (Eds.), *Syntax and semantics. Vol. 3: Spech acts*. New York: Academic Press, 1975.

Grice, H. Meaning. *Philosophical Review*, 1957, *66*, 377–388.

Grice, H. Logic and conversation. In P. Cole & J. Morgan (Eds.), *Syntax and semantics. Vol. 3: Speech acts*. New York: Academic Press, 1975.

Halpern, R. The bivalence of neg-raising predicates. *Studies in the Linguistic Sciences*, 1976, *6*(1), 69–81.

Hooper, J., & Thompson, S. On the applicability of root transformations. *Linguistic Inquiry*, 1973, *4*, 465–491.

Horn, L. *On the semantic properties of logical operators in English*. Unpublished doctoral dissertation, University of California at Los Angeles, 1973.

Horn, L. Neg-raising predicates: Toward an explanation. *Papers from the Eleventh Regional Meeting of the Chicago Linguistic Society.* Chicago: Chicago Linguistic Society, 1975.

Horn, L. *Presuppositions: Variations on a theme.* In preparation.

Karttunen, L. Presuppositions of compound sentences. *Linguistic Inquiry,* 1973, *4,* 169–193.

Karttunen, L. Presuppositions and linguistic context. *Theoretical Linguistics,* 1974, *1,* 182–194.

Kasher, A. Mood implicatures: A logical way of doing generative pragmatics. *Theoretical Linguistics,* 1974, *1,* 6–38.

Kuno, S. Three perspectives in the functional approach to syntax. In R. Grossman, L. San, & T. Vance (Eds.), *Papers from the parasession on functionalism.* Chicago: Chicago Linguistic Society, 1975.

Kuno, S. Subject, theme, and the speaker's empathy—A reexamination of relativization phenomena. In C. Li (Ed.), *Subject and topic.* New York: Academic Press, 1976.

Lakoff, G. Presupposition and relative well-formedness. In D. Steinberg & L. Jakobovits (Eds.), *Semantics: An interdisciplinary reader.* Cambridge: Cambridge University Press, 1971.

Lakoff, G. Linguistics and natural logic. In D. Davidson & G. Harman (Eds.), *Semantics of natural language.* Boston: D. Reidel, 1972.

Lakoff, G. Fuzzy grammar and the performance/competence terminology game. In C. Corum, T. Smith-Stark, & S. Weiser (Eds.), *Papers from the Ninth Regional Meeting of the Chicago Linguistic Society.* Chicago: Chicago Linguistic Society, 1973.

Lakoff, G. Pragmatics in natural logic. In E. Keenan (Ed.), *Formal semantics of natural language.* Cambridge: Cambridge University Press, 1975.

Lakoff, R. A syntactic argument for negative transportation. *Papers from the Fifth Regional Meeting of the Chicago Linguistic Society,* Chicago: Chicago Linguistic Society, 1969. (b)

Lakoff, R. Some reasons why there can't be any *some-any* rule. *Language,* 1969, *45,* 608–615. (a)

Lakoff, R. The logic of politeness; or, minding your p's and q's. *Papers from the Ninth Regional Meeting of the Chicago Linguistic Society,* Chicago: Chicago Linguistic Society, 1973.

McCawley, J. Remarks on the lexicography of performative verbs. In A. Rogers, R. Wall, & J. Murphy (Eds.), *Proceedings of the Austin Conference on Performatives, Presuppositions and Implicatures.* Arlington, Va.: Center for Applied Linguistics, 1977.

Montague, R. Pragmatics and intensional logic. In D. Davidson & G. Harman (Eds.), *Semantics of natural language.* Boston: D. Reidel, 1972.

Morgan, J. *Presupposition and the representation of meaning: Prolegomena.* Unpublished doctoral dissertation, University of Chicago, 1973.

Morgan, J. Some interactions of syntax and pragmatics. In P. Cole & J. Morgan (Eds.), *Syntax and semantics. Vol. 3: Speech acts.* New York: Academic Press, 1975.

Morgan, J. *Pragmatics, common sense, and the performative analysis.* Paper presented at the Twelfth Regional Meeting of the Chicago Linguistic Society, Chicago, 1976.

Morgan, J. Conversational postulates revisited. *Language,* 1977, *53,* 277–284.

Morgan, J. *Two types of convention in indirect speech acts* In P. Cole (Ed.), *Syntax and Semantics. Vol. 9: Pragmatics.* New York: Academic Press, 1978.

Morris, C. Foundations of the theory of signs. *International Encyclopedia of Unified Science,* 1938, *1, 2,* 1–59.

Nunberg, G., & Pan, C. Inferring quantification in generic sentences. In R. Grossman, L. San, & T. Vance (Eds.), *Papers from the Eleventh Regional Meeting of the Chicago Linguistic Society.* Chicago: Chicago Linguistic Society, 1975.

Ross, J. On declarative sentences. In R. Jacobs & P. Rosenbaum (Eds.), *Readings in English transformational grammar.* Waltham, Mass.: Ginn, 1970.

Sadock, J. Whimperatives. In J. Sadock & A. Vanek (Eds.), *Studies presented to R. B. Lees.* Edmonton: Linguistics Research Inc., 1970.

Sadock, J. *Toward a linguistic theory of speech acts.* New York: Academic Press, 1974.

Sadock, J. The soft, interpretive underbelly of generative semantics. In P. Cole & J. Morgan (Eds.), *Syntax and semantics. Vol. 3: Speech acts.* New York: Academic Press, 1975.

Sadock, J. Methodological problems in linguistic pragmatics. In *Problems in linguistic metatheory*. East Lansing: Department of Linguistics, Michigan State University, 1976.

Sag, I., & Liberman, M. The intonational disambiguation of indirect speech acts. In R. Grossman, L. San, & T. Vance (Eds.), *Papers from the Eleventh Regional Meeting of the Chicago Linguistic Society*. Chicago: Chicago Linguistic Society, 1975.

Schegloff, E. Sequencing in conversational openings. In J. Gumperz & D. Hymes (Eds.), *Directions in sociolinguistics*. New York: Holt, Rinehart & Winston, 1972.

Schmerling, S. Assymetric conjunction and rules of conversation. In P. Cole & J. Morgan (Eds.), *Syntax and semantics. Vol. 3: Speech acts*. New York: Academic Press, 1975.

Schmerling, S. *Aspects of English sentence stress*. Austin: University of Texas Press, 1976.

Schweller, K. G. *The role of expectation in the comprehension and recall of direct and indirect requests*. Unpublished doctoral dissertation, University of Illinois at Urbana, 1978.

Searle, J. *Speech acts*. New York and London: Cambridge University Press, 1969.

Searle, J. Indirect speech acts. In P. Cole & J. Morgan (Eds.), *Syntax and semantics. Vol. 3: Speech acts*. New York: Academic Press, 1975.

Searle, J. Review of J. Sadock, Toward a linguistic theory of speech acts. *Language,* 1976, *52*, 966–971.

Shatz, M. *The comprehension of indirect directives: Can two-year-olds shut the door?* Paper presented at the summer meeting of the Linguistic Society of America, Oswego, N.Y., 1974.

Sinha, A. How passive are passives? *Papers from the Tenth Regional Meeting of the Chicago Linguistic Society*. Chicago: Chicago Linguistic Society, 1974.

Stalnaker, R. Pragmatics. In D. Davidson & G. Harman (Eds.), *Semantics of natural language*. Boston: D. Reidel, 1972.

Stampe, D. Meaning and truth in the theory of speech acts. In P. Cole & J. Morgan (Eds.), *Syntax and semantics. Vol. 3: Speech acts*. New York: Academic Press, 1975.

Stanley, J. *Passive motivation*. Paper presented at the Fourth Southeastern Conference on Linguistics, 1971.

Strawson, P. Meaning and truth. In *Logico-linguistic papers*. London: Methuen & Co., 1971.

Weiser, A. Deliberate ambiguity. *Papers from the Tenth Regional Meeting of the Chicago Linguistic Society*. Chicago: Chicago Linguistic Society, 1974.

Weiser, A. How not to answer a question: Purposive devices in conversational strategy. *Papers from the Eleventh Regional Meeting of the Chicago Linguistic Society*. Chicago: Chicago Linguistic Society, 1975.

Ziv, Y. *On the communicative effect of relative clause extraposition in English*. Unpublished doctoral dissertation, University of Illinois at Urbana, 1976.

6 Syntax Beyond the Sentence: Anaphora

Bonnie Lynn Webber
Center for the Study of Reading,
Bolt Beranek and Newman Inc.

INTRODUCTION

In understanding language understanding and, in particular, reading comprehension, it is almost a truism to say that one cannot stop at the analysis of
single sentences. In comprehending text, the import of each successive
sentence must be determined within, and integrated into, an incrementally
growing model of the discourse. One can then ask: What devices in the text
aid that integration, either by indicating connections or by lightening memory
load? That is, what intersentential devices carry over to text that most
important function of sentence-level syntax that Huggins (Chapter 4, this
volume) describes as "a way of maximizing the rate of transfer of meaning
from a language producer to a language receiver, taking into account the
limitations of memory of the receiver?" What sorts of knowledge and
processing heuristics must be possessed by the language receiver to handle
such devices? What would result from their absence?

One such intersentential device, *anaphora,* is the subject of this survey.
Anaphoric expressions comprise pronouns, pro-verbs, some definite noun
phrases, and ellipses. They epitomize a device for "maximizing the rate of
transfer of meaning": for example, one short syllable, "it," can evoke in the
language receiver's mind a complex theoretical construct or an entire chain of
events leading to some conclusion.

It was christened by Feynmann "the eight-fold way."
In the end, *it* drove Lear mad.

There are certain fundamental assumptions about anaphora in which this survey is grounded. First, it is assumed that there are differences in syntactic and semantic properties that divide anaphora into two basic classes—*deep* and *surface* (Hankamer & Sag, 1976). Second, it is assumed that each discourse participant is incrementally *synthesizing* his or her own *model* of both the discourse and the external situation. In the case of definite pronouns—*he, she, it, they,* even *s/he*—the pronoun's *referent* is an entity within the speaker's current model. In using a definite pronoun, the speaker presumes that its referent corresponds to a *similar* entity in the listener's current model. Moreover, he or she presumes that it is accessible to the listener via the minimal cues of pronominal reference.

Third, it is assumed that entities have *descriptions,* that is, purely linguistic constructs, which allow the discourse participants to reason about them. Any of these descriptions may be the *antecedent* of a definite pronoun if it has been suggested by the immediately preceding text. The relationship between the discourse or external situation, on the one hand, and the referents of deep anaphora, on the other, is thus an indirect one, mediated by the discourse participants' models. The discourse serves as one possible source of antecedent descriptions, and thus, indirectly, as one possible source of referents within these models.

A line is being drawn here between the separate notions of anaphora and deixis (Rubin, Chapter 17, this volume). Deixis, as a linguistic device for *pointing* to things, shares with anaphora the previously mentioned function of allowing a language producer to maximize the rate of information flow out to a language receiver. However, deictic expressions are seen as pointing to things within the *shared spatial* and/or *temporal context* of the discourse participants, whereas anaphoric expressions are seen as pointing to entities within their discourse models. An *effect* of deictic pointing—*You see that chair there?*—is to engender model-based entities that may then be addressed anaphorically: *Well, I paid almost 200 dollars for it.*

I see several reasons for discussing anaphora here as an illustration of intersentential devices in reading comprehension. First, if a reader cannot handle an anaphoric expression as the writer intended, there is no way that he or she can correctly update his or her discourse model in response to it. Second, as recent research in artificial intelligence, psychology, and linguistics has shown, choosing between possible antecedents may demand very sophisticated syntactic, semantic, pragmatic, inferential, and evaluative abilities on the reader's part. As I point out later, such abilities are even required to identify those possibilities. One might suspect, therefore, that anaphora might easily be a source of comprehension difficulties. Third, research on children's comprehension of anaphora has been hampered by unsubstantiated and often incorrect assumptions. By bringing together research on anaphora from various disciplines, a more sophisticated view of its comprehension processes may emerge to the benefit of reading researchers and theoreticians alike (also see Webber, 1978).

There is at least one major topic relevant to anaphora of which space limitations preclude a discussion. That is a survey of computer-based attempts to handle anaphoric expressions. Such attempts are documented in Bullwinkle (1977), Burton (1976), Charniak (1972, 1973), Grosz (1977), Hobbs (1976), Klappholz & Lockman (1975), Levin (1976), McDermott (1974), Norman & Rumelhart (1975), Rieger (1974), Rosenberg (1976), Wilks (1975), Winograd (1972), Woods (1977), and Woods, Kaplan, and Nash-Webber (1972). Such systems are only first- or second-order attempts at handling anaphora, but they do point to real problems that any more sophisticated systems must overcome.

Finally, it must be emphasized that the formal view of language that guides this survey of anaphora is not only compatible with other, more pragmatically oriented viewpoints (Morgan, Chapter 7, this volume) but is entirely complementary. To see this, consider the following example: When asked to recommend John Smith for a vacant position, his advisor writes *Mr. Smith has a lovely wife*. Viewing this sentence pragmatically will assign it an import that damns Mr. Smith with irrelevant praise. On the other hand, viewing it formally will identify those entities that the sentence evokes into the listener's discourse model: John, John's wife, the descriptions "lovely wife" and "wife," and the predicate "having a lovely wife." All of these are accessible pronominally or elliptically in subsequent sentences, which may of course continue to reflect the speaker's beliefs about Mr. Smith. For example,

Moreover, *her* father attended this university.
   or
Moreover, *his* brother *does too.*
   or
His previous *one* was quite ugly.

In the first section of this chapter, I sketch out answers to three important questions about the antecedents and referents of anaphoric expressions. These are:

1. What is it that is accessible to anaphora?
2. What is the role of text *vis a vis* antecedents and referents?
3. What is the role of inference?

In the next section I discuss how the need to account for successful anaphoric expressions places constraints on models for human memory. The next section presents some factors that have been proposed as functioning in anaphor resolution. Finally, in the last section, I discuss past and possible future research on skill acquisition, in view of the approach to anaphora outlined here.

ANTECEDENTS AND REFERENTS

What Is Accessible to Anaphora?

Probably the most important thing to understand about the referent of a definite pronoun is that it is not an element *in* the text but one suggested *by* it, one of the concepts evoked into the reader's discourse model. That is, the referent of *it* in

1(a). Mary gave Sue a T-shirt.
1(b). She thanked her for *it*.

is not the string *a T-shirt* but the entity describable as "the just-mentioned T-shirt that Mary gave Sue." This description is the antecedent of *it*.

Given this observation, an important question becomes: What does English allow one to access anaphorically? Obviously, not everything is a possible antecedent or referent in English; there is, for example, no anaphor whose antecedent is an adjective, a string of adjectives, an adverb, a preposition, or a quantifier. For example, there is no way to get around saying "all except three" in

2(a). All except three boys love their mothers.
2(b). ... girls do too.

So what types of antecedents and referents does English allow and what do they demand of a reader?

Examples 3 and 4 show two types of referents: ones that are *individual concepts* and ones that are *sets of individuals*.

3(a). Mary took her nieces to Design Research, where
3(b). *she* bought each of *the girls* a T-shirt.
3(c). *They* thanked *her* for *them*.
4(a). John met Mary and Alice at Logan airport.
4(b). *They* took a taxi home.

The referent of both *she* in 3(b) and *her* in 3(c) is the explicitly mentioned woman, Mary. On the other hand, the referents of *they* (and *them*) in sentences 3(c) and 4(b) are each a set of objects. However, the three sets differ radically with respect to how they come about. In 3(c), the referent of *they* can be described as the explicitly mentioned set of Mary's nieces, that of *them* as the set of T-shirts, each of which Mary gave to one of her nieces. This set is not given explicitly but must be *derived* from one T-shirt per niece and several nieces. The referent of *they* in sentence 4(b) is the set of John, Mary, and Alice, a set that again is not given explicitly in the text but must be constructed. (Notice that if this example were *John didn't meet Mary and Alice at Logan. They took a taxi home,* one would not infer the set of three people—*they* is probably just Mary and Alice.)

Notice that such individual concepts also include continuous entities (mass concepts) as well as particular quantities of them, as in Examples 5 and 6.

5(a). Water constitutes 76% of the earth's surface.
5(b). *It* occurs as a solid in icebergs, as a gas in the atmosphere, and as a liquid in rootbeer.
6.   Whenever John brings beer home, his brother drinks *it* up.

In 5(b), the referent of *it* is the mass concept, water, and in 6, the quantity of beer that John just brought home.

Example 7 shows a third type of referent: ones that are *generic* or *class concepts.*

7(a). A German shepherd bit me yesterday.
7(b). *They* are really vicious beasts.

The referent of *they* is the generic concept *German shepherds,* which the reader is assumed to be able to derive from the particular one doing the biting. I am asserting that, as a class, they are vicious beasts.

Predicates constitute a fourth class accessible to anaphoric reference, in which a *predicate* is anything that can be thought of as a property of something or as a relationship between things. Syntactic verb phrases, for example, may be understood as predicates. Predicates may be asserted or questioned as in,

John is a doctor.
Did John meet a lama in Nepal?

in which the predicate *being a doctor* can be taken to be asserted of John in the first sentence and that of *meeting a lama in Nepal* can be taken to be asked about John in the second. Alternatively, the second sentence can be read as questioning whether the predicate *John meeting a lama in place X* is true of Nepal, or whether the predicate *Y meeting Z in Nepal* is true of John and some lama. The fact that sentences *rarely* have a single interpretation as to what is being predicated of what is extremely important to anaphoric reference, as is discussed later.

In addition to being asserted, questioned, or even ordered (e.g., *Be a good girl.*), predicates may also be used descriptively to specify one or more members of the class of which the predicate is true. Consider the phrase "A green tie-dyed T-shirt that Mary bought at DR." There are four simple predicates here—*green, tie-dyed, T-shirt,* and *which Mary bought at DR*—all of which are true of any object denoted by this phrase. Note that one or more of these *simple* predicates can be composed into a single *complex* predicate, such as *tie-dyed T-shirt, green tie-dyed T-shirt, T-shirt which Mary bought at DR,* and so on. Complex predicates, as well as simple ones, can function as antecedents, and again comprehension requires the ability to recognize and manipulate them.

Examples 8, 9, and 10 all contain instances of anaphora whose antecedents are predicates.

8(a). Mary bought a green tie-dyed T-shirt.
8(b). Fred bought *one* too, though he wanted a red *one.*
9(a). I can walk and I can chew gum.
9(b). Jerry can $\emptyset$ too, but not at the same time.
10(a). Garth beats his wife.
10(b). Fred does $\emptyset$ too, though she hits him back.

The antecedent of the first instance of *one*-anaphora in 8(b) is the complex predicate *green tie-dyed T-shirt,* which is true of what Fred bought. It is probably not the same T-shirt as the one Mary bought (though that is a pragmatic inference, not one derivable linguistically). The antecedent of the second *one* is the predicate *tie-dyed T-shirt,* from which the more complex predicate *green tie-dyed T-shirt* has been composed. Because this latter predicate is incompatible with the predicate *red,* which is also true of what Fred bought, it cannot be the antecedent of *one* in this case.

Examples 9 and 10 illustrate ellipsed verb phrases, indicated by $\emptyset$. The antecedent of such an anaphor is always a predicate—in Example 9, it is the complex predicate *walk and chew gum.* Note that this predicate was not given explicitly in the text but had to be derived from the two simpler forms *walk* and *chew gum,* which were earlier predicated separately of me. In Example 10, the antecedent of the ellipsed verb phrase is ambiguous: It is either the predicate *beats his wife,* asserting that Fred also beats his own wife, or the predicate *beats Garth's wife,* asserting that Fred beats her, too. (Discussion of examples similar to these can be found in Bresnan [1971], Grinder & Postal [1971], Partee [1972], Sag [1976], under such labels as "sloppy identity" and "identity of sense anaphora.")

Events, actions, and *states* may also serve as referents, as in

11. John dunked Mary's braids in the inkwell. Because *it* made her cry, he apologized for doing *it*.
12. Sam is a male chauvinist, and he's not ashamed to admit *it*.

In the first example, both the event corresponding to John's dunking Mary's braids in the inkwell (the specific incident that made her cry), as well as the action, dunking Mary's braids in the inkwell (what John apologized for *doing*), are available referents. In example 12, being a male chauvinist can serve as a referent for *it*.

Another type of referent comprises entities that are introduced contextually through the writer and reader's shared knowledge of the world. For example, in

13(a). John's room was a mess.
13(b). His sneakers were dangling from *the chandelier!*

The referent of *the chandelier* is the one in John's room. Such *context-definite noun phrases* are discussed at great length in Chafe (1976), Charniak (1972, 1973), Clark (1975), Grosz (1977), Haviland & Clark (1974), Hobbs (1976), Klappholz & Lockman (1975), McDermott (1974), Rieger (1974), and Rosenberg (1976).

Finally, as a consequence of the claim that anaphoric expressions refer to entities in the discourse participants' models, there is no need for such entities to exist in any real sense. Thus, a hypothetical individual, set, event, and so on may also serve as the referent of an anaphoric expression. For example,

14(a). John wants to catch a trout for dinner.
14(b). He plans to eat *it* with sauteed almonds.

Here the referent of *it* is that entity describable as "the trout John will have if his desire to catch one is fulfilled." Issues of reference and existence are discussed in Bartsch (1976), Edmondson (1976), Karttunen (1976), Lakoff (1970), Webber (1978), Nash-Webber & Reiter (1977), and Partee (1972).

To summarize this section, I have presented what I believe is a partial answer to the relevant question, *What is accessible to anaphoric expressions in English?* It should be clear now that pronouns do not just "stand for" nouns, and that just being capable of constructing possible antecedents and referents for anaphoric expressions presumes complex cognitive abilities on the part of any understander.

What Is the Role of the Text?

As Hankamer and Sag (1976) point out, certain anaphoric expressions are not anchored linguistically but are controlled by aspects of the nonlinguistic environment shared by the speaker and listener. Thus, if I'm eating a mushroom and you say to me, *Do you realize that it's hallucinogenic?*, the referent of *it* is the mushroom that I am eating, which neither of us has mentioned but which both of us are aware of. Most often in reading, the writer and the reader have little or no shared nonlinguistic environment, so that most anaphoric expressions will have antecedents and referents derived from the text.

In the previous section, I mentioned several different types of antecedents and referents—individuals, sets, events, predicates, and so on. Obviously not every stretch of text will evoke instances of each type, though it is entirely possible for an entity presumably evoked in one way to be later interpreted in another (see Woods, Chapter 3, this volume). Thus, it may not be a profitable question to ask what antecedents and referents can be evoked by a particular piece of text. On the other hand, it is profitable to ask which of them *cannot*. It is to this question that some recent research in linguistics has been addressed.

For example, Kuno (1970) and Karttunen (1976) have pointed out that predicate nominative phrases do not evoke individual referenceable entities. That is, in Example 15(a), *he* may only refer to Bert and not a Maori (or the Maori that Bert is), whereas in 15(b), *he* may refer to either Bert or the Maori he met yesterday.

15(a). Bert is a Maori. *He* lives in New Zealand.
15(b). Bert met a Maori yesterday. *He* lives in New Zealand.

However, both instances of the phrase *a Maori* evoke generic entities (Example 16) and can serve as antecedents for *one*-anaphora (Example 17).

16(a). Bert is a Maori. *They* are indigenous to New Zealand.
16(b). Bert met a Maori yesterday. *They* are indigenous to New Zealand.
　　　(*they* = the generic class of Maoris)
17(a). Bert is a Maori, and Fred is *one* too.
17(b). Bert met a Maori yesterday, and Fred met *one* today.
　　　(*one* = a Maori)

In another paper, Kuno (1975) has also pointed out that no single entity introduced in a noun phrase of "exhaustive listing" may serve as an individual referent of a pronoun, though the entity evoked by the entire phrase may. Thus, in Example 18,

18(a). It was Mary, John, and Marsha who flunked Comp. Sci. 112.
18(b). *He also flunked AM261b.
18(c). They played bridge every night of the term.

John, who was introduced in a noun phrase of "exhaustive interpretation,"
cannot be the referent of he, although the whole group can be the referent of
they. (Obviously, if John had been introduced earlier in the discourse, as well
as being mentioned in this noun phrase, one could refer to him as he.)

Karttunen (1976) also notes that existential noun phrases do not introduce
individual referents when they occur in certain negative contexts as in
Examples 19 and 20.

19(a). Bill doesn't have a car.
19(b). *It is black.
20(a). John failed to find an answer.
20(b). *It was wrong.
21(a). Bill didn't marry a blonde.
21(b). She had red hair.

Both the simple explicit negative in Example 19 and the implicitly negative
verb fail in Example 20 should keep the reader from creating an entity that
could serve as an individual referent—the car Bill does not have or the answer
John failed to find. Both existential phrases, of course, could evoke
antecedents for one-anaphora: that is, 19(a) could sensibly be followed by
Frank has one, and 20(a) by Bill made one up. However, a primary problem
with negation in English is that it may not be clear from the given sentence just
what is being negated, in particular, whether or not the existential is within
the scope of negation. Thus in Example 21, the existential noun phrase does
introduce an individual referent, the female Bill married: What is denied is her
blondness, not the existence of such a woman. However, we cannot know this
from sentence 21(a) alone. Only when it becomes necessary to justify a
referent for she in sentence 21(b) is a particular scoping forced on us.

Before concluding this section, I would like to point to one interesting case
of textual evocation of referents. Several linguists (Bresnan 1971; Grinder &
Postal 1971; Hankamer & Sag 1976; Sag 1976) have pointed out that even
when ellipsed, a verb phrase may be a source of referents for anaphora. This
they have called the missing antecedent phenomenon (using the term
"antecedent" in a much looser sense than here). For example:

22(a). Because Fred didn't bake a cake for Mary's birthday, John did ∅.
22(b). She couldn't eat it though because it was chocolate.

If the first sentence is assumed to arise from

> 23(a). Because Fred didn't bake a cake for Mary's birthday, John baked a cake for Mary's birthday.

from which can be derived a referent for *it*—namely, the entity describable as "the just-mentioned cake that John baked for Mary's birthday"—then it appears that material deleted before a sentence "reaches the surface" can evoke referents as well as can material explicitly here. The problem is the range of this phenomenon—whether all types of anaphora may harbor "missing antecedents," or, if not, what accounts for the discrepancy. Examples like 24 and 25 illustrate the problem.

> 24(a). Although Fred couldn't bake a cake for Mary's birthday, John managed *it*.
> 24(b). ?She couldn't eat *it* though because *it* contained chocolate.
> 25. ?Although Fred didn't sink a boat carrying a gorilla, John sank *one*, and *it* drowned.

In example 24(b), *it* is meant to refer to the cake John baked for Mary's birthday, and in Example 25, to the gorilla in the boat that John sank. Neither antecedent is explicit—they seem rather to come from the material anaphorized as *it* in 24(a) and *one* in 25. Because judgments of acceptability vary on such examples, Bresnan (1971) has suggested that those people who accept these examples are actually inferring a referent rather than being given one linguistically. I have more to say about this in the next two subsections.

What Is the Role of Inference?

I will be using the term *inference* with respect to antecedents and referents to describe any type of reasoning process that can augment the set of available antecedents and referents. Most research in this area has dealt with examples such as:

> 26. John found a shop manual for his Fiat, but *the page* specifying the dwell angle was missing.

This research has shown that inferences embodying general world knowledge are needed to provide referents for those definite noun phrases, that, out of context, would have no unique referent and therefore make no sense. In Example 26, the shop manual John found provides a context in which *the page* ... may denote a unique individual, that is, the page from that shop manual. John's Fiat likewise provides a context in which *the dwell angle* denotes an unique individual—the dwell angle of the distributor shaft of John's Fiat. What this research seems to lead us to conclude is that there is probably no general world knowledge that would not be needed to justify a referent for *some* definite noun phrase.

Because so much has been written about this one class of inferences, often in the context of *frames,* I omit any further discussion of it. (The reader is referred to Bullwinkle, 1977; Chafe, 1976; Charniak, 1972, 1973; Clark, 1975; Grosz, 1977; Haviland & Clark, 1974; Hobbs, 1976; Klappholz & Lockman, 1975; Rieger, 1974; Rosenberg, 1976.) However, there are many other types of inferences that should be mentioned in order to show the range of capabilities expected of any language receiver through the language producer's use of anaphora. (A discussion of some types of inferences needed for *resolving* anaphora is given in a later section.)

In the following discussion, the types of inferences mentioned are presented in order of veracity, ranging from purely structural, always valid inferences to more contingent ones. It is probably the case that the more contingent an inference becomes, the more that judgments on the consequent existence of an antecedent or referent will vary from person to person. This can be seen in how often a sentence containing an anaphoric reference to one of these is judged nonsensical or bizarre. In evaluating reading comprehension, this point might be taken into account: that people might vary as to the amount of effort they will expend inferring an antecedent or referent or as to whether they will expend any effort at all! (This discussion is necessarily brief and informal. For a more rigorous and extensive presentation of material, the reader is referred to (Nash-Webber, 1977; Webber, 1978; and Nash-Webber & Reiter, 1977).

The first set of inferences involves purely structural rules, which are independent of the content of the sentence to which they apply. One such rule is applicable whenever a nonnegative sentence contains an existentially quantified noun phrase within the scope of a universally quantified one, for example

27(a). Mary gave each girl a T-shirt.

In such a circumstance, there will be available as a referent for *they* or *them* a set of things evoked by the existentially quantified noun phrase. Each member of this set is associated with one (or possibly more) of the things associated with the universally quantified noun phrase, for example

27(b). She bought *them* at Design Research.

Here, *them* refers to the discourse entity describable as "the set of T-shirts, each of which Mary gave to some girl." The qualification that there be no negation around is needed to account for the inapplicability of this rule to sentences like: "Mary didn't give each girl a T-Shirt" or "Mary refused to give each girl a T-shirt." Neither of these could sensibly be followed by 27(b).

Another such inference rule accounts for conjoined predicates as antecedents, in which only simple ones have been given explicitly. This rule explains the existence on the predicate *walk and chew gum*, which is the antecedent of the ellipsed verb phrase in Example 9 (repeated here).

9(a). I can walk and I can chew gum.
9(b). Jerry can ∅ too, but not at the same time.

The reason for mentioning such simple inference rules, when the examples I have given to illustrate them are so obvious to a skilled understander, is to point out that these antecedents and referents are not explicit and that reasoning is involved in constructing them. If a reader does not possess or does not apply these inference rules, he or she will fail to understand related anaphoric expressions and consequently fail to understand the text.

A third type of inference rule yields generic or class referents from a mention of a member of the class, as illustrated in Example 7 earlier (repeated here).

7(a). A German shepherd bit me yesterday.
7(b). *They* are really vicious beasts.

It is interesting to note that the only sets that may be inferred in this way are ones denoted by the given lexical items. Thus, in Example 7, the only possible referent for *they* is the class "German shepherds" and not "dogs" or "mammals," and so on, which are also classes to which a German shepherd belongs.

To end this section on inference, antecedents, and referents, I would like to mention another phenomenon that has been discussed in the linguistics literature (Bresnan, 1971; Lakoff & Ross, 1972; Ross, 1971) and is exemplified by:

28. John became a guitarist because he thought *it* was a beautiful instrument.
29. Max knifed me before I even realized he had *one*.

In Example 28, the referent of *it* is the guitar (understood generically), and in Example 29, the antecedent of *one* is "a knife." The simplest account for such examples seems to involve antecedents and referents being somehow evoked by nearby "morphologically related" (Lakoff and Ross' term) lexical items. Although Bresnan notes, I think correctly, that they are inferred rather than grammatically assigned, it is not at all clear just what kinds of inferences are acceptable to what people in these circumstances. For example, it seems possible to infer a "morphologically related" generic referent from a given lexical item, but it does not seem possible to infer a specific individual one, as in,

30. *John was a guitarist before he lost *it* on the subway.

in which *it* is meant to refer to Johns's guitar. Also, it does not seem possible to infer an antecedent that is morphologically more complex than the lexical item it is related to, for example,

31. *After John lost his guitar on the subway, he gave up being *one*.

in which *one* is meant to stand for "a guitarist."

MEMORY

In the section on Antecedents and Referents, I claimed that the referents of definite pronouns are not the elements in a text, but those suggested by it— that is, entities in a discourse model. Because anaphoric expressions are capable of accessing those discourse entities, characterizing aspects of the anaphor–referent relation should shed light on the organization of human memory. Conversely, any theory purporting to model human memory organization should account for what is known about anaphora.

What sort of things are of concern here? First, consider two entites that are known equally well by the language receiver. In a given state of the discourse, it may be the case that one, but not the other, can be referred to pronominally. Consider for example:

32(a). I saw your mother at the Led Zeppelin movie last night.
32(b). She seemed to be enjoying it. *But he looked rather ill.

Although *she* is meant to refer to your mother and *he* to your father, the former reference will succeed and the latter will probably fail. This cannot be because your father is unknown or less known to you. To account for this dichotomy, Chafe (1974, 1976) has introduce the notion of *consciousness*. Only entities that the speaker or writer assumes to be in the consciousness of the addressee can be referred to pronominally (or with diminished stress). (Currently consciousness is described only by the phenomena it is meant to explain, so further research by linguists and psychologists in this area is obviously needed.)

Second, consider the following short paragraph.

34. While driving through the game reserve, I passed a pregnant zebra, though I almost didn't notice her. Then on past several enormous termite nests and a river full of hippopotami, before I came to our camp. *She* looked like a distended Moire pattern.

Even after a single intevening sentence, the referent of *she* seems difficult to find. To account for this, Chafe attributes consciousness with a limited capacity, with old items being pushed out as new ones come in. For example, my *pregnant zebra* remained in your consciousness long enough for you to make sense of *I almost didn't notice her* but not long enough, possibly, for *she looked like a distended Moire pattern.* Chafe notes that "the question of what causes the speaker to believe that an item has left the addressee's consciousness needs systematic examination " (Chafe, 1976, p. 32) but speculates that the factors influencing an item's stay include the number of intervening sentences in which it was not mentioned, as well as such discourse boundaries as change of scene. Recent work by Grosz (1977) has shown that in task-oriented dialogues, whose structure closely parallels that of the task being performed, the participants' consciousness of an item is strongly influenced by the task structure. Viewing transcripts of actual dialogues between an apprentice trying to reassemble an air compressor and an expert whose advice he can request, Grosz notes several instances of pronoun references skipping over pieces of dialogue, in which, in each case, the piece skipped over was a whole segment relating to some distinct subtask or subtasks.

Also substantiating Chafe's speculation that "change of scene" may influence an item's stay in consciousness is a survey of the use of "discourse links" in newspaper articles done by Rosenberg (1976). After charting the thematic structure of several articles from *The New York Times,* Rosenberg notes that in his sample there were no instances of pronominal reference that crossed thematic boundaries. Even though this sample was small, it is probably the case that such cross-overs really are rare.

There is one more thing I would like to take up before concluding this section on anaphora and memory and that is again the problem of "missing antecedents." Reconsider Example 25 (repeated as follows).

25. ? Although Fred didn't sink a boat carrying a gorilla, John sank *one,* and *it* drowned.

Many people cannot find an appropriate referent for *it* in this example. (The boat that John sank may suggest itself but will be rejected on the grounds that boats do not drown.) However, it is the same as that for *the gorilla* in:

25'. Although Fred didn't sink a boat carying a gorilla, John sank one, and *the gorilla* drowned.

I don't agree with Bresnan (1971) that this is a case of people's varying capacity to infer a referent. I see this as a problem that will be solved when we understand the partner to Chafe's question mentioned previously. That is, what causes the speaker to believe an item, in this case a gorilla, has entered the listener's consciousness in the first place?

ANAPHORA RESOLUTION

Resolving an anaphoric expression, be it a pro-form or a definite noun phrase, refers to the process of determining its intended antecedent or referent. Many factors have been suggested as influencing a reader's or listener's choice in the matter, more than I can adequately survey in the limited space available. What I do instead is present a short piece of text containing several anaphoric expressions and mention factors that have been discussed in the literature as applicable to their correct resolution. In many cases, the examples may not seem to justify hypothesizing these factors as an appropriate level of explanation. Interested readers are advised to consult the original sources to discover the range of phenomena each is meant to account for.

33(a). Fred left his niece at home and went to the zoo with Mary and John.

33(b). *It* had not yet opened, so *they* sat down on the grass outside.

33(c). Suddenly near John *he* saw a snake.

33(d). *The girl* saw *it* too, as did John.

33(e). Fred admired John because *he* reacted so quickly.

33(f). John regretted not having a stick, since *he* could have used *it* to bash the snake.

One simple factor influencing the choice of a referent for *they* in Sentence 33(b), as well as *he* in Sentence 33(c), is that, in English, most pronouns are marked for number and gender. So, in Sentence 33(b), *they* must refer to something interpretable as a set of more than one item, whereas in 33(c), *he* must refer to an animate entity that is not explicitly marked "female." (That *they* is taken to refer to Fred, Mary, and John would result from deriving such a set.)

In Sentence 33(c), the fact that *he* refers to Fred and not to John could be explained by the interaction of three factors that have been discussed in the linguistics literature (aside from the fact that Fred was the only other male around). The first is a syntactic constraint blocking John from being the referent of *he* based on factors such as relative depth of embedding and left–right ordering. This has been rendered in various forms in the literature by Culicover (1976), Langacker (1966), Postal (1966), Ross (1967), and Reinhart (1976).

The second and third explanations for Fred being the referent of *he* are based on notions of *theme* (Kuno, 1976) and a simple cognitive strategy in which the roles of the participants in a discourse are changed as little as possible (Maratsos, 1973). Both would point to the fact that Fred is the subject of sentence 33(a), the opening sentence of the discourse. A thematic explanation would say that Fred is the theme of the discourse and therefore most easily pronominalizable, being what the reader is most conscious of. The latter, "inertial," explanation would say that because Fred is in the subject role in a previous sentence, the reader will interpret subsequent sentences, if possible, with him in that same role. (One of Maratsos' experiments to show the existence of this strategy is discussed in the next section.)

In Sentence 33(b), the fact that *it* refers to the zoo and not to Fred's home may be explained on semantic grounds, that a zoo is more likely to open than a home. Such *semantic selectional restrictions* have been used in several computer-based natural language understanding systems in resolving anaphora (Burton 1976; Wilks 1975; Winograd 1972; Woods et al., 1972).

In sentence 33(d), *the girl* is understood as referring to Mary, even though two girls have been mentioned, Mary and Fred's niece. *Recency*—Mary being the last female mentioned—might be one factor influencing this assignment. But it might also be the case that Chafe's notion of change of scene is at work here; of the two, only Mary participates in the park scene. (Note that the fact that Mary is a girl rather than, say, a woman falls out of the anaphor–referent assignment; it is not known for certain prior to this point. If sentence 33(d) had been *the woman saw it too,* Mary would still have been assumed to be the referent, with the fact that she was a woman now emerging. This issue of anaphor resolution resulting in a further characterization of a known entity is discussed at length in Rieger [1974].

In sentence 33(e), *he* would normally be understood as referring to John. This cannot be the result of syntactic factors or recency because in similar sentences such as,

34. Fred phoned John because he needed help.

he would probably be understood as referring to Fred. Garvey, Caramazza, and Yates (1974) attribute both these choices to a factor that they call *implicit causality*, which biases the assignment of a referent toward the candidate "primarily responsible for instigating the action or state denoted by the antecedent clause." In sentence 33(e), John· would be held responsible for Fred's admiration, whereas in Sentence 34, Fred would be responsible for the phone call. The authors conclude from their experiments that this factor is not an all-or-none thing but only a bias, which may be attenuated by such other factors as passivization (which overtly marks the surface subject noun phrase as the topic of the sentence), negation (which alters the sense of causality), and the relative status of the candidates.

In sentence 33(f), the referent of *it* is the stick John would have in the (set of) possible world(s) in which he had one. That is, *it* refers to a nonexistent entity. However, the clause in which *it* occurs may also be understood as referring to that same (set of) possible worlds. (This would not be the case if *it* occurred in a sentence such as *He used it to bash the snake*, which would require the referent of *it* to exist in the current world.) Different possible worlds are associated with different hypothetical contexts (future and modal worlds), as well as different peoples' beliefs and desires. *Possible worlds* as a factor influencing anaphor–referent assignments is discussed in Karttunen (1976), Kuno (1970), Lakoff (1970), and Webber (1978).

The previous short text does not provide a framework for discussing all of the factors that have been proposed as operative in anaphor resolution. Other factors include task structure in task-oriented dialogues, emphatic stress (Akmajian & Jackendoff 1970), and empathy (Kuno 1975, 1976). With all these proposed factors, it is important to note that no one has tried to model how these factors might interact in human anaphor resolution.

SKILL ACQUISITION

It has only been fairly recently that language acquisition research has moved from the study of purely intrasentential phenomena to phenomena that cross sentential boundaries. As part of this trend, there is a small but growing body of studies concerning children's developing abilities to produce and comprehend anaphoric expressions. In particular, researchers have observed children of various ages regarding:

1. their ability to comprehend different types of anaphoric expressions, e.g. definite pronouns, "sentential it" anaphora, relative pronouns, etc. (Bormuth, Manning, Carr & Pearson, 1970; Lesgold, 1974):
2. the effect of syntactic complexity on this ability (Richek, 1976–77);
3. their knowledge of which syntactic and prosodic devices either imply that a particular text string is associated with some anaphoric expression or ban it from that association (Chomsky, 1969; Flahive, 1976; Maratsos, 1973);
4. their knowledge of particular semantic or pragmatic (social) properties required of the referent of a given pronoun (Chipman & deDardel, 1974; Flahive, 1976; Hollos, 1977; Tanz, 1977).

In some cases, the goal is to discover, for particular aspects of these skills, a hierarchy of comprehension difficulty or an order of acquisition that instructional material can then take into account (Bormuth et al., 1970; Richek, 1976–77; Waryas, 1973).

In all cases, however, this research has been undertaken with assumptions about anaphora that cannot withstand close scrutiny. For example, although it is never stated directly, it is taken for granted that the antecedent of an anaphoric expression is a string of text (usually to be found in the same sentence as the pronoun or else in a previous one). This is tied in with the assumption that anaphora is a single phenomena—that we comprehend all types of anaphoric expressions in the same way and that children do so as well. I propose on the other hand: (1) that at least in *adult* language there are differences in syntactic and semantic properties that divide anaphora into two basic classes (Hankamer & Sag, 1976); (2) that these classes may require different comprehension and production skills; (3) that reasoning (inference) based on sentential structure and/or content accounts for the antecedents and referents of many anaphoric expressions; and (4) that an adequate account of the properties displayed by one class is precipitated by adopting the position that its members refer to entities in a *model* of the discourse and not the discourse itself. (It is certainly possible that all anaphoric expressions are used and understood by children purely as surface phenomena and that children only acquire the previously-mentioned sophisticated characteristics later. That is something that we do not know and would of itself be an important thing to discover.)

The most obvious point to make is that hypotheses about both the skills involved in anaphora and how they interact are going to be very different, depending on whether a direct text–text position on anaphora or an indirect model-based one is adopted. For example, one persuasive view of text understanding is in terms of model-based inference (Bobrow & Brown, 1975; Collins, Brown, & Larkin, Chapter 16, this volume). According to this view, the main function of inference when applied to text understanding is to aid in the synthesis of an underlying model that organizes and augments the explicitly present material. Though I am more concerned with the role of the input text in the model-synthesis process than I am with inference per se, the point is that a model-based approach to anaphora ties its comprehension into the primary understanding process rather than seeing it as a separate text-based activity. The development of skills in model-synthesis is thus directly relevant to anaphor comprehension. With a purely text-based approach to anaphora, this would not be so.

Another point about this model-based position is that (1) by assuming reference is to model-based entities, and (2) by allowing both linguistic and perceived input to evoke entities into the model, things in the external situation are referenced anaphorically that have never been mentioned linguistically. (More exactly, it allows that model-based entity *corresponding* to the external one to be referenced anaphorically.) Put another way, it allows anaphoric pronouns to be "pragmatically controlled" (Hankamer & Sag, 1976). As a consequence, an external object or event that has been both perceived *and* mentioned may establish its correspondent in the listener's model on the basis of *either* the perception or the explicit language or, in some way, both. This may be taken as a critique of some results reported in very interesting papers by Chipman and de Dardel (1974) and Tanz (1977).

These studies evaluated young children's (3-7 years old) understanding of pronominal reference to different types of items based on the children's responses to the following task. Placed in front of a table on which several items were prominantly arrayed, each child was required to respond to instructions like:

There is a box with five marbles. Give it to me.
There are flowers on the table. Give them to me.

Both studies claimed a purely linguistic ability was being tested: Tanz states that her study concerns "children's knowledge of some details of how anaphoric pronouns *map onto their discourse antecedents*" (emphasis mine), whereas Chipman and de Dardel claim to be interested in "the anaphoric use of the pronoun 'it' where 'it' *replaces a surface noun phrase*" (emphasis again mine). However, if one accepts that an external object that has been both perceived and mentioned may evoke a discourse entity on either or both bases, then it is not as clear that these studies were testing what they intended.

That is, by presenting their material visually as well as linguistically, it is not clear that the child's discourse model reflects only a *linguistically* evoked entity. In the initial statement of a sentence pair—*There is x on the table—x* may have acted simply as a key word focusing the child on some kind of item on the table. What entered the child's model may have been a result of language, visual perception, or some combination of both. And we certainly are not yet able to characterize a person's conceptualization of a particular external environment based on pure visual perception, much less how that conceptualization might be altered by simultaneous linguistic description of aspects of it.

A third point raised by the approach to anaphora advocated here concerns the assumption that anaphora is not a single phenomenon and that for adults at least there may be vastly different recovery strategies for the two basic classes. This suggests that attempts reported in Bormuth et al. (1970) and Lesgold (1974) to identify a single "difficulty ordering" for anaphoric syntax (i.e., an ordering by comprehension difficulty of syntactically characterized anaphor–antecedent pairs) cannot really achieve what was intended.

Given the approach advocated here, it would not be appropriate to ask whether certain anaphoric forms are more or less easy for children to comprehend per se. Rather, for deep anaphora, one would first consider whether a child could update his or her discourse model in response to a new sentence in a way that validates that sentence and that is 'inhabited" by a similar population of discourse entities as an adult's model would be. One would then ask whether the child was able to take the anaphoric expression in its given linguistic context, know to what kinds of things it could refer, and then find the most appropriate of them in his or her current (updated) model. For surface anaphora, one would consider whether the child knows what kind of unit can form its antecedent (i.e., whether he or she understands what is being anaphorized), whether he or she can derive that unit from the previous text under light processing loads, and whether it is so well-entrenched that heavy processing loads do not affect performance to a significant degree.

One final point raised by this approach concerns the reasoning required to derive antecedents for anaphoric expressions. This is especially significant for successful reading comprehension. I showed previously, albeit briefly, that inference based on the *form* of a sentence rather than its content was required in many places to identify antecedents for anaphoric expressions. If, as it has been noted (Rubin, Chapter 17, this volume), a child finds it difficult to recognize sentence structure in written discourse (i.e., in the absence of prosodic cues), he or she may find it correspondingly difficult to identify those antecedents that are derived from structural inference.

Before closing this section on skill acquisition, I want to mention briefly several studies on a child's development of adult conventions for pronoun use. One is by Chomsky (1969) on syntactic structure and coreference. She found that it was not until children were well over 5 years old that they learned that coreference is blocked syntactically in sentences such as *He will be very happy if Pluto wins the race* but not *If Pluto wins the race he will be very happy.*

Another study is by Maratsos (1973) on emphatic stress and coreference. He found that at an age when children can successfully identify the referent of an unstressed pronoun in a context like,

35. John hit Harry and then Sarah hit him.

they cannot yet do so when the pronoun receives emphatic stress. (For adults, emphatic stress would indicate role reversal.)

Finally, a third study is by Hollos (1977) on social rules in pronoun selection. She investigated the ability of children taken from two different social backgrounds to: (1) recognize which person a given pronoun would refer to when used by some specified other person in a particular social context; and (2) use appropriate pronouns when role-playing those same situations. The children she studied ranged in age from 7 to 9 years old, 15 from an isolated rural Hungarian background, 15 from the nearby town. She found that their different degrees of social exposure made a less significant difference in their comprehension abilities than it did in their ability to use this knowledge in role-taking. She concluded that the latter ability requires the child to have already acquired a "cognitive operation" that enables him or her to switch perspectives with others.

To summarize this section, then, a model-based approach leads one to distinguish several components involved in understanding anaphora:

1. whether the child conceptualizes the world as does an adult;
2. whether the child can process text and synthesize an appropriate discourse model—one that reflects both a mature conceptualization of the world *and* the text as given;
3. whether the child has and can apply the syntactic, semantic, and pragmatic (social) knowledge required to resolve anaphoric expressions;
4. whether the child has the real-time capacity to apply both these interpretive and model-building skills.

Obviously, these are not independent properties; for example, anaphoric expressions that occur in the discourse must themselves be understood correctly vis a vis their antecedents or referents in order for the listener to construct a valid model for the discourse. Many other ties can be seen between them as well. However, distinguishing them, as I have tried to show, leads to a different set of questions, as well as a different interpretation of the current set, that might produce more stable and useful results.

CONCLUSION

In this chapter, I have tried to bring together a variety of ideas on the subject of anaphora. The problems raised by anaphora impinge on several fields: In philosophy, anaphora touches on issues of reference and possible worlds; in psychology, on issues of memory organization and language acquisition; in linguistics, on issues of general syntactic constraints and sentence generation and interpretation; and in artificial intelligence, on the use of diverse sources of knowledge and the control of inferential processing. To summarize the point of this survey, I believe that a characterization of anaphora that unifies relevant work from all these fields will benefit us both theoretically and practically.

ACKNOWLEDGMENT

This research was supported by the National Institute of Education under Contract No. MS-NIE-C-400-76-0116.

REFERENCES

Akmajian, A., & Jackendoff, R. Coreferentiality and stress. *Linguistic Inquiry.* 1970, *1*, 124–126.

Bartsch, R. Syntax and semantics of relative clauses. In R. Bartsch, J. Groenendijk, & M. Stokhof (Eds.), *Amsterdam papers on formal grammars.* The Netherlands: University of Amsterdam, 1976.

Bobrow, R., & Brown, J. S. Synthesis, analysis and contingent knowledge in specialized understanding systems. In D. Bobrow & A. Collins (Eds.), *Representation and understanding.* New York: Academic Press, 1975.

Bormuth, J. R., Manning, J., Carr, J., & Pearson, D. Children's comprehension of between- and within-sentence syntactic structures. *Journal of Educational Psychology,* 1970, *61,* 349–357.

Bresnan, J. A note on the notion "identity of sense anaphora." *Linguistic Inquiry,* 1971, *2,* 589–597.

Bullwinkle, C. Levels of complexity for anaphora disambiguation and speech act interpretation. *Proceedings of 5-IJCAI,* August 1977, 43–49.

Burton, R. *Semantic grammar: An engineering technique for constructing natural language understanding systems* (BBN Report No. 3433). Cambridge, Mass.: Bolt Beranek and Newman Inc., 1976.

Chafe, W. Language and consciousness. *Language,* 1974, *50,* 111–113.

Chafe, W. Givenness, contrastiveness, definiteness, subjects, topics and points of view. In C. Li (Ed.), *Subject and topic.* New York: Academic Press, 1976.

Charniak, E. *Towards a model of children's story comprehension* (Technical Report 226). Cambridge, Mass.: MIT Artificial Intelligence Laboratory, 1972.

Charniak, E. Context and the reference problem. In R. Rustin (Ed.), *Natural language processing.* New York: Algorithmics Press, 1973.

Chipman, H., & de Dardel, C. Developmental study of the comprehension and production of the pronoun "it." *Journal of Psycholinguistic Research,* 1974, *3,* 91–99.

Chomsky, C. *The acquisition of syntax in children from 5 to 10.* Cambridge, Mass.: MIT Press, 1969.

Clark, H. Bridging. In B. Nash-Webber & R. Schank (Eds.), *Theoretical issues in natural language processing.* Cambridge, Mass.: Association for Computational Linguistics, 1975.

Culicover, P. A constraint on coreferentiality. *Foundations of Language,* 1976, *14.*

Edmonson, J. A. Semantics, games and anaphoric chains. In R. Bartsch, J. Groenendijk, & M. Stokhof (Eds.), *Amsterdam papers on formal grammars.* The Netherlands: University of Amsterdam, 1976.

Flahive, D. The development of pronominalization in children 5–9. In S. Mufwene et al. (Eds.), *Papers from the 12th Regional Meeting of the Chicago Linguistics Society,* 1976, 199–207.

Garvey, C., Caramazza, A., & Yates, J. Factors influencing assignment of pronoun antecedents. *Cognition,* 1974, *3,* 227–244.

Grinder, J., & Postal, P. Missing antecedents. *Linguistic Inquiry,* 1971, *2,* 269–312.

Grosz, B. *The representation and use of focus in dialog understanding.* Doctoral dissertation, University of California at Berkeley, 1977.

Hankamer, J., & Sag, I. Deep and surface anaphora. *Linguistic Inquiry,* 1976, *7,* 391–428.

Haviland, S., & Clark, H. What's new? Acquiring new information as a process in comprehension. *Journal of Verbal Learning and Verbal Behavior*, 1974, *13*, 512–521.

Hobbs, J. *A computational approach to discourse analysis*. (Research Report 76-2). New York: City College, City University of New York, Department of Computer Science, December, 1976.

Hollos, M. Comprehension and use of social rules in pronoun selection. In S. Ervin-Tripp & C. Mitchell-Kernan (Eds.), *Child Discourse*. New York: Academic Press, 1977.

Karttunen, I. Discourse referents. In J. McCawley (Ed.), *Syntax and semantics* (Vol. 7). New York: Academic Press, 1976.

Klappholz, A., & Lockman, A. Contextual reference resolution. *American Journal of Computational Linguistics*, 1975, *4*, microfiche 36.

Kuno, S. Some properties of non-referential noun phrases. In R. Jakobson & S. Kawamoto (Eds.), *Studies in general and oriental linguistics*. Tokyo,: TEC Company Ltd., 1970.

Kuno, S. Three perspectives in the functional appraoch to syntax. In Grossman, San, & Vance (Eds.), *Papers from the parasession on functionalism*. Chicago: Chicago Linguistics Society, 1975.

Kuno, S. Subject, theme and the speaker's empathy: A reexamination of relativization phenomena. In C. Li (Ed.), *Subject and topic*. New York: Academic Press, 1976.

Lakoff, G. *Counterparts, or the problem of reference in transformational grammar* (Report No. NSF-24, pp. 23–36). Cambridge, Mass.: Harvard Computation Laboratory, 1970.

Lakoff, G., & Ross, J. R. A note on anaphoric islands and causatives. *Linguistic Inquiry*, 1972, *3*, 121–127.

Langacker, R. Pronominalization and the chair of command. In D. Reibel & S. Schane (Eds.), *Modern studies in English*. Englewood Cliffs, N.J.: Prentice-Hall, 1966.

Lesgold, A. Variability in children's comprehension of syntactic structures. *Journal of Educational Psychology*, 1974, *66*, 333–338.

Levin, J. A. *Proteus: An activation framework for cognitive process models* (Working Paper WP-2). Marina del Rey, Calif.: Information Sciences Institute, 1976.

Maratsos, M. The effects of stress on the understanding of pronominal co-reference in English. *Journal of Psycholinguistic Research*, 1973, *2*, 1–8.

McDermott, D. *Assimilation of new information by a natural language understanding system* (AI Technical Report TR-291). Cambridge, Mass.: MIT Artificial Intelligence Laboratory, 1974.

Nash-Webber, B. L. Inference in an approach to discourse anaphora. In M. Stein (Ed.), *Proceedings of NELS-8*. Amherst: University of Massachusetts, 1977.

Nash-Webber, B. L., & Reiter, R. *Anaphora and logical form: On formal meaning representations for English* (CSR-36). Center for the Study of Reading, University of Illinois, and Bolt Beranek and Newman Inc., 1977. (Also in *Proceedings of 5-IJCAI*, 22–25, August 1977, 121–131.)

Norman, D., & Rumelhart, D. *Explorations in cognition*. San Francisco: W. H. Freeman, 1975.

Partee, B. Y. Opacity, coreference and pronouns. In Harman & D. Davidson (Eds.), *Semantics of natural language*. The Netherlands: D. Reidel, 1972.

Postal, P. On so-called 'pronouns' in English. In D. Reibel & S. Schane (Eds.), *Modern studies in English*. Englewood Cliffs, N.J.: Prentice-Hall, 1966.

Rieger, C. U. *Conceptual memory*. Unpublished doctoral dissertation, Stanford University, Department of Computer Science, 1974.

Reinhart, T. *The syntactic domain of anaphora*. Unpublished doctoral dissertation, MIT, Department of Foreign Literatures and Linguistics, 1976.

Richek, M. Reading comprehension of anaphoric forms in varying linguistic contexts. *Reading Research Quarterly*, 1976–77, *12*, 145–165.

Rosenberg, S. *Discourse structure* (Working Paper 130). Cambridge, Mass.: MIT Artificial Intelligence Laboratory, 1976.

Ross, J. R. *Constraints on variables in syntax.* Unpublished doctoral dissertation, MIT, 1967.

Ross, J. R. The superficial nature of anaphoric islands. *Linguistic Inquiry,* 1971, *2,* 599–600.

Sag, I. *Deletion and logical form.* Unpublished doctoral dissertation, MIT, Department of Foreign Literatures and Linguistics, 1976.

Tanz, C. Learning how "it" works. *Journal of Child Language,* 1977, *4,* 224–235.

Waryas, C. L. Psycholinguistic research in language intervention programming: The pronoun system. *Journal of Psycholinguistic Research,* 1973, *2,* 221–237.

Webber, B. L. *A formal approach to discourse anaphora.* New York: Garland Press, 1978.

Wilks, U. A preferential, pattern-seeking semantics for natural language. *Artificial Intelligence,* 1975, *6,* 53–74.

Winograd, T. *Understanding natural language.* New York: Academic Press, 1972.

Woods, W. A. *Semantics and quantification in natural language question answering.* (BBN Report 3687). Cambridge, Mass.: Bolt Beranek and Newman Inc., 1977.

Woods, W. A., Kaplan, R. M., & Nash-Webber, B. L. *The lunar sciences natural language information system: Final report* (BBN Report 2378). Cambridge, Mass.: Bolt Beranek and Newman Inc., 1972 (NTIS No. N72-23155).

7 Discourse and Linguistic Theory

Jerry L. Morgan
Center for the Study of Reading,
University of Illinois, Urbana-Champaign

Manfred B. Sellner
University of Salzburg

The importance of the text in the reading process is obvious; yet it is not well understood what properties of texts are crucial nor how such properties are to be characterized beyond the obvious variables like word frequency and gross aspects of syntactic complexity. Recently, two elusive notions have been pointed to as fundamentally important properties of texts, and some suggestions have been made for theoretical accounts of them, often in terms of linguistic theories of discourse, sometimes called *text grammars*. In this chapter we sketch some of these suggestions, explore a few in detail and examine their implications, and discuss generally the relation between discourse and linguistic theory. In the first section we present a brief survey of some of the pertinent literature. In the second section try to draw out clearly the theoretical issues to which this literature is addressed, and in the third section we examine a few well-known proposals in light of these issues. In the last section we draw some general conclusions and suggest some directions for theoretical development.

SOME PREVIOUS WORK ON DISCOURSE IN LINGUISTICS

Linguistic theories of discourse are a relatively recent development in linguistics. It was not until the 1960s that texts or discourse generally came to be considered an object of (rather than merely a source of data for) linguistic analysis. Discourse analysis and theories of the organization of discourse (text grammars) were developed in the work of Zellig Harris and his colleagues at the University of Pennsylvania, in the "tagmemic" school of linguistic analysis, and in the work of the "Prague School" in Czechoslovakia. Elaborations have come from a number of scholars. In this section, we describe some of this work, in a more or less chronological order.

The first American linguist to attempt the analysis of connected discourse as discourse was probably Fries (1952). This work, an analysis of telephone conversations, explored connections among sentences in texts and, in a limited way, the distribution of sentence types within a text but did not propose any theoretical schemes of text analysis.

Harris' work, begun in the 1950s, was more theoretically oriented. It was an attempt to apply the methodology of American structural linguistics (including Harrris' notion of "transformation") to the analysis of connected prose. Although it received some attention in Europe, Harris' work on discourse has not received much attention in this country. Harris (1970, p. 13) proposed "a method for the analysis of connected speech and writing," which extended the "formal," structural methods used for sentence analysis to the analysis of connected discourse. Harris' methods were designed to avoid the necessity of referring to the "meanings" of the morphemes or the sememes of text chunks containing them. According to Harris (1970), the goal was "to discover the particular interrelations of the morphemes of the text as they occur in that one text; and in doing so, we discover something of the structure of the text, of what is being done in it. [p. 313]." What Harris proposed was an extension of the use of structural discovery procedures such as substitution and opposition to mechanically arrive at morphemic *equivalence chains*.

Because stylistic variations of the sentences of a text might limit the applicability of the equivalence operations, Harris introduced the concept of *transformation* to structural linguistics. The function of transformations was to make possible the most general application of the equivalence operations. The end product of the analysis is a tabular arrangement of all the equivalence classes found in successive sentences. On the vertical axis of the table are those classes found in successive sentences; on the horizontal axis, those found within the sentences. Such a segmentation is a representation of the structure of the text under analysis.

Another major thread of discourse analysis is the work of scholars of the familiar framework of tagmemic theory, associated primarily with Kenneth Pike and Robert Longacre and their coworkers (see Pike, 1967, and Longacre, 1968, 1972). In this framework the attempt is made to apply the slot-filler-tagmeme mode of syntactic description to the description of discourse at the level of sentence, paragraph, and discourse, yielding a hierarchical analysis in terms of form and function. Attempts are made at classifying types of discourse (narrative, hortatory, expository, etc; see Longacre, 1972, Chapter 5) as a first step toward analyzing the form-function relation in discourse and, within this taxonomy, relating discourse function to grammatical form. This approach includes an abstract "deep structure" of the discourse and rules relating this structure to grammatical structure in terms of intersentential relations and grammatical devices, making use also of case-like concepts such as *agent, instrument,* and so on. The bulk of tagmemic work on discourse structure has been on languages of New Guinea and the Philippines.

The work of Grimes, as exemplified in Grimes (1975), is closely associated with the tagmemic school but is different in certain ways. He appears to be mildly skeptical of grammars built on constituency relations as models for discourse (and perhaps for sentences as well). His interesting book contains a wealth of illustrative detail but is nonetheless programmatic, suggesting theoretical directions rather than developing them. He argues for a number of distinctions to be made in the description and classification of discourse, for example, between events and nonevents, and, within the latter category, distinguishes *setting, background, evaluation,* and *collateral.* He discusses *constituency* in discourse and suggests alternatives to the usual sort of hierarchical "trees." He also discusses briefly a number of other topics but not in any detail. He proposes no general theoretical apparatus.

The Prague School of text-linguistics, which organizes discussion of texts around the principles of *functional sentence perspective* (FSP) (Daneš, 1970, 1974) and *communicative dynamism* (Firbas, 1964), has its roots in the observation by Mathesius that in unemphatic, normal discourse the *theme* (in his interpretation, roughly the information that has been mentioned, given earlier in the discourse) precedes the *rheme* (roughly, that which is new information).

Although there are various conceptions of FSP within this school of linguistics, their general assumptions are that it is possible to draw a distinction between "new" and "old" information in a sentence, that there are segments that are dependent on previous and subsequent discourse, and that there are segments that are of greater communicative importance than others.

Research in FSP goes back to the work of Mathesius and other linguists of the Prague School on the syntax of Slavic languages. Slavic languages generally have more highly developed case-marking systems and, probably as a result, considerably more freedom of word order than English. But in studying variations in word order, Prague linguists noticed that word order is constrained by discourse factors. Elements expressing "known" or "old" information generally precede elements expressing "unknown" or "new" information. The primary difference in this respect between English and Slavic languages is that, in English, word-order changes are brought about by rules that also change grammatical relations—passivization, for instance. Firbas (1964, 1966, 1971) has written in detail on the relation of English word order to information distribution.

From these origins there has arisen an extensive literature of discourse notions like *topic, foucs, comment, given/new, new/old information,* and *communicative dynamism.* Although there are differences among the various proponents of FSP, there is a common theme—close attention to language as a communication system (as opposed to the recent American bias toward description of language as an abstract formal system); in particular, there is a growing interest in reflections in linguistic forms of discourse properties. Generally speaking, FSP linguists have a three-level approach: the level of semantic structure, the level of grammatical (roughly, syntactic) structure, and the level of the *organization of the utterance* (see Daneš, 1974, for discussion). The third level is described in terms of discourse-functional properties and their reflection in grammatical form.

Firbas (1966) defines *communicative dynamism* (CD) as "the extent to which a particular sentence element contributes to the development of the communication [p. 27]." Difference in degree of communicative dynamism, Firbas says, is the interplay of two factors:

1. The tendency to raise the degree of CD from the beginning to the end of the sentence.
2. The semantic structure of the sentence.

Firbas claims that "new" information carries more communicative dynamism than "old" information and that the degree of communicative dynamism may differ among the elements that convey new information. He identifies the theme as the element that contains the lowest degree of communicative dynamism. The *rheme* is the element that carries the highest degree of communicative dynamism. This is reflected in word order, Firbas claims, in that in neutral utterances the *theme* occurs first and is followed by transitional elements and the *rheme.*

Daneš' (1974) main concern, however, is not the organization of the sentence but the organization of the text, as reflected in his discussion of *thematic progression:*

> text connexity is represented, *inter alia* by the thematic progression (TP). By this term we mean the choice and ordering of utterance themes, their mutual concatenation and hierarchy, as well as their relationship to the hyperthemes of the superior text units (such as paragraph, chapter, . . .) to the whole text, and to the situation. Thematic progression might be viewed as the skeleton of the plot [p. 114].

Daneš distinguishes between the *micro structure* of an utterance that reflects "the distribution of different degrees of the communicative dynamism over sentence elements [p. 114]" and the *macro structure* of a text. This latter structure is determined by the *thematic* and the *rhematic* part of the utterances, but "without specifying the central, peripheral and transitional elements (p. 114)."

The *macro-structure* of texts is described as consisting of a certain type of *thematic progression* (TP). Daneš distinguished three basic types of TP: *simple linear progression; thematic progression with a continuous (constant) theme;* and *thematic progression with derived themes.* For example, according to Daneš (1974), the following text has a simple theme–rheme structure in which the original rheme becomes the second theme, which takes a new rheme, which in turn becomes the new theme, and so on. "The first of the antibiotics was discovered by Sir Alexander Flemming in 1928. He was busy at the time investigating a certain species of germ which is responsible for boils and other trouble [p. 118]." Graphically this is represented as shown below:

$$T_1 \rightarrow R_1$$
$$\downarrow$$
$$T_2 (> R_1) \rightarrow R_2$$

etc.

The determination of thematic progression was intended to be achieved through a procedure of asking *wh-questions:*

> Generally speaking, we assume that it is possible to assign to any sentence (taken as a grammatical unit) a set of wh-questions, representing all possible types of context in which a given sentence is applicable, and consequently, revealing all possible FSP-structures which it can acquire. In this way we are also able to find out, indirectly the theme of the given utterance. The procedure seems workable, since it is objective, purely linguistic, and involves both the contextual and the thematic aspect of FSP [pp. 114–115].

The second type of TP, thematic progression with a continuous theme, has an abstract macro-structure that represents the skeleton of the plot that is graphically representable in this way:

$$T_1 \rightarrow R_1$$
$$\downarrow$$
$$T_1 \rightarrow R_2$$
$$\downarrow$$
$$T_1 \rightarrow R_3$$

Here, the theme of the first sentence consists of a theme-rheme nexus. The first theme is taken up again and joined by a new rheme. The same old theme is taken up again in the subsequent sentence and joined by a new rheme, again. Daneš (1974) offers the following text as an example of this type:

> The Rousseauist especially feels an inner kinship with Prometheus and other Titans. He is fascinated by any form of insurgency... He must show an elementary energy in his explosion against the established order and the same time a boundless sympathy for the victims of it... Further the Rousseauist is every ready to discover beauty of soul in any one who is under the reprobation of society [p. 119].

Thematic progression with derived themes is derived from a hypertheme, roughly what the whole paragraph or section is about. From this hypertheme, sub-theme-rheme-nexuses branch off as shown.

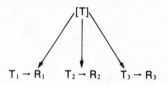

This organization is exemplified in a text such as this:

> New Jersey is flat along the coast and southern portion; the northwestern region is mountainous. The costal climate is mild, but there is considerable cold in the mountain areas during the winter months. Summers are fairly hot. The leading industrial production includes chemicals, processed food, coal, petroleum, metals, and electrical equipment. The most important cities are Newark, Jersey City, Paterson, Trenton, Camden. Vacation districts include Asbury Park, Lakewood, Cape May, and others [p. 120].

We expect that many of the concepts of FSP theory, especially *topic, new/old information,* and the insight that these matters at least partially condition some syntactic properties will be of great importance in understanding the role of linguistic form in the interpretation of content structure.

The main problem with this approach (and all theories that deal with these matters) is that crucial, intuitively appealing notions such as topic, given/new, theme, rheme, and so forth, even though central to the theory, are not clearly and explicitly defined or described, so that it is not clear how to apply them in any but the simplest cases. This makes it difficult to test the predictions. Although we find Kuno's (1972) innovations intuitively very appealing, there are serious problems in evaluating them. The crucial notions theme, contrast, exhaustive listing, and neutral description are not adequately defined and are consequently difficult to test.

A second European school concerned with discourse is sometimes called the "text grammar" school of linguistics. But the blanket use of this term hides important differences in theoretical orientation within this group. These orientations can be loosely grouped into three main categories.

The first is structural text grammar, exemplified by the work of Koch (1965, 1966, 1970) and Harweg (1968, 1977). Second, there are a number of groups working independently within frameworks suggested by generative grammar. These include the East European generativists Heidolph (1966), Lang (1973, 1976, 1977), Petöfi (1971a, 1971b, 1972a, 1972b, 1973), Rieser *(1973, 1976), as well as Dressler (1970), van Dijk (1972, 1973, 1975, 1977), and van Dijk, Ihew, Pet*öfi, and Rieser (1972). Their work is based on the view that the goal of linguistic theory is to provide a mechanism for the generation of well-formed text as opposed to the generation of well-formed sentences. Thus, van Dijk (1972) requires that a generative text grammar "enumerate all and only the grammatical text of the language (p. 17)." Third, there are the use-oriented text-grammarians, such as Brinker (1973), Klein (1972), Sandig (1973), Schmidt (1973), and Wunderlich (1970, 1971, 1972). This group regards the text as a communicative unit that occurs in and depends on a socio-communicative context.

We discuss representative work from each of these groups, beginning with Harweg's substitutional model of text grammar.

The basic tenets of Harweg's substitutional linguistics were set forth in his 1968 book *Pronomina und Textkonstitution,* recently hailed as "without doubt a pioneering work" in text linguistics (Gulich & Raible, 1977, p. 124). There are three components of Harweg's text model: (1) the substitutional component; (2) the macrosyntactic component, which determines the text structure; and (3) a speaker-hearer component, which takes account of intonational factors. This theory is constructed on the basis of a specific interpretation of the concepts of *syntagmatic substitution, substituendum,* and *substituens.*

Harweg (1977) takes substitution to be the most important innovation in the development of text-linguistics. Thus he defines text as "a succession of linguistic units, (or more precisely of grammatical sentences) that is built up by an uninterrupted chain of syntagmatic substitutions [p. 148]." According to Harweg, a substituendum is a linguistic unit that can be replaced by a substituens. He illustrates the concept with this example: "I asked *a policeman,* and *the policeman* told me. *He* was very friendly [p. 250]." Of this example, Harweg says: "Not only *he,* but also the antecedent *the policeman* functions as a syntagmatic substituens and the only expression in this sequence to be interpreted as a (syntagmatic) subsituendum in the expression *a policeman:* for *the policeman* could, paradigmatically be replaced by *he; a policeman,* however, could not [p. 250]." The uninterrupted chain of substitution that Harweg refers to can be linked, he says, by pairs of homonyms (this woman:a woman), and similarity substitutions (a mechanic: the repairman; a boy:he; an airplane:that fast bird powered with kerosene), as well as by different types of associative substitutions (a defeat:the victory; a flash of lightning:the thunder; a train:the conductor). It thus appears that Harweg's system requires supplementation by some kind of encyclopedic dictionary that would include not only the vocabulary of a language but also every possible synonym, association, and metaphorical expression. Harweg speaks of concatenation through syntagmatic substitution as a left-to-right process. This process is supposed to determine the "textiness" of a stretch of sentences. Left-to-right concatenation is in turn complemented by a top to bottom concatenation that determines the particular text type. This means that the text type "classical drama" is characterized in terms of notions that had been developed by classical rhetoric, such as thesis, protasis, and so on. Harweg refers to this abstract structure as the *macro-structure* of the text.

The speaker–hearer component originated as an addendum to Harweg's standard theory of syntagmatic substitution to resolve certain problems in determining substituendum and substituens. Harweg hypothesized that all substituenda were stressed. Thus, if the proper name "Karl" was found to be stressed in a conversation, it had to be a substituendum. If it was not stressed, it had to be a substituens. This observation apparently grew out of Harweg's descriptive work on conversations and was problematic for his distinction between "Grossraumtext" and "Kleinraumtext." A Grossraumtext arises when identical groups of persons meet in certain intervals and at the same place, such as family breakfasts, and the conversation of the previous day or week is taken up again; a Kleinraumtext is more-or-less the ordinary conception of texts (paragraphs, books, speeches, etc.).

The work of Weinrich (1971) bears some similarity to that of the FSP linguists. Weinrich's approach to the analysis of text consists of (1) setting up a two-dimensional matrix called *text partition* (*Textpartitur*) and (2) determining similarity of transitions between sentences on the basis of information contained in the verb. *Textuality* is then explained as a phenomenon of transition *(Ubergangsphanomen).* This means that each verb in a text is analyzed and marked as to what syntactic information it contains, for example, if it is negated, if it is singular or plural, third person, first person, and so on. In case the information thus obtained from the sentences of a text is of the same order, then we have obtained an equivalent transition. If the information is not the same, we have a nonequivalent transition. Equivalent transition is claimed to be the basic text-contributing phenomenon. In addition, there are also other connectives. that can also contribute to the making of a text, such as conjugations, certain adverbs, and syntactic and semantic proforms. Weinrich adopts the term *text-thematics* when referring to the sum of the equivalent transitions and of *text-rhematics* when referring to the sum of the nonequivalent transitions. Textuality is described in terms of the relation between text-rhematics and text-thematics. It is not obvious, however, that such a strictly morphological technique can adequately characterize either the structure or the connectedness of texts.

There is a related school of thought, exemplified by Halliday and Hasan (1976) that attempts to define texthood in terms of *cohesion*: "A text is any passage, spoken or written of whatever length, that does form a unified whole [p. 1–2]." In Halliday and Hasan's (1976) book-length treatment of this subject, they try to find coherence *in* the text via *connectives* that form ties in a text. For them, cohesion is a semantic matter:

> The concept of cohesion is a semantic one; it refers to the relations of meaning that exist within the text, and that define it as a text. Cohesion occurs where the *interpretation* of some element of discourse is dependent on that of another. The one presupposes the other, in the sense that it cannot be effectively decoded except by recourse to it. When this happens, a relation of cohesion is set up, and the two elements, the presupposing and the presupposed are thereby at least potentially integrated into a text [p. 4].

The ties Halliday and Hasan mention include reference, substitution, ellipsis, reiteration, collocation, and conjuction. Their approach is discussed later in this chapter.

Generative text grammar developed as an outgrowth of conventional generative sentence grammar. Dressler (1970) was a pioneer in this effort. He proposed *text-generating* rules that resembled the phrase structure rules of early generative grammar. Dressler tried to capture the wholeness of a sequence by proposing recursive rules capable of generating *text*. The rules that Dressler proposed were of the following sort:

$$\text{Text} = \begin{cases} \text{sentence} \\ \text{sentence + connector + text} \end{cases}$$

$$\text{Connector} = \text{continuity intonation + conjunction +} \\ \text{(syntactic anaphor) + (textual restrictions)}$$

$$\text{syntactic anaphor} = \begin{cases} \text{explicit anaphor} \\ \text{elliptic anaphor} \end{cases}$$

This set of rules, once fully developed, was intended to be capable of generating one-sentence texts as well as texts of indefinite length.

A considerable amount of research was spawned by proposals such as this and is reported in the publications of linguists like Petöfi (1971a, 1971b, 1972a, 1972b, 1973), Rieser (1973, 1976), van Dijk (1972, 1973, 1975, 1977), van Dijk & Petöfi (1977) and van Dijk et al. (1972). European generative text grammarians have attempted to develop a mathematical system that would generate texts rather than just sentences.

The classic generative text grammar, van Dijk (1972), had the following outline. The aim of van Dijk's (1972) text was to enumerate all and only the grammatical texts of language [p. 17]." Towards this goal, van Dijk proposed substituting as the initial symbol of the grammar T (for text) in place of the traditional S (for sentence) of sentence grammar, and postulated the function of the grammar as follows:

1. Instead or producing all the grammatical sentences of a language, the grammar now assigns structural descriptions to all and only the grammatical texts of a language.
2. Instead of assigning structural descriptions to sentences, a text grammar now assigns a structural description to each of the generated texts.

The grammar would then make use of the following kinds of rules:

1. Rules to form and relate semantic structures to texts rather than independent sentences.
2. Rules and conditions for the well-formed concatenation of pairs, triples, etc. of the text which controls the intersentential properties of sentences, i.e., sequence signals, boundary signals, linkage, etc. (These describe the micro-structure of the text).
3. Rules and/or a formalism for describing the macro-structure of the text.
4. Transformational rules relating such macro-structures to the sentential structures of the text.

We discuss van Dijk's work in greater detail later in this chapter.

There are also theories of text that are founded on the notion of *communication*. Communicative text theory, according to Schmidt (1973), has as its goal the development of an "explicit theory of linguistic communication [p. 15]." *Text* in Schmidt's framework is defined as "the linguistic part of a communicative act in a communicative interaction [p. 150]." Or, according to Dressler (1973), a text is "a linguistic unit completed according to the intentions of the sender(s) and receiver(s) following rules of grammar [p. 1]."

One approach that might prove useful in characterizing rhetorical structure makes use of the notion of speech acts as developed by Searle (1969). This approach attempts to show that texts (oral and written) have an information structure that consists of a hierarchy of speech acts and the illocutionary roles that are embedded in a text according to the function of the text. Such an approach has been sketched by researchers such as Schmidt (1973), Breuer (1974), Sandig (1973), and Sinclair and Coulthard (1975).

In addition to the linguistic literature, there have been a number of proposals for text structure in other fields, beginning at least as long ago as the work of Vladimir Propp (1928) on Russian folktales and continuing to fairly recent work by literary scholars and psychologists on story grammars as an approach to narrative structure. Although these large literatures are outside the scope of this chapter, we take up a couple of interesting examples—Prince (1973) and Rumelhart (1975)—in the following section.

THE ISSUES

The main issue is quite simple and is roughly the same for the problem of understanding discourse comprehension as for constructing a reasonable linguisic theory. It is this: How much of the competence that underlies the ability to understand and construct discourse is specifically linguistic, and how much is just the manifestation, in *use* of language, of mental systems more general than linguistic competence? Stated from a different viewpoint, how much of discourse competence should be accounted for in linguistic theory? Such a question can only be answered if we have a clear conception of what a linguistic theory is.

Given an understanding of "language" in the broad colloquial sense, a reasonable goal for a theory of language is that it provide an account for the human ability to use language for the multitude of purposes it serves. Such a theory would have to account for the ability to read and understand traffic signs, compose poetry, solve problems by means of internal monologues, make puns, appreciate Wallace Stevens, imitate an Italian accent, talk baby-talk to an infant, learn a second language, write letters, and tell by the third or fourth page that one has read a certain Maigret novel before, to say nothing of the prosaic utilitarian task of understanding what one is told and saying what one means.

A naive view of things might be that an account of all this is precisely an account of language, the domain of a single unified theory that one might call a general theory of language. But it has become clear that the overall ability such a general theory addresses is a complex function of many different skills and kinds of knowledge—the ability to reason, knowledge of social norms, encyclopedic knowledge, mastery of grammatical systems, and so on.

For reasons embedded in the intellectual and social history of the field, recent American linguistics has taken as its primary goal not the construction of such a general theory of language but the construction of what generative linguists mean by "linguistic theory": a theory that treats those parts of human knowledge that are involved only in knowledge of language (and its acquisition), rather than being instances of the application of more general cognitive abilities. An accompanying assumption, of course, is that this partitioning of knowledge reflects some significant property of the mind, as opposed to, say, a partitioning between knowledge about things that are blue and all other knowledge.

The distinction between linguistic and nonlinguistic knowledge is a crucial one, for both theoretical and practical reasons. The general theory of language as we have described it is probably indistinguishable from a theory of the mind. Then, one of the most important empirical questions for the general theory for solutions to applied problems such as reading comprehension, and for linguistics as a field is, what, if any, are the purely linguistic aspects of language ability? Is there an isolatable language faculty? If so, what kind of theory provides the best account of it? These are the questions that are the domain of linguistic theory, as distinguished from a general theory of language.

In regard to discourse, then, the application of this general question is, how much of the ability to understand discourse is to be accounted for in linguistic theory? A couple of examples might help to clarify what we mean. A clear case is the inferential system that gives rise to conversational implications or indirect speech acts as in the work of Grice (1975), Searle (1975), Sadock (1975), and others. A good amount of meaning (in the loose sense) is conveyed, according to this picture of things, by means of inferences about the speaker's intentions and purposes. But if Grice is right, these inferential principles are just the application, to use of language, of principles that are quite general, and found in other areas of human interaction. Insofar as this is true, the mental systems underlying indirect speech acts are not linguistic systems, hence not in the domain of linguistic theory. Then the answer to the frequent question, "Where do these things fit in the grammar?" is "Nowhere at all."

A second clear case is word order. Knowledge that, in English, the determiner precedes the noun (as opposed to many languages with the opposite order) seems to follow from no other fact of the psychology, culture, and so on of the people who speak English. It seems to be, then, a strictly linguistic piece of knowledge and, as such, in the domain of linguistic theory. There are sure to be unclear cases, as well as knowledge that it is hard to classify as linguistic or nonlinguistic. But the existence of hard cases does not diminish the importance of the distinction.

In fact, there have been several recent proposals that explicitly or inexplicitly attempt to extend linguistic theory to account for discourse problems. These proposals seem to have wide appeal, and we will discuss a few of them at length in the next section. Their appeal, it seems to us, stems from two sources: First, the assumption that linguistic ability is an isolatable, relatively small component of the mind offers hope for limited solutions to discourse problems, both theoretical and practical. Second, the existence of properties of discourse that seem similar to well-known properties of sentences makes plausible the proposal that discourse and sentence properties should be treated in the same terms by the same *linguistic* theory. The points of similarity are these: People have intuitions of well-formedness about texts/discourses (we will use these terms interchangeably) just as they do about sentences. Moreover, it makes good sense to speak of texts as having internal structure of some kind, just as sentences do. It also makes sense to speak of texts as having "meaning," on some construal of the term, just as sentences have "meaning" in some sense. Finally, certain properties of grammatical systems seem to have some kind of discourse function—topic markers, pronouns, beginning/ending markers like *amen,* and so forth. From observations such as these, the conclusion is drawn that sentences and texts are the same kind of thing, to be described in the same terms in some general *linguistic* theory of discourse that accounts both for entire discourses and for smaller units such as sentences, words, and phonemes.

We argue in considering some of these proposals that this conclusion is unfounded and that the similarity between text properties and grammatical properties is an artifact of superficial inspection, an illusion that disappears on careful scrutiny. The notions we will be looking at most closely are coherence and text structure.

SOME PROPOSALS

In this section we examine a handful of recent proposals for treating discourse properties as linguistic properties, or language-like properties. We take up first Halliday and Hasan's (1976) treatment of cohesion as a linguistic property contributing to coherence. Then we review the proposals of Prince (1973) and Rumelhart (1975) for treating story structure in terms that suggest a linguistic treatment. Finally, we will consider van Dijk's (1977) ambitious proposal for a comprehensive linguistic theory of discourse.

Halliday and Hasan (1976) propose the concept of cohesion as a factor in what is generally called coherence. They state their goals as follows:

> If a speaker of English hears or reads a passage of the language which is more than one sentence in length, he can normally decide without difficulty whether it forms a unified whole or is just a collection of unrelated sentences. This book is about what makes the difference between the two.

The word TEXT is used in linguistics to refer to any passage, spoken or written, or whatever length, that does form a unified whole. We know, as a general rule, whether any specimen of our own language constitutes a TEXT or not...

This suggests that there are objective factors involved—there must be certain features which are characteristic of texts and not found otherwise.... We shall attempt to identify these, in order to establish what are the properties of texts in English, and what it is that distinguishes a text from a disconnected sequence of sentences. As always in linguistic description, we shall be discussing things that the native speaker of the language "knows" already [p. 1].

Though this seems the kind of property of texts that is commonly referred to as coherence, Halliday and Hason (1976) prefer the term *texture*: "The concept of TEXTURE is entirely appropriate to express the property of "being a text." A text has texture, and this is what distinguishes it from something that is not a text. It derives this texture from the fact that it functions as a unity with respect to its environment [p. 2]." Texture, say Halliday and Hasan, is the combination of semantic configurations of two kinds: register and cohesion. Register is an unclear notion, but seems to include content as a subpart. According to Halliday and Hasan (1976), cohesion, on the other hand, is *not* a matter of content:

Cohesion does not concern what a text means; it concerns how the text is constructed as a semantic edifice [p. 26].

Cohension, say Halliday and Hasan, "occurs when the INTERPRETATION of some element in the discourse is dependent on that of another [p. 4]." They present a taxonomy of cohesion relations in four main groups: reference, including antecedent–anaphor relations, *the,* and demonstrative pronouns; substitution, including such various pronoun-like forms as *one, do, so,* etc. and several kinds of ellipsis; conjunction, involving words like *and, but, yet,* etc.; and lexical cohesion, which has to do with repeated occurrences of the same (or related) lexical items. Halliday and Hasan (1976) see these relations as linguistic relations, as one can see at several points in the book:

If a passage of English containing more than one sentence is perceived as a text, there will be certain linguistic features present in that passage which can be identified as contributing to its total unity and giving it texture [p. 2].

Cohesion is part of the system of a language [p. 5].

Halliday and Hasan take the position that cohesion is some kind of linguistic property distinct from content:

...One can construct passages which seem to hang together in the situational-semantic sense, but fail as texts because they lack cohesion [p. 23]

Where there is continuity of subject-matter within a text, as we typically find it, the texture is not necessarily the result of this; the following example is about mathematics, but cohesion is provided, especially in the last sentence, more by the lexical patterns of *complicated... difficult... easy* and *greater time... long ...short* than by any linking of specifically mathematical concepts [p. 25].

The example they give is a paragraph on the history of mathematics and complexity of calculation. Their point seems to be that mere coherence of content does not suffice to make a text coherent; rather, there is some additional *linguistic* property that contributes to the coherence of a text. Halliday and Hasan's (1976) position is made quite clear when they refer to "lexical cohesion" as "relatedness of form [p. 304]." This is an important hypothesis, if correct. One might have assumed that the coherence of a text was a matter of content, which would have, of course, linguistic consequences. In a coherent biography of Churchill, for example, one would expect frequent mention of Churchill; one would therefore expect frequent expect frequent occurrence of words like *Churchill, he, him, his,* and so on. The source of coherence would lie in the content, and the repeated occurrence of certain words would be the *consequence* of content coherence, not something that was a *source* of coherence. It would be a serious mistake to construe this linguistic manifestation as cause rather than effect. But this is just the mistake Halliday and Hasan have made. On careful inspection it is clear that cohesion, insofar as any sense can be made of Halliday and Hasan's description of it, is an epiphenomenon of content coherence. This can be seen in Halliday and Hasan's (1976) very first example:

Let us start with a simple and trivial example. Suppose we find the following instructions in the cookery book:

Wash and core six cooking apples. Put them into a fireproof dish.

It is clear that *them* in the second sentence refers back to (is ANAPHORIC to) the *six cooking apples* in the first sentence. This ANAPHORIC function of *them* gives cohesion to the two sentencs, so that we interpret them as a whole; the two sentences together constitute a text. Or rather, they form part of the same text; there may be more of it to follow.

The texture is provided by the cohesive RELATION that exists between *them* and *six cooking apples.* It is important to make this point, because we shall be constantly focusing attention on the items, such as *them,* which typically refer back to something that has gone before; but the cohesion is effected not by the presence of the referring item alone but by the presence of both the referring item and the item it refers to [p. 2].

There is a confusion here that reflects Halliday and Hasan's quite general confusion on matters of meaning.[1] *Them* does not refer back to something that has gone before. It refers (more accurately, the writer *uses* it to refer) to six cooking apples, not to the noun phrase *six cooking apples*. The sentence is an instruction to put apples, not words, into a dish. It is not the apples that have "gone before," but the act of referring to the apples by using certain words. Then there are two ways to construe the mysterious relation Halliday and Hasan (1976) have in mind. One might take it to be the relation of reference, between *them* and the apples *them* is used to refer to. But the relation, then, is not one between elements in a text. Or, one might take the cohesive relation to be the relation of *co*reference, the used-to-refer-to-the-same-thing relation between the expression *six cooking apples* and *them*. But Halliday and Hasan give no reason to believe that this secondary kind of relation plays any direct role in understanding texts or determining properties such as coherence. Furthermore, they are mistaken in taking the coherence relation in this example as a clear, objective fact. They say it is clear that *them* refers to the six cooking apples. But how can we know what *them* refers to? What forces the conclusion that *them*, in fact, is intended to refer to the apples and not, say, to the author's children? It is not knowledge of language that supplies this conclusion. It is our knowledge of cooking and of the author's purpose, our ability to reason, and the assumption that the recipe is coherent. Without this latter assumption, we have no way of knowing what *them* is intended to refer to; the *recipe* might have been written by a madman or produced by a computer. It is because we *assume* the text is coherent that we infer that *them* is intended to refer to the apples. All of the Halliday and Hasan's examples are misconstrued in this way—taking certain aspects of linguistic form as cause, rather than effect, of coherence. This shows up most sharply in their discussion of lexical cohesion. This type of cohesion arises, according to Halliday and Hasan, from the repetition of some lexical items or from occurrences of lexical items that are *related* in certain ways. It is clear that Halliday and Hasan (1976) mean this as a case of a relation of linguistic form: "It is not by virtue of any referential relation that there is a cohesive force set up between two occurrences of a lexical item; rather, the cohesion

---

[1]Some quotations to illustrate this point:

What is the MEANING of the cohesive relation between *them* and *six cooking aples?* The meaning is that they refer to the same thing [p. 3].

A third person form typically refers anaphorically to a preceding item in the text [p. 48].

An occurrence of *he* typically presupposes a singular masculine common or proper noun somewhere in the vicinity [p. 49].

Plural forms may refer anaphorically... to sets that are plural in meaning [p. 62].

A social context is a much more abstract conception, a kind of semiotic structure in which meaning takes place [p. 305].

exists as a direct relation between the forms themselves [p. 284]." But Halliday and Hasan provide no reason to believe that this formal notion has any explanatory value as cause, rather than effect. The notion collapses entirely when they extend the notion of lexical cohesion to instances of chains of related lexical items in a text, like *mountaineering-Yosemite-summit peaks-climb-ridge*. It is clear that a text containing these lexical items is likely to be coherent insofar as their use is symptomatic of a common overall topic. Halliday and Hasan's position, though, is that there is an independent *linguistic* notion of cohesion that cannot be reduced to this factor, and the burden is clearly theirs to show that it has some explanatory value. But they do not provide a single persuasive argument for their position. Halliday and Hasan (1976) anticipate this criticism, but their defense of it is hard to interpret.

> This seems to suggest that what we are calling lexical cohesion carries no meaning; that it is simply an incidental consequence of the fact that discourse does not wander at random from topic to topic but runs on reasonably systematic lines with a certain consistency of topic and predictability of development. In general, of course, this is true; most discourse is well organized, and the patterned occurrence of lexical items is a natural consequence of this. But this does not imply that lexical cohesion has no meaning. Without our being aware of it, each occurrence of a lexical item carries with it its own textual history, a particular collocational environment that has been built up in the course of the creation of the text and that will provide the context within which the item will be incorporated on this particular occasion. This environment determines the "instantial meaning," or text meaning, of the item, a meaning which is unique to each specific instance [pp. 288–289].

As far as we can see, there is no evidence for cohesion as a linguistic property, other than as an epiphenomenon of coherence of content.

The situation is similar, we think, in the case of text structure. It is clear that the mind does impose some kind of structure on a text, but the exact nature of this structure is not well understood. One proposal is that it is a *linguistic* structure, a proposal that seems to be supported by some analyses of text structure in terms of a theoretical apparatus much like Chomskyan syntactic theory. But, on close examination, the seeming parallels disappear. To show this we shall examine two works of unusual clarity that attempt to bring out such parallels, implying (perhaps unintentionally) the possibility of a linguistic account of text structure.

Much of the recent work on text structure has to do with the structure of stories. This work is descended from a common ancestor: the classic work of the Russian Formalist Vladimir Propp on Russian folktales (Propp, 1928/1958). Propp's work grew out of his attempt to classify Russian folktales. His solution was to classify them by the presence of certain functions, which he defines as "an act of dramatis personae, defined from the point of view of its significance for the course of action [p.20]." Propp's functions are:

1. One of the members of a family absents himself from home.
2. An interdiction is addressed to the hero.
3. The interdiction is violated.
4. The villain makes an attempt at reconnaissance.
5. The villain receives information about his victim.
6. The villain attempts to deceive his victim in order to take possession of him or of his belongings.
7. The victim submits to deception and thereby unwittingly helps his enemy.
8. The villain causes harm or injury to a member of a family.
8a. One member of a family either lacks something or desires to have something.
9. Misfortune or lack is made known: the hero is approached with a request or a command; he is allowed to go or is dispatched.
10. The seeker agrees to or decides upon counteraction.
11. The hero leaves home.
12. The hero is tested, interrogated, attacked, etc., which prepares the way for his receiving either a magical agent or helper.
13. The hero reacts to the actions of the future donor.
14. The hero acquires the use of a magical agent.
15. The hero is transferred, delivered, or led to the whereabouts of an object of search.
16. The hero and the villain join in direct combat.
17. The hero is branded.
18. The villain is defeated.
19. The initial misfortune or lack is liquidated.
20. The hero returns.
21. The hero is persued.
22. Rescue of the hero from pursuit.
23. The hero, unrecognized, arrives home or in another country.
24. A false hero presents unfounded claims.
25. A difficult task is proposed to the hero.
26. The task is resolved.
27. The hero is recognized.
28. The false hero or villain is exposed.
29. The false hero is given a new appearance.
30. The villain is punished.
31. The hero is married and ascends the throne.

Propp groups these functions into subgroups; 1 through 7, for example, are *preparation.* These functions are fulfilled by seven *spheres of action,* each of which, save number 4, concerns the actions of one character:

1. The villain
2. The donor
3. The helper
4. The princess (a sought-for person) and her father
5. The dispatcher
6. The hero (seeker or victim)
7. The false hero

He generalizes over all Russian folktales in terms of these functions, and the structural analysis that they give rise to:

1. Functions of characters serve as stable, constant elements in a tale, independent of how and by whom they are fulfilled. They constitute the fundamental components of a tale.
2. The number of functions known to the fairy tale is limited.
3. The sequence of functions is always identical.
4. All fairy tales are of one type in regard to their structure [pp. 21, 22, 23].

One can see how this schema can be used to impose a structure on a story; sequences within the story can be grouped under one of Propp's functions, and these perhaps subgrouped under higher categories, yielding a hierarchical organization of the plot: a plot structure.

Work such as Propp's (1928/1958) that brings out the *structure* of stories has led some analysts to see strong parallels between linguistic structure and story structure and to propose story grammars that draw on the conceptual apparatus of syntactic theory. Prince (1973) and Rumelhart (1975) are clear examples. Prince, writing from the point of view of the literary scholar, borrows heavily (and explicitly) from the works of Chomsky on syntactic theory. He sees parallels between tacit knowledge of syntax in a Chomskyan view of language and knowledge of what makes a story.

Everybody may not know how to tell good stories but everybody, in every human society known to history and anthropology, knows how to tell stories, and this at a very early age.... Furthermore, everybody distinguishes stories from non-stories, that is, everybody has certain intuitions—or has internalized certain rules—about what constitutes a story and what does not [p. 9].

He set up requirements for a story grammar that are strongly reminiscent of a Chomskyan syntax.

A grammar of stories is a series of statements or formulas describing these rules or, rather, capable of yielding the same results. A grammar should be explicit. It should indicate, with a minimum of interpretation left to its user, how a story can be produced by utilizing a specific set of rules and assign to such a story a structural description. It should also be complete and account for all and only possible stories.... It could also specify their degrees of grammaticalness. (p. 10)

The parallel is complete with the use of terminology such as *simple story, kernel story,* and *complex story,* and especially the *grammar* he proposes to use with story structure. For simple and kernel stories, he provides what looks like a context-sensitive phrase grammar; its first two rules, for example, are:

1. M St → E + CCL + E + CCL + E
   {E stat/#__}
2. E → {E stat/__#}
   {E act   }

The claim Prince (1973) wishes to embody in his story grammar is this:

A minimal story consists of three conjoined events. The first and third events are stative, the second is active. Furthermore, the third event is the inverse of the first. Finally, the three events are conjoined by three conjunctive features in such a way that (a) the first event precedes the second in time and the second precedes the third, and (b) the second event causes the third [p. 31].

From these minimal stories Prince derives kernel stories by the addition of rules that allow for complex event structures he calls *episodes*; to these certain *singulary transformations* can apply, for example, to rearrange the order of episodes to produce flashbacks. Complex stories are derived by the application of generalized transformations that can embed one story within another, just as the generalized embedding transformations of early transformational grammar embedded one clause within another.

Rumelhart (1975), like Prince, borrows heavily from the terminology and conceptual apparatus of syntactic theory. For example: "The grammar consists of a set of syntactical rules which generate the constituent structure of stories and a corresponding set of semantic interpretation rules which determine the semantic representation of the story [p. 213]." Some examples from his rewriting rules:

Rule 1: Story → Setting + Episode
Rule 2: Setting → (State)*
Rule 3: Episode → Event + Reaction

And their corresponding "semantic" rules:

Rule 1′: ALLOW (Setting, Episode)
Rule 2′: AND (State, State...)
Rule 3′: INITIATE (Event, Reaction)

Rumelhart's paper has been taken up by psychologists. Stein and Glenn (1978), for example, although it abandons Rumelhart's semantic/syntactic distinction, is essentially an extension and refinement of his system, apparently adopting his assumptions about the nature of story structure.

But is there any substance to the seeming parallels between story structure and syntactic structure?

To begin the criticism, we return to Propp (1928/1958).

As we pointed out previously, Propp's system can be interpreted as yielding a hierarchical organization of the plot: a plot structure. Propp's functions are all matters of the *content* of the story, with the possible exception of his generalization 3, that "the sequence of functions is always identical [p. 22]." As it stands, this could be construed in two ways: regarding either the content alone or imposing a constraint both on the content of the story and the way in which that content is presented by the storyteller. That is, generalization 3 might be construed to mean that the events in the plot must relate chronologically according to the order of his list, such that, for example, the false hero must present unfounded claims (24) *before* a difficult task is presented to the hero (25), regardless of the order in which these two events are presented in narrative. Flashbacks might be used, or other literary devices, that result in the order of presentation not being a mirror of the order of events in the plot. On such a construal, Propp's generalization 3 affects only the content of the story, not the way it is told. A stricter construal would be one that dictated that 24 must not only precede 25 in the plot but must also be presented in narration before 25.

This points up an important three-way distinction that is often confused in story grammars, a distinction that is absolutely essential if any sense is to be made of story structure. (It should be kept in mind, though, that these three matters are only necessary, not sufficient, for an understanding of what makes a story. They do not themselves provide an account of the difference between stories and nonstories, nor between good and bad stories.)

First, and most obviously, stories have *content*: the facts and events that make up the "world" of the story. Included among these facts are relations among the events of the story; not functional relations, but just the kind of relations that hold between the facts and events of the real world: temporal order, relations of causation, motivation, and so on. The most appropriate system for describing this aspect of story content, then, is a system for describing facts and events in the world. The reader/hearer constructs a "model" of the story world.

A second and very different aspect of the content of a text is *the manner* in which the world is described: the storyteller's choices concerning which points of content to present explicitly and which to leave to the hearer to infer; what order events should be presented in; and so on. We shall call this *presentational structure* (cf. Brewer, Chapter 9 this volume). Recovering this kind of content from a text entails the reader/hearer's inferring what kind of *plan* the storyteller has followed in presenting the story and how each choice that the teller has made advances toward the goal that motivates that plan. A typical question for the reader to resolve is what the function or purpose is of a given stretch of text, or of a choice or other subsentential elements. The most appropriate system for describing this aspect of story content is a system for describing intentions, goals, purposes, and plans; a full-fledged theory of acts would be a start. Note that this aspect of a story is not a matter of linguistic form.

The third aspect of a story (or of a telling of a story) is its linguistic form: the linguistic elements and relations that make up the means used to express the story.

Though these three kinds of properties are distinct, they are of course not entirely independent. The content of the story will determine many matters of presentational structure and linguistic form. This is trivially true in the case of lexical items, for example. Again, if one is telling a story about Winston Churchill, one is likely to use the linguistic form "Winston Churchill." If one decides to present event *A* before event *B,* then the linguistic forms used to present event *A* will precede the linguistic forms used to present event *B,* and so on. There are nontrivial relations among the three as well. One well-known case is the fact that order of presentation tends to mirror the order of events. Typically, the reader/hearer will assume that events in the plot occur in the order in which they are presented, given no evidence to the contrary. Thus the need arises for linguistic and literary devices to signal deviations from this simple correlation between plot and presentation. But such influences notwithstanding, the three kinds of structure are logically independent. Thus, order of presentation will not always mirror the order of events, causes will sometimes be told after presenting the events they cause, important events may be left to the reader/hearer to infer, and so on.

Armed with this three-way distinction, we turn again to Prince (1973) and Rumelhart (1975).

There are two aspects of Prince's model that, on close examination, show that the parallel between syntactic structure and story structure is an illusion. First, there is a confusion on the distinction between content and presentational structure. Prince derives stories in which order of presentation does not match order of occurrence of events by *transforming* one order into the other. But if the two orderings are logically distinct, therefore independent of each other, then the transformational approach makes no sense. In syntactic theory, there is an abstract relation of order that can hold between elements in a string. A reordering transformation is hypothesized when the analyst wishes to claim that at one level two elements bear the ordering relation $R(a, b)$, but at another level bear the *very same* relation, but in the opposite order, $R(b, a)$. But in Prince's case, it is not a single relation between two elements at two levels but between two *different* pairs of elements; that is, between two events, *a* and *b*, and between their presentation, $p(a)$ and $p(b)$. Thus, in the case of a flashback we have (in which *P* stands for the relation "precedes in time") $P(a, b)$ but $P[p(b), p(a)]$. One might even wish to argue that there are two distinct kinds of precedence relations involved here rather than simply one. At any rate, Prince's transformational treatment of such cases is a mistake. There is no reason not to treat these matters as questions of different properties at a single level of description rather than the same property at different levels.

Second, the parallel disappears when we consider just what it is that his story grammar generates. It is not "stories" in the obvious sense, that is, linguistic objects (texts, say) that when understood by a speaker of the language can be interpreted as expressing stories. Rather, for Prince (1973), a story is a more abstract kind of entity:

> Stories may be expressed in a variety of ways. As a matter of fact, any given story may be rendered through language, film, pantomime, and so on.... Consequently, it can be said that neither the substance (sounds, images, gestures, etc.) nor the form (certain specific English sentneces, for instance) of the expression of a story defines it as a story rather than a non-story. This is why a grammar of stories does not have to be concerned with the description of the expression side of stories [p. 13].

Then a story is a matter of content, abstracted away from any particular means of expression of that content. A story is a complex of events, which might be related verbally or conveyed in entirely nonverbal ways. We find this view appealing and consider it a promising approach. But its adoption leads quickly to certain consequences for Prince's theory that he seems to have overlooked. First, if the story is independent of its mode of expression, then his *transformations* are irrelevant to the definition of storyhood, because they have to do not with the content of the story but with the way it is expressed. Second, the empirical status of Prince's story grammar is quite different from that of a Chomskyan sentence grammar. In a syntactic theory, the objects generated are strings of words, each with an associated structural description. The grammar, by virtue of its mathematical properties, makes unambiguous claims about possible strings of words and about what structural description is associated with a given sentence, from which the analyst can proceed to empirical test, which may be difficult but is, in principle, possible. The case with Prince's story grammar is not so simple. Because it is not linguistic forms but abstract entities (plots, roughly) that are generated, the progression to empirical test is rather difficult. A particular plot cannot be identified with any particular linguistic or other expression of it. Then how are we to talk about plots? In particular, how can we come to agree or disagree on whether or not a given plot is embodied in a certain text, film, and so on? We must rely on the analyst's intuition alone to supply this missing link, a very subjective matter. Prince's theory supplies no solution to this problem, nor does any other that we know of.

Rumelhart, like Prince, is inconsistent on whether a story is a text or something more abstract that can be expressed by a text. Throughout his chapter, he fails to distinguish among the three types of structure we have discussed. He speaks, for example, of inferring "the causal relationship between the propositions." But events cause events; propositions are not the kind of thing that can cause or be caused. Such small errors become a serious problem when they occur often enough. The same error seems to underlie Rumelhart's (1975) claim that: "the structure of stories is more than pairwise relationships among sentences. Rather, strings of sentences combine into psychological wholes [p. 213]." The same confusion between the three types of structure can be seen in his complaint that: "no one has ever been able to specify a general structure for stories that will distinguish the strings of sentences which form stories from strings which do not [p. 211]." From this one would expect Rumelhart's theory to be one that generated stories as strings of sentences, with associated structural descriptions that captured the "story structure" of the generated text. But in fact, Rumelhart's grammar is like Prince's in that it generates abstract structures rather than texts. The structures generated seem to be a mixture of plot and presentational structure, in that they are specified in terms of structures of events in particular orders. It is not made clear whether this order is to be interpreted as order of events, order of presentation, or both. As with Prince (1973), no explicit method is provided for applying the grammar to particular texts. It is up to the analyst's intuition, just as with Prince's grammar, to determine which plot structures the grammar assigns to a particular text. In demonstrating the application of his grammar to particular stories, Rumelhart merely presents a structural analysis, with discussion. He does not say how one goes about deciding what plot structure is assigned. In both Prince's and Rumelhart's theories this matter goes undiscussed, left entirely to the subjective judgments of the analysts. And there is no discussion of the question of ambiguity: Can a given text be associated with more than one plot structure?

Rumelhart's (1975) borrowings from syntactic theory are well worth examination. He clearly has in mind some close parallel between his rewriting rules and phrase structure grammars in syntax, but is the parallel substantive? Apparently it is not. The distinction between syntactic and semantic rules in the standard theory of grammar hinges on the fact that the categories of syntax are categories of *form*, the semantic structure's representations of meaning. A noun phrase is a noun phrase, as a matter of form, independently of what its semantic role is, and independently of its grammatical relations to other elements in the sentence. But in Rumelhart's system, the categories of his syntax are not categories of form, in two ways. First, they are actually relational terms, not category terms. The same event might be a reaction in one story, an episode in another. These notions really have to do with the functional relations among the parts of the story, not with the form of the parts. Second, whatever their interpretation, it is clear that they have to do with the content of the text, its plot, and perhaps presentational structure, not its linguistic form. In fact, the question arises of the need for Rumelhart's two separate systems, because both are really systems of content, not form. Is it possible, for example, that the terms of the syntax might be not primitive but definable, in terms of the notions of the semantics? If so, the syntactic rules may well be entirely superfluous. Both would be needed, of course, if one were really a grammar of plot structure, the other of presentational structure. But this does not appear to be the distinction Rumelhart has in mind.

There are insights to be found in these two works, but the story grammar metaphor is inappropriate and ultimately misleading. Our goal is an adequate *theory* of text structure. Using the notational machinery of syntactic theory gives the appearance of a rigorous formal theory and suggests detailed answers to important questions. On close examination, this appearance turns out to be an illusion. Moreover, this use of syntactic apparatus has the unintended effect of confusing and obscuring what the real issues are. From the homely observation that stories have structure, we should be led to ask questions such as: "What is a story?" "What kind of 'structure' is this structure that stories have?" By using the analogy with syntactic theory, one suggests the far-reaching answer, "It is like syntactic structure," with the quite detailed notion of structure that that implies, and the question is pursued no further. But we see that there is so far no reason to believe that it is at all like syntactic structure. There are similarities between syntactic structure and story structure only insofar as both involve structure. But probably every human activity has some kind of structure, so the similarity is a trivial one. We are left with no answers for the important questions. Even though there is some intuitive appeal to the ideas behind these works, their theoretical treatment is inadequate, due mainly to lack of understanding of the concepts involved.

There are two insights that are a motif in these two works and others on the structure of stories that are, though rather confused at times, worth pursuing. The first is the idea that there is some sort of schema for stories; the second, that a crucial property of stories is the types of events in them and the relations among them. We will argue that insofar as there are story schemata, they are really a function of several factors, rather than anything like a syntactic structure. We will also claim that most of the insights about events and their relations should follow naturally from an understanding of what stories are for, *not* from any kind of internalized schema. We will begin by trying to reconstruct the essence of one kind of story in its simplest form, pointing out how certain important consequences can be derived.

What is it that makes a story a story? None of the things discussed so far distinguish stories from other kinds of connected discourse. Any discourse can be described in terms of content, presentational structure, and linguistic form. Many nonstories involve the description of events and their interrelations. What then sets stories apart? If we had to tell a Martian what a story is, how would we go about it?

What makes a story a good or a bad story? If we leave aside the more subtle pleasures of sophisticated literary tradition, sticking to gut-level judgments of stories that might be made by children, or by adults of a television culture, the answer seems to relate to the presence of a mild cathartic effect. The impression one gets from story schema literature is usually that a good story is one that fits well with some story schema, as if the enjoyment and judgment of stories were derived from trying to fit events into schemata. But this misses the point entirely. The essence of a story is the imaginary experience it evokes in the reader or hearer. People enjoy stories via the experiences that they derive from understanding the story, not through the sensual pleasures of fitting information structures into an abstract schema. Typical rudimentary stories involve a conflict of some kind, with the result of an increasing feeling of tension, which is released when the conflict is resolved. This is hardly a new idea.

But from just this much we can see how some common story properties follow as a natural consequence. First, if there is to be a conflict and resulting increase in tension, there must be events. States-of-affairs in themselves will not have the right effect. Second, the events that lead to or constitute the conflict and resolution must involve a tension that a human being can experience, at least in imagination; therefore, there must be at least one character, human or human-like, who is the focus of the tension—the one endangered, or thwarted, or whatever—with whom the reader can, at least to some extent, identify. A description of how pressure builds up inside a popcorn kernel until it pops may be fascinating, but it is not a story; there is no human experience to be vicariously experienced by the reader. Third, the conflict cannot be *too* real; it must be removed at least in time from the world of the real present. If we tell you that a bull is charging at you, then that someone has shot him, there is a rise and release of tension, but it is hardly a story. And if we tell you all the exciting details of your friend's dramatic death just this afternoon, you will not consider it a story at all, though a stranger might consider it a good one. There is a point of intention to be made here. A mark of a story is that the main intention in telling it is *not* just to inform the reader of the events in the story. Rather, it is to provide an enjoyable imaginary experience for the reader.

There are a couple of consequences we can derive from the fact that the story cannot be too real. First, the characters in the story are likely to be unfamiliar, (i.e., not too close to the real world), either imaginary characters, or real ones in another time. Then it is not surprising that stories (at least rudimentary stories) often begin with a setting. It is pragmatically necessary to provide enough background material for the reader/hearer to be able to construct the world of the story from the semantics of the sentences used by the storyteller; that is, to figure out in what relevant respects the story world differs from the real world of the present, to have the information necessary for understanding deictics, referring expressions, and so on.

Another instance is the order of narrative, which generally mirrors the order of events. This fact follows from the *purpose* of narrative. Insofar as that purpose is to evoke in the hearer an imaginary experience, it follows that the events should be related in order of occurrence, because that is how the events would be experienced firsthand.

Our point, then, is that many properties of stories that might be taken as exotic kinds of learned mental structures are actually best understood functionally, as properties that are necessary for something to have the *effect* of a story—namely, to evoke certain kinds of imaginary experiences for the hearer. Insofar as a story lacks one or more of these properties, it will be less likely to evoke an enjoyable experience in the imagination of the hearer. Take, for example, a story whose sole source of potential enjoyment is a rising level of suspense and a sudden, surprising resolution. If the outcome is told first, then the story may well be judged as "bad" or "ill-formed," because for the hearer, who already knows the outcome, the following events produce no suspense. There is the added problem, of course, that the story may be so poorly constructed that the hearer is unable to reconstruct from the narrative the order in which the narrated events occurred or even the events themselves. And it may be that the hearer has enough intelligence to see how a badly constructed story could be repaired in one or more ways so that it has more nearly the *effect* one expects from a story. But this in itself does not argue for any kind of story schema. Neither the ability to distinguish a story from other kinds of text (or good stories from bad) nor the ability to repair stories provides any evidence for the existence of abstract story schemata; all one need know to make the relevant judgments is whether (or to what degree) the putative story produces an enjoyable experience, the effect one expects of a story. Expectations about effect are surely a matter of experience and may vary from culture to culture; but this is not a matter of story schemata.

From this description of rudimentary stories we can see how things can go wrong in the telling. First, the hearer can fail to construct in imagination a coherent picture of the story world. This could happen if the teller provided insufficient setting or presented events in an order that did not correspond to order of occurrence without saying so, and so on. And, as we pointed out earlier, the right flashback can ruin a story as well. If the resolution is presented first, even clearly labeled so that the hearer can recover the order of events easily, the resulting experience will, in this kind of story, likely be less enjoyable, because the tension will be less if one knows ahead of time how it will be resolved.

Another way presentation can go wrong is by violations of the principle of relevance. If we assume that the storyteller's purpose in telling a story is to provide whatever we mean by "enjoyment," then it follows that everything he or she does in presenting the story should serve to advance toward that purpose. Given no evidence to the contrary, hearers will assume this is so and, if irrelevant events are described, will try to interpret them as relevant by inferring what the narrator's goals are and what the story world would have to be like for them to be relevant. Thus they will be likely to construct a story world different from the one the teller has in mind, and the story is likely to fail. As a consequence of the teller observing the principle of relevance, then, the facts and events of the story will all be related to each other in some way or another: causes, consequences, motivations, links in a chain of events, rhetorical relations, and so on. The possible relations are limited only by the requirement that they jointly contribute to producing the right kind of imaginary experience for the reader. There will necessarily be chains-of-events, because the tension has to grow rather slowly. One cannot take the hero immediately to the danger of the shark's jaws; one has to lead up to it, or the story is no fun. And if the reader is to identify with a protagonist, even to experience vicariously what the protagonist experiences in the story, he or she must have some inkling of the character's motivations for his actions. If it is hard to understand why the hero does what he does, it is hard to identify with him. But from the fact that people dislike or do not understand stories that lack these properties, we cannot conclude that they have internalized any schema about the relations between events in stories.

So far we have discussed stories from the viewpoint of a Martian with no prior experience with stories, arguing that once the main purpose of stories is made clear, many story properties follow naturally without the need for anything like story schemata. But most people are unlike Martians in that they have considerable prior experience with stories. Accordingly, they may have certain expectations, based on experience, about what they will encounter in stories. These expectations may follow not from the purpose of stories but from accidents of individual experience. Although a story in which the "good guy" wins may be more satisfying, for obvious reasons, it is not a necessary property of stories. But a person who has heard only such stories may come to expect that in stories the good guy will win (or that there will be a witch, or a fairy princess, or that it will begin with a setting). In themselves, such expectations about story content are not very interesting, but they point to the possibility that such expectations may harden into literary convention (implicit or explicit) in particular cultures. Here, if anywhere, is found a set of data for which story schemata may be an appropriate descriptive tool. There clearly are such conventions, as seen, for example, in the work of Propp (1928/1958). But we doubt that it is this kind of convention that is involved in the recent psychological literature on story grammars.

It is worth pointing out that such conventions about story content are clearly not *linguistic* conventions, except possibly in the case of conventions governing the use of particular expressions (e.g., *Once upon a time, . . . amen,* etc.) in terms of discourse function. And even here there are arguments that there are conventions of *usage,* as opposed to conventions of language proper; see Morgan (1978) for a fuller discussion of the distinction.

We conclude, then, that the notion story grammar, insofar as it makes any sense at all, provides no basis for concluding that there are nontrivial parallels between discourse structure and linguistic structure.

A similar mistake can be found, it seems to us, in the work of van Dijk (1972, 1977). In these works van Dijk attempts two versions of a complete *linguistic* theory of discourse. Van Dijk's work is vulnerable to many technical and theoretical criticisms (see, in this regard, Dascal & Avishai, 1974a, 1974b, Elffers-van Ketel et al., 1973), especially (despite prolific use of fancy notations) the criticism that it is so vague as to have little content. But here we are interested mainly in his view of the relation between discourse and linguistic theory, the spirit of which is easy to discern.

Although there are a number of technical differences between these two attempts, van Dijk makes the same mistake in both by misconstruing problems of content as linguistic problems. In his first book (1972), his proposal is for the replacement of the familiar kind of grammatical theory by a theory of text grammar. According to van Dijk, "the only valid natural domain of a theory of language is an infinite set of discourses [p. v]." Grammars of the familiar sort, then, are to be replaced by text grammars that generate texts in a fashion analogous to the generation of sentences by transformational grammars. Besides generating texts, the text grammar assigns to each text a kind of meaning representation van Dijk calls a *macrostructure.* These are essentially abstracts or summaries. Further, van Dijk (1972) states:

> Text grammars must enumerate formally the abstract objects, called "texts,"
> underlying these discourses, and assign structural descriptions to the texts they
> generate.... Moreover, it will be shown that text grammar is the only adequate
> framework for the description of sentence structure [p. v].

As it turns out, van Dijk provides no persuasive argument for the latter claim. There is nothing anywhere in his work that could be considered an explication of syntactic properties in terms of discourse properties.

It is quite clear that van Dijk (1972) intends his theory to be taken as a *linguistic* theory of discourse (as well as of sentence grammar): "We explicitly claim that macro-structures (and rules) have a strictly linguistic status. They are not merely aspects of performance, e.g. as non-linguistic cognitive strategies [p. 6]." The most important flaws in van Dijk's first attempt are his notion of "ungrammatical" text and his "macro-structures" as representations of text meaning.

In van Dijk's view, texts, considered as "*n*-tuples of sentences," can be considered "grammatical" or "ungrammatical," just as for sentences: "We will require of any adequate grammar to predict which combinations (pairs, triples, ..., *n*-tuples) of sentences are grammatical and ungrammatical [p. 41]." As examples of ungrammatical texts, van Dijk (1972) offers sentence pairs such as these:

> We will have guests for lunch. Calderon was a great Spanish writer [p. 39].

> The old woman was buried in her native village. She is dying of virulent pneumonia [p. 82].

The ungrammaticality of the latter text van Dijk attributes to the fact that it is "ungrammatical to predicate something about an individual of which the (actual) non-existence has been asserted [p. 83]." But surely what is wrong with the two examples just given has nothing at all to do with the language in which they are expressed. In fact, there is no reason to believe that they are at all deviant as texts; in the second example, it is just that the events described are bizarre. By van Dijk's (1972) approach, any accurate narrative of a bizarre chain of events would be labeled "ungrammatical." In the first example, it is hard (though not impossible) to see any relation of relevance between the two sentences. But van Dijk gives no reason to believe that relevance is a linguistic matter. One can produce the same kind of irrelevance in nonlinguistic domains, for example, by the right selection of scene changes in a movie. Van Dijk's mistake is in failing to distinguish texts that are unusual in some way because of their content from the possible case of texts that are deviant for linguistic reasons. In all his examples of ungrammatical texts, there is not one convincing case of a text that is ungrammatical for linguistic reasons, that is, in which what is "wrong" with the text is to be explained in linguistic terms (for example, as a matter of the relation between the form of the text and its intended content) rather than in terms of bizarreness of content.

But the most glaring flaw in his program is his notion of macro-structure as a representation of the meaning of a text. This macro-structure is essentially an abstract of the text or, rather, a hierarchical structure of abstracts, abstracts of abstracts, and so on, "derived" from the meanings of the sentences of the text in some mysterious way. This notion has a certain appeal in that the ability to summarize or abstract is often taken as an indication of understanding; but to take that summary as what is being understood (the meaning of the text) is a mistake for two reasons. First, the most profound and fascinating fact about text understanding, which we assume is what van Dijk is attempting to account for, is that the meaning of the whole text is far more than just the meanings of the parts. In van Dijk's (1972) system, the macro-structure contains *less* information than the text itself; for him the meaning of the whole seems to be less than the meaning of the parts. Second, it is a mistake to construe the ability to summarize, to abstract this kind of macro-structure, as a strictly linguistic matter. Surely one would come up with roughly identical summaries of an event directly observed and of the same event narrated in language. Summarization or abstracting has to do with interpreting the world, and the world can be observed directly or vicariously through narrative. Summarization is *not* a linguistic operation performed on texts to recover content. Summarization may be a mark of understanding but it is not itself either understanding or what it is that is understood.

By the time he wrote his second book (1977), van Dijk had apparently become aware of some shortcomings of his approach and had, with the rest of the field, discovered the importance of pragmatics to understanding connected discourse. His second book, then, "aims at providing some corrections by establishing a more explicit and more systematic approach to the linguistic study of discourse [p.vii]." By way of being more explicit, van Dijk offers the reader an introductory course in mathematical logic. Unfortunately, he makes no systematic use of the systems he presents, save an occasional use of just the notation. Nor does he make use of the tremendous potential of pragmatics for explanation of discourse phenomena, except for occasional lip service to the need for consideration of speech acts, and so on. Rather, van Dijk (1977) continues the approach of the first book, wherein, for example, "connectedness" is defined in terms of semantic relations between meaning of words in sentences rather than, say, pragmatic relations between speech acts, and "topic" is "some specific proposition (or set of propositions) entailed" by the "set of available information [p. 50]." The improved version retains macro-structure summaries as representation of text meaning, and macro-structure is still construed as a linguistic concept:

> It should be emphasized again that macro-structures are not merely postulated in order to account for cognitive information processing. The hypothesis is that they are an integral part of the meaning of a discourse, and that, therefore, they are to be accounted for in a semantic representation [p. 143].

Again it is clear that, insofar as macro-structures are intended as a representation of the meaning of a text, van Dijk's approach has the meaning of the whole to be considerably less than the sum of the parts. He attempts (not very successfully) to provide clear statements of rules to derive macro-structures from the meanings of lower-level stretches of discourse by "deleting" information. For example, he proposes the following rule to delete "accidental" (as opposed to "essential") properties [p. 144]:

$$fx \ \& \ gx \rightarrow fx$$

This rule would apply to a case like "town (a) & little (a)" to derive "town (a)"; that is, in a text about a little town, the fact that it was little would be deleted and hence not present in macro-structure.

In his second book, van Dijk seems to have abandoned the notion "ungrammatical text" but makes a similar error in considering the notion "coherence," which he takes to be a semantic matter. He speaks of the "acceptability" of, say, "she drank her inkwell [p. 99]." as a continuation of:

> Clare Russell came into the *Clarion* office on the following morning, feeling tired and depressed. She went straight to her room, took off her hat, touched her face with a powder puff and sat down at her desk.
>   Her mail was spread out neatly, her blotter was snowy and her inkwell was filled. But she didn't feel like work [p. 98].

It is a mistake to consider matters like this to be in the domain of a theory of discourse at all. What is at issue here is what kinds of events in the world are considered bizarre, not what makes a coherent text. Again, if this is the approach taken to coherence, then any clear and accurate narrative of a strange series of events would count as an incoherent text. The proper business of a discourse theory is to say what makes a *text* successful or not, clear or not, coherent or not, in terms of the relation between the text and the intended content. But what kind of things or events count as strange is surely not the business of a theory of discourse, much less of linguistic theory. As far as we can see, van Dijk's (1977) second book does not succeed in avoiding the fundamental mistakes of the first.

CONCLUSION

At this point the only thing that is clear is the kind of approach to discourse that is likely to fail—that is, a strictly linguistic approach that attempts to put all the burden of text comprehension on the language faculty. In fact, such an approach is prima facie implausible. Given the powerful common-sense abilities that are brought to bear in just making sense of the world and other people, it is thoroughly implausible to suppose that these abilities are suppressed when texts are encountered in favor of some arcane, strictly linguistic mechanism whose sole function is to process and understand discourse. Surely the mind employs all available resources in interpreting discourse. The question is, then, how to begin to factor out those aspects of text competence that are just the application to this task of general abilities, in order to reach an understanding of (at the theoretical level) how much of this competence is to be accounted for in linguistic terms, how much in more general terms, and (at the practical level) whether reading comprehension difficulties can be attributed to "local," especially linguistic, problems, as opposed to more global deficiencies in intelligence, differences in culture or experience, and so on.

We think it is important to abandon the idea that the meaning of a text is some kind of summary of it. The proper analysis of this problem would be one in which the ability to summarize or abstract *presupposed* an understanding of the text, rather than being identified with understanding. Further, it seems most plausible that the ability to summarize is not a linguistic skill at bottom (except insofar as one has to put the summary into words); the process of constructing a summary is based on an understanding of what the (perhaps imaginary) world is like, not a kind of linguistic processing. We would expect, then, that the ability to summarize movies or direct observation is the same ability that is involved in summarizing texts. Likewise, with at least some types of text structure, the ability to impose some kind of organizational structure on the events narrated in a story is most likely the same ability one uses in imposing structure on observed reality. In fact, it is tempting to suppose that what is called "pragmatics" is just the application, to verbal problems, of very general abilities for interpreting the everyday world (see Morgan, 1978, for fuller discussion). It seems to be a fact that people automatically understand the behavior of other humans in terms of notions such as intention, belief, purpose, desire, and so on. And a good deal of what has been discussed under the rubric "pragmatics" is most reasonably seen as the interpretation of *linguistic* behavior in these terms. We suggest that this is the most promising avenue to explore for an understanding of apparently linguistic matters such as coherence, relevance, topic, comment, text structure, and so on.

In the case of text structure, for example, there are at least two kinds of structure involved. One is the structure the mind unconsciously imposes on the events that are being narrated; this structure will, of course, also influence the interpretation of what the events are that are being narrated. But there is another kind of organization to texts that might fruitfully be viewed as a kind of plan structure—for example, that the author has completed one subgoal and begun another. A judgment as to what the speaker is trying to do in a discourse will influence the interpretation of what he or she says. Here, also, is a likely place for the definition of one kind of relevance. For example, if we understand that the speaker's present purpose is to tell us how to get to San Francisco, and in the midst of speaking he tells us that the price of gold has risen on the Paris market, we will likely label this utterance "irrelevant" unless we can construct some way of relating it to his goal of giving us directions. This kind of relevance, then, would be most insightfully considered not as some kind of semantic entailment relation between sentences but as relations of purpose between speech acts, relative to some goal.

Lacking even a partially explicit theory of plans, actions, and inference in which to state such hypotheses, though, our proposals are little more than speculation. But we think this line of research is more likely to bear fruit than that of constructing ever more exotic linguistic units and levels and accounts of discourse comprehension.

ACKNOWLEDGMENTS

Our work on this topic has been strongly influenced by the work of William Brewer, Chip Bruce, and Georgia Green, who nonetheless are not responsible for our distortions of their ideas. We also owe much to discussions with Herb Clark and Robert Kantor, who likewise bear no blame for our mistakes. This work was supported in part by the National Institute of Education under Contract No. US-NIE-C-400-76-0116.

REFERENCES

Breuer, D. *Einfuehrung in die Pragmatische Texttheorie.* Muenchen: Wilhelm Fink Verlag, 1974.

Brinker, K. Zum Textbegriff in der heutigen Linguistik. In H. Sitta & K. Brinker (Eds.), *Studien zur Texttheorie und zur Deutschen Grammatik.* (= Sprache der Gegenwart 30, Festgave H. Glinz). Duesseldorf: Schwann, 1973.

Daneš, F. One instance of Prague School methodology: Functional analysis of utterance of text. In P. Garvin (Ed.), *Theory and method in linguistics.* The Hague: Mouton, 1970.

Daneš, F. *Papers on functional sentence perspective.* Prague: Publishing House of the Czech Academy of Sciences, 1974.

Dascal, M., & Avishai, M. A new revolution in linguistics—"Textgrammars" vs. "Sentence grammars." *Theoretical Linguistics,* 1974, *1,* 195–213(a)

Dascal, M., & Avishai, M. Text grammars—a critical view. *Papiere zur Textlinguistik,* 1974, *5,* 81–134(b)

Dressler, W. Towards a semantic deep structure of discourse grammar. In M. A. Campbell et al. (Eds.), *Papers from the Sixth Regional Meeting, Chicago Linguistic Society.* Chicago: University of Chicago, Department of Linguistics, 1970.

Dressler, W. Einführung in die Textlinguistik. München: Max Niemeyer.

Elffers-van Ketel, E., de Haan, S., & Klooster, W. Een [+ fantastischel] macrostructuur. *Spektator,* 1973, *3,* 581–600; 1973, *4,* 53–74.

Firbas, J. On defining the theme in functional sentence analysis. *Travaux Linguistique de Prague,* 1964, *1,* 267–380.

Firbas, J. Non-thematic subjects in contemporary English. *Travaux Linguistiques de Prague,* 1966, *2,* 239–256.

Firbas, J. On the concept of communicative dynamism in the theory of functional sentence perspective. *Sbornik praci filosoficks fakulty brnanake university,* 1971, *A = 19,* 135–144.

Fries, C. *The structure of English.* New York: Harcourt, 1952.

Grice, H. Logic and conversation. In P. Cole & J. Morgan, (Eds.), *Syntax and semantics, Vol. 3: Speech acts.* New York: Academic Press, 1975.

Grimes, J. *The thread of discourse.* The Hague: Mouton, 1975.

Gulich, E., & Raible, W. *Linguistische Textmodelle: Grundlagen und Möglichkeiten.* Muenchen: Wilhelm Fink Verlag, 1977.

Halliday, M., & Hasan, R. *Cohesion in English.* London: Longman, 1976.

Harris, Z. *Papers in structural and transformational linguistics.* Dordrecht: D. Reidel, 1970.

Harweg, R. *Pronomina und Textkonstitution.* Muenchen: Wilhelm Fink Verlag, 1968.

Harweg, T. Substitutional textlinguistics. In W. Dressler (Ed.), *Current trends in textlinguistics.* New York: Walter de Gruyter, 1977.

Heidolph, K. Kontextbeziehungen zwischen Saetzen in einer generativen Grammatik. *Kybernetika Cislo,* 1966, *3,* 273–281.

Klein, W. Text. *Linguistik und Didaktik,* 1972, *3,* 161–180.

Koch, W. Preliminary sketch of a semantic type of discourse analysis. *Linguistics,* 1965, *12,* 5–30.

Koch, W. *Recurrence and a three-modal approach to poetry.* The Hague: Mouton, 1966.

Koch, W. *Vom Morphem zum Textem.* Hildesheim: Olms, 1970.

Kuno, S. Functional sentence perspective. *Linguistic Inquiry,* 1972, *3,* 269–320.

Lang, E. Ueber einige Schwierigkeiten beim Postulieren einer Textgrammatik. In F. Kiefer & N. Ruwet (Eds.), *Generative grammar in Europe.* Dordrecht: D. Reidel, 1973.

Lang, E. Erklaerungstexte. In F. Danes & D. Viehweger (Eds.), *Probleme der Textgrammatik.* Berlin: Akademie Verlag, 1976.

Lang, E. *Semantik der koordinativen Verknuepfungen.* Berlin: Akademie Verlag, 1977.

Longacre, R. *Discourse, paragraph and sentence structure in selected Phillipine Languages.* Santa Ana, Calif.: Summer Institute of Linguistics, 1968.

Longacre, R. *Hierarchy and universality of discourse constituents in New Guinea languages.* Washington, D.C.: Georgetown University Press, 1972.

Morgan, J. Two types of convention in indirect speech acts. In P. Cole (Ed.), *Syntax and semantics, Vol. 9, Pragmatics.* New York: Academic Press, 1978.

Petöfi, J. Probleme der ko-textuelle Analyse von Texten. In J. Ihew (Ed), *Linguistik und Literaturwissenschaft.* Frankfurt: Athenaeum, 1971(a)

Petöfi, J. *Transformationsgrammatik und eine ko-textuelle Texttheorie.* Frankfurt: Athenaeum, 1971.(b)

Petöfi, J. "Generativity" and "Textgrammar." *Folia Linguistica,* 1972, *5,* 277–309.(a)

Petöfi, J. Zu einer grammatischen Theorie sprachlicher Texte. *Linguistik und Literatur,* 1972,*5,* 31–58.(b)

Petöfi, J. Towards an empirically motivated grammatical theory of verbal texts. In J. Petöfi & H. Rieser (Eds.), *Studies in text grammar.* Dordrecht: D. Reidel, 1973.

Pike, K. *Language in relation to a unified theory of the structure of human behavior.* The Hague: Mouton, 1967.

Prince, E. Discourse analysis in the framework of Zellig S. Harris. In W. Dressler (Ed.), *Current trends in textlinguistics.* New York: Walter de Gruyter 1977.

Prince, G. *A grammar of stories.* The Hague: Mouton, 1973.

Propp, V. *Morphology of the folktale.* Bloomingdale: Indiana University Research center in Anthropology, Folklore, and Linguistics, 1958.

Rieser, H. Probleme der Textgrammatik II. *Folia Linguistica,* 1973, *6,* 28–46.

Rieser, H. *On the development of text grammar.* Unpublished manuscript, Bielefeld University, 1976.

Rumelhart, D. Notes on a schema for stories. In D. Bobrow & A. Collins (Eds.), *Representation and understanding.* New York: Academic Press, 1975.

Sadock, J. *Toward a linguistic theory of speech acts.* New York: Academic Press, 1975.

Sandig, B. Beispiele pragmalinguistischer Textanalyse. *Der Deutschunterricht,* 1973, *25,* 5–23.

Schmidt, S. *Texttheorie. Probleme einer Linguistik sprachlicher Kommunikation.* Muenchen: Wilhelm Fink Verlag, 1973.

Schmidt, S. J. Some problems of communicative text theories. In W. Dressler (Ed.), *Current trends in textlinguistics.* New York: Walter de Gruyter, 1977.

Searle, J. *Speech acts.* London: Cambridge University Press, 1969.

Searle, J. Indirect speech acts. In P. Cole & J. Morgan (Eds.), *Syntax and semantics, Vol. 3, Speech acts.* New York: Academic Press, 1975.

Sinclair, J., & Coulthard, R. *Toward an analysis of discourse.* London: Oxford University Press, 1975.

Stein, N., & Glenn, C. An analysis of story comprehension in elementary school children. In R. Freedle (Ed.), *Discourse processing: Multidisciplinary perspectives.* Norwood, N.J.: Ablex, 1978.

van Dijk, T. *Some aspects of text grammars.* The Hague: Mouton, 1972.

van Dijk, T. Text grammar and text logic. In J. Petöfi & H. Rieser (Eds.), *Studies in text grammar*. Dordrecht: D. Reidel, 1973.

van Dijk, T. (Ed.). *Pragmatics of language and literature*. Amsterdam: North Holland, 1975.

van Dijk, T. *Text and context: Explorations in the semantics and pragmatics of discourse*. London: Longman, 1977.

van Dijk, T., Ihew, J., Petöfi, J. S., & Rieser, H. Two text grammatical models. *Foundations of language*. 1972, *8*, 499–545.

van Dijk, T., & Petöfi, J. (Eds.). *Grammars and descriptions*. Berlin: de Gruyter, 1977.

Weinrich, H. *Tempus, Besprochene und erzaehlte Welt*. Stuttgart: Kohlhammer, 1971.

Wunderlich, D. Die Rolle der Pragmatik in der Linguistik. *Der Deutschunterricht, 1970, 22,* 5–41.

Wunderlich, D. Pragmatik, Sprechsituation, Deixis. *Zeitschrift fuer Literaturwissenschaft und Linguistik, 1971, 1,* 153–190.

Wunderlich, D. *Linguistische Pragmatik*. Frankfurt: Athenaeum, 1972.

8
Psychological Correlates of Text Structure

Ernest T. Goetz
Bonnie B. Armbruster
Center for the Study of Reading,
University of Illinois, Urbana-Champaign

INTRODUCTION

In this chapter, we attempt to review what is known of the psychological correlates of text structure; that is, we examine research that has investigated how variations in text structure influence the way people read, comprehend, and remember text. Those not familiar with this literature might expect that a review so brief as ours would barely be able to scratch the surface. Clearly, this is an area of broad and vital concern to both education and psychology. Because reading *always* involves text, it seems certain that the analysis of text structure and its effects on comprehension and memory must by now have generated a rich, complex, highly advanced domain of inquiry. Sadly, this is not the case. The existing literature is almost embarrassingly meager and rudimentary, given the import and complexity of the area.

The first question we must address, then, is why is there so little to report. Several answers are possible. One reason has been the long-standing neglect of connected discourse by linguists. The notion that the single sentence is the only proper domain of the linguist has had a long, pervasive history. Only recently has there dawned a growing awareness that many problems of semantics and pragmatics can only be addressed at the discourse or broader contextual level. To date, little or no work on text structure has appeared in the mainstream of linguistics in this country. As further progress is made on this linguistic frontier, it may be hoped that at least some additional benefits will accrue to educators and psycholinguists interested in psychological consequences of text.

A second reason for the lack of knowledge about the psychological effects of text structure is that only in the last few years has text become the subject of extensive psychological research. Until very recently, psychology was almost totally dominated by behaviorism. "Mentalistic" language and theorization were shunned, and texts were avoided both as too complex and as too contaminated by "meaning" and contact with prior "knowledge" to be studied. Thus, although texts have been studied by a few daring and adventurous psychologists since the time of Binet and Henri (1894; Thieman & Brewer, 1978), only recently has text become an accepted area of psychological investigation. Although text has been employed in a sizable number of studies in the educational psychology literature, these studies for the most part have been directed at issues other than text structure, or else they have not been sufficiently theoretically motivated to have made much real headway.

A problem that pervades the research into the psychological correlates of text structure is the confounding of text structure with text content. Ideally, text structure would be studied by comparing comprehension of and memory for texts that had the same content or meaning but different structures or linguistic embodiments. This ideal, however, has proved unattainable, because any change in structure seems to entail a change in meaning. In fact, most of the research that has investigated the effect of text structure has compared texts or portions of texts without any attempt to control content. If the problem of text structure were not already difficult enough, this confounding with content would still ensure headaches for future investigators.

A final reason for the lack of progress is that nearly all of the existing research has been conducted under the implicit assumption that text structure and content are inherent in the text. This approach is an example of the meaning-in-the-text position that is outlined by Spiro (Chapter 10, this volume). We are convinced that the psychological utility of this approach is severely limited by the failure to come to grips with the constructive, interactive nature of comprehension and memory.

What, then, is known of the psychological correlates of text structure? We have divided our review into three sections, covering what we feel are the three major findings.

1. Text represents a higher level of psychological structure or organization than less integrated verbal materials such as collections of sentences or lists of words.
2. Within a text, readers will find some elements more important than others, and, if tested, they will be more likely to remember the important elements.

3. The linguistic and extra-linguistic context in which a text appears and the knowledge, interest, and perspective of the reader are important determinants of the psychological structure and meaning of text.

WHAT IS SO CONNECTED
ABOUT CONNECTED DISCOURSE?

The most obvious characteristic of text is its connectedness. The term *connected discourse* emphasizes the distinction between texts and unrelated collections of sentences or lists of words. Because experimental psychology had long busied itself with the study of word lists, it is not surprising that many of the first studies of texts included comparison of memory for *discourse order* versus *scrambled order* word lists (e.g., Brent, 1969; Dooling & Lachman, 1971; Lachman & Dooling, 1968; Montague & Carter, 1973; Pompi & Lachman, 1967; Yuille & Paivio, 1969). It is even less surprising that texts, even when presented word by word, were better recalled in their normal order than as scrambled lists.

The advantage of psychological unity at the discourse level has also been demonstrated in experiments comparing the memorability of regular texts to lists of unrelatd sentences or texts with sentence order scrambled. For example, in the educational psychology literature, a number of studies (e.g., Frase, 1969; Myers, Pezdek, & Coulson, 1973; Perlmutter & Royer, 1973; Yekovich & Kulhavy, 1976) have demonstrated the effect of sentence order on descriptive texts in which each of several objects is described in terms of several attributes. These texts were presented with all the sentences specifying the attributes of a given object grouped together, with the sentences describing the attribute values of a given attribute for all the objects grouped together, or in random orders. Both of the rational organizations were remembered better than the random order.

Although there is by now a great deal of evidence that text is both easier to learn and better remembered than lists of words or sentences, the explanation of this fact has received relatively little attention. There are, however, several possible interpretations, three of which are considered here.

Connectedness and Representation in Memory

The first possibility is that connected discourse permits the construction of a highly integrated or interconnected representation in memory that is both easier to construct and more efficient at retrieval. This point can be illustrated by several current models of memory (e.g., Anderson & Bower, 1973; Kintsch, 1972, 1974; Rumelhart, Lindsay, & Norman, 1972). In these models, information is represented in memory as a network of interconnected or linked nodes. The nodes represent concepts and the links between nodes represent the relationships between the concepts. In connected discourse, the same concepts (people, objects, events) will be referenced in many sentences so that there will be fewer different concepts to represent than in a list of unconnected sentences of equal length. By this analysis, unrelated sentences are harder to learn than connected discourse because the construction of a new node is more difficult (or occurs with a smaller probability) than adding additional links to existing nodes. The representation constructed from connected discourse is more efficient for retrieval because the many interconnections between concepts increase both the number of nodes that can be accessed from a single node and also the number of potential paths for access to a given node.

There is some evidence supporting this analysis. For example Levin (1970) studied the learning of a word list embedded in sentences and varied the degree of integration by using either a single long connected sentence (a short story) or up to 12 unrelated sentences. Fourth- and fifth-graders were able to learn the list more rapidly when it appeared in one or two sentences than when it was used in several unrelated sentences. De Villiers (1974) manipulated the use of articles (e.g., *a, the*) in a loosely knit passage about the adventures of a small boy. When definite articles *(the)* were used, the subjects assumed that referents were shared across sentences, and they were more likely to treat it as a story and construct an integrated representation. With indefinite articles *(a)*, subjects assumed that referents varied across sentences and thus were more likely to treat the passage as a list of unrelated sentences. The manipulation was not entirely successful, but deVilliers used postexperimental questioning to determine how subjects had treated the passage and analyzed his data with subjects sorted as a function of their answer. The subjects who treated the passage as a story recalled more than did those who treated it as a sentence list.

Several studies have directly manipulated the number of concept repetitions in order to test the prediction that such repetitions will make texts easier to learn and remember. Kintsch, Kozminsky, Streby, McKoon, and Keenan (1975) constructed brief (about 70 word) texts that contained either few concepts with many repetitions and many interconnections or many concepts with fewer repetitions and interconnections. They found that the less connected passages required more reading time. When reading time was restricted and equated for the two passage types, the less connected passages were more poorly recalled. Manelis and Yekovich (1976) controlled both the number of words and concepts while varying the number of repetitions in sentences of about 10–15 words and found that the sentences with fewer interconnections took longer to read. When reading time was fixed, immediate recall of less connected sentences was inferior. Finally, they compared three sentence texts in which concept repetitions were either included (e.g., *Arnold lunged at Norman. Norman called the doctor. The doctor arrived.*) or deleted (e.g., *Arnold lunged. Norman called. The doctor arrived.*). The stories that contained repetitions were better recalled, even though they were longer. They were also much better recalled than stories of the same length in which different concepts rather than repetitions occurred (e.g., *Arnold lunged at Brian. Norman called the doctor. The police arrived.*).

Connectedness and the Processing of Text

A second explanation of the advantage of connected discourse is that there may exist important differences in the way subjects process sentence lists and connected discourse. The levels-of-processing analysis of R. C. Anderson (1970; 1972), Craik and Lockhart (1972), and Craik, (1973) suggests that connected discourse may be remembered better because it is processed more deeply. In the levels-of-processing analysis, processing of verbal material is said to progress from processing of surface orthographic and/or phonological features to elaborate representation of meaning. Each successive level of processing leaves its own memorial representation, with deeper levels producing more durable codes, as evidenced by the fact that the verbatim form of verbal material is more rapidly forgotten than meaning (e.g., Fillenbaum, 1966; Sachs, 1967). Further, Craik and Lockhart's conception of the reader/hearer of discourse as a limited-capacity information processor implies that the more cognitive effort is expended upon encoding at one level, the less information will be retained at other levels. Thus, if subjects reading connected discourse are more likely to engage in deep, meaningful encoding than are subjects who read sentence lists, then they should retain more information about the meaning and less about the form of the sentences involved.

There is some empirical support for this prediction. For example, White and Gagné (1976) compared recognition memory for changes in wording with recall of the meaning of the text after subjects read and answered questions either about sentences concerning a single topic (i.e., connected discourse) or a list of sentences selected from each of the different and unrelated topics. They found that connected discourse resulted in better memory for meaning but poorer memory for exact wording. Thorndyke (1977) has also found better recognition for the verbatim form of sentences by subjects who read scrambled stories than by those who read well-ordered stories. A similar result was obtained by Pezdek and Royer (1974), who presented sentences either with a context paragraph or in isolation. In addition, J. Anderson (1974) conducted two studies of verification latencies for sentences, one in which subjects studied connected discourse and the other in which subjects read sentence lists. The verification targets were either repeated verbatim from the study materials or changed in voice (active or passive). It was found that immediate verification was faster for unchanged sentences, regardless of which type of materials subjects had studied. When verification was delayed 2 minutes, the effect of sentence form only reached significance for the scrambled sentence condition.

That subjects are more likely to encode connected discourse deeply is supported by another line of evidence: Subjects who read sentence lists seem to employ the shallow rehearsal or recycling strategies typically employed in learning lists of unrelated words, whereas the order of words and sentences in text provides a useful and meaningful organization that obviates such shallow processing. DeVilliers (1974) observed that subjects who treated his passage as a sentence list tended to output the last sentence or two first in recall, similar to the "dumping" strategy observed in immediate free recall of word lists (e.g., Glanzer & Cunitz, 1966). Deese and Kaufman (1957) had previously noted that subjects recalling discourse do not employ a dumping strategy. They reported a study that compared discourse recall with recall of a word list. For discourse, recall order was essentially perfectly correlated with input order. With word lists, however, subjects tended to recall last-presented items first. Dumping in the recall of sentence lists has also been found in the studies of short-term memory for proverbs by Glanzer and Razel (1974).

Another prediction is possible if the depth-of-processing notion is expanded to include inference and constructive processes. If subjects are more likely to process normal connected discourse at a deep, meaningful level, then they should be more likely to engage in inferential and constructive processes. This prediction follows from the position that inference and constructive processes are a vital component of the comprehension of and memory for discourse (cf. Spiro, Chapter 10, this volume; R. C. Anderson & Shifrin, Chapter 13, this volume). Thorndyke (1977) has obtained empirical support for this prediction: Subjects who read stories in the normal order were more likely to falsely recognize statements reflecting inferential constructions from the story than were subjects who read stories that had been scrambled.

Connectedness and Contact with Existing Knowledge

The third explanation of the better learning and memory of connected discourse, compared to less integrated verbal material, is that readers are better able to relate text to what they already know. The psychological unity of connected discourse may derive from the fact that the reader's knowledge, beliefs, and expectations permit him or her to organize and interrelate elements in the text.

When contact with existing knowlede is minimal, texts will be difficult to learn and remember. Thus, an advanced text on nuclear physics may seem to be "disconnected" discourse to the reader who is totally unfamiliar with the topic. This point was dramatically illustrated by Dooling and Lachman (1971) and Bransford and Johnson (1972), who showed that a vague, opaquely written passage, which in isolation seemed nonsense and was very poorly recalled, became perfectly sensible and easily recalled when a title or picture preceded it, establishing contact with the subjects' prior knowledge. Although the texts used in these studies were contrived, they provide striking demonstration of the effect.

Recently, the structure and function of knowledge has received a great deal of attention, and many variants of schema and frame-like notions have been developed (cf. Rumelhart, Chapter 2, this volume). In addition to these general knowledge models, story grammars (e.g., Rumelhart, 1975) have been developed to represent people's presumed knowledge and expectations about the structure of simple stories. Such story-specific knowledge will obviously be of little or no help if the reader is presented with a list of unrelated words or sentences or if the text is so thoroughly scrambled as to destroy all traces of connectedness. If, however, a story is only slightly scrambled, for example, with paragraphs remaining intact or with only a single event being displaced, the existing knowledge structures may permit reordering of the story in order to conform to expectations.

Kintsch and van Dijk (1975; see also van Dijk and Kintsch, 1976) randomized the paragraph order of stories, while leaving paragraphs intact. They found that subjects took longer to read scrambled stories than to read intact stories. The story summaries produced by the two groups were, however, indistinguishable as the readers of the scrambled stories were able to impose the missing but expected order. Studies by Rumelhart (1976) and Stein (1976) have demonstrated that when an event is displaced from its normal position, readers tend to recall the story in more normal order.

If the reader's knowledge is an important determinant of the comprehension and memory of texts, then texts that describe familiar or well-structured events should produce better, more structured recall or summarization. Kintsch and van Dijk (1975) found greater agreement between the summaries produced by readers of a "conventional" story, the organization of which matched their expectations, than among summaries produced by readers of an "unconventional" story, which did not conform to their expectations. Kintsch and Greene (1978) found better recall of a conventional story (a Grimm fairy tale) than of an unconventional story (an Apache Indian tale). Kintsch, Mandel, and Kozminsky (1977) presented a well-structured and a less well-structured story in normal or scrambled paragraph order. The well-structured story had strong underlying causal connections between events, whereas the less well-structured story did not. Subjects who read the scrambled well-structured story were able to successfully reorganize it, so that their summaries were not noticeably different from those who read the normal order version. Subjects who read the scrambled, less well-structured stories were less likely to produce summaries that matched the normal order version.

R. C. Anderson, Spiro, and Anderson (1978) report a study in which college students read a story about a couple who were either grocery shopping or dining at a fine restaurant. The same foods were mentioned in identical order and associated with the same person in both stories, and the two stories were otherwise as much alike as possible. Because people's stereotype for a meal at a fancy restaurant is more constrained than the stereotype for grocery shopping, it was predicted that the restaurant story would be better remembered. In particular, the restaurant story was found to increase the number of food items recalled and the likelihood that those food items recalled would be attributed to the correct character, as predicted. Although there was a trend for subjects who had read the restaurant story to more accurately recall the order of the food items, this effect did not attain significance.

Related experiments using pictures alone or pictures with a narrative have lead to similar conclusions about children's use of their knowledge of logical story organization in comprehension. Brown and Murphy (1975) presented four-year-olds with sets of pictures that portrayed events in either an arbitrary sequence or a logical sequence in normal or scrambled order. During test trials, subjects were given the pictures again in random order and asked to reconstruct the order of presentation after a lag of zero, two, or 5 other series. For immediate reconstruction, performance was very high for both logical and arbitrary sequences. After two and five other series, however, reconstruction of well-ordered logical sequences was better than for scrambled logical sequences or arbitrary sequences. Apparently the children understood the logical structure of the pictures and were able to draw on their prior structural knowledge to improve memory. Another experiment showed that the arbitrary sequence of pictures was better reconstructed when accompanied by a narrative providing a meaningful structure.

In a similar experiment (Brown, 1975), kindergarteners and second-graders either viewed sets of pictures accompanied by logically or arbitrarily sequenced narratives or were asked to invent their own story to aid their memory. On a posttest of recognition, reconstruction, or recall, performance was worse for arbitrarily than for logically ordered narratives. Performance was equally good for the self-constructed stories as for the logically ordered sequences.

Poulson, Kintsch, Kintsch, and Premack (1979) presented sets of 15–18 logically or randomly ordered pictures depicting a story of 4- and 6-year-olds. After viewing the complete set, the children were asked to describe the pictures one at a time; their descriptions were compared to adults' descriptions. Some of the children's responses could be classified as "story propositions" that could only be generated by understanding the pictures as representing a structured story. The children, particularly the 6-year-olds, added story propositions to the normal story. The 6-year-olds also added story propositions to the randomly ordered stories, apparently in an attempt to interpret the pictures as a coherent story. After the children had described the pictures, they were asked to recall the story without pictures. Recall was best for descriptions that had been successfully integrated into a story.

In sum, there is a great deal of evidence that adults and even children as young as 4 years old have knowledge of logical relationships and the structures underlying simple stories that greatly influences their comprehension and memory for narratives. Recall is superior for passages organized according to an underlying logical structure than for arbitrarily ordered passages. Also, text deviating from the idealized schema will tend to be reorganized to conform to the schema. It is not clear, however, that story grammars or story-specific knowledge structures are necessary to account for these results. General knowledge about such things as temporal and causal sequences and plans (see Bruce, Chapter 15, this volume) would seem to suffice.

Finally, although we have raised three possible explanations for the memorability of connected discourse, we do not view them as competing hypotheses. Rather, it seems that each may contain an element of truth and all may be needed to provide an adequate account. One reason for suspecting that this may be the case is that the three accounts can be easily combined to form a connected discourse: People remember connected discourse better because their prior knowledge and expectations permit them to form a highly interconnected representation, a process that requires deep semantic processing.

RECALL OF IMPORTANT VERSUS UNIMPORTANT MATERIAL IN TEXT

Importance as Theme Relatedness

One of the first findings of the early research on prose recall was that when a group of people are presented with a text and then asked to recall it, some portions of the text are recalled by nearly everyone whereas other portions are recalled by almost no one. The early prose investigators noted that the most commonly recalled portions of the text were the most important sections of the text, or those sections most central to the theme of the text. Much of the prose research that has been reported to date has substantiated this relationship between the importance and memorability of text elements.

Newman (1939) tested story recall after an 8-hour period of sleep or waking activity. He found that "essential" material was much better recalled than "nonessential" material after either type of retention interval, and that although considerable forgetting of the nonessential material occurred as a result of waking activity, essential material was equally well recalled after either sleep or waking activity. Gomulicki (1956) investigated the immediate recall of prose passages, that varied in length from 15 to 200 words. He found that although the subjects were able to recall the shorter passages verbatim, they were only able to recall the more important aspects of the longer passages. Gomulicki noted that the recall protocols for the longer passages resembled abstracts. In fact, judges given both recalls and abstracts performed only slightly above chance at discriminating the two.

Johnson (1970) developed a direct method of measuring perceived theme-related importance. Subjects were presented with a text that had previously been segmented into pausal units (units between which pauses would be acceptable) and told that some of the units were central and essential to the passage whereas others were of lesser importance and could be deleted with little or no damage to the passage. The subjects were then told to indicate those units that were least important and could therefore best be deleted. Different groups of subjects were told to delete ¼, ½, or ¾ of the pausal units; the number of subjects who deleted a given unit was the measure of importance. Importance was found to be a strong determinant of recall over retention intervals ranging up to 63 days.

More recent developmental studies have also demonstrated the relationship between the importance of idea units and recall of those units. Brown and Smiley (1977) had third-, fifth-, and seventh-graders and college students rate the importance of linguistic units of prose passages in the manner of Johnson. Sensitivity to levels of importance as measured by the deletion task was found to develop over time: Third-graders were unable to distinguish any of the four levels; fifth-graders could differentiate the most important from the rest; seventh-graders could distinguish the most and least important but had trouble with the middle levels of importance; and college students could differentiate all levels. It is possible that this rating task proved difficult for the younger students and masked their sensitivity to importance. Despite the varying ability to make editorial decisions about importance, recall for all subjects was strongly affected by importance at each grade level; that is, more important units were better recalled than less important units when the adult importance measure was used.

Recently it has been shown that the effect of importance extends to implied as well as stated information. Goetz (1979) reports that increasing the importance of an inference in a story will increase the probability that the inference will be made. When the consequences of an inferred event (e.g., a woman stops to talk to her son before leaving on a busines trip) were made important (the woman misses a plane that crashes into the mountains), readers were more likely to correctly infer the event than when it had less dire consequences (the woman arrives at the airport behind schedule to await a plane that is even further behind schedule.)

Importance in Text Structure Analyses

Recent research in prose memory has seen the development of increasingly formal accounts of text structure. The development of text structure analysis and text grammars has provided a new method for determining the importance of text elements and has again demonstrated that important text elements are better recalled.

Meyer and McConkie (1973) used a simple, informal method of discourse structure analysis to examine the relationship between importance and recall. They had graduate students outline a passage and then converted the outlines to tree structures. From these tree structures, three measures of the importance of an idea unit in the structure of the passage were developed: a hierarchy depth score, which measured how high in the hierarchy the unit occurred; a units beneath score, which measured the number of units that were beneath the given unit in the hierarchy; and a combined hierarchy score, which combined the two previous measures. Important units were better recalled than unimportant units on all three measures. Further, when significant effects of serial position and rated importance were found, these were shown to be largely due to the correlation of those factors with hierarchical importance.

The effect of importance has been replicated using more formal models and analyses of text structure (e.g., Kintsch, 1972, 1974; Meyer, 1975). Kintsch and Keenan (1973) presented subjects with a set of sentences, each of which was 14–16 words in length. The sentences were analyzed into hierarchical propositional representations, in which each proposition essentially consisted of a verb or adjectives and their attendant nouns. Both propositional rank (analogous to Meyer and McConkie's hierarchy depth score) and number of descendant propositions (analogous to Meyer and McConkie's units beneath score) affected recall: The higher in the hierarchy a proposition occurred, or the more propositions directly beneath it in the hierarchy, the more likely it was to be recalled. However, the two measures were highly correlated and when propositional rank was controlled, no effect of number of descendants remained. The effect of propositional rank was replicated by Kintsch, Kozminsky, Streby, McKoon, and Keenan (1975), for both immediate and 24-hour delayed recall of historical passages (approximately 20 or 65 words long).

McKoon (1977) has shown that importance, as measured by the level of a proposition in the hierarchical representation, affects both the speed and accuracy of verification. A sentence containing propositions that were either high or low in the propositional hierarchy were presented at either the beginning or end of a passage. Both short (about 50 words) and long (about 200 words) passages were employed. No differences occurred when a sentence derived from the text was presented for immediate verification, but when verification occurred after a 25-minute delay, those probes based on the important text sentences were verified more accurately than less important probes. Neither passage length nor position (beginning or end) of the sentence had any effect.

Importance in Story Grammars

A different formalization of text structure is represented in the story grammar research, briefly discussed previously. According to this view, readers comprehend a narrative by selecting and verifying a prototypical structure assumed to underlie simple stories. Although a story grammar analysis differs from the text structure analyses discussed previously in that the structures described are general to a large, potentially infinite set of stories of a given type rather than specific to particular text as they are in structural analysis, there are many similarities between the two approaches. For example, Stein and Glenn (1978) state that research on story grammars is guided by three assumptions:

1. Stories have an internal structure.
2. This structure can be depicted as a hierarchical network of units of information serving different functions in the story structure and the logical relations existing among these units.
3. The hierarchical structure corresponds to some extent to the way people comprehend and store imformation in stories.

In addition, the recent research employing story grammars shows that importance as defined by height in the hierarchical network predicts recall.

Rumelhart (1976), van Dijk and Kintsch (1976), and Thorndyke (1977) examined recall protocols and summaries of adult subjects who read narratives. The consistent findings were, in general, that upper-level, more structurally central propositions were better recalled and more often included in summaries than were lower-level propositions. These studies have all replicated the similarity between abstracts and recall of text reported by Gomulicki (1956). Similarly, in a developmental study including first-grade, fourth-grade, and university-level subjects, Mandler and Johnson (1977) found that "basic," upper-level nodes were better remembered than "elaborative" or lower-level nodes for all age groups.

Explaining the Effect of Importance on Memory

Although the effect of importance on memory for text is by now well established, only recently have the reasons for this effect been investigated. Meyer (1975, 1977) has sought to test three possible sources of the effect of importance. Important material may be better remembered because it is: (1) more likely to be encoded during reading; (2) less susceptible to loss through forgetting; or (3) easier to access or more retrievable.

Meyer (1977) has reported some preliminary evidence for the encoding process explanation. Subjects were given a free recall test immediately after reading a passage in which the target paragraph was high (important) or low (unimportant) in the content structure. As soon as subjects had completed their free recall, they were given cues (a list of content words from the passage) and instructed to write a second recall. Preliminary inspection of the results for the free recall task indicated that the target paragraph was better recalled when important. The introduction of cues aided the recall of both important and unimportant target segments but did not reduce the advantage of important versions. Meyer argued that this result supports the encoding hypothesis, because if the poor recall of unimportant material was due to retrieval failure, the introduction of cues should decrease this deficit by reducing the difficulty of the retrieval task.

In the earlier study just mentioned (Meyer, 1975), support was found for the hypothesis that important material is better remembered because it is less susceptible to loss through forgetting. In this study, subjects read and immediately recalled a passage. One week later they were given a second free recall test followed by a cued recall test, using the content word list as cues. When loss scores were computed by subtracting the second free recall from the first, passages in which the target paragraph was important showed less forgetting. The introduction of cues produced much better recall than the second free recall, but it did not reduce the advantage of important versions. Thus, the greater forgetting of the unimportant material seems to be due to its loss from memory, because if it had been equally retained and was simply less accessible, the introduction of cues should have reduced this deficit.

As with the superior recall of connected compared to unconnected discourse, one possible explanation of the superior recall of important information is offered by the levels-of-processing approach. The skilled reader, realizing that he or she has a limited processing capacity and can not deeply encode all the information in or implied by the text during reading (Frederiksen, 1972, 1975a, 1975b), identifies an abstract or core of important material for deep encoding and elaboration. Because important elements are more deeply encoded, they are less subject for forgetting, an advantage that increases with the retention interval (e.g., Newman, 1939; Meyer, 1975).

What such an account obviously lacks is an explanation of how readers (or psycholinguists, for that matter) identify what is important in text. Although linguistic devices employed by authors such as repetitions, highlighting (e.g., use of phrases such as "the main point is . . . "), and sequencing are no doubt important, we concentrate, in the next section, on the effect of the readers' own knowledge, interest, and perspective on what he or she considers important.

STRUCTURE AS AN INHERENT ASPECT
OF TEXT: SOME SNAGS

A common feature of the discourse structure analyses to date is that text structure is treated as though it were an inherent, immutable attribute of the text, interpreted in the same manner by all readers. Thus, the importance of an element of text is determined by the position of that element in *the* structure of the text. This approach is representative of the "meaning-in-the-text" position discussed by Spiro (Chapter 10, this volume). Such an approach can only be psychologically adequate if the meaning of text is, in fact, invariant across subjects and contexts. An alternative position is the constructivist view outlined by Spiro. In the constructivist view, the emphasis shifts from the structure of text as an independent, immutable entity to structure and meaning as imposed on the text by the reader. It is assumed that although text constrains the possible meanings, readers with different knowledge, interests, and perspectives, or the same reader in different contexts, may construct quite different interpretations. This section discusses the research supporting the constructivist approach to text structure—studies investigating the effect of context and perspective on interpretation of text.

The effect of context on the meaning of text has been demonstrated by a growing body of research. As noted previously, Dooling and Lachman (1971) and Bransford and Johnson (1972) have shown that the same passage can seem nonsense or perfectly interpretable, depending on the context. Schallert (1976) showed that the same ambiguous passage could be given two very different meanings when preceded by different title contexts. Sulin and Dooling (1974) showed that when brief biographical passages were written so that the main character was a famous person, subjects tended to falsely recognize statements of well-known information about the famous person that were not contained in the passage. Subjects who read the same passages with fictitious names substituted as the main characters were unlikely to falsely recognize such statements. Brown, Smiley, Day, Townsend and Lawton (1977) have demonstrated similar effects in the memory for stories of grade school children. In the first of two experiments, context was varied by telling the children that the central character of a story about an escape was either a convict or the chimpanzee hero of the television series, *Planet of the Apes*. Children who were told that the story was about a *Planet of the Apes* chimpanzee were more likely to falsely recognize foils based on the television series. In the second study, context for a story about a fictitious tribe was varied by depicting the tribe as either Eskimos or desert Indians. Children produced intrusions in their recalls consistent with the presented context. In sum, studies manipulating context have shown that the meaning of text is not invariant.

Another line of research has demonstrated the influence of reader interest and perspective on the interpretation and structure of discourse. For example, Anderson, Reynolds, Schallert, and Goetz (1977) used ambiguous passages similar to those of Schallert (1976) to show the effect of reader interest and knowledge on the interpretation of text. They found that with an ambiguous passage describing either a card game or a musical quartet practice, music students were far more likely to construct the latter interpretation than were physical education students. The subjects' interpretations were indicated by intrusions and disambiguations in free recall, choices made in disambiguating recognition tests, and responses to a postexperimental debriefing questionnaire.

Pichert and Anderson (1977) have demonstrated the effect of reader perspective on the rated importance and recall of idea units in text. One of their passages was a story about two boys who played hookey from school and went to play at the home of one of the boys. The passage contained some information that would be of special interest to a prospective home buyer (e.g., information about a new house siding, a fireplace, and a damp and musty basement), and other information that would be more likely to interest a potential burglar (e.g., information about the existence and location of 10-speed bicycles and a color television, and the fact that no one was home on Thursdays). A rating study was conducted in which different groups of subjects were asked to read the passage and rate the importance of idea units from the perspective of a home buyer or from the perspective of a burglar. A control group was told nothing about perspective. If importance is indeed an inherent aspect of text, as implied by existing text analysis systems, then assigned perspective should have no effect on rated importance; the rank order correlation of the rated importance of idea units between groups should approach one. This prediction was clearly disconfirmed by low intergroup correlation. In a second study, subjects who had been assigned to one of the perspective conditions read the passage and later recalled it. The importance ratings from a given perspective were the best predictors of the recall of subjects who read the passage from that perspective.

Evidence for the effect of reader perspective on retrieval processes has been developed by Anderson and Pichert (1978). Subjects read and recalled stories under perspective instructions identical to those just described. After completing recall, however, half of the subjects were told of the alternative perspective (i.e., the perspective different from the one under which they read and recalled the story) before attempting a second recall. These subjects were able to recall information relevant to their new perspective that they had failed to recall in their initial attempt. When compared to subjects who were not informed of the alternative perspective before the second recall, the informed subjects recalled more information relevant to their new perspective.

In sum, research on the effect of context, interest, and knowledge on interpretation has invalidated the conception that meaning and structure are inherent, invariant aspects of text and has provided support for the constructivist approach. It would seem that an account of text structure must reflect different interpretations imposed by the reader in order to be of any real utility as a model in psychology and education.

CONCLUSIONS AND EDUCATIONAL IMPLICATIONS

The experimental literature on the psychological correlates of text structure is still in its infancy and has thus far produced just three major findings. The first is that connected discourse is much easier to learn and remember than collections of unrelated sentences or lists of words and that, among texts, those that are more highly organized or more congruent with the reader's knowledge and expectations are better remembered. The second finding is that within a text, a reader will identify important elements that will then be more likely to be remembered. The third finding is that the reader and the context in which text occurs interact with the text itself in the construction of the psychological structure of text. We briefly consider a few of the more salient educational implications of these three findings.

The fact that connected discourse is better remembered than words or sentences suggests that when students must learn a list such as state capitals or chief exports of foreign countries, learning may be facilitated by embedding the list in a meaningful and interesting story context. The use of "narrative chaining" (Bower & Clark, 1969) to learn word lists is a mnemonic device that has had long favor with memory virtuosi but still may have untapped potential in the classroom.

Certainly the texts children read and the lectures they hear should be as clearly and consistently organized as possible, and ties to the existing knowledge of the students should be stressed. Similarly, if the connections between different learning activities are stressed so that the student perceives an organized, connected pattern of related activities rather than a random array of unrelated action, learning may be facilitated.

The research on memory for important information suggested that it is probably unrealistic for teachers to expect students to remember all the details of any particular lesson. Memory for the gist or main points of a text seems a more realistic objective. Further, adults are readily able to identify and concentrate on important portions of a text, but research suggests that without special guidance, children are less able to identify and utilize important elements as aids to study. It therefore seems likely that highlighting important information in a text by means of underlining, instructional objectives, or the like should enhance learning in young children. Teaching such students to identify the important portions of text should have the same beneficial effects and greater transfer.

Finally, we reviewed recent research that has shown that considerations of text structure in isolation are incomplete and untenable. The linguistic and nonlinguistic context in which a text occurs and the knowledge, expectations, and purposes of the reader interact with the text itself to determine the interpretation and the structure of the memorial representation that the reader will construct. We are convinced that future research on the psychological correlates of text structure will make real progress only when this interaction, rather than the structure "in" the text, becomes the object of study. The educational implications of the position have been discussed in some detail in two recent papers by R. C. Anderson (1977; Anderson et al., 1977). One implication is that teachers should realize that different students may interpret the same text differently and that tests must be designed to reveal not only whether or not a student has understood, but *what* that student has understood.

We wish to close this review on a note of optimism. The study of the psychological correlates of text structure has only recently received attention that is in any way commensurate with its importance and complexity. Though there is little known now, the level and quality of current research efforts assures us that it is one of the most promising areas of psychological inquiry and one which may someday have most important educational implications.

ACKNOWLEDGMENTS

The authors would like to thank Linda Baker for her many helpful comments on an earlier draft of this paper. The development of this paper was supported by the National Institute of Education under Contract No. US-NIE-C-400-76-0116.

REFERENCES

Anderson, J. R. Verbatim and propositional representation of sentences in immediate and long-term memory. *Journal of Verbal Learning and Verbal Behavior, 1974, 13,* 149–162.

Anderson, J. R., & Bower, G. H. *Human associative memory.* New York: John Wiley, 1973.

Anderson, R. C. Control of student mediating processes during verbal learning and instruction. *Review of Educational Research, 1970, 40,* 349–369.

Anderson, R. C. How to construct achievement tests to assess comprehension. *Review of Educational Research,* 1972, *42,* 145–170.

Anderson, R. C. The notion of schemata and the educational enterprise. In R. C. Anderson, R. J. Spiro, & W. E. Montague (Eds.), *Schooling and the acquisition of knowledge.* Hillsdale, N.J.: Lawrence Erlbaum Associates, 1977.

Anderson, R. C., & Pichert, J. W. Recall of previously unrecallable information following a shift in perspective. *Journal of Verbal Learning and Verbal Behavior,* 1978, *17,* 1–12.

Anderson, R. C., Reynolds, R. E., Schallert, D. L., & Goetz. E. T. Frameworks for comprehending discourse. *American Educational Research Journal,* 1977, *14,* 367–382.

Anderson, R. C., Spiro, R., & Anderson, M. C. Schemata as scaffolding for the representation of information in connected discourse. *American Educational Research Journal,* 1978, *15,* 433–440.

Binet, A., & Henri, V. La mémoire des phrases (Mémoire des idées). *L'Anée Psychologique,* 1894, *1,* 24–59.

Bower, G. H., & Clark, M. C. Narrative stories as mediators for serial learning. *Psychonomic Science,* 1969, *14,* 181–182.

Bransford, J. D., & Johnson, M. K. Contextual prerequisites for understanding: Some investigations of comprehension and recall. *Journal of Verbal Learning and Verbal Behavior,* 1972, *11,* 717–726.

Brent, S. G. Linguistic unity, list length, and rate of presentation in serial anticipation learning. *Journal of Verbal Learning and Verbal Behavior,* 1969, *8,* 70–79.

Brown, A. L. Recognition, reconstruction, and recall of narrative sequences by preoperational children. *Child Development,* 1975, *46,* 156–166.

Brown, A. L., & Murphy, M. D. Reconstruction of arbitrary versus logical sequences by preschool children. *Journal of Experimental Child Psychology,* 1975, *20,* 307–326.

Brown, A. L., & Smiley, S. S. Rating the importance of structural units of prose passages: A problem of metacognitive development. *Child Development,* 1977, *48,* 1–8.

Brown, A. L., Smiley, S. S., Day, J. D., Townsend, M. A. R., & Lawton, S. C. Intrusion of a thematic idea in children's comprehension and retention of stories. *Child Development,* 1977, *48,* 1454–1466.

Craik, F. I. M. A "levels of analysis" view of memory. In P. Pliner, L. Krames, & T. Alloway (Eds.), *Communication and affect: Language and thought.* New York: Academic Press, 1973.

Craik, F. I. M., & Lockhart, R. S. Levels of processing: A framework for memory research. *Journal of Verbal Learning and Verbal Behavior,* 1972, 11, 671–684.

Deese, J., & Kaufman, R. A. Serial effects in recall of unorganized and sequentially organized verbal material. *Journal of Experimental Psychology,* 1957, *54,* 180–187.

deVilliers, P. A. Imagery and theme in recall of connected discourse. *Journal of Experimental Psychology,* 1974, *103,* 263–268.

Dooling, D. J., & Lachman, R. Effects of comprehension on retention of prose. *Journal of Experimental Psychology,* 1971, *88,* 216–222.

Fillenbaum, S. Memory for gist: Some relevant variables. *Language and Speech,* 1966, *9,* 217–227.

Frase, L. T. Paragraph organization of written materials: The influence of conceptual clustering upon the level and organization of recall. *Journal of Educational Psychology,* 1969, *60,* 394–401.

Fredericksen, C. H. Effects of task-induced cognitive operations on comprehension and memory processes. In J. B. Carroll & R. O. Freedle (Eds.), *Language comprehension and the acquisition of knowledge.* Washington, D.C.: Winston, 1972.

Fredericksen, C. H. Acquisition of semantic information from discourse: Effects of repeated exposures. *Journal of Verbal Learning and Verbal Behavior,* 1975, *14,* 158–169. (a)

Fredericksen, C. H. Effects of context-induced processing operations on semantic information acquired from discourse. *Cognitive Psychology,* 1975, *7,* 139–166. (b)

Glanzer, M., & Cunitz, A. R. Two storage mechanisms in free recall. *Journal of Verbal Learning and Verbal Behavior*, 1966, *5*, 351-360.

Glanzer, M., & Razel, M. The size of the unit in short-term storage. *Journal of Verbal Learning and Verbal Behavior*, 1974, *13*, 114-131.

Goetz, E. T. Infering from text: Some factors influencing which inferences will be made. *Discourse Processes*, 1979, *2*, 179-195.

Gomulicki, B. R. Recall as an abstractive process. *Acta Psychologica*, 1956, *12*, 77-94.

Johnson, R. E. Recall of prose as a function of the structural importance of the linguistic units. *Journal of Verbal Learning and Verbal Behavior*, 1970, *9*, 12-20.

Kintsch, W. Notes on the structure of semantic memory. In E. Tulving & W. Donaldson (Eds.), *Organization of memory*. New York: Academic Press, 1972.

Kintsch, W. *The representation of meaning in memory*. Hillsdale, N.J.: Lawrence Erlbaum Associates, 1974.

Kintsch, W. & Greene, E. The role of culture specific schemata in the comprehension and recall of stories. *Discourse Processes*, 1978, *1*, 1-13.

Kintsch, W., & Keenan, J. Reading rate and retention as a function of the number of propositions in the base structure of sentences. *Cognitive Psychology*, 1973, *5*, 257-274.

Kintsch, W., Kozminsky, E., Streby, W. J., McKoon, G., & Keenan, J. M. Comprehension and recall of text as a function of content variables. *Journal of Verbal Learning and Verbal Behavior*, 1975, *14*, 196-214.

Kintsch, W., Mandel, T. S., & Kozminksy, E. Summarizing scrambled stories. *Memory and Cognition*, 1977, *5*, 547-552.

Kintsch, W., & van Dijk, T. A. Recalling and summarizing stories (Comment on se rappelle et on résumes des histoires). *Languages*, 1975, *40*, 98-116.

Lachman, R., & Dooling, D. J. Connected discourse and random strings: Effects of number of inputs on recognition and recall. *Journal of Experimental Psychology*, 1968, *77*, 517-522.

Levin, J. R. Verbal organizations and the facilitation of serial learning. *Journal of Educational Psychology*, 1970, *61*, 110-117.

Mandler, J. M., & Johnson, N. S. Remembrance of things parsed: Story structure and recall. *Cognitive Psychology*, 1977, *9*, 111-151.

Manelis, L., & Yekovich, F. R. Repetitions of propositional arguments in sentences. *Journal of Verbal Learning and Verbal Behavior*, 1976, *15*, 301-312.

McKoon, G. Organization of information in text memory. *Journal of Verbal Learning and Verbal Behavior*, 1977, *16*, 247-260.

Meyer, B. J. F. *The organization of prose and its effects on memory*. Amsterdam: North-Holland, 1975.

Meyer, B. J. F. The structure of prose: Effects on learning and memory and implications for educational practice. In R. C. Anderson, R. J. Spiro, & W. E. Montague (Eds.), *Schooling and the acquisition of knowledge*. Hillsdale, N.J.: Lawrence Erlbaum Associates, 1977.

Meyer, B. J. F., & McConkie, G. W. What is recalled after hearing a passage? *Journal of Educational Psychology*, 1973, *65*, 109-117.

Montague, W. E., & Carter, J. F. Vividness of imagery in recalling connected discourse. *Journal of Educational Psychology*, 1973, *64*, 72-75.

Myers, J. L., Pezdek, K., & Coulson, D. Effects of prose organization upon free recall. *Journal of Educational Psychology*, 1973, *65*, 313-320.

Newman, E. B. Forgetting of meaningful material during sleep and waking. *American Journal of Psychology*, 1939, *52*, 65-71.

Perlmutter, J., & Royer, J. M. Organization of prose materials: Stimulus, storage, and retrieval. *Canadian Journal of Psychology*, 1973, *27*, 200-209.

Pezdek, K., & Royer, J. M. The role of comprehension in learning concrete and abstract sentences. *Journal of Verbal Learning and Verbal Behavior*, 1974, *13*, 551-558.

Pichert, J., & Anderson, R. C. Taking different perspectives on a story. *Journal of Educational Psychology*, 1977, *69*, 309–315.

Pompi, K. F,. & Lachman, R. Surrogate processes in the short-term retention of connected discourse. *Journal of Experimental Psychology*, 1967, *75*, 143–150.

Poulson, D., Kintsch, E., Kintsch, W., & Premack, D. Children's comprehension and memory for stories. *Journal of Experimental Child Psychology*, 1979, *28*, 379–403.

Rumelhart, D. E. Notes on a schema for stories. In D. G. Brown & A. Collins (Eds.), *Representation and understanding: Studies in cognitive science*. New York: Academic Press, 1975.

Rumelhart, D. E. Understanding and summarizing brief stories. (Tech. Report No. 58). San Diego, Calif.: Center for Human Information Processing, University of California, San Diego, 1976.

Rumelhart, D. E., Lindsay, P. H., & Norman, D. A. A process model for long-term memory. In E. Tulving & W. Donaldson (Eds.), *Organization and memory*. New York: Academic Press, 1972.

Sachs, J. S. Recognition memory for syntactic and semantic aspects of connected discourse. *Perception and Psychophysics*, 1967, *2*, 437–442.

Schallert, D. L. Improving memory for prose: The relationship between depth of processing and context. *Journal of Verbal Learning and Verbal Behavior*, 1976, *15*, 621–632.

Stein, N. L. *The effects of increasing temporal disorganization on children's recall of stories*. Paper presented at the Psychonomic Society Meetings, St. Louis, Missouri, November 1976.

Stein, N. L., & Glenn, C. G. An analysis of story comprehension in elementary school children. In R. Freedle (Ed.), *Discourse processing: Multidisciplinary perspectives*. Hillsdale, N.J.: Lawrence Erlbaum Associates, 1978.

Sulin, R. A., & Dooling, D. J. Intrusion of a thematic idea in retention of prose. *Journal of Experimental Psychology*, 1974, *103*, 255–262.

Thieman, T. J., & Brewer, W. F. Alfred Binet on memory for ideas. *Genetic Psychology Monographs*, 1978, *97*, 243–264.

Thorndyke, P. W. Cognitive structures in comprehension and memory of narrative discourse. *Cognitive Psychology*, 1977, *9*, 77–110.

van Dijk, T. A., & Kintsch, W. Cognitive psychology and discourse: Recalling and summarizing stories. In W. U. Dressler (Ed.), *Trends in text linguistics*. New York: deFruyter, 1976.

White, R. T., & Gagné, R. M. Retention of related and unrelated sentences. *Journal of Educational Psychology*, 1976, *68*, 843–852.

Yekovich, F. R., & Kulhavy, R. W. Structural and contextual effects in the organization of prose. *Journal of Educational Psychology*, 1976, *68*, 626–635.

Yuille, J. C., & Paivio, A. Abstractness and recall of connected discourse. *Journal of Experimental Psychology*, 1969, *82*, 467–471.

9

Literary Theory, Rhetoric, and Stylistics: Implications for Psychology

William F. Brewer
Center for the Study of Reading,
University of Illinois, Urbana-Champaign

The purpose of this chapter is to show that literary theory, rhetoric, and stylistics can provide an important source of theoretical ideas for experimental psychologists studying discourse. I think that recourse to these disciplines can be seen as the continuation of a long-term trend in the experimental investigation of linguistic materials by psychologists. In 1885, in the first experimental study of memory, Ebbinghaus contrasted memory for nonsense syllables with memory for narrative poetry. He argued that in order to gain experimental control over the phenomena it was necessary to use the nonsense material, since this would reduce or eliminate the complex effects of syntax and meaning that are characteristic of actual linguistic discourse. Ebbinghaus' arguments were accepted by most experimental psychologists, and research on memory for linguistic material focused on the nonsense syllable. However, in the 1960s, there was a dramatic change in this picture due to the impact of Chomsky's work in linguistics. Experimental psychologists discovered syntax and the sentence, and began a systematic exploitation of constructs from linguistics. These new ideas from linguistics resulted in a large body of work on sentence memory, sentence comprehension, and sentence production (cf. reviews in Fillenbaum, 1973; Greene, 1972). Recently there has been growing realization that the study of sentences in isolation may be very misleading, since actual exposure to language tends to be in discourse settings (hearing a conversation, reading a book, remembering a lecture). This movement has led to some interesting new work (see Goetz & Armbruster, Chapter 8, this volume) but has been hampered by the fact that research on discourse is just beginning in linguistics. Since it will be some time before linguistics provides a substantial body of theory, it seems to me that psychologists must look to see if there are other disciplines that already have an established framework that can be of help in developing the psychological study of discourse.

LITERARY THEORY, RHETORIC, AND STYLISTICS

The academic disciplines that have the best developed body of knowledge about written discourse are: literary theory (e.g., Wellek & Warren, 1962); rhetoric (e.g., Brooks & Warren, 1970); poetics (e.g., Culler, 1975); and stylistics (e.g., Enkvist, 1973). Each of these areas has a long tradition of scholarly work on some aspects of discourse.

The remainder of this chapter is an attempt to survey these areas to see whether the constructs that have been developed can be of help in developing a psychological theory of discourse. Most of the work in these areas comes out of the humanistic tradition of scholarship, and this causes a number of difficulties. Frequently the nature of the problem, the methods of argument, and the standards of evidence are very different from those that prevail in experimental psychology. Another problem is how to deal with the theoretical constructs that have been developed in these other disciplines. When psychologists first came into contact with generative-transformational linguistics, an attempt was made to convert it directly into a psychological theory (e.g., Miller, 1962). After about a decade of work it became evident that linguistic theory could not be used in a simple fashion as a psychological theory (cf. Greene, 1972). In more recent work, psycholinguists have adopted the more cautious approach of taking some of the apparently relevant insights and constructs from linguistics and using them to attempt to build an independent psychological theory of language. It seems to me that in opening up a new set of intellectual exchanges with these areas in the humanities, we should try to avoid the mistake made in the initial enthusiasm with linguistics and adopt the more cautious approach that now characterizes the relationship of psychology and linguistics.

TYPES OF DISCOURSE

A fundamental issue is: What is there to study? What are the types of discourse? The very different viewpoints of the authors from the various humanistic disciplines make for a great variety of answers to this question. Thus, Wellek and Warren (1962) suggest fiction, drama, and poetry. Brooks and Warren (1970) suggest exposition, argument, description, and narration. D'Angelo (1976) suggests expressive, persuasive, literary, and referential. An analysis of these and other classification schemes provides insight into the characteristics of discourse, but the humanistic perspective of these authors leads them to focus on somewhat different issues from those of interest to a cognitive psychologist. The humanistic writers often wish to include historical material in their classification, they want to consider the quality of a given form of discourse, and they tend to work with the very rare masterpieces of world literature. The goals of current psychology are somewhat less ambitious. For the cognitive psychologist, the classification of discourse is intended to help develop an understanding of how ordinary people comprehend, remember, and produce the types of discourse with which they come into contact. Therefore, the next section of this chapter attempts to develop a theory of discourse types that arises out of the traditional work in rhetoric and literary theory, but is designed to serve the purposes of cognitive psychology.

A PSYCHOLOGICAL CLASSIFICATION
OF WRITTEN DISCOURSE TYPES

Underlying Structure

The overall classification scheme is based on the cognitive structure underlying written discourse and the force of the discourse. Structure is discussed first. I propose that there are three basic types of written discourse: description, narration, and exposition. These three types are distinguished by the cognitive structure that is hypothesized to underlie each type. *Descriptive discourse* is discourse that attempts to embody in linguistic form a stationary perceptual scene. Since vision is by far the most frequently involved sense, the underlying cognitive representation will be considered to be visual-spatial. *Narrative discourse* is discourse that attempts to embody in linguistic form a series of events that occur in time. Actually, a much more subtle definition is needed. The sheer occurrence of events in time is not enough to constitute a coherent narrative (e.g., *The boy saw a dandelion on Monday. On Tuesday, the periscope jammed. On Wednesday, twins were born*). The events underlying a narrative must be related through a causal or thematic chain (eg., *The boy saw a dandelion. He picked the dandelion. He gave the dandelion to his mother*). Thus, the cognitive structure underlying narrative is the mental representation of a series of temporally occurring events that are perceived as having a causal or thematic coherence. *Expository discourse* is discourse that attempts to represent in linguistic form the underlying abstract logical processes. The underlying mental processes presumably involve such things as induction, classification, and comparison.

In this initial classification, the different types of discourse have been defined in terms of their underlying nonlinguistic cognitive structure. The differences between them can also be seen by attempting to translate each of the types into some other form of representation. Thus, typical descriptive passages can be represented by a picture. Typical narratives can be represented by a motion picture. Expository passages cannot be represented by pictures or movies; they could best be converted into some abstract form of representation, such as a particular logical notation. This classification is restricted to prose forms; for present purposes, the highly complex issues raised by poetry will not be discussed.

Force

In addition to cognitive structure, the classification of discourse types requires a construct of discourse force. Discourse force is taken to be analogous to sentence force as it has been used in the theory of speech acts (Searle, 1969). The discourse force of a particular instance of discourse is an interaction of the communicative intent of the author and the perception of the reader. However, for the present I will consider only the viewpoint of the author. I propose that there are four basic discourse forces: to inform, to entertain, to persuade, and literary-aesthetic (English does not seem to have an appropriate verb for this force). In *informative discourse* the intent of the author is to give information about something. In *entertaining discourse* the author's intention is to entertain, in the broader sense that includes amuse, frighten, and excite. In *persuasive discourse* the author's intention is to convince or persuade the reader to take a particular course of action or to adopt a particular set of ideas. In *literary-aesthetic discourse* the purpose of the author is to provide an aesthetic experience for the reader, to have the reader approach the discourse as a work of art.

Classification by Structure and Force

Since discourse structure and discourse force are largely independent of one another, it is possible to reflect the four forces (inform, entertain, persuade, literary-aesthetic) across the three structures (description, narration, exposition) and produce a classification scheme with 12 categories. Table 9.1 gives the psychological discourse classification with some examples of traditional types of discourse (genres) in each of the cells. Reading across the rows gives examples of discourse types that are based on the same discourse structure. Thus, discourse types based on events occurring in time (newspaper stories, instructions, novels) are classified together. The columns give examples of discourse types that have similar forces. Thus, advertisements, parables, editorials, and sermons are classified together under persuasive force.

There are many complexities that are not revealed in this relatively global classification. For example, some of the types of discourse under a given genre label are not really internally homogeneous. Within a genre such as

TABLE 9.1

A Psychological Classification of Written Discourse Types

Discourse (Underlying Structure)	Discourse Force			
	Inform	*Entertain*	*Persuade*	*Literary-Aesthetic*
Description (Space)	technical description botany geography	ordinary description	house advertisement	poetic description
Narrative (Time-Events)	newspaper story history instructions recipes biography	mystery novel western novel science fiction novel fairy tale short story biography 'light' drama	'message novel' parable fable advertisement drama	literary novel short story 'serious' drama
Exposition (Logic)	scientific article philosophy abstract definition		sermon propaganda editorial advertisement essay	

Note: This global classification of genres omits much of the actual complexity. See text for details.

225

"science fiction," some novels have a clear entertain force ("space opera") while others have a clear persuade and/or literary-aesthetic force ("new wave"). A number of additional problems and complexities with the classification scheme will be discussed in the next section of this chapter. Nevertheless, this classification scheme brings some order out of the confusion of discourse types and attempts to find the order along psychologically revealing dimensions.

Surface Structure Cues

Both the discourse structure and the discourse force are reflected to some extent in the surface structure of the discourse. Descriptive discourse based on underlying spatial structure tends to be organized with locatives such as *near, above, to the right of,* and *behind.* Narrative discourse based on an underlying series of events in time tends to be organized with terms such as *before, then,* and *while.* Expository discourse based on an underlying logical structure tends to be organized with terms such as *thus, because,* and *since.* The surface cues for discourse force are not as clear, but there are some examples in vocabulary choice. Thus, if a scene is described as *a stand of coniferous saplings on a 50-meter moraine,* the discourse force is almost certain to be to inform. If the same scene is described as *a sublime sylvan knoll,* the discourse force is almost certain to be literary-aesthetic. If it is described as *a little old molehill dressed up fit to kill with pine trees,* the discourse force is almost certain to be to entertain.

Literary-Aesthetic Force

The literary-aesthetic force is somewhat different from the other forces, but seems to me to be a very necessary component of the classification scheme. It is required to account for the distinction, made with some fervor by those in belles-lettres, between popular novels and serious literature, between "greeting card" verse and serious poetry. This force appears to be predominantly a product of schooling and exposure to written discourse, whereas the other forces are probably acquired quite early in the child's acquisition of the spoken language. Culler (1975) makes a very powerful case for the position that understanding literary discourse requires a "literary competence" that must be developed by exposure to the historical literary tradition. He suggests that this force is the result of readers adopting a "rule of significance," which is the assumption by the reader that the writer of a literary work is attempting to say something about the human condition. Thus, no matter how banal the surface structure of a literary work appears, the reader should attempt to find something significant in it. This accounts for the fact that individuals who have a well-developed sense of the literary-aesthetic force will interpret a passage one way if told it is from a popular novel and quite a different way if told the passage is from a literary work. All in all, it appears that including literary-aesthetic force as one of the discourse forces goes a long way toward resolving the problem of what is "literature" and accounts for a wide range of phenomena that would otherwise not be covered.

DISCOURSE CLASSIFICATION: PROBLEMS AND COMPLEXITIES

The classification of discourse types has been discussed as if whole works (e.g., novels) were internally homogeneous. In practice, a large piece of discourse is usually composed of smaller units of different types of discourse. The level of analysis required for homogeneity is quite variable. There can be homogeneity for whole paragraphs, or for several consecutive sentences, or for single sentences, and sometimes only within the parts of a complex sentence. Description, for example, rarely occurs as free-standing discourse. It is found embedded in narrative in segments as large as paragraphs and as small as single sentences.

In a similar fashion, large segments of discourse are frequently composed of segments with different discourse forces. Thus, a mystery novel with an overall entertain force may contain a long segment about the poisonous nature of a particular plant with inform force. A sermon with an overall persuade force may contain a segment of history with inform force and a segment of narrative with entertain force.

The fact that actual discourse is quite complex should not be too surprising or discouraging. For purposes of analysis and experimentation, it is easy to find or write segments of discourse that are homogeneous.

Underlying Structure

Another problem with the proposed classification scheme is one that almost always arises when an attempt is made to categorize the world. Some types of discourse seem to fall between the categories. For example, it is hard to classify a passage in which a narrator is moved through space and describes the static scene as it passes by. Is this an example of description or narration? If there are experimental consequences of the classification scheme, as will be suggested later, it may be possible to turn this question into an empirical issue. In experiments, do passages of this kind behave like descriptive passages, like narrative passages, or somewhere in between?

A more serious problem with the classification in terms of underlying structure is the restriction of the description category to descriptions with an underlying visual-spatial component. What about descriptions through the other sensory modalities? What about descriptions of internal psychological states? It is simply not clear what underlying form of representation should be postulated for descriptive passages such as these. Again, however, it may be possible to reformulate these issues as empirical questions.

Another difficulty with the classification scheme is that it omits important distinctions in defining narrative as discourse that embodies a series of events that occur in time and are related through a causal or thematic chain.

Although this definition of a minimal narrative enables it to cover such diverse types of discourse as instructions, history books, and novels, it is not sufficient to account for the more complex construct of story or plot. Since Aristotle's time it has been recognized that a (good) story has more structure than is suggested by the definition of narrative given previously. Consider for example the following discourse: *Jack made out his will. He slipped on his 'New York is fun city' T-shirt. He gathered up his roll of wire. Then he got into the car and drove south. He got out and took the elevator.* Although this is a fairly coherent piece of narrative discourse, it is a lousy story. It does not build up to a climax. It does not seem to have a natural ending. It does not seem to have a point. However, if it were to continue with *He threw the wire to the other side and then slowly and carefully became the first human being to walk a wire between the World Trade Center towers,* the discourse has the makings of a minimal story with a beginning and end, a build-up of tension, and a climax. A number of recent investigators (Mandler & Johnson, 1977; Rumelhart, 1977) have made a promising start in attempting to account for the special qualities of a narrative that produce a story. However, we need much more work on the structure of events and the conventions for representing a particular set of events as a story before we will know how to give an account of the underlying cognitive structure of stories.

Discourse Force

There are also a number of problems associated with the notion of discourse force as it was outlined earlier. It appears that there is not always a one-to-one relation of type of discourse and discourse force. Some types of discourse can have several simultaneous forces. A biography can be designed to inform and entertain at the same time, a fable to persuade and entertain, a scientific article to inform and persuade. In these instances it is not the case that one segment of the discourse has one force and another segment another force, but that the same segment of prose gives rise to the two forces.

Satire is a very interesting form of discourse in this regard. Satire is a type of discourse with a force that combines aspects of the entertain and persuade forces. The intriguing thing about satiric force is that it appears to be hierarchically related to the original force of the discourse. In other words, when an author writes a piece of satire, the author leaves enough characteristics of the original discourse so that it can be understood but then places a satiric force over it. Thus, in writing a satire of scientific writing, the author leaves many aspects of the original discourse, but exaggerates the pompousness and triviality of the genre in order to entertain and to suggest that scientists should avoid this style of writing. The hierarchical nature of the satire force leads to an interesting property. If the satire is subtle, it is easy for the reader to read the discourse and derive the original force but miss the satire force altogether.

A final complexity relating to discourse force is the interaction of the writer and the reader. Thus far, the discussion of discourse force has focused on the force intended by the author of the discourse. However, the overall force extracted from a piece of discourse is actually a complex interaction of the intention of the author and the intentions and assumptions of the reader. The author uses the various literary devices at his or her command in order to convey the intended force. However, the force as perceived by the reader may or may not match that intended by the author. Thus, a child reading *Gulliver's Travels* may extract the entertain force but not the satiric force of the book. If the reader of a classic piece of bureaucratic prose begins to find it funny and starts reading it to enjoy the sheerness awfulness of the style, then the author's original intent to inform actually gives rises to the entertain force. In general, the assumptions and intentions of the reader can cause the resulting force of a passage of discourse to be very different from that intended by the authors.

A final issue relating to the classification scheme is the degree of differentiation needed for a psychological classification of discourse types. For the purposes of breaking up the universe of discourse into manageable chunks, the global classification that has been proposed seems a good first step. However, for many purposes, a framework that classifies instructions and newspaper stories together must be too general. The fact that mysteries and western novels are classified together seems a little less troublesome, but even here the conventions about content and structure are quite different. The problem is to decide just how detailed the analysis need be in order to capture the general psychological findings. For example, is it necessary to include in a general psychological analysis of discourse the fact that fables are typically about animals or is this just to be treated as an irrelevant historical fact relating to Western literature?

Although this section has revealed a large number of problems with the psychological classification of discourse types, none seem fatal to the scheme. Instead, the analysis points out the complexity of discourse and the need for much more detailed theory development.

RHETORICAL LITERARY STRATEGIES

In the preceding section of the paper I argued that there were three basic types of discourse structure (description, narrative, and exposition), each determined by the nonlinguistic cognitive processes that were hypothesized to underlie them. In writing a piece of discourse, an author must attempt to capture in sequential linguistic form the nonlinguistic information that underlies that particular type of discourse. In attempting to bridge the gap between the linguistic medium and the underlying information, the author has available a wide variety of options—these options will be referred to as rhetorical strategies. The rhetorical strategies are available for each of the different types of discourse structure, but the detailed nature of the strategies differs depending on the particular discourse structure involved. For example, the underlying structure of narrative consists of events in time, and the corresponding written discourse consists of a linguistic description of events. For narrative discourse, the writer can embody the underlying events in the linguistic surface structure in the same order as the events occur in the underlying event structure or the author can place one or more events out of order in the linguistic surface structure. In fact, it is possible for the linguistic surface order to be completely the reverse of the underlying order of events. For example, a series of events such as MAN SEES BROKEN GLASS ON ROAD—MAN TRIES TO SWERVE CAR—CAR RUNS OVER GLASS—TIRE GOES FLAT—MAN JACKS UP CAR, can be expressed in completely reverse order by a narrative such as: *John was jacking up the car. He remembered the sickening thump-thump sound as the tire went flat. Right before he ran over the glass he had tried to swerve the car. Now he certainly wished he had been paying more attention and had seen the glass in the road soon enough to have missed it.*

Discussion of the various rhetorical strategies can be found in standard introductory rhetoric books (Brooks & Warren, 1970; Kane & Peters, 1966); in how-to-write books (Surmelian, 1969); and in works on literary theory. In literary theory, the Russian Formalists made a number of important early contributions (cf. Lemon & Reis, 1965, for a selection of translated papers). In more recent times this work has been reviewed and extended by authors such as Chatman (1971b), Culler (1975), and Rutherford (1975).

The basic rhetorical strategies available to an author of written discourse are: (1) to vary the surface order from some underlying order; (2) to select how much detail of the underlying material is to be represented in the surface material; (3) to vary how "visible" the narrator is in the discourse; and (4) to vary the amount of information available to the narrator (especially the internal psychological state information and the spatial-sensory information).

The existence of the rhetorical devices leads to an important distinction in the analysis of the comprehension of discourse. One of the major tasks of the reader is to use the surface linguistic information in order to derive the underlying structure. However, many of the rhetorical devices can be used to withhold certain information or to give information out of order, in order to lead the reader to make certain hypotheses. Thus, the reader's moment-to-moment comprehension of a piece of discourse may be very different from the knowledge that the reader has at the end of the process after all the work has been done. In one sense, the work of the artist in writing a piece of discourse can be viewed as manipulating the reader's moment-to-moment comprehension processes. Thus, in the classic mystery novel the author presents the events in an order designed to build up suspense, or in some branches of modern literature the author uses the rhetorical devices to distort the surface information to such a degree that it is impossible for the reader to develop a single clear underlying representation. The next sections of this chapter discuss some of the types of rhetorical devices available for each of the three basic modes of discourse.

Description

Since the underlying information for a description has been hypothesized to be a visual-spatial representation, the author of a piece of descriptive discourse is faced with a problem—how to represent in sequential linguistic form the complex set of relations found in a spatial scene. A standard strategy adopted by authors is to give the information from near to far, from top to bottom, or from left to right. Because of the enormous information available in most real-life scenes, the author usually has to select rather drastically what information is to be presented in the linguistic discourse. For example, the author, in describing an apartment, might tell you that there was a ring around the bathtub and the bed was unmade and leave to your imagination the possibility that there was dust under the bed and dishes in the sink. If the description of a scene gives a relatively prosaic straightforward account, the reader gains little information about the narrator and tends to ignore the obvious fact that someone (a narrator) must be describing the scene. Thus, if the descriptive passage says *There were a couple of concrete pink flamingos on the front lawn,* we simply accept the facts (if we are sophisticated readers we might wonder why the narrator told us this fact rather than that there were trees on the front lawn). However, if the passage says *There were a couple of garish concrete pink flamingos on the front lawn,* we become aware that there is a narrator describing the scene and that, in this case, the narrator is the type of individual who does not think concrete pink flamingos are tasteful lawn decorations. Another important option available to the author of a descriptive passage is the location of the narrator with respect to the scene being described. If the description of a town is written as *The train tracks divided the town in half, the only high school was in the center of the northern half, while the southern half was surrounded by forest,* the narrator appears to be located high above the town. If the narrator describes the underside of a table in an office, the narrator appears to be located in the office under the table. In effect, the author of a descriptive passage has available all the spatial options that the director of a motion picture has (plus some). Finally, the literary point of view used to describe the scene can vary in a number of highly complex ways (these options will be discussed in the subsection on narrative).

Narrative

The author's options with respect to surface order of narrative material are quite open. The author can choose to present the events in the surface in the same order as the events occur in the underlying order, or the author can distort the surface order in any permutation desired. Also, the author has the option of representing several independent underlying series of events simultaneously. The independent underlying sequences of events can be interwoven at will and in any order desired. The author can use rhetorical devices to indicate the shifts of surface order, or the author can let the underlying logic of the event be the only cue as to the correct underlying order. In writing the narrative, the author has the option to select the events to be explicitly mentioned in the surface discourse. Thus, the author can tell the reader that a particular character got into a car and drove away, or the author can tell the reader that the character opened the door of the car, got in, turned the key, and so on. For most well-structured events this type of selection will cause the reader little difficulty, since the reader will easily fill in the gaps from his or her knowledge of the world.

The problem of narrator's presence and literary point of view is much too complex to be outlined here (see Booth, 1961; Culler, 1975; Friedman, 1955); however, a few examples can demonstrate the possibilities. First, the author may vary the "visibility" of the narrator. Thus, the narrator can announce his or her presence: *I am your narrator and I am about to tell you a wonderful story...* In this case, the narrator's presence will frequently be indicated by surface pronouns. However, by using various other devices, the author can build up a very complete narrator without any first-person pronouns ever appearing. The author can have the narrator make evaluative comments (*It was a cute little hat, if you like that sort of thing*) or have the narrator give extraneous information (*He was quite awkward, as are most boys that age*). Another aspect of point of view is the author's decision about where the narrator is with respect to the underlying events. The narrator can be a nonparticipant viewing the events from outside the world of the events, or the narrator can be one of the participants in the underlying events. The narrator can be the protagonist or a minor character who never takes part in the events. Another option is the author's choice of how much information the narrator is to have about the internal psychological states of the characters. The narrator can be omniscient and have access to every character's mental states; the narrator can have access to only one character's internal states; or the narrator can have no access to any of the characters' internal mental states. Finally, the author can choose for the narrator to have access to various types of spatial information. Thus, the narrator may be able to fly around the world of the underlying events and narrate events from various viewpoints (miles high over the scene, inside someone's pocket, etc.) or the narrator's knowledge of the world may be limited to those aspects of the world available to the sensory experiences of a single character.

Exposition

Although exposition is usually considered to be quite different from narrative and descriptive discourse, it seems to me that the rhetorical devices available to the author are very similar. Since the underlying organization for exposition has been hypothesized to be abstract logical mental processes, the author's options in the surface linguistic form are with respect to those structures. The author can present the evidence first and then the conclusions, or the conclusions first and then the evidence. In the selection of degree of detail the author has considerable freedom. The author may skip obvious (or not so obvious) steps in an argument. The author can bring to bear on an argument every possible piece of evidence that he or she can think of, or just use the most powerful pieces of evidence. The author can choose to present evidence from both sides of an argument, or just evidence from one side. The "narrator" of a piece of exposition is usually thought to be the author. However, since the author may be deliberately writing to make you think that he or she has one opinion, when he or she actually has another, perhaps it would be safer to call the "narrator" in exposition the implied author. Like the narrator in narrative prose, the implied author in exposition may be made quite "visible" or may keep a low profile. Thus, the implied author of a piece of exposition may tell you who he or she is and what his or her opinions are. Or the implied author may be revealed by evaluative comments such as "power-mad dictator" or more subtly by choice of lexical items such as "murder" versus "assassinate" or "Red China" versus "China." In certain styles of writing, such as history texts and scientific articles, the preferred style has traditionally been to try to make the implied author as invisible as possible.

In looking over the rhetorical devices available to the author in each of the three basic types of discourse, it appears that there are some very general strategies (order, selection, narrator) which are possible and that the details of how they function are determined by the particular form of discourse involved. It seems clear that these rhetorical devices play a very powerful role in both the ease of comprehension and the artistic success of a piece of discourse.

STYLISTICS

In addition to the choice of rhetorical devices discussed previously, the author of a piece of discourse has a wide variety of other lexical and syntactic options. The style of a discourse is the set of lexical and syntactic choices made by an author trying to express a particular underlying discourse content. The study of this aspect of discourse has traditionally been referred to as stylistics and has generated a large literature (cf. Chatman, 1971a; Enkvist, 1973; Sebeok, 1960). Sometimes a particualr style is used by the literary authors of a particular time period (e.g., a literary genre such as Victorian romantic prose). Sometimes a particular style is used by authors writing within a particular content domain. Thus, if a passage contains words such as "hereunto," "whereof," and "the undersigned," it is almost certainly discourse dealing with legal content. In addition to the style found in groups of authors, there are also some individual writers who have rather obvious styles (Hemingway vs. Faulkner). Complex statistical analyses of such things as word frequency and sentence length have shown consistent style differences between samples of discourse by different authors, even when they intuitively appear to be quite similar (Mosteller & Wallace, 1963).

Originally, many of the styles may have been related to a particular discourse function. The use of the passive construction in scientific discourse was designed to hide the narrator and make the prose look more objective. The use of short sentences and repetition by the authors of first-grade readers was an attempt to use an implicit psychological theory to make the discourse easier to read. Over time, the styles become conventional, and so lexical and syntactic selections not in keeping with the conventions violate the reader's stylistic intuitions. It may be that the style of a discourse is evaluated with respect to some norm of discourse (spoken language?) such that newspaper style and mystery novels are less deviant than a legal contract or a poem by e. e. cummings.

The stylistic aspects of discourse also play an important role in comprehension and artistic success. The author can choose or is forced to choose vocabulary and syntax that can ease or hinder the reader's recovery of the underlying structure.

IMPLICATIONS FOR EXPERIMENTAL PSYCHOLOGY

Types of Discourse

The classification of discourse proposed in this chapter points out the need for a much more systematic approach in theory and experimentation in this area. Recent experiments on memory and comprehension of discourse have used a variety of materials: expository discourse (Meyer & McConkie, 1973); short stories (Kintsch & van Dijk, 1975); folktales (Mandler & Johnson, 1977; Rumelhart, 1977); hierarchically organized exposition (Frederiksen, 1975; Thorndyke, 1977). The experimenters have tended to focus their experimental and theoretical efforts on one type of discourse without consideration of how the theory or results fit into the larger universe of discourse types (see Goetz & Armbruster, Chapter 8, this volume, for a review of some of these experiments). Regardless of the merits of the particular classification of discourse proposed in this chapter, the attempt certainly reveals the need to take a broader look at the problems. Are the findings and theoretical account of a particular experiment unique to the specific passages used? Restricted to the genre studied? Or are the findings general across discourse types?

The specific proposal for classification of discourse by underlying cognitive structure has a number of implications. The results of studies on discourse types will have to be consistent with our knowledge of the nonlinguistic cognitive structures postulated to underlie each type of discourse. Currently, our knowledge of the nonlinguistic structures is fairly limited and does not place strong constraints on studies of discourse, but as cognitive psychology matures this should change. As current debates about the nature of the cognitive structures underlying visual-spatial imagery (Kosslyn & Pomerantz, 1977; Pylyshyn, 1973) are resolved, the resulting theory will have to mesh with our understanding of description.

If the proposals about the nature of the cognitive structures underlying the various types of discourse are correct, then experiments showing that coherent discourse is easier to remember than random sentences (see Goetz & Armbruster, Chapter 8, this volume) will probably better be interpreted in terms of the underlying cognitive structures that are built up by the discourse than by the linguistic characteristics of the discourse. The present classification also makes predictions about the nature of the inferences in the comprehension and recall of the different types of discourse (e.g., spatial inferences in description, logical inferences in exposition).

The concept of discourse force also suggests a number of theoretical and empirical issues. What are the relations of the traditional forces of utterances (Searle, 1969) and the discourse forces postulated here? It should be possible through scaling and various measures of reader comprehension to explore some of the problems raised in the discussion of discourse force. If satire is hierarchically related to the other forces, it should be possible to show that some readers understand the basic force of a passage, but not the satiric force. The acquisition of the discourse forces raises a number of interesting questions. Are the forces learned at different ages? What is the relation of spoken versus written discourse in developing discourse force? Is literary-aesthetic force somehow special? Does it develop later and in different ways from the other forces? Thus, the proposed scheme for classification of discourse in terms of structure and force raises a wide range of theoretical and empirical issues.

Rhetorical Strategies

The rhetorical strategies form a particularly interesting area for experimental investigation. Many of the strategies are essentially techniques for expressing the same underlying information. Thus, each strategy can be studied to see what effect the particular strategy has on the moment-to-moment comprehension of the information (see Rumelhart, Chapter 2, this volume; Woods, Chapter 3, this volume) and on the overall comprehension and memory of the material. Through this type of investigation, the hypotheses developed in the various humanistic disciplines can be used to help construct an experimental rhetoric.

Manipulation of the order of presentation is one of the most important rhetorical strategies and one of the most interesting to study empirically. In our laboratory at the University of Illinois, we have carried out a preliminary series of experiments on descriptive passages which show that the rhetorical device of describing a scene in terms of spatially contiguous parts improves comprehension. Manipulation of the order of narrative passages is a very complex issue. The effect of the order manipulation appears to interact with the degree of logical constraint of the underlying plot and the use of rhetorical devices (e.g., flashbacks, tense markers) to indicate shifts in order. Although much of the work is yet to be carried out, Stein & Nezworski (1978) have found effects of narrative order manipulation on children's memory for stories, and we have preliminary results that show effects of order manipulation on comprehension and memory for narrative in adults. The rhetorical device of mapping the surface order of events onto the underlying order of events appears to result in narrative passages that are easiest to comprehend. Manipulation of the order of elements in expository passages should also produce effects on the comprehension and memory of this type of discourse.

Manipulation of how much information is given in the surface discourse may also be open to experimental study. It is impossible to make everything explicit in the surface discourse, yet, if too much is left out, the inferences required become too hard (see Huggins & Adams, Chapter 4, this volume). Thus, it should be possible to study what combinations of linguistic information and inferences produce the best comprehension.

It should also be possible to carry out experimental studies of narrator visibility and reliability. The fact that there is a narrator between the reader and the information suggests one possible line of research. As cues appear in the discourse that the narrator is unreliable (e.g., biased, drunk, insane), the reader should make adjustments in his or her belief in the information being read. What are the effects of various types of information about narrator reliability on reader belief? Do readers remember the narrator reliability information over time, or do they forget this while remembering aspects of the original content?

The complex problems of point of view raise a number of questions. What are the psychological consequences of the various possible points of view? Are some points of view harder to comprehend than others? What are the effects of shifting points of view versus consistent points of view? Does the reader keep track of where the information comes from? There is also the problem of how the literary points of view are learned. Are some points of view learned in spoken discourse, while others are acquired through exposure to written discourse?

It seems obvious from this brief look at the prospect for empirical research in the area of written discourse that the development of an experimental rhetoric is not only possible, but is already beginning. Given the directions of current cognitive psychology, the initial studies will be directed at the issues of comprehension and memory for written discourse. In the longer run, psychologists may attempt to study some of the more affective aspects of literature and attempt to carry out experiments on issues such as what makes a particular work interesting or what underlies literary critics' judgments about the quality of a given work.

IMPLICATIONS FOR READING COMPREHENSION

The successful development of an experimental rhetoric will be required if the practice of reading instruction is to be given a scientific foundation. Currently, the materials used in reading instruction appear to be selected on the basis of the (frequently conflicting) opinions of writers, publishers, and teachers. Many of these opinions stand as hypotheses ready to be evaluated. For example, one book on writing for children (Berry & Best, 1947) suggests the following rules for children's discourse:

1. Use simple plots for young readers.
2. In narratives for young children, keep the surface order of events consistent with the underlying order of events.
3. If the order of events in narrative for children is to be varied, mark the shifts with obvious rhetorical devices.
4. The older the child, the less explicit the written discourse has to be and the more the ability to make inferences can be assumed.
5. For younger readers use a consistent viewpoint.

Clearly, each of these rules for writing can be interpreted as a hypothesis to be tested.

Eventually, an experimental rhetoric should be able to tell us how difficult a particular form of discourse is and how the difficulty varies with the age and competence of the reader. This information, along with a developed psychology of instruction, should make it possible to provide a scientifically designed curriculum for instruction in reading comprehension.

ACKNOWLEDGMENTS

This research was supported by the National Institute of Education under Contract No. US-NIE-C-400-76-0116 and by Grant MH 29562 from the National Institute of

Mental Health. I would like to thank several of my colleagues in the humanities, Dennis Baron, Larry Grossberg, and Joanna Maclay, for commenting on an earlier draft of this chapter. However, they certainly should not be held responsible for what I have had to say since they were unanimous in warning me that I have captured only little of the true complexity of literary discourse.

REFERENCES

Berry, E., & Best, H. *Writing for children.* New York: Viking Press, 1947.

Booth, W. C. *The rhetoric of fiction.* Chicago: University of Chicago Press, 1961.

Brooks, C., & Warren, R. P. *Modern rhetoric* (3rd ed.). New York: Harcourt, Brace & World, 1970.

Chatman, S. (Ed.). *Literary style: A symposium.* New York: Oxford University Press, 1971. (a)

Chatman, S. The structure of fiction. *The University Review* (Kansas City), 1971, *37*, 199–214 (journal title changed to *New Letters*). (b)

Culler, J. *Structuralist poetics.* Ithaca, N.Y.: Cornell University Press, 1975.

D'Angelo, F. J. The search for intelligible structure in the teaching of composition. *College Composition and Communication,* 1976, *27*, 142–147.

Ebbinghaus, H. *Memory.* New York: Dover, 1964. (Originally published, 1885).

Enkvist, N. E. *Linguistic stylistics.* The Hague: Mouton, 1973.

Fillenbaum, S. *Syntactic factors in memory?* The Hague: Mouton, 1973.

Frederiksen, C. H. Acquisition of semantic information from discourse: Effects of repeated exposures. *Journal of Verbal Learning and Verbal Behavior,* 1975, *14*, 158–169.

Friedman, N. Point of view in fiction: The development of a critical concept. *PMLA,* 1955, *70*, 1160–1184.

Greene, J. *Psycholinguistics.* Baltimore: Penguin, 1972.

Kane, T. S., & Peters, L. J. *A practical rhetoric of expository prose.* New York: Oxford University Press, 1966.

Kintsch, W., & van Dijk, T. A. Comment on se rappelle et on résumes des histoires. *Langages,* 1975, *40*, 98–116.

Kosslyn, S. M., & Pomerantz, J. R. Imagery, propositions, and the form of internal representations. *Cognitive Psychology,* 1977, *9*, 52–76.

Lemon, L. T., & Reis, M. J. (Eds.). *Russian formalist criticism: Four essays.* Lincoln, Neb.: University of Nebraska, 1965.

Mandler, J. M., & Johnson, N. S. Remembrance of things parsed: Story structure and recall. *Cognitive Psychology,* 1977, *9*, 111–151.

Meyer, B. J. F., & McConkie, G. W. What is recalled after hearing a passage? *Journal of Educational Psychology,* 1973, *65*, 109–117.

Miller, G. A. Some psychological studies of grammar. *American Psychologist,* 1962, *17*, 748–762.

Mosteller, F., & Wallace, D. L. Inference in an authorship problem. *Journal of the American Statistical Association,* 1963, *58*, 275–309.

Pylyshyn, Z. W. What the mind's eye tells the mind's brain: A critique of mental imagery. *Psychological Bulletin,* 1973, *80*, 1–24.

Rumelhart, D. E. Understanding and summarizing brief stories. In D. LaBerge & S. J. Samuels (Eds.), *Basic processes in reading: Perception and comprehension.* Hillsdale, N.J.: Lawrence Erlbaum Associates, 1977.

Rutherford, J. Story, character, setting, and narrative mode in Galdós's *El amigo Manso.* In R. Fowler (Ed.), *Style and structure in literature.* Ithaca, N.Y.: Cornell University Press, 1975.

Searle, J. R. *Speech acts.* London: Cambridge University Press, 1969.

Sebeok, T. A. (Ed.). *Style in language.* Cambridge, Mass.: MIT Press, 1960.

Stein, N. L., & Nezworski, T. The effects of organization and instructional set on story memory. *Discourse Processes,* 1978, *1,* 177–193.

Surmelian, L. *Techniques of fiction writing.* Garden City, N.Y.: Anchor, 1969.

Thorndyke, P. W. Cognitive structures in comprehension and memory of narrative discourse. *Cognitive Psychology,* 1977, *9,* 77–110.

Wellek, R., & Warren, A. *Theory of literature* (3rd ed.). New York: Harcourt, Brace & World, 1962.

III
LANGUAGE, KNOWLEDGE OF THE WORLD, AND INFERENCE

The chapters in the preceding section on "Text Structure" emphasized that language comprehension cannot be understood by any solely linguistic analysis of the text by itself. Comprehension involves going beyond both the information contained in text and the logical implications of that information. The chapters on "Language, Knowledge of the World, and Inference" explore the contextual factors that contribute to comprehension, with particular emphasis on the processes by which knowledge structures organize understanding and permit extensions beyond that which is explicit in text.

Chapter 10 by Spiro provides an historical overview of the movement toward an orientation to language comprehension that stresses the construction of meaning. Spiro illustrates the importance of various types of context (e.g., linguistic, attitudinal, situational) as a basis for extensions beyond the literal content of text. The processes by which preexisting knowledge interacts with information in text receive special attention. Similarities between the constructive processes involved in comprehending and remembering text are discussed.

The importance of preexisting knowledge has been *repeatedly* emphasized in this volume. How is that knowledge organized? What processes are involved in utilizing knowledge structures? Chapter 2 by Rumelhart provided a global framework for answering such questions. Several of the chapters in this section adopt a more narrow focus and attempt to specify in hard detail how specific types of knowledge structures are used. Chapter 11 by Mervis compares two prominent theories of the categorization of concrete objects and the empirical support for each. She concludes that category representation is a function of an object's relation to "best examples" of a concept, rather than being determined by an object's possession of critical attributes of the concept. On the basis of research on the development of categorization, Mervis suggests possible implications for the construction of texts for children.

Shoben, Chapter 12, is concerned with the development of theories of sentence comprehension based on models of the representation of words and their interrelations in "semantic memory." Shoben argues for a research strategy that involves restricting the domain of inquiry to the relationship between world knowledge and the processing of words in sentences. He suggests that this approach should lead to greater specificity and precision and thus may permit decisive empirical validation or disconfirmation. Additionally, we would hope that the development of models for restricted units of analysis might facilitate the search for *comprehensive* generalizations concerning the processes of interaction between text and knowledge.

Dictionary definitions are often inadequate in characterizing the meaning of words and expressions in their natural contexts. Chapter 13 by Anderson and Shifrin and Chapter 14 by Ortony deal with aspects of this problem. Anderson and Shifrin argue that words do not have fixed meanings. Rather, words can take on many meanings depending on their context of occurrence. Analysis of the processes by which one uses knowledge of the world to particularize the meaning of a word in a given context provides a microcosmic view of the operation of constructive processes.

Not only do words take on different shades of meaning in different contexts, but sometimes they (and the expressions of which they are a part) are used to refer to entities totally different from those they typically denote. Such metaphoric use of language is the topic of Ortony's chapter. He discusses the processes involved in the comprehension of metaphor and speculates about the theoretical mechanisms underlying those processes. He also argues for a central role for metaphor in learning new concepts.

The understanding of virtually all stories is dependent on a successful interpretation of the purposes for the actions described therein. In Chapter 15, Bruce analyzes actions in stories as steps in, or reactions to, plans. He examines the skills needed to understand plans, emphasizing the manner in which plans are related to one's knowledge and beliefs about the world. A detailed plan analysis of the episodes in a children's story is provided.

Finally, Chapter 16 by Collins, Brown, and Larkin synthesizes many of the concepts from this section in analyzing the *ongoing* processes of text understanding. They conceive of comprehension as a model-building activity. Early parts of a text suggest preliminary models of what a text is "about," including information about which preexisting knowledge schemata are relevant. As reading of a text proceeds, the models become increasingly refined as questions left unanswered in earlier versions of the model are resolved. The development of more refined models guides, in turn, an even more constrained search for "missing" information. Eventually, all important information in the text should "fit" a final model. Collins et al. elicited reports by readers of the processes they were employing at varying stages in the reading of stories. These reports resulted in a catalogue of strategies used in the evaluation and revision of text models.

Thus, this section provides evidence on the interactions of language and knowledge of the world from the level of the individual word up to the level of the reader's overall model of the text.

10 Constructive Processes in Prose Comprehension and Recall

Rand J. Spiro
Center for the Study of Reading,
University of Illinois, Urbana-Champaign

INTRODUCTION AND OVERVIEW

The physical world and the world of ideas are infinitely rich in their actual and potential contents, subtleties, and nuances. The question arises as to how language is able to convey this richness. The most obvious answer is that natural language systems possess characteristics that are sufficient in themselves for the task. Whether or not this may be correct in any abstract or logical sense, it is obviously incorrect in terms of what people actually do. Examples of extratextual extension in natural language processing are abundant. The kinds of extensions beyond the explicit content of discourse that will be illustrated in this chapter are typical at all levels of analysis of language functioning. The view of language comprehension that emerges is one in which the comprehender is a far more active participant than was thought by psycholinguists of the 1960s under the influence of Chomsky and Katz.

Meaning does not reside in words, sentences, paragraphs, or even entire passages considered in isolation. It will be argued that if connected discourse is analyzed at each of those levels taken out of context, the result is an incomplete understanding of that level's meaning in use. What language provides is a skeleton, a blueprint for the creation of meaning. Such skeletal representations must then be enriched and embellished so that they conform with the understander's preexisting world views and the operative purposes of understanding at a given time. This process of knowledge-based, contextually influenced, and purposeful enrichment in comprehending language is what is referred to as "construction."

Constructed meaning is the interactive product of text and context of various kinds, including linguistic, prior knowledge, situational, attitudinal, and task contexts, among others. It applies to the changes in the meaning of a single word embedded in different sentences, and to the meaning of an entire discourse when context dictates that the discourse should be assimilated to one rather than another preexisting knowledge base. In other words, the meaning of language in use is insufficiently characterized by solely linguistic or logical analyses.

This is a paper with a beginning and an end, but no middle. As the first chapter in a section on *Language, Knowledge of the World, and Inference*, its main purpose is to provide a general and somewhat elementary introduction to the constructive orientation to prose understanding in its historical context, prior to a more detailed treatment in the remaining chapters of this section. Because I found it difficult to limit myself to the past, the final part of this paper skips ahead to the future, with a discussion of some unresolved issues and suggestions for research directions. So, the reader will find the past and future represented somewhat to the neglect of the present, ample discussions of which may be found in the succeeding chapters of this section. In a sense, these others chapters would form the proper middle for the present one.

In the next section the development of the constructivist orientation, primarily in the psychological literature, is traced and compared to "meaning in the text" positions, focusing on Bartlett's (1932) notion of effort after meaning. The role of context as a basis for effort after meaning is discussed in the third section, and the variety of impinging contexts is illustrated. Two particular kinds of context, the preexisting knowledge of the world brought to bear when processing language, and the tasks and purposes of reading are given special attention. Remembering is briefly discussed in the fourth section, stressing the similarities between processes involved in comprehension and memory. Finally, as promised, some shortcomings of current thinking about constructive processes and directions for future research are outlined in the last section.

DEVELOPMENT OF THE CONSTRUCTIVE ORIENTATION IN CONTEMPORARY COGNITIVE PSYCHOLOGY

The contemporary constructive view of language comprehension, with its attendant emphasis on the role of contextual factors, has many historical antecedents in psychology (e.g., Binet & Henri, 1894; Buhler [see Blumenthal, 1970]). The major influence is, however, undoubtedly Bartlett (1932). In his book, *Remembering*, marred as it was by ambiguity and lack of precision, he pointed to virtually all the aspects of constructive processing currently discussed. However, in the behaviorist-associationist climate in psychology at that time, Bartlett's highly mentalistic orientation was quite radical and was virtually ignored for over 30 years (exceptions include the British psychologist Zangwill and his students, [see Zangwill (1972) for a review of this work] and an occasional American psychologist such as Paul, 1959).

The heart of Bartlett's argument was that cognitive research focusing on nonsense syllables in the Ebbinghaus tradition was subject to the criticism that it simplified stimuli without simplifying the responding organism, thereby leading to artificiality. When he used more meaningful stimulus materials such as connected prose, he found substantial evidence of errors in reproduction. Bartlett's (1932) conclusion was that comprehension consisted of an "effort after meaning." "Speaking very broadly, such effort is simply the attempt to connect something that is given with something other than itself [p. 227]." The comprehender used prior knowledge of the world, organized in holistic cognitive structures called schemata, to "conventionalize" what was read in terms of one's preexisting world views. Unfortunately, as was mentioned earlier, Bartlett's views were submerged for many years. The path to their growing acceptance is now traced.

It was recognized fairly early that what is comprehended and stored is something other than the literal content of prose. Many studies from the early part of this century presented evidence that surface form is not stably represented verbatim; rather, the "logical" or "ideational" gist is stored (see the review by Welborn & English, 1937 and Cofer, 1941). In a refinement of this early work, Sachs (1967) demonstrated that when the surface form of presented prose is altered while maintaining functional relations such as logical subject and object, such changes have very low likelihood of being detected. Jarvella (1971) later showed that surface information is primarily used only until a semantic interpretation of each clause is derived. Clearly then, comprehension was seen to entail some transformation of linguistic stimuli. However, such transformations did not alter the semantic content "carried" by the linguistic objects; rather, they resulted in stored paraphrases (Sachs, 1967).

There remained at least tacit acceptance of the notion that the meaning is "in the text." In other words, all that is needed for complete semantic description of a sentence is contained in that sentence. This point of view was embodied in Chomskyan transformational grammar (Chomsky, 1965; Katz & Fodor, 1963; Katz & Postal, 1964), which was widely accepted by psychologists in the l960s (e.g., Clark, 1969; Miller, 1962). Surface structures are transformations of deep structures. These deep structures receive interpretation in a semantic component. The interpretive procedure consists primarily in a look-up of fixed work meanings in an internal lexicon followed by applying preexisting projection rules from a finite set which, in combination with the functional relations specified in the deep structure, yield the one and only semantic interpretation of a given sentence (or, if ambiguous, the set of semantic interpretations). The meaning is solely derivable from the sentences in isolation with context involved only in the occasional case where a choice must be made between the structural descriptions of an ambiguous utterance. Thus, according to Katz and Postal (1964), a semantically interpreted deep structure of a sentence, where the interpretive procedure is a *purely linguistic* one, provides "a full analysis of its cognitive meaning [p. 12]."

Two lines of research can be identified that finally led to a fairly widely accepted repudiation of the "meaning is in the text" position. An example of the first line is an experiment by Bransford, Barclay, and Franks (1972) in which sentences such as (1) and (2) were presented.

1. Three turtles rested *beside* a floating log, and a fish swam beneath them.
2. Three turtles rested *on* a floating log, and a fish swam beneath them.

Subjects were then given recognition tests which included foils such as (3).

3. Three turtles rested *(beside/on)* a floating log, and a fish swam beneath *it*.

Bransford et al. (1972) argued as follows:

> According to the interpretive theory Ss store only the linguistic information underlying the input sentence. Hence Ss hearing either sentence (1) or (2) above should be equally likely to detect the pronoun change in sentence (3). The constructive theory makes a different set of predictions, however. Ss are assumed to construct wholistic semantic descriptions of situations. If they forget the information underlying the input sentence they should not be reduced to guessing, but should base their recognition ratings on the complete semantic descriptions presumably acquired. Given this view, Ss hearing sentence (1) should still reject sentence (3) since it is neither consonant with the actual input sentence nor the complete semantic description constructed. Ss hearing sentence (2) should be quite likely to think they heard sentence (3), however, since the latter sentence is consonant with the complete semantic description presumably acquired [p. 194].

The results supported the constructive hypothesis. This study served as a prototype for what was to become a near avalanche of demonstrations that inferential elaborations are a part of the process of comprehending prose.

The other line of research involved demonstrations of the important role in comprehension of superordinate notions of the theme or context of prose passages, i.e., what they are about. Pompi and Lachman (1967) concluded that such "surrogate structures" are present in comprehension when they found that individuals falsely recognized words that were related to the theme of a passage at a far greater rate than words not related to the theme. That such contextual information can be necessary for comprehension to occur at all was shown by Dooling and Lachman (1972) and by Bransford and Johnson (1972). In both studies, passages perfectly comprehensible when contextual support was provided (by titles in the former study and by pictures in the latter) were nonsensical without that support. Once again, the meaning cannot be considered to be in the text alone.

Even in linguistics, the "meaning is in the text" view is falling out of favor. Four examples can be cited out of many. Text grammarians posit as a basic condition for text grammars that they should constrain acceptable utterances in a discourse as a function of the context of preceding discourses (Van Dijk, 1973). Linguistic consequences of the distinction between old, redundant, or shared information and newly presented information have been demonstrated (Chafe, 1972; Halliday, 1970). Even that seemingly most context-independent bastion of linguistics, sentential well-formedness, has been shown to be influenced by factors such as beliefs and knowledge of the world (Lakoff, 1971). Consider sentences that employ co-referential noun phrases.

1. Richard Nixon lost his cool, but the former president soon regained it.
2. Richard Nixon lost his cool, but the current president soon regained it.

If both sentences were spoken at the present time, only (1) would be considered well-formed, and the judgment would require the knowledge that Richard Nixon is a former president and not a new one. Lakoff (1971) concluded that:

> One must speak of relative well-formedness and/or relative grammaticality; that is in [some] cases a sentence will be well-formed only with respect to certain presuppositions about the nature of the world. In these cases, the presuppositions are systematically related to the form of the sentence, though they may not appear overtly. Given a sentence, S, and a set of presuppositions PR, we will say, in such instances, that S is well-formed only relative to PR [p. 320].
>
> Suppose that S is well-formed only relative to PR. Then a speaker will make certain judgments about the well-formedness or ill-formedness of S which will vary with his extralinguistic knowledge. If the presuppositions of PR do not accord with his factual knowledge, cultural background, or beliefs about the world, then he may judge S to be "odd", "strange", "deviant", "ungrammatical", or simply ill-formed relative to his own presuppositions about the nature of the world. Thus, extra-linguistic factors very often enter in judgments of well-formedness. This is a matter of performance. The linguistic competence underlying this is the ability of a speaker to pair sentences with the presuppositions relative to which they are well-formed [p. 329].

Finally, there is the work in the general area of pragmatics (e.g., Austin, 1962; Gordon & Lakoff, 1971; Grice, 1975; Morgan, 1975; Searle, 1975; see Chapter 5 by Morgan & Green in this volume).

The discussion of context effects in the next section provides further support for the constructivist position. All things considered, the constructivist position seems unassailable. The cognitive meaning of discourse, what the prose means to the individual reading or hearing it, is something more than can be derived by any linguistic or logical analysis of the linguistic objects "in the text." The text is obviously part of the meaning-creating process. However, it must be considered in concert with the contextual settings and the activities of the reader/hearer who, by making an effort after meaning, will attempt to construct a comprehension product that makes sense within his or her individual view of the world.

It should also be emphasized that we consider constructive extensions beyond inferences about the speaker/writer's intent to be within the domain of language comprehension. It might be argued that the domain has thus been too broadly conceived. Part of the reason is that if you allow too many unintended extensions as comprehension products, it can lead to absurd outcomes (e.g., the utterance "The ground is rumbling" partly meaning "The ground is like my Uncle John" because his stomach rumbles). Furthermore, it makes the study of language comprehension far more complex and difficult to manage. However, consider the utterance "The ground is rumbling" spoken by an individual living on the San Andreas fault. Few non-Chomskyans would dispute that some inference about the possibility of an earthquake is a valid part of the comprehension of that utterance. On the other hand, if the same utterance in the same situation was made by a child who did not know about earthquakes, and the hearer knew that, the inference about earthquakes would be excluded from the study of language comprehension because it was not part of the speaker's communicative intent. However, the inference about earthquakes seems to be as natural and automatic a part of the comprehension process when talking to the child as in the other case. How can this dilemma be resolved?

It is here that the distinction between typical listening and reading situations has an important ramification. When comprehending utterances in conversations, the speaker's intent is all that is attempted to be communicated. If that intent is apprehended, the goal of *communication* is met and the communicative act is "understood." The case of reading comprehension in schools, particularly if one considers expository texts, is not quite the same. A specific "author's intent"like the speaker's intent in oral communication can be identified and is certainly relevant. However, there is a broader, more general sense of intent beyond that which could be specified explicitly. It is intended that the reader use the text to contribute to the growth of the reader's knowledge structures for the text's topic. This involves an intended assimilation with the reader's relevant preexisting knowledge of the topic that could not be completely anticipated in any explicit way. It involves an intention that the new information should not be understood in isolation.

For example, a chapter in a sixth-grade text about the Civil War may involve a specific author's intention to inform on the war's causes. But the writer will know that the reader already knows something about earlier American history and wars in general. If the reader's understanding of the war's causes includes inferences based on knowledge concerning problems with late 18th-century confederation attempts in the United States, such an inference would be considered part of the author's intentions for the ideal reader's activities although the specific inference may not have been foreseen. In other words, the author of an expository text for children intends something more than communication. He or she intends knowledge acquisition, growth, and integration beyond the confines of text material and intentions specifically related to that material in isolation. Given these educational goals, the broader conception of constructive language processing exposed in this chapter would seem to be most relevant to reading comprehension in schools.

CONTEXT AS A BASIS FOR
EFFORT AFTER MEANING

Given that the meaning of discourse goes beyond the explicit language with which it is expressed, where does the rest of what is understood come from? What are the other contributors to the constructive process, contributors that permit implicit meanings to be transmitted and apprehended with uniform regularity? The answer lies in the fact that language is for communication, and communication does not occur in a vacuum. Discourse is contextually embedded, and the contexts in which it occurs (as well as those intentionally brought to bear) guide extra-textual construction. Interpretation is shaped by the temporally neighboring linguistic messages that precede (and succeed). The reader/hearer encounters discourse in some situation that will affect the perceived purpose of understanding the discourse and the nature of that understanding itself. As reader/hearers we have our own purposes, attitudes, and interests that shape the constructive process. Finally, we possess, in varying degrees, knowledge related to the context of discourse that may be used to extend interpretation beyond the literal, as well as knowledge about the writer/speaker's knowledge (and interests and purposes), his or her knowledge about our knowledge, etc. Thus there are a variety of contexts: the other neighboring discourses any given one may be embedded in; the perceived task requirements of a given situation; the situation itself; and the interests, attitudes, and preexisting knowledge of the comprehender. As you can see, the contextual web is quite complex, and from those complexities arise the complexities of the understanding process (of which we have more to say in a later section). For now we would merely like to illustrate the magnitude of the effects on the meaning of discourse that the various contexts may have.

Consider the following passage (very loosely adapted from Bransford & Johnson, 1972).

> John Smith is responsible for a unique idea. He was seen outside of apartment houses on Main Street playing a guitar. It was hooked up to an amplifier suspended many stories above by a balloon. A second balloon held aloft a monkey carrying a cup that was held out to the inquisitive tenants by their windows.

Consider now some of the constructive extensions that might be incorporated into the final product of comprehension (what the passage means to the reader) as a function of the following impinging contextual factors. An expert on monkey behavior might have prior knowledge indicating the likely response of the monkey in that situation and incorporate that as an equal partner with the actual presented description of the situation in his or her semantic representation of the passage. Imagine the different senses in which the passage would be understood had it appeared in *People Magazine, Electricians' News,* an article about unemployed electrical workers in the business and finance section of *Newsweek,* or in the *ASPCA Weekly.* In the first case, it might be understood fairly literally as an anecdote about an interesting person with an unusual idea. In the second case, it might be understood and stored as a passage about some technological advance, with imported inferences about those procedures that must have been involved but were not mentioned, and notions about how the advance might relate to the reader's previously formed plans to create a floating blue light for cocktail parties. In the third case, the passage might be considered to be a commentary on the economy and be integrated with related notions from prior knowledge about Federal Reserve monetary policy and inferences about why electrical workers might be running into job trouble. In the fourth case, the reader might just worry about monkeys floating around in the air and understand it as an article about cruelty to animals. Parallel consequences for effort after meaning might have occurred if, instead of encountering the passage in those magazines, it had been opened to randomly in a waiting room by an electrician, an economist, or an animal lover. Similar effects might also occur if the passage had been preceded by an introductory paragraph discussing interesting people, electronics, the economy, or cruelty to animals.

What if you were shopping and your butcher went out of his or her way to show the passage to you accompanied by a regretful expression? Its broad meaning might then be "times are bad and my prices will have to go up again." Alternatively, if you showed it to your butcher the message might be "times are bad and your prices are too high." If a subordinate in a corporation was shown the passage by a bossy superordinate not given to idle chatting, the subordinate might see the passage as containing a kind of instruction or order, perhaps to be more creative in approaching some enterprise that is not working out well.

In all these cases, it is not being suggested that the explicit descriptive content of the passage is not processed and understood. Rather, it is contended that the extratextual extensions are at least equally valid parts of a holistic semantic representation of what is understood or comprehended when the passage is read in the various contexts.

Although the preceding illustrations have focused on the text as a whole, many kinds of context effects can also be identified at the micro level. For example, the interpretation of anaphora (e.g., "it" in sentence 3) is obviously dependent on the preceding linguistic context (see Chapter 6 by Webber). The interpretation of the second sentence will include some tag about incompleteness because the activity described does not provide a complete description of an activity that the first sentence had led the reader to expect would be "unique." At the word level, the meaning of the word "balloon" in the third sentence will certainly be particularized to a far greater extent than the dictionary entries for any sense of that word; since it is supporting an amplifier, it is likely to be understood to be a large balloon filled with something that gives it a tendency to rise, rather than the run-of-the-mill party balloon, for example.

The two types of context that perhaps have had the greatest research attention devoted to them, as well as having important implications for the problems that face the child learning to read with comprehension, are the quality and quantity of the relevant prior knowledge possessed by the comprehender and the perceived task or purpose of comprehending a given discourse. A brief discussion of research with skilled readers concerning each of these follows.[1]

---

[1]Discussion of the literature on the development of constructive processes is beyond the scope of this paper. Suffice it to say that the volume of work far exceeds the number of useful generalizations it has generated. The findings can be summed up as follows: Most of what adults do children do, but less efficiently. If tasks demands are made simpler, children's processing more closely resembles that of adults. For a review, see Baker and Stein (1978). Among the more useful directions being taken related to the constructive processes of prose understanding in children involve investigation of the acquisition of the knowledge structures themselves (e.g., Nelson, 1977) and of the relationship between prose processing and metacognitive knowledge (e.g., Brown & Smiley, 1977; see also Chapter 19 by Brown in this volume).

Prior Knowledge as a
Context for Comprehension

Of all the types of context alluded to thus far, the largest share of experimental work has investigated the role of prior knowledge. We only try to provide the flavor of some of the paradigms employed in these investigations and the typical results obtained. One paradigm investigates the incorporation of pragmatic implications as a part of comprehension. Pragmatic implication may be contrasted with justified logical inference in that the former deals with states of affairs that would be expected to be true with a high probability given some other state of affairs (determined by one's knowledge of the world), but are not necessarily true. For example, if one flicks on a light switch, a light usually goes on, but not necessarily. The bulb may not work, for example. Johnson, Bransford, and Solomon (1973) presented sentences in an acquisition set and then presented pragmatic implications of those sentences in a recognition test. Subjects tended at very high rates to incorrectly identify the implication items as having been presented earlier. Similar results have been found by Brewer (1977) with recall rather than recognition. Harris (1974) found that subjects presented with sentences of the form "X said Y" falsely recognize the sentence "Y" as having been presented, making the pragmatic inference that what one says is true. Anderson and his associates have demonstrated in a series of studies (reviewed in Chapter 13 of this volume) that the semantic representation of words involves a process of instantiation or particularization as a function of the sentence context in which they occur and pragmatic knowledge of the world. The conclusion: In the process of comprehending discourse, what is understood and stored frequently includes not only what is directly stated, but also what seems to follow from that information (probabilistically or necessarily).

Sometimes the operative prior knowledge context will not be general knowledge of the world, but specific knowledge (e.g., about a given individual). For example, Sulin and Dooling (1974) found that when subjects read passages about Helen Keller, they later tended to falsely recognize that the sentence "She was deaf, dumb, and blind" had been presented. That sentence was not falsely recognized if the passage was purported to be about a character with an arbitrary name. Clearly, when possible, information in text is assimilated to specifically relevant prior knowledge, even when there are no clues in the text that such assimilation is necessary for understanding. For complete understanding, most passages about Helen Keller will require activated prior knowledge of her disabilities.

This suggests some implications for the recent research that has attempted, using analysis schemes of varying sophistication, to demonstrate how structural characteristics of text lead to selective processing of the most important semantic elements (e.g., Meyer, 1975). Spiro (1975, 1977) has argued that because comprehension is an interactive product of semantic content directly stated or logically derivable in text and some contribution from the comprehender's prior knowledge, the text structural approaches are misleading in their implications for psychological process models (although quite useful for other purposes, such as measurement of text complexity and for scoring recall protocols). Again, the "meaning in the text" fallacy seems to be operating. It might be argued by advocates of such approaches that psychological validity has been demonstrated by patterns in recall data supportive of the structural analysis scheme. However, Spiro (1975, 1977) has pointed out that conventional memory experiments are subject to demand characteristics that minimize interaction with and assimilation to prior knowledge and thus maximize the variability that factors "in the text" will account for by default. Under conditions where prior knowledge characteristics are less restricted in their operation, the possibility must be confronted that anchoring patterns from preexisting cognitive structures (Ausubel, 1968) may be at variance with those structural charcteristics of text purported to determine importance of semantic components (besides increasing the probability that semantic components not present in or inferable from the text will be added [Spiro, 1977]). A demonstration in support of these suppositions was provided by Anderson, Reynolds, Goetz, and Schallert (1976), who presented texts to wrestlers or music majors. Recall of the text evidenced different selectivity patterns as a function of the group's prior knowledge and interests. In a related vein, Pichert and Anderson (1976) found that determinations of a text component's structural importance in isolation were overridden as a function of the perspective of the reader. Clearly, importance of text elements is the result of some interaction between characteristics of the text and the context.

Attitudinal contexts also have profound effects on comprehension. Spiro and Sherif (1975) found that an individual's selectivity patterns are a somewhat predictable function of ego-involvement with the issue discussed, favorability of statements vis-à-vis the issue, and whether the statements are agreed or disagreed with. More basic to the issue of comprehension, the Sherifs (e.g., Sherif & Hovland, 1961; Sherif, Sherif, & Nebergall, 1965) have repeatedly demonstrated that individuals with a strong stand on issues that they are ego-involved with will interpret statements about that issue differently than individuals without a stand on the issue. For example, the former typically see statements that the latter judged to be neutral as being favorable to the stand opposite theirs. Statements that are moderately acceptable are assimilated to their position and judged more favorable to it than is actually the case. Once again, the cognitive impact of prose incorporates an aspect contributed by the comprehender and not derivable from the text itself—in this case an evaluative aspect.

Throughout this discussion, effects of prior knowledge have been described without any indication of the cognitive structures that are the basis for the effects. Although this issue is not addressed in detail here (see Chapter 2 by Rumelhart in this volume), some suggestions can be made about the direction likely to be most productive. Construction is assumed to move toward a conventionalization of to-be-comprehended prose, an attempt to fit the message as much as possible with one's knowledge of the world. Knowledge structure representations for such conventionalized world knowledge have been developed under the rubrics frame (Charniak, 1975; Minsky, 1975), script (Schank & Abelson, 1977), and schema (Anderson, 1977; Bartlett, 1932; Rumelhart & Ortony, 1977; Spiro, 1977). These knowledge structures are generally thought to have slots with variable names that are instantiated by information provided in the course of perceiving or comprehending, and to specify relations between the slots. The structures are holistic in that they generally specify all the variables and relations involved in a stereotyped situation or concept. If variables are not instantiated, they may possess default values. Hence, if information in discourse leads to the selection of a given schema as appropriate, and, in turn, to the instantiation of those variables specified in the discourse, those variables that are not instantiated will be assigned their default values. It is the default assignment process that probably forms the basis for a large part of construction in comprehension. Once a schema is selected, everything in that schema can be part of the final comprehended product. This could occur even though only a small part of the schema is instantiated by information expressed "in the text." Because schemata can be conceived as existing at various levels of abstraction, the same processes could apply at various levels of analysis, from the instantiation of word meanings in context to the intrusion of theme-related information.

Most of the research on schemata has been conjectural, without attempts at experimental validation (of course, these concepts have been tested in artificial intelligence research, e.g., Schank & Abelson, 1977). However, Anderson, Spiro, and Anderson (1978) have found evidence that the restaurant script developed by Schank and Abelson (1975) is operative as a context for understanding stories taking place in restaurants. Similar support for the psychological reality of scripts has been found by Bower, Black, and Turner (1979).

Degree of Effort After Meaning

The extent to which constructive extensions will go on is clearly variable. One can simply form a minimal plausible semantic representation or one can make elaborate extensions (as in the update of the organ-grinder's monkey passage discussed earlier). In fact, several experiments concerned with depth of processing and prose memory demonstrate consequences of the extent of effort after meaning.

Mistler-Lachman (1972) found that sentence processing varies qualitatively as a function of the task requirements. Subjects either had to judge whether sentences were meaningful, judge whether they were appropriate given preceding context, or generate a contextually appropriate next sentence. Whether or not subjects processed sentences sufficiently to resolve ambiguity of various kinds depended on the type of task being performed. For example, ambiguity was not resolved when judgments of meaningfulness were made, but generally was resolved when contextual appropriateness had to be decided. In a similar vein, Schallert (1976) found that context was used to disambiguate polysemous prose passages only if instructions induced a set for "deeper" semantic processing.

The extent to which inferences are made as part of the comprehension process is largely dependent on the task context. For example, Frederiksen (1975) found a far larger proportion of various kinds of inferential elaboration at the time of comprehension by subjects who were in a problem-solving set while reading than those subjects given conventional prose learning instructions. Brockway, Chmielewski, and Cofer (1974) scaled inferences generated from stories for their "closeness" to the stories. When the scaled generated statements were used in a recognition test, the likelihood of acceptance as a function of closeness varied across manipulated accuracy sets. Inferences scaled further away from the presented stories were "recognized" more often when less importance was explicitly placed on accuracy.

Task context also can affect structural characteristics of the cognitive representations of what is read. This is illustrated by Zajonc's (1960) experiments on cognitive "tuning." This research is a direct descendent of the Wurzburg School's concern with the directing influence of *Aufgabe* (task assignment) on cognition, as well as some of the research on topics like "set" and orienting attitudes (see the Zajonc article for references). All subjects read a paragraph supposedly describing a job applicant. Some subjects were then told that they were going to have to communicate the information in the paragraph to another group. In a second condition, subjects were told that they were going to receive more information about the applicant later. Immediately following the tuning instructions, the subjects were asked to indicate what they knew about the applicant. Subjects wrote down all the characteristics of the applicant that they remembered (one per index card).

The results indicated that the "transmitters" recalled more characteristics than the "receivers," had cognitive structures representing the applicant that were more "complex" (i.e., a greater amount of subdivision of characteristics as indicated by the subjects' judgments of natural groupings), had a higher degree of "unity" (i.e., the extent to which subjects judged that change in one characteristic would lead to changes in other characteristics—a measure of the "extent that one part or a cluster of parts dominates the whole").

Although Zajonc's mesures of cognitive structure may be faulted, the magnitude and reliability of the differences make the results striking. Zajonc attributed the results to a more general and abstract encoding (supposedly more flexible) by those who expected to receive more information. It also seems possible that although the "receivers" had less internal structure (i.e., structures dealing with relationships among the characteristics), they may have had greater "external" structure (i.e., structures dealing with relationships between the characteristics and prior knowledge).

The extent to which effort after meaning proceeds has broad ramifications for theory and practice related to reading comprehension. First, it can be assumed that in a given situation, some amount of effort after meaning will be optimal (sufficient extensions without diminishing returns on their value). Little is known, however, about the processes involved in initiating, directing, and terminating construction. It seems they are usually, but not necessarily, tacit. An initial guess is that there is some monitoring device which is tuned by the operative purposes or functions of reading at a given time and resonates to satisfied functions until a sufficient number are satisfied (given the level of tuning), at which time a click of comprehension occurs and effort after meaning ceases.

A BRIEF NOTE ON REMEMBERING AS A CONTEXT-BASED CONSTRUCTIVE PROCESS

A tradition in cognitive psychology, following Bartlett, has come increasingly to view remembering as a process similar to comprehending. I am referring to those who see memory as a reconstructive process (see Spiro, 1977, for a review of this literature). Rather than retrieving stored traces of past experience as the heart of remembering, the past is inferentially reconstructed in much the same manner as a paleontologist uses his knowledge of anatomy and physiology to reconstruct a dinosaur from its bone fragments. Similarly, the ingredients of reconstructive memory are stored fragments of the past (specific memories) and knowledge of the world. The assumption is made by the rememberer that the past is orderly, and an attempt is then made to enrich the fragmentary specific memories in such a way as to produce a complete and coherent account of that in the past which is the target of the activity. (The sparseness of specific memories is given considerable attention in the section on cognitive economy of representation.) In other words, part of the answer to the question "What is remembered?" is "What is needed." The process is often below the level of conscious awareness: Under certain conditions (see Spiro, 1977 for a discussion of those conditions), reconstructed memories may be inaccurate, but when erroneous importations and distortions serve to produce coherence, individuals are unable to distinguish them from accurate memories (Spiro, 1980). The nature of what is remembered is as much affected by the variety of impinging contexts as is comprehension. Furthermore, remembering is usually subject to the influence of a richer context because all the contextual factors that influenced original comprehension will have an effect, but relevant additions to or alterations of the context can occur during the interval between initial exposure and subsequent retrieval. Further still, as specific memories are lost over time, other knowledge must be relied on more to fill out the picture of the past. Returning, then, to the similarity between remembering and comprehending alluded to at the beginning of this section, it is that both processes involve the combining of data (information in text for comprehension, specific memories for remembering) with contextual knowledge toward the goal of understanding—in the case of memory, an understanding of the past.

PROBLEMS AND NEW DIRECTIONS

The constructive orientation, with its attendant emphasis on the importance of what one already knows in determining what one will come to know, must be considered an improvement over the narrow bottom-up conceptions that earlier dominated thinking about reading. Nevertheless, if the usefulness of schema theories to those interested in children's reading comprehension is not to quickly reach a point of diminishing returns, I believe more research will have to be initiated in several areas that are currently being neglected. In this section I sketch my personal view of what those needed directions are. It should not be surprising that much of my own current research falls in the areas I discuss (why undertake work that one thinks is unimportant?). Thus more detailed discussions of many of the topics discussed in the following section are available, and these are cited where appropriate.

Specification of Component Processes and Their Patterns of Co-Occurrence in Less Able Readers

I sometimes get the impression that people think the main implication of schema approaches is that if a child is having problems with comprehension, they are caused by a deficiency of requisite knowledge. The solution, then, is merely to build in that knowledge. Clearly, availability of appropriate schemata is necessary for comprehension, and many reading problems may be traceable to mismatches between background knowledge presumed in a given text and that actually possessed by the reader. However, schema availability is not a sufficient condition for comprehension. Schemata may be available but not accessed appropriately or efficiently. Even when an appropriate schema is brought to bear while reading, it is not automatically the case that it will be *used* appropriately. More attention needs to be paid to top-down processing difficulties that go *beyond schema availability*. We have to say more than that prior knowledge matters. How is prior knowledge used? It is very possible that there are a variety of things that can go wrong in top-down processing. However, unless we know better what *should* be occurring, it will be difficult to precisely determine what is going wrong. Thus we need to identify and model the components of the process by which preexisting knowledge affects the acquisition of new knowledge. Toward this end, let me suggest, at a very general level, several aspects of the total process that may form a useful taxonomy to guide further study.

1. *Schema acquisition.* Where do our knowledge structures come from in the first place? This question continues to puzzle developmental psychologists. Cognitive psychologists of the last 20 years have had little to say about learning. (This topic receives further attention later.) However, various difficulties could result from problems of schema acquisition. If schemata are not acquired in great enough quantity, they may tend to be frequently absent, leading a child to think that his or her knowledge is not relevant even in those cases where it might be (see the following discussion of "general" schema unavailability). Or if the schemata tend to be insufficiently general and overly tied to personal experience, they may not be readily enough applicable to a sufficiently wide range of situations. Even when an individual has a rich store of schemata, it is unreasonable to think he or she will have a prepackaged knowledge structure for every situation that may be encountered. Sometimes knowledge structures will have to be built (or at least altered) to fit the demands of a given situation (see the following discussion of generic cognitive economy of representation). It should be noted, however, that the demands on writers and speakers to be "cooperative" (Grice, 1975) suggest that this problem may not occur as often as one might think; if it is expected that readers or hearers will not have appropriate prior knowledge to understand a discourse, cooperative communicators are expected to provide it.

2. *Schema selection.* How does one know which knowledge structure to bring to bear in a given situation (including those situations for which a directly relevant schema does not exist, so that a structurally similar one must be selected and used by analogy)? If a schema is inaccessible, it has the same consequences as if it was not available. If it is not readily and effortlessly accessible, the flow of other aspects of the process may be disrupted (see the section on top-down processing efficiency).

3. *Schema instantiation and refinement.* As discourse proceeds, the variables or slots in generic structures must receive specific instantiation. That is, we start off with a general model of what a discourse is about, and that model must be progressively refined as more information is received. We probably understand this aspect better than any of the others; see Chapter 2 by Rumelhart and Chapter 16 by Collins et al. in this volume.

4. *Schema change and maintenance.* Again, as discourse proceeds, different schemata will have to be brought to bear at different times, depending on signals from the text. What may be less obvious is that a schema which has had its relevance clearly signaled at one point in a text will often continue to be relevant long past the point of the original explicit signal. In these cases there may be problems of schema maintenance, which in turn produce problems of information integration across segments of text (Spiro, Boggs, & Brummer, 1979, demonstrate the existence of just such a problem in some children with comprehension difficulty).

5. *Schema combination.* In some cases, perhaps most, individual knowledge structures will not suffice for understanding a given part of a discourse. Rather, schemata will have to be combined. Furthermore, the result of that combination may issue in a product not inferable by an additive combination of its schema parts. Needless to say, such issues of emergence are still poorly understood in psychology.

6. *Nonanalytic aspects of schema-based processing.* (These are discussed in the last section of this paper.)

If there are problems with any of these types of processes, reading difficulities may ensue. Unfortunately, we know very little about how they all work. For some, it may even be too much to expect answers to be forthcoming in the near future, because they get at basic questions of cognitive functioning that have resisted solution by philosophers and psychologists since the beginning of recorded thought: What is insight, creativity, thinking? How do these phenomena occur? After all, we now realize that comprehension is a kind of problem solving, but we still are in the primitive stages of discovering where the solutions to complex problems come from.

Once the component processes are identified and we know how they operate, we can then ask more precise questions about what might go wrong in children having difficulty comprehending. Do they generate too many hypotheses about what a text is about (i.e., which schemata are appropriate for its understanding)? Too few? None? Once hypotheses are generated, are they characterized by inflexibility when they have to be changed? By inertia? Do they access their schemata too early, prematurely locking themselves into interpretations that are not warranted by the data of the text? Or do they wait too long, and by the time a schema is selected much of the previously read information has been forgotten because it lacked an organizing framework? Is text content appropriately mapped onto generated hypotheses? Are hypotheses inappropriately evaluated, with little or no checking to see if subsequent parts of the text fit (see Chapter 19 by Brown in this volume) When we better understand what comprises the process, we can then systematically attack the important question of where the *seams* in the process are. What problems tend to co-occur, forming unified deficiency syndromes? (This is a question that has been asked before, e.g., in the various factor analytic approaches. The problem is that a component model corresponding to schema-based processing has never been incorporated into such an analysis.) To what extent are breakdowns idiosyncratic? Does the same individual tend to have the same or different breakdown patterns across situations, types of material, levels of difficulty of material, etc.

Naturally, the recommended attention to the components of knowledge-based processes must be complemented by further investigation of the composition of the knowledge structures themselves. In particular, it would be nice to know what is in common across the efficient representation of knowledge in the various subject area domains, and how the representations of individuals can be assessed.

In a sense, each of the remaining sections also deal with deficiencies in our knowledge of the specifics of the contribution of prior knowledge to comprehension. They differ from this section in that they deal with particular problems; the current section was intended to argue for a more detailed inquiry into the components of the entire process and their interaction.

Individual Differences in Comprehension Style

Clearly there are differences in the component skills of individual readers that affect their prerformance. However, a theoretically distinct question that can be asked is whether individuals with comparable reading skills all read the same way. Here the question is not so much concerned with differences between more and less able readers, as with differences in comprehension *styles*. Despite the fact that constructive processes in comprehension have been the subject of continuous investigation for over 10 years now, there has been next to no consideration of individual differences in that vein. If someone who accepted the constructivist premise were to ask whether everyone did it in the same way, there would be no basis for a reply. This is particularly surprising given the relatively nonmechanistic approach of constructivism, with its emphasis on personal contributions of the comprehender, and the emphasis on more natural and personally relevant sorts of stimuli that have characterized the movement away from the isolated materials of the verbal learning tradition.

Recent work has shown, however, that everybody does *not* process text the same way. Rather, individuals differ in the way they allocate their limited-capacity processing resources. As we have repeatedly seen demonstrated, reading comprehension is an interactive process (see Chapter 1 by Adams in this volume). What we already know informs in top-down fashion information from text that is being processed from the bottom up. ("Top down" may be loosely equated with "knowledge based", "bottom up" with "text based.") At the most general level, some individuals seem to rely more on the contributions of text to understanding; others stress processes based on what they already know. This is true of adult skilled readers (Spiro & Tirre, 1980) and of children who are far from maturity as readers (Spiro, Tirre, Freebody, & DeLoache, 1979). For the former, the pattern is frequently one of an optimal distribution of processing in a preferred direction, with little effect on success of performance. For the latter, the problem sometimes appears to be more serious, with maladaptive patterns of *overreliance* manifest.

The instructional implications of such findings, if the interpretation continues to be validated by future research, appear to be profound. Common sense would suggest that the most effective strategies for remediating the problems of individuals with one type of style would be exactly the opposite of what would most help children wtih the other type of style. For example, if a child is overreliant on the text, instruction should seek to enlighten the child as to the importance of using prior knowledge as a context for understanding. However, the child who is not paying *enough* attention to the text will find his or her problem reinforced by instruction that stresses using prior knowledge more! Hence a failure to consider individual differences in reading comprehension styles in the classroom may lead either to helping some while hurting others or, if a middle road is adopted, providing optimal help for nobody.

The story on discourse processing styles does not stop with the dichotomy just discussed, however. One must also consider the etiology of an individual's style (Spiro, 1979). A given style can result from a variety of causes, and each might imply its own preferred treatment. Consider the case of overreliance on text-based (or bottom-up) processing:

1. A child may lack the requisite schema for understanding particular passages. Clearly, in those cases where knowledge is not available, it cannot be applied. I call this *local schema unavailability*. On the other hand, a child may tend to be knowledge-deficient across a range of situations, which I refer to as *general schema unavailability*. When such is the case, a text-based reading style may develop.

2. As we have already indicated, skills and styles are considered to be part of a two-tiered model of individual differences. That is, skills are not considered to be perfectly determinate of styles or vice versa. In general, a given skill deficiency should be able to result in either processing style depending on whether the child perseveres in the problem area or attempts to escape and compensate. For example, consider a child who is slow and effortful at word identification. Such a child may persevere at decoding, utilizing so much of available processing capacity that other, higher order, comprehension processes may suffer from the ensuing "bottleneck" (Perfetti & Lesgold, 1978). On the other hand, a child with such a problem may try to escape from the unpleasant task for which he or she possesses so little skill by

doing other things to compensate. Here the child may come to rely on top-down processing to guess at many of the words in a text.

3. Some children seem to have a misconception about reading (Canney & Winograd, 1979; Spiro & Myers, 1979). They think that reading is a bottom-up process, and top-down, extratextual activities are inappropriate. Such a child may develop a bottom-up bias because that is what the child thinks he or she is *supposed* to do. We know very little about children's conceptions of reading and even less of their causes. However, reasonable candidates with respect to bottom-up biases include code emphases in early reading instruction, insular and irrelevant reading texts, and tests that stress literal content at the expense of its integration with relevant preexisting knowledge.

4. Some individuals seem to have general cognitive processing styles that dictate their discourse processing style. For example, some people have difficulty overcoming the closure of a geometric stimulus configuration in order to detect a memorized target configuration within it. These people are said to be stimulus-bound, lacking in freedom from Gestaltbindung (Thurstone, 1942), or field dependent (Witkin, Moore, Goodenough, & Cox, 1977). This style of stimulus-boundedness generalizes to a variety of situations (Witkin et al., 1977). Does it generalize to text, where a structure from memory (a schema) must be superimposed on a more external stimulus structure (that of the text)? Spiro and Tirre (1980) found that to indeed be the case. College students scoring lower on an embedded figures test (with vocabulary scores statistically removed) used their prior knowledge less in the performance of a discourse processing task.

5. Sometimes there may be small areas of breakdown or "bugs" in a child's processing routine that create the appearance of an overreliance on the text. For example, we have found (Spiro, Boggs, & Brummer, 1979) that some children have difficulties with schema maintenance across sentences. However, top-down processes within sentences are carried out adequately. Hence their top-down processing apparatus is intact and operative, but a bug keeps them from demonstrating it to full effect. I would call such instances "pseudo-styles."

The pilot study by Spiro et al. (1979) found that three of these etiological factors (decoding skill, cognitive style, and general schema availability) were predictive of discourse processing style in fifth and sixth grade children. However, all of the preceding discussion must be considered conservatively. More work needs to be done to demonstrate the reliability, validity, and range of application of these findings across types of tasks and texts. Their potential practical importance, however, should make the study of individual differences from a constructive viewpoint a major priority in reading research.

Efficiency of Top-Down Processing

A point often overlooked in schema-theoretic research is that individuals may be able to execute the various processes of comprehension under some set of ideal conditions, but have difficulty under the real-time constraints of reading in natural settings because some of the processes are not executed *efficiently*. Efficiency is a topic that has received considerable attention with respect to bottom-up processes following the paper by LaBerge and Samuels (1974) on automaticity (see also the demonstration by Perfetti & Hogaboam (1975) of the importance of rapidity of decoding). Unfortunately, there has been almost total neglect of aspects of top-down processing efficiency, despite the fact that inefficient top-down processing can, in principle, contribute as much to reading deficiency as inefficiencies in word identification. In this section we consider several aspects of top-down processing efficiency: automaticity,[2] cognitive economy of representation (episodic and generic), and cognitive economy of resourse deployment. As a general point, any of the processes discussed earlier in the section on components should be capable of efficient or inefficient execution. For example, schemata can be selected rapidly and without requiring conscious awareness, or selection may occur only after a process of effortful, self-conscious consideration.

Automaticity. The point for reading instruction again involves our limited capacity as information processors. There is a limit on the number of things we can devote conscious attention to at a given time. If much of this capacity must be used for processes of word identification, a bottleneck will be created that inhibits other important comprehension processes. On the other hand, to the extent that word identification can proceed without requiring conscious attention (or at least rapidly), more capacity will be freed to do such things as think about what one is reading. Note, however, that much top-down processing may also be automatic (with similar ramifications vis-à-vis limited processing capacity). As adults, if we read that "The child was carelessly playing with the delicate pitcher and it suddenly fell to the floor," an inference about it probably breaking will typically be made without requiring any conscious effort. As an exercise, read a prose passage as you would normally do. Think about what it all meant when you are done. Then go back and see how much additional meaning you imported to the text without having been at all aware of doing it. Such examples of automatic top-down

---

[2]Technically, automatic processes are those that do not require conscious attention. However, for the purposes of the following highly condensed discussion, we will be somewhat more general in the use of our terms. Thus by automaticity we may sometimes be including rapidly executed processes that do require some conscious attention.

processing are ubiquitous. We tend to no longer be aware of it because of the high level of skill we have achieved. But a child may not be doing as much automatic top-down processing as we take for granted.

Any of the components of schema-based processing that were discussed in an earlier section can be executed automatically or not. For example, where we would automatically select a schema to inform our understanding of a given text, an inefficiently comprehending child might have to labor over the question of what the text is about, what already possessed knowledge must be brought to bear to understand it, etc. Such conscious attention to what could be an automatic top-down process can have as severe consequences for the flow of text processing as laborious decoding. (Note however that it is not necessarily the case that more attention to one process will produce interference with other processes—mutual facilitation is always another possibility.) Unfortunately, we know little about how processes below the level of consciousness operate, perhaps because their unavailability to introspection make them more difficult to form hypotheses about and subsequently investigate in rigorous fashion. Philosophers have devoted some attention to the question (e.g., Polanyi, 1966). Some speculations based on psychological models are possible (e.g., default nodes in schemata may be activated whenever their superordinate structures are; (see Schank & Abelson, 1977, and Spiro, Esposito, & Vondruska, 1978). In general, however, there is little we can say conclusively on this matter.

Issues get fuzzier still when one thinks of a special kind of automaticity—immersion. Often when we are reading we become so involved that we forget that we are reading, much like we sometimes forget that we are driving. Yet, as with driving, if we pay more attention to the details of our reading, the process suffers. This is the commonly experienced feeling colloquially expressed as "getting into" something. Although it seems intuitively obvious that there are advantages of such a processing mode, we have little idea of what they may be, much less how the ability to immerse develops, its preconditions, or even what is going on when you are immersed that is not going on when you are not. I would venture one speculation: It is something more than the benefits of freed-up information-processing capacity. Rather, there seems to be a greater sense of directly experiencing what is being read. One "feels" it more. The role of such feelings in cognitive processing, an unexplored topic since Bartlett proposed his concept of attitudes, is discussed in a later section.

Cognitive Economy of Representation.   Much of the information that we encounter is at least imperfectly derivable from other information already represented in memory. Does such derivable information receive its own durable representation in long-term memory? Results of an experiment by Spiro & Esposito (1977) indicate in the negative. For example, if skilled reading adults read that a karate champion hit a block during a demonstration, and they then read that the block broke, the latter information can be shown not to be explicitly represented in memory shortly after reading. When information is subsequently presented in the story that vitiates the force of the derivability of the predictable information (e.g., the karate champion was having trouble concentrating because of a fight with his wife that day), thus *blocking* its derivation if it was not stored, skilled reading adults tend to say either that it did not say in the story whether the block broke or that the block did *not* break. Furthermore, they are as certain about these errors as they are about accurate memories. Such errors do not occur when the target information is made less predictable, and they can be shown to not be due to representing the predictable information and subsequently modifying that representation when the vitiating information is encountered.

I would argue that minimizing representation where possible contributes to efficient discourse processing. Much of the information we take in will either be used infrequently in the future or not at all. In that case it is more economical to lessen the cognitive effort expended toward complete en-coding. If information may be derived from already encoded information (even imperfectly), then leave it to be derived later if it is needed (see the earlier discussion of reconstructive processes in remembering) rather than devoting time and processing capacity to elaborately encoding it. This has the advantages of not cluttering up mental representations (perhaps facilitating the retrieval of information) and, more importantly, of freeing time and capacity for thinking more about what one is reading rather than thinking about how to remember what one has read! It is possible that some children's apparent discourse processing problems may be traceable to uneconomical representation strategies (see, for example, the earlier discussion of text-biased processing styles). The cost of cognitive economy is occasional inaccuracy in remembering. As a matter of fact, some children may have representations that are too sparse. That is, they *overestimate* the future derivability of information. Consider the often heard plaint that material that seemed solidly encoded when studying for a test was a blank when the test actually arrived. Although we have no data yet on the existence of such a strategy, it would fit with a commonly observed tendency even in the most skilled of information processors to make inappropriate use of existing knowledge to estimate the future likelihood of events (Kahneman & Tversky, 1973). Particularly relevant is the finding of Fischoff (1975) that individuals presented with answers to questions tend to overestimate the probability that they would have been able to generate the answers themselves had they not been provided. Might not, in similar fashion, some readers tend to erroneously think that explicit information in text, once encountered, was "obvious," and thus may be superficially processed?

One thing that enables accurate cognitive economy of representation is the development of highly ramified knowledge structures. The larger the cluster of mutually implied information, the greater the number of opportunities to leave information to be derived later if needed. Again, poor readers may have difficulties capitalizing on potential cognitive economies, now because of the way their knowledge is organized.

I call the kind of storage economies just discussed *episodic* cognitive economy. That is, they concern the representation of particular, detailed information. A related phenomenon can be called *generic* cognitive economy of representation. First some background. Much of the modeling of knowledge structures has taken the direction of proposing precompiled, i.e., already assembled, packages of information. For example, there are the scripts of Schank and Abelson (1977). It does seem to be the case that holistic sorts of knowledge are brought to bear to understand, for example, a trip to a restaurant; it is what permits the episode to be appreciated as a connected activity and enables missing elements to be imported in the constructive manner that is the topic of this paper. Also, the claim has been confirmed in psychological experiments (Anderson, Spiro, & Anderson, 1978; Bower, Black, & Turner, 1979). However, to say that knowledge may be brought to bear as a whole is not the same as to say that that knowledge is represented in compiled fashion when not being used. An alternative is that knowledge is stored in more fragmented form and is assembled when (and as is) needed, a kind of ongoing programming of prior knowledge (Schank, 1979). A virtue of such an organizational principle is that it answers a critical question often asked of schema theories: How can you have a prepackaged knowledge structure in your head for all the situations you will encounter? The answer then becomes that you don't. Rather, the knowledge structures are *(re-)built* to fit the needs of the subtly changing variety of situations that they must help inform, thus permitting greater flexibility in their application. The efficiency point here, besides whatever advantages may accrue from lessening storage requirements, is that the quality of fit between the need for understanding in some situation and the knowledge brought to bear for that purpose varies. The more degrees of freedom available for adjusting the knowledge context, the greater the potential for more optimal fit. An analogy may be drawn to posture, which is endlessly fluid, yet very accurately recognized. We have knowledge structures that permit us to take the variety of external signals that we receive and integrate them to form a background for an understanding of the current "postural scene." If rigid knowledge structures had to be used to recognize the infinity of postures, in their infinity of preceding contexts, the process could not work nearly as well as it does. Perhaps then, similarly for text understanding, as well as any other activity in which humans demonstrate their characteristic symbolic flexibility. It is interesting to note that the schema model of postural recognition proposed by Head (1920) was an important antecedent of Bartlett's theory.

How is knowledge organized to permit such flexibility? Obviously, we have little idea at this time. A simple hypothesis may, however, be proposed. Knowledge structures that are used as wholes (e.g., knowledge about trips to restaurants) are composed of aspects or scenes of two types: those fairly unique to the event (e.g., ordering food) and those that are in common with other events (e.g., eating food). Those aspects that are shared across types of events might then be stored in a single common location, rather than being repeatedly represented with each of type of event (artificial intelligence programs operating on this principle are being developed by Schank, 1979). Each of the events that share the structure would have pointers to the shared location where more information is available. Generic event knowledge would then be compiled by combining those aspects of the decomposed knowledge structure that are unique with those shared ones that are *needed*. Note that for events that are less routinized than going to a restaurant there would be more degrees of freedom for adaptive flexibility in the way the "ongoing *construction* of prior knowledge" occurs.

What would be the implications of such a reconceptualization of the nature of knowledge organization for reading instruction? For one thing, it might suggest an emphasis on *knowledge assembly,* in addition to that already placed on knowledge availability. The problems one looks for are constrained by one's theories. What new problems might be suggested by a theory of decomposed schemata that are assembled in ongoing fashion? Two come immediately to mind. Some children may store too much generic knowledge in rigidly precompiled form, reducing the ability to adapt flexibility to the subtleties and nuances of difference from one superficially similar situation to the next. If a given text does not fit the tightly prescribed formulas inscribed in memory, it will be less than optimally understood. For other children perhaps there is inappropriate generic cognitive economy; i.e., knowledge is decomposed in such a manner that recomposition is inhibited. Finally, some children may lack the processing apparatus to handle the increased demands placed on compiling knowledge when and as is needed.

Economical Deployment of Resources. This is an area of reading efficiency that has received some considerable research attention and therefore is not discussed here. Very briefly, the important aspects include selectivity—paying appropriate amounts of attention to different parts of text as a function of contextual factors (Reynolds, Standiford, & Anderson, 1978), as well as the computability/derivability of information (Spiro, Esposito, & Vondruska, 1978)—and interactive flexibility (e.g., shifting resources between bottom-up and top-down processes as a function of such characteristics of text and context as familiarity, syntactic complexity, etc.).

Learning

The movement away from behaviorism in cognitive psychology, for all its virtues, has had an unfortunate consequence. We are now able to talk about states of knowledge and processes that operate on those states; the unfortunate concomitant to this static orientation is that there has been almost no new thinking in the constructive paradigm about the process of moving to new structural states, i.e., *learning*. It is suggested that, in addition to the attention we have been paying to how knowledge affects the processing of text, we need to be concerned with how the processing of text affects the development of new knowledge. Two aspects of the neglected topic of learning will be discussed: trans-situational integration and conceptual change.

Trans-Situational Integration. When you are reading the latest install-ment in *Newsweek* about the energy crisis, if you have been following it in the past you will probably not endeavor to form a complete insular representa-tion of the article as your goal of understanding. Rather, your goal will probably be to integrate what you are reading with what you already know of the subject, with special attention to information that is new. That is, your goal of reading is to *update* your knowledge. Knowledge updating is not totally automatic; it is under strategic control. Sometimes, rather than integrating related information across the situations in which they are encountered, information is *compartmentalized* by acquisition situation. This tends to happen with material to be remembered in memory experiments under conventional instructions and with the typical esoteric and/or useless prose materials employed (Spiro, 1977). The danger is that it may also be happening in the schools. This would not be very surprising given the fact that the kinds of tests that are most convenient to construct, administer, and grade also tend to reward compartmentalization. There are situations, of course, where it is desirable to maintain the particular identity of a given text. For example, law students must try not to blend various cases that bear on a given issue. However, in many school situations, a knowledge updating mode would seem to be preferred. A child is exposed to information about the Civil War on many occasions during his or her schooling. I doubt if many educators would want the information about the Battle of Gettysburg contained in a seventh grade history text to receive its own insular representation rather than being integrated with other knowledge already possessed about that battle, the Civil War, war in general, and perhaps interpersonal relations and the plight of man. The questions that must be addressed include: How is trans-situational integration promoted? Answers provided by experimental psychology up to this point are minimal, e.g., that using the same wording promotes integration—see Hayes-Roth & Thorn-dyke, in press. When should it be promoted? What are the costs of integration (these will certainly include a certain amount of forgotten detail not sharing the organizing principle of the body of information with which it is integrated)? What are the consequences of failures to integrate? Beyond the obvious consequences of compartmentalization, e.g., that knowledge of a given topic will be hopelessly diffuse and that specific information may be harder to locate if more locations are potential repositories (see the earlier discussion of efficiency and cognitive economy of representation), failure to integrate may lead an individual to miss some crucial connections between information that is necessary for conceptual change to occur, a topic we now consider.

Conceptual Change. There are a variety of kinds of learning. One kind that cognitive psychology is fairly adept at dealing with is the type that involves incorporating new information into existing structures without thereby substantially altering those structures. This is like what Piaget has called assimilation. Arguably, a more interesting kind of learning in the educational process involves the radical restructuring of existing knowledge as a result of encountering new information, what might be called conceptual change or, after Piaget, accommodation. Becoming more expert in any domain involves more than the mere accretion of information (Bransford, Nitsch, & Franks, 1977). We have already seen that we understand via mental frameworks or schemata. One thing that characterizes experts is that their frameworks are qualitatively different from novices (Chase & Simon, 1973). Such qualitative conceptual change typically brings with it these character-istics, among others: The signficance or interpretation of new information changes (much as it does in science when paradigms change; Kuhn, 1962); more efficient patterns of selectivity develop; more processing becomes tacit (see the next section), accompanied by greater immersion; and information is processed in larger chunks. We know next to nothing about the processes of conceptual change. It is a question that has resisted solution since (and before) Plato's paradoxes of the *Meno*. Piaget has described the differences between cognitive states children pass through but has not proposed a satisfactory explanation of how those changes transpire. Neither has anyone else. Perhaps metaphor, with its capability of describing something new in terms of what is already known plays an important role (Ortony, 1975). Unfortunately, it is probably the case that psychology will have to undergo its own "conceptual change" if an understanding of that essential learning phenomenon is ever to ensue.

What Does a Schema "Feel" Like?: Nonanalytic Aspects of Knowledge Structures

Given the avalanche of research triggered by the revival of interest in Bartlett's (1932) thinking about constructive processes, it is remarkable that a central aspect of that thinking has been totally ignored. I refer to his concept of the "attitude." Perhaps part of the problem was his choice of terms, so easily confusable with the social psychological concept. One's position on abortion is not an attitude in Bartlett's sense. Rather he meant "a general impression of the whole... a complex state or process which it is very hard to describe in more elementary psychological terms... very largely a matter of feeling or affect [pp. 206–207]." Such attitudes were given a central place in the constructive process. For example, recall is described as "a construction, made largely on the basis of this attitude, and its general effect is that of a justification of the attitude [p. 207]." If our knowledge of the past includes such attitudes, then those aspects of *comprehension* that depend on prior knowledge must also be subject to attitudes' effects. (It is worth noting that Bartlett is not the only person to place feelings at or near the center of analysis of cognitive activity. One should see, for example, the philosopher Pepper's (1942) discussion of the contextualist's construct of "quality." The idea is not even original with Bartlett in cognitive psychology, being very similar to Wundt's "Gesamtvostellung" (see Blumenthal, 1970), among others. Neurophysiological work on differences in specialization of the cerebral hemispheres suggests a similar role for the right hemisphere (see Ornstein, 1972, for an introduction to this area). Among educators, Bruner (1962) is one prominent individual who has considered the importance of such phenomena. Another is Broudy (1977).

What are these "summary feelings" (eschewing the confusing term "attitude")? Obviously we do not know. However, a speculative line might proceed as follows. Consider the act of holding a specific object, such as a ball, on one's hand. Our experience of that act has diverse aspects. One of those aspects is the one that could take the form of a verbal description of the ball: It in one's hand. Our experience of that act has diverse aspects. One of those etc. Such descriptions seem inadequate however. They miss the "existential" aspect of the act: what the experience of holding the ball in the hand *feels* like, what enables us to refer *metaphorically* to some entity's "texture," "color," or "flavor." It is proposed, then, that experiences possess qualities, such as texture, that permit of being "felt." Likewise, they have properties amenable of verbal description. However, no verbal description could ever capture the quality of an experience's existential feel, except as a very rough approximation (and vice versa). Now, my proposal is that the preceding dichotomy of aspects of the experience of holding a ball in the hand is extendable by analogy to the "holding" of a concept in the mind! Cohesive concepts, however complex, have properties that can be decomposed and analytically examined. However, they also are *experiences,* and as such they have textural, gestalt-like properties that can only be felt. (A distinction should be made between feelings related to the experience of having an idea and feelings related to the content of the idea; within the latter a further distinction can be made between more and less analytical verbally describable properties, like, e.g., the white color versus the smooth feel of the ball).

Work in the schema-theoretic tradition has focused on the structure of knowledge that must be analyzed, rather than on the texture that must be felt. Accordingly, there is very little to be offered as support for these views. However, a body of data concerned with meaning at the level of the individual word is suggestive. Clearly, word meanings have an analytic aspect, which is what lexicographers and semanticists study. However, words also have been shown to additionally have psychological meaning of a far different kind from that studied analytically. I am thinking about the results of research using the semantic differential (Osgood, Suci, & Tannenbaum, 1957), which have demonstrated that much of the variability in judgments concerning words is due to their evaluative connotations. For an exemplary review of other research that suggest a central role for affect viz-à-viz cold cognition, see Zajonc (1979). (Please note, however, that the concept of feeling under discussion, while including affect, encompasses other nonaffective aspects).

Assuming one accepts the preliminary phenomenological evidence for summary feelings, one might still inquire as to their utility. What is a feeling good for? Many things, it seems to me. First there is the role designated for attitudes in Bartlett's theory. They are like durable "signatures" of past events, preceding and facilitating the retrieval of detailed information ("I don't quite remember what happened in the situation you refer to, but I know it was something sort of unpleasant and puzzling.") In an evolutionary sense, it would appear to be adaptive to remember for the future those situations in which you experienced fear, pleasure, gratification, etc. The attitudes or feelings then remain active in monitoring the reconstructive process; for example, forming the basis for rejection of generations that do not fit ("It sounds like that might have happened, but it does not feel right— I have a feeling that it did not happen.")

However, their constraining function may be more general. As Langer (1967) has pointed out, we need both models of how things work and images of how they "appear" (by which she meant something similar to what I have been referring to as that aspect of knowledge structures that is holistically felt.) Our models of things (including the mind) too often perpetuate new paths and directions that we are deluded into thinking are correct by their systematic fit with that which preceded them. We need the holistic image to be able to detect when our models of how things work no longer fit the "look" (feel) that the system was supposed to analytically describe. It is what enables us to say that something that does not appear to create any logical inconsistencies or to violate any of our explicit knowledge of the world nevertheless "does not feel right."

Summary feelings may also have various kinds of efficiency benefits. They are single units or chunks, thought of all at the same time, and they are often thought of rapidly (as when somebody says they have had a "gut reaction"), thus making more parsimonious use of our limited processing capacity. There is another, perhaps more important, sense in which such a mode of processing may be efficient. Where it is not possible to think analytically about two things at the same time, it may be possible to think about one thing while simultaneously *feeling* several others, as when Broudy (1977) talks of "knowing with" or Bransford et al. (1977) speak of thinking "in terms of" some context. (Of course, this begs the question of what potential informational value is carried by a feeling—again). Perhaps feelings are more amalgamable than more analytic entities. If so, feelings and the characteristics of knowledge that enable them may be an appropriate place to start looking for the answer to that most important question of conceptual change posed earlier. It may be in the rapid interplay of feelings (so much like the combinatorial idea play that Einstein spoke of) that the source of the creation of ideas, later to receive their analytic flesh and bones, may be found. If so, how sad it would be if it were discovered that the real problem of many readers is that their instruction so automatizes them that they do not develop a feeling for what they read or use the feelings available to them in the development of new understandings from reading.

ACKNOWLEDGMENTS

Preparation of this paper was supported by Contract No. US-NIE-C-400-76-0116 to the Center for the Study of Reading from the National Institute of Education and by Grant AP Sloan Fdn 79-4-8 to Yale University. Final revisions of this paper were completed while I was being graciously hosted at Yale by Roger Schank and Robert Abelson. Helpful discussions with them and with Jerry Samet are gratefully acknowledged.

REFERENCES

Anderson, R. C. The notion of schemata and the educational enterprise. In R. C. Anderson, R. J. Spiro, & W. E. Montague (Eds.), *Schooling and the acquisition of knowledge.* Hillsdale, N.J.: Lawrence Erlbaum Associates, Inc., 1977.

Anderson, R. C., Reynolds, R. E., Goetz, E. T., & Schallert, D. L. *Frameworks for comprehending discourse* (Tech. Rep. No. 12). Urbana, Ill.: Center for the Study of Reading, University of Illinois at Urbana-Champaign, 1976.

Anderson, R. C., Spiro, R. J., & Anderson, M. C. Schemata as scaffolding for the representation of information in discourse. *American Educational Research Journal,* 1978, *15,* 433-440.

Austin, J. L. *How to do things with words.* Oxford: Oxford University Press, 1962.

Ausubel, D. P. *Educational psychology: A cognitive view.* New York: Holt, Rinehart & Winston, 1968.

Baker, L., & Stein, N. L. *The development of prose comprehension skills.* (Tech. Rep. No. 102). Urbana, Ill.: Center for the Study of Reading, University of Illinois at Urbana-Champaign, 1978.

Bartlett, F. C. *Remembering.* London: Cambridge University press, 1932.

Binet, A., & Henri, V. La mémoire des phrases. *L'Ann. Psychology,* 1894, *1,* 24–59.

Blumenthal, A. L. *Language and psychology.* New York: Wiley, 1970.

Bower, G. H., Black, J. B., & Turner, T. J. Scripts in memory for text. *Cognitive Psychology,* 1979, *11,* 177–220.

Bransford, J. D., Barclay, J. R., & Franks, J. J. Sentence memory: A constructive versus interpretive approach. *Cognitive Psychology,* 1972, *3,* 193–209.

Bransford, J. D., & Johnson, M. K. Contextual prerequisites for understanding: Some investigations of comprehension and recall. *Journal of Verbal Learning and Verbal Behavior,* 1972, *11,* 717–726.

Bransford, J. D., Nitsch, K. W., & Franks, J. J. Schooling and the facilitation of knowing. In R. C. Anderson, R. J. Spiro, & W. E. Montague (Eds.), *Schooling and the acquisition of knowledge.* Hillsdale, N.J.: Lawrence Erlbaum Associates, Inc., 1977.

Brewer, W. F. *Memory for the pragmatic implications of sentences.* (Tech. Rep. No. 65). Urbana, Ill.: Center for the Study of Reading, University of Illinois at Urbana-Champaign, 1977.

Brockway, J., Chmielewski, D., & Cofer, C. N. Remembering prose: Productivity and accuracy constraints in recognition memory. *Journal of Verbal Learning and Verbal Behavior,* 1974, *13,* 194–208.

Brown, A. L., & Smiley, S. S. Rating the importance of structural units of prose passages. *Child Development,* 1977, *48,* 1–8.

Broudy, H. S. Types of knowledge and purposes of education. In R. C. Anderson, R. J. Spiro, & W. E. Montague (Ed.s), *Schooling and the acquisition of knowledge.* Hillsdale, N.J.: Lawrence Erlbaum Associates, 1977.

Bruner, J. S. *On knowing.* New York: Atheneum, 1962.

Canney, G., & Winograd, P. *Schemata for reading and reading comprehension performance.* (Tech. Rep. No. 120). Urbana, Ill.: Center for the Study of Reading, University of Illinois at Urbana-Champaign, 1979.

Chafe, W. L. Discourse structure and human knowledge. In J. B. Carroll & R. O. Freedle (Eds.), *Language comprehension and the acquisition of knowledge.* Washington, D.C.: V. H. Winston, 1972.

Charniak, E. Organization and inference in a frame-like system of common knowledge. In *Proceedings of theoretical issues in natural language processing: An interdisciplinary workshop.* Cambridge, Mass.: Bolt Beranek and Newman Inc., 1975.

Chase, W. G., & Simon, H. A. Perception in chess. *Cognitive Psychology,* 1973, *4,* 55–81.

Chomsky, N. *Aspects of the theory of syntax.* Cambridge, Mass.: MIT Press, 1965.

Clark, H. H. Linguistic processes in deductive reasoning. *Psychological Review,* 1969, *76,* 387–404.

Cofer, C. N. A comparison of logical and verbatim learning of prose passages of different lengths. *American Journal of Psychology,* 1941, *54,* 1–20.

Dooling, D. J., & Lachman, R. Effects of comprehension on retention of prose. *Journal of Experimental Psychology,* 1972, *88,* 216–222.

Fischoff, B. Hindsight does not equal foresight: The effects of outcome knowledge on judgment under uncertainty. *Journal of Experimental Psychology: Human Perception and Performance,* 1975, *1,* 288–299.

Frederiksen, C. H. Acquisition of semantic information from discourse: Effects of repeated exposures. *Journal of Verbal Learning and Verbal Behavior,* 1975, *14,* 158–169.

Gordon, D., & Lakoff, G. Conversational postulates. In *Papers from the Seventh Regional Meeting, Chicago Linguistic Society,* 1971.

Grice, H. P. Logic and conversation. In P. Cole & J. L. Morgan (Eds.), *Sytax and semantics* (Vol. 3: Speech Acts). New York: Academic Press, 1975.

Halliday, M. A. Language structure and language function. In J. Lyons (Ed.), *New horizons in linguistics.* Harmondsworth, Middlesex, England: Penguin Books Ltd., 1970.

Harris, R. J. Memory and comprehension of implications and inferences of complex sentences. *Journal of Verbal Learning and Verbal Behavior,* 1974, *13,* 626–637.

Hayes-Roth, B., & Thorndyke, P. W. Integration of knowledge from text. *Journal of Verbal Learning and Verbal Behavior,* in press.

Head, H. *Studies of neurology.* Oxford: Oxford University Press, 1920.

Jarvella, R. J. Syntactic processing of connected speech. *Journal of Verbal Learning and Verbal Behavior,* 1971, *10,* 409–416.

Johnson, M. K., Bransford, J. D., & Solomon, S. K. Memory for tacit implications of sentences. *Journal of Experimental Psychology,* 1973, *98,* 203–205.

Kahneman, D., & Tversky, A. On the psychology of prediction. *Psychological Review,* 1973, *80,* 251–273.

Katz, J. J., & Fodor, J. A. The structure of a semantic theory. *Language,* 1963, *39,* 170–210.

Katz, J. J., & Postal, P. M. *An integrated theory of linguistic descriptions.* Cambridge: MIT Press, 1964.

Kuhn, T. S. *The structure of scientific revolutions.* Chicago: University of Chicago Press, 1962.

LaBerge, D., & Samuels, S. J. Toward a theory of automatic information processing in reading. *Cognitive Psychology,* 1974, *6,* 293–323.

Lakoff, G. On generative semantics. In D. D. Steinberg & L. A. Jakobovits (Eds.), *Semantics.* Cambridge, England: Cambridge University Press, 1971.

Langer, S. K. *Mind: An essay on human feeling.* Baltimore: Johns Hopkins University Press, 1967.

Meyer, B. J. *The organization of prose and its effects on memory.* Amsterdam: North-Holland Publishing Co., 1975.

Miller, G. A. Some psychological studies of grammar. *American Psychologist,* 1962, *17,* 748–762.

Minsky, M. A framework for representing knowledge. In P. H. Winston (Ed.), *The psychology of computer vision.* New York: McGraw-Hill, 1975.

Mistler-Lachman, J. L. Levels of comprehension in processing of normal and ambiguous sentences. *Journal of Verbal Learning and Verbal Behavior,* 1972, *11,* 614–623.

Morgan, J. Some interactions of syntax and pragmatics. In P. Cole & J.L. Morgan (Eds.), *Syntax and semantics* (Vol. 3: Speech Acts). New York: Academic Press, 1975.

Nelson, K. Cognitive development and the acquisition of concepts. In R. C. Anderson, R. J. Spiro, & W. E. Montague (Eds.), *Schooling and the acquisition of knowledge.* Hillsdale, N.J.: Lawrence Erlbaum Associates, Inc., 1977.

Ornstein, R. E. *The psychology of consciousness.* San Francisco: Freeman, 1972.

Ortony, A. Why metaphors are necessary and not just nice. *Educational Theory,* 1975, *1,* 45–54.

Osgood, C. E., Suci, G. J., & Tannenbaum, P. H. *The measurement of meaning.* Urbana: University of Illinois Press, 1957.

Paul, I. H. Studies in remembering: The reproduction of connected and extended material. *Psychological Issues,* 1959, *1,* Monograph #2.

Pepper, S. C. *World hypotheses.* Berkeley: University of California Press, 1942.

Perfetti, C. A., & Hogaboam, T. The relationship between single word decoding and reading comprehension skill. *Journal of Educational Psychology,* 1975, *67,* 461–469.

Perfetti, C. A., & Lesgold, A. M. Discourse comprehension and individual differences. In P. Carpenter, & M. Just (Eds.), *Cognitive processes in comprehension.* Hillsdale, N. J.: Lawrence Erlbaum Associates, 1978.

Pichert, J. W., & Anderson, R. C. *Taking different perspectives on a story* (Tech. Rep. No. 14). Urbana, Ill.: Center for the Study of Reading, University of Illinois at Urbana-Champaign, 1976.

Polanyi, M. *The tacit dimension.* Garden City, N.Y.: Doubleday, 1966.

Pompi, K. F., & Lachman, R. Surrogate processes in the short-term retention of connected discourse. *Journal of Experimental Psychology,* 1967, *75,* 143–150.

Reynolds, R. E., Standiford, S. N., & Anderson, R. C. *Distribution of reading time when questions are asked about a restricted category of text information.* (Tech. Rep. No. 83). Urbana, Ill.: Center for the Study of Reading, University of Illinois at Urbana-Champaign, 1978.

Rumelhart, D. E., & Ortony, A. The representation of knowledge in memory. In R. C. Anderson, R. J., Spiro, & W. E. Montague (Eds.), *Schooling and the acquisition of knowledge.* Hillsdale, N.J.: Lawrence Erlbaum Associates, Inc., 1977.

Sachs, J. Recognition memory for syntactic and semantic aspects of connected discourse. *Perception and Psychophysics,* 1967, *2,* 437–442.

Schallert, D. L. Improving memory for prose: The relationship between depth of processing and context. *Journal of Verbal Learning and Verbal Behavior,* 1976, *15,* 621–632.

Schank, R. C. *Reminding and memory organization.* Unpublished manuscript, 1979.

Schank, R. C., & Abelson, R. P. Scripts, plans and knowledge. In *Advance Papers of the Fourth International Joint Conference on Artificial Intelligence.* Tbilisi, Georgia: USSR, 1975. Pp. 151–157.

Schank, R. C., & Abelson, R. P. *Scripts, plans, goals, and understanding.* Hillsdale, N.J.: Lawrence Erlbaum Associates, 1977.

Searle, J. R. Indirect speech acts. In P. Cole & J. L. Morgan (Eds.), *Syntax and semantics* (Vol. 3: Speech Acts). New York: Academic Press, 1975.

Sherif, M., & Hovland, C. I. *Social judgment.* London: Yale University Press, 1961.

Sherif, C. W., Sherif, M., & Nebergall, R. E. *Attitude and attitude change: The social judgment-involvement approach.* Philadelphia: Saunders, 1965.

Spiro, R. J. *Inferential reconstruction in memory for connected discourse* (Tech. Rep. No. 2). Urbana, Ill.: Center for the Study of Reading, University of Illinois at Urbana-Champaign, 1975.

Spiro, R. J. Remembering information from text: Theoretical and empirical issues concerning the "State of Schema" reconstruction hypothesis. In R. C. Anderson, R. J., Spiro, & W. E. Montague (Eds.), *Schooling and the acquisition of knowledge.* Hillsdale, N.J.: Lawrence Erlbaum Associates, Inc., 1977.

Spiro, R. J. Accommodative reconstruction in prose recall. *Journal of Verbal Learning and Verbal Behavior,* 1980, *19,* 84–95.

Spiro, R. J. Etiology of reading comprehension style. In M. Kamil & A. Moe (Eds.), *National Reading Conference Yearbook,* 1979, *28,* 118–122.

Spiro, R. J., Boggs, J., & Brummer, R. *Schema maintenance and reading comprehension ability.* Unpublished manuscript, 1979.

Spiro, R. J., & Esposito, J. Superficial processing of explicit inferences in text. (Tech. Rep. No. 60). Urbana, Ill.: Center for the Study of Reading, 1977.

Spiro, R. J., Esposito, J., & Vondruska, R. The representation of derivable information in memory: When what might have been left unsaid is said. In D. Waltz (Ed.), *TINLAP: Theoretical issues in natural language processing II.* New York: Association for Computing Machinery & Association for Computational Linguistics, 1978.

Spiro, R. J., & Myers, A. *Children's misconceptions about the role of knowledge-based processes in reading comprehension.* In preparation, 1979.

Spiro, R. J., & Sherif, C. W. Consistency and relativity in selective recall with differing ego-involvement. *British Journal of Social and Clinical Psychology,* 1975, *14,* 351–361.

Spiro, R. J. & Tirre, W. C. Individual differences in schema utilization during discourse processing. *Journal of Educational Psychology,* 1980, *72,* 204–208.

Spiro, R. J., Tirre, W. C., Freebody, P., & DeLoache, J. *Reading style etiology and preferences for bottom-up versus top-down processes.* Unpublished manuscript, 1979.

Sulin, R. A., & Dooling, D. J. Intrusion of a thematic idea in retention of prose. *Journal of Experimental Psychology,* 1974, *103,* 255–262.

Thurstone, L. L. *A factorial study of perception.* Chicago: University of Chicago Press, 1942.

van Dijk, T. A. Text grammar and text logic. In J. S. Petofi & H. Rieser (Eds.), *Studies in text grammar*. Dordrecht: Reidel, 1973.

Welborn, E. L., & English, H. Logical learning and retention: A general review of experiments with meaningful verbal materials. *Psychological Bulletin*, 1937, *34*, 1–20.

Witkin, H. A., Moore, C. A., Goodenough, D. R., & Cox, P. W. Field-dependent and field independent cognitive styles and their educational implications. *Review of Educational Research*, 1977, *47*, 1–64.

Zajonc, R. B. The process of cognitive tuning in communication. *Journal of Abnormal and Social Psychology*, 1960, *61*, 159–167.

Zajonc, R. B. *Feeling and thinking: Preferences need no inferences*. Manuscript submitted for publication, 1979.

Zangwill, O. L. Remembering revisited. *Quarterly Journal of Experimental Psychology*, 1972, *24*, 123–138.

11 Category Structure and the Development of Categorization

Carolyn B. Mervis
Center for the Study of Reading,
University of Illinois, Urbana-Champaign

A category exists whenever two or more distinguishable objects or events are treated equivalently. This equivalent treatment may take any number of forms, such as labeling distinct objects or events with the same name or performing the same action on different objects. For example, a person might indicate the category "dog" by calling a German shepherd, a beagle, a cocker spaniel, and a chihuahua each "dog." Or the person might indicate the category "things that can be thrown" by throwing a ball, a rock, and a stick.

Because the world consists of an infinite number of discriminably different stimuli, categorization is essential. A person who treated each object or event in the world as unique would rapidly be overwhelmed by the complexity of the environment. By categorizing, a person is able to render the unfamiliar familiar. And because one is able to generalize about an object based on knowledge about its category, one is also able to know more about the object than just what can be ascertained by looking at it.

The purpose of the present chapter is to discuss the structure of categories and the development of the processes of categorization with regard to concrete objects. Because one needs to know something about the nature of categories in order to consider how categorization develops, the chapter begins with a section in which the two major theories of categorization and category structure are discussed. In the second section, the development of categorization is discussed in light of the findings of the previous section. In the third section, implications of categorization theory and research for facilitating reading development—in particular, implications for constructing children's readers—are discussed.

THEORIES OF CATEGORY STRUCTURE

In this section, the evolution of the best-example theory of category structure is described. The section begins with a description of the traditional theory of category structure. This description is followed by a discussion of some of the major researches that pointed to problems with the traditional theory and that led to the development of the best-example theory. Finally, the best-example theory is considered.

The Traditional Theory

According to the traditional theory of categorization, a category is defined by a (set of) criterial attribute(s). (Hull, 1920, was one of the first psychologists to propose this idea.) A criterial attribute is an attribute that all the members of the category being defined possess and that is not possessed by any nonmember of that category. The criterial attribute definition is as brief (i.e., minimal) as possible. Thus, it includes only those attributes that are necessary to set off the category being defined from other categories that might be confused with it. As an example, consider a "pretend" world composed only of squares of various colors and sizes. If one were to divide these squares according to color, then the criterial attribute of each category would be the color of the squares in that category. So the criterial attribute of the category "red squares" would be "red." No mention of size or shape would be made because neither is relevant to separating members of the category "red squares" from the other categories in this pretend world. If, however, one were to introduce circles of various colors and sizes (corresponding to the colors and sizes of the squares) into this world, then the criterial attribute definition for "red squares" would no longer simply be "red" because this definition would admit red circles into the category. A combination of criterial attributes would be needed; in particular, "red plus square." Again, size is an irrelevant attribute and is therefore left out of the definition.

The boundaries (limits) of these categories are well defined. Thus, an object either meets the criterial attribute definition of a category and is therefore included in the category, or else the object does not meet the criterial attribute definition and is accordingly excluded from the category. Once a person knows the criterial attribute definition of a category, he or she will always be able to decide whether or not a given object belongs in the category. Thus, in our pretend world, a person who knows the criterial attribute definition of "red squares" would be able to decide, for any object presented to him or her, whether or not it belonged in the category "red squares." There would be no objects that the person would be unsure whether to include.

Once it is determined that an object meets the criterial attribute definition of a category, that object is automatically included as a full and equal member. Thus, no category member exemplifies its category better than any other member. In our pretend world, all objects admitted into the category "red squares" would be considered to be equally "red plus square."

The real world as conceived by the traditional theory corresponds to what Garner (1974) called a "total set." That is, all the values of any attribute present in the world occur equally often in combination with each other value of every other attribute present. No particular combination of attributes is any more likely to occur than is any other combination. Therefore, the attribute structure of the world provides no basis for deciding how to divide the objects in the world into categories, so the decision must be made arbitrarily. Consider our pretend world again. If it included two colors (red and blue), two shapes (square and circle), and two sizes (large and small), then the set of objects in this world would consist of equal numbers of large red squares, small red squares, large red circles, small red circles, large blue squares, small blue squares, large blue circles, and small blue circles. There is no obvious ideal way to divide these objects into categories. One could divide them into two categories based on shape, two different categories based on color, two different categories based on size, eight categories based on each of the different combinations of values for the three attributes, and so on. None of these schemas is any more reasonable in general than is any other.

The traditional theory as I have presented it is primarily Bourne's (1968) theory. The general form of traditional theory, however, is not unique to psychology. Parts (at least) of the theory have been included in theories of category structure in such fields as philosophy, linguistics, anthropology, and education. For example, over 2,000 years ago Aristotle (*The Metaphysics*, translated 1933) argued that categories were composed of essence and accident. The essence of the category was defined as that which *is* the category—as the attribute(s) that all category members possess. Accident, on the other hand, was defined as those attributes that are possessed by some, but not all, of the category members. The idea of essence is very similar, although not identical, to the idea of a combination of criterial attributes.

Several educational psychologists (e.g., Klausmeier, 1976a, 1976b; Markle, 1975) have argued that categories are defined by criterial attributes. According to these researchers, the goal of category concept instruction should be to teach children these criterial attribute definitions and how to apply them to determine the status of potential category members.

Some of the fairly recent theories of category structure in both linguistics and anthropology have included the idea of fixed boundaries, with all category members having full and equal status. In addition, the goal of these theories has been to describe the categories studied using the minimum number of attributes necessary to distinguish a particular category from other similar categories. The most obvious examples of these theories are distinctive feature theory (e.g., Chomsky & Halle, 1968; Katz & Fodor, 1963;

Katz & Postal, 1964) within linguistics and componential analysis (cf. Tyler, 1969) within anthropology.

Finally, the argument that the division of the world into categories is arbitrarily based has been made by Leach (1964), an anthropologist. And the "world" that the educational psychologist Vygotsky (1962) devised in order to study categorization was constructed as a total set.

The Research Questioning Traditional Theory

Just as the proponents of the traditional theory of categorization represent many different disciplines, so the researchers whose work points to problems with this theory also represent diverse fields. The following review of research will therefore be multidisciplinary.

The tenets of the version of traditional theory that I have presented are the following:

1. A category is defined by a set of criterial attributes.
2. This set should be the smallest one that will serve to differentiate the category under consideration from other categories.
3. Category membership is full and equal for all objects that meet the category definition.
4. The boundaries of a cateogry are absolute.
5. The world of objects is constructed as a total set.

The research contradicting each of these tenets will be described in order, except that tenet (2) will be considered before tenet (1). Note that the five tenets are not necessarily dependent on one another and, thus, invalidation of any given one would not invalidate the theory; rather, such invalidation would only require modification of the theory.

The research aimed at contradicting the tenet that a category should be defined by the smallest possible set of criterial attributes has focused primarily on the nonpsychological reality of defining a category in this manner. Smoke (1932) argued that the more one learns about a category, the richer one's knowledge of that category becomes. Therefore, one's definition should also become richer—which is contradictory to using the smallest possible number of attributes to define a category. Within linguistics, it has been pointed out (Grimes, personal communication, 1969) that, although it is possible to differentiate all English phonemes from one another without using the feature "nasal," the resulting definitions of nasal phonemes do not seem intuitively reasonable. Thus, although the feature "nasal" is redundant, it seems to be psychologically necessary to a reasonable definition of nasal phonemes. Finally, Bolinger (1965) has carried the argument even further, saying that these definitions are not only psychologically unrealistic, but that they are also logically impossible to make, because in the real world it is impossible to determine whether or not any given attribute is criterial for a given category.

Bolinger's work points out one of the arguments against categories being defined by criterial attributes—the apparent impossibility (in the real world, as opposed to in the laboratory) of determining whether or not any given attribute is criterial for any given category. The argument has also been advanced that for some categories, there is no criterial attribute that is common to all category members. Thus, Smoke has argued that "common elements" in Hull's (1920) sense are probably a fiction. Wittgenstein (1953) has claimed that categories may be structured as "family resemblances." According to Wittgenstein, a family resemblance occurs when members of a category are related by a series of overlapping attributes (e.g., member 1: *ab;* member 2: *bc;* member 3: *cd*) but do not all share a criterial attribute. Recently, Rosch and Mervis (1975) have shown that many common superordinate categories (e.g., furniture) are indeed structured as family resemblances.

The tenet that all category members are full and equal has been attacked by a number of researchers who have shown that people do not treat (or respond to) all category members in the same manner. Lakoff (1972) has shown that any given linguistic "hedge" is applicable to some, but not all, category members. Thus, it is reasonable to say "A penguin is *technically* a bird," but it is not reasonable to say "A robin is *technically* a bird." Similarly, although it makes sense to say "A robin is a bird *par excellence,*" it does not make sense to say "A penguin is a bird *par excellence.*" Rosch (1973a) studied subjects' responses to sentences of the type *An X is a Y* (e.g., *An apple is a fruit*). She found that although adult subjects tended to be equally accurate for all category members tested, the subjects consistently responded faster when asked about certain exemplars than when asked about others. Wertheimer (1950) has argued that certain numbers function as "reference points" for the entire number system. Thus, people consider it reasonable to say "97 is nearly 100," but not reasonable to say "100 is nearly 103," even though the difference between the two numbers is the same in both cases. Rosch (personal communication, 1973b) has shown that even for the types of categories typically used in a traditional-theory experiment, subjects will often consider one category member to be "better" than the others. Thus, if the category to be learned is "red plus square" and the members of this category are of various sizes, subjects find it reasonable to pick a "most representative" member—usually the middle (mean)-sized one.

There have been a number of demonstrations that category boundaries are not absolute. Berlin and Kay (1969) have shown that the boundaries of color categories are extremely variable. Thus, a speaker of Hebrew would not agree with a speaker of English concerning the boundaries of the category "red" ("adom" in Hebrew). But the disagreement is not limited to speakers of different languages. Two speakers of English would probably disagree concerning the boundaries of "red." And the same person, queried on separate occasions, is like to disagree with himself or herself. All of these subjects, however, would probably pick the same color red as most representative of the category. Thus, people agree on best examples but not on boundaries. Rosch and Mervis have demonstrated this same phenomenon—that people agree on best examples but disagree on boundaries—for both superordinate semantic categories such as furniture or animal (Rosch, 1975a; Mervis, 1978) and for lower level semantic categories such as chair (Rosch & Mervis, 1975). Labov (1973) has shown that the boundaries of the category "cup" vary not only from person to person but also from situation to situation. For example, whether or not a thing is a cup depends partly on what is inside the thing.

The remaining tenet, that the world of objects is structured as a total set, has been contradicted by Garner (1974), who has argued that the world of objects is constructed as a subset. By "subset," Garner means that all possible attribute combinations are not equally likely. Instead, an attribute tends to co-occur only with a limited set of other attributes. Often the presence of a few of these correlated attributes is enough to predict almost perfectly the presence of the rest of the correlated cluster. Rosch and Mervis (Rosch, Mervis, Gray, Johnson, & Boyes-Braem, 1976) have provided several empirical examples of this subset phenomenon—for example, that creatures with feathers are very likely to have wings, to have beaks, to have hollow bones, to lay eggs, and to be able to fly, whereas creatures who have fur are very likely *not* to have feathers, wings, beaks, or hollow bones, are likely not to lay eggs, and are likely not to be able to fly. Instead, these creatures with fur are likely to have either four legs or else two legs and two arms, to have a mouth rather than a beak, to have solid bones, to bear their young alive,and to be able to suckle their young. All these researchers have argued that the subset structure of the world provides reasonable bases for dividing objects into categories and that, therefore, these divisions are nonarbitrary.

Thus, four of the five tenets of the traditional theory have been empirically contradicted. The remaining tenet, that a category is defined by criterial attributes, can never be empirically contradicted. I have, however, cited research that offers alternatives to criterial attribute definitions. There are three more problems—problems of omission—with the theory that should be mentioned. The first (orginally pointed out by Smoke, 1932) is that the definitions provided do not include relational information. Thus, a traditional criterial attribute definition of chair might be "four legs plus seat plus back." This definition does not provide any information about how to put these attributes together to form a chair. A more adequate definition (according to Smoke) would be something like "four legs forming the vertical sides of a rectangular solid, with a seat attached perpendicular to the legs and at their top, and a back attached perpendicular to the seat and at its rear."

The second problem has to do with function. In addition to describing a category in terms of perceptual attributes, it is possible to describe it in terms of functional attributes—what the category can be used for, and (for animate categories) what the category can do. Smoke has again pointed out that the traditional theory has not considered the role function plays in determining categorization; in fact, the traditional theory experiments have almost always used "functionless" categories. Because real-world categories almost always have both form and function, it seems incumbent upon a categorization theory to consider both, at least until one might be shown to be irrelevant.

The third problem has to do with levels of categorization. Because, according to the traditional theory, category divisions are arbitrary, the theory does not discuss the different levels of generality (e.g., rocking chair vs. chair vs. furniture) at which objects may be categorized. All these levels are implicitly treated as the same; no one level is more reasonable than another. Recently, however, arguments have been advanced that these levels are not equivalent and that categorization at one (the basic) level is more fundamental than categorization at any other level. Thus, Berlin, Breedlove, and Raven (1973) have argued that the plant world can be categorized at six different levels of generality but that one of these levels is more basic than the others. They have shown that this "basic" (in their term, "generic") level is the first level of categorization to be labeled in the botanical system when a language is acquiring botanical nomenclature. The level is also the most general one at which an object can be classified on a Gestalt basis, rather than by a feature analysis (Hunn, 1975). Rosch and Mervis (Rosch et al., 1976) have advanced a similar argument for both biological and nonbiological categories. They have claimed that the basic level of categorization is the one at which the division of objects into categories best corresponds to the perceived correlated attribute structure of the objects in the world. This basic level has been shown to be the most general level for which people are able to list large numbers of attributes that (most) category members share, for which people are able to form a concrete image, and for which people use the same motor programs to interact with (most) category members. The argument that one level of categorization is more fundamental than the other levels will be discussed further in the next part of this section.

The Best-Example Theory

Although the traditional theory of categorization accounts well for the data of many laboratory categorization studies, it is unable to account for the data from more ecological studies. The particular problems and omissions of traditional theory were described in the previous section. Some of these criticisms were raised many years ago (e.g., Smoke, 1932; Wittgenstein, 1953), before the advent of ecological categorization research. However, although present in the literature, these criticisms went unnoticed until very recently. For example, Smoke, who argued against many of the tenets of the traditional theory and who pointed out two of the major omissions of the theory, is frequently cited (e.g., Anglin, 1977) as a major proponent of that theory. Thus, although some of the bases for best-example theory were discussed many years ago, the theory itself is primarily a very new one. It was developed in response to the results from the large number of ecological studies of categorization done starting in the late 1960s; much of this research was generated by the intuitions and introspections of the researchers concerning how real-world categories really are structured.

According to the best-example theory, categories are not necessarily delineated by a criterial attribute—that is, an attribute shared by all category members but not by any nonmember. In fact, members of a category need not share even a single relevant attribute (e.g., an attribute more specific than animate–inanimate)—let alone one that all nonmembers do not possess. Instead, category members may be related by overlapping series of attributes—the "family resemblance" described in the previous subsection. It should be noted that, although there is often no attribute shared by all category members, there may be several attributes shared by the best examples (see later) of a category. For example, the best examples of the category furniture—chairs, (dining) tables, and couches—all have rigid frames (assuming for the moment that beanbag chairs are not really chairs), all serve as support for objects (either people or things), and all are fairly large. Thus, if one considers only the best examples of the category, it may appear as though at least one attribute (whether criterial or not) is shared by all category members. Perhaps this accounts for the ease with which criterial attribute delineations of categories have often been accepted. However, when one begins to consider the poorer examples, exceptions to each of the attributes shared by the good examples will almost always be found. Thus, returning to the furniture example, such items as floor pillows and rugs do not have rigid frames. Things like lamps do not serve as support for other objects, and things like stacking tables, vases, and many types of floor pillows are quite small.

As alluded to in the previous paragraph, proponents of the best-example theory do not agree that all category members are equal. Some of the members are more representative (more "typical") of their category than are others. For example, an apple is more typical of "fruit" than is a cantalope. Similarly, a "typical" overstuffed chair is more representative of the category "chair" than is a swivel chair. The most typical members of a category form its core (cluster of best examples). The category then radiates out from this center toward poorer and poorer examples of the category. (The core of a category has often been referred to as the *prototype*. It should be noted that *prototype* has been used in the literature in two different ways: as the best-example [real] object(s) of a category and as an idealized [nonreal] best example. In the present chapter, the term will be avoided in order to prevent confusion.)

Several principles have been proposed (e.g., Rosch, 1975b; Rosch & Mervis, 1975) to account for the internal structure of a category—that is, to account for why certain members are "better" (more typical of the category) than are others. Two of the most important are the principles of family resemblance and of contrast set. According to the family resemblance principle, the better examples are those that have larger numbers of attributes that are widely shared with other category members. These attributes may describe parts of the object, what the object does, what it is used for, and so on. Correspondingly, the poorer category members are those that have fewer attributes shared with other category members. For example, in the (*ab, bc, cd*) family resemblance structure mentioned previously, the second member would be considered to be better than either the first or the third. This is because the second shares one attribute with each of the other two category members, whereas the first and the third share one attribute with the second member but also possess an attribute that is not shared by either of the other category members.

According to the contrast set principle, the good examples of a category are those that have few (if any) attributes that are commonly present in members of other similar categories. In other words, categories form in such a manner as to make their cores as different as possible from each other. The family resemblance principle and the contrast set principle may be combined to make predictions about which category members are most likely to be the best examples—those that have many of the attributes that are shared with many other category members while at the same time having very few attributes that are shared with members of other related categories. (In the discussion so far, it has been assumed that all attributes are equally important. This assumption may often be incorrect. The theory discusses the differential importance of attributes in terms of their relative salience; the family resemblance and contrast set principles may easily be modified to take into account the differences in relative salience among attributes.)

The boundaries of a category are fuzzy, rather than clear-cut. This follows from the fact that category membership is not determined by criterial attributes. Poor examples of related categories may have many attributes in common. The number and salience of these attributes will vary along a continuum so that there is no obvious break between the categories. Similarly, because degree of similarity to the category core is also a continuum, there is no straightforward answer to the question of how dissimilar from the category's core an object must be before being excluded from the category. For these two reasons, the assignments of poor examples to categories will vary from person to person and will vary for a given person on different occasions.

Several methods for determining the cut-off for category membership might be used by a person. For example, the cut-off might be determined by use of a feature list expressing degree of family resemblance to the category, by comparison to an (idealized) "image" of the category, or by comparison to a few of the members of the category core. The theory does not at present specify which of these (or other) processes is used (but see the next section for constraints concerning the processes used by young children) or whether different processes might be used, depending on the circumstances.

Because the real world is a subset rather than a total set, the division of objects into categories is determined by the attribute structure (as determined by the perceiver) of the world. All possible combinations of attribute values are *not* equally likely to occur. Certain combinations are very likely to occur, whereas certain others are very unlikely to occur or never do occur. As mentioned in the previous subsection, creatures with feathers are very likely to also have wings, beaks, and hollow bones, and to be able to fly. Creatures that have fur are very like *not* to have wings, beaks, or hollow bones, and *not* to be able to fly (the bat is an exception). They *are* likely to have either four legs or two arms and two legs, to have a mouth (rather than a beak), to bear their young alive, and to be able to suckle their young. The division of these two types of objects into categories would be made by using each of the two obviously different attribute clusters (sets of correlated attributes) as the basis for one category. Thus, the decision of how to categorize these objects would not be arbitrary but, rather, would be determined by natural breaks between these clusters. In learning to categorize, the child's task would be to notice and utilize these natural breaks; presumably a much simpler task than learning a set of arbitrarily determined categories.

Although the natural breaks between correlated attribute structures may be perfect or almost perfect, the breaks between the actual categories will not be perfect (at least for related categories) once all (or most) of the exemplars in each category are considered. That is, although the correlated attribute clusters of the categories will often not overlap, the sets consisting of all attributes possessed by at least one category member will almost certainly overlap. (Note that if these sets did not overlap, it would be possible to define categories by criterial attributes.) The best exemplars of a category are those whose attribute structures most closely correspond to those of the correlated attribute structure of the category (see the family resemblance principle), which at the same time correspond very poorly (or not at all) to the correlated attribute structure of other related categories (see the contrast set principle). The poorest exemplars of a category are those whose attribute structures least correspond to those of the correlated attribute structure of the category; their attribute structures may also be similar to (may overlap) those of poor exemplars of related categories. Thus, the natural breaks between the two categories will appear most perfect when considering good examples of each category and least perfect when considering certain poor examples of related categories.

An object may be categorized at each of several different levels. These levels form a category hierarchy, or taxonomy. Categories at lower levels in a taxonomy are based on specific similarities; members of these categories tend to share many attributes in common and tend to look at least somewhat similar to each other. Categories at higher levels in a taxonomy are formed by combining lower level categories based on more general similarities. These higher level categories are formed based on the few attributes that all (or most) of the subsumed categories share. For example, members of the lower level category "bus" share many common attributes—overall shape, holds lots of people, has an engine, many wheels, gas and brake pedals, a steering wheel, etc. In addition, buses can be used to take people or things to places. Members of the lower level category "bicycle" share many attributes in common—overall shape, holds one or two people, moves by people power (rather than gas or diesel power), has two wheels, and so on. In addition, bicycles can be used to take people or things to places. The higher level category "vehicle" combines lower level categories such as buses and bicycles by ignoring the differences between the categories and concentrating on the similarity—"takes people or things to places."

Ethnobotanists (e.g., Berlin et al., 1973) have described six levels of categories within botanical hierarchies. These levels are best illustrated with an example. A cutleaf sumac tree (varietal level) is a type of staghorn sumac tree (specific level), which in turn is a type of sumac tree (generic level). A sumac tree is a type of leaf-bearing tree (intermediate level), which is a type of tree (life-form level), which is a type of plant (unique beginner). The five levels other than the intermediate one are well-documented in the ethnobotanical literature. Intermediate categories are relatively rare, may occur between any pair of the other five levels (Dougherty, 1978), and usually do not have labels (although the taxonomy that I have described includes an intermediate-level taxonomy to which English speakers have assigned a name). Although the maximum number of levels in an ethnobotanical hierarchy is six, many types of plants are members of shorter hierarchies. For example, bamboo (generic) is not subsumed under any intermediate or life-form categories. It is very rare for the varietal level to be named unless the particular type of plant is culturally significant.

Although the same six-level hierarchies are theoretically possible for other categories of concrete objects, their use is uncommon. In talking about concrete objects, psychologists tend to consider only three levels: subordinate (corresponding to specific), basic (corresponding to generic), and superordinate (corresponding roughly to life form). Thus, a rocking chair (subordinate) is a kind of chair (basic), which is a kind of furniture (superordinate).

Both psychologists working within the best-example theory (in considering a three-level hierarchy) and ethnobotanists (in considering a six-level hierarchy) have argued that there is a "basic" level of categorization—a level that is more fundamental than the remaining levels.

Rosch et al. (1976) have suggested that the principle underlying the concept of basic level is that categories at this level should provide a person as much information as possible, while allowing him to use as little cognitive effort as possible. That is, on the one hand, it is important for a person to be able to predict as many additional properties of an object as possible, based on knowledge of only one of its properties (often, the important property of the category name). This situation would lead to the formation of large numbers of categories, with very fine discriminations among categories. However, it is also important for a person to reduce the infinite differences among stimuli to cognitively and behaviorally usable proportions. This requirement means that it is important not to make finer discriminations than those necessary for a particular purpose. The combination of these two rules leads to a definition of the basic level as the most inclusive level at which categories delineate significant real-world correlational structures (attribute clusters).

Attribute clusters can occur at any level within a hierarchy. The clusters that occur at the highest levels consist of only a few attributes, whereas the clusters that occur at the lowest levels include a large number of attributes. Empirically (Rosch et al., 1976), if one starts at the most general level of a hierarchy and descends the hierarchy level by level, one finds a level at which the number of attributes in the correlated cluster increases dramatically, as compared to the next higher level. As one descends the hierarchy further, the number of attributes added to the cluster increases very slowly.

One can consider the derivation of the basic level in terms of the total category cue validity of categories at each of these levels. The total category cue validity has been defined as the sum of the cue validities (the conditional probabilities of an object being in the given category, based on the presence of a certain attribute), summed across each of the attributes of the category. Note that category cue validity is not a probability. (For further discussion of category cue validity, see Rosch & Mervis, 1975, or Rosch et al., 1976.) At the highest levels in a hierarchy, the cue validities of the categories are low, because members of these categories share very few attributes relative to the number of attributes shared by members of categories at lower levels. At the basic level (usually one of the middle levels) the cue validities of the categories are high, because members of these categories share relatively large numbers of attributes that are not generally shared by other basic (middle) level categories. At the lower levels, cue validities are low, because many of the attributes shared by members of a subordinate category are also shared by members of other subordinate categories subsumed under the same basic level category. The level at which categories have the highest cue validities is by definition the level at which categories are most differentiated from each other. This level corresponds both theoretically and empirically to the most general level at which categories look similar to one another and where a person uses similar motor programs for interacting with category members. Rosch et al. argue that this fundamental level of categorization is the basic (middle) level. Berlin et al. (1973) argue that this level is the generic level.

Although the basic level of psychologists and the generic level of ethnobotanists generally refer to the same category (e.g., chair), there are exceptions. Thus, for example, psychology experiments with Americans have yielded "tree" as a basic level term. As mentioned previously, however, ethnobotanists generally consider "tree" a life-form term, but consider types of trees (e.g., birch, sumac) to be generic (basic) terms. Ethnobotanists usually study the plant taxonomies of cultures for whom the plant world is culturally significant; it is based on results from such cultures that "tree" is assumed to be a life-form term whereas "sumac" is a generic term. However, when ethnobotanists later studied Americans, results indicated that "tree" is a generic term. Thus, the results of both the psychologists and the ethnobotanists agree, once they are considering the same population.

It is important to note (as Dougherty, 1978, has done) that the basic level must be relative rather than fixed. Although the basic level is indeed the level described by the two principles just given, and by Hunn's Gestalt categorization, the application of these principles is dependent on which attributes of the objects are noticed. In cultures in which trees are important (for something other than shade), people are likely to pay more attention to specific types of trees and therefore to notice similarities within a type and differences across types. For these people, there will be large clusters of correlated attributes and the highest category cue validities at the "birch" level. Different types of trees will be categorized at the Gestalt level. For cultures in which trees are not important, people are not likely to pay attention to specific types. Rather, people will compare trees to shrubs, grasses, and so on. Large clusters of correlated attributes and the highest category cue validities will occur at the "tree" level. "Tree" will be categorized at the Gestalt level, but different types of trees will have to be identified by specific features, if indeed they can be identified at all.

Thus, which level in a hierarchy is basic is determined not simply by the objectively available attribute structure of the world but by the subset of that structure that people actually notice. Although "experts" may have a basic level subordinate to the basic level of the population-at-large for their particular area of expertise, the basic level is generally the same level for all members of a given population. Although it may vary across populations, the principles used to determine the basic level and the characteristics of basic level categories are expected to be universal.

The view of best-example theory I have presented is primarily the one that Rosch and Mervis have developed. As with the traditional theory, best-example theory is not limited to psychology. Parts of the theory are included in theories of categorization in linguistics, and especially in anthropology. These parts have already been discussed, in this subsection and in the previous one, and so are not described further here.

THE DEVELOPMENT OF CATEGORIZATION

Category development is not a particularly new area of research. Over the past 40 years or so, there have been several studies that have compared adult and child categorizations. Almost all of these studies considered only superordinate categories, and almost all have found differences in categorization between children and adults. The general conclusion was simply that children categorize differently from adults. In the absence of a theory of categorization, or in the presence of only the traditional theory, this conclusion is not surprising.

A theory of categorization is not only necessary to understanding the results of previous studies, however. The theory also serves to make predictions and to point out questions that are worthwhile to investigate. In this section, I use best-example theory to predict how categorization ability might develop and to suggest specific areas of category development that need to be investigated. When relevant, I reinterpret the results of previous studies in terms of how their results fit with predictions made by best-example theory. It is important to keep in mind that, while we are testing the predictions of best-example theory with regard to development, we are testing the validity of the theory itself. An adequate theory of categorization should be able to explain category development as well as category structure and adult categorization.

The Role of Basic Level Categories in Development

According to best-example theory, there exists a basic level categorization in which categories "make sense." That is, there exists a basic level that is the most general level at which categories are formed according to large, naturally occurring attribute clusters. Categories at this level are more differentiated from each other than are categories at any other level. Thus, basic level categories are the most obvious way of dividing the world.

Given the special status of basic level categories in categorization in general, one would predict that basic level categories would be the easiest and also the most useful ones for children to learn. Thus, one would predict that children would learn to name objects at the basic level before learning to name them at either the subordinate or superordinate levels, and that children would be able to sort objects into basic level categories before they could sort them into subordinate or superordinate level categories. Even after they learn superordinate and subordinate level names for objects, children should prefer to name the objects with basic level terms. Finally, when asked specifically to name objects for their children, parents should be more likely to use basic level names than names at other levels.

Several of these predictions have recently been tested empirically. The hierarchical level of a child's initial naming of objects has been studied by both psychologists and anthropologists. Rosch et al. (1976) analyzed Brown's (n.d.) transcripts of Sarah's early speech. They found that almost all of the object names that Sarah used were basic level terms. This was true even though her mother tended to use certain superordinate terms (such as *toy* and *clothes*). Stross (1973) investigated the acquisition of ethnobotanical nomenclature by Tzeltal Mayan children and found that the typical Tzeltal child began to acquire botanical terminology by learning basic level names for culturally significant plants. (Basic level in Tzeltal is equivalent to subordinate level in English, for the plant taxonomy; see the discussion in the previous section.) Dougherty (1978) investigated the acquisition of ethnobotanical nomenclature by American children. Her subjects also first learned to name plants at the basic level (equivalent to the superordinate level in Tzeltal, for the plant taxonomy).

Rosch and Mervis (1977; Rosch et al., 1976) tested the prediction that children would be able to divide objects into basic level categories before being able to divide them into superordinate levels categories by asking children to put together the two pictures (out of three) that "go together, that are the same kind of thing." The pair that was the "same kind of thing" consisted either of two pictures of objects from different subordinate categories but the same basic level category (e.g., sports car, large 4-door sedan), or of two pictures of objects from different basic level categories but the same superordinate category (e.g., car, train). Both the 3-year olds and the 4-year-olds were able to correctly sort the basic level sets; however, only the 4-year-olds were able to correctly sort the superordinate level sets. (Given the previously available data, one might be surprised that the 4-year-olds were able to correctly sort the superordinate level sets; reasons for the discrepancy in results will be discussed in the next subsection.) This experiment has not yet been tried using pictures of objects from the same subordinate level category. In order to be certain that the middle level is the easiest level for a child to sort at, one would want to test children using sets of pictures in which two were from the same subordinate category and one was from a different subordinate category of the same basic level category, in addition to the sets described previously. If the basic level is more fundamental than the subordinate level, then children should at some point be able to sort taxonomically by basic level categories but be unable to sort taxonomically by subordinate categories. Such sets were not included in the experiment just described because the original purpose of the experiment was simply to show that preschoolers were capable of sorting objects taxonomically at all. (Previous studies [e.g., Goldman & Levine, 1963; Olver & Hornsby, 1966] tended to conclude that young children were incapable of sorting objects taxonomically; see the next part of this section.)

In order to determine how young children label pictures, Mervis (reported in Rosch et al., 1976) asked preschoolers to name a variety of pictures. Each picture could theoretically be named at either the subordinate, basic, or superordinate level; however, all the labels given by the children (whether correct or incorrect) were at the basic level. Posttest questioning indicated that the child usually knew appropriate superordinate labels for the pictures, although they often did not know the appropriate subordinate level names. Thus, the children usually knew at least two appropriate labels for each picture but always chose to use the basic level name.

In order to determine how parents name pictures for their children, Anglin (1977) asked parents to name a wide variety of pictures as though they were naming them for their children. He found that nearly all the names given were at the basic level.

Thus, basic level categories do play a special role in category development, as predicted by the best-example theory. The data so far, however, have not completely ruled out the (unlikely) possibility that the basic level plays a special role only because parents choose to name objects at this level (that is, because the parents recognize the basic level as something special), rather than because the child naturally divides objects into basic level categories as opposed to categories at another level of abstraction. In order to be certain that young children would naturally divide objects into basic level categories, there is an obvious (but difficult) experiment to perform. That is, have children learn to categorize "artificial" objects that have been patterned after naturally occurring categories into either subordinate, basic, or superordinate level categories. If the basic level is really the most natural one, children will find it easier to learn basic level categories than to learn categories at either of the other two levels.

The Structure of Children's Concrete Object Categories

In this subsection, three issues are discussed. The first concerns whether young children (usually interpreted as children younger than about 8 years) are able to form taxonomic categories. The second deals with the relationship between the child's structure and the adult's structure for any given category. The third concerns the relationship between the typicality of the first exemplar that a child learns is a member of a given category and the concordance of the child's early category structure with that of the adult. Within the framework of the third question, the issue of how young children represent categories is briefly considered.

The question of whether young children are able to form taxonomic categories has interested psychologists for more than 4 decades. Until recently, all the evidence concerning the question was obtained from either picture or object sorting tasks, and all the commonly cited studies concluded that the answer was either "no" or "hardly ever." Thus, Thompson (1941), Goldman and Levine (1963), Inhelder and Piaget (1964), and Olver and Hornsby (1966) all found that children formed groups to correspond to concrete situations (e.g., bunny and carrot go together—bunnies eat carrots) rather than to taxonomic categories (e.g., bunny and cow go together—they are both animals). Annett (1959) found that young children sometimes formed taxonomic categories but that these categories were almost never exhaustive (for example, the child might put tree and flower together, but not include apple and toadstool).

While accepting these sorting studies as valid measures of children's performance abilities concerning the formation of taxonomic categories, a few researchers have recently argued that the competence to form taxonomic categories is present in even very young children. Goldberg, Perlmutter, and Myers (1974) found that 2-year-olds show better recall for short lists if the words are members of the same superordinate category than if they are chosen from unrelated categories. Mansfield (1977) found that when children listened to a sentence and then were asked whether a given word had been included in the sentence, they were more likely to be confused if the distractor word was a superordinate of one of the words in the sentence than if the distractor bore a part–whole relationship to one of the words. Confusion was measured both by length of response time and by number of errors.

The predictions of best-example theory go beyond the competence argument just advanced. Best-example theory predicts that young children should also show performance abilities to form taxonomic categories, at least at the basic level. This is because basic level categories are considered to be formed to best correspond to the correlated attribute structure of the world (to have the highest category cue-validity), and young children are presumed to notice and to use this structure as a natural basis for grouping objects together.

There have been only two sorting studies done in which the pictures used allowed for the formation of basic level categories. Rosch and Mervis (1977; Rosch et al., 1976) showed that children as young as 3-years-old (the youngest age tested) were able to group together items from the same basic level category. In this study, children were given sets of three pictures and were asked to put together the ones that were "the same kind of thing." Greenfield, Reich, and Olver (1966) reported an experiment in which Eskimo children (age unspecified) were given a set of 44 animal pictures and asked to put together "those that go together." The children tended to divide the pictures perfectly into basic level categories (e.g., seals, chickens, sheep, dogs, whales) rather than dividing them into groups according to concrete situations (e.g., putting a whale and a seal together because both are found in the water). Unfortunately, this study is never mentioned when the issue of children's ability to form taxonomic categories is discussed. The available evidence indicates clearly that very young children are able to sort taxonomically according to basic level categories.

Best-example theory does not predict an exact age at which children should be able to group objects taxonomically into superordinate categories. The theory does predict, however, that certain sets of stimuli should be easier to sort taxonomically than other sets. In particular, sets should be easier to sort taxonomically if all the stimuli are of typical exemplars of their category than if they are all of atypical exemplars, or if some are of typical exemplars and some are of atypical ones. The reason for this prediction is simple and is discussed further in the next part of this section. Basically, there are many categories for which young children agree that the good exemplars are category members but do not agree that the poor exemplars are category members. Presumably, children can only be expected to sort taxonomically as adults do if the children consider all the presented objects to fit into the same categories to which adults assign them.

Annett (1959) is the only author who has described any of the cases in which children assigned objects to taxonomic categories but left out some of the purported members. For all the cases described, the children included the typical category members and excluded the atypical ones.

Mervis and Judd (unpublished manuscript) have explicitly tested the prediction that good-exemplar sets should be easier to sort taxonomically than mixed-exemplar sets. The researchers found that, as predicted, first-graders were much more likely to sort the good-example sets taxonomically than to sort the mixed-exemplar sets taxonomically.

Although the next point to be made is important, it is not directly relevant to best-example theory; rather, it is relevant to methodological issues. It turns out that 4-year-olds are the youngest children who will consistently sort pictures taxonomically into superordinate categories (Rosch et al., 1976). These positive results were obtained using oddity problems and asking the children to put together the ones that were "the same kind of thing"—a direct request for taxonomic groupings. The results of this study are in conflict with the results of the studies discussed at the beginning of the section. The reasons for the conflict are obvious: Previous studies used mixed-exemplar sets, used large numbers of stimuli (at least 16, and usually more than twice that many), and used ambiguous directions—put together the ones that "go together." Thus, the task that the children were asked to perform was unnecessarily difficult. It appears that young children are able to group taxonomically into superordinate categories (and into basic level categories at an even younger age) if one designs a fair test—that is, if one uses an optimally designed set of stimuli and unambiguously worded directions.

The next issue to be considered concerns the relationship between the child's category structure and the adult's category structure, for a given category. Because of space limitations, I discuss only research concerned with children who were at least 5 years old. [There are basically three theories concerning the category structures of younger children—see Clark, 1973; Nelson, 1974a; Bowerman, 1978. Bowerman's theory might be considered a type of best-example theory.]

There are four likely relationships between the child's and the adult's category structures. First, the category structures could be the same. Second, the child might undergeneralize the category; that is, he might exclude some exemplars that almost all (or all) adults include. Third, the child might overgeneralize the category; that is, he might include all the exemplars adults include, plus some additional items that adults hardly ever (or never) include. Fourth, the child's category might overlap the adult's; that is, the child might leave out some exemplars that adults almost always include and include some exemplars that adults almost always exclude. If the child's category structure is related to the adult's by either undergeneralization or overlap, than the items that children exclude might be typical exemplars, middling exemplars, or atypical exemplars of the given (adult) category. In the cases of overgeneralization or overlap, the "additional" items might similarly be either typical, middling, or atypical exemplars of their "correct" (according to adults) category.

Best-example theory does not predict which of the four possible relationships will hold between children's and adults' structures for any given category. The theory does predict, however, that the child's structure will usually be quite similar to the adult's structure (for exceptions, see the next part of this section). In particular, both adults and children should include the typical exemplars in their category structures, because these exemplars are both the most representative of their own category and the least similar (in general) to members of related categories. Disagreements should be focused on the poor exemplars, which are least representative of their own category and often are similar to poor exemplars of other related categories. In the case of undergeneralization, the children should exclude poor examples of the category; in the case of overgeneralization, the children should include poor exemplars of related categories; if the overgeneralization is extreme, the children may include both poor and good exemplars of very related categories. The familiarity of an item should be irrelevant to its correct classification.

These predictions have been directly addressed in only three studies (plus one to be described in the last part of this section); however, the results of a few other studies may be reexamined to determine how well their data accord with these predictions.

Mervis, Catlin, and Rosch (1975) investigated the structure of the eight basic chromatic color categories (delineated by Berlin and Kay, 1969) for 5-year-olds, 8-year-olds, and adults. They found that, for seven of the eight color categories, all three age groups chose the same color chip (out of 320 chips representing the entire spectrum) as the "best example" of the category. For the remaining category, both groups of children chose the same color chip; adults chose an almost identical one. However, the three groups disagreed concerning the boundaries of the categories. In particular, the 5-year-olds overgeneralized most of the color categories along the hue dimension while undergeneralizing along the brightness and saturation dimensions as compared to the adults. Even within an age group, there were disagreements concerning the poorer exemplars, although these disagreements were generally minor compared to those between age groups. When the children overgeneralized a color category, the overgeneralized chips were either poor members of an adjacent (in spectral terms) color category or else were not considered to be members of any category at all. Similarly, whenever the children undergeneralized a color category, the colors that were excluded were poor exemplars by adult standards. When age group members disagreed among themselves, the colors in question were almost always poor members of either the given category or an adjacent category. Thus, the data fit the predictions of best-example theory perfectly.

Anglin (1977) examined the structure of children's and adults' categories, for several superordinate categories, by asking subjects to indicate whether or not a given picture belonged to the category in question. He attempted to systematically vary familiarity and typicality of exemplars in order to find out which was more important in determining children's category judgments. Anglin found that the more typical an item was of its category, the more likely a child was to correctly classify it. Familiarity was irrelevant. Again, children often disagreed with adults concerning the poorer exemplars of the categories, and subjects within a single age group often disagreed among themselves concerning the poor exemplars. The results of this study, including the irrelevance of familiarity, are again those predicted by best-example theory. Unfortunately, Anglin has not adequately proven that familiarity is irrelevant. In order to consider an item "unfamiliar" to a child, two things are necessary. First, the item should be one that the child has not seen before. Second, the child should realize that he or she does not know what the item is and should therefore refuse to assign it to a basic level category. Anglin's stimuli met the first criterion but not the second. Most of the children willingly labeled the "unfamiliar" items with "familiar" names. For example, the wombat was frequently labeled "bear." To the extent that the child believed the wombat was a bear, the wombat must be considered familiar rather than unfamiliar to the child. To determine whether familiarity is irrelevant, Anglin's experiment must be repeated using exemplars that children will not assign (either correctly or incorrectly) to any basic level category.

Rosch (1973b) examined children's and adults' category structures using a completely different procedure—that of sentence verification. Subjects were asked to indicate the truth of sentences of the *An X is a Y* type (e.g., *An apple is a fruit*). The typicality of the X's was varied systematically. Rosch found that for correct responses, both adults and children responded more rapidly to sentences in which X was a typical exemplar than in which X was a poor exemplar. Children also made far more errors when X was a poor exemplar than when X was a typical exemplar. Thus, children appear to learn the good exemplars of a category before learning the poor exemplars.

The results of several studies that did not directly address the predictions of best-example theory may be reinterpreted in light of the theory. Two of these studies utilized sorting paradigms, whereas the others asked children to produce exemplars of various categories. The sorting studies are considered first. Saltz, Soller, and Siegel (1972) asked children to pick out all the exemplars of a given category from a large deck of pictures. After the child made his choices, the pictures were returned to the deck and the task repeated. This process was continued until the child had chosen exemplars for six superordinate categories. In analysing their results, the authors considered "core" members (those chosen by 75% of the children, combined across age groups) separately from noncore members. They found that all the core members that were included by the youngest group (5-6-year-olds) were also included by the older groups (8-9-year-olds and 11-12-year-olds). The older children added items to the younger children's core but did not subtract any. Similarly, the older groups included more noncore members than did the youngest group. The authors present a brief item analysis; from this analysis it appears that the "core" members are in fact the most typical members, according to goodness-of-example norms. It also appears that the younger children were undergeneralizing the categories relative to the older children, and that the undergeneralizing was confined primarily to poorer exemplars.

Neimark (1974) replicated this study, using different age groups (second-graders, sixth-graders, and adults) and using only two of Saltz et al.'s (1972) six categories. The purpose of the replication was to show that young children do not necessarily undergeneralize categories relative to adults. Neimark found that her youngest subjects undergeneralized the category "food" and overgeneralized the category "clothing" relative to adults. In both cases, the children's categories were very similar to the adults'. Once again, the items in question appears to be poorer exemplars or else exemplars of related categories (e.g., the disagreement over clothing was whether or not to include jewelry).

Children's production of category members was examined by both Nelson (1974b) and Rosner and Hayes (1977). Nelson asked her subjects (5-year-olds and 8-year-olds) to list members of nine common superordinate categories. She found that, for all nine categories, the children tended to include those exemplars that adults would consider most typical. She found evidence for both undergeneralization and overgeneralization; in general, for any given category, all subjects tended to show the same response pattern—whether undergeneralization or overgeneralization—if their lists were different from those expected from an adult. For example, "furniture" was frequently overgeneralized to include anything that might be found in a house; "animal" was often undergeneralized to include primarily mammals—the best examples of animals, according to adult norms.

Rosner and Hayes (1977) followed the same procedure as Nelson, except that their subjects were 5-year-olds and 10-year-olds, and four categories rather than nine were used. The authors also asked adults to indicate whether they considered each item listed by the children to be a member of the relevant category. They found that on the average, over 90% of the adults agreed that the items listed were indeed category members. Despite this extremely high agreement figure, Rosner and Hayes argued that the younger children's categories included relatively fewer good exemplars of the categories and relatively more poor exemplars than did the older children's. This argument is, of course, in conflict with the predictions of best-example theory. However, the validity of the argument can be questioned on several grounds. First, for three of the four categories, over 85% of the exemplars provided by the younger children were considered to be category members by at least 92% of the adults. Second, the children were not given an opportunity to review and amend their lists. Younger children are more likely to get carried away with listing irrelevant items than are older children; however, even young children are capable of correctly "editing" their lists. If such editing had been permitted, the disparity between the two age groups might well have been eliminated. Finally, the adults seemed to have misinterpreted some of the items listed, and in particular, many of the items listed by the younger children. For example, many of the children said "beanbag," meaning "beanbag chair," when asked to list furniture. Most of the adults, however, did not interpret "beanbag" correctly and, therefore, said it was not furniture; however, almost all of the adults agreed that "beanbag chair" was furniture. Thus, the results of this study need to be carefully reanalyzed before the validity of the author's arguments can be determined. Tentatively, the results seem to support best-example theory in that most of the exemplars listed by the children are considered to be category members by most adults—thus, it appears that the adult and child categories are not very different.

The final issue to be considered is the effect of the typicality of the first-learned exemplar on the ease with which a child learns the correct category structure for a given category.

Best-example theory would predict that categories should be learned more easily and more accurately if the initial exemplar identified as a category member is an atypical exemplar than if the initial exemplar is an atypical member. This prediction is made because the typical exemplars are at the same time both most representative of their own category and least representative of other similar categories and, thus, these typical exemplars should provide an ideal basis for accurate generalization. The atypical exemplars, on the other hand, are not only the least representative members of their own category but are often similar to poor examples of related categories. Thus, it would be difficult to learn to correctly generalize a category if the initial exemplar was an atypical one. This prediction has been directly addressed in only one series of studies (Mervis, 1976). The purpose of the research was to test the developmental implications of best-example theory; thus, the research addressed, and confirmed, all the developmental implications discussed previously in this section. The present issue was tested in two different situations. The first was designed to mimic the real-world situation in which a child has already learned one exemplar of a category and is now being exposed to novel exemplars. The second mimicked the real-world situation in which a child had not previously been exposed to any exemplar of the category. When he is shown an object for the first time, he asks "What's that?" and is given the object's name. He then tries to apply the name appropriately to other category members. Because the categories had to be completely novel, it was necessary to use artificial stimuli. The object categories constructed were designed as basic level categories, were structured according to the same principles as are real-world categories (see the first section), and were designed to be interesting for young children. Six categories of objects, each with four exemplars ranging in typicality from excellent to poor, were used. The children in the experiment were 5-year-olds. Children in the first situation learned the name of one exemplar (either the most typical or the least typical) from each category and were then asked both to name a series of novel exemplars and to point out which novel exemplars belonged to which of the previously learned categories. Children in the second situation were shown one exemplar (either the most typical or the least typical) of each category and were told its name once. They were then given the same test as the subjects in the first situation. The procedure in the second situation was repeated once a day until the subject correctly named and pointed out all the objects or until he had been tested for 5 days (whichever occurred first). Results from both experiments indicated that category learning based on initial experience with a typical exemplar is much easier than learning based on initial experience with an atypical exemplar. In the first experiment, children in the good-example condition tended to either generalize the categories correctly or else to undergeneralize them slightly (by leaving out the poorest exemplar). In contrast, children in the poor-example condition tended to either refuse to generalize to any other objects (that is, they insisted that none of the novel objects were the same kind of thing as any of the previously learned objects) or to generalize incorrectly (almost always by overlapping or overgeneralizing). In the second experiment, the initial responses of children in the good-example condition were the same as the responses described for the first experiment. By the end of the last session, all but one child was able to correctly generalize all six categories. The initial responses of children in the poor-example condition were almost always refusals to generalize. Even after five sessions, none of the children had learned to generalize all six categories correctly, and all the children were still refusing to generalize at all for at least one category.

The anecdotal evidence also supports the best-example theory prediction. Children in the poor-example condition often complained that what they had to do was very difficult, whereas children in the good-example condition thought that their game was easy. The best evidence, however, comes from a little girl in the poor-example condition. For four sessions, she insisted that none of the novel objects were the same kind of thing as any of the familiar objects. In the fifth session, she suddenly realized how to generalize four of the categóries. As soon as she had shown me which objects went together, she handed me the best examples of each of the four categories and somewhat plaintively asked me why I had not told her the names for these, because that would have made it much easier to learn the categories.

Although nothing within best-example theory would automatically constrain the form of a person's category representation (see the first section), there is some recent evidence available that indicates that the category representations of young children may not be feature-lists but rather may be something analogous to an image (which may include visual, auditory, tactile, etc. components). Shepp (1978) has found that dimensions that are easily perceived by adults as separable are perceived by young children as integral. Therefore, children might have difficulty dividing an object into features but would find it easy to deal with some more analogical representation, such as an image. One of the subjects in the second Mervis (1976) experiment provided anecdotal evidence in favor of images—in particular, images similar to the best examples—as category representations. This boy was a subject in a control condition in which all the members of the category were named. After the first session, he told me that this game was very easy. All you had to do was make pictures of the categories in your head and then match the objects to the pictures. You assigned the object to the category whose picture was most similar to the object. When I asked him what these pictures were like, he at first told me that I must be stupid not to know. When I finally convinced him that I did not know, he said he would show me what his pictures were like. He then went over to the array of objects and picked out the most typical exemplar of each category.

IMPLICATIONS FOR THE CONSTRUCTION OF CHILDREN'S READING BOOKS

The research previously described has implications for designing both the texts and illustrations of children's readers. These implications will be discussed separately for each of the three major conclusions from the previous section.

The first conclusion is that when children begin to refer to objects, the names used are almost always basic level ones. Furthermore, although a very young child may know the basic level name for an object, he or she may not learn the appropriate superordinate and/or subordinate names for that object until he or she is in the middle elementary school grades or even later. This finding implies that authors of children's books should be wary of using superordinate or subordinate terms, unless either the author is sure that the children who will read the book already know these terms or unless he or she wishes to introduce the children to a new term. If the author chooses to introduce such a term, he or she should be certain that the word's meaning is made clear. As is pointed out later, these new terms should be represented by their good exemplars rather than their poor ones.

The second conclusion is that children tend to agree that good exemplars are category members before agreeing that poor exemplars are category members. It is therefore important that illustrations in early readers show good exemplars of a category rather than poor exemplars. For example, if one were to illustrate the sentence *Jean was sitting in a chair,* the chair should be either a typical armchair or a typical straight-backed chair rather than a beanbag chair. This is because most young children do not consider beanbag chairs to be chairs—thus, for these children, the illustration will not correspond to the text. Similarly, authors should be careful when using anaphoric references, because not all statements that are anaphoric for adults are also anaphoric for children. For example, consider the following story. "Jimmy was sitting in the kitchen eating a candy bar. His mother walked in and saw Jimmy. She got very angry. 'Didn't I tell you not to have any more food before dinner?', she asked." This story makes sense to an adult, because adults consider candy bars to be food. However, it probably would not make sense to a young child, because most young children do not consider candy bars food. Thus, when using a higher-level term to refer back to a lower-level term, the author should make sure that the lower-level term is a good example of the higher-level term. Of course, the use of poor examples, whether in illustrations or in stories like the one described, may sometimes be justified as a device to expand the child's knowledge of a concept. This is only reasonable, however, if the child reads well enough to have confidence that he actually read the sentence correctly—that, for example, the sentence about a chair really said "chair," rather than "cushion."

It should be noted that the best exemplars of a category are often not the members with the highest word frequency. In fact, the correlation between word frequency and goodness-of-example for members of common superordinate categories is almost always nonsignificant (Mervis, Catlin, & Rosch, 1976). Therefore, in choosing category exemplars, authors should not consult word frequency norms; instead, goodness-of-example norms (now available for several categories; see Rosch [1975a] or Mervis [1978]) should be used. Children are far more likely to agree with adults about the category membership of the good examples of a category than about the category membership of the most frequent examples (as measured by word frequency norms).

The third conclusion is that children learn concepts best if the concepts are introduced using good exemplars rather than poor exemplars. Therefore, when authors wish to present new concepts (for example, types of animals, such as coelenterates), these concepts should be described and illustrated by good members. This procedure should enable the child to generalize the concept accurately, whereas description and illustration by poor members is likely to lead the child to generalize the concept incorrectly, if he or she generalizes at all.

It is clear that the results from categorization research have substantive implications for the construction of children's readers. In order to establish how best to make suggestions for actual improvements in children's readers, the extent to which these books already fit the present suggestions must be determined. The answer to this question is unknown, but there are three immediately obvious ways to study it. First, one could analyze a large number of children's readers for their correspondence to the suggestions made. Second, one could test the intuitions of authors and illustrators with regard to what children of various ages know about categories and category members. Finally, one could explicitly ask authors and illustrators to describe how they make the decisions discussed in this section—for example, which exemplar to illustrate, which exemplar to use to demonstrate or illustrate a new concept, or when to use a higher-level term to refer back to a lower-level term.

ACKNOWLEDGMENTS

Parts of the research reported here were supported by a National Science Foundation Special Projects Grant (SOC75-21717 to Carolyn Mervis and Jack Catlin, by a Grant-in-Aid from Sigma Xi (The Scientific Research Society of North America) to Carolyn Mervis, and by grants to Eleanor Rosch (under her former name Eleanor Rosch Heider) by the National Science Foundation GB-38245X, by the Grant Foundation, and by the National Institutes of Mental Health 1 RO1 MH24316-01. Carolyn Mervis was a National Science Foundation predoctoral fellow during the conduct of the research.

I would like to thank John Pani for his thoughtful criticism of previous drafts of this paper.

REFERENCES

Anglin, J. M. *Word, object and conceptual development.* New York: Norton, 1977.
Annett, M. The classification of instances of four common class concepts by children and adults. *British Journal of Educational Psychology,* 1959, *29,* 223–236.
Aristotle. *The metaphysics* (H. Tredennick, trans.). Cambridge, Mass.: Harvard University Press, 1933.
Berlin, B., Breedlove, D. E., & Raven, P. H. General principles of classification and nomenclature in folk biology. *American Anthropologist,* 1973, *75,* 214–242.
Berlin, B., & Kay, P. *Basic color terms: Their universality and evolution.* Berkeley: University of California Press, 1969.
Bolinger, D. The atomization of meaning. *Language,* 1965, *41,* 555–573.
Bourne, L. E. *Human conceptual behavior.* Boston: Allyn & Bacon, 1968.
Bowerman, M. The acquisition of word meaning: An investigation of some current conflicts. In N. Waterson & C. Snow (Eds.), *Development of communication: Social and pragmatic factors in language acquisition.* New York: Wiley, 1978.
Brown, R. *Transcripts of Sarah's early speech.* Unpublished manuscript, Harvard University.
Chomsky, N., & Halle, M. *The sound pattern of English.* New York: Harper & Row, 1968.
Clark, E. V. What's in a word? On the child's acquisition of semantics in his first language. In T. E. Moore (Ed.), *Cognitive development and the acquisition of language.* New York: Academic Press, 1973.
Dougherty, J. W. D. Relativity and salience in categorization. *American Ethnologist,* 1978, *5,* 66–80.
Garner, W. R. *The processing of information and structure.* New York: Wiley, 1974.
Goldberg, S., Perlmutter, M., & Myers, W. Recall of related and unrelated lists by 2-year-olds. *Journal of Experimental Child Psychology,* 1974, *18,* 1–8.
Goldman, A. E., & Levine, M. A developmental study of object sorting. *Child Development,* 1963, *34,* 649–666.
Greenfield, P. M., Reich, L. C., & Olver, R. R. On culture and equivalence: II. In J. S. Bruner, R. R. Olver, P. M. Greenfield et al., *Studies in cognitive growth.* New York: Wiley, 1966.
Grimes, J. Personal communication, November, 1969.
Hull, C. L. Quantitative aspects of the evolution of concepts. *Psychological Monographs,* 1920, *28,* No. 1.

Hunn, E. *Cognitive processes in folk ornithology: The identification of gulls* (Working paper No. 42). Berkeley: Language Behavior Research Laboratory, University of California, 1975.

Inhelder, B., & Piaget, J. *The early growth of logic in the child: Classification and seriation.* New York: Harper & Row, 1964.

Katz, J. J., & Fodor, J. A. The structure of a semantic theory. *Language,* 1963, *39,* 120–210.

Katz, J. J., & Postal, P. M. *An integrated theory of linguistic description.* Cambridge, Mass.: MIT Press, 1964.

Klausmeier, H. J. Conceptual development. In J. R. Levin & V. L. Allen (Eds.), *Cognitive learning in children: Theories and strategies.* New York: Academic Press, 1976. (a)

Klausmeier, H. J. Instructional design and the teaching of concepts. In J R. Levin & V. L. Allen (Eds.), *Cognitive learning in children: Theories and strategies.* New York: Academic Press, 1976. (b)

Labov, W. The boundaries of words and their meanings. In C. J. Bailey & R. Shuy (Eds.), *New ways of analyzing variation in English.* Washington, D. C.: Georgetown University Press, 1973.

Lakoff, G. Hedges: A study in meaning criteria and the logic of fuzzy concepts. *Papers from the Eighth Regional Meeting: Chicago Linguistics Society.* Chicago: University of Chicago Linguistics Department, 1972.

Leach, E. Anthropological aspects of language: Animal categories and verbal abuse. In E. H. Lenneberg (Ed.), *New directions in the study of language.* Cambridge, Mass.: MIT Press, 1964.

Mansfield, A. Semantic organization in the young child: Evidence for the development of semantic feature systems. *Journal of Experimental Child Psychology,* 1977, *23,* 57–77.

Markle, S. M. They teach concepts, don't they? *Educational Researcher,* 1975, *4*(5), 3–9.

Mervis, C. B. *Acquisition of object categories.* Unpublished doctoral dissertation, Cornell University, 1976.

Mervis, C. B. *Goodness of example norms: Animal.* Unpublished manuscript, University of Illinois, 1978.

Mervis, C. B., Catlin, J., & Rosch, E. Development of the structure of color categories. *Developmental Psychology,* 1975, *11,* 54–60.

Mervis, C. B., Catlin, J., & Rosch, E. Relationships among goodness-of-example, category norms, and word frequency. *Bulletin of the Psychonomic Society,* 1976, *7,* 283–284.

Mervis, C. B., & Judd, S. A. *The role of goodness-of-example in children's sorting and memory clustering.* Unpublished manuscript, University of Illinois.

Neimark, E. D. Natural language concepts: Additional evidence. *Child Development,* 1974, *45,* 508–511.

Nelson, K. Concept, word, and sentence: Interrelations in acquisition and development. *Psychological Review,* 1974, *81,* 267–285. (a)

Nelson, K. Variations in children's concepts by age and category. *Child Development,* 1974, *45,* 577–584. (b)

Olver, R. R., & Hornsby, J. R. On equivalence. In J. S. Bruner, R. R. Olver, P. M. Greenfield et al., *Studies in cognitive growth.* New York: Wiley, 1966.

Rosch, E. On the internal structure of perceptual and semantic categories. In T. E. Moore (Ed.), *Cognitive development and the acquisition of language.* New York: Academic Press, 1973. (a)

Rosch, E. Personal communication, June, 1973. (b)

Rosch, E. Cognitive representations of semantic categories. *Journal of Experimental Psychology: General,* 1975, *104,* 192–233. (a)

Rosch, E. Universals and cultural specifics in human categorization. In R. Brislin, S. Bochner, & W. Lonner (Eds.), *Cross-cultural perspectives on learning.* New York: Halsted Press, 1975. (b)

Rosch, E., & Mervis, C. B. Family resemblances: Studies in the internal structure of categories. *Cognitive Psychology,* 1975, *7,* 573–605.

Rosch, E., & Mervis, C. B. Children's sorting: A reinterpretation based on the nature of abstraction in natural categories. In R. C. Smart & M. S. Smart (Eds.), *Readings in child development and relationships.* (2nd ed). New York: MacMillan, 1977.

Rosch, E., Mervis, C. B., Gray, W. D., Johnson, D. M., & Boyes-Braem, P. Basic objects in natural categories. *Cognitive Psychology,* 1976, *8,* 382–439.

Rosner, S. R., & Hayes, D. S. A developmental study of category item production. *Child Development,* 1977, *48,* 1062–1065.

Saltz, E., Soller, E., & Siegel, I. E. The development of natural language concepts. *Child Development,* 1972, *43,* 1191–1202.

Shepp, B. From perceived similarity to dimensional structure: A new hypothesis about perceptual development. In E. Rosch & B. B. Lloyd (Eds.), *Cognition and categorization.* Hillsdale, N.J.: Lawrence Erlbaum Associates, 1978.

Smoke, K. L. An objective study of concept formation. *Psychological Monographs,* 1932 (Whole No. 191).

Stross, B. Acquisition of botanical terminology by Tzeltal children. In M. Edmonson (Ed.), *Meaning in Mayan languages.* The Hague: Mouton, 1973.

Thompson, J. The ability of children of different grade levels to generalize on sorting tests. *Journal of Psychology,* 1941, *11,* 119–126.

Tyler, S. A. (Ed.) *Cognitive anthropology.* New York: Holt, Rinehart & Winston, 1969.

Vygotsky, L. S. *Thought and language.* New York: Wiley, 1962.

Wertheimer, M. Numbers and numerical concepts in primitive peoples. In W. D. Ellis (Ed.), *A source book of Gestalt psychology.* New York: The Humanities Press, 1950.

Wittgenstein, L. *Philosophical investigations.* New York: MacMillan, 1953.

12

Theories of Semantic Memory: Approaches to Knowledge and Sentence Comprehension

Edward J. Shoben
Center for the Study of Reading,
University of Illinois, Urbana-Chapaign

Early models of reading comprehension analyzed the reading process as a high-level form of perception. Early theories (Gough, 1972) consequently were very concerned with the perception of individual words, and many relatively recent theories (Smith, 1971) have dealt extensively with the Reicher (1969) and Wheeler (1970) finding that single letters were perceived more accurately in the context of words than in the absence of context.

In marked opposition to this extremely "bottom-up" viewpoint, many of the chapters in this volume view reading as a problem in language comprehension. There is now considerable evidence to suggest that knowledge interacts with one's processing of text. Although these effects of schemata, or other higher order structures, are important, a complete theory of reading comprehension must include a theory of individual sentence comprehension. Although reading the sentence *The bird landed after the cat left* will facilitate processing of *The robin began eating worms* (Garrod & Sanford, 1977), the contextual information in the first sentence does not explain how meaning is extracted from the second.

An explicit model of sentence comprehension is needed to explain how meaning is extracted from a surface representation. This subset of reading comprehension is an extremely difficult problem, as evidenced by the absence of theories in this area. As a consequence, this chapter focuses on one aspect of the comprehension problem with an eye toward the generality of the theories. Specifically, we examine the requirements for an adequate theory of semantic memory, focusing specifically on the comprehension of simple, categorical statments such as *Robins are birds*.

Hopefully, by working at this more microcosmic level, our theories can aspire to a greater degree of precision. This greater precision will enable us to derive more explicit predictions and perform more explicit tests than are otherwise possible. One important virtue of these more limited theories is that one can reasonably expect to find psychological evidence that will support one theory over another. With vaguer, more global theories (e.g., Schank & Abelson, 1977), such evidence is much less likely to be obtained.

It can also be argued that a theory of sentence comprehension is the cornerstone of a theory of reading. The basic processes that underlie sentence comprehension are, without doubt, employed in the comprehension of every sentence. Higher level operations, such as frames (Minsky, 1975) or scripts (Schank & Abelson, 1977) may not be operative at all times. Moreover, if we had a complete theory of sentence comprehension, it might be the case that these higher level constructs might simply direct, rather than alter, the processes of sentence comprehension.

Thus, the study of individual sentence comprehension is not only a logically necessary part of any theory of reading comprehension, but it also provides us with an area in which our theorizing can be much more precise and explicit. The psychological approach to semantic memory is an important subset of sentence comprehension, and our examination of this area will enable us to see some of the basic theoretical choices that must be made in constructing theories of sentence comprehension.

Psychological research on memory prior to the 1970s was almost exclusively concerned with the learning of new information. A typical psychological experiment involved reading a list of nonsense syllables, words, or rarely, sentences to a subject and studying the conditions that facilitated or retarded acquisition of the material. Subjects were tested either by their recall of the material or by their recognition judgments. In this latter testing procedure, subjects decided if a particular item was among the stimuli that they were asked to learn. Notice that this recognition paradigm is not really a test of recognition at all but rather a test of list discrimination. Everyone will recognize the word *cat*, but it is a different task to determine if *cat* was on the to-be-learned list of material.

Several characteristics of this early research on memory are immediately apparent. First, it is clear that this kind of reserach bears little relationship to language comprehension and hence to reading. In fact, the vast majority of these studies assumes that the material got into the system; items not remembered are assumed to have been forgotten. Second, what must be remembered about the presented information is not its content so much as its circumstance. Specifically, one need not recall that a cat is a small, domesticated mammal but rather that it occured on the list in this particular laboratory. Put another way, what must be remembered about the information is its temporal circumstance.

Semantic memory deals with what appears to be a completely different type of information. In a typical experiment, subjects might be asked to decide if *sparrows are birds*. The dependent variable of interest is how rapidly subjects decide that this assertion is true. Notice here that the memory involved is part of our world knowledge and does not depend on the temporal context. What psychologists try to infer from such experiments is the structure of the stored knowledge and the processing capabilities that operate on the stored information.

The differences between these two different avenues of memory research led Tulving (1972) to propose a distinction between semantic and episodic memory. Tulving argued that episodic memory contains information that is fundamentally autobiographical and temporally marked; semantic memory contains facts that do not depend on a particular circumstance. Whether this definition of semantic memory is meant to include all our world knowledge or only our knowledge of the language is a complicated issue that is addressed later.

There are several advantages to adopting the more restrictive definition. First, such a definition would allow us to make contact with the interpretative school of linguistics (Katz, 1972). Although this approach has run into problems (Bolinger, 1965), it would enable us to look at meaning in a very precise way, trying to identify that set of primitives that uniquely specifies each lexical item. In addition, this definition would enable us to borrow the concept of production rules as well, thereby generating some hypotheses about the process of semantic composition. This definition of semantic memory as knowledge of the language also has the inherent advantages of being more restrictive.

Despite these advantages, there are distinct disadvantages that lead us to adopt the broader definition here and view semantic memory as that store of information that corresponds to our knowledge of the world. First, adoption of the more restrictive view would exclude a large amount of semantic memory research involving information that cannot be construed as knowledge of the language. Second, the narrower definition forces us to believe that there is a valid distinction between knowledge of the language and knowledge of the world. Although such a distinction may exist, it has not fared well in linguistics (cf. Bolinger's [1965] comments on Katz & Fodor [1963]), and it would seem foolish to choose a definition on so tenuous an assumption.

Thus, the decision to include in semantic memory information that can be classified as world knowledge means that the difference between semantic and episodic memory is not equivalent to the difference between analytic and synthetic truth (Quine, 1953). The truth of synthetic as well as analytic statements may be determined by reference to semantic memory, and this analytic/synthetic distinction does not address the issue of temporal marking.

Although it will be argued later that the distinction between episodic and semantic memory is a useful one, it should be pointed out that the boundary between the two memory systems is a fuzzy one and should not be viewed as a dichotomy. Consider the following sentences.

1. Christopher Columbus discovered America in 1492.
2. Fred Wharton tripped on a roller skate yesterday.
3. James McCord was caught in the Watergate on June 17, 1972.

Sentence 1, although certainly not an analytic truth, can be confirmed on the basis of general world knowledge in semantic memory. On the other hand, I have no relevant world knowledge[1] on which to base my decision about statement 2. The statement refers specifically to a particular time period, and episodic memory must be consulted to determine if this particular event occurred. Although it was possible to classify these first two statements unambiguously, 3 is problematic. Certainly, when I first heard of the Watergate break-in, this information was stored in episodic memory with other temporally marked events. The question about sentence 3 is whether this particular piece of information has become part of my general world knowledge. This problem leads us to notice that all information must originate in episodic memory, and that one of the very difficult problems facing us is the determination of how temporally marked information is transformed into general knowledge. Although no answer to this important question is offered in the present chapter, it does seem safe to conclude for the present that there is no strict dividing line between episodic and semantic memory.

RELATIONSHIP TO COGNITIVE PSYCHOLOGY

One can view the relationship of semantic memory to cognitive psychology in a number of ways. It can be viewed as a subset of concept formation and one can examine how people determine that *robins are birds* or that *bears have hairy legs*. It is obvious that the determination of the truth of such statements depends in large part on the nature of our concepts of *bird and hairy-legged things*. Although such an approach is a fruitful one (see Mervis, Chapter 11, this volume; Rosch, 1973; Smith, Rips, & Shoben, 1974) it is not the approach adopted in this chapter. Instead, semantic memory is viewed as a subset of language comprehension.

---

[1]This example also points out the autobiographical nature of episodic memory in that the verification of this statment requires personal knowledge about the event.

In this approach, the major focus of interest is on how people decide if a particular statement is true or false. Although our domain is restricted to the semantic rather than episodic truth of the statements, the goals of a theory of semantic memory reflect this emphasis on comprehension. More specifically, an adequate theory must specify at least five processes, four of which have been noted earlier by Smith (1978). First, it must specify the nature and outcome of the process of retrieving the meanings of individual words. Second, an adequate theory must specify the process by which these individual meanings are combined in order to form a semantic representation of the entire sentence. Third, a theory should explain how this overall meaning is compared to one's stored knowledge in order to determine the truth or falsity of the statement. Fourth, the theory should say something about the inferences that can be drawn from these semantic interpretations. In addition to these four goals, I would like to add a fifth goal: the theory should be able to account for contextual effects. A viable theory of semantic memory should state how (if at all) the performance of these retrieval and combinatorial operations on sentence A will affect these same operations on sentence B.

The most straightforward approach to developing a taxonomy of semantic memory models is to examine their approach to each of the five goals just outlined. Unfortunately, the area of semantic memory is still in a nascent state, and few, if any, theories address all of these goals in sufficient detail to permit a reasonable evaluation. Consequently, the focus will be on the goal of describing the representation and the goal of specifying the sequential effects, two problems that most theories of semantic memory do consider. Hopefully, the approaches taken by the various theories will enable us to discern two distinct classes of semantic memory models. Before examining this question, however, it is instructive to consider earlier classifications of the theories.

KINDS OF SEMANTIC MEMORY MODELS

The only previous classification of semantic memory theories has run into problems (Smith, Shoben, & Rips, 1974). Smith et al. distinguished between network models and set models, in which network models view semantic memory as an interconnected group of words connected in a graph–theoretic structure, whereas set models view semantic memory as an unconnected group of terms denoted by a set of attributes or features. Although Hollan (1975) has argued that there may be no formal distinction between these two classes in that one may always be able to translate one into the other, the set/net distinction may be heuristic in examining the differences among models that are highly correlated with this set/net distinction (Shoben, Rips, & Smith, 1978). More specifically, it may be the case that one can distinguish models on a basis that parallels the set/net distinction rather closely. Although one can translate one type of model into the other in a formal sense, it seems that a distinction between models that emphasize the pre-storage of information (network models) and those that require most information to be computed (set models) will allow us to group the various proposals.

To illustrate these differences, let us consider two simple models that will be called the attribute model and the hierarchical model. Both will be examined in terms of their handling of simple statements. The former was initially proposed (though not espoused) by Meyer (1970). In this set model, a concept is represented as a set of defining attributes, that is, the set of all attributes that are individually necessary and jointly sufficient to define a concept's meaning. In deciding if, for example, *robins are birds,* one must see if the attributes of *robin* contain all the attributes of *bird.* More specifically, subjects must first retrieve the attributes for the two terms from memory. They must then compare them and match all the attributes of the predicate noun in order to verify the categorical relation. Meyer initially attributed differences in verification time to differences in the number of predicate attributes, because under standard processing assumptions,[2] an increase in the number of attributes to be matched will increase the time required to perform the matching. For example, there are good linguistic reasons to believe that higher order superordinates, such as *animal,* have fewer defining attributes than their subordinates, for example, *bear,* because a *bear* must logically have all the attributes of an *animal* plus those attributes that make it a *bear.*

As an example of a simple network model, let us consider the hierarchical model. This model has not been proposed by anyone. Although it bears some resemblance to Collins and Quillian's (1969) original formulation, the hierarchical model is an oversimplification of both Quillian's (1968) original proposal and Collins and Quillian's (1969) adaptation. Concepts are represented as nodes in a hierarchical graph structure, interconnected by directed links. Using the same examples as before, the verification of the statement *robins are birds* is made by locating *robin* and *bird* in the hierarchy and checking to see if there is a path pointing from *robin* to *bird.* In several more complex network models (Rumelhart, Lindsay, & Norman, 1972), this path is given the explicit label *isa,* denoting the subset model. More explicitly, according to the hierarchical model, the subject retrieves the two nouns of a categorical statement, determines if there is a pathway indicating subset

---

[2]Following Meyer (1970), it is assumed here that even a parallel comparison process will be slowed by an increasing number of components because, in most parallel models, the time required is determined by the slowest comparison operation. If we increase the number of operations that must be performed, then we will also increase the average duration of the longest operation.

relation between them, and, finally, compares the information retrieved from memory with the test sentence and responds accordingly.

Although the set/net distinction may fail in a formal sense, it does seem that these two simple models are quite different from each other.[3] These differences are most readily apparent when examining the nature of the verification process. Most important, the truth of a statement must be computed in the attribute model. Operations must be performed on the attributes of the concept in order to ascertain the truth of the sentence. In contrast, the truth of the sentence can be determined by a search of memory according to the hierarchical model. In this latter case, the information is already present in memory, and once it is found, no further operations are necessary. The distinction here is between computation models, such as the attribute model, and pre-storage models, such as the hierarchical model. There are two corollaries to this computation–pre-storage distinction. The first related distinction deals with the emphasis placed on retrieval or comparison processes. Variations in verification time are explained by the difficulty of retrieval according to the hierarchical model and by the difficulty of comparison in the set model. An additional correlated distinction centers on the necessity of expanding terms. In the hierarchical model, concepts are represented as nodes in the network, and no further expansion is necessary. In the attribute model, comparison must be performed on the attributes of a concept and thus the concept must be expanded before the critical comparison operations can begin.

The major postulate in this taxonomy is the distinction between computation and pre-storage models. Computation models imply that even simple categorical relations are derived by some procedures, whereas pre-storage models claim that these relations are confirmed by finding the appropriate information. Put most concretely, pre-storage models claim that *robins are birds* is a fact that is stored in memory. People can confirm this statement merely by finding the fact. In contrast, computation models deny the storage of this fact and argue that the truth of this statement is determined by a computational procedure.

It is important to note that this distinction must not be carried to a ridiculous extreme. More explicitly, there is some pre-storage in every computational model, and there is some computation in every pre-storage model. In the case of the attribute model, it is necessarily the case that the attributes are pre-stored or there would be nothing with which to compute. The computational aspect of the pre-storage model is not such a logical necessity, in that a pre-storage model could assert that all semantic facts are stored in memory and that verification is exclusively the process of retrieving

---

[3]A detailed discussion of this issue appears in Shoben, Rips, and Smith (1978).

them. However, it seems quite ridiculous to assume that facts like *George Washington had an arm,* or *collies are living things* are stored directly in memory. We may never have used this information before, yet we can readily determine its truth. From an artificial intelligence perspective, it is certainly uneconomical to require that every possible true statement be stored uniquely.

The solution to this problem for pre-storage models is to allow some computation in the form of inferences. In the hierarchical model, these inferences are transitive relations. For example, we can determine the truth of *collies are living things* by retrieving the following facts: *collies are dogs; dogs are mammals; mammals are animals;* and *animals are living things.* From these facts, one can infer (because transitivity holds) that *collies are living things.* Although this inference procedure is not very similar to the computation in the attribute model, it does constitute a departure from the strictly pre-storage character of the model. Although the information on which the computations are performed is pre-stored (as it must be), the inferences themselves are not.

Thus there is some fuzziness to this distinction in that there is some computation in the simplest of pre-storage models and some pre-storage in a very simple computation proposal. Despite this blurring of the distinction, it does seem that the computation–pre-storage distinction does reflect a fundamental difference in belief about how people confirm simple statements. At some basic level, computational models believe that comprehension involves deriving the relationship among the sentence's constituents, whereas pre-storage models view comprehension as locating the information.

This distinction between computation and pre-storage perspectives is pervasive in cognitive psychology. For example, the current dispute in linear orders reflects this distinction. The imagery position (e.g., Moyer & Bayer, 1976) contends that one decides which of two objects is larger by comparing analogue representation of them. Variations in decision times are attributed to variations in the difficulty of this comparison. In contrast, the discrete code view of linear orders (Banks, 1977) argues that in comparing the size of two objects, a discrete code is retrieved and that decisions are (usually) made on the basis of the retrieved information.

An even clearer example of this computation–pre-storage distinction is in the area of recognition memory. According to one point of view (Atkinson & Juola, 1974), subjects decide if a word is on a memorized list by comparing its familiarity to some criterion. In another view (Anderson & Bower, 1973), people will recognize test stimuli if they are able to retrieve the information that the particular stimulus was on the test list. According to this latter model, recognition is the act of finding the requisite information; if the information is not present, the subject will respond erroneously. In the computation model, on the other hand, the subject's response will depend on a computation in which the familiarity value of the stimulus is compared to a criterion; stored information is inherently insufficient to make a response.

An important correlate of this distinction between computation and pre-storage models is the distinction between retrievel processes and comparison processes. More explicitly, computation models emphasize comparison processes, and pre-storage models emphasize retrieval processes. It should be noted at the outset that both kinds of processes are needed in both kinds of models; the distinction rests on the emphasis placed on these processes. More important, from a psychological point of view, computation models attribute differences in comprehension difficulty in changes in the number or difficulty of comparison operations, whereas pre-storage models attribute such changes to changes in the number or difficulty of retrieval operations.

This distinction is best understood in the context of our two simple models. In the attribute model, verification of a statement such as *collies are dogs* is accomplished by first retrieving each of the set of defining attributes for the subject and predicate nouns. The critical operation is the comparison of attributes to see if each of the defining attributes of the predicate is among the defining attributes of the subject noun. To see the emphasis on comparison processes, let us examine a second example: *collies are mammals.* In this example, the predicate *mammals* will have fewer defining attributes than the concept *dogs.* As noted earlier (Bierwisch, 1971; Meyer, 1970), *dogs* must have all the defining attributes of *mammals* plus some others that make them *dogs.* The important consequence of this argument is that higher order superordinates (such as *mammals*) must have fewer defining attributes than their subordinates. As a result, when we change from *collies are dogs* to *collies are mammals,* then, according to the attribute model, it will be easier to match all the defining attributes of the predicate *mammal* because it has fewer attributes. As verification depends on matching all defining attributes of the predicate, it will be easier (and faster) to verify *collies are mammals* than *collies are dogs.* Thus the difference in the difficulty of these two statements lies in the number of comparison operations that must be performed.

Although computation models attribute differences in comprehension difficulty to variations in the comparison process, pre-storage models attribute these differences to variations in the retrieval process. Considering the same two simple statements as before, the hierarchical model claims that verifying *collies are dogs* requires only that the fact be retrieved from memory. Because *dogs* is presumably a direct superordinate of *collie,* this fact is stored directly in memory and only a single retrieval operation is required. In the case of *collies are mammals,* an inference is required; because *mammal* is not the direct superordinate of *collie,* this particular relation is not stored directly and must be inferred. More specifically, the subject must retrieve the fact that *collies are dogs* and that *dogs are mammals* and finally infer that *collies are mammals.* For this sentence, two retrieval operations are required, and hence, according to the hierarchical model, *collies are mammals* will be more difficult than *collies are dogs*. Although this prediction is exactly opposite to the one derived from the attribute model, this difference is not important for the present purpose. What is important is that, where our example of a computation model attributed differences in verification difficulty to variations in the number of comparison operations, our example of a pre-storage model attributes these differences to variations in the number of retrieval operations required.

There is one other distinction that is also correlated with the distinction between computation and pre-storage models. Computation models always provide for the expansion of concepts whereas pre-storage models do not. Expansion is virtually a logical necessity of computation models as the components on which the computational procedures operate must be obtained beforehand. In the case of the attribute model, expansion occurs when the attribute sets are retrieved for the subject and predicate nouns. In contrast, pre-storage models do not require decomposition before retrieval operations can proceed. Although many later pre-storage models do have attributes, retrieving superordinates or making inferences about them can proceed from the concepts themselves. In the hierarchical model, the word itself is represented in the graph–theoretic structure, and components or attributes are entirely superfluous to the operation of the model.

The three distinctions proposed earlier permit us to see some clear differences in approach between the hierarchical model and the attribute model. As both of these models are very rudimentary proposals, it remains to be seen if our distinctions will shed any light on the differences in approach among more complicated and more modern models. In what follows, little attempt is made to evaluate the models because detailed critiques are widely available (Collins & Loftus, 1975; Glass & Holyoak, 1975; Smith, 1978). Instead, the emphasis is on the differences in the models' approach to comprehension as illuminated by the distinctions just proposed. Subsequently, we can examine some current problems and see how these different kinds of semantic memory models might approach them.

Consideration of length compel a high degree of selectivity in examining models in any detail. As a result, detailed discussion is limited to one computation model, the feature comparison model (Smith, Shoben, & Rips, 1974), and one pre-storage model, the marker search model (Glass & Holyoak, 1975). Finally, some comments are offered on the most widely known hybrid model, the spreading activation proposal of Collins and Loftus (1975). Such a classification leaves out the global memory models (Anderson, 1976; Anderson & Bower, 1973; Norman & Rumelhart, 1975) and the older, less often cited, semantic memory models (e.g., Schaeffer & Wallace, 1969).

Feature Comparison Model

The feature comparison model (Smith, Shoben & Rips, 1974) assumes that concepts are represented as sets of semantic attributes or features. These components differ from those assumed by the attribute model in that the feature comparison model's attributes can be differentiated into those that are relatively more essential or *defining* of a concept's meaning and those that are more incidental or *characteristic* of it. Put another way, some features are more important than others.

According to this model, simple category statements are processed by a comparison of attributes. More specifically, the subject retrieves the feature sets of the subject and predicate nouns. All features are then compared without respect to their definingness. This heuristic comparison operation determines the proportion of the predicate's features that are shared by the subject noun. If this index of feature overlap is very high, the subject can verify the statement immediately. Conversely, the subject can disconfirm the statement if the level of feature overlap is very low. Finally, if the level of overlap is intermediate, then no immediate decision can be made and a second comparison must be performed.

In this second stage of the model, the relatively more defining features of the predicate are isolated, and the subject checks to see if each of these features is present among the features of the subject noun and verifies the statement only if all features can be matched. This second stage of the model is very similar to the attribute model in that an algorithmic matching of defining features is performed.

With respect to our three distinctions, the model is quite easily classified. First, the model is a computational one. It assumes that categorical relations are not stored but that they are derived from a comparison of semantic components. If our assertion about correlated distinctions is correct, then the model should allow for expansion of terms and also emphasize comparison operations. Both of these correlations are borne out in the feature comparison model. Concepts must be expanded in order to obtain the sets of semantic features, as there are not mechanisms in the model to deal with concept labels themselves. Similarly, the feature comparison model accounts for differences in verification difficulty by variations in the comparison process. According to the model, the average time required to verify a statement will depend on the proportion of the time that first-stage processing is sufficient. For example, in the statement *robins are birds, robins* and *birds* have very similar defining and characteristic features because *robins* are very typical *birds* (see Mervis, Chapter 11, this volume, for a fuller discussion of typicality). This high degree of feature overlap suggests that the rapid first-stage comparison will be sufficient to yield a correct response. On the other hand, a statement such as *penguins are birds* will be more difficult to verify because, although penguins have all the essential features of *birds, penguins* are atypical exemplars and share few of the characteristics features of *birds.* As a consequence the measure of feature overlap derived in the first stage will usually be insufficient to make a response and hence the time-consuming second stage will have to be executed.

The feature comparison model is thus quite unequivocal with respect to our three distinctions. It is a computational model, which requires expansion of concepts and which attributes differences in comprehension difficulty to variations in the comparison process. The marker–search model, on the other hand, is a pre-storage model that does not allow expansion of terms and that attributes comprehension differences to variations in retrieval processes.

Marker–Search Model

The marker–search model (Glass & Holyoak, 1975) assumes that concepts are represented in a semantic network with each concept denoted by markers. For example, the term *bird* is represented as [avian], in which [avian] means "possessing the essential properties of a bird." This notion of semantic markers is adapted from Katz's (1972) formal theory of semantics, and much of the model has the flavor of Katzian theory. These markers are interconnected in an implicational way so that there exist paths from [robins] to [avian] and from [avian] to [animate]. From these two paths, one can infer that *robins are animals.* So far, the model is very difficult to differentiate from the hierarchical model. However, the model has two additional structural assumptions. First, it is assumed that shortcut paths may exist. That is, there may be a direct connection between [chicken] and [animate], so that the connection between these two markers may be accessed directly without going through the marker [avian]. Finally, the paths are labeled; this last assumption deals exclusively with the processing of false statements and need not concern us further here.[4] All four of these assumptions are evident in Fig. 12.1, in which the concepts *robin, chicken, bird,* and *animal* are depicted. Notice that there is a direct path between [chicken] and [animate] but not between [robin] and [animate].

The processing assumptions of the model are simpler. When one is presented with a statement such as *A robin is a bird,* the defining markers entailed by the two concepts are retrieved. The subject then searches until a path is found that indicates that the defining marker of the predicate is

---

[4]A more detailed evaluation of how the marker search model handles the disconfirmation of false statements may be found either in Smith (1978) or in Shoben, Rips, and Smith (1978).

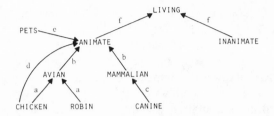

FIG. 12.1.   An illustration of the Glass and Holyoak (1975) model. Lower case letters designate the labels on relations.

implied by the defining marker of the subject; in other words, until a path is found from [robin] to [avian].

The model is able to account for typicality effects in terms of variations in search order. For example, as noted in the discussion of the feature comparison model, it is easier to verify a statement such as *A robin is a bird* than *A chicken is a bird*. This typicality effect was explained by similarity of characteristic features in the feature comparison model. In the marker-search model, this finding is explained by differential search order. More specifically, it is assumed that the first path to be searched from [robin] will be the path leading to [avian]. In contrast, the first path emanating from [chicken] to be searched may be [animate], not [avian]. This situation is depicted in Fig. 12.1. Although the small number of concepts necessarily oversimplifies the situation, it does illustrate how one might be slower in verifying *A chicken is a bird,* because the path between these two concepts might not be the first one to be searched.

We can now examine how the model lines up with our three distinctions. First of all, the model is clearly of the pre-storage type in that all the information needed to make the verification decision is stored in the memory structure. There is no provision for any kind of computational system. Variations in the ease of verification are attributable to variations in the difficulty of retrieval. In the example shown in Fig. 12.1, *a robin is a bird* is easier than *A robin is an animal,* because two retrieval operations are required in the latter whereas only one is necessary in the former. Similarly, some variations are attributable to the order in which the paths are searched. For example, *A chicken is an animal* may be easier than *A chicken is a bird,* because the path from [chicken] to [animate] may be searched before the path from [chicken] to [avian]. In both cases, variation in verification difficulty results directly from variations in the ease of retrieving the requisite information. With respect to our last distinction, the model does not allow for expansion of terms; all of the retrieval processes operate on the defining markers themselves. Although it might seem that the reference to defining markers implies a kind of expansion in and of itself, it should be remembered that the defining markers are not really components of the concepts. On the contrary, the defining markers actually denote the concept and the processing routines of the model would be unaffected if concept names were substituted for the defining markers in the marker–search model.

Thus our distinctions seem to separate these more developed semantic memory models as well as the simpler ones. It is also interesting to note that, despite their formal nonidentifiability (Hollan, 1975), the two models that were classified as computational, emphasizing comparison processes and allowing for expansion of terms, were originally formulated in terms of set theory. In contrast, the two models classified as pre-storage emphasizing retrieval processes and not allowing for expansion of terms, were formulated in terms of a semantic network. Thus, this set/net distinction may capture the difference between these two different approaches to semantic memory, although the set theory versus network choice of representation may be a byproduct and not a determinant of that approach.

Before turning to some current problems, it is important to note that our three distinctions do break down in the case of the only existing hybrid model. The spreading activation model of Collins and Loftus (1975) is a hybrid model in the true sense in that it allows for multiple procedures in verifying statements. The model has its theoretical roots in the seminal work of Collins and Quillian (1969), which, in its psychological form at least, was a pre-storage model. In the spreading activation model, verification can occur by finding a pathway from the subject noun to the predicate noun in memory. This aspect of the model is similar to the hierarchical model in that the necessary information is pre-stored, the critical operation is retrieval, and no expansion of concepts is required. However, another verification strategy in the spreading activation model is a comparison strategy in which one matches features of the two concepts. This procedure is quite similar to the feature comparison model and, in this aspect, the spreading activation model is clearly computational, emphasizes comparison processes, and requires the expansion of terms. The model is therefore a true hybrid in the sense that it combines procedures and structural assumptions from both classes of models. Our three distinctions should not be abandoned because we cannot place all of this model on one side or the other. Instead, the usefulness of our three distinctions is enhanced by their utility in identifying component parts of this hybrid model.

Although our distinctions seem useful in distinguishing two different approaches to semantic memory, it remains to be seen what these distinctions will tell us about the future of these two approaches. More explicitly, semantic memory models are currently facing a number of questions of sufficiency, and these distinctions may give us a clue as to the response of the models and, perhaps, how successful their responses will be. Most of these sufficiency questions are of the form "How does the model handle____?" An obvious example is "How does the model handle more complicated sentences?" Although this question is an important one, no answers are provided here (see Rips, Smith, & Shoben, 1978, for the approach of the feature comparison model). Instead, the focus is on two related questions: the question of access and the question of context.

Context and Spreading Activation

Although these two questions are separable, there is a very definite relation between them. Pre-storage models typically account for context effects through differences in access time. More specifically, context allows for more efficient retrieval of related concepts. Although computation models do attempt to deal with the effects of context, they do not use the concept of access in order to do so.

Besides its relationship to semantic memory models and to context, the question of access is important in its own right. The basic question here is whether the processing of one term will facilitate the subsequent processing of a semantically related term. Most of the evidence on this question comes not from tasks requiring semantic decisions but from research on lexical decisions. The lexical decision task requires a subject to decide whether an orthographic string is a word or not. The relationship of this task to the sentence verification task is discussed later. The basic finding of relevance from the lexical decision literature is that one's decision that *doctor* is a word is easier if it is preceded by *nurse* than by *butter*. Usually, these pairs of strings are presented close together, and there is some evidence that this lexical facilitation effect declines rapidly over time (Meyer & Schvaneveldt, 1976). Although the temporal parameters of this finding need not concern us here, the basic result certainly does establish a *prima facie* case for retrieval facilitation.

Meyer and Schvaneveldt (1976) and Collins and Loftus (1975) have interpreted these findings in terms of spreading activation. Both versions of this hypothesis claim nouns are organized in a semantic network and that when one concept node is activated (i.e., processed), other nearby concept nodes are also activated. Activation spreads outward from the original node such that nodes that are close in semantic distance to the processed concept receive more activation than those nodes that are further removed from the original concept. If we assume further that any node requires a threshold for firing, then activated nodes will be accessed more rapidly.

The concept of spreading activation will fit with any retrieval model. Although Glass and Holyoak (1975) do not attempt to apply their marker-search model to these data, the assumption of spreading activation would certainly enable them to account for the lexical facilitation effect. In their terms, the defining markers [nurse] and [doctor] are certainly closer in the network than [butter] and [doctor], and thus subjects will more rapidly identity *doctor* as a word in this latter case.

In each of these cases, we have treated spreading activation as if it were an automatic process, that is one that requires little or no conscious processing. Such a mechanism is difficult to implement in a computational model. In either the feature comparison model or the attribute model, such activation would have to spread via the semantic components because the concepts are not, in and of themselves, connected. If we permit activation to spread through these features or attributes, then we must argue that what produces the facilitation is a more rapid retrieval of semantic components. Such a procedure would change the fundamental character of the models in that this activation of features would emphasize a retrieval rather than a comparison process; it would shift the emphasis from computation to pre-storage, and it would make both models sound like semantic networks, because we must now talk of activation flowing from one construct to another along some kind of path.

There are several alternatives to such a radical alteration in the character of these models. The first is to argue that the results in the lexical decision task are due not to an automatic spreading of activation but to a sophisticated guessing strategy. The second alternative is to argue that the results in question are specific to lexical decisions and do not generalize readily to a semantic task. Each of these hypotheses is reasonable, and we examine each in turn.

Although the unconscious, spreading activation explanation of the lexical facilitation effect is intuitively compelling, some have attempted to explain this phenomenon in terms of a conscious guessing strategy (Becker, 1976). In its most simple terms, the guessing hypothesis assumes that when a string like *nurse* is presented, the subject generates as many plausible associates of *nurse* as possible. If one of the associates does appear, it is recognized as a word much faster than an unassociated word. Thus the lexical facilitation effect is due to subjects' anticipations and not to an automatic activation process.

However, this explanation answers one question but poses another. One might reasonably ask whether the associates were not generated by an automatic activation process, thereby reducing the difference between the two accounts to one of theoretical style rather than substance. In fact, however, the generation of associates can be handled quite elegantly by a semantic feature theory that postulates that associates are generated by minimal changes in the semantic features. Although the details of this account are beyond the scope of this chapter, the interested reader is advised to consult Clark (1972) for a full discussion.

Although there have been attempts to discriminate between the two accounts of the lexical facilitation effect (Neely, 1977), the question remains unresolved and there are articulate exponents on both sides (Becker, 1976; Meyer & Schvaneveldt, 1976). The issue is important for semantic memory in that the lexical facilitation effect constitutes some of the most direct evidence for a spreading activation model. However, the conscious guessing–automatic activation debate is resolved, it may be that the facilitation effect in question is specific to lexical decision tasks.

One straightforward paradigm in which to look for a similar facilitation effect is the same–different task, introduced by Schaeffer and Wallace (1969). In this task, subjects are given a pair of words and are asked to decide if both members belong to the same category. For example, in the studies by Schaeffer and Wallace (1969, 1970), subjects were given a pair *rose–tulip* and had to decide if both nouns were members of the category *living things*. The results were consistent with the results observed in the lexical decision task, in that pairs close in meaning (*rose–tulip*) were judged same more readily than words distant in meaning (*rose–canary*), although in both pairs the two exemplars are members of the category *living things*.

Subsequent research has cast doubt on the generality of this finding. Rips, Shoben, and Smith (1973) presented pairs of nouns and asked subjects to judge if both words were members of the category *birds*. Contrary to earlier findings, they found that the similarity or association value of the two terms to each other (as measured by ratings) did not predict the ease of the verification judgment. Instead, the typicality of each of the instance with respect to *bird* was the best predictor of the results. Shoben (1976) extended this result to other categories and, perhaps more important, extended the result to different judgments. He showed that the association or similarity between the two members of the pair predicted neither the same results nor the different results. In contrast, the similarity between each of the exemplars and the target category was a good predictor of pair difficulty for both same and different pairs. Recent findings (Gellatly & Gregg, 1977) in a related paradigm cast further doubt on the generality of the spreading activation hypothesis.

These studies suggest that the same–different task can be most aptly characterized as two separate semantic decisions in which subjects initially categorize the first item in the pair and then check to see if the second item is a member of the same category. Strong evidence for this view comes from the finding (Shoben, 1976) that different pairs like *bear–goose* and *goose–bear* are reliably different in difficulty. Although the lexical decision data provide a strong base for a differential access point of view, an alternative explanation of this phenomenon is available, and it seems that the critical result does not generalize to the semantic domain in a straightforward way. Thus, it seems that a random access position is tenable at least with respect to the semantic domain. Such a view is very comfortable for computational models, but it leaves these models without a way to account for effects of context. Although it has been argued that the context effects frequently studied in the lexical decision task do not generalize to the semantic domain, it would seem inconceivable that context plays no role in comprehension (see Anderson & Shifrin, Chapter 13, this volume).

One simple example of an effect of context that is intuitively compelling involves the emphasis on certain aspects of meaning. For example, it should be easier to comprehend *pianos are furniture* when it is preceded by a context that accents the furniture-like qualities of a piano, such as *pianos are hard to lift*. In contrast, *pianos are furniture* might be more difficult when preceded by *pianos need to be tuned*, because this statement emphasizes the musical aspect of pianos. Although this kind of context effect has been shown with respect to the likelihood that subjects will recall the categorical statement (Barclay, Bransford, Franks, McCarrell, & Nitsch, 1974), it is not clear whether the relevant context aids in the memory of the categorical statement or in the comprehension of it. Moreover, there is some evidence to suggest that these memorization techniques may be relatively poor measures of semantic memory (Shoben, Wescourt & Smith, 1978). Although the empirical basis for the context effect in semantic memory is somewhat tenuous, it would seem foolish to deny the existence of such an effect, and we would be justly skeptical of the viability of any semantic memory model that had no provision for effects of context.

As noted earlier, pre-storage models account for effects of context in terms of spreading activation. For example, given a context sentence, *some foods are birds,* activation presumably spreads from foods to many different kinds of foods. If the test sentence is *chickens are birds,* then it should be fairly easy to comprehend because *chicken* will have been activated from *food.* No such facilitation will occur if the test sentence is *robins are birds,* because *robins* are not *food.* This hypothetical result is the opposite of the one obtained for these two sentences when they are presented in the laboratory without explicit context. Under the circumstances, *robins are birds* is comprehended more readily than *chickens are birds.*

For computational models, the most promising explanation appears to involve the weighting of semantic attributes or components. In our discussion of the feature comparison model, we noted that the semantic features varied in terms of how essential or defining they were to a concept's meaning. In accounting for the effects of context, we will allow these definingness weights to enter into our computation of feature overlap in the first stage of the model and, in addition, we will allow context to alter the definingness weights themselves.

To take a specific example, let us again consider the case in which *some foods are birds* precedes the sentence *chickens are birds.* Although we do not discuss in detail how the feature comparison model accounts for the verification of this quantified context sentence (see Rips, 1975, for a full discussion), we assume that the processing of the first sentence will alter the definingness weights of the concept *bird*. Specifically, those features that are food-related (those that related to a bird's fleshiness, or boniness, for example) will increase in definingness relative to other features that are unrelated to the food aspect (such as those relating to wings, or voice). Thus, our assumption leads us to the fact that, after the processing of the context sentence, the definingness weights of the *bird* features will be different from those associated with *bird* in the absence of specific context. In deciding whether *a chicken is a bird,* we must invoke our second assumption; in executing the first stage, the amount of feature overlap is determined from a comparison of all features of the subject and predicate nouns weighted by definingness. Thus, the more defining features count more in the determination of the amount of overlap. Consequently, the increase in the definingness weights of the food-related features (as a result of context) will result in a high amount of feature overlap between *chicken* and *bird*. This increase in definingness has just the opposite results in the verification of the test sentence *a robin is a bird;* because *robin* and *bird* mismatch on many of the food-related features, the weighted amount of feature overlap is quite low. Because the amount of overlap is directly related to the ease of comprehension according to this model, this differential weighting procedure allows this computational model to handle potential effects of context on comprehension.

It is also important to note that this proposal does not alter the nature of the model with respect to the three distinctions proposed earlier. The revised model remains computational in that the comprehension of a statement requires the computation of the relationship between the lexical items. Moreover, variations in comprehension difficulty are explained in terms of variations in the comparison process. No additional assumptions about retrieval have been added; only an assumption about the weights of the elements that are compared. Finally, the model still requires the expansion of terms.

These three distinctions allow us to distinguish two fundamentally different approaches to comprehension. The three distinctions further guide us in how these two classes of models may approach new problems in semantic memory, as exemplified by their approaches to access and context.

One question that invariably arises with these relatively detailed, formal models is whether they are capable of being extended to more complicated sentences and to actual texts. This question is particularly current, given the interest in more global constructs such as schemata and scripts (Rumelhart, Chapter 2, this volume; e.g., Schank & Abelson, 1977). The work on context effects provides a first step in the right direction. It seems clear that a kind of interface is needed between the higher level processes and the fundamental processes involved in sentence comprehension. The question is not whether these higher order processes have an effect but how they influence more basic reading processes. A logical prerequisite to this question is some knowledge of the basic processes involved, and that certainly includes choosing between the theoretical perspectives outlined here.

ACKNOWLEDGMENT

This research was supported by the National Institute of Education under Contract No. US-NIE-C-400-76-0116.

REFERENCES

Anderson, J. R. *Language, memory, and thought.* Hillsdale, N.J.: Lawrence Erlbaum Associates, 1976.
Anderson, J. R., & Bower, G. H. *Human associative memory.* Washington, D.C.: Winston, 1973.
Atkinson, R. C., & Juola, J. F. Search and decision processes in recognition memory. In D. H. Krantz, R. C. Atkinson, R. D. Luce, & P. Suppes (Eds.), *Contemporary developments in mathematical psychology.* San Francisco: Freeman, 1974.
Banks, W. P. Encoding and processing of symbolic information in comparative judgments. In G. H. Bower (Ed.), *The psychology of learning and motivation* (Vol. 8). New York: Academic Press, 1977.
Barclay, J. R., Bransford, J. D., Franks, J. J., McCarrell, N. S., & Nitsch, K. Comprehension and semantic flexibility. *Journal of Verbal Learning and Verbal Behavior,* 1974, *13,* 471–481.
Becker, C. A. Allocation of attention during visual word recognition. *Journal of Experimental Psychology: Human Perception and Performance,* 1976, *2,* 556–566.
Bierwisch, M. On classifying semantic features. In D. D. Steinberg & L. A. Jakobovits (Eds.), *Semantics: An introductory reader in philosophy, linguistics, and psychology.* Cambridge: Cambridge University Press, 1971.
Bolinger, D. The atomization of meaning. *Language,* 1965, *41,* 555–573.
Clark, H. H. Word association and linguistic theory. In J. Lyons (Ed.), *New horizons in linguistics,* Baltimore: Penguin, 1972.
Collins, A. M., & Loftus, E. F. A spreading activation theory of semantic processing. *Psychological Review,* 1975, *82,* 407–428.
Collins, A. M., & Quillian, M. R. Retrieval time from semantic memory. *Journal of Verbal Learning and Verbal Behavior,* 1969, *8,* 240–248.
Garrod, S., & Sanford, A. Interpreting anaphoric relations: The integration of semantic information while reading. *Journal of Verbal Learning and Verbal Behavior,* 1977, *16,* 77–90.
Gellatly, A. R. H., & Gregg, V. H. Intercategory distance and categorization times: Effects of negative probe relatedness. *Journal of Verbal Learning and Verbal Behavior,* 1977, *16,* 505–518.
Glass, A. L., & Holyoak, K. J. Alternative conceptions of semantic memory. *Cognition,* 1975, *3,* 313–339.
Gough, P. B. One second of reading. In J. F. Kavanaugh & J. G. Mattingly (Eds.), *Reading by ear and by eye: The relationships between speech and reading.* Cambridge, Mass.: MIT Press, 1972.

Hollan, J. D. Features and semantic memory: Set theoretic or network model? *Psychological Review*, 1975, *82*, 154–155.

Katz, J. J., & Fodor, J. A. The structure of a semantic theory. *Language*, 1963, *39*, 170–210.

Katz, J. J. *Semantic theory*. New York: Harper & Row, 1972.

Meyer, D. E. On the represenation and retrieval of stored semantic information. *Cognitive Psychology*, 1970, *1*, 242–299.

Meyer, D. E., & Schvaneveldt, R. W. Meaning, memory structure, and mental processes. In C. N. Cofer (Ed.), *The structure of human memory*. San Francisco: Freeman, 1976.

Minsky, M. A framework for representing knowledge. In P. H. Winston (Ed.), *The psychology of computer vision*. New York: McGraw-Hill, 1975.

Moyer, R., & Bayer, R. H. Mental comparison and the symbolic distance effect. *Cognitive Psychology*, 1976, *8*, 228–246.

Neely, J. H. Semantic priming and retrieval from lexical memory: Roles of inhibitionless spreading activation and limited-capacity attention. *Journal of Experimental Psychology: General*, 1977, *106*, 226–254.

Norman, D., & Rumelhart, D. E. *Explorations in cognition*. San Francisco: Freeman, 1975.

Quillian, M. R. Semantic memory. In M. Minsky (Ed.), *Semantic information processing*. Cambridge, Mass.: MIT Press, 1968.

Quine, W. V. O. Two dogmas of empiricism. In W. V. O. Quine (Ed.), *From a logical point of view*. Cambridge, Mass.: Harvard University Press, 1953.

Reicher, G. M. Perceptual recognition as a function of meaningfulness of stimulus material. *Journal of Experimental Psychology*, 1969, *81*, 275–280.

Rips, L. J. Quantification and semantic memory. *Cognitive Psychology*, 1975, *7*, 307–340.

Rips, L. J., Shoben, E. J., & Smith, E. E. Semantic distance and the verification of semantic relations. *Journal of Verbal Learning and Verbal Behavior*, 1973, *12*, 1–20.

Rips, L. J., Smith, E. E., & Shoben, E. J. Semantic composition in sentence verification. *Journal of Verbal Learning and Verbal Behavior*, 1978, *17*, 375–402.

Rosch, E. On the internal structure of perceptual and semantic categories. In T. E. Moore (Ed.), *Cognitive development and the acquisition of langauge*. New York: Academic Press, 1973.

Rumelhart, D. E., Lindsay, P. H., & Norman, D. A. A process model for long-term memory. In E. Tulving & W. Donaldson (Eds.), *Organization and memory*. New York: Academic Press, 1972.

Schaeffer, B., & Wallace, R. Semantic similarity and the comparison of word meanings. *Journal of Experimental Psychology*, 1969, *82*, 343–346.

Schaeffer, B., & Wallace, R. The comparison of word meanings. *Journal of Experimental Psychology*, 1970, *86*, 144–152.

Schank, R. C., & Abelson, R. P. *Scripts, plans, goals, and understanding*. Hillsdale, N.J.: Lawrence Erlbaum Associates, 1977.

Shoben, E. J. The verification of semantic relations in a same–different paradigm: An asymmetry in semantic memory. *Journal of Verbal Learning and Verbal Behavior*, 1976, 365–379.

Shoben, E. J., Rips, L. J., & Smith, E. E. *Issues in semantic memory: A response to Glass and Holyoak*. (Tech. Rep. No. 101). Center for the Study of Reading, University of Illinois, 1978.

Shoben, E. J., Wescourt, K. T., & Smith, E. E. Sentence verification, sentence recognition, and the semantic/episode distinction. *Journal of Experimental Psychology: Human Learning and Memory*, 1978, *4*, 304–317.

Smith E. E. Theories of semantic memory. In W. K. Estes (Ed.), *Handbook of learning and cognitive processes* (Vol. 6). Hillsdale, N.J.: Lawrence Erlbaum Associates, 1978.

Smith, E. E., Rips, L. J., & Shoben, E. J. Semantic memory and psychological semantics. In G. H. Bower (Ed.), *The psychology of learning and motivation* (Vol. 8). New York: Academic Press, 1974.

Smith, E. E., Shoben, E. J., & Rips, L. J. Structure and process in semantic memory: A featural model for semantic decisions. *Psychological Review,* 1974, *81,* 214–241.

Smith, F. *Understanding reading.* New York: Holt, Rinehart & Winston, 1971.

Tulving, E. Episodic and semantic memory. In E. Tulving & W. Donaldson (Eds.), *Organization and Memory.* New York: Academic Press, 1972.

Wheeler, D. D. Processes in word recognition. *Cognitive Psychology,* 1970, *1,* 59–85.

13 The Meaning of Words in Context

Richard C. Anderson
Zohara Shifrin
*Center for the Study of Reading,
University of Illinois, Urbana-Champaign*

People understand words they know in an unbounded range of sentences. To account for the generality of understanding, it is usually assumed that every word must have a fixed, abstract meaning. However, a close look at most words in ordinary use will show shifts in meaning from context to context. Variations in meaning are readily appreciated in the uses of *game* (Wittgenstein, 1953, *cup* (Labov, 1973), *eat* (Anderson & Ortony, 1975), *red* (Halff, Ortony, & Anderson, 1976), and *held* (Anderson, Pichert, Goetz, Shallert, Stevens, & Trollip, 1976), for instance. The changes in the sense of the word *kick* and the reference of the word *ball* in the following sentences provide further intuitively clear cases.

1. The punter kicked the ball.
2. The baby kicked the ball.
3. The golfer kicked the ball.

A different sort of ball is, loosely speaking, implied by each sentence. The punter is kicking a football and the golfer a golfball. Although a baby could be kicking either of these kinds of ball, this is not the inference that will be drawn by most readers. Instead, a ball a baby is likely to kick will be hypothecated—perhaps, a brightly colored, inflated, plastic ball.

Kick has different senses in the three sentences. Compare the smooth, powerful kick of a punter with the hesitant, uncoordinated, possibly accidental kick of a baby. Golfers ordinarily do not kick their balls; this fact lead to the supposition that this one was angry or maybe cheating.

Rather than having a fixed, abstract meaning, a word can be conceived to have a "family" of potential meanings (Wittgenstein, 1953). Let us explore this analogy. There are varying degrees of resemblance among the members of a human family. Two members can be alike in one respect, and each like a third member in an entirely different respect. Though each is recognizable as a member of the same family, there need be no single attribute that all share. The relation among the various uses of a word can be aptly characterized as "family resemblance." Many theorists have supposed that words are defined by a *fixed* set of semantic components (Bierwisch, 1970; Katz & Fodor, 1963). The contrasting view presented for consideration here is that the set of salient or critical properties *shifts* from use to use. A property that is distinguishing in one case may be unimportant or even absent in another. Extending the position of Smith, Shoben, and Rips (1974), we propose that few words have any absolutely defining features but only characteristic ones.

A word considered without context permits many interpretations. When considered in context, its meaning is further articulated in a process of inferential interpolation based on knowledge of the world. Usually the scope of reference is constrained to a subset of the cases that otherwise would be denoted or even to a single real or imagined case. We have called this process *instantiation* (Anderson & McGaw, 1973; Anderson et al., 1976).

Words vary in the extent to which, without context, they constrain interpretation. At one limit are pronouns and very general terms such as *thing, did,* and *somebody.* At the other extreme are singular expressions such as *Grand Canyon* and *Buckingham Palace.* However, context can influence the meaning of even singular terms. Notice what happens to the intension of *Chicago* in the following three sentences.

4. Chicago has a new mayor.
5. A blizzard has engulfed Chicago.
6. There were serious riots in Chicago last night.

In Sentence 4 Chicago is a political entity, in 5 a geographical entity, in 6 a social entity. It is the same city, but different aspects are made salient in the three contexts.

Without context, every word places some boundaries on possible instantiations. But these boundaries taken one word at a time generally are too loose to account for the precision, richness, and detail of the mental representation to which connected discourse gives rise. Thus, the meaning of an utterance could not consist of the abstract core meanings of its constituent words coordinated on the basis of grammatical rules.

Every theorist recognizes the need to provide different readings for categorically distinct meanings of words, as in *ball*—a round thing, *ball*—a formal dance, or *ball*—a good time. We are simply proposing to extend this principle to the uses of a term that would be said to involve the "same" sense, that is, to the more subtle forms of polysemy illustrated with the sentences about balls being kicked and Chicago. The usual gambit to deal with polysemy is to postulate a different reading to handle each recognizable variation in sense. This works for categorically distinct uses. But a word can have a slightly different meaning in indefinitely many of the sentences in which it might appear. A theory will become unmanageable and will lose its generative power if there are different readings in the subjective lexicon for most uses (see Anderson & Ortony, 1975; Weinreich, 1966).

The information about, for instance, the kind of ball that a punter is likely to kick is not a semantic fact to be found in the subjective lexicon listed under *punter, ball,* or *kick.* Rather it is a part of knowledge of the world. It follows that an adequate theory of language comprehension will necessarily entail an account of how extralinguistic knowledge is brought to bear. A message is only a cryptic recipe for the construction of a meaning; the message itself does not contain all of the ingredients; much must be supplied by the hearer or reader from knowledge of the world and analysis of context.

It is not our claim that people always instantiate. In the first place, people must be able to deal with expressions such as *All men are mortal.* In the second place, we regard instantiation as a fallible or uncertain process that people do not always follow through to completion. Instantiation entails "deep" processing, but people sometimes are content to process discourse at a "shallow" level.

Full comprehension of most utterances requires people to form a representation that is more particularized than could be generated solely on the basis of the abstract semantics of the constituent words. Our reasoning is similar to Lees' (1960). He said that even when we

> confine our attention to nouns which are names of things, it is clear that no extant lexicon contains anywhere near enough expressions of this kind to suffice even for ordinary daily life. We cannot get along with any single common noun to refer to a familiar object, but must have at every moment modifiers with which to construct new, more complex names to use for all the specific instances of that object which we encounter and talk about [p. xvii].

Carrying Lees' analysis of a step further, in actual practice linguistic descriptions are seldom, if ever, adequate to uniquely discriminate a thing, event, or property from all others in the universe. To illustrate, *the redhead* is an imprecise description in an unbounded domain, but it will uniquely identify an individual in many contexts. People could not understand the truncated descriptions to which they are constantly exposed unless they are instantiated on the basis of their knowledge of the context and the world.

The remainder of this chapter contains a review of selected empirical research on the meanings of words in context. The next section examines studies involving adults. The following sections deal with the development of word meanings in children.

INSTANTIATION AMONG ADULTS

Several studies using an indirect cued recall paradigm have suggested that people tend to instantiate the general terms encountered in discourse. Anderson and McGaw (1973) presented sentences containing general concrete nouns listed in the Battig and Montague (1969) norms. The most probable exemplars of the general terms are the ones named by the most frequent associates in the norms. For instance, one of the sentences was *The clothing caught on the lock. Shirt* is the most frequent associate of *clothing* so, if the hypothesis is correct, there probably will be an instantiation in the form of a shirt. Also selected from the norms were two equally probable, low associates of the general term, one signifying a case bearing a greater resemblance than the other to the predicted instantiation. In the case of *clothing,* the two low associates were *jacket* and *slacks.* A shirt is more like a jacket than like slacks, thus it was reasoned that *jacket* would make a better retrieval cue for the clothing sentence than *slacks.* In two experiments, among a pair of low associates, the one referring to a case that resembled the most probable exemplar of the category named by the general term evoked the greater recall of the rest of the sentence.

To give an idea of the magnitude of the difference, in Experiment 2, the probability of responding correctly to the low associate naming a case that was *like* the expected instantiation of the general term (given recall to the general term itself) was .79, whereas the comparable figure for the low associate naming a case *unlike* the predicted instantiation was .59. These results suggest that people use exemplars to represent the meanings of pronouns encountered in sentences. It is improbable that uncontrolled properties of the low associates explains their differential effectiveness as cues. The pairs were: (1) equally likely to be evoked as associates by the general term; (2) equally likely to evoke the general term as an associate; and (3) equally frequent in the Thorndike-Lorge (1944) norms.

Whereas Anderson and McGaw were able to predict instantiations using tables of norms, their materials were designed to minimize the effects of context. Context ordinarily has a strong influence on instantiation. Evidence that this is the case has obtained by Barclay, Bransford, Franks, McCarrell, and Nitsch (1974), and Anderson and Ortony (1975). In the latter study, subjects saw, for instance, either *The container held the apples* or *The container held the cola* and then received in counterbalanced orders both *basket* and *bottle* as retrieval cues. *Basket* was a much more effective cue for the first sentence, *bottle* for the second. Another example from this study illustrates an inference about an instrument not expressly mentioned in a sentence. *Hammer* was a better cue than *fist* for recall of *The accountant pounded the stake,* but less effective for recall of *The accountant pounded the desk.*

It might be admitted that people make inferences about details, while at the same time maintaining that the essence of the representation for an encoded utterance consists of core meanings. The details people apparently incorporate into their representations could be nothing more than optional embroidery. Anderson et al. (1976) sought to test the stronger view that instantiation is integral to sentence comprehension and memory. Sentences were constructed with general terms in the subject noun position. The rest of each sentence was designed to cause a certain instantiation of the general term. Here is an example: *The fish attacked the swimmer.* Especially after the movie *Jaws,* most people will think of this fish as a shark. Later the cues *fish* and *shark* were presented. In three experiments, the particular terms naming the expected instantiations were substantially better cues for recall of the last words in the target sentences than the general terms contained in these sentences. This fact is difficult to square with any theory that presumes that it is the fixed core meanings of terms that are encoded and stored.

These experiments were designed to try to preclude the interpretation that the particular terms were better cues because of stronger associations to the constituent words. The technique was to write control sentences that contained the same words as a target sentence but did not constrain the interpretation of the subject noun to a certain exemplar. For example, the sentence *The fish avoided the swimmer* is less likely to produce a shark instantiation than its companion target sentence, yet, given the control sentence, *swimmer* would be recalled to the cue *shark* if the association between these two words were of overriding importance. Also included in two of the experiments were controls for the other instantiation–guiding words in the target sentences, for example, *The Communists attacked the village.* Recall of target sentences given particular cues was about twice as great as recall of the control sentences given these cues. It was concluded that associative interpretations give a poor account of the data.

Gumenik (1979) found that several different particular terms made better cues than a general terms that had actually appeared in a sentence. For instance, *barracuda* as well as *shark* led to better recall of the sentence about the fish attacking the swimmer. Gumenik wanted to conclude that this was inconsistent with the instantiation hypothesis. He maintained that ordinarily a person wouldn't think of both a shark and a barracuda when reading the sentence, yet he argued that that is what would be required in order for both words to be good cues. Gumenik has construed the instantiation hypothesis in too limited a fashion. In their most cautious statement of the hypothesis, Anderson et al (1976, p. 667) indicated that any narrowing of the sense and reference of a term counts as instantiation. Thus, in the case being used for illustration, a delimitation of fish to aggressive man-eaters is instantiation. Both sharks and barracudas are members of this smaller class and, thus, both *shark* and *barracuda* will be effective cues. It must be acknowledged, though, that according to a bolder and more interesting version of the instantiation hypothesis, when the context is rich, readers ought to commit themselves to quite specific interpretations of general terms. In this latter view, it is to be assumed that many readers did think of the fish as a shark. Even under this assumption *barracuda* would still be a good cue. Indeed, it can be argued that it is conceptually closer to *shark* than *fish* is (see Medin & Schaffer, 1978). The conclusion is that Gumenik's results are compatible with the instantiation hypothesis, whether it is given a cautious or a bold interpretation.

Several experiments have shown substitutions in recall that are consistent with the instantiation hypothesis (see Schweller, Brewer, & Dahl, 1976). Gentner (1975) has obtained some especially clear evidence for context-guided instantiation. She prepared stories that made likely the substitution of the particular verbs *pay* or *loan* for the more general verb *gave* in recall of a common last sentence *Max finally gave Sam the ten dollars.* In one story, Max was described as owing money to Sam. In the other, Sam simply asked Max for some money. Neither story contained *pay* or *loan.* Among those who heard the version that involved owing money, 30% reproduced *gave* when recalling the last sentence, whereas 47% substituted *paid* or *paid back,* and none used *loaned.* Subjects who had heard the story that involved asking for money recalled the last sentence quite differently: 33% repeated *gave,* 34% used *loaned,* whereas none substituted *paid* or *paid back.*

Anderson et al. (1976), in the studies previously described, also investigated substitutions of particular terms for general terms in free recall. Such substitutions occurred in only 11% of the cases in which sentences were recalled at all. They concluded that there must have been some sort of representation of the general term, quite likely of its surface form. Their explanation for the low percentage of particular term substitutions was as follows: Assume that every stage of processing leaves a memorial trace. Remembering begins with retrieval of the semantic representation, usually— it was presumed—an instantiation. Then the representation is coded into language and there is a check to see whether there is a trace for this surface form. If there is a match, the response is made. If not, depending on demand characteristics, a search is made for the original word. The demand characteristics of the Anderson et al. (1976) studies may have predisposed subjects against substitutions of particular terms. Every target sentence contained a subject noun obviously more abstract than the basic level of description (see Rosch, Mervis, Gray, Johnson, & Boyes-Braem, 1976). It would have been easy to edit output according to the rule that the subject noun must be more abstract than the name of the presumably specific concept generated from memory.

Garnham (1979) found that contextually appropriate specific verbs were better cues than general verbs that were contained in a series of to-be-recalled sentences. For instance, *fried* was a better word than *cooked* for recall of the *Housewife cooked the chips.* (The study was completed in Great Britain. In British English, french fries are called chips.) However, on a recognition test subjects chose the version containing the general verb 72% of the time but selected the one in which the specific verb had been substituted only 22% of the time. This result is consistent with the hypothesis that some information about the surface form of words is retained in memory.

Using a different paradigm, Halff et al (1976) showed that context serves to narrow the possible representations of a term. Subjects judged whether the red object mentioned in each of 19 sentences was redder, less red than, or could be equally as red as the red object mentioned in each of the other sentences. The ratings of redness systematically varied according to sentence context. The rating data could be satisfactorily characterized in terms of an interval order but not a semiorder or full order. This indicates that the meaning of *red* in each context could not be represented as a point-value—that is, as a single, precise shade of red—but, rather, had to be represented as an interval or band whose width also depended on context. The general implication is that, rather than having fixed meanings, terms have variable meanings partitioned according to shifting context-sensitive boundaries.

Labov (1973) has completed some especially provocative work illuminating the shortcomings of the "categorical view" of word meaning. According to Labov, this view defines words in terms of discrete, invariant categories, which are qualitatively distinct, conjunctively defined, and composed of atomic primitives. Labov's experiments suggest that the rather vague and hedged definitions found in ordinary dictionaries—replete with *usually, often, sometimes*—are in closer agreement with actual language use than the fixed, all-or-none definitions assumed in most linguistic and psychological models. Labov showed subjects drawings of permutations of a standard cup. The width, height, contents, material of construction, and number of handles were all factors in determining whether a drawing of an object would be called a *cup, mug, bowl, vase,* and so on. A most interesting finding was the interaction of characteristics of an object with context. For instance, a vessel of a given width was more likely to be labeled a cup if it was said to contain coffee than if it was said to contain soup. Labov's research demonstrates the fuzziness of the concept cup and its dependence on context for resolution.

In summary, research with adult subjects involving diverse tasks and measures indicates that word meanings are context-sensitive. A pervasive effect of context is to allow people to narrow or focus the encoded representation of a word, a process that we have termed instantiation.

INSTANTIATION AMONG CHILDREN

In this section, the following questions are asked: Do children instantiate? When a child hears or sees the word *father,* for example, does he think about his own father, or is it a general, abstract representation that comes into his mind? If children do instantiate, is their process of instantiation similar to adults'? If it is different, what are the differences?

Anderson, Stevens, Shiffrin, and Osborn (1978) have completed the one study of instantiation of word meanings in children of which we are aware. Twenty pairs of sentences were written. Both members of each pair contained a word whose instantiation depended upon the sentence context. For example, one pair of sentences was *Sally looked at the clock in her bedroom* and *Sally looked at the clock in her classroom.* Four line drawings were done for each pair of sentences. Two pictures represented the expected instantiations of the target word in the two sentences, one picture represented another possible instantiation of the target word, and the fourth picture was of a completely unrelated object that served as a distractor. For the clock sentences, the four pictures showed a typical electric alarm clock, a standard classroom-type wall clock, a grandfather clock, and a sponge. The sentences were read to 30 first-graders and 30 fourth-graders. For each sentence the child was instructed to point to the picture that best fit the sentence. Overall, the first-graders picked the expected picture 92% of the time, and the fourth-graders did so 97% of the time.

The logic of the experiment was that, if the child were endcoding an undifferentiated sense for a target word, he or she would be equally likely to choose any of the pictured examples. If this were so, the hit rate would be about 33% because there were three examples for each target word. It is clear, therefore, that the children were not simply bringing to mind abstract concepts but were instantiating specific concepts for the target words.

Although the study that has just been described surely demonstrates that children *can* draw inferences in instantiation, it may give an overly optimistic picture of the likelihood that they *will* draw them. There is considerable evidence that young children do not always make even obvious inferences. For example, Paris and Lindauer (1976) constructed sentences in which the instrument that would be used to accomplish some action was obvious—for instance, *The workman dug a hole in the ground (with a shovel).* Sentences were presented to first-, third-, and fifth-graders, with the instrument explicitly stated, or unstated and, therefore, left implicit. Then the names of the instruments were presented as cues and the children were asked to recall the remainder of each sentence. Fifth-graders recalled almost as many sentences when the cue was implicit as when it was explicit. The explicit–implicit difference was much larger for third-graders and larger still for first-graders.

Although the Paris and Lindauer study, as well as a number of others (e.g., Trabasso, Riley, & Wilson, 1975), show that children as young as 6 or even younger (Macnamara, Baker, & Olson, 1976) can make inferences of various sorts, there is a clear developmental trend: The older the child, the more likely the inference. Instantiation has been hardly studied at all in children, but it is reasonable to guess that the process parallels inferencing of other types. Thus, we would be surprised if the tendency to engage in instantiation did not show about the same developmental time course as hypothecating an unstated instrument.

Why are young children apparently less likely to draw an inference than older children and adults? One general reason is suggested in a further experiment of Paris and Lindauer (1976). Asking first-graders to act out each sentence resulted in an overall enhancement of memory and, more interesting, brought performance with implicit cues up to the level observed with explicit cues. This indicates that the children were now making inferences while processing the sentences. Evidently, first-graders are able to make inferences of instantiation but they do not always do so spontaneously.

Brown's (1975) excellent review and synthesis indicates that young children do not approach memory tasks, nor perhaps even comprehension tasks, with deliberate, planful processing strategies. Techniques such as having children act out the episode described in a sentence appear to cause them to engage in processing activities that they would not otherwise undertake. Process-invoking cover tasks make a big difference with young children, ordinarily less difference with older children and adults, presumably because most of the latter process in a functional manner without prompting.

Helpful context can have a huge effect on children's comprehension, memory, and problem solving. Many studies have shown that placing a verb between two nouns to form a meaningful sentence, such as *Roses like rain,* makes the noun pair much easier to learn for young children (Rohwer, 1967). But the same procedure has little effect with adults, or even a negative effect when compared to a condition in which the person constructs in his own sentence (Bobrow & Bower, 1969). Again, the reason seems to be that adults spontaneously elaborate noun pairs into meaningful configurations; so, furnishing a sentence does not help. Children are less likely to elaborate; thus, providing a sentence is facilitative.

In young children, context can support inference drawing. Hildyard (1976) has studied three-term series problems. The following is an example of her materials: *The policeman was in front of the clown. The garbageman was behind the clown.* The problem for the child was to infer whether the policeman was in front of or in back of the garbageman. Other children heard an alternate form of the passage (Hildyard, 1976):

> The policeman, on his hosrse, was in front of the clown so that he could clear a way for the parade. The garbageman was behind the clown collecting the candy wrappers from the candies the clowns gave to the kids on the sidewalk [p. 8]

First-graders did much better with the augmented version whereas third- and fifth-graders did only slightly better. Notice that the context did not change the logic of the problem. Instead it appears to rationalize the spatial arrangement of the characters, perhaps inviting the child to construct a veridical mental configuration. Once this has been done, solving such problems is easy (Barclay, 1973).

To summarize what we have said so far, young children are less likely to draw inferences involving discourse—including, probably, inferences of instantiation—because they have yet to acquire sophiscated metacomprehension and metamemorial knowledge and skill (Brown, 1975). Another reason for poor inferencing on the part of young children may be their lack of understanding of certain complex linguistic forms, a matter that is considered in the next section.

DEVELOPMENT OF WORD SEMANTICS
IN CONTEXT

That there is general improvement through the school years in children's ability to use and understand language seems obvious, though perhaps the point should be documented because of the widely heralded claim that language acquisition is essentially completed by age 5. Entwisle and Frasure (1974) found that 6-, 7-, 8-, and 9-year-olds were equally poor at reproducing random word strings such as: *Confused falling brightly the clock children.* The 6-year-olds were little better with grammatically acceptable but anomolous strings such as *The brightly falling clock told customers* and meaningful sentences such as *The gently ticking clock told time.* However, there were year-by-year increases in the accuracy with which the syntactically well-formed strings were repeated and even bigger increases in the reproduction of meaningful sentences. The 9-year-olds were about twice as likely to correctly reproduce a syntactically acceptable string and three times as likely to reproduce a sentence as they were to correctly repeat a random word string. The data show that the ability to use syntactic and semantic information increases over the early school years. In this experiment, Entwisle and Frasure (1974) failed to replicate a small, unpublished, but often cited experiment by McNeil (1965), who had found no improvement in reproduction of anomolous by syntactically acceptable strings in children 6 to 8 years of age.

Turning now to analyses of specific deficits in linguistic understanding, E. Clark (1973) has marshaled an array of evidence in support of the proposition that the meaning a young child has for a word is likely to be more global, less differentiated than that of an older person. With increasing age, the child makes more and more of the distinctions an adult would make. Clark has couched her treatment of the growth of word meanings in the language of semantic feature theory: When first learned, a child's definition of a word need not include all of the features of the adult concept. Eventually, the missing features will be added.

The most subtle evidence for the progressive differentiation view is the manner in which the meaning of pairs of dimensional adjectives develops. The pioneering study was done by Donaldson and Balfour (1968). They questioned 3-year-olds about which of two cardboard apple trees contained more or less apples. To their surprise, the children responded as though they thought *less* was synonymous with *more*. That is, whether asked to pick the tree with more apples or the tree with less apples, the children consistently chose the one with more. Donaldson and Wales (1970) examined the children's understanding of *same* and *different* and also several other pairs or relational terms. The results paralleled those obtained with *more* or *less*.

We should note in passing that the Donaldson and Balfour (1968) finding that "less is more" for 3-year-olds has been replicated; the finding appears to be robust over several variations in procedure (Palermo, 1974). However, Glucksberg, Hay, and Danks (1976) discovered an artifact in the study by Donaldson and Wales (1970) and, contrary to their finding, demonstrated that 2½-year-old children do not understand the word *same* to mean *different*. Instead, children of this age interpret these terms appropriately in the same fashion as adults.

Contrasting dimensional adjectives often form what are called "marked-unmarked" pairs. In English, the unmarked term can be used to refer to the dimension of concern as well as the positive end of this dimension. Consider the pair *strong-weak*. You could ask "How strong is the door?" without implying that the door is strong. However, asking "How weak is the door?" suggests that the door is on the weak side of average. Both the unmarked and marked term can be used contrastively (*The door is strong, The door is weak*). But only the unmarked term can be used nominally, that is, to refer to the dimension.

Applying these notions to the development of the meanings of *more* and *less*, E. Clark (1973; see also, H. Clark, 1970) argues that *more* is first understood simply to mean "amount" or "quantity of." This is the nominal sense, so if the analysis is correct, no particular amount, large or small, is understood. The reason that this is the first stage of understanding is, she says, that "the dimension itself has to be there before one can talk about greater or lesser extent along that dimension [p. 90]." At this stage, *less* is not differentiated from *more* so it too is understood in the nominal sense. Why are both terms applied as though they meant "more?" E. Clark's answer "that having extent is always best exemplified by the object with the *most* extent [p. 90]." At the last stage, *more* and *less* can be understood in the contrastive sense, and *less* is differentiated for *more*.

Brewer and Stone (1975) have presented a somewhat different analysis of the development of understanding of dimensional adjectives, which they tested with contrasting pairs of spatial terms such as *tall–short* and *wide–narrow*. Their theory is that children learn the concept represented by positive or unmarked terms before learning the underlying dimensions. The second aspect of Brewer and Stone's theory is that the differentiated senses of *long, wide, tall* and so forth evolve from an amorphous concept of bigness. Finally, Brewer and Stone assume, as others have, that the meaning of positive terms is acquired before the meanings of the corresponding marked, negative terms. Four-year-olds were presented arrays of four objects—for example, a tall object, a short object, a wide object, and a narrow object—and were asked, for instance, to "touch the wide one." According to the Clarks' theory that the underlying dimension is learned first, confusions should have been between, for example, *wide* and *narrow*. However, the results showed that errors more often involved confusing positive terms with positive terms and negative terms with negative terms. For instance, if a child made a mistake with *wide,* he was more likely to choose the tall object than the narrow object. Thus, the results were consistent with Brewer and Stone's theory.

The acquisition of the distinctions entailed in sets of related verbs has been an active area of inquiry in recent years. For example, Gentner (1975) examined verbs of possession. Her theoretical analysis indicated that *buy, sell,* and *spend* entail a more complex set of distinctions than *give* and *take*. The terms *pay* and *trade* were determined to be intermediate in complexity. The grounds for the claim that, for instance, *sell* is more complex than *give* can be appreciated without tracing Gentner's entire analysis. Giving involves the transfer of something from one person to another. Selling likewise involves the transfer of something from one person to another but it involves an additional transaction as well, the transfer of money from the buyer to the seller.

Gentner expected children to acquire the meanings of terms in order of complexity. Children ranging from 4 to 8 years of age were asked to make dolls act out transactions from directions involving each verb. For example, the children were requested to "make Ernie sell Bert a (toy) car." The four-year-olds performed flawlessly with directions containing *give* and *take* but never correctly executed instructions that involved *spend, buy,* or *sell.* The 8-

year-olds exhibited nearly perfect understanding of every direction except the ones containing *sell*. Overall, the results were exactly as expected: The meanings of verbs of possession are acquired in order of complexity.

Gentner's error analysis suggested that the younger children treated the complex verbs as though they were simple ones. She says:

> the commonest incorrect response was some form of one-way transfer. . . . It is noteworthy that for all five complex verbs the erroneous one-way transfers are in the correct direction. . . . For example, the young child acting out *buy* and *sell* completely disregards the money transfer that should be a part of their meanings, yet performs the object transfer in the correct direction. He reacts to *buy* as if it were *take*. He treats *sell* as if it were *give* [p. 242]."

When asked to "make Bert spend some money," even the youngest child correctly handles the money transfer, but he neglects to have Bert get anything for the money he "spends." The child treats *spend money* as though it meant give money away.

Although there are some differences in theoretical interpretation and some findings appear to hinge on procedural details, most of the research done to date points to the conclusion that there is progressive differentiation of word meanings with increasing age and experience. However, it has been argued that this cannot be the whole story. Notably, Nelson (1974, 1977) has theorized that children learn the meanings of most words by learning their significance in familiar "scripts." A script is generic knowledge about a common life episode. A child will acquire scripts for such mundane events as eating a family dinner, getting ready for bed, and going on a shopping trip, for instance. The script consists of the knowledge about the roles certain people play in these episodes and the typical sequence of events. The child will also learn the vocabulary appropriate for talking about the objects and actions in scripted episodes. Nelson's hypothesis is that the young child's understanding of words in context initially is bound to the particular circumstances of the common episodes in which the words were acquired. As he or she grows older, the child eventually is able to use and understand words without as much contextual support.

Based on reasoning similar to Nelson's, Richards (1976) argued that young children's apparent failure to comprehend certain words might be due to a dependence on context rather than lack of knowledge of the adult distinctions entailed by words. Richards studied children's understanding of the verb pairs *come-go* and *bring-take*. These verbs have "deictic content"; that is, their meanings are relative to the position of the speaker or addressee. Children of 4 to 8 years of age had to use the appropriate verbs in play situations in which they were active participants. For instance, *come* and *go* were elicited in a game in which the child "lived" in one of several "houses."

An experimenter would hold up a vividly painted cardboard "flame" behind one of the houses. The child was the "firewatcher" whose job was to call the other experimenter to *come* or *go* to the house to put out the fire. The correct response was to say *come* when the fire was at the child's own house and *go* when it was at one of the other houses. In this situation, even the youngest children used the verbs perfectly. The children made more mistakes using *bring* and *take* in a similar game, but, again, the 4- and 5-year-olds did nearly as well as the older children.

Richards' results contrast sharply with those obtained by Clark and Garnica (1974). Withoug going into detail, these investigators assessed understanding of *come-go* and *bring-take* in tasks that involved identifying the perspectives of toy animals situated in different locations. The results suggested, among other things, dramatic increases in comprehension of the verbs from 4 to 9 years of age. However, when the task is simplified, as Richards did, so that only one's own perspective is critical, then the young child performs almost as well as the older child.

To summarize this section, children's competence at using and understanding important but common words improves from early childhood through the primary school years. It is only reasonable to suppose that some of this improvement is attributable to acquiring finer distinctions in the senses of the words (of course, it is obvious that during this period children also will be learning new words and concepts). But, in addition, there are concurrent changes in language functioning. Children become increasingly able to use words in a depersonalized and decontextualized fashion.

To the extent that development does involve progressive differentiation of word meanings, what implications does this have for the process of instantiation? It implies, first, that a child's instantiations of words often will be less finely articulated than an adult's, for no one can employ a distinction he does not possess. However, whether a person has a more or less differentiated meaning for a word has nothing to do with the likelihood he will instantiate. Consider the child who takes *sell* to mean that an object is transferred from one person to another without a complimentary transfer of money. To say that this child's understanding of *sell*, in an actual use, is somehow more "abstract" than that of a person who knows the full, adult meaning is simply an odd and confusing way of speaking. Another example will further illuminate the point. Suppose there is a child who at a certain stage calls all adult males *Daddy*. Usually, when he uses the term, the child will mean a specific man, his father. On other occasions he will mean different, but still specific men. It is only reasonable to assume in addition that upon hearing *Daddy*, the child usually will understand a specific man—and that is what we mean by instantiation. To be sure, because he is assumed to possess a general term, the child sometimes may intend when speaking, and understand when hearing, a comment as about more than one adult male, but that is another matter.

IMPLICATIONS FOR EDUCATION

The preceding sections surveyed arguments and evidence pointing to the conclusion that people tend to instantiate the words encountered in discourse. Although the evidence is meager, it appears that children beginning school are able to instantiate but that they are less likely to do so than older persons. Probably the chief reason is that children do not spontaneously draw inferences to flesh out that which is literally given in a message. Adults know that "reading between the lines" is ordinarily required for full comprehension. Furthermore, when they do instantiate, the constructions children place on semantically complex words may be impoverished because they do not make all of the adult distinctions.

Developing lesson materials and teaching techniques to speed development of instantiation skills should not be difficult. Paris and Lindauer (1976), in the study outlined earlier, obtained dramatic results from simply instructing children to perform the actions described in sentences. If the parallel with other metacomprehension processes holds true, the problem will not be so much one causing a child to make an instantiation inference on a particular occasion as one of insuring that he continues to make them on his own when the facilitative cover tasks, hints, and helpful context are withdrawn (Campione & Brown, 1976). This suggests the need for an educational regimen that supports maintenance and generalization.

We take it as nearly axiomatic that most children come to school quite capable of instantiation. Otherwise they would comprehend almost nothing of the language they hear. It would be incredible to suppose, for instance, that a normal first-grader who heard *Put on a shirt* would be systematically unable to conceive of specific objects that appropriately fit the description. However, instantiation of oral language is one thing, instantiation of printed language another. As Olson (1977) has argued, prose is not written in the "mother tongue." It differs from oral language in a number of respects (see Rubin, Chapter 17, this volume). A most important difference is that a context is less rich with instantiation-guiding information. A boy told *Put on a shirt* knows it must be a shirt suitable for him, no doubt one he owns already, probably one appropriate for a certain activity or occasion that the unstated context makes clear. He will know a particular, concrete shirt that meets these requirements. Contrast this rich context with the lean context supplied in a story when there is mention of a character putting on a shirt.

Oral language ordinarily is an instrument in the service of some purpose. The purpose brings with it a motivation to understand and criteria for determining whether understanding has occurred. The purpose of reading prose is often more obscure. Often it is simply to be "read."

The demand characteristics of school may lead children in the early grades to believe that "simply reading" is more a matter of correct pronunciation than complete comprehension. On the other hand, too much emphasis on using context and prior knowledge to augment the message may have the unfortunate side effect of leading children to ignore the print. It is known that poor readers frequently make wild guesses at words after incomplete and unsuccessful attempts to decode (Biemiller, 1970). Thus, we are cautious in our endorsement of the principle that reading is a "psycholinguistic guessing game" (Goodman, 1967). Closer to the truth is the characterization of reading as a difficult balancing act. Text and extratext information both must be applied, in the proper portions, at the right times.

ACKNOWLEDGMENT

The preparation of this paper was supported by the National Institute of Education under Contract No. US-NIE-C-400-76-0116.

REFERENCES

Anderson, R. C., & McGaw, B. On the representation of the meanings of general terms. *Journal of Experimental Psychology,* 1973, *101,* 301–306.

Anderson, R. C., & Ortony, A. On putting apples into bottles—A problem of polysemy. *Cognitive Psychology,* 1975, *1,* 167–180.

Anderson, R. C., Pichert, J. W., Goetz, E. T., Shallert, D. L., Stevens, K. W., & Trollip, S. R. Instantiation of general terms. *Journal of Verbal Learning and Verbal Behavior,* 1976, *15,* 667–679.

Anderson, R. C., Stevens, K. C., Shifrin, Z., & Osborn, J. Instantiation of word meanings in children. *Journal of Reading Behavior,* 1978, *10,* 149–157.

Barclay, J. R. The role of comprehension in remembering sentences. *Cognitive Psychology,* 1973, *4,* 229–254.

Barclay, J. R., Bransford, J. D., Franks, J. J., McCarrell, N. S., & Nitsch, K. Comprehension and semantic flexibility. *Journal of Verbal Learning and Verbal Behavior,* 1974, *13,* 471–481.

Batting, W. F., & Montague, W. E. Category norms of verbal items in 56 categories: A replication and extension of the Connecticut category norms. *Journal of Experimental Psychology Monograph,* 1969, *80*(3, pt. 2).

Biemiller, A. The development of the use of graphic and contextual information as children learn to read. *Reading Research Quarterly,* 1970, *6,* 75–96.

Bierwisch, M. Semantics, In J. Lyons (Ed.), *New horizons in linguistics.* Baltimore: Penguin Books, 1970.

Bobrow, S. A., & Bower, G. H. Comprehension and recall of sentences. *Journal of Experimental Psychology,* 1969, *80,* 455–461.

Brewer, W. F., & Stone, B. J. Acquisition of spatial antonym pairs. *Journal of Experimental Child Psychology,* 1975, *19,* 299–307.

Brown, A. L. The development of memory: Knowing, knowing about knowing, and knowing how to know. In H. W. Reese (Ed.), *Advances in child development and behavior* (Vol. 10). New York: Academic Press, 1975.

Campione, J. C., & Brown, A. L. Memory and metamemory development in educable retarded children. In R. V. Kail, Jr. & J. W. Hagen (Eds.), *Perspectives on the development of memory and cognition.* Hillsdale, N.J.: Lawrence Erlbaum Associates, 1976.

Clark, E. V. What's in a word? On the child's acquisition of semantics in his first language. In T. E. Moore (Ed.), *Cognitive development and the acquisition of language*. New York: Academic Press, 1973.

Clark, E. V., & Garnica, O. K. Is he coming or going? On the acquisition of deictic verbs. *Journal of Verbal Learning and Verbal Behavior*, 1974, *13*, 559–572.

Clark, H. H. The primitive nature of children's relational concepts. In J. R. Hayes (Ed.), *Cognition and the development of langauge*. New York: Wiley, 1970.

Donaldson, M., & Balfour, G. Less is more: A study of language comprehension in children. *British Journal of Psychology*, 1968, *59*, 461–471.

Donaldson, M., & Wales, R. J. On the acquisition of some relational terms. In J. R. Hayes (Ed.), *Cognition and the development of language*. New York: Wiley, 1970.

Entwisle, D. R., & Frasure, N. E. A contradiction resolved: Children's processing of syntactic cues. *Developmental Psychology*, 1974, *10*, 852–857.

Garnham, A. Instantiation of verbs. *Quarterly Journal of Experimental Psychology*, 1979, *31*, 207–214.

Gentner, D. Evidence for the psychological reality of semantic components: The verbs of possession. In D. A. Norman,. & D. E. Rumelhart, & the LNR Research Group, *Explorations in cognition*. San Francisco: Freeman, 1975.

Glucksberg, S., Hay, A., & Danks, J. H. Words in utterance contexts: Young children do not confuse the meaning of same and different. *Child Development*, 1976, *47*, 737–741.

Goodman, K. S. Reading: A psycholinguistic guessing game. *Journal of Reading Specialist*, May 1967, 126–135.

Gumenik, W. E. The advantage of specific terms over general terms as cues for sentence recall: Instantiation or retrieval. *Memory and Cognition*, 1979, *1*, 240–244.

Halff, H. M., Ortony, A., & Anderson, R. C. A context-sensitive representation of word meanings. *Memory and Cognition*, 1976, *4*, 378–383.

Hildyard, A. *Children's abilities to produce inferences from written and oral material*. Unpublished doctoral dissertation, University of Toronto, 1976.

Katz, J. J., & Fodor, J. A. The structure of semantic theory. *Language*, 1963, *39*, 170–210.

Labov, W. The boundaries of words and their meanings. In C. J. Bailey & R. Shuy (Eds.), *New ways of analyzing variation in English*. Washington, D.C.: Georgetown University Press, 1973.

Lees, R. B. *Grammar of English nominalizations*. Bloomington, Ind.: University of Indiana Press, 1960.

Macnamara, J., Baker, E., & Olson, C. L. Four-year-olds' understanding of *pretend, forget*, and *know*: Evidence for propositional operations. *Child Development*, 1976, *47*, 62–70.

McNeil, D. *Is child language semantically consistent?* Unpublished manuscript, Harvard University, Center for Cognitive Studies, 1965.

Medin, D. L. & Schaffer, M. M. Context theory of classification learning. *Psychological Review*, 1978, *85*, 207–238.

Nelson, K. Concept, word and sentence: Interrelations in acquisition and development. *Psychological Review*, 1974, *31*, 267–285.

Nelson, K. Cognitive development and the acquisition of concepts. In R. C. Anderson, R. J. Spiro, & N. W. E. Montague (Eds.), *Schooling and the acquisition of knowledge*. Hillsdale, N. J.: Lawrence Erlbaum Associates, 1977.

Olson, D. R. The language of instruction: The literate bias of schooling. In R. C. Anderson, R. J. Spiro, & N. W. E. Montague (Eds.), *Schooling and the acquisition of knowledge*. Hillsdale, N.J.: Lawrence Erlbaum Associates, 1977.

Palermo, D. S. Still more about the comprehension of "less." *Developmental Psychology*, 1974, *10*, 827–829.

Paris, S. G., & Lindauer, B. K. The role of inference in children's comprehension and memory for sentences. *Cognitive Psychology*, 1976, *8*, 217–227.

Richards, M. R. *Come* and *Go* reconsidered: Children's use of deictic verbs in contrived situations. *Journal of Verbal Learning and Verbal Behavior,* 1976, *15,* 655–665.

Rohwer, W. D. *Social class differences in the role of linguistic structures in paired-associate learning: Elaboration and learning of proficiency* (Final Report, Project 5-0605, Contract No. OE-6-10-273). Washington D.C.: U.S. Office of Education, 1967.

Rosch, E., Mervis, C. B., Gray, W. D., Johnson, D. M., & Boyes-Braem, P. Basic objects in natural categories. *Cognitive Psychology,* 1976, *8,* 382–439.

Schweller, K. G., Brewer, W. F., & Dahl, D. A. Memory for illocutionary forces and perlocutionary effects of utterances. *Journal of Verbal Learning and Verbal Behavior,* 1976, *15,* 325–337.

Smith, E. E., Shoben, E., & Rips, L. J. Structure and process in semantic memory: A featural model of semantic decisions. *Psychological Review,* 1974, *31,* 214–241.

Trabasso, T., Riley, C. A., & Wilson, E. G. The representation of linear order and spatial strategies in reasoning: A developmental study. In R. Falmagne (Ed.), *Psychological studies of logic and its development.* Hillsdale, N.J.: Lawrence Erlbaum Associates, 1975.

Thorndike, E. L., & Lorge, I. *The teacher's word book of 30,000 words.* New York: Teacher's College, 1944.

Weinreich, U. Explorations in semantic theory. In T. A. Sebeok (Ed.), *Current trends in linguistics* (Vol. 3). The Hague: Mouton, 1966.

Wittgenstein, L. *Philosophical investigations.* (G. E. Anscombe, trans.). New York: Macmillan, 1953.

14 Metaphor

Andrew Ortony
Center for the Study of Reading,
University of Illinois, Urbana-Champaign

INTRODUCTION

The phenomenon of metaphor is much more complicated than it might seem. One looks to the dictionary to discover the standard account of metaphor as simply the use of a word or expression to refer to an object that it does not normally denote; and that, one might think, would be that. However, a good case can be made, and I think has been made, for supposing that such a conception of metaphor is inadequate (e.g., Ortony, Reynolds, & Arter, 1978a; Reddy, 1969; Van Dijk 1975). The questions such an account raises far outnumber those it answers. The most obvious of these questions is: If a word or expression is not being used in the normal way, how does a hearer or reader discover in what way it is being used? The answer to this question is far from clear. Some (e.g., Kintsch, 1974) have suggested that it is done by transforming the metaphor into a simile. So, for example, the metaphor *Mary is a block of ice* would be transformed into the simile *Mary is like a block of ice.* However, not all metaphors can be so transformed. Furthermore, the processes involved in the comprehension of similes themselves constitute a nontrivial problem (Ortony, 1979a; 1979b). A more general approach in the same vein is to argue that metaphors are really implicit analogies. According to this view, the metaphor is really an analogy that could be expressed, perhaps, something like this: "The relationship between Mary and her amorous exploits is the same as the relationship between a block of ice and its temperature." There may be some merit in this approach, but it has little explanatory value until one can work out the systematic relationships between metaphors, similes, and analogies, a problem that I am not about to

349

tackle here but that receives an excellent treatment in G. Miller (1979). A further problem with this kind of approach is that it presupposes that analogies themselves cannot be metaphorical. I suspect that this presupposition is incorrect (see Ortony, 1979a).

The question of how metaphors are understood is a question of central concern in this paper. I wish to highlight two reasons for dwelling on the topic; there are other reasons that will receive little or no attention. First, metaphors are widespread in both the written and oral language to which young children are exposed; they are there, and children are doubtless from time to time expected, required, or assumed to be able to understand them. Second, as I have argued elsewhere (Ortony, 1975; 1976), metaphors may be necessary communicative devices—unique and powerful ways of expressing the new in terms of the old. In other words, it may be the case not only that they are there but that sometimes they have to be there. This chapter has three parts. The first is primarily concerned with the comprehension processes. In particular, some of the literature on the development of the capacity to comprehend metaphors in children is discussed. The second part speculates about some theoretical mechanisms whereby the comprehension of metaphor might take place. Finally, the third part is concerned with the effects of metaphor on learning, particularly with respect to the role of metaphors in text.

THE COMPREHENSION OF METAPHOR AND ITS ONTOGENY

The terms in a metaphor are usually called the *topic* and the *vehicle*. The topic (sometimes also called the *tenor*) is the principal subject to which the metaphorical term or vehicle is being applied. So, if one says that an A is a B where A is not literally a B, then A would be the *topic* and B the *vehicle,* that is, the term being used metaphorically. Furthermore, insofar as the topic and the vehicle have something in common, the term *ground* is usually employed to refer to the relationships between the topic and vehicle that capture that commonality. One other technical terms needs to be introduced before we can proceed: the metaphorical *tension.* The tension in a metaphor is, or at least results from, the conceptual incompatibility between the topic and the vehicle (interpreted literally). Thus, to show the application of all these terms (first proposed by Richards, 1936) in another example, consider *The man is a wolf* uttered by someone intending to speak metaphorically. The topic is *man,* the vehicle is *wolf,* the ground is the comparative relationship between the two, and the tension is, or is caused by, the literal incompatibility between men and wolves. Thus, there is a sense in which the total meaning is exhausted by the conjunction of the ground and the tension of a metaphor.

Several theories of metaphor have been proposed since the time of Aristotle to modern times. Although not wishing to embark on a lengthy discussion of these theories and their defects (see, Ortony et al., 1978a, for such discussions), a few components do seem necessary by way of stage-setting. Roughly speaking there are three "theories," perhaps better called "views." The first is the *substitution view*, which alleges that metaphors are dispensable linguistic devices, almost frivolous in nature. They are dispensable because they can always be replaced by a literal paraphrase whose meaning lacks the mystery and enigma of the metaphor. They are frivolous because, for example, according to R. Miller (1976), they serve to surreptitiously obscure what could have been clearly stated; thus they seem to be convenient ways of disguising ignorance and uncertainty. The second view is usually called the *comparison view*. This view, well characterized by Alston (1964), alleges that a metaphor is an implicit comparison. Indeed, Alston claims that an important and noticeable similarity between the terms being (implicitly) compared is a necessary condition for a successful metaphor. Such a view fits well with the approach that Kintsch (1974) proposes, which I mentioned a the outset. The third general theory of metaphor is somewhat more complicated. Called the *interaction view* and espoused most notably by Richards (1936) and by Black (1962; 1979), it rests on the idea that the knowledge associated with the terms in the metaphor interacts to produce something new.

Rather than committing myself to any of these views, I shall offer a definition of metaphor that I think does justice to the facts. Furthermore, it is a definition that avoids the problems of the standard account mentioned at the outset because, unlike that account, it is based on the fact that not all metaphors are what one might call "part-sentence" metaphors. This means that they do not all involve an unconventional use of a particular word in such a way as to make a literal interpretation of the sentence in which the word or phrase appears either nonsensical, impossible, or false. Some metaphors are metaphors only because the contexts in which they appear force a metaphorical interpretation. In other contexts, the very same sentence might make a perfectly good, literal, sense. These kinds of metaphors I call "whole-sentence" metaphors. For example, consider a context in which a battle between some Indians and a wagon train is described. In such a context, one might find the sentence *The Indians were on the warpath*. Such a sentence is not semantically anomalous. However, the same sentence could occur in a context describing the wrath of some children toward an unyielding babysitter. Perhaps the babysitter threatened them and they decided to get their own back. Such a context could easily support the sentence about the Indians, and it would then be the whole sentence that required a metaphorical interpretation rather than just a part of it.

Given that it is a fact of linguistic life that there are both part-sentence metaphors and whole-sentence metaphors, we need a definition of metaphor that is sensitive to each. The definition that I propose is that a metaphor is any contextually anomalous utterance, intended to be such by a speaker or writer, that has the characteristic that the tension is, in principle, eliminable. "Contextually anomalous" means with respect to a literal interpretation within the discourse context. Grice (1975) has suggested that there are implicit conventions governing linguistic (and in general, social) interactions. These conventions include mutual expectations between the participants that they will be sincere (i.e., they mean what they say), that they will be relevant, and a couple of others that need not detain us here. In the particular case of metaphors, there is an apparent violation of both the expectation to be sincere (as there also is with, for example, irony and sarcasm) *and* the expectation to be relevant. So the contextual anomaly of a literal interpretation must be so for both of these reasons if the anomalous expression is to be a metaphor, otherwise metaphor becomes indistinguishable from irony, sarcasm, indirect speech acts (see, Searle, 1975; Davison, 1975) and all sorts of other things. I believe that this definition has both theoretical and empirical consequences that make it superior to the more standard approach, provided only that we can independently characterize "tension elimination." The theoretical virtues lie in the fact that it seems to include all types of metaphor while excluding semantic anomaly; its empirical virtues lie in the fact that it offers good prospects for investigating the psychological processes involved in the comprehension of metaphor. I will not elaborate here on either the definition or its justification and merits, because the elaboration can be found in Ortony et al., (1978a). However, a cautionary note is called for. This definition of metaphor serves only to distinguish metaphors from nonmetaphors. It does not follow from the definition that the psychological processes underlying comprehension map onto it.

We can now return to the main questions. How does a reader know how to interpret a linguistic expression that cannot be plausibly interpreted literally? Do children who are beginning to master reading and have already largely mastered the oral language know how to interpret metaphors? If they do not, why do they not? There are at least three possible answers to this last question, answers that can be expressed by three hypotheses; the metalinguistic knowledge deficit hypothesis, the world-knowledge deficit hypothesis, and the cognitive processes deficit hypothesis. The first of these, the metalinguistic knowledge deficit hypothesis, reflects the possibility that young children simply do not understand that it is possible or (in some sense) permissible to use language for anything other than "saying what you mean" (i.e., they equate language use with literal language use). The world-knowledge deficit hypothesis would explain an inability to understand metaphors by young children in terms of their having insufficient knowledge about the topic and, especially, the vehicle to permit them to figure out the ground of the metaphor or possibly even to perceive the tension. The cognitive processes deficit hypothesis would claim that children lack some (special) language-processing abilities required to comprehend metaphors.

The world-knowledge deficit hypothesis is perhaps not quite appropriately named, for it is intended to capture the possibility not only that the reader has an inadequate appreciation of certain facts about the world but that he or she may also not know the meaning of certain words, and so on. The distinction between these two is not a very sharp one, especially when considering concrete nouns. It is not unreasonable to suppose that there is a close connection between the richness of one's knowledge about something and the degree to which one could be said to know the meaning of the word that designates that thing. The rather broad sense of "world-knowledge" that I am using should not be overlooked. The world-knowledge deficit hypothesis does not, in fact, constitute a very interesting explanation of the inability of young children to comprehend metaphors. If someone fails to understand a metaphor because the appropriate world-knowledge required is not present, we do not have a finding that is psychologically very interesting, although it could well be educationally interesting. The hypothesis is important for a rather different reason. Many of the experimental studies designed to investigate the comprehension of metaphors in children are confounded because the investigators failed to control for world-knowledge (see Ortony et al., 1978a, for a more detailed critique). Many of the developmental trends reported in the literature seem to be consistent with the view that, as children grow older and learn more about the world in which they live and the words used to describe it, so their ability to understand metaphors increases. For example, in a classic study, Asch and Nerlove (1960) investigated the development of words such as *sweet, hard, cold,* and so on, which they called "double function" terms. Adults readily apply such terms both to physical objects and to personality characteristics. Believing that the application of such terms in the psychological domain constituted evidence of metaphoric processing, Asch and Nerlove found that young children failed to agree that the terms could be applied to people. They concluded from this that the capacity to deal with metaphor does not emerge until adolescence. In the context of the current discussion, the point to be emphasized is that even if one were willing to concede a highly questionable assumption, namely that Asch and Nerlove were indeed investigating metaphors, a child's inability to agree with the application of these double function terms to people could be explained in terms of an impoverished understanding of the nature and subtleties of human personality traits. This would then be an example of the effects of a world-knowledge deficit. It says no more about the ability of children to understand nonliteral uses of langauge than it does about their ability to understand literal uses.

More recently, a study reported by Billow (1975) attempted to show that the development of the ability to comprehend what he called "similarity" metaphors was related to the ability to deal with concrete operations. Using children ranging in age from 5 to 13, he examined performance on these similarity metaphors. Similarity metaphors, he claimed, are those in which disparate objects are compared on the basis of shared attributes. An example would be *The branch of the tree was her pony*. In fact, this particular example of Billow's hardly satisfies his criterion because the only way in which a branch and a pony can share the attribute he suggests, namely that of being ridden, is if the branch is "ridden" metaphorically. In any event, metaphors of this kind were contrasted with "proportional" metaphors such as *Summer's blood is in ripened blackberries*. In these cases, four or more elements are compared proportionally rather than directly and Billow correctly predicted that children would show evidence of poorer comprehension for them. For the similarity metaphors, Billow found that when they were accompanied by pictures even 5-year-olds were able to explain some 30% of them correctly. Seven-year-olds were performing with about 75% accuracy and 11-year-olds were virtually perfect. But he also found that the stable use of concrete operations was not a prerequisite for comprehending similarity metaphors. To test his other hypothesis, Billow only used children aged 9 through 12. There he did find a high correlation between their ability to explain proportional metaphors and the development of formal operational thought. Again, some of these findings can probably be explained in terms of the world-knowledge deficit hypothesis. As should be evident from the examples of the items I have cited, the kind of knowledge required to understand the similarity metaphors is much less sophisticated than that required to understand the proportional metaphors. Looking at the materials leads one to speculate that some of the younger children might have performed very well on some of them, such as *Anger ate him up*. Unfortunately, this cannot be determined from Billow's paper, but if it is right, it would again suggest that the type of materials used vary along an uncontrolled but influential dimension, namely, existing knowledge pertaining to the concepts and relationships involved.

A third study in which the results are open to a world-knowledge deficit explanation is one by Winner, Rosenstiel, and Gardner (1976). Winner et al. postulated various levels of metaphoric comprehension relating to age. These were, first, the magical level, second, the metonymic level, third, the primitive metaphoric level, and finally, genuine metaphoric comprehension. A child was deemed to have interpreted a metaphor at the magical level if he interpreted it literally, thereby implicitly constructing a magical world in which what was stated was literally possible. A metonymic interpretation was one wherein the child invented a situation in which the two terms were sensibly juxtaposed but not appropriately so. Primitive metaphoric interpretations were held to be those in which the child focused on incidental aspects of one of the terms. Finally, genuine metaphoric interpretations were held to be those in which the child focused on the appropriate aspects of the terms, at least appropriate by adult standards. Children between the ages of 6 and 14 heard simple sentences containing metaphors. *The prison guard was a hard rock* is an example. There were two tasks, a selection task and a production, or explication, task. In the selection task, each child was asked to choose his interpretation; the experimenters assigned these choices to one of the four postulated levels of comprehension. In the explication task, children were asked to explain the meaning of the sentence. Responses were scored primarily in terms of the four postulated stages. The authors concluded that the results tended to confirm the hypothesized stages. The world-knowledge deficit explanation for these findings relates closely to the hypothesis that the authors set out to test. Every teacher and parent knows that, as readers grow older, the nature of the texts that they encounter changes. In particular, young children are exposed to a much greater proportion of fairy stories and the like than are older children. In other words, the materials to which younger children are exposed are heavily represented by "magical worlds," so it would be consistent with much of their experience for children to select a magical interpretation. By contrast, older children know more abut the world, they know more about what can really happen in it, and the material they read is not so likely to be predominantly "magical" in character. The problem is that an inadequate control over the preexisting knowledge of the subjects in this and in many of the developmental studies that have been carried out to date renders their results open to different interpretations than those their authors favor.

The studies cited so far typically suggest that the development of a genuine metaphoric comprehension capacity emerges long after a child has mastered the rudiments of language comprehension. At the same time, these studies, and others like them, often contain a hint that there is some perhaps inadequately developed capacity quite early on, and certainly by 5-years-old. So, when one takes into account the complexity of the tasks the children are usually asked to perform, the variation in the complexity of the materials, both linguistically and conceptually, and the relative lack of a full, rich, and varied understanding of world around them, one cannot help but wonder whether the experimental work on the development of the comprehension of metaphors is in fact concerned with metaphors at all. Perhaps it merely catalogues the fact that as children grow older they learn more and become correspondingly smarter. It is undoubtedly true that the comprehension of metaphors, as of most other things, improves with the acquisition of increasing knowledge about the world and consequently with age. It would, however, be a depressingly uninteresting finding were there nothing more to it.

In order to establish that a lack of appropriate knowledge cannot alone account for the relatively poor performance of younger children, experimental techniques have to be employed that have at least the following two characteristics: First, there must be no doubt that the child is thoroughly (or at least adequately) conversant with the domains of the topic and vehicle. Second, the child has to be given the chance to exercise the appropriate metaphoric comprehension processes, if he has them. It might be, for example, that young children, although cognitively capable of comprehending metaphors, have a preference for literal interpretations, so that, for example, selecting a magical or metonymic interpretation in the Winner et al. (1976) study might merely be the manifestation of a response bias. One study that begins to avoid some of these difficulties is reported in Gentner (1977). Although it is not obvious that she was investigating the capacity of children to comprehend metaphor as opposed to their capacity to handle spatial analogies, the study is exemplary with respect to its avoidance of some of the standard pitfalls of research in this area. Furthermore, unlike most other studies, very little emphasis was placed on the child's ability to explain his or her response. It is well known that the skill to verbally explain one's comprehension of something develops later than the ability to actually comprehend (see, e.g., Brainerd, 1973; Brown, 1978; Kuhn, 1974). The demands place on such metacognitive skills are quite widespread in developmental research and it is not a very promising way of uncovering the true capabilities of children.

Gentner used quite young subjects, ranging in age from 4 to 5½-years-old; she also used college sophomores as controls. She had subjects map either body parts or facial features on pictures of cars, trees, and mountains. Here, there is no "knowledge" problem. It is reasonable to assume that a child knows enough about the relative positions of the limbs on the body, or the ears, eyes, nose, and mouth on the face, to be confident that the domain is a familiar one (and of course, it is easy enough to test). Similarly, subjects were required to know rather little about the target domains, for they needed only to know what the appropriate shape (or pictorial symbolic representation) of it would be. Subjects were shown a line drawing of, say, a mountain, and asked: "If the mountain had a nose, where would it be?" Gentner scored her data in terms of reversals of positions of the mapped features on the new domain, and she found that the children performed as well as adults, thus weakening the position that young children lack metaphorical ability and consequently weakening the cognitive processes deficit hypothesis.

Previously in this section, I indicated an unwillingness to discuss in any detail the relationship between metaphors, similes, and anologies, and I am not about to renege on that. However, if one thinks of analogies as comparisons between relations and if one concedes that the process of making or discovering similarities is part of what is involved in comprehending metaphors, then anecdotal observations that children can see similarities and make comparisons, and the experimental evidence that under certain circumstances they can handle analogies, suggests the possibility that much of the cognitive machinery required to comprehend metaphors may be present quite early on. There is, perhaps, too much attention given to questions about the age at which children become able to engage in genuine metaphoric comprehension and what kind of comprehension they engage in before "metaphoric maturity." The problem with this emphasis is that such questions presuppose that there is a stage, after command of the oral language has been achieved, during which children cannot make good sense of metaphors. The consequence is that the experimental tasks that are used tend to embody these presuppositions and then the results often reveal a preference for less sophisticated comprehension (by the adult experimenter's standards). Instead of this, perhaps one should ask whether, given every opportunity, a child can show an ability to comprehend metaphors, just as Gentner showed that given every opportunity to show evidence of analogical reasoning, children show it.

One way to investigate the issue is to set up little stories and determine that the children understand them. One can then create a set of whole-sentence metaphorical targets and pretest the children on their comprehension of those targets when embedded in contexts that would induce literal interpretations of them. These preliminary stages would largely eliminate the world-knowledge deficit hypothesis as an account of any differences that might turn up between the comprehension of metaphorical and literal language. The main experiment would then involve using the contexts (already established as being intelligible to the subjects) as little stories on the basis of which the child would have to select the most appropriate sentence satisfying some criterion or other (continuation of the story, point of the story, or whatever). The child would be faced with a series of sentences (i.e., well formed, semantically acceptable, literal sentences), all of which were known to be intelligible as literal statements but none of which would make sense in the context if so interpreted. One of them, however, would make good sense under a metaphorical interpretation. Now, the child is known to have the requisite knowledge of the pertinent domains, so the question becomes, can he or she select the sentence that makes sense under a metaphorical interpretation? Suppose that this experiment were run with second-grade children and the results revealed that, for the most part, they were selecting their choices on a random basis. One would then be in a better position to conclude that those children lacked the appropriate cognitive capacity. Furthermore, a variation on such an experiment might even enable us to distinguish the cognitive-deficit hypothesis from the metalinguistic deficit hypothesis. The variation would involve transforming the targets from metaphors into similes. The simile would do two things that the metaphor would not. First, it might make the determination of the topic of the metaphor easier, because an explicit reference to it, albeit anaphoric, appears in the simile. Second, the explicit sytnactic signal that some kind of comparison was being made (through the use of lexical items such as "like" or "as though") might serve to facilitate the nonliteral interpretation. An approach of this kind suggests that, although research in the area is difficult, it is possible to devise ways of determining whether and when children can handle nonliteral uses of language, and if not, why not. And these, I think, are the first questions that need to be answered.[1]

In some cases of the comprehension of metaphor, a reader or hearer recognizes that a literal interpretation gives rise to problems. A reader perceives, for example, that a sentence, literally interpreted, is irrelevant, given the context. This irrelevance has to be resolved; it has to be rendered only apparent. The process of tension elimination is one way to do this. The conceptual incompatibility between the topic and the vehicle is eliminated by predicating of the topic only those contextually salient attributes of the vehicle that are consistent with the topic. It would seem, then, that an important component is the recognition that "something is wrong." This requires a reader to monitor his own comprehension, something that children are probably not very good at doing. We now can see emerging a possible program of research. If it transpires that children lack the appropriate cognitive processes, it should be possible to determine whether the problem lies in the metacomprehension skills required or in the tension elimination. As we have already seen, Gentner's data might suggest that research concentrates on the former rather than the latter.

METAPHOR AND SCHEMA THEORY

Our concern with the child's ability to deal with metaphor is motivated by the importance of metaphor in reading and learning, topics that are discussed more in the next section. There are, however, many questions that need to be investigated with respect to the end state; what are the processes involved in the comprehension of metaphors by adults? Some recent work in this area is reported in Ortony, Schallert, Reynolds, and Antos (1978b). In a reaction-time experiment, they found that sentences following contexts that required them to be interpreted metaphorically took significantly longer to understand than those same sentences following contexts inducing their literal inter-retation *only* when the preceding contexts were very short (e.g., a phrase or short sentence). A second experiment revealed an interesting contrasting effect for the comprehension of idioms such as *chew the fat* or *let the cat out of the bag*. Here again, there was an effect for type of context, literal inducing or

---

[1]This paper was originally written early in 1977 and is, in certain respects, out of date. For example, Ralph Reynolds and I have already successfully employed the paradigm for developmental research suggested in this section (see Reynolds & Ortony, in press).

idomatic inducing. But this time it was in the other direction; idioms were understood faster than were the same expressions used literally. I do not want to discuss the conclusions that can be drawn from these results here, save to say that the context-length by context-type interaction found in the experiment with metaphors is very amenable to a schema-theory treatment. What I plan to do now is to speculate (perhaps fantacize is a better word) as to how schema theory might handle the comprehension of metaphor. I do not present here a lengthy account of schema theory. Such an account can be found in Rumelhart and Ortony (1977) and in various places in this volume and elsewhere. The overall perspective, however, is worth reiterating.

Schemata are complex interacting structures of knowledge (rather than definitions) that have variables and that can be at various levels of abstraction. Because schemata have variables, the same schema can be used as an interpretive framework for a variety of different instances of the same phenomenon. In schema theory, the comprehension process involves the selection of appropriate or "best-fitting" schemata to "account for" the input. Episodic memory representations are created from more or less complete records of instantiated schema. The relationship between comprehension and memory in schema theory has not been well worked out, although Ortony (1978) attempts to provide an account of sorts.

Any theory that claims to account for the nature of human language comprehension has to be able to account for nonliteral as well as literal uses of language; this is true for both linguistic and psychological theories insofar as they are concerned with the realities of language and language comprehension. In speculating about how schema theory might handle metaphor, there are several dangers. Foremost among these is the fact that schema theory is so general that it readily lends itself to ad hoc accounts of almost any phenomenon. In such a situation, the best that can be hoped for is that the conjunction of such accounts is, at least, consistent if not compelling. A second and related problem is that any account so offered may itself be too vague and too general to have any interesting empirically testable consequences. So, we may be able to do little more than to suggest that the theory is not incapable of accounting for the phenomenon.

With the excuses now made, how might schema theory deal with the comprehension of metaphor? In a sense, what we need is a theory of the comprehension of metaphor that can be cast in schema-theoretic terms. Ortony (1975) proposes that the comprehension of metaphor involves predicating of the topic those salient aspects of the vehicle that are not incompatible with it. In schema-theoretic terms, it is clear that the selection of the schemata for the topic and vehicle does not, in general, constitute a problem. If it is asserted of some man, say Smith, that he is an ox, the two schemata, SMITH and OX, can be readily accessed, primarily through the operation of bottom-up processes (see Rumelhart, Chapter 2, this volume).

Now normally, with the literal use of an expression of this form, say, *Smith is a man,* comprehension is achieved by subsuming the MAN schema as a subschema under the SMITH schema. (In the present context, I mean by "subsume" that the subsumed schema appears in the subsuming schema as a token in a type; it does not refer to the set/superset relation). In the example of the literal use of *Smith is a man,* we might assume that the point is to designate Smith as a male rather than as a female. Thus, I am assuming that it is already known that Smith is a person and that the PERSON schema appears as a subschema within the SMITH schema. The role of the MAN schema would be to provide the value of the sex variable in the subsumed PERSON schema. This is easily brought about because MAN has PERSON as a subschema of its own with MALE as the value of the sex variable. Consequently, the SMITH-PERSON relation can easily be augmented to SMITH-PERSON (SEX = MALE). Of course, this accounts only for the attribution of maleness to Smith, but the same principle could be used to attach other man-related predicates as the particular context might suggest.

What is needed for the comprehension of metaphor is that the inappropriate predicates find no "points of attachment." Thus, when it comes to attributing four legs to Smith when he is said to be an ox, the existing schema and associated schemata should not allow the value of the number of legs a person has to be overridden. In other words, in metaphor, values have to be assigned to variables by taking them from the vehicle, or subschemata within it, as long as they do not conflict. But this leads to a difficult problem. How and when should established values not be overridden? After all, if one were to say literally and truthfully that Smith was a very strange fellow in that he has four legs, the value of the number of legs possessed by the person Smith ought to be changed from two to four. In such a case, however, four-leggedness should become a salient property of Smith. Its effect on the distribution of the value of the "number of legs" variable in the general PERSON schema would be insignificant. If we already have the SMITH-PERSON relation incorporated into the SMITH schema and if the context has already enabled the appropriate schema to be selected, then on encountering *Smith is an ox,* a conflict is discovered. One has to assume that rather than overriding the SMITH-PERSON relation for which strong evidence exists within the schema, only the salient subschemata of OX that do not conflict would be tied into the SMITH schema. This would only happen in the absence of explicit information to the effect that the statement was meant literally or that the existing SMITH schema needed some fundamental changes.

One theoretical tool that might be useful for restricting the set of candidate subschemata to be used in the metaphoric comprehension process (and in literal comprehension for that matter) is that of a context-sensitive spreading activation mechanism (see Collins & Loftus, 1975; Ortony, 1978). One might conceive of the primary input concepts (e.g., SMITH and OX) with contextually active concepts initiating a spread of activation to other schemata such as STRENGTH, WORK, and so on. In this way, it would, in principle, be possible for candidate subschemata to be activated in a top-down fashion; further, those activated schemata would be more likely to be related to the ground of the metaphor (through intersection) than they would to those schemata that gave rise to the metaphoric tension, because these latter schemata would receive less accumulating activation from different sources.

A final observation in the context of metaphor and schema theory seems appropriate. In schema theory, an important component of the comprehension process is the selection of a schema or set of schemata that best accounts for the input. This means that the schemata should not only "fit" the input but that where the fit is not good there should be minimal "violation" to those schemata employed. Thus, although constraints on values of variables in schemata are rarely absolute, there do exist more probable and preferred values. In the comprehension of metaphor, one might suppose that staying within reasonable limits (both literally and metaphorically) would be one of the chief controlling factors. That is why such a system would have to reject the subsumption of the OX schema under the SMITH schema (the literal interpretation); alternative accounts of the input would result in less disastrous repercussions.

This is not the place to attempt a detailed, well-worked-out account of the processing and structural aspects of metaphoric comprehension in schema theory, nor do I think that such an account is yet possible; but perhaps the few suggestions I have made may pave the way for someone else to explore the issue, if only to show that there are much better ways of handling it.

SOME OBSERVATIONS ON METAPHOR AND LEARNING

Metaphor is more than a linguistic and psychological curiosity. It is more than rhetorical flourish. It is also a means of conveying and acquiring new knowledge and of seeing things in new ways. It may well be that metaphors are very closely related to insight. Anecdotal evidence for this abounds in the history of science. Newton's apple and Kekulé's snakes are but two famous examples. In the field of mathematical discovery, Hadamard (1949) provides a fascinating discussion of others.

Metaphors, then, can be a way of knowing and a way of coming to a new understanding. They are wide in scope, extending from the highest pinnacles of scientific endeavor to the most lowly explanations in the classroom or introductory texts. In other words, metaphors are an important ingredient in learning and understanding. As I have argued in Ortony (1975, 1976), they also constitute a powerful pedagogical tool if used judiciously.

One of the more interesting questions that arises concerns whether or not metaphors in texts facilitate learning from them. A first attempt at investigating this question is described in Arter (1976). She constructed two parallel passages about the Sasquatch (Yeti, Bigfoot, or Abominable Snowman). One version, hereafter called the "metaphor passage," contained metaphors. In the other version, the "literal passage," the metaphors were replaced with literal expressions conveying, as far as possible, the same meaning. Thus, for example, in discussing the consequences of discovering that the Sasquatch was real, the metaphor passage reported that "it would be like finding out that Santa Claus exists," whereas the literal passage claimed that "it would be an exciting discovery, unexpected by many." Sixth-grade children read one of the passages and were then given comprehension tests. The children also received a posttest to determine whether or not they possessed the requisite knowledge of the metaphorical vehicles in order to permit comprehension. One of the most interesting findings was a trend for improved performance on questions about the unmanipulated portion of the passage for subjects receiving the metaphor passage. This trend was significant for the low verbal ability group. It was in the same direction for the medium and high verbal ability groups. This may mean that the presence of metaphors in a text somehow facilitates the comprehension of the text in a rather general way. Arter's (1976) finding parallels that of Mayer (1975), who found that the use of of what could be called "metaphorical models" facilitated low ability subjects in learning about computer programming. Pearson, Raphael, Te Paske, and Hyser (1979) report a study based on Arter (1976). Using a different passage and oral recall, they found a marked increase in the probability of children remembering the metaphors in the passage over the probability of their remembering their literal equivalents.

It seems to me to be important to investigate some of the issues in this kind of seminaturalistic manner. However, there are some persistent problems associated with it. One of these pertains to the production of good literal equivalents of "naturally occurring" metaphors. For example, in one popular introductory social studies text for 5- and 6-graders, it is said of Ghandi that "he looked into the face of a two thousand year old despair and stared it down." If one is interested, as one might be, in determining what a child learns from this when he reads it, some basis of comparison is helpful. But then, how does one construct a good literal equivalent of such a metaphor? Part of its very effectiveness lies in its resistance to paraphrase. How else could it be succinctly expressed unless by another, different metaphor? A large part of the problem with this particular example lies in the fact that it is a part-sentence metaphor. It tends to be much easier to make up good paraphrases for whole-sentence metaphors. Nevertheless, if some of the power of metaphors lies in their ability to express what is literally inexpressible, then it would follow that the problem may be a more general one. One can only hope that in attempting to use literal paraphrases of metaphors in context, researchers will try to minimize the information lost in the translation.

To conclude, I am going to revert to the question of insight. If man has any innate intellectual capacities, the ability to perceive similarities and differences (at some level) is likely to be one of them. Now, let us suppose that, with respect to any individual, there are two kinds of similarity that can exist between two compared entities. There is "preexisting" similarity and there is "discovered" similarity. For any individual, preexisting similarities were acquired, either by being pointed out or by being discovered. In calling them preexisting similarities, the point is not to imply that the similarities exist somehow "out there" but rather that at some level the individual already knows or believes that the two entities are indeed similar.

It may be that this difference underlies the distinction between two views of metaphor mentioned at the outset of this paper, namely, the comparison view and the interaction view. Thus it might well be that some metaphors for some people are "interaction" metaphors. Comparison metaphors would be those based on preexisting similarities, and it might be that they are intended to point to the relationship(s) between topic and vehicle. Thus, consider again the example *Smith is an ox*. If this is uttered in a situation in which it is obvious that enough is known about both Smith and oxen for nothing new to be said, then, the metaphor would be based on a preexisting similarity. So if Smith were a huge, strong wrestler seen picking up his 250-lb. opponent, the point of the metaphor might well be to say something about the relationship between Smith and oxen. By contrast, suppose that little is known about Smith by the hearer or reader. Suppose, further, that the speaker or writer knows that this is true. In this situation, in saying or writing *Smith is an ox,* the author intends the hearer or reader to discover something about Smith that was not previously known. Smith is thus seen in a new way and we would then have some of the characteristics of an interaction metaphor. The person who understands this metaphor has a new insight; he or she has learned something that, in the general case, might not have been so rich if it had resulted from a literal account. That this is true may not be so obvious from the Smith example, for its simplicity, although useful for explanatory purposes, tends to eliminate some of the more subtle aspects of the effects of metaphor. If we now recall the example of Ghandi, however, it may become more obvious. Another good example from a widely read 5th and 6th grade social studies text (on Exploring Latin America and Canada) is: *Coffee became king in Brazil.* The richness of this metaphor lies in the fact that it does far more than assert the supreme importance of coffee in Brazil. It seems also to say a lot about the controlling influence of it over the economy, it carries implications of "respect" for and pride in coffee that Brazilians might be expected to have. Thus, a child who reads such a sentence might come to see both coffee and Brazil in a new light. Consequently, metaphors that involve the discovery of similarities for their comprehension do, by virtue of that fact, provide new insights for the comprehenders in much the same way as Kekulé's vision of snakes chasing their tails led him to "see" the benzene ring.

There are many theoretical and empirical questions concerning figurative language that still need to be asked and answered. What, for example, is the role of imagery in the production and comprehension of metaphor? What roles do metaphors play in texts? Are those that occur in early reading texts generally comprehensible to the target population or not? Does figurative language really facilitate comprehension, at least under ideal circumstances? If so, how? If not, why not? Do comprehensible metaphors make a text, or at least its import, more memorable? Questions such as these make the area potentially a rich and fertile one for research. I suspect that if one learns something through a metaphor, one learns it well, not only because of additional processing required to understand it, but also because of its relative vividness and imageability. On the other hand, if one fails to understand a metaphor in a text, it might well be that the overall level of comprehension of that text deteriorates. Metaphors are like jokes; good ones can be very successful, but bad ones can be disastrous.

ACKNOWLEDGMENTS

This research was supported by the National Institute of Education under Contract No. US-NIE-C-400-76-0116 and by a Spencer fellowship awarded by the National Academy of Education.

REFERENCES

Alston, W. P. *Philosophy of language.* Englewood Cliffs, N.J.: Prentice-Hall, 1964.

Arter, J. L. *The effects of metaphor on reading comprehension.* Unpublished doctoral dissertation, University of Illinois, 1976.

Asch, S., & Nerlove, H. The development of double function terms in children: An exploration study. In B. Kaplan & S. Wapner (Eds.), *Perspective in psychological theory.* New York: International University Press, 1960.

Billow, R. A cognitive developmental study of metaphor comprehension. *Developmental Psychology,* 1975, *11,* 415–423.

Black, M. Metaphor. In *Models and metaphors: Studies in language and philosophy.* Ithaca, N.Y.: Cornell University Press, 1962.

Black, M. Metaphor revisited. In A. Ortony (Ed.), *Metaphor and thought.* Cambridge: Cambridge University Press, 1979.

Brainerd, C. J. Order of acquisition of transitivity, conservation, and class inclusion of length and weight. *Developmental Psychology,* 1973, *8,* 105–116.

Brown, A. L. Knowing when, where and how to remember. In R. Glaser (Ed.), *Advances in instructional psychology.* Hillsdale, N.J.: Lawrence Erlbaum Associates, 1978.

Collins, A. M., & Loftus, E. F. A spreading activation theory of semantic processing. *Psychological Review*, 1975, *82*, 407–428.

Davison, A. Indirect speech acts and what to do with them. In P. Cole & J. L. Morgan (Eds.), *Syntax and semantics* (Vol. 3): *Speech acts.* New York: Academic Press, 1975.

Gentner, D. On the development of metaphoric processing. *Child Development*, 1977, *48*, 1034–1039.

Grice, H. P. Logic and conversation. In P. Cole & J. L. Morgan (Eds.), *Syntax and semantics* (Vol. 3): *Speech acts.* New York: Academic Press, 1975.

Hadamard. J. *An essay on the psychology of invention in the mathematical field.* Princeton, N.J.: Princeton University Press, 1949.

Kintsch, W. *The representation of meaning in memory.* Hillsdale, N.J.: Lawrence Erlbaum Associates, 1974.

Kuhn, D. Inducing development experimentally: Comments on a research paradigm. *Developmental Psychology*, 1974, *10*, 590–600.

Mayer, R. E. Different problem solving competencies established in learning computer programming with and without meaningful models. *Journal of Educational Psychology*, 1975, *67*, 725–734.

Miller, G. A. Images and models, similes and metaphors. In A. Ortony (Ed.), *Metaphor and Thought.* Cambridge: Cambridge University Press, 1979.

Miller, R. M. The dubious case for metaphors in educational writing. *Educational Theory*, 1976, *26*, 174–181.

Ortony, A. Why metaphors are necessary and not just nice. *Educational Theory*, 1975, *25*, 45–53.

Ortony, A. On the nature and value of metaphor: A reply to my critics. *Educational Theory*, 1976, *26*, 45–53.

Ortony, A. Remembering, understanding, and representation. *Cognitive Science*, 1978, *2*, 53–69.

Ortony, A. Beyond literal similarity. *Psychological Review*, 1979, *86*, 161–180. (a)

Ortony, A. The role of similarity in similes and metaphors. In A. Ortony (Ed.), *Metaphor and Thought.* Cambridge Cambridge University Press, 1979. (b)

Ortony, A., Reynolds, R. E., & Arter, J. A. Metaphor: theoretical and empirical research. *Psychological Bulletin*, 1978, *85*, 919–943. (a)

Ortony, A., Schallert, D. L., Reynolds, R. E., & Antos, S. J. Interpreting metaphors and idioms: Some effects of context on comprehension. *Journal of Verbal Learning and Verbal Behavior* 1978, *17*, 465–477. (b)

Pearson, P. D., Raphael, T., TePaske, N., & Hyser, C. *The function of metaphor in children's recall of expository passages* (Tech. Rep. No. 131). Urbana: University of Illinois, Center for the Study of Reading, July, 1979.

Reddy, M. J. A semantic approach to metaphor. In *Chicago Linguistic Society, Collected Papers*, 1969.

Reynolds, R. E., & Ortony, A. Some issues in the measurement of children's comprehension of metaphorical language. *Child Development*, in press.

Richards, I. A. *The philosophy of rhetoric.* London: Oxford University Press, 1936.

Rumelhart, D. E., & Ortony, A. The representation of knowledge in memory. In R. C. Anderson, R J. Spiro, & W. E. Montague (Eds.), *Schooling and the acquisition of knowledge.* Hillsdale, N.J.: Lawrence Erlbaum Associates, 1977.

Searle, J. Indirect speech acts. In P. Cole & J. L. Morgan (Eds.), *Syntax and semantics* (Vol. 3): *Speech acts.* New York: Academic Press, 1975.

van Dijk, T. A. Formal semantics of metaphorical discourse. *Poetics*, 1975, *4*, 173–198.

Winner, E., Rosenstiel, A. K., & Gardner, H. The development of metaphoric understanding. *Developmental Psychology*, 1976, *12*, 289–297.

15 Plans and Social Actions

Bertram C. Bruce
Center for the Study of Reading,
Bolt Beranek and Newman Inc.

INTRODUCTION:
A FUNCTIONAL VIEW OF LANGUAGE

Viewing an action as a step in a plan provides an organizational schema for events in the social world just as the concept of physical causality does for events in the purely physical world. Because the perception of plans plays a central role in our structuring of reality, it may be an important component of the reading comprehension process.The person who has difficulty in recognizing plans and social actions in the behavior of others will have difficulty in understanding episodes related in written form. The person who can understand episodes in daily life may still have difficulty in understanding the connection between purposeful behavior and its conventional linguistic expression. The person who does not understand the communicative intent of a text will likewise have a serious comprehension problem. Thus, the recognition of plans has implications for understanding the actions of characters in a narrative as well as understanding the action performed by an author.

Plans and social actions have been the focus of work in social psychology (Heider, 1958), cognitive psychology (Miller, Galanter, & Pribram, 1960), cognitive-social psychology (Schmidt, 1976), developmental psychology (Piaget, 1932; Sedlak, 1974); philosophy (Austin, 1962; Searle, 1969, 1975a, 1975b, 1976), psycholinguistics (Clark & Lucy, 1975), sociolinguistics (Sudnow, 1972), linguistics (Gordon & Lakoff, 1971; Sadock, 1974), and artificial intelligence (Bruce, 1975; Cohen & Perrault, 1976; Schmidt & Sridharan, 1976). This work has shown: (1) that understanding plans is a critical part of understanding actions; (2) that the ability to understand plans is one of the most complex inferential tasks that people accomplish; and (3) that children require many years to develop these complex skills.

This chapter sketches some of the components of a model for the understanding of plans and social actions. The model is first applied to narrative text, wherein actions of characters need to be interpreted as social actions. The emphasis on social actions and plans leads to a distinction between *story analysis* and *story model analysis* (i.e., analysis of a reader's model for the story). Next, the model is applied to texts in general, wherein the author's action of writing needs to be interpreted as an action done to achieve a social goal. Finally, the chapter discusses implications for teaching and further research.

INTERPRETING ACTIONS

A person learns to interpret events in the world in many different ways. A given event may have, for example, both a physical and a biological interpretation. When the events are actions performed by people, additional explanatory systems become relevant. In particular, conventional interpretations of personal actions go beyond physical and physiological levels to include notions such as "rule," "goal," and "intention." In this chapter, we will be most concerned with the levels of explanation for personal action that include these latter notions. The following example should clarify what is meant here.

Imagine that you observe a person named Susie perform an action. At one level, you might describe her action as *Susie moved her arm up and down causing a paint brush to move while in contact with a chair until the chair was covered with paint.* At a second level you might describe her action in terms of an organizing concept; for example, you could say *Susie is painting the chair,* thus both summarizing and reinterpreting the action just described. You could also describe Susie's action as *helping Martha paint* if it satisfies a set of rules that constitute the definition of *help.* That *help* must be defined by a set of rules about beliefs becomes clear when we consider what it is about Susie's action that makes us view it as a helping action. Certainly it is more than just the physical–physiological facts or even the propositional content of her act, for the same action could also be seen as a *harming,* or an *exploiting.* We have to know that Martha had a goal of painting the chair, that this goal satisfied some want or need of Martha, that Susie believed that Martha had the painting of the chair as a goal, and so on.

The three levels previously outlined are merely indicative of the different ways to view actions. A *moving of a paint brush,* a *painting,* and a *helping* are not differen⁺ acts but different ways of conceptualizing the same act (cf.

Bobrow & Winograd, 1977; Moore & Newell, 1973). The concept of *moving a paint brush* differs from the concept of *helping* in that the rules for its use are primarily physical–physiological, whereas the rules for *helping* are primarily social. This is not to say that there are no physical–physiological correlates of a particular instance of *helping* but only that the concept summarizes a set of beliefs about the goals and beliefs of an actor. The level of beliefs cannot, in principle, be reduced to the physical–physiological level, but even if it could, it appears that people's reasoning about actions (and hence the language they use to discuss actions) does not make that reduction. Some definitions of actions at the intentional level are given in Bruce (1975).

One implication of the different aspects of actions is that, to understand a story, one needs to link together actions at different levels. The connectivity of an action to the main line of a story depends on appropriate understanding of the levels. Children may have difficulty in the interpretation of an action at a given level or in the connections to be made to other actions. They may even have difficulty in determining what action (at the social level) is being carried out. For example, a speaker might be asking a question, giving an order, or making a statement; a painter might be helping or harming.

The ability to interpret actions in terms of their presumed purpose begins to develop early in one's life but improves over many years. In fact, the *expression* of intention begins before a child begins to speak (Bruner, 1966, 1973), is evident at the single-word utterance stage (Dore, 1974), and is elaborated over many years of development to the complexities of adult language use (Shatz, 1977; see also the analysis of "promise" in Searle, 1969). With regard to the *interpretation* of intentions, Piaget (1932) noted that younger children appear to make blame and praise judgments more on outcomes of actions than on the apparent intention behind them, whereas older children rely more on the intent. This observation may reflect a difference in perceived intentions. Some recent studies (Feldman, Klosson, Parsons, Rholes, & Ruble, 1976; Sedlak, 1974) suggest that the complexity of problem solving required to perceive intentions, and therefore the memory and processing demands on the child, results in such differences.

Other studies (Berg-Cross, 1975; Gutkin, 1972) have shown, however, that the complexities of the experimental task have made possible differences in the processing ability appear to be qualitative differences in the under-standing of intentions. It appears that younger children can perceive intentions and do use that perception in evaluating actions, but they may have difficulty in constructing the elaborate hypotheses about plans that are sometimes needed.

. The reason why our ability to interpret actions (or taken on other roles) takes time to develop is still an open question. Given the complexity of the necessary skills (discussed later), it is not surprising that the development of the ability to understand intentions takes years to develop. Furthermore, the knowledge required must be accumulated from a variety of sources, including one's own experience with plan formulation and interactions with others.

In order to interpret actions at the intentional level, one needs the *ability to plan,* that is to formulate a sequence of actions leading to a goal (Sacerdoti, 1975) and to recognize the actions of others in terms of their presumed goals. One needs to know how certain social actions are typically carried out (e.g., *giving* often involves a physical transfer) and what the preconditions and outcomes of actions are. One also needs knowledge of the normative behaviors associated with social actions and situations, and knowledge of social situations and the roles people take. One needs the ability to distinguish one's beliefs from one's beliefs about another's beliefs; also, the ability to handle possibly inconsistent data about the beliefs and plans of others. Finally, one needs knowledge of *social action patterns,* that is, the sequences of actions that typically occur. Some of these needs are discussed in the next section.

UNDERSTANDING IN TERMS OF PLANS AND SOCIAL ACTIONS

Plans and Goals

We learn early in life to interpret actions in terms of their purposes. What must we know to understand the purpose behind someone's behavior? Heider (1958) answers with the postulate that deciding that a person has performed (caused) an action (or outcome) commits us to the judgments that he or she can cause the action (or outcome) and is motivated to do so:

$$\text{cause } (p,x)) \Rightarrow \text{can } (p,x) \ \& \ \text{try } (p,x)$$

in which p is a person and x is an action. "Motivation" should be taken here in the general sense that the outcome (as perceived by the actor) facilitates (in the actor's mind) the attainment of some goal of the actor. For example, if someone who is observed to be holding a box that is wrapped in fancy paper with a ribbon places that box in someone else's hands, then we may assume that the first person *gave* a present. Symbolically, if the persons are labeled $p1$ and $p2$, and the box, b, we would have:

$$\text{cause } [p1, \text{ give } (p1,p2,b)] \Rightarrow \text{can } [p1, \text{ give } (p1,p2,b)]$$
$$\& \text{ try } [p1, \text{ give } (p1,p2,b)]$$

Rules for the *try* component of Heider's axiom essentially resolve to common-sense notions of why people do things (Schmidt, 1976), because it is at that level at which persons reason about the actions of others.

The *can* component of Heider's axiom says that if a person causes an action, then he or she can do that action. Being able to do something may mean that certain physical and skill conditions are met. But it may also mean that these conditions can be brought about. Thus we may infer that *Henry can go to the store* if he can drive his car there; he can drive his car if he can find the keys; he can find the keys if he can find the pants he left them in, and so on. In other words, we want to say that a person can do something if he or she can do it directly or can do some other action that enables it to be done directly.

But the problem is even more complicated. Someone else may be able to enable the action. In that case, the first person will succeed if he or she can motivate (cf. the *try* component) the second person to enable the action. This means that the perception of a purposeful act may require the observer to simulate the planning process of the actor, and, in so doing, simulate the planning process of a third party. Plan perception and plan generation are thus inextricably linked.

In order to do plan recognition (and hence, simulation of the planning behavior of others), a reader must possess a set of well-elaborated types of knowledge and processing abilities (Schmidt & Sridharan, 1976). The coordination of these abilities forces a reader into a hypothesis-based mode of comprehension (cf. Goodman, 1973) in which perceived plans are constantly being evaluated and refined.

Social Actions

Recognizing a social action involves knowing its typical realizations as well as its internal structure. For example, *buying* implies beliefs about ownership and free exchange, and it has a typical realization in terms of money and object transfers. Understanding an action also implies knowing what conditions are appropriate for an action to occur (the *preconditions*) as well as what is typically true afterwards (the *outcome conditions*). Children may fail to discover the structure of a story if they fail to generate all the outcomes of an action, including the implications of outcomes. For example, *Sally made the third out* has as one of its outcomes the fact that the inning is over. They may also have trouble if they fail to generate all preconditions of an action. This example presupposes that Sally is playing a game of baseball. Finally, one must discover connections between preconditions and outcomes of actions in order to construct a connected sequence of actions that follow from one another. The section on story model analysis shows that these links between actions are crucial for understanding even a simple story.

A special case of actions that require interpretation at the intentional level is the *speech act,* or more broadly, the *linguistic act.* Like other social actions, speech acts can be described at various levels. At the physical–physiological level we have the "utterance act" (Searle, 1969). For example, an utterance act might have the description

> Betsy uttered the sounds,
> /'th a t/ /'p l a n t/ / i s/ /'s i k/

A speech act also can be given a propositional description. Continuing our example, we could say that Betsy's statement refers to *that plant* and predicates *is sick*.

Speech acts also have intentional descriptions, or in Austin's (1962) terminology, "illocutionary force." If we believe that Betsy believes her statement, that she believes she has evidence for it, that she believes that it is not obvious to her listeners that the statement is true, that she wants her listeners to believe the statement, and perhaps other conditions, then we might describe her act as "asserting." At yet another level, we might describe her action in terms of its role in a larger plan, for example, as the answer to a question or as part of a general informing plan. As is the case for social actions in general, there are higher level descriptions for speech acts that depend more and more on beliefs and social conventions.

Recent work (Schweller, Brewer, & Dahl, 1976) has shown that people tend to remember the underlying illocutionary force of an utterance, often at the expense of its literal form. In fact, even the prelocutionary effects (e.g., if I "threaten" you, you may become "frightened") may lead to false recognition errors. Processing at the intentional level is thus apparently automatic at times. It is not known how successful children are at this intentional processing, particularly with respect to text, where the cues become more abstract and subtle, where the complexity in terms of actors and goals increases, and where very indirect forms need to be interpreted in terms of multiple intentions.

Beliefs

In order to recognize another's intentions, we need to take his or her perspective on the world. Selman (1971) has shown that role-taking is correlated with the ability to make sophisticated moral judgments (i.e., judgments based on the perceived purpose of an action). Yussen (1976), studying subjects in grades 9, 10, 12, and college, found that differentiation among social roles increases even at those ages.

Taking another's perspective demands a flexibility in memory organization. One problem is how to take another's perspective when that perspective may entail taking our perspective again. Another is to know when to stop, for example, how many levels of perspective-taking are there (Schiffer, 1972; Strawson, 1964). A representation for perspective-taking must include notions such as the dependence of one belief on another and differing certainties about beliefs. One approach to this representation problem is to postulate a memory in which items become true ("visible") in certain contexts (Cohen & Perrault, 1976). For example, that Boston is cold in January may be true in my world and in my view of your world, but perhaps not in my view of your view of my world. See the section on Story Model Analysis for a further discussion of embedded beliefs.

Patterns of Behavior

One way in which a person can cope with the complexities inherent in social action (and speech act) recognition is to look for patterns of interactional behavior. Patterns recur because the outcomes and preconditions of certain actions match each other. As a sequence of actions unfold, the conditions for subsequent actions to occur may change. Thus previous actions play an important role in determining the environment for later ones. Action patterns represent summaries of many sequences of action; thus, they are efficient through occasionally faulty mechanisms for predicting or accounting for behavior. Some patterns have a simple and explicit goal-orientation, but others (like the teaching–learning pattern discussed later) may not. Abelson (1975) uses the term *script* for the general pattern and *plan* for the goal-directed pattern.

There are a multitude of action patterns that fit the description just given. One special type includes patterns that have become ritualized, often embedded in the language. It is not difficult to imagine a grammar that generates many of the patterns we use (cf. Becker, 1975). Furthermore, it is clear that the words in these patterns have lost much of their original significance. We usually do not want a graphic answer to the greeting "How are you?." Instead, the phrase is serving as an unanalyzed symbol in the "greeting" grammar. Fillmore (1975) shows, however, that even these rituals can only be heuristics for action and not conditioned responses.

A richer example of a behavior pattern is one that might be observed in a school or other teaching and learning situation. This pattern includes talking, writing on paper or a blackboard, and possibly a lot of gesturing or silences for thinking. Furthermore, the content of the talking and writing is constrained. We might expect many questions and answers by both the teacher and the student. On the other hand, commands might be less common. See Hall and Guthrie (Chapter 18, this volume) and Hall and Freedle (1975) for a discussion of these conventions and the difficulties they may cause.

An important feature of any behavior pattern is that it cannot be applied in all situations, that is, that there are implicit constraints on its applicability. The greeting pattern occurs only upon meeting someone; a waiter–customer pattern exists only in a restaurant; a boss–employee pattern exists only in the work situation; and even the teaching–learning pattern applies only when we infer certain conditions. But the pattern also changes the conditions for interaction in that mutual recognition of a pattern leads to shared expectations and beliefs about the interactions. The importance of social learning is evident here as a prerequisite to effective use of these action patterns in comprehension.

UNDERSTANDING NARRATIVE TEXT

Story Analysis

The connectivity of a story can be illustrated via a *story grammar* in much the same way that the structure of a single sentence can be illustrated by a sentence grammar. Rumelhart (1975) and others (Mandler & Johnson, 1977; Stein & Glenn, 1977; Sutton-Smith, Botvin, & Mahony, 1976) have shown that such grammars can account for the relative salience of parts of a story. In this section I want only to sketch the use of story grammars (or *story schemas*) and to point to both their usefulness and limitations.

For the purpose here, we will use the following story adapted from the first Winston reader (Firman & Maltby, 1918):

The Fox and the Rooster

1. Once a dog and a rooster went into the woods.
2. Soon it grew dark.
3. The rooster said, "Let us stay here all night. I will sleep in this tree-top. You can sleep in the hollow trunk."
4. "Very well," said the dog.
5. So the dog and the rooster went to sleep.
6. In the morning the rooster began to crow, "Cock-a-doodle-do! Cock-a-doodle-do!"
7. Mr. Fox heard him crow.
8. He said, "That is a rooster corwing. He must be lost in the woods. I will eat him for my breakfast."
9. Soon Mr. Fox saw the rooster in the tree-top.
10. He said to himself, "Ha! ha! Ha! ha! What a fine breakfast I shall have! I must make him come down from the tree. Ha! ha! Ha! ha!"
11. So he said to the rooster, "What a fine rooster you are! How well you sing! Will you come to my house for breakfast?"
12. The rooster said, "Yes, thank you, I will come, if my friend can come, too."
13. "Oh yes," said the fox. "I will ask you friend. Where is he?"
14. The rooster said, "My friend is in this hollow tree. He is asleep. You must wake him."
15. Mr. Fox said to himself, "Ha! ha! I shall have two roosters for my breakfast!"
16. So he put his head into the hollow tree.

17. Then he said, "Will you come to my house for breakfast?"
18. Out jumped the dog and caught Mr. Fox by the nose [pp. 44–48].

One story grammar that has been proposed (Rumelhart, 1975; see also Rumelhart, 1977) can be read roughly as follows: A story consists of a setting and an episode (we might generalize this for the dog and rooster story to "episodes"). Each episode comprises an event and a reaction to the event. Events can be episodes themselves, changes of state, actions, or pairs of events. And so on. When we apply the grammar to a story, we get a *tree* structure representation. The portion of the resulting tree for segments 8–11 of "The Fox and the Rooster" is shown in Fig. 15.1.

Given a grammatical representation for a story, one can make predictions about recalls and summaries based on the structural relevance of parts of the story. For example, segments coded as internal responses and deeply

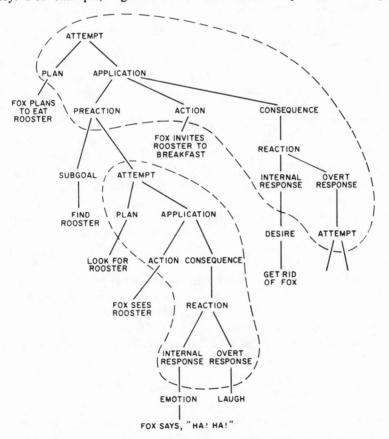

FIG. 15.1. A portion of a story grammar analysis of "The Fox and the Rooster."

embedded segments may be less easily remembered. Stein and Glenn (1977) and Mandler and Johnson (1977) have done work along these lines. Rather than consider that work in detail, I want to point out some general characteristics of a story grammar analysis. The section on Story Model Analysis presents a complementary type of analysis that addresses some of the following problems.

When one attempts to apply a story grammar, it soon becomes apparent that the interpretation of a segment of the story can vary. For example, I coded Segment 11, inviting the rooster to breakfast, as an action to achieve the overall goal stated in 8, eating the rooster; but it could have been viewed as part of the overt response to 9, finding the rooster. Furthermore, the choices made by the "grammar applier" in assigning structures are evident only in the final product, the tree representation. For purposes such as predicting free prose recall performance, the alternative structures given by the grammar may be equivalent. If our goal, however, is to account for variations in a child's model of a story, then we need a representation system that makes more of these choices explicit.

In a story such as "The Fox and the Rooster", which has two protagonists, we see a repeated pattern in the tree analysis (the dashed lines in Fig. 15.1). This pattern appears whenever one character acts in response to an action of the other. In dialogues or, in general, stories whose characters have independent but interacting plans, one would expect to find this pattern. Unfortunately, we cannot view here the entire tree structure for our example story, for in it one could see the flow of these patterns, each showing <plan>—<action>—<internal response>—<overt response>—<plan>— and so on. The story grammar is a reasonable way to label this flow, but it says nothing about the processes that generate it. The reason is that each character's plan is based on that character's beliefs about ways to attain his or her goals. Thus, the processes that account for a <plan>—<action>— <internal response>—<overt response> sequence must be explained in terms of a model of the character, not just the story itself.

A final point is that the story grammar cannot show how elements of a setting or an internal response are linked to the plans and actions of the characters. I would expect that setting and internal response information is easily lost unless it is critical to the account of a plan. A representation that made these links explicit could be used to predict relative salience of those nonaction parts of a story.

Story Model Analysis

The preceding section discusses a method of story analysis that explains some important features of stories. The method has an important limitation in that it simply ignores the internal structure of plans and, hence, of the beliefs of characters about actions that occur. The best way to show this is to present an alternative analysis that explicitly incorporates the structure of plans, beliefs, and social actions.

For comparison purposes, we will again use "The Fox and the Rooster." What we find after just a cursory analysis is that the elements of the story (facts, actions, presuppositions, etc.) must be relativized with respect to the reader. Different readers have different prior beliefs and expectations about foxes, roosters, dogs, and stories. For example, a reader who knows of foxes in stories as sly and greedy can use that knowledge in reading. In order to represent beliefs of different readers, we need to have propositions of the form, Reader-believes (P), in which P is a proposition such as *roosters are good to eat*. Furthermore, many of the reader's beliefs are, in turn, beliefs about beliefs of the characters. The reader must recognize, for example, that the fox believes that he wants to convince the rooster that the fox wants the rooster as a guest for breakfast (and not as the main course). Thus, we need to represent a proposition of the form, Reader-believes (Fox-believes (Fox-wants (Rooster-believes (Fox-believes (Fox-wants (P)))))), in which P is *the rooster comes as a guest for breakfast*.

Figure 15.2 shows a partial and somewhat superficial analysis of part of this story. In fact, it shows only propositions that are embedded within the reader's beliefs about the fox's beliefs and wants. A complete analysis would show the reader's beliefs about the dog's and the rooster's beliefs, as well as the reader's "absolute" beliefs. In this story, as in many others, part of the interest lies in the discrepancies between the reader's model of the world defined in the story and his or her models of the characters' models. Here, it is critical for the reader to recognize differences between the fox's model (as shown in Fig. 15.2) and the rooster's.

To take just one example, consider the belief, *Rooster is-easy-to-catch-and-eat*. We might hypothesize that the support for this belief consists of at least the two beliefs, *lost-animals-are-easy-to-catch-and-eat* and *Rooster is-lost-in-woods*. The fox's subsequent actions are most easily interpreted in terms of his belief that he can easily catch and eat the rooster. Conflict in the plot is provided by the belief that the rooster believes that he is neither lost, nor easy to catch and eat.

The fox's belief that the rooster will be easy to catch provides support for his belief that he can satisfy his top-level want, *Fox eat-breakfast*. This want becomes the impetus for the fox's actions. As readers, we might imagine that he begins to formulate a plan as follows:

1. In order to eat the rooster, he must be holding him.
2. Therefore, the rooster must be near the fox.
3. This will happen if the rooster descends from the tree.
4. He will come down if he wants to.

FOX BELIEVES

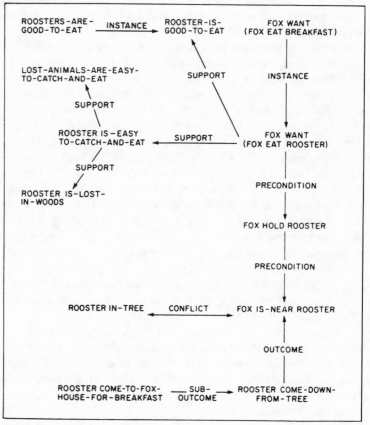

FIG. 15.2. A portion of an analysis of "The Fox and the Rooster" in terms of plans and beliefs.

5. He will want to if he wants to join the fox for breakfast.
6. He may want to do that if he trusts the fox and if the fox asks him nicely.
7. The invitation will be more successful if it is accompanied by flattery.

Acting on the basis of this plan, he says,

What a fine rooster you are! How well you sing! Will you come to my house for breakfast?

Note that these utterances make sense only if we recognize a plan of the sort sketched in 1–7 just given. Furthermore, recognition of this plan reinforces a classic schema about foxes in fables, that is, that they are clever and deceitful but often not clever enough. Schemas like this allow a reader to cope with the otherwise unmanageable mass of information found in stories.

In addition to formulating his own plans, the fox must simulate the plan formulation of the rooster in order to account for the rooster's actions. Figure 15.2 shows a few of the beliefs he might have about the rooster's plans. Note that (from the fox's point of view) the rooster's actions are both understandable and desirable. Thus the fox believes his deception is working, a belief essential to the development of the plot.

Figure 15.2 does not even show all of the fox's beliefs. For example, the fox could infer that the rooster's friend is a rooster from certain "rules of conversation." His reasoning might go as follows:

1. The friend of a rooster is probably a rooster (so the fox believes).
2. A different kind of friend would be highly unusual.
3. One should include in an utterance (or conversational turn) highly unusual, yet relevant information.
4. Without contrary indications, the rooster can be assumed to be following the rules of conversation.

The method of analysis that considers a reader's beliefs is clearly not just *story* analysis but *story model* analysis; that is, we analyze the model a "typical" reader constructs for the story. Ideally, we would like to be able to analyze a particular reader's model and compare it to other models, looking for differences in beliefs to account for differing interpretations. It also makes explicit the issue of conflicting beliefs and shows how the plans of different characters can interact. Finally, it gives a way of integrating speech acts (even multiple speech acts) with other actions. One important drawback is, of course, that such an analysis (like a story grammar analysis) is far from automatic and, to be done well, requires detailed examinations of stories and readers.

We asked children to read a version of "The Fox and the Rooster" and found striking differences in their ability to understand. One child (age 11), who happened to be a very good reader, had no trouble with the story, easily recognizing the flattery and trickery aspects of the plot. He volunteered a description of a schema for foxes in stories of this type, in which the fox is seen to be greedy or villainous, plotting to gain his evil ends, ultimately tricking himself, and so on. Furthermore, he recognized that this characterization applies not to foxes but only to *foxes in stories of this type,* that is, he knew that he was reading a particular kind of story, intended to be entertaining, perhaps to impart a moral, but not to persuade, inform, criticize, or any of a number of other social actions an author could be performing. A second child (age 10), who happened to have had trouble with previous stories, had difficulty with this one well. Not surprisingly, she gave little indication of knowing either the fox schema mentioned previously nor that schema as instantiated by this story. We can only speculate about the reasons for the differing abilities we observed; but it is clear that understanding the purpose of the story played an important role in recognizing what higher level schemata to apply and hence to understand the story itself. The importance of understanding the author's purpose is discussed further in the next section.

UNDERSTANDING THE AUTHOR'S INTENTIONS

An important step in the comprehension process is understanding what the discourse is about and what the writer's intentions are. To some extent, the writer can signal intentions via the structure of the text. However the lack of a one-to-one correspondence between text structure and purpose requires the reader to infer intentions on the basis of knowledge of the writer in much the same way as he or she infers intentions of characters in a story. Failure to understand the author's intentions can cause problems for all levels of comprehension, from that of "getting the main idea" to the subtle insights expected of skilled readers.

At the crudest level, a reader must divine enough of the purpose of a passage to know what questions should be asked or what schemata to apply in comprehending. It is a commonplace observation that the best readers know more about the process they are engaged in when reading and see elements more quickly in a text in terms of their larger functional role, for example, descriptive passage as a stage setter. The extent to which these abilities are automatic rather than evidence of meta-comprehension is still not clear.

In cases in which a reader does understand adequately, the ability to perceive the author's intentions can still make the difference between minimally sufficient comprehension and deep understanding of a text. This difference has implications for the accumulation of knowledge from text, but, more important, for motivation and development of critical reading, writing, and thinking. One example (from a technical article) should illustrate the skill that is needed; we can say little at this time, however, about how a reader acquires this skill.

In the article, the author states that a particular theory of semantics is perhaps useful for the computerization of language but not as part of a general theory of language. Some readers of this article interpreted the statement (and the supporting discussion) as a "suggestion," that is, that the author was distinguishing two possible applications of the theory he was discussing and then suggesting the more appropriate application. A discussion held among several people who read the article concluded with a contrary interpretation. The statement was seen not as a serious suggestion but rather (or more important) as a "criticism." The readers, applying their beliefs about the beliefs of the author and the creators of the semantic theory, concluded that the statement was saying that the purported general theory could be applied only in the "vain" attempt to computerize language. Their beliefs about the author's beliefs indicated that this would be a quite damning criticism and not just a friendly suggestion.

The issue is not whether these readers were correct, for a text can always be reinterpreted in the light of different beliefs. The important points are: (1) The group discussion convinced several readers that the criticism interpretation was more valid, thus enriching their understanding of the article; and (2) in order to reach the criticism interpretation, they had to apply a great amount of knowledge about the author, his use of a word like "computerize," and his purpose in writing. A general theory of reading comprehension should ultimately give an account of this process, a process in which the structural and "context-free" (if such there be) meaning aspects of language are embedded in the social function the language serves.

IMPLICATIONS FOR TEACHING

We simply do not know the extent to which children may differ in their understanding of social actions and plans, but the cultural differences could be significant. Furthermore, serious comprehension difficulties can result when there is a mismatch between the beliefs of a writer and those of a reader. A test designer should assume that an "error" may reflect differences between the reader and the writer regarding what counts as a given social action or what prerequisites there are to inferring a particular goal. It is an open question whether cultural differences with respect to social actions are greater or less than the corresponding differences with respect to general world knowledge.

If it is true that we can best understand a linguistic act (whether spoken or written) as a social action, then an adequate test of reading comprehension should distinguish between a reader's skill at building a model for a text and his or her knowledge of social roles, social behavior patterns, and the relevant linguistic conventions. It is also important for the test to identify differences between the writer's and the reader's beliefs about the world. That most reading comprehension tests ignore these issues is a statement on the potential cultural bias inherent in the tests. It may also provide an explanation for the limited success of attempts to select culture-free items for tests.

The previous discussion might suggest that we teach social actions and plans directly. A better idea would be to encourage a child to treat written language as the skilled reader does, as a tool with a purpose. This leads one to ask questions such as: What is the author trying to say? What makes you think so? Is the text convincing?

Skilled readers do not look for details without reasons, yet that is often suggested implicitly by exercises such as "find the word in paragraph 3 that means a device for carrying water." We might instead ask the student to formulate an interpretation of a text and then to support that interpretation, stating details where appropriate. Similarly, a student should not just look for actions of characters in a story but for *why* characters act as they do. This suggests a deemphasis of training for literal comprehension. Skilled reading may even be hampered by an overreliance on the explicitly stated actions and beliefs in a story.

FURTHER RESEARCH

The issues discussed in this paper are only beginning to be explored. We are not much beyond the anecdotal stage in describing how prior beliefs and organizing schemas are used in recognizing plans. We can say even less about how people manage the complex hypothesis formation task they are given by a story or dialogue.

We do know some ways of dealing with complexity of this sort. One can store frequently used patterns, for example, "Can you . . . ?" often signifies a request for action and not information about ability. But how are these conventions learned? How do we know when one has failed? What are the forms for the discourse rather than the sentence level?

The models discussed herein stress the building of representations for the plans and beliefs of characters in stories and for those of authors. They provide an account for connectivity in discourse and perhaps for some reading comprehension difficulties. But how do we examine a person's beliefs, not to mention their beliefs about the beliefs of others? If a person builds the "correct" model for a text, we may be able to discover that, but incorrect models may rest on beliefs that are obscure even to the reader.

In order to answer these questions, we need more research on how children first learn and use language, especially on their models of language function. We need better analyses of texts that consider more directly the alternative readings implied by different beliefs. We should study the beliefs that children have about social relationships and the use of language. We also need more work on how the apparently well-developed skills children have for oral discourse transfer to, interefere with, or are orthogonal to the corresponding skills for written material. Finally, we need a better model of how knowledge about linguistic forms, prose structure, social relationships, and purposeful action can be integrated to impose structure on a text.

ACKNOWLEDGMENTS

The research described herein was supported in part by the National Institute of Education under Contract No. US-NIE-C-400-76-0116. I would like to thank Andee Rubin, Maryl Gearhart, and Denis Newman for valuable discussions and extensive comments.

REFERENCES

Abelson, R. P. Concepts for representing mundane reality in plans. In D. G., Bobrow & A. Collins (Eds.), *Representation and understanding: Studies in cognitive science.* New York: Academic Press, 1975.

Austin, J. L. *How to do things with words.* London: Oxford University Press, 1962.

Becker, J. D. The phrasal lexicon. *Proceedings of the Workshop on Theoretical Issues in Natural Language Processing,* Cambridge, Mass., 1975.

Berg-Cross, L. G. Intentionality, degree of damage, and moral judgments. *Child Development,* 1975, *46,* 970–974.

Bobrow, D. G., & Winograd, T. An overview of KRL, a knowledge representation language. *Cognitive Science,* 1977, *1,* 3–46.

Bruce, B. C. Belief systems and language understanding. BBN Report No. 2973, Bolt Beranek and Newman Inc., Cambridge, Mass., 1975.

Bruner, J. On cognitive growth I and II. In J. Bruner, P. Oliver, & P. Greenfield (Eds.), *Studies in cognitive growth.* New York: John Wiley and Sons, 1966.

Bruner, J. S. The ontogenesis of speech acts. *Journal of Child Language,* 1973, *2,* 1019.

Clark, H. H., & Lucy, P. Understanding what is meant from what is said: A study in conversationally conveyed requests. *Journal of Verbal Learning and Verbal Behavior,* 1975, *14,* 56–72.

Cohen, P. R., & Perrault, C. R. Preliminaries for a computer model of conversation. *Proceedings CSCSI National Conference.* Vancouver. August 1976.

Dore, J. A pragmatic description of early language development. *Journal of Psycholinguistic Research,* 1974, *3,* 343–350.

Feldman, N. S., Klosson, E. C., Parsons, J. E., Rholes, W. S., & Ruble, D. N. Order of information presentation and children's moral judgments. *Child Development,* 1976, *47,* 556–559.

Fillmore, C. J. Santa Cruz lectures on deixis. Lecture notes, 1971 (reproduced by the Indiana Linguistics Club, Indiana University, 1975.

Firman, S. G., & Maltby, E. H. *The Winston readers: First reader.* Philadelphia: Winston, 1918.

Goodman, K. S. Psycholinguistic universals in the reading process. In F. Smith (Ed.), *Psycholinguistics and reading.* New York: Holt, Rinehart & Winston, 1973.

Gordon, D. & Lakoff, G. Conversational postulates. *Papers from the Seventh Regional Meeting.* Chicago Linguistic Society, 1971, 63–84.

Gutkin, D. The effect of systematic story changes on intentionality in children's moral judgments. *Child Development,* 1972, *43,* 187–195.

Hall, W. S., & Freedle, R. O. *Culture and language; The black American experience.* Washington, D.C.: Hemisphere, 1975.

Heider, F. *The psychology of interpersonal relations.* New York: Wiley, 1958.

Mandler, J. M., & Johnson, N. S. Remembrance of things parsed: Story structure and recall. *Cognitive Psychology,* 1977, *9,* 111–151.

Miller, G. A., Galanter, E., & Pribram, K. *Plans and the structure of behavior.* New York: Holt, 1960.

Moore, J., & Newell, A. How can MERLIN understand? In L. Gregg (Ed.), *Knowledge and cognition.* Hillsdale, N.J.: Lawrence Erlbaum Associates, 1973.

Piaget, J. *The moral judgment of the child.* London: Kegan Paul, 1932.

Rumelhart, D. E. Notes on a schema for stories. In D. Bobrow & A. Collins (Eds.), *Representation and understanding: Studies in cognitive science.* New York: Academic Press, 1975.

Rumelhart, D. E. Understanding and summarizing brief stories. In D. LaBerge & J. Samuels (Eds.), *Basic processes in reading: Perception and comprehension.* Hillsdale, N.J.: Lawrence Erlbaum Associates, 1977.

Sacerdoti, E. D. Nonlinear nature of plans. *Proceedings of the Fourth International Joint Conference on Artificial Intelligence.* Tbilisi, Georgia, U.S.S.R. September 1975.

Sadock, J. M. *Toward a linguistic theory of speech acts.* New York: Academic Press, 1974.

Schiffer, S. *Meaning.* London: Oxford University Press, 1972.

Schmidt, C. F. Understanding human action: Recognizing the plans and motives of other persons. In J. Carroll & J. Payne (Eds.), *Cognition and social behavior.* Hillsdale, N.J.: Lawrence Erlbaum Associates, 1976.

Schmidt, C. F., & Sridharan, N. A. The representation of plans: Rules of consistency for plan recognition. *Proceedings AISB Summer Conference.* Edinburgh, Scotland: July 1976.

Schweller, K. G., Brewer, W. F., & Dahl, D. A. Memory for illocutionary forces and perlocutionary effects of utterances. *Journal of Verbal Learning and Verbal Behavior,* 1976, *15,* 325–337.

Searle, J. R. *Speech acts: An essay in the philosophy of language.* Cambridge: Cambridge University Press, 1969.

Searle, J. R. Indirect speech acts. In P. Cole & J. L. Morgan (Eds.), *Syntax and semantics* (Vol. 3). *Speech acts.* New York: Academic Press, 1975. (a)

Searle, J. R. A taxonomy of illocutionary acts. In K. Gunderson (Ed.), *Minnesota studies in the philosophy of language.* Minneapolis: University of Minnesota Press, 1975. (b)

Searle, J. R. The rules of the language game. *Times Literary Supplement,* September 10, 1976.

Sedlak, A. J. *An investigation of the development of the child's understanding and evaluation of the actions of others* (Tech. Rep. No. NIH-CBM-TR-28). New Brunswick, N.J.: Department of Computer Science, Rutgers University, May 1974.

Selman, R. The relation of role taking to the development of moral judgment in children. *Child Development,* 1971, *42,* 79–91.

Shatz, M. On the development of communicative understandings: An early strategy for interpreting and responding to messages. In J. Glick & A. Clarke-Stewart (Eds.), *Studies in social and cognitive development.* New York: Gardner Press, 1977.

Stein, N., & Glenn, C. G. An analysis of story comprehension in elementary school children. In R. Freedle (Ed.), *Multidisciplinary approaches to discourse comprehension.* Norwood, N.J.: Ablex, 1977.

Strawson, P. F. Intention and convention in speech acts. *The Philosophical Review,* 1964, *5,* 73.

Sudnow, D. *Studies in social interaction.* New York: The Free Press, 1972.

Sutton-Smith, B., Botvin, G., & Mahony, D. Developmental structures in fantasy narratives. *Human development,* 1976, *19,* 1–13.

Yussen, S. R. Moral reasoning from the perspective of others. *Child Development,* 1976, *47,* 551–555.

16 Inference in Text Understanding

Allan Collins
John Seely Brown
Kathy M. Larkin
Center for the Study of Reading,
Bolt Beranek and Newman Inc.

INTRODUCTION

When people understand a text, they do not simply connect the events in the text into a sequential structure. Rather, they seem to create a complex scenario or model within which the events described might plausibly occur (Bransford & Johnson, 1973). This model-based view suggests that we cannot characterize inference procedures soley in terms of finding connections between elements in a text. But it in turn raises a number of unanswered questions about how people understand texts. For example:

1. What precisely is meant by a model of the text?
2. How do people synthesize these models?
3. How do people revise their initial models?
4. Why do people select one model over another?

In order to study how people construct and revise models, we gave subjects five difficult-to-understand texts and recorded protocols of the processing they went through to make sense of the texts. The results indicated that skilled readers use a variety of strategies for revising and evaluating different models, finally converging on a model that best accounts for the events described in the text. These strategies concern the ways that skilled readers deal with the difficulties that arise in comprehension. By making these strategies explicit, we can possibly provide less-skilled readers with strategies for what to do when they do not undertstand a text.

Text-Based Versus Model-Based Inference

Classically, in cognitive psychology and artificial intelligence, inference is thought of as filling in the missing connections between the surface structure fragments of the text by recourse to context and knowledge about the world. This text-based view of inference stresses the notion that the inference process looks for meaningful relations between different propositions in the text. Such a view permeates semantic network theory (Quillian, 1969; Rumelhart, Lindsay, & Norman, 1972), conceptual dependency theory (Rieger, 1975; Schank, 1972), demon-based approaches (Charniak, 1972), and cognitive psychology (Anderson & Bower, 1973; Frederiksen, 1975; Kintsch, 1974).

An alternative model-based view argues that a central purpose of inference is to synthesize an underlying model, which organizes and augments the surface structure fragments in the text. In this view, inference is controlled by a target structure that specifies the a priori constraints on the kind of model to be synthesized. This target structure acts as an organizational principle for guiding a set of inference procedures.

If this target is a nongenerative structure, then this view is extremely similar to the view that the purpose of inference is to select and fill out a set of frames (Charniak, 1975; Minsky, 1975; Winograd, 1975) or scripts (Lehnert, 1977; Schank & Abelson, 1975) or schemas (Bobrow & Norman, 1975; Rumelhart & Ortony, 1977). If, however, the target is a generative structure, such as a grammar, it can produce a potentially infinite number of possible models. In the latter case, the control exercised by the target structure is more subtle, requiring the growing of the target structure in conjunction with filling in the variables of the model (Bobrow & Brown, 1975).

Methodology for Studying Model-Based Inference

We studied the four questions given in the first section by reading five short but difficult-to-understand passages to four different subjects. We recorded the subjects' protocols after they had heard the entire text. The subjects were asked to describe how they processed the text, whether they had any intermediate hypotheses along the way, whether they were satisfied or dissatisfied with any of these hypotheses, and why. Subjects could ask to have the text reread if they wanted. The texts ranged from a fragment of a mystery story to a recipe for an unspecified food. Analysis of these protocols suggests some initial answers to the four questions.

Two of the texts we used follow. We describe our theory of text understanding in terms of how two of the subjects dealt with these texts. At the same time we try to point out other cases in which the same phenomena occurred in other protocols. It will help the readers to think about and remember their own processing as they read these texts:

Window Text

He plunked down $5 at the window. She tried to give him $2.50, but he refused to take it. So when they got inside, she bought him a large bag of popcorn.

Boating Text

John and Bill were sailing on Mystic Pond, and they saw a coffee can floating in the distance. Bill said, "Let's go over and pick it up." When they reached it, John picked it up and looking inside said, "Wow, there are rocks in the can." Bill said, "Oh, I guess somebody wanted the can to float there."

Because the passages were difficult to understand, subjects were able to give us valuable clues to their model-synthesis process. Equally revealing were the unsatisfactory hypotheses that people discarded along the way, and the reasons why they decided to do so. The theory described in the following section is our interpretation of the processing revealed by these subjects' protocols.

A PROGRESSIVE-REFINEMENT THEORY OF TEXT UNDERSTANDING

Overview of the Theory

We outline our theory briefly first. Then we expand each of these ideas in more detail. The theory states that text understanding proceeds by progressive refinement from an initial model to more and more refined models of the text. The target structure guides the construction process, constraining the models to the class of well-formed, goal-subgoal structures that *means-ends analysis* (Newell & Simon, 1963) produces. The initial model is a partial model, constructed from schemas triggered by the beginning elements of the text. Successive models incorporate more and more elements from the text. The models are progressively refined by trying to fill the unspecified variable slots in each model as it is constructed. As the questions associated with the unfilled slots in more refined models become more and more specific, the search for relevant information is constrained more and more. The overall process is one of *constraint satisfaction* (Fikes, 1970; Waltz, 1975).

The refinement process makes use of a variety of general-purpose problem solving strategies. These include rebinding a variable when its binding leads to a conflict, trying different variable bindings when there are a number of possible alternatives, questioning the bindings on other variables that lead either directly or indirectly to a conflict, questioning any default assumptions when there is a conflict, and focusing on another part of the problem when you are not getting anywhere. People pursue this refinement process until it converges on a solution that satisfies a number of conditions for a plausible model.

The Target Structure

The theory states that people try to understand the actions and events in a text in terms of characters applying means-ends analysis (Newell & Simon, 1963) to solve the problems that occur in the text. Means-ends analysis operates as follows: If there is a method to reach a goal directly and its preconditions are met, then apply that method. If the preconditions for the method are not met, then generate a subgoal to satisfy these preconditions. When a subgoal is generated, apply means-ends analysis recursively to reach that subgoal. If there is no way to satisfy the preconditions for that method, then look for another method that can be applied to reach that goal, and so on. Means-ends analysis thus puts certain constraints on the permissible structures that interrelate events in the text. For example, a subgoal must be a means to satisfy the preconditions for a method applicable to a higher goal. Failures in trying to apply a method must lead to application of other possible methods for obtaining the same goal or a higher goal. But within these constraints there is still a potentially infinite set of plans or solutions to a problem depending on the particular subgoals and methods generated.

Story grammars (Mandler & Johnson, 1977; Rumelhart, 1975, 1977b) are an attempt to specify the class of well-formed target structures in the domain of stories. But the target structures for other domains pertinent to text understanding can also be characterized as goal–subgoal structures. For example, the recipe used in our study consists of a set of steps for mixing ingredients and then steps for cooking. Subjects attempted to understand the recipe by figuring out the overall goal of the recipe, from the set of subplans specified in the recipe. These target structures are a kind of tacit knowledge that guides people to make sense of texts in terms of goals and subgoals.

What is missing from story grammars but is crucial to the way a target structure guides the construction of models is a notion of *planning knowledge* (Brown, Collins, & Harris, 1978). In the domain of stories, this planning knowledge consists of knowledge about social goals and deltacts (i.e., acts to reduce differences between present states and goal states), about specific methods for achieving particular deltacts, about the ordering on these methods, and about the preconditions and results of each method (Abelson 1975; Schank & Abelson, 1977). This planning knowledge places enormous constraints on the way people construe stories; for example, giving somebody money is a method for getting that person to give you possession of something, but it is not a method for conveying information to them. In order to construct a model of the text, the comprehender must identify events in the story with different methods, determine the goals that those methods are being used to achieve, identify whether those methods succeed or fail, bind successes to satisfy preconditions for higher goals, and relate failures to alternative plans to achieve the same higher goals. In the next subsection we try to indicate how this planning knowledge is invoked in constructing a model of the window text.

Constructing an Initial Model of the Text

We can best illustrate the process by which subjects construct a model in terms of the window text, because this text almost always leads people down a false path. The following protocol shows the kind of mistake subjects make initially in interpreting this text.

When you said he plunked down $5 at the window, I thought he was at the racetrack, because I decided it was a betting window. The amount of money really didn't tell me anything. I didn't think the $5 was what you bet on a horse or anything like that, but somehow the window part of it; I don't think of the movie theater as having a window; I think of it as a box office. And the only place I can think of as a window is a betting window. So I thought that was a racetrack.

So then when you said "she," I thought that was the person behind the window. And when she tried to give him $2.50 back, I thought that was his change. When he said he wouldn't accept it, I started wondering. Because I can't imagine anyone not accepting his change from a bet at a horsetrack. If the next sentence had been something like he gave her $.50 because that had really been $3 instead of $2.50, then that whole hypothesis would have fit together. I prepared myself for that; I had that expectation that there was going to be some sort of exchange of how much the bet really was. I was trying to hang on to my original hypothesis, which was that he was at a racetrack.

The second sentence was harder to integrate into that hypothesis, because it said that she tried to give him $2.50 back—it didn't say back, I guess. She tried to give him $2.50 but he refused. I was trying to integrate that into the racetrack hypothesis. And in order to do that, I had to believe that the $2.50 was his change and that he refused because it was the incorrect amount, but I was suspicious at that point, because that seemed a little strange; that didn't quite fit in.

Then when you said "when they got inside"—I believe it was the next sentence—I realized that I was wrong because there was no reason for him and the woman behind the window to be going anywhere together. I realized that the person he'd given the money to was not the same as "she" in the second sentence, and in fact they meant he and the "she" who had tried to give him the money, and suddenly I realized that she must have been his date, and it's hard to say if I really realized it at that point or at the point where you said, "so she bought a big bag of popcorn," or whatever the rest of it was. But then I had to reinterpret where the $2.50 had been coming from and it all made sense; it came from his date and she wanted to go dutch and he didn't, and so she bought the food when they got inside.

Here we see the phrase *he plunked $5 down at the window* very quickly triggers the idea of a racetrack bet. For other subjects, it triggered a bank window or a theater window. Thus many subjects apparently make a fast jump to a specific hypothesis that may or may not be correct (Rubin, 1975).

How does such a phrase converge on one of these hypotheses? What should be emphasized about this process is that the "racetrack-betting schema," "the theater-going schema," and "the bank-teller schema" all exist as prior knowledge structures for the subjects (see Schank and the Yale AI Project 1975, or Lehnert, 1977, for descriptions of a restaurant-going schema, or Charniak, 1975, for a description of a grocery-store-going schema). These schemas function as highly constrained structures that are competing to fill their slots most successfully. This is a *top-down process.* Simultaneously, the words in the text trigger a number of potential inferences. For example, *$5* suggests the notion of buying or giving; *window* suggests a house, office, car, bank, theater, or racetrack window. These inferences are the kind with which text-based theories have been concerned (see section on Text-Based Versus Model-Based Inference). This is a *bottom-up* process. The selection of a particular schema, such as the racetrack-betting schema, depends on the conjunction of these two processes (Adams & Collins, 1978; Rumelhart, 1977a; Rumelhart & Ortony, 1977).

In the protocol, each new piece of data from the text was assimilated to the initial model in order to construct more refined models of the text. Thus, the *she* in the second sentence was identified as the only other person necessary in the racetrack-betting schema (or the bank or theater-going schema), that is, the receiver of the money. When *she tried to give him $2.50,* people understood this as *change,* which can be a subschema in any of the three schemas people selected (though not so easily in the bank-teller schema). But the man's refusal of the $2.50 causes trouble for the notion of change; subjects try to explain the refusal as a result of wrong change, but this seems shaky to them because outright refusal is not the usual way to deal with wrong change. Such a model is in worse trouble when *they* get inside. It is possible for the person behind the window to go inside with the man but highly unlikely. Many subjects probably introduced a third person at this point. But when she buys him popcorn, all the subjects abandoned this incorrect model and jumped to the notion of a date. Thus, all the subjects drastically revised their initial models in order to accommodate them to the information in the text.

Figure 16.1 shows the top-level structure of the model that the subject constructed while processing the first two phrases of the window text. In a more complete representation of the model, each box in the diagram would be expanded into its underlying semantic components (Norman & Rumelhart, 1975; Schank, 1972) and all the variable bindings (which are represented by arrows) would be shown. The arrows coming out of any box represent the variable slots in the schema for that concept (Norman & Rumelhart, 1975). These slots must be specified in the conceptual representation of any schema,

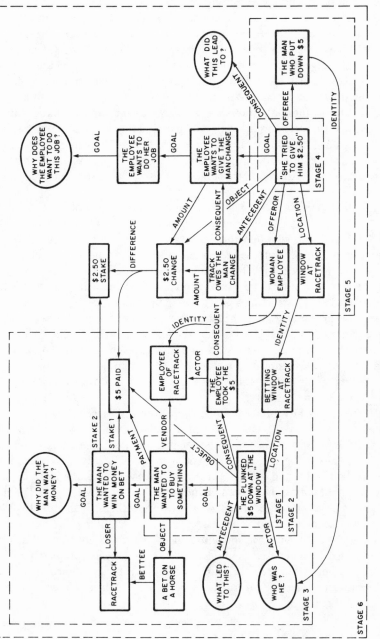

FIG. 16.1. Stages in constructing a model.

such as putting, buying, or betting. We have represented unbound variables as pending questions in circles and bound variables as concepts in boxes. As the model develops over time, pending questions turn into bound variables.

The figure attempts to show the progressive stages of understanding and how these stages encompass the goals and intentions of the characters. The first stage consists of a set of pending questions that arise from the man putting down $5, such as "Who was he?," "Why did he do it?," "Where was he?" Many of these questions are answered as the subject's understanding progresses. The second stage reflects the notion that the man is putting down money toward the goal of buying something for which the money is payment. The third stage reflects the full notion that the man's goal is betting on a horse at a racetrack. At this point the subject has constructed an initial model of the text.

The next three stages show how new information is assimilated to the initial model. Stage 4 again consists of a set of pending questions about who tried to give whom $2.50, why they did it, and how this event is connected with the first event. Stage 5 proposes some tentative interrelations between the two events: *she* must be the racetrack employee who received the $5, and *him* must be the man who plunked down $5. In stage 6, the new information is fully assimilated by constructing a goal for the employee of returning change to the man. This presupposes that the employee took the $5 and that the amount of the bet must have been $2.50. Thus the initial model is modified slightly to change the betting stake from $5 to $2.50. In general, assimilation of new information is accomplished by filling in intervening structures based on the characters' goals and intentions and making modifications to the original structures when necessary.

Figure 16.2 shows how a model is restructured when new information cannot be assimilated, which happened at the end of the window text. The new structure preserves a few of the original bindings: The plunking down $5 is still a "buying" event, the man who is offered $2.50 is still the man who plunked down $5, and there is still an employee who takes the $5. But most of the original bindings have been abandoned: A new character (i.e., the man's date) has been introduced, and it is she who offers the $2.50 in order to pay for her own ticket to the movie. The process of rebinding all the variables probably started with the introduction of this third character. Each new binding led to other new bindings until the model was completely restructured. However, the process occurred too quickly for the subject to describe; it is best seen in the next protocol in which another subject was trying to make sense of the boating text.

The Questions Arising Out of a Model

Any model that the subject constructs raises a number of questions that the subject tries to answer. For example, in constructing a model for the window

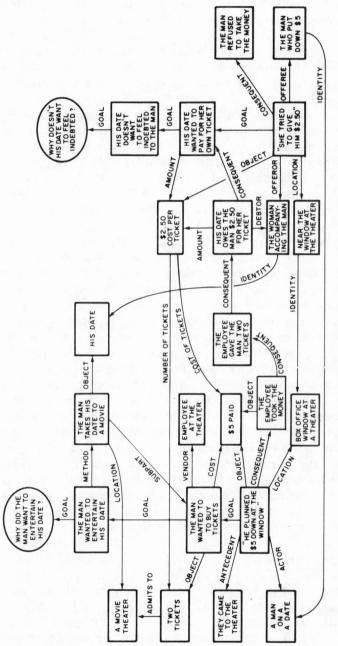

FIG. 16.2. Restructured version of the partial model in Fig. 16.1.

393

text, the subject considered the following questions: "Where were they?"; "Why did the man plunked down $5?"; "Who was the *she* that tried to give him $2.50?"; "Why did she try to give him $2.50?"; "Why did he refuse the $2.50?"; "Why did she go inside with him?"; and "Why did she buy him popcorn?" Failure to answer any of the questions can lead to restructuring the model. Answering any of these questions leads to a more refined model and puts additional constraints on the answers to the other questions.

These questions derive from the unfilled variable slots in the world knowledge schemas that are triggered by the understander's attempt to construct a coherent goal–subgoal structure. This is seen most clearly in a segment from a protocol on the boating text: "Well if it was an open can it might not float, if water got into it. Maybe if it was a closed can... " Here the subject is considering possible values for the "lid" variable in the "coffee can" schema. However, in most cases in which the coffee can schema might be needed to understand a text, it would never lead to a question about the lid variable. Why does it in this text? The reason is that the lid variable is crucial to finding a method for the goal of keeping the can afloat, which is a basic problem that arises out of the statement of the text. The subject eventually decided the can was closed. By fixing the variable in this way, she constrained the model in order to help her converge on a solution.

Sometimes questions arise out of the answers to other questions. For example, one of the subjects given the boating text was working on the question "What was the function of the rocks?" In doing so he considered the possibility that the rocks were lighter than water and that their function was displacement of water. This solution led in turn to two kinds of questions: "Are there lighter-than-water rocks?" and "What kept the rocks in the can?" The existence of pumice answers the first question, but in turn leads to questions such as "Would there be pumice around Mystic Pond?" The second question can be answered in terms of a lid, but this raises the question of "How does water get into the can for the rocks to displace?" These examples show how binding a new schema to a slot in order to answer one question can lead to other questions about how that schema interacts with the rest of the model. However, at some point, the process must converge because subjects usually do find a model that is satisfactory to them.

Constraint Satisfaction

The process by which people converge on a model that answers these questions involves *constraint satisfaction* (Bobrow & Brown, 1975; Fikes, 1970; Waltz, 1975). Constraint satisfaction occurs frequently in human problem solving. For example, consider cryptarithmetic problems, such as Fikes (1970) or Newell and Simon (1972) analyzed. The problem is to determine how to assign the digits (0–9) to letters so that the addition is correct:

        DONALD
      + GERALD
        ROBERT

In this problem once the problem solver sees that E must be equal to 9 or 0, this constrains A to be either 4 or 5. To solve the problem, subjects make initial default assignments (such as $E = 9$) and see if the constraints imposed by the assignments converge on a solution. Like means–ends analysis, constraint satisfaction is a pervasive part of cognitive processing.

Constraint satisfaction also arises in understanding scenes made up of toy blocks (Waltz, 1975). The problem is to identify the individual blocks making up the scene. In such scenes, there are different patterns of edges that occur both at corners of blocks or where one block occludes another. The interpretation of one pattern is constrained by the interpretations of the adjacent patterns involving the same edges. In interpreting such scenes, the convergence time depends on the amount of ambiguity in the possible interpretations. As Winston (1977, p. 59) points out, if the process starts at the edge of a scene where there is less ambiguity, it converges much faster than if it starts in the middle of the scene. Similarly, if humans focus on the center of a scene, they find it much harder to identify the individual blocks, suggesting that human vision depends on a process similar to constraint satisfaction.

In understanding text, people try to answer the questions that arise out of the models they construct. When any question is answered, it constrains the solutions to other questions. Thus, the bottom-up search for relevant information becomes more and more constrained as solutions to other questions are proposed. Sometimes the entire process converges too quickly for subjects to use introspection, as when the occurrence of *popcorn* caused a very fast restructuring of the answers to all the questions about the window text. Other times, the process converges quite slowly, as is detailed later for the boating text. But we doubt that the slow convergence is a special case; rather, we suspect it reveals the processing that occurs when disconfirming evidence as well as confirming evidence is encountered.

REVISING A MODEL

Problem-Solving Strategies

In revising their model of a text, subjects bring to bear a variety of problem-solving strategies. We can best describe these strategies in terms of their similarity to solving crossword puzzles. In the following list, we show some common strategies that people use to solve crossword puzzles. The column or row space in which a word can be inserted in a puzzle is called a *slot* to emphasize its schema-theoretic correlate. In schema-theoretic terms, the words inserted in the puzzle are the values assigned to variable slots.

1. If the word generated for a slot leads to a conflict, then generate a new word for that slot. (*Rebinding*)
2. If you cannot think of a word that satisfactorily fills a slot, then try to find another interpretation of the clue. (*Question Default Interpretation*)
3. If the word generated for a slot leads to a conflict with a crossing word, then question if that crossing word is correct. (*Question Direct Conflict*)
4. If the word generated for a slot leads to a conflict with a crossing word, then question the words that led to the selection of that crossing word. (*Question Indirect Conflict*)
5. If you cannot think of a word that satisfactorily fills a slot, then shift focus to find a crossing word to constrain the current slot. (*Near Shift of Focus*)
6. If you cannot think of a word that satisfactorily fills a slot, then shift focus to find a noncrossing word to constrain words crossing this word. (*Distant Shift of Focus*)
7. If there are a small set of possible words to fill a slot, try each one to see how they fit with possible crossing words. (*Case Analysis*)
8. If there are several possible words to fill a slot, tentatively try the most likely word. (*Most Likely Case Assignment*)

There are two aspects of these strategies we should explain. First, the two strategies we have referred to as "Indirect Conflict" and "Distant Shift of Focus" can be more or less indirect or distant. It depends on the number of steps between the new slot and the old slot in terms of crosswords. For example, a conflict or a shift can be one step removed to a slot that intersects a crossing word or two steps removed to a slot that intersects the one-step-removed slot, and so on. A shift of focus of several steps is usually tried only when a whole area is causing difficulty. Second, what we have called "Question Default Interpretation" is tied to a whole set of strategies for most skilled crossword puzzlers. For example, one such strategy is to view the clue as a verb if you have been viewing it as a noun. But these strategies are highly domain specific and do not concern us here. What is important for our purposes is how the eight strategies just listed appear to be domain independent.

A Subject's Protocol for the Boating Text

Most of these problem-solving strategies can be seen in the following protocol for the boating text. Because of the length of the protocol, we have extracted only the most relevant segments:

1. Well immediately it doesn't make sense. I mean a can with rocks wouldn't float. I am going back. Mystic Pond, I don't think that could be anything other than a regular pond, unless it's a fairy tale in which anything could happen. I'm wondering if there is any other kind of coffee can it could be other than the round ones I'm thinking of. And I was wondering if there was any other kind of rocks there could be except the usual ones.

2. Well I thought about halfway through maybe they were ice sailing, but that wouldn't make sense that a can with rocks would float on ice, so I don't think they were ice sailing. It could be such salty water that a can with rocks would float in it. I think there is such a one out in Salt Lake City.

3. Somebody wanted it to float, so they put rocks in it. Well if it was an open can, it might not float if water got into it. Maybe if it was a closed can and there was air in it, it would float, but if it was closed why would they put rocks in it. I mean if it was closed and there was air in it, it doesn't seem like you would need rocks to keep it afloat. I'm baffled.

4. No, I wouldn't settle on anything I've said; nothing I've said really explains it.

5. Well the can was either opened and then somebody closed it using a plastic lid or some other kind of lid, in which case if they didn't open it, then I don't see how they could have gotten the rocks into it, so they must have opened it.

6. Maybe they put in a few rocks. Maybe that would make it drift, not drift as far, but I don't know whether that's true or not. Well if something's heavier, it won't move as fast with the same amount of force applied to it, so maybe thay put a few rocks in.

7. Yeah, it says float *there,* not just float, so maybe they put a few rocks in to keep it relatively stable and then the rest was filled with air. I think that's what I would settle on.

8. Well, I am assuming that there's currents, oh it's a pond. OK, I'm assuming that there's currents or wind. Well, there must have been some wind because they went sailing so maybe if it was light like a leaf it would get blown all over the place because an empty coffee can would be pretty light I would imagine. I think if they put a few rocks in, though, it might not sink and that would weight it down a bit, so that it wouldn't get blown as far. That's what I would guess.

The questions that this subject was trying to answer were foremost "Why didn't the can sink?" and "What was the function of the rocks?" Other subjects addressed different questions, as we show. The protocol shows abandonment of several answers to the first question, then a solution to it, (there were only a few rocks), and then a turning to the second question and a solution to it, (the rocks functioned as an anchor). The subject did not, in fact, arrive at the same solution as the one found by Bill in the story. Bill's solution was that the rocks functioned as ballast to keep the open can upright, and hence afloat. But the protocol does illustrate most of the different kinds of problem-solving strategies that occur in the protocols collected.

Strategies in Revising a Model

The subjects were using the problem-solving strategies listed earlier in order to determine the meaning of the texts. Examples from the protocols of each of the strategies follow.

Rebinding. The most common strategy seen in the protocols (e.g., in segments 2, 5, and 8) involves rebinding the current slot. The strategy is simply: If a value that is bound to a variable slot leads to a conflict, then try another binding for that variable. A clear case of the subject rebinding a previous solution to the question "Why didn't the can sink?" occurs in the second fragment. There she adopted a high-density-of-water solution by considering the water as ice. But this solution produced an immediate conflict: The coffee can was said to be floating. To patch this high-density solution, she thought of another way (salt water) that water could be dense enough to hold up a rock-filled can. In segment 5, the subject considers the possibility that the can had never been opened. This leads to a conflict with the fact that the can had rocks in it, so the subject resumes the assumption that the can had been opened. In segment 8, there was a patch of the anchor solution in which the subject abandoned the notion that the can was anchored against currents and instead decided it was anchored against winds. Rebinding involves keeping most of the model constructed up to the present point and changing only the last variable bound.

Figures 16.3 and 16.4 depict two of the attempts at rebinding by the subject: Fig. 16.3 shows the unsuccessful attempt in segment 2, and Fig. 16.4 shows the successful attempt in segment 8. In each case, the model constructed in attempting to answer a particular question had an unbound slot that needed to be filled to make the model plausible. (We have depicted the models here as a metaphorical image that may not be too different from the kind of model people actually have.) A first attempt at binding the slot failed on the basis of the evaluation strategies described later. In Fig. 16.3 the second binding also failed, leading to abandonment of that particular model. In 16.4, however, the rebinding succeeded and the subject decided that the entire model was plausible.

Questioning a Default Interpretation. When subjects are not getting anywhere, they often begin to question their default assumptions. This can be seen most clearly in the first segment, in which the subject considered changing her initial default assumptions that: (1) this is the real world; (2) it is a standard coffee can; and (3) these are normal rocks. Some subjects elaborate these possibilities by creating a fairy tale in which the lake is only a little pond and the can rests on the bottom or by assuming the rocks are lighter than water and their function is displacement of water. This is an important

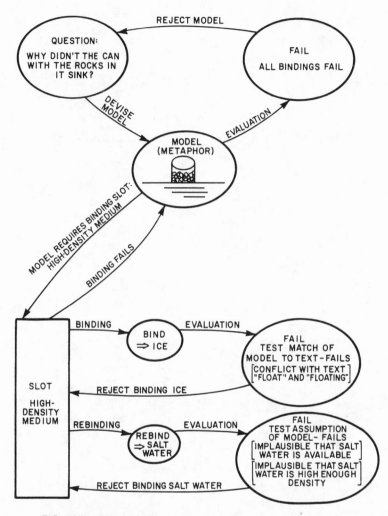

FIG. 16.3.   Rebinding the slot for a high-density medium (protocol segment 2).

problem-solving strategy, because assuming the wrong default values can often prevent subjects from finding the correct solution, which happened to the subjects who decided the coffee can was closed.

Questioning a Direct or Indirect Conflict.   The strategy of questioning a direct conflict can best be seen in the earlier protocol on the window text. There the subject had bound the *she* in the text as the person who received the money behind the window. However, when *she* went inside with the man, this

400   COLLINS, BROWN, LARKIN

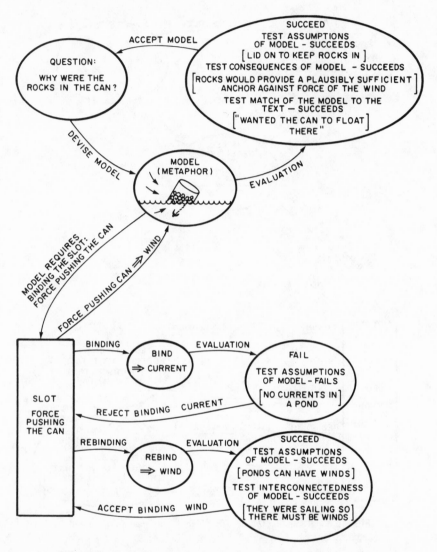

FIG. 16.4.   Rebinding the slot for the force pushing on the can (protocol segment 8).

led the subject to question her earlier binding of *she* to the person behind the window. This questioning of previous bindings is rather prevalent in dialogues.

Sometimes the questioning of a particular binding may only occur through a chain of inferences that are needed to support a particular binding. For example, one subject had decided the coffee can was covered with an air-tight plastic lid. This binding was made when he initially heard in the text that the coffee can was floating in the distance. Later, when he was considering the question about the function of the rocks, he considered the possibility that the rocks were lighter than water (e.g., pumice) and their function was to displace water. In order to displace water, water had to be able to get into the can without the rocks getting out. This led the subject indirectly to question the earlier lid binding: What he needed was a leaky lid. Thus through a whole chain of bindings the subject was led to question a binding made much earlier.

Near or Distant Shift of Focus. Subjects in the protocols sometimes move from a question they cannot solve to a different question. Often the new question is closely related to the old question. For example, between segment 2 and segment 3 of the protocol shown for the boating text, the subject changed the question she was addressing from "Why didn't the can sink?" to "What was the function of the rocks?" Then, during segment 3, she changed to the related question "Was the can open or closed?" Another subject, when he was not getting anywhere with the question about the function of the rocks, considered the more distantly related question "What was the intention of the people who put the rocks in the can?" By addressing a different question when in trouble, the subject frees himself of some of the assumptions he has made in constructing his current model. It gives the subject a new perspective by allowing him to start binding variables in a different part of the structure (see paragraph on constraint satisfaction in vision).

The reason this strategy works is that the answer to one question constrains the answers to other questions. For example, the subject's solution in fragment 6 that the can floated because there were only a few rocks apparently suggested the anchor solution to the function question. Another subject, when he heard the ballast solution, answered the question about the intention of the people who put rocks in the can as follows: They must have been kids who wanted the can to float, and to prevent it from floating on its side, they put rocks in. Addressing different questions in order to constrain other variables helps the subject converge on a solution from a different angle.

Case Analysis and Most Likely Case Assignment. Often subjects make tentative assignments as a deliberate strategy to constrain the possible solutions so that the process will converge. Case analysis is the systematic consideration of all alternative cases. This is what the subject did in segment 3, when she considered whether the can was open or closed. Then, in segment 5, she elaborated her model by making several likely case assignments: that the can was closed, that a plastic lid was used, and that it was empty except for the rocks. But these were tentative assignments of variables; they were chosen only because they were the most plausible values. Hypothetical reasoning on cases (i.e., choosing *either* the most likely *case,* or the case that might

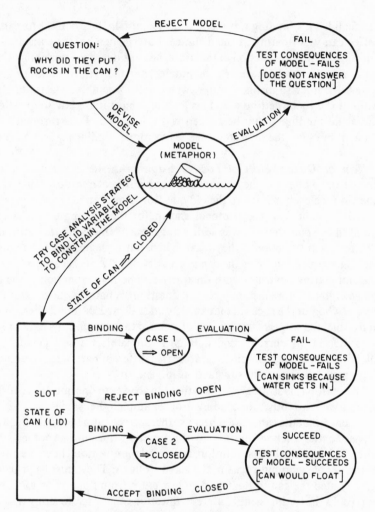

FIG. 16.5.   Case analysis for the lid variable (protocol segment 3).

constrain the model the most) is a standard technique in constraint satisfaction. By pinning these variables down to their most likely values, the subject hoped to impose enough constraint so that the process would converge (see subsection on constraint satisfaction).

Figure 16.5 depicts the case analysis strategy used by the subject in segment 3. There, the subject tried to bind the lid variable in order to constrain her model. The first binding failed but the second succeeded at the level of the particular slot it filled. However, the entire model failed, because it did not answer the basic question about the function of the rocks. This illustrates how the evaluation strategies described later are applied at different levels in testing the plausibility of any model.

Evaluating the Model

The protocols showed that subjects evaluated a number of models while trying to make sense of the texts. There are a number of *strategies* they applied in order to evaluate the models, and these strategies are linked to the *conditions* they used to either accept or reject a model. The evaluation process is a complex one, but we think we can specify at least four different tests that subjects applied in evaluating the plausibility of the models they constructed. The evidence from all these tests appears to be weighed together in evaluating the plausibility of any model.

1. The Plausibility of the Assumptions and Consequences of the Model. In constructing any model, it is necessary to fill a number of slots in the model with default values. Furthermore, the model has certain consequences that follow from it. There are a number of places in the protocols in which subjects clearly are testing the plausibility of the model's default assumptions and consequences. For example, in segment 2 of the protocol, the subject tried to test the likelihood that Mystic Pond might be salty. To do this, she tried to think of cases of salt water lakes and she came up with the Great Salt Lake in Utah. Apparently, in part, because of the relative *unavailability* (Tversky & Kahneman, 1973) of salt water lakes among the lakes she knew, she decided it was fairly implausible that the Mystic Pond was salty. She may also have found it implausible that salt water would hold up a can filled with rocks. In the last segment, she spent considerable effort elaborating the anchor model to see if she could think of some force (e.g., currents or winds) that the rocks would anchor the can against. All of these are tests of parts of the model against the subject's world knowledge. They make use of the wide variety of strategies people have for evaluating plausibility (Collins, 1978; Collins, Warnock, Aiello, & Miller, 1975).

2. The Completeness of the Model. Models are evaluated in terms of how well the assumptions and consequences of the model answer all the different questions that arise. For example, the salt-water-lake notion answers the question "Why didn't the can sink?" but it does not answer the questions "What was the function of the rocks?" and "What were the intentions of the people who put the can in the lake?" Thus, the salt-water model seems shaky because it does not answer important questions that arise with respect to the text.

3. The Interconnectedness of the Model. The assumptions or consequences of a model are weighed with respect to how they fit together with other aspects of the model. When particular assumptions are unsupported by other parts of the model, the whole model seems shakier. For example, when the subject was considering currents and winds as forces acting on the can, she rejected currents because they did not fit with the fact that it was a pond. But she accepted winds because the people were sailing, which requires winds. In her final model, then, winds enter in two ways: to sail the boat and to provide a force to anchor the can against. Subjects appear to put more belief in the plausibility of the model if the different pieces tie together in more than one way.

4. The Match of the Model to the Text.   Very often, subjects seem to weigh the model in terms of how well its assumptions or consequences match particular aspects of the text. For example, in segment 2, the subject decided that "sailing" on the lake could be "ice sailing," but that if the can was held up by ice, it would not really be "floating." Thus, we see a careful matching (Collins & Loftus, 1975; Smith, Shoben, & Rips, 1974) of the concepts implied by the model against surface aspects of the text.

In making judgments about the plausibility of a model, subjects weigh all these different factors against each other. Sometimes, each particular aspect of the model may be acceptable in and of itself, but taken together the whole thing seems shaky. This may have been why one subject rejected the salt-water model and another subject rejected the lighter-than-water-rocks (e.g. pumice) model. However, these four tests are not exhaustive; they merely encompass the major factors the subjects expressed concern about in the protocols.

In the subjects' evaluation of models, there appears to be a parallel to the distinction in science between a model's ability to explain prior data and its ability to predict new data. For the most part, in the protocols, the subjects are evaluating prior data. But in segment 7, there is a striking case in which the subject's model led to a prediction that was confirmed by referring to the text (test 4 given previously). Her model implied that the function of the rocks was to keep the can stationary. Then, looking at the text again, she found in Bill's remark a *there,* which could be interpreted as meaning "in that one place." This confirmation of a prediction from the model seemed to give her much more confidence in her model. There is no way to tell for sure, but this suggests that making a successful prediction may act to increase confidence more than finding a successful account of prior data.

IMPLICATIONS FOR READING COMPREHENSION

In our schools, we do not typically teach children what to do when they cannot comprehend a text. Furthermore, the strategies children have developed to deal with comprehension difficulties in conversation (e.g., ask a question or look puzzled) do not apply in reading (Rubin, Chapter 13, this volume). At this point, children need to develop a whole new set of strategies for what to do when they do not understand. It is just such strategies that we see so ubiquitously in the protocols of the adults we studied.

One failure that occurred in the adult procotols is perhaps revealing of what may go wrong when a child cannot understand a text. One of the subjects, in dealing with the boating text, apparently failed to make much sense of it because she tried to answer the wrong questions about the text. First she dealt with the question "Who were John and Bill?" Because she quickly determined who John and Bill were, she thought the problem for the reader in understanding the text was going to be to figure out their identities, just as in a mystery story. Bill's remark at the end then violated her expectations about the point of the story. This in turn led her to ask the question "Why didn't Bill explain what the rocks were doing in the can?" This too is a reasonable question about Bill's intentions, but it does not help find answers to the major questions posed by the text, that is, "Why didn't the can sink?" and "What was the function of the rocks?" She did not ignore these questions altogether, but she did not focus on them enough to find a solution. Nor was she exceptional. Another subject, who focused on the question "What was the intention of the people who put the rocks in the can?" which seems from Bill's remark to be the correct question, also failed because the question leads down blind alleys. It brings up issues such as: "Who were the people who put rocks in the can?"; "What were they trying to accomplish?" (e.g. catching lobsters or raindrops); "Were they playing some game, doing some job, or trying to confuse John and Bill?" These examples suggest that one of the most critical skills may be to choose the right questions upon which to focus one's problem-solving skills. But the protocols do not tell us how people make these choices.

The theory outlined here provides a framework for studying specific questions about text understanding; for example: How do skilled readers formulate questions about a text? What strategies do they use to revise the models they construct to answer these questions? How do they evaluate those models? These questions address the strategies essential for dealing with difficult texts. By pinpointing the strategies that skilled readers use for dealing with difficulties in understanding, it should become clear what strategies unskilled readers must learn.

ACKNOWLEDGMENTS

The research described herein was supported by the National Institute of Education under contract No. MS-NIE-C-400-76-0116. We thank Andee Rubin, Sally Goldin, and the editors for their comments on earlier drafts of the paper, and Sally Goldin for pointing out how subjects question their default assumptions.

REFERENCES

Abelson, R. P. Concepts for representing mundane reality in plans. In D. G. Bobrow & A. Collins (Eds.), *Representation and understanding: Studies in cognitive science.* New York: Academic Press, 1975.

Adams, M. J., & Collins, A. A schema-theoretic view of reading. In R. Freedle (Ed.), *Discourse processing: A multidisciplinary perspective.* Norwood, N.J.: Ablex Publishing Co., 1978.

Anderson, J. R., & Bower, G. *Human associative memory.* Washington, D.C.: Winston & Sons, 1973.

Bobrow, R. J., & Brown, J. S. Syntheses, analysis, and contingent knowledge in specialized understanding systems. In D. Bobrow & A. Collins (Eds.), *Representation and understanding: Studies in cognitive science.* New York: Academic Press, 1975.

Bobrow, D. G., & Norman, D. A. Some principles of memory schemata. In D. G. Bobrow & A. Collins (Eds.), *Representation and understanding.* New York: Academic Press, 1975.

Bransford, J. D., & Johnson, M. K. Consideration of some problems of comprehension. In W. G. Chase (Ed.), *Visual information processing.* New York: Academic Press, 1973.

Brown, J. S., Collins, A., & Harris, G. Artificial intelligence and learning strategies. In H. F. O'Neil (Ed.), *Learning strategies.* New York: Academic Press, 1978.

Charniak, E. *Toward a model of children's story comprehension.* Unpublished doctoral dissertation, Massachusetts Institute of Technology, 1972. (Also MIT Artificial Intelligence Laboratory Tech. Rep. AI-TR, 266, 1972).

Charniak, E. Organization and inference in a frame-like system of common knowledge. In R. C. Schank & B. L. Nash-Webber, (Eds.), *Theoretical issues in natural language processing.* Cambridge, Mass.: Bolt, Beranek and Newman Inc., 1975.

Collins, A. Fragments a theory of human plausible reasoning. In D. L. Waltz (Ed.), *Theoretical issues in natural language processing—2.* Urbana: University of Illinois, 1978.

Collins, A., & Loftus, E. F. A spreading activation theory of semantic processing. *Psychological Review,* 1975, *82,* 407–428.

Collins, A., Warnock, E. H., Aiello, N., & Miller, M. L. Reasoning from incomplete knowledge. In D. Bobrow & A. Collins (Eds.). *Representation and understanding: Studies in cognitive science.* New York: Academic Press, 1975.

Fikes, R. E. REF-ARF: A system for solving problems stated as procedures. *Artificial Intelligence,* 1970, *1,* 27–120.

Frederiksen, C. H. Representing logical and semantic structure of knowledge acquired from discourse. *Cognitive Psychology,* 1975, *7,* 371–458.

Kintsch, W. *The representation of meaning in memory.* Hillsdale, N.J.: Lawrence Erlbaum Associates, 1974.

Lehnert, W. Human and computational question answering. *Cognitive Science,* 1977, *1,* 47–73.

Mandler, J. M., & Johnson, N. S. Remembrance of things parsed: Story structure and recall. *Cognitive Psychology,* 1977, *9,* 111–151.

Minsky, M. A framework for representing knowledge. In P. H. Winston (Ed.), *The psychology of computer vision.* New York: McGraw-Hill, 1975.

Newell, A., & Simon, H. A. GPS, a program that simulates human thought. In E. A. Feigenbaum & J. Feldman (Eds.), *Computers and thought.* New York: McGraw Hill, 1963.

Newell, A., & Simon, H. A. *Human problem solving.* Englewood Cliffs, N.J.: Prentice-Hall, 1972.

Norman, D. A., Rumelhart, D. E., & the LNR Research Group. *Explorations in cognition.* San Francisco: W. H. Freeman, 1975.

Quillian, M. R. The teachable language comprehender: A simulation program and theory of language. *Communications of the ACM,* 1969, *12,* 459–476.

Rieger, C. J. Conceptual memory and inference. In R. C. Schank (Ed.), *Conceptual information processing.* New York: American Elsevier, 1975.

Rubin, A. D. *Hypothesis formation and evaluation in medical diagnosis* (Report AI-TR-316). Cambridge, Mass.: Artificial Intelligence Laboratory, MIT., 1975.

Rumelhart, D. E. Notes on a schema for stories. In D. Bobrow & A. Collins (Eds.), *Representation and understanding: Studies in cognitive science.* New York: Academic Press, 1975.

Rumelhart, D. E. Toward an interactive model of reading. In S. Dornic (Ed.), *Attention and Performance VI.* London: Academic Press, 1977. (a)

Rumelhart, D. E. Understanding and summarizing brief stories. In D. LaBerge & J. Samuels (Eds.), *Basic processes in reading: Perception and comprehension.* Hillsdale, N.J.: Lawrence Erlbaum Associates, 1977. (b)

Rumelhart, D. E., Lindsay, P. H., & Norman, D. A. A process model for long-term memory. In E. Tulving & W. Donaldson (Eds.), *Organization of memory.* New York: Academic Press, 1972.

Rumelhart, D. E., & Ortony, A. Representation of knowledge. In R. C. Anderson, R. J. Spiro, & W. E. Montague (Eds.), *Schooling and the acquisition of knowledge.* Hillsdale, N.J.: Lawrence Erlbaum Associates, 1977.

Schank, R. C. Conceptual dependency: A theory of natural language understanding. *Cognitive Psychology,* 1972, *3,* 552–631.

Schank, R. C., & Abelson, R. P. Scripts, plans and knowledge. *Proceedings of the Fourth International Joint Conference on Artificial Intelligence.* Tbilisi, Georgia, U.S.S.R.: 1975.

Schank, R. C., & Abelson, R. P. *Scripts, plans, goals, and understanding.* Hillsdale, N.J.: Lawrence Erlbaum Associates, 1977.

Schank, R. C., & the Yale A. I. Project. SAM—A Story understander (Res. Rep. 43). New Haven, Conn.: Yale University, Department of Computer Science, August 1975.

Smith, E. E., & Shoben, E. J., & Rips, L. J. Structure and process in semantic memory: A featural model for semantic decisions. *Psychological Review,* 1974, *81,* 214–241.

Tversky, A., & Kahneman, D. Availability: A heuristic for judging frequency and probability. *Cognitive Psychology,* 1973, *5,* 207–232.

Waltz, D. Understanding line drawings of scenes with shadows. In P. H. Winston (Ed.), *The psychology of computer vision.* New York: McGraw-Hill, 1975.

Winograd, T. Frame representations and the declarative–procedural controversy. In D. G. Bobrow & A. M. Collins (Eds.), *Representation and understanding: Studies in cognitive science.* New York: Academic Press, 1975.

Winston, P. H. *Artificial intelligence.* Reading, Mass.: Addison-Wesley, 1977.

IV EFFECTS OF PRIOR LANGUAGE EXPERIENCES

Long before they read, most children have conversations, watch television, hear lectures from their parents, talk on the telephone, listen to records, and have other experiences of language. That these experiences are the base for the acquisition of reading comprehension skills is obvious; a more surprising possibility is that they may be a potential source of problems in learning to read as well. An understanding of reading requires an analysis of how it is like or unlike these other prior language experiences and of how the similarities or differences affect one's learning.

Most of the research on reading vis-a-vis other forms of communication has focused on written versus oral comprehension. One line of work has stressed the similarities between reading and hearing the same material. Generally speaking, experiments in this tradition have suggested that the person who has troubles comprehending written words has similar difficulties with the same words in spoken form. This is not surprising given the known importance of vocabulary and general knowledge in the comprehension of language. A second line of work, however, has focused on differences between written and spoken language. Differences between the syntax of children's oral language and the syntax of the texts they encounter are emphasized (Huggins, Chapter 4, this volume). The general approaches appear to be contradictory.

Rubin's Chapter 17 considers apparent inconsistencies such as this and comes to the conclusion that a broader framework is needed to account for the relationship between reading and other forms of communication. There is not a simple "oral language–written language" dichotomy. Reading is not achieved by just adding decoding skills to oral language skills. She argues that, instead, we should consider a multidimensional view of language activities or experiences. Written and oral language will appear similar if we contrast one pair of these experiences, say, listening to a textbook being read aloud versus reading the textbook, but will appear dissimilar if we contrast another pair, say, having a conversation versus reading a story without pictures. Comparing two written language experiences may even reveal more differences than comparing a particular oral–written pair. When the experiences are similar, decoding alone may be the principal difference. When the experiences are dissimilar, many skills may be needed in one that are not needed in the other. Rubin argues that we should focus our attention on these many and varied dimensions of language experiences as well as on that of modality (phonemic vs. orthographic).

A striking aspect of the differences between many of the oral language experiences and the typical written language experiences is that the language itself (the vocabulary, the syntax, the topic) is different. This is particularly true for precisely those groups who have the greatest difficulties with formal education. Although good and poor readers can be found in every subculture of our society, a disproportionate number are found among groups with lower socio-economic status, such as inner-city Blacks and rural Chicanos. These groups also have English dialects that differ most from that found in standard school books. The transition from ordinary conversation to reading, which, as Rubin shows, is one requiring the acquisition of many new skills, is almost certainly made more difficult by the additional demands of dialect change.

Hall's Chapter 18 considers the effects of dialect differences on learning to read. First, he reviews the work on dialect as phonological variation and concludes that such things as pronunciation differences have not been shown to be the critical factors. Then, he examines vocabulary, syntax, and finally language use and function. He argues that it is differences in the use of language that may account for the greatest problems for speakers of nonstandard English. Thus Hall arrives at the same point Rubin does from a different perspective: In addition to the traditional approaches to reading, we must explore the ways people use language in different situations, their mode of involvement with a topic, the way in which they interact with the speaker (or writer), their use of contextual information, and their understanding of the purposes of communication experiences.

17

A Theoretical Taxonomy of The Differences Between Oral and Written Language

Andee Rubin
Center for the Study of Reading,
Bolt Beranek and Newman Inc.

INTRODUCTION

Children come to the task of reading with a set of well-developed oral language comprehension skills. This linguistic skill, remarkably obtained in just a few years, obviously facilitates reading and learning to read. One view is that oral and written language comprehension represent essentially the same process; reading a passage simply involves decoding the orthographic symbols to a phonemic representation, then comprehending that as if it were speech. Huey's (1908/1968) often-cited statement expresses this view: "The child comes to his first reader with his habits of spoken language fairly well formed and these habits grow more deeply set with every year. His meanings inhere in this spoken language and belong but secondarily to the printed symbols [p. 123]." An alternative point of view is that, although the two processes share significant subparts, they also differ in crucial ways. For example, Kolers (1970) contends that "the questions of interest to the student of reading are not whether all [symbol–sound] correspondences can be characterized by rules, for they can, but whether reading is merely their application. Here the answer is decisively negative [p. 116]."

Advocates of the first position contend that reading comprehension = oral comprehension skills + decoding. Those who espouse the second claim that the equation contains many more terms and that some of the coefficients might even be negative, indicating skills that must be unlearned in the transition from oral comprehension to reading.

In this chapter, I emphasize and explore the differences among various forms of oral and written language rather than their similarities. The

411

discussion is based on the claim that it is misleading to compare the broad class "oral language" with all "written language," because differences within these classes can be much greater than any general distinction between them. In fact, the simple oral versus written dichotomy on which much research has focused corresponds to only *one* of several dimensions of language experience that I develop here. Although it is clear that the necessity for visual decoding is a difference between children's oral language and reading comprehension, I contend that it is but one of a great many distinctions, all of which may well present stumbling blocks for children learning to read. Recognizing the multifaceted manner in which a child's language skills must develop, we can see that the cognitive leaps we expect children to make are enormous and can perhaps be broken down into more manageable steps.

The major portion of this chapter introduces a taxonomy of the differences between children's typical oral language experiences and the experience of reading a book. The section on the taxonomy explores these distinctions and then considers some implications of this taxonomy for teaching reading and doing research in reading comprehension. (These issues are discussed further in Rubin 1978a and Rubin 1978b). The next section discusses, from the perspective of the taxonomy developed in this chapter, some experimental work that purports to investigate the "same process" hypothesis exemplified by Huey's statement. In addition to the problems identified, the major criticism of this research is that it ignores the differences I consider most crucial to a child's transition from listening to reading comprehension. As an example of an alternative type of research question that the taxonomy developed here might provoke, the final section explores the difficulties that deictic words, whose meanings are sensitive to the time, place, and context of the utterance, may present to children when these terms are used in written text. The discussion of deixis illustrates the potential complexity of comparing text and speech according to the taxonomy presented here.

A THEORETICAL TAXONOMY OF THE DIFFERENCES BETWEEN ORAL AND WRITTEN LANGUAGE

If we wish to truly understand the contribution of children's oral language skills to their learning to comprehend what they read, we must carefully specify the conceptual differences between their earlier language experiences and the new one they are trying to master. The following taxonomy attempts to go far beyond the traditional emphasis on decoding skills and identifies a much more comprehensive set of differences. It should be viewed primarily as a specification of the processes children must learn (and unlearn) to become competent reading comprehenders but is also useful as a framework for specifying which variables are really being tested in listening–reading experiments such as those described later, and as a suggestion for teaching the totality of reading comprehension by making progress along one dimension at a time.

A child's oral language experiences may be described as interactive conversations in which the child participates as both speaker and listener. All the participants share a spatial, temporal, and situational context and their verbal communication is augmented by intonation, facial expression, and gestures. I have divided the differences between this situation and that of a child reading a story into two large subcategories: those having to do with the communicative *medium* and those dealing with the *message;* each of these subcategories is further divided into dimensions. I describe these in detail in the following sections. Because the emphasis here is on the consequences of these distinctions for a child learning to read, I also attempt to indicate what kinds of modifications must happen to a child's comprehension processes in the complex transition to reading comprehension. Although I have chosen to designate the goal language experience in this analysis as "reading a story," it is important to realize that there are other language experiences that differ even more from children's conversations, for example, reading a textbook or technical paper. Because the kinds of texts to which children are first and most frequently exposed are stories, I concentrate on these first and discuss differences between stories and textbooks in the section on message-related dimensions.

Medium-Related Dimensions

I have formulated seven dimensions along which the communicative medium of a language experience can be placed. The medium here is expressed in experiential terms and does not represent just the vehicle for the message; for example, the contrast is made between being in a conversation and watching a play rather than between a conversation and a play. If we were to think of a space defined in terms of these seven dimensions, a child's oral language experience, as described previously, would lie on the opposite end of a long diagonal from reading stories, with one point being $(0,0,0,0,0,0,0)$, the other $(1,1,1,1,1,1,1)$. For simplicity, I treat these dimensions here as two-valued, although it is clear that some of them do not divide language experiences neatly into two parts; a further refinement of the theory would be to consider intermediate values on some dimensions.

In any such dimensionalization, it is often unclear when a dimension should be listed separately and when it should be combined with some other related dimension with which it may occasionally covary. I have, at least informally, used the following criterion for identifying a dimension: If I could think of a minimal pair, that is, two language experiences that differed in terms of medium only along the dimension in question, that dimension was considered to be independent and was therefore included in the list.

The medium-related dimensions are: modality, interaction, involvement, spatial commonality, temporal commonality, concreteness of referents, and separability of characters.

Modality.   Is the message written or spoken? This dimension is the one on which most research on the relationship between listening and reading has focused. In fact, it has mainly concentrated on only one aspect of this distinction: the added necessity of visual decoding in reading. Even in this single dimension, however, there are other differences that impinge substantially on the processing demands of the comprehension task. These are briefly reviewed here; a more extensive discussion of the components of modality may be found in Schallert, Kleiman, and Rubin (1977).

Spoken language has as one of its most salient aspects the use of stress, intonation, and other prosodic features. Temporal characteristics of speech such as pauses and changes in speed often provide clues for the chunking of words into larger constituents. In general, pauses and breaths occur at syntactic boundaries (Henderson, Goldman-Eisler, & Skarbek, 1965, 1966). Similarly, a more quickly spoken set of words often indicates an appositive phrase or something that is not germane to the top-level structure of the sentence. In a relevant experiment, Friedman and Johnson (as reported in Sticht, 1972) found that pauses at phrase boundaries in speech increased its comprehensibility. We rely on stress in oral language as an indicator of such discourse organizing topics as given versus new. Compare the following two sentences, for example.

> I sent *Adam* the book.
> I sent Adam *the book.*

In the first sentence, the book has already been mentioned (is given), although the information that it was sent, specifically, to Adam is new. The situation is reversed in the second sentence.

In addition, stress on pronouns helps to disambiguate their referent as in the familiar:

> John hit Peter and then *Mary* hit him.
> John hit Peter and then Mary hit *him.*

In the first sentence, the referent of *him* is definitely *Peter,* whereas in the second, it is *John*. Intonation, yet another feature found solely in speech, is often used as an indication of the illocutionary force of an utterance. For example, *It's cold in here* could be a statement or a question, depending on the intonation pattern.

These prosodic features are a great help for everyone—and especially children—in understanding speech, as they facilitate the detection of syntactic and discourse structure. (See Adams, Chapter 1, this volume, for further discussion). The transition to text requires the development of alternate strategies to compensate for the disappearance of these features.

Text does have some compensatory aspects. A partial analogue of many prosodic features is punctuation. Although our limited set of punctuation marks does not reflect all the nuances possible with speech, it frequently indicates illocutionary force (. ? !), pauses (;), lists (, : ;) and related statements (;), among others. In contrast with speech, segmentation of the message into words and sentences is correctly indicated in written text and is not a task that must be performed by the reader. In addition, certain devices that are used solely in text can help specify the larger structure of the message. The demarcation of paragraphs is such an organizational aid. Textual devices such as underlining and italicizing may be used to emphasize or contrast words and phrases. Effective reading involves the recognition of the function of these aids and the development of processes to take the best advantage of them.

Another characteristic of text that can be an asset in its comprehension is its permanence. Readers can use this fact by looking back over passages they have previously read, rereading a sentence that was misparsed the first time around or rereading an entire paragraph whose point became clear only at the last sentence. Effective readers often glance ahead at the next few sentences or skim chapter and section headings. A major strategy a child must develop in making the transition from oral to written language is a method for using the permanence of text to compensate for some of its differences from speech. One such strategy, for example, is to keep some high-level structure of the text in mind to facilitate looking back to check a specific point or answer a specific question; in an interactive oral language situation, people more commonly just ask for clarification.

Interaction. Is the hearer–listener able to interact with the speaker–writer? Clearly, in a conversation, each participant has a chance to speak and often uses this opportunity to indicate that he or she has not understood the speaker. Thus, in a conversation that is "working," the hearer can verify his or her hypotheses quickly, making the maintenance of competing hypotheses less necessary.

Being in a conversation also requires the listener to make an active attempt to understand what is being said in order to respond appropriately. In noninteractive media such as books and TV, this impetus is absent. Being able to participate in this way requires knowledge of the rules by which conversations are conducted; Grice (1957) and Searle (1969) have codified some of the assumptions that underlie conversational interactions. Being able to actively participate also implies having an effect on the course of a conversation. Keenan and Schieffelin (1976) have represented the establishment of discourse topic as a dynamic process that includes feedback from both the speaker and the hearer. Participatory language experiences are, in addition, highly individualized; each participant has some model of the other's beliefs and knowledge and composes utterances taking this model into account. Thus, the language with which a child comes into contact in conversations is more tailored to his or her knowledge than the language in a multi-recipient object such as a book.

Involvement. Is the communication directed to the reader–listener? The inclusion of this dimension reflects the fact that certain language experiences are directed toward the reader–listener, whereas in others, he or she is essentially "eavesdropping." One clue to locating a language experience along this dimension is the use of second-person pronouns. An "involving" communication will use *you* to refer to the reader–listener, sometimes even in the imperative. If a "noninvolving" communication contains *you* at all, the referent will be a character in the story or a generalized person (e.g., *You never know what's going to happen next.*). Involvement in a communication act usually implies that the writer–speaker knows who the reader–listener is; consistent with this implication is the fact that most written communications of this sort are derived from oral situations (e.g., letters).

Spatial Commonality. Do the speaker and listener (reader and writer) share a spatial context? This dimension really comprises two different questions. The first might be phrased: Can the participants see one another? The second: Can the participants use the same spatial deictic terms because they are in the same place?

The first question is primarily one of extralinguistic communication. Gestures, facial expressions, and pointing can all be used to facilitate communication. A nod of the head may denote agreement; a puzzled look may communicate a lack of understanding, causing the speaker to restructure the utterance. Pointing may aid in specifying referents for pronouns or noun phrases such as *that dog over there.* Keenan and Schieffelin (1976) cite the following example of two 34-month-old children eating dinner:

David: (looking at his bowl of food) what's zis?
Toby: Kamoniz
David: No macaroniz. Sketiz [p. 364].

In this case, David's eye movements were necessary for Toby to understand the referent of *zis.* A developmental movement away from this early dependence on extralinguistic communication has been noted by de Laguna (1927/1970): "Th evolution of language is characterized by a progressive freeing of speech from dependence on the perceived conditions under which it is uttered and heard, and from the behavior which accompanies it [p. 107]."

The second aspect of spatial commonality has to do with the use of deictic words such as *here, there, come, go,* and so on. (see the last section for a definition and discussion of deixis). If the two participants are in the same place, they can understand such words without translating them to account for the other person being in a different place. (Of course, such words as *right* and *left* must always be interpreted relative to each person's *own* position.) The permanence of written language and the existence of modern tele-communications have created situations in which the two participants can be separated in space, thus making it necessary for the listener to interpret spatial deictic terms in the speaker's context.

Temporal Commonality. Do the participants share a temporal context? This again is a deictic issue involving the use of such words as *now, today, last Sunday,* and verb tense markers. The correct interpretation of such words when the participants are separated in time requires the reader–listener to take the point of view of the speaker–writer. A child's oral language experience does not often require this ability to switch the temporal context of utterances. Although it is certainly possible for a mother to address the following remark to her child, *Remember I told you yesterday, "You can go out to play tomorrow,"* it appears that this type of demand for temporal context-switching is seldom imposed on a child in oral conversations.

Concreteness of Referents. Are objects and events referred to visually present? Early conversations deal almost exclusively with concrete objects that a child can see—Mommy, Daddy, clothes, food—or objects that the child has at least seen previously and that therefore have some concrete reality to him or her—Grandpa's dog, friend Jackie, carrots we had for dinner last night. In reading or listening to stories, a child is often required to make up an object or event given only an incomplete, verbal description, a process that may take additional cognitive sophistication. The child may also have to integrate several partial descriptions of the same object and remember the composite description without the aid of an external referent.

Separability of Characters. Is the distinction between different people's statements and points of view clearly indicated? In a normal conversation, such distinctions are obvious, as each person makes his or her own statements; each point of view has a physical "anchor." Even so, for a young child, the parallel maintenance of several distinct points of view may be confusing. In a book, this problem is compounded, as the child must not only "construct" the individuals involved (see concreteness of referents, discussed previously) but must parcel out comments, feelings, and motivations to each

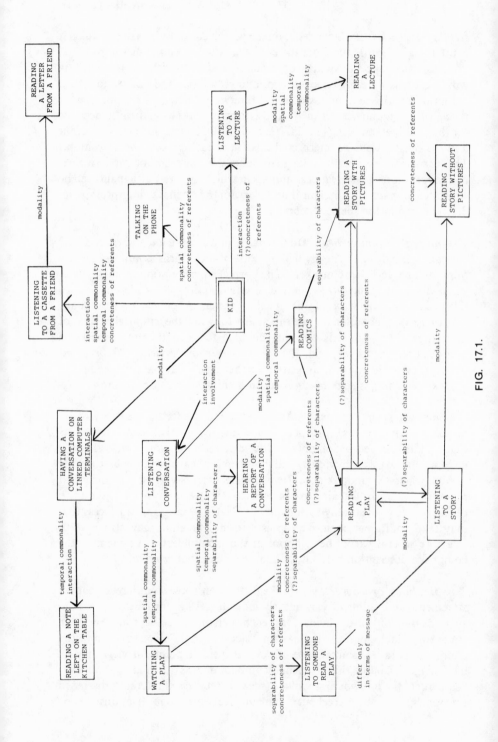

FIG. 17.1.

418

of them on the basis of more subtle clues: punctuation, paragraph structure, and inferences based on some consistent model of each of the characters.

Points in the Medium Space

Although these seven dimensions have been identified and discussed by contrasting two extremes—children's oral conversations and reading a story—there are many language experiences that lie between the two. A dimensionalization such as the one presented here defines a space within which language experiences may be compared and inspires a search for the uninstantiated possibilities. We can think of each language experience to be described as a point in seven-dimensional space. At first, the space appears to be only sparsely filled but, in fact, we can come up with quite a few intermediate points by teasing apart the dimensions we have listed.

Figure 17.1 illustrates the relationships among several different experiences, presented as labeled rectangles. Lines connecting the rectangles are labled with the dimension(s) along which the two experiences diverge. The rectangle in the center of the page, labeled KID, represents a child's language experiences as previously described; the goal of early reading teaching—the ability to read a story—is near the bottom of the figure. Arrowheads indicate a movement away from a child's normal oral language experiences toward the other end of the space—reading a story. Notice that in some cases two opposing arrows connect two adjacent rectangles. This is an indication that one of the two is closer to oral conversations along one dimension, whereas the other is closer along another.

The complexity of the figure should immediately suggest that there are many more conceptual transitions involved between these two language experiences than an emphasis on decoding would imply. This figure attempts to pinpoint these transitions, focusing on the divergent cognitive demands different langauge experiences impose on a child. For example, according to this analysis, a child talking on the telephone faces the potential problem of incorrectly interpreting words such as *here* because of the spatial context shift necessary to interpret the word; there is, in fact, anecdotal evidence that this confusion occurs. An additional hindrance implied by the "spatial commonality" dimension is the lackof extralinguistic communication, made impossible by the limited communicative medium. Objects referred to in the conversation that are in the speaker's spatial context are probably not immediately visible or accessible to the child. For the child who relies on these aids to comprehend speech, their absence may necessitate additional

---

FIG. 17.1. *(Opposite page)* Differences among language experiences as communicative media. The box labeled "KID" represents a child's typical oral language experience; the other boxes show experiences that differ along one or more dimensions.

processing and/or lead to comprehension difficulties. The point is that this additional processing is precisely the type that is necessary in reading stories as well. Although there is no suggestion that a child must pass through all or any of the intermediate stages in learning to read, language experiences between the two extremes may be useful in teaching reading and diagnosing children's reading problems.

Although an attempt has been made to keep these medium-related dimensions binary, some language experiences clearly lie midway on some dimension rather than at one end or the other. This is indicated in the figure by question marks in front of dimension names; in these sentences, the two adjacent rectangles may differ only marginally along that dimension. For example, the clues to separating characters' points of view are somewhat clearer in reading a play than in reading a story (the demarcation of characters' lines helps in this respect) but are less obvious than in watching a play.

Many children's most common source of language input—watching television—is not included in this figure because, in many respects, it cuts across the distinctions made here. A child can listen to a lecture, conversation, or story or watch a play on television. As both a visual and an auditory medium, television can combine characteristics of both modalities by presenting material to be read as well as listened to (although except for the "Sesame Street" family of programs, it seldom uses any written text). On the other hand, television is not an interactive medium, as are everyday conversations, so it lacks the individual tailoring that is an integral part of such communicative episodes and places few demands on the child to respond in an appropriate way. In this sense, television may be considered a passive rather than an active medium in terms of the obligations it imposes on the child.

Finally, it is appropriate to consider this dimensionalization as a departure point for analyzing language experiences rather than as the final product. For one thing, most communicative acts are not "pure"; they are, instead, mixtures of several media. Many language experiences change in the course of time, wandering from point to point in the medium space. For example, a common occurrence for a child might be to listen to and watch a conversation, occasionally becoming an active participant. A parent might carry on a direct conversation with a child at various points during reading a story aloud. The designation of medium can also become more complicated when communication originally composed for one situation is delivered in another. Reading a transcript of a lecture is one example of a language experience that is more difficult to classify in terms of medium. Most important, as mentioned previously, there is an entire other set of dimensions along which communicative acts vary and that exhibits marked contrasts between conversations and stories: the message itself.

Message-Related Dimensions

The medium dimensions detailed earlier capture only some of the differences between a child's typical oral language experiences and typical school reading experiences. There are also wide gaps between the two in terms of the *topic* of the communication, its *structure,* and its *function.* I have grouped these three aspects of linguistic communication in the category *message*—intuitively, the "meat" of the interaction, in contrast to its communicative channel. Changes along message dimensions necessitate developments in a child's language comprehension abilities that must occur in parallel with the emergence of skills to effectively handle the medium-related differences discussed previously. Unlike those, message dimensions cannot be considered two-valued, or designations of characteristics of which communicative acts can be said to have more or less. When two messages are compared in terms of structure, for example, the results will be that they have different structures rather than that one has more or less structure than the other.

Although medium and message dimensions are examined separately, they are far from independent aspects of communication. Certain medium characteristics are most appropriate for particular types of messages and, in some instances, the choice of medium essentially determines some aspects of the message. A potentially interactive medium will tend to push the structure of the message toward that of a conversation. Parents could deliver expository lectures to their children, but few do (thank goodness); it would be a poor use of face-to-face communication. Similarly, the syntax of oral interactive language is generally "ungrammatical" because of the characteristics of the communicative medium. Stated another way, it is not really possible to randomly choose values on each of the medium and message dimensions and be sure of finding a natural language experience that fits that set of choices. Yet, even if some of the message distinctions singled out later are consequences of medium differences, looking at them separately may enable us to discover which ones are the most critical roadblocks for children learning to read. In the following discussion of various message dimensions, I first define the dimension, then indicate the effect a choice of medium has on the location of a language experience along this dimension, then contrast children's typical oral language experiences with reading with respect to this dimension.

Some attempts have been made to classify oral and written language per se along these message dimensions. For example, Danks (1977) reports that other experimenters found college sophomores' oral productions, when compared to written ones on the same topic, to contain longer and more difficult words and more verbs. Although it is tempting to generalize this result, the data do not support judgments about anything more general than college sophomores talking and writing about a particular topic in a particular communicative situation. Surely their oral productions in a conversation about a technical topic would differ significantly from oral productions about their social lives. There is actually little to learn from this experiment which is relevant to children learning to read, for their typical oral and reading experiences do not match those in the experiment along a number of other dimensions. It is important to keep this caution in mind in reading the sections that follow.

Structure exists at many different levels of a message: word, sentence, paragraph, and the entire message, to name the most obvious. At the word level, the question of structure is really one of vocabulary. Words have been rated with respect to difficulty and abstractness; for any individual child, however, the crucial issue may be familiarity—whether or not they have heard, read, or used the word before. Because children are participants in the conversations that constitute the major portion of their linguistic experience, the words they hear tend to be familiar to them. Clearly, a typical children's book will contain words that are not familiar to a child from everyday conversation and more sophisticated written material such as textbooks may be densely populated with unknown words. This makes it necessary for the child not only to learn new words but also to develop strategies for hypothesizing about unfamiliar words when he or she encounters them in reading.

At the sentence level, we note syntactic differences among language experiences. The structure of individual sentences may be more or less complex: on the other hand, sentences may not even be "grammatical" or complete. In interactive communications, incomplete sentences frequently occur as answers to questions ("Where did you see her?" "Canoeing on the Charles."). Because it is produced on the fly, speech tends to wander off into run-on sentences and baroque structures. Redundancy and repetitions are common compensations for the nonpermanence of speech. Anyone who has transcribed a conversation can vouch for the looseness of the syntax. In an experiment investigating children's story comprehension, one 10-year-old offered the following comment on a story she had just read: "I don't know, I think it was some book like that she wasn't allowed to read as though it were a really Christian home or something and you weren't allowed to read a book about, I don't know, dirty or something." (Rubin, Bruce, & Brown, 1976). Another example of the lack of formality in spoken language is Allen's (1966) observation that perfect tense (e.g., "had been closed") are often replaced by simple tenses (e.g., "was closed") in conversation. Thus, because children's experience is with oral, interactive conversations, they may have to learn new syntactic rules for reading. Even if the syntactic structures are the same, however, speech provides additional clues to the discovery of syntactic structures, as explained in the description of modality differences given previously; the lack of such clues in writing presents an additional new challenge to children.

Larger-than-sentence-level structure has not been investigated until more recently and, as a consequence, has been less clearly defined. Conversational structure is characterized by utterances that are very context-sensitive, taking advantage of the fact that speaker and listener can interact. (Notice that the word "conversation" here refers to a language experience that makes use of an interactive medium, not just to an experience that has that potential, such as a lecture delivered in a one-to-one situation.) One frequent sequence that has been identified in conversations is [question]–[answer]; another is [question]–[request for additional information]–[response to request]–[answer to original question]. "Sequences" tend to be short and misunderstandings are cleared up in short order because of the interactive nature of the medium. The structure of conversations continues to be examined and formalized by Schegloff (1972), Dore (1977), and Grosz (1977), to name just a few.

The structure of stories has also recently been examined by people such as Rumelhart (1975) and the grammars generated differ greatly from those built for conversations, containing such constructs as "episode," "setting," and "theme" (see Bruce's Chapter 15 in this volume for an example of the application of story grammars). Expository texts differ in yet other ways from conversations with concepts such as "thesis," "supporting evidence," and even "topic sentence" being relevant. Olson (1974) characterizes the most common current use of language in scientific and technical texts as "an extended logical essay—an assertion examined and re-examined to determine all of its implications in a single coherent text [p. 23]."

The child learning to read is clearly the victim of these differences. Even though lucky children may hear oral stories from their parents and may even be exposed to expository structure when they demand to know why boys and girls are different, their typical oral language experiences are conversations. They are accustomed to asking and answering questions ("Where are you going?"), or relating their experiences ("Well, first I fell into the mud puddle and then . . . "), but are not as familiar or comfortable with other structures. These differences require the child to develop a new set of structures and procedures to comprehend stories; still other skills will be necessary for understanding history texts and lectures.

The *topic* of a language experience is, informally, what it is about. Children, in general, talk about everyday objects and situations—their pets, friends, parents, games, things that are relevant to their own lives. The speaker and listener usually share a background of experiences and knowledge that makes possible references such as "The dog looked a little like Uncle Oscar." In such conversations, the speaker has a relatively complete and accurate model of the listener and thus the listener will find comprehension facilitated. Contrast this with the situation of a child reading a book. The story is likely to be about a child or animal in an unfamiliar situation. In fact, it is clear that one of the fascinations of reading is this very capacity to introduce the reader to characters and situations that might otherwise be unattainable. Yet, this source of excitement is also a potential source of problems for a young reader unused to such language experiences. In addition, a book's author certainly does not know his or her audience personally and thus can not tailor the story to their knowledge and beliefs. This mismatch of background assumptions between cultures has been postulated as one source of difficulty for minority children learning to read. We have discovered in informal experiments that an important component of comprehending a story is understanding the characters' goals and interpreting their actions in light of these goals; without this connective tissue, the story falls apart. Understanding a story about other people requires the reader to be able to assume the characters' points of view; this "standing in another's shoes" is difficult when certain basic assumptions are not shared.

As a child gets older, the topics he or she reads in school also tend to become more abstract; the child must progress from the dogs and friends of his or her childhood to democracy and the periodic table of chemical elements.

These shifts along the topic dimension are somewhat predicted by the shift from interactive to noninteractive language experiences. Children play a large role in the choice of topic in conversations with their parents and peers and, thus, it is more likely to be familiar and relevant to them. On the other hand, there are interactive language experiences—for example, a technical conversation between two nuclear physicists—which, in terms of topic, are closer to reading a text book than to participating in a typical child's conversation.

Finally, we may contrast the *function* of children's conversations with that of stories. Children learn to speak initially because mastering this skill is most useful in having one's needs filled. Just getting a parent's attention may be the first motive a child acts upon in learning to speak. Later, his or her language capabilities are more differentiated, and a child can get father to pour some juice or ask mother to fix a broken toy. As children get older, the functions of conversations remain somewhat constant: to persuade, to obtain information (often relevant to some task), to express some emotion, to acquire some object or action, or sometimes just to interact and maintain contact. This function is often consistent with the child's goals, especially if the child has initiated the conversation. Stories and texts, on the other hand, often have as their function to describe, to entertain, to excite, or to evoke (see Brewer, Chapter 9, this volume). Early reading may even submerge all of these functions in service of the goal of teaching the child certain words and letter-sound correspondences. Not only are these functions different from those normally associated with conversations, but they may not correspond very well to a child's goals. Certainly, many children have asked their teachers and parents, "Why should I read?"; very few have asked, "Why should I talk?"

An additional difference between the functional fabric of children's conversations and that of stories is the duration of goals. In conversations, a

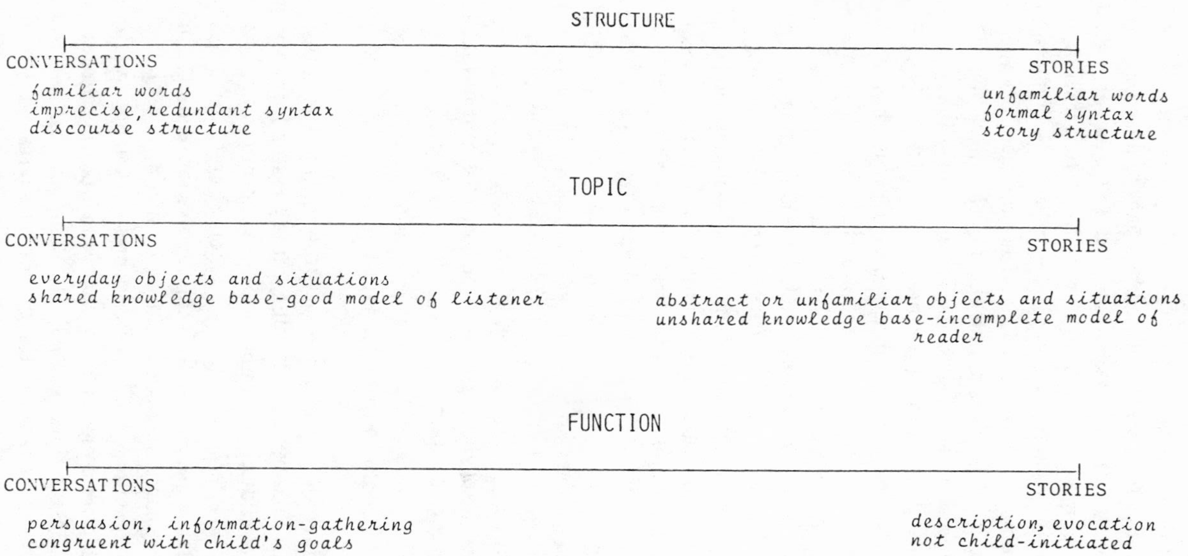

STRUCTURE

CONVERSATIONS ————————————————————————— STORIES

familiar words   *unfamiliar words*
imprecise, redundant syntax   *formal syntax*
discourse structure   *story structure*

TOPIC

CONVERSATIONS ————————————————————————— STORIES

everyday objects and situations   *abstract or unfamiliar objects and situations*
shared knowledge base-good model of listener *unshared knowledge base-incomplete model of*
                                               reader

FUNCTION

CONVERSATIONS ————————————————————————— STORIES

persuasion, information-gathering   *description, evocation*
congruent with child's goals   *not child-initiated*

FIG. 17.2. A contrast of children's typical oral language experiences (conversations) and the experience of reading a story on three message-related dimensions.

single exchange may satisfy a goal and the focus will shift to another topic. In stories, we see more sustained purposes, as one of the goals of even a lengthy book may be to evoke a single emotion.

These message differences are affected by medium differences in some of the same ways structure and topic are influenced. In particular, a child's active participation in a conversation makes it more likely that it will satisfy his or her goals for the interaction. A child often prevents a conversation from "sticking to the subject" by introducing another topic and another goal. In a sense, many message differences are an effect of the interactive nature of the children's language experiences and the resulting possibility of the child's affecting the course of the communication.

Figure 17.2 summarizes the contrasts drawn earlier between children's typical oral language experiences and the experience of reading a story. When these differences are combined with the medium-related distinctions discussed previously, it is clear that the path from oral language comprehension to reading comprehension is full of difficult steps and that learning to decode written words to meaning is but one of them. We see that neither of the models alluded to at the beginning of this chapter (that reading and listening are either the same or completely divergent processes) makes sense in the framework developed here. What is supported in their stead is the view that each language experience involves its own set of cognitive skills, each of which is shared with many other language experiences. The dimensions identified here provide a first pass at indicating which cognitive skills are involved in a particular language experience; much more work needs to be done to specify at a more detailed level the cognitive processes involved in understanding language in different situations.

Implications for Teaching and Research

The model presented here clearly diverges from the more traditional view of the crucial steps a child must go through in progressing from oral language comprehension to reading. One implication of the proliferation of differences is that there may be intermediate steps in teaching children to read that will require the use of some but not all the skills involved in reading. For example, two children might carry on a conversation by writing notes or by typing on linked computer terminals; this exercise preserves many of the message properties of children's conversations and even some of the medium-related properties (e.g., interaction, spatial and temporal commonality) while varying the modality. Reading aloud to children shares many medium- and message-related aspects with children's reading themselves yet differs in modality. Computer technology can be used to provide language experiences that would not be easily available otherwise. For example, in order to combine interaction with the normally noninteractive reading process, one could build a computer program that we could whimsically call *Huh?*. The terminal could include a special *Huh?* key that, when pressed, would explain a specified piece of text more completely or simply, thus preserving some of the feedback properties of conversational situations. An increased understanding of the relationship between children's comprehension of conversations and stories will be valuable as an indicator of which reading skills not transferred from the oral situation should be explicitly trained and where children might have "bugs" that derive from a too-general transfer of oral language skills. Such a model would also be useful in devising diagnostic measures for individual children to determine if their reading difficulties are reading-specific, general to both language modalities, or are evidence of an even more general deficiency in problem-solving skills.

In terms of research, this model can be useful in more precisely understanding what experiments are actually investigating. The following brief survey of experiments exploring the relationship between listening and reading comprehension is included to demonstrate that work has often focused only on changes in modality and has, in general, ignored the other distinctions among naturally occurring language experiences. The relevance of these experiments to children learning reading comprehension is tenuous precisely because of this narrow focus. In the last section, I outline an alternative approach to research in reading comprehension based on the theory developed here.

EXPERIMENTAL INVESTIGATION OF THE RELATIONSHIP BETWEEN ORAL AND WRITTEN LANGUAGE

The purpose of the following admittedly incomplete sample of experiments is to give the flavor of past and current experimentation in the relationship between oral and written language comprehension. If any conclusion is supported, it is that certain aspects of oral comprehension may be prerequisites for reading comprehension; that is, certain shared skills that facilitate both types of comprehension can be tested in certain listening situations and used as predictors for certain reading situations. Sticht (1972) notes that "it is to be desired and expected that with readers beyond the learning to decode–read stage, learning by listening and learning by reading should be highly correlated [p. 295]." When the material is held constant, this intuition is generally supported. In general, though, these experiments tell us little about the skills children must acquire in learning to understand what they read.

Relevant Experiments

Experiments investigating the relationship between oral and written comprehension usually proceed in one of the following six ways:

Comparing Comprehension of the Same Passage Presented as Both Text and Speech or of Passages Produced Differently (as Text or Speech), but Presented in the Same Modality. Durell (1969) found, in presenting the same material in both oral and written form to first- through eighth-graders, that sentence–paragraph comprehension in listening surpassed that in reading in first-graders. However, in eighth-graders, reading comprehension was 12% superior to listening comprehension. For Durrell, this change was evidence against a simple unitary-process hypothesis. In related work, Sticht (1972) demonstrated equal comprehension of the same passage presented to adults as speech or text and commented that "men who score low on the Armed Forces Qualifications Test and are of marginal literacy may learn equally poorly by listening as by reading [p. 288]." Both of these experiments varied only the *modality* of the language experience examined. Durrell's results are most likely due to children's increasing competence in decoding and the advantage of the permanence of written text. However, neither looked at conversations or any type of interactive language experience; one wonders, for example, how Sticht's subjects would have done has they been allowed to ask questions while they were listening.

In a different approach, DeVito (1965) asked writers to describe orally topics from their published papers. These oral productions, when transcribed, were understood as well as the original passages when subjects read both. This would suggest that these particular oral passages did not make excessive use of features of oral language that would be lost in their transcription to written form or that such losses were compensated for by such features of text as its permanence. Here again, we gain little insight into children's reading problems, as children do not, in general, read transcriptions of oral productions and, in writing down an oral passage, we in fact produce a somewhat anomalous language experience.

Demonstrating That Practiced Listening Skills Aid Reading Comprehension. A form of experiment that bears most directly on the hypothesis that skills are shared between comprehension of text and speech is exemplified by Tatham (1970). Using "frequent" (e.g., subject-verb-object) and "infrequent" (e.g., subject-verb-manner adjective) syntactic patterns from children's *oral* language, she demonstrated that the frequent patterns were more easily comprehended in *written* form than the infrequent ones. Although this type of experiment could indicate a transfer of skills from one modality to the other, it could also be the case that the frequent syntactic patterns used were frequent precisely because they were easier to comprehend in any modality, perhaps due to the semantic complexity of the concepts they represented. Studies along these lines would be more useful if they looked at other frequent patterns in children's conversations (e.g., discourse structure) and pinpointed how texts do or do not require the same skills.

Investigating the Transfer of Trained Listening Skills to Reading. Other experiments investigate the possibility of skill transfer by actually training listening skills and then testing their manifestations in reading. Lewis (1952) trained general listening skills such as determining the main idea, noting details, and drawing conclusions and inferences; the results did not show clear transfer to reading achievement. Sticht (1972) presents a possible explanation for this failure in noting that such organizing skills are often taught in conjunction with reading but not with listening. Thus, training people to "think" while listening may produced improvement in oral comprehension but may not transfer to reading if they are already proficient readers. This insight fits easily into the framework developed previously, with the thinking skills referred to here seen as a consequence of the message-related distinctions between conversations and stories. In other studies, however, reading did benefit from listening training. Jenkins and Pany, Chapter 24, this volume, report that 10 out of 12 studies they surveyed reported improvement in reading following training to improve listening skills. The effect was seen in training to recall events, ideas and details, to predict outcomes, draw conclusions or inferences, or follow directions—in other words, in thinking skills. We may integrate these seemingly contradictory results by postulating that the subjects in Lewis' study had more successfully learned "thinking" skills in connection with reading than the subjects in other studies; therefore, their improvement in listening comprehension was not accompanied by an improvement in reading comprehension.

Comparing Listening Comprehension of "Good" Versus "Poor" Readers. Some experimenters have looked at performance differences among differently skilled readers on oral comprehension tests. Perfetti and Goldman (1976) found that less-skilled readers could recall a recent word less successfully in a listening task than more highly skilled readers. Pike (1976) asked children in fifth and sixth grades to repeat three types of strings of words: random lists, syntactically well-formed but semantically anomalous sentences, and meaningful sentences. She found that, although the two groups performed equivalently on the random lists, better readers were more successful in their performance on structural strings than poorer readers, indicating a greater ability on their part to make use of syntactic and semantic structure. She concludes that "the ability tested by the experimental task could be a performance-limiting factor in learning to read [p. 8]." Neither of these experiments tells us much about the relationship between listening and reading; the subjects could have read the stimulus materials instead of listening to them and the results would most likely have been similar. What they seem to indicate is that one skill important in any kind of language comprehension is the ability to structure the sentences one reads, to make a list of words into a structured, meaningful object. I would extend this thought to texts bigger than sentences; understanding a story means reading it as something other than a list of sentences.

Investigating What Disrupts Reading for "Good" Versus "Poor" Readers. Oaken, Wiener, and Cromer (1971) studied the differential effect on good and poor readers of a tape or a transcript of a poor reader reading aloud. Good readers' listening comprehension was unaffected by hearing a poor reader, although their reading comprehension decreased when they read a transcript of the tape. In contrast, poor readers' listening comprehension went down when they listened to a tape of a poor reader. This suggests that poor readers' strategies for listening comprehension are somehow disrupted by a lack of cues in the poor readers' tape (e.g., fewer prosodic cues for syntax). Such a result suggests that poor readers may rely on certain features of oral language that do not exist in written language and have not learned strategies to compensate for this loss.

Considering The Relationship of Both Oral and Written Language Comprehension to Independent Measures. Sticht (1972) discovered that reading and listening comprehension scores were equally good predictors of job performance in nonreading jobs. He concludes from this and related statistics that "the measurement of comprehension by reading includes the measurement of comprehension by language (by listening in the present case) [p. 292]." Again, this experiment looked only at a change in modality: The material presented and the manner in which it was presented do not differ otherwise. The not-so-surprising conclusion to be derived from this experiment is that comprehension is affected much more by factors *other* than modality, by skills related to other aspects of the medium and the message.

Problems With These Experiments

Several considerations make it difficult to interpret these experimental results or to pinpoint their relevance to children learning to read.

The Materials Themselves. In the bulk of the experiments described so far, materials differ only in the modality of presentation. All of the other dimensions of the taxonomy developed in this paper remain the same. In addition, several experiments use anomalous language experiences such as listening to a passage that was to be read or reading a talk that was meant to be spoken. We hardly ever encounter these in nonexperimental situations, and they are certainly not comparable to reading text or participating in a conversation. Thus, many of the experiments that purport to compare comprehension across these modes are difficult to interpret. Those experiments that only test comprehension of sentences in isolation may be less sensitive to this criticism, but they suffer from yet another problem—the tenuous relationship between understanding isolated sentences and comprehending entire written or oral passages.

Presentation Conditions. Two of the striking differences between oral and written language are the speed at which they may be presented and the permanence of the display. The normal rate of reading is commonly two to three times that of speech. Some experiments attempt to pace subjects' reading or compress speech in order to equalize these variables, but it is unclear what other effects these variations have. Similarly, some experiments present only a small portion of the written input at a time to simulate the nonretrievability of speech. Although this method may make the two comprehension situations more comparable, it destroys a difference between oral and written language that might be crucial in teaching children to read.

Subject Characteristics and Comprehension Measures. Danks (1977) points out that the use of subjects of different ages in different experiments makes comparison difficult, as we know little about the developmental aspects of either reading or oral language comprehension. In addition, he points out several difficulties with comprehension measures. He notes that free-recall and question–answering techniques may be hard to compare and that the necessity of delay before comprehension is tested in both of these approaches may confound results. Comprehension measures that are simultaneous with processing may avoid the delay problems but disturb the comprehension process itself.

Methodological Fallacies. The discovery of a factor (e.g., impaired listening comprehension) that occurs more frequently among poor readers than good readers cannot be interpreted as indicating that the factor causes poor reading. First, poor readers tend to score lower on a wide variety of tasks and one can not determine which factors are intimately related to reading. Second, a causal relation is never established simply by a correlation; more complex analyses are necessary.

The Relationship of the Comprehension Process to Experimental Results. It is always difficult to infer a process from looking at its output. Even if we were to consistently obtain the same results on comprehension tasks in both oral and written language, we would have no proof that the comprehension processes were the same. Even showing that a component (e.g., syntactic analysis) is operational in both modes of language comprehension does not specify the relationship of that component to the rest of the process: when it is activated, what its input is, and how much time, space, and attention are devoted to its operation.

Error Analysis. Few of the experimenters mentioned earlier looked carefully at their subjects' errors; they did not follow Goodman [1973], who built his theory primarily on "miscue" analysis. One exception among the research reported here is Pike (1976); she noted that, in the string memory task described previously poorer readers seemed to be using a strategy appropriate for serial-list tasks even for the structured strings. Their responses had a list-like quality and their errors were most often omissions. The better readers tended to transpose or substitute words; they would generally answer using a normal intonation pattern that indicated they were attempting to use syntactic and semantic structure to remember the words. This type of data suggests that more complete, even if therefore less quantitative, analyses of experimental results might provide more insight.

In some sense, though, all these experiments miss the point in regard to children learning to read. Although it may be true that many of the same processes come into play in the comprehension of the same material presented visually or aurally, children's early conversational language and the books they read can hardly be considered the same material. By focusing on the modality of language experiences at the expense of other characteristics, these experiments have missed some of the crucial differences between conversational experiences and reading stories. This is not a criticism of these experiments per se, for their purpose was in fact to investigate modality isolated from other factors. What is wrong is the extrapolation of these findings to the equation of reading comprehension with the sum of oral language comprehension + decoding and to the concomitant emphasis in schools on teaching decoding. In order to better understand reading comprehension, we need to look at material that differs in terms of other dimensions—structure of the message, interaction, and topic, to name a few. The following section is just the beginning of a potential investigation of two of these dimenions (without any claim that they are somehow most important or primary): temporal and spatial commonality.

UNDERSTANDING OF DEICTIC TERMS
IN ORAL AND WRITTEN LANGUAGE

The effect of the permanence of text on certain terms has been discussed before by linguists. Olson (1974) notes: "Written materials are ordinarily portable and preserved over time; hence the writer must use language in such a way as to permit the text to preserve its meaning across space and time [p. 15]." This shift in the text poses new problems for a child, whose previous exprience has been with language experiences in which speaker and listener share spatial and temporal contexts. This section provides a preliminary look at these *deictic terms,* as they are called by linguists, and considers how they may be a source of confusion for children learning to read.

Definitions of Deixis

In general, deictic terms are those whose interpretation relies on the context of the utterance. Fillmore (1971) gives an intuitive feel for context-sensitive terms with the following example: Imagine finding a bottle afloat in the ocean holding a piece of paper with these words: "Meet me here at noon tomorrow with a stick about this big." Clearly, no one could fill that request without more information!

Weinreich (1963) divides deixis into four categories:

1. Person Deixis.   Terms whose interpretation requires knowledge of the speaker and/or hearer. The most common words in this category are first- and second-person pronouns.

> May I hold hands with you?
> Have you seen my octopus?

2. Time Deixis.   Terms whose meaning depends on the time at which the utterance occurred. Time adverbs such as *now* and time phrases such as *a week ago* fall into this category. Tense indicators on verbs may also be considered examples of time deixis.

> Now you see it, now you don't. (Note the two different uses of "now" in this sentence.)
> John came to stay last Sunday, but I'm going to ask him to leave tomorrow.

3. Place Deixis.   Terms that depend on the spatial position of the speaker and/or hearer. The adverbs *here* and *there* as well as certain motion verbs (e.g., *come*) are in this category.

> Is Johnny there? (refers to the hearer's position)
> Put that knife over here. (refers to the speaker's position)

4. Discourse Deixis.   Terms that depend on the previous discourse for their interpretation. Anaphoric reference may be included here, as well as such phrases as *in the next chapter* [see Webber, Chapter 6, this volume, for further discussion of anaphora].

> I drove the car to the bus station and left it there.
> In the next paragraph, you will read about social deixis.

Fillmore (1971) adds a fifth category.

5. Social Diexis.   Terms that are sensitive to the social relationships between the participants in the conversation. Examples of such words are more common in Japanese, in which many pronouns include an assumption about the social class of the people referred to. In French, the second-person pronouns "tu" and "vous" are differentially used depending on the relationship between the speaker and hearer.

Experimental Work on
The Understanding of Deictic Terms

Few experiments have been done on the effect of deictic terms in language understanding. Harris and Brewer (1973) demonstrated that subjects' recall of sentences such as *All California had felt the earthquake* was frequently "All California felt the earthquake," suggesting that the lack of specific reference to the implicit second time reference (before which California felt the earthquake) rendered the *had* meaningless and thus prone to omission. Similar experiments in Brewer and Harris (1974) indicated the same phenomenon with other deictic elements not anchored in the experimental context. Such experiments could be explored to provide more insight on the effect of context on the interpretation of deictic terms.

Not much work has been done either concerning children's acquisition of the ability to produce or understand deictic terms. Lyons (1975) claims, on the basis of linguistic arguments, that "the grammatical structure and interpretation of referring expressions . . . can be accounted for in principle on the basis of a prior understanding of the deictic function of demonstrative pronouns and adverbs in what might be loosely described as concrete or practical situations [p. 251]." Although Lyons makes no reference to actual observations of children, he recognizes the primacy of deixis in a child's development of speaking and listening skills. One developmental point he makes is that a child must learn the distinction between referring to a place and referring to an entity, for example, the difference between *That's the park* and *There's the park*.

Fillmore (1971) reports an experiment by Herb Clark in which preschool children gave each other instructions to assemble blocks without being able to see one another. Clark recorded the following conversation:

"Put this block on top of that one."
"You mean this one."
"Yes."

These children did not yet understand the deictic nature of *this* and *that;* the assumption is that they were still too egocentric to realize the discrepancy in the conversation.

In some related experiments, Krauss and Glucksberg (1977) showed that children often do not appreciate the fact that the person they are speaking to does not share their knowledge and assumptions. The experimenters separated children by a screen, then asked the speaker to describe the design on blocks as he or she stacked them. The listener's task was to select the correct blocks from a randomly ordered collection and stack them in the same order. Children through the fifth grade gave noncommunicative descriptions such as "My Daddy's shirt," which were usually misunderstood. Adults, of course, made up suitable descriptions and had no trouble with the task.

Tanz (1976) found that the order of acquisition in *speech* of deictic terms by a group of 40 children between the ages of 2 and 6 was as follows: personal pronouns (in back of/in front of), demonstratives and locatives (this/that, here/there), deictic verbs (come/go, bring/take). Some of her techniques might be extensible to research on reading. Tanz notes the connection between deixis and what psychologists have commonly called egocentrism: "Children's use of diectic terms without sufficient linguistic or extra-linguistic anchoring is one of the clearest symptoms of cognitive egocentrism to be visible in ordinary interactions [p. 228]." She also hints that the kinds of cognitive processes inherent in a child's decentering may pave the way for a child to stand in other people's shoes and see the world from their personal and motivational point of view—a crucial skill in understanding stories.

Deictic Terms in Text

What happens to deictic terms in text? For one thing, they are most likely used less frequently. Fillmore (1971) distinguishes three types of uses of deictic place terms: gestural (*I want you to put it there*), symbolic (*Is Johnny there?*) and anaphoric (*I drove the car to the lot and left it there*). Only the third really translates easily into the written situation. The other two make sense only as quoted utterances, that is, as written records of conversations.

Let us examine one example of such a use of deixis in text.

Sally said to Jill, "Come to my house tomorrow."

Two words in this sentence have deictic content: *my* and *tomorrow*. If a child were to hear the quoted sentence, he or she would understand that *my* referred to the speaker and *tomorrow* referred to the day after the utterance. In reading this sentence (or in hearing it read), he or she must interpret *my* as "Sally's" and *tomorrow* as the day after Sally's remark to Jill. For a child, this changing of context may not be easy. Similarly, if the child read *"I want you to put it there," said Jack, pointing to the card table,* he or she would have to realize the correspondence between *there* and *the card table* rather than the common correspondence between *there* and a place in their own spatial context. Not all deictic references in texts are quoted conversations. For example:

John looked to the left.

Again, a child must be able to switch contexts in reading this sentence to realize that John's left, not the reader's left, is indicated.

Of course, each of the previous sentences could have been spoken. My claim, though, is that such sentences are much more common in text than in speech and further that they might provide some difficulty for children in the transition from speech to reading comprehension. To support this claim, more research is necessary into children's use and understanding of deictic terms in speech, the occurrence of deixis in children's books, and children's understanding of these terms when they read. As a start, here are some examples of the uses of deixis in *My First Picture Dictionary* (Greet, Jenkins, & Schiller, 1970):

1. You wear a glove on your hand.
2. You blow air into a baloon.
3. (Accompanied by a picture of a boy watching a sunrise)
   The sun is rising.
   Dan was up when it rose yesterday.
   It has risen later every day.
4. (Accompanied by a picture of a mother, a girl looking at her, a girl holding a doll, and a boy holding an airplane)
   Mother is giving me a birthday present.
   She gave my sister one last month.
   She has given my brother his present [p. 62].

Although it is true that dictionary definitions are not the most natural form of text, children certainly read and hopefully understand them. An investigation into just how much and how they *do* understand should provide some insight into the general relationship between the comprehension of oral and written language.

In sum, a new approach to investigating the contribution of children's oral language comprehension skills to their learning to read has been proposed here. It rejects the traditional equation that claims that skilled reading is the sum of oral comprehension and decoding skills for two reasons: (1) It is impossible to compare oral and written language in general without further specifying the medium and message of the language experience; (2) The relevant experiences for children learning to read are conversations (oral) and stories (written), and there are many more differences between these than the application of decoding skills could overcome. Attempting to dimensionalize the distinctions among language experiences leads us to a scrutiny of linguistic factors, such as deictic terms, to a new experimental approach and, hopefully, to better ways to teach children how to read.

ACKNOWLEDGMENTS

This research was supported by the National Institute of Education under Contract No. MS-NIE-C-400-76-0116. I would like to thank Chip Bruce for inspiration and idea-sharing throughout the development of this chapter. I also thank Allan Collins, Glenn Kleiman, Denis Newman, Diane Schallert, and Brian Smith for helpful comments and discussions on this manuscript, and Angela Beckwith for numerous retypings in responding to their suggestions.

REFERENCES

Allen, R. L. *The verb system of present-day American English.* The Hague: Mouton, 1966.
Brewer, W., & Harris, R. Memory for deictic elements in sentences. *Journal of Verbal Learning and Verbal Behavior,* 1974, *13,* 321–327.
Danks, J. H. *Comprehension in listening and reading: Same or different?.* Submitted for the report of the Interdisciplinary Institute in Reading & Child Development, University of Delaware, June–July 1977.
deLaguna, G. *Speech: Its function and development.* College Park, Md.: McGrath Co., 1970. (reprint of 1927 edition.)
DeVito, J. A. Comprehension factors in oral and written discourse of skilled communicators. *Speech Monographs,* 1965, *32,* 124–128.
Dore, J. "Oh Them Sheriff": A pragmatic analysis of children's responses to questions. In S. Ervin-Tripp and Mitchell-Kernan (Eds.), *Child discourse.* New York: Academic Press, 1977.
Durell, D. D. Listening comprehension versus reading comprehension. *Journal of Reading,* 1969, *12,* 455–460.
Fillmore, C. J. *Santa Cruz Lectures on deixis.* Lecture notes, 1971 (Reproduced by the Indiana Linguistics Club, Bloomington, 1975).
Goodman, K. S. Psycholinguistic universals in the reading process. In F. Smith (Ed.), *Psycholinguistics and reading.* New York: Holt, Rinehart & Winston, 1973.
Greet, W. C., Jenkins, W. A., & Schiller, A. *My first picture dictionary.* New York: Scott, Foresman & Co., 1970.
Grice, H. P. Meaning. *Philosophical Review,* 1957, *66,* 377–388.
Grosz, B. J. *The representation and use of focus in dialogue understanding.* Doctoral dissertation, University of California at Berkeley, Computer Science Department, May 1977.
Harris, R. J., & Brewer, W. Deixis in memory for verb tense. *Journal of Verbal Learning and Verbal Behavior,* 1973, *12,* 590–597.
Henderson, A., Goldman-Eisler, F., & Skarbek, A. Temporal patterns of cognitive activity and breath control in speech. *Language and Speech,* 1965, *8,* 236–242.
Henderson, A., Goldman-Eisler, F., & Skarbek, A. Sequential temporal patterns in spontaneous speech. *Language and Speech,* 1966, *9,* 207–210.
Huey, E. B. *The psychology and pedagogy of reading.* Cambridge, Mass.: MIT Press, 1968. (Original Edition: The Macmillan Company, 1908.)
Keenan, E., & Schieffelin, B. Topic as a discourse notion. In Li (Ed.), *Subject and topic.* New York: Academic Press, 1976.
Kolers, P. A. Three stages of reading. In H. Levin & J. P. Williams (Eds.), *Basic studies on reading.* New York: Basic Books, 1970.
Krauss, R. M., & Glucksberg, S. Social and nonsocial speech. *Scientific American,* 1977, *236,* p. 100–106.
Lewis, M. S. The effect of training in listening for certain purposes upon reading for these same purposes. *Journal of Communication,* 1952, *2,* 81–86.

Lyons, J. Deixis as the source of reference. In E. Keenan (Ed.), *Formal semantics of natural language.* Cambridge: Cambridge University Press, 1975.

Oaken, R., Wiener, M., & Cromer, W. Identification, organization, and reading comprehension for good and poor readers. *Journal of Educational Psychology,* 1971, *62,* 71–78.

Olson, D. *From utterance to text: The bias of language in speech and writing.* Paper presented to the Epistemics Meeting at Vanderbilt University, Nashville, February, 1974.

Perfetti, C., & Goldman, S. Discourse memory and reading comprehension skill. *Journal of Verbal Learning and Verbal Behavior,* 1976, *14,* 33–42.

Pike, R. *Linguistic development as a limiting factor in learning to read.* Paper presented at the First Annual Boston University Conference on Language Development, 1976.

Rubin, A. D., Bruce, B. C., & Brown, J. S. A process-oriented language for describing aspects of reading comprehension (Tech. Rep. No. 13), Urbana: Center for the Study of Reading, University of Illinois, April, 1976.

Rubin, A. D. A taxonomy of language experiences. In *Reading: Disciplined inquiry in process and practice.* Clemson, South Carolina; The National Reading Conference, Inc., 1978. (a)

Rubin, A. D. *A framework for comparing language experiences.* Proceedings of Theoretical Issues in National Language Processing-2, New York: Association for Computing Machinery, 1978. (b)

Rumelhart, D. E. Notes on a schema for stories. In D. Bobrow & A. Collins (Eds.), *Representation and understanding: Studies in cognitive science.* New York: Academic Press, 1975.

Schallert, D. L., Kleiman, G. M., & Rubin, A. D. *Analyses of differences between written and oral language.* Tech. Rep. No. 29), Urbana: Center for the Study of Reading, University of Illinois, April 1977.

Schegloff, E. A. Notes on a conversational practice: Formulating place. In D. Sudenow (Ed.), *Studies in social interaction.* New York: The Free Press, 1972.

Searle, J. R. *Speech acts: An essay in the philosophy of language.* Cambridge: Cambridge University Press, 1969.

Sticht, T. Learning by listening. In J. Carroll & R. Freedle (Eds.), *Language comprehension and the acquisition of knowledge.* Washington, D.C.: V. H. Winston & Sons, 1972.

Tanz, C. *Studies in the acquisition of deictic terms.* Doctoral dissertation, University of Chicago, Department of Psychology, August 1976.

Tatham, S. M. Reading comprehension of materials written with select oral language patterns: A study at grades two and four. *Reading Research Quarterly,* 1970, *5,* 402–426.

Weinreich, U. On the semantic structure of language. In J. H. Greenberg (Ed.), *Universals of language.* Cambridge,: Mass.: MIT Press, 1963.

18 On the Dialect Question and Reading

William S. Hall
Larry F. Guthrie
Center for the Study of Reading,
University of Illinois, Urbana-Champaign

This chapter has a twofold purpose. The first is to describe studies on dialect variation and to discuss the implications of these studies for reading performance. The second is to raise some relevant questions for research that are suggested by the current state of affairs in the area. The dialect variant to be described is Vernacular Black English (VBE). The levels of analysis to be considered are: (1) phonological; (2) grammatical; and (3) lexical and content. In the process of discussing the implications of these data for reading performance, we suggest reasons for the equivocal nature of many of the existing findings. Finally, we suggest questions toward which further research might be directed.

PHONOLOGICAL INTERFERENCE

A sizable body of literature exists on phonology and grammar as they relate to reading interference among black dialect speakers. Generally speaking, the distinction between grammatical and phonological features of black dialect is not clear-cut. Simons' (1973) categorization of VBE features illustrates the difficulty of making this distinction:

> First, there are features that are wholly phonological such as consonant cluster simplification in monomorphemic words, e.g., "test"–"tess," "desk"–"dess." Second, there are features that are phonological in origin but intersect with consonant cluster simplification in words with past tense morphemes, e.g., "liked"–"like," "passed"–"pass," etc. Third, there are features that are clearly grammatical such as the invariant "be" [p. 3].

In a study that considered the question of phonological interference, Melmed (1971) investigated the major phonological features in which VBE differs from Standard English (SE)—"r-lessness," "l-lessness," consonant cluster simplification, weakening of final consonants, and vowel variations. He compared third-grade black children with third-grade white children on their ability to discriminate these phonological features auditorily, to produce them, to comprehend them in oral reading, and to comprehend them in silent reading. He found that the blacks differed from the whites both in auditory discrimination and production of the selected features. The blacks failed to discriminate the features more often than the whites and they also produced them more often than the whites. This difference was taken as a demonstration that the blacks were dialect speakers and the whites were not. If phonological interference exist, the speakers who exhibited the most dialect features (in this study, the black subjects) should do less well on the reading measures than those who exhibited fewer dialect features (here, the white subjects). If there is no phonological interference, then there should be no difference on the reading measures. The latter was found to be the case for Melmed's subjects. Although the black subjects differed in auditory discrimination and production of the selected phonological features, they did not differ in their ability to comprehend them in oral and silent reading.

Rystrom (1970) conducted another study that considered the question of phonological interference. He compared the effect of training in the production of SE phonology on the reading achievement of VBE speakers. The experimental group received training in producing SE phonology; the control group received language arts training without particular emphasis on SE. Reading instruction for both groups was equally divided between basal reader and phonics approaches. He found that neither training in SE phonology nor type of reading instruction produced significant differences in reading achievement on four measures of reading achievement.

In another study, Rentel and Kennedy (1972) investigated the effects of pattern drill in SE on first-grade Appalachian dialect speakers and its influence on reading achievement. They employed the same research strategy as Rystom to test the hypothesis of phonological and grammatical interference. They compared the reading achievement of three experimental classes who received pattern drill on the phonological and grammatical features of SE that conflict with Appalachian dialect with three control classes who received no special training. Thus, in the same way as Rystom, they attempted to manipulate the amount of dialect to see if it affected reading achievement. If dialect interferes, the group that receives training in SE should experience less interference and do better in reading than a comparable group who have no training and experience more dialect interference. Employing a posttest design, Rentel and Kennedy found no difference in reaching achievement between the experimental and control groups.

Further indirect evidence on the question of phonological interference is provided by Osterberg (1961), who studied reading acquisition in a dialect area of Sweden. He conducted an experiment in which a group of first-grade children were taught for the first 10 weeks of the school year with books especially written to conform to the phonological features of the dialect area in which they lived. A control group received instruction using standard texts that conformed to the standard Swedish speech. If phonological interference with learning to read exists, then teaching students to read with texts that conform to their phonological system should reduce this interference and thus increase reading achievement. Assuming this line of reasoning is correct, then the experimental group in the Osterberg study should have learned to read better than the control group, all other things being equal. Osterberg found that the experimental group was superior to the control group on various measures of reading achievement after 10 weeks and at the end of one year.

Taken as a whole, the evidence just cited is not convincing in regard to the question of whether phonological interference in learning to read exists. It is not clear in several works (Melmed; Rental & Kennedy; Rystrom) whether subjects were actually dialect speakers or whether children were assumed to be dialect speakers because they were from lower Socio-economic Status (SES) groups. In the Melmed study, in particular, it is unlikely that the third-grade children were pure dialect speakers. At the very least they should have been mixed dialect speakers. It is quite unlikely that a child could have experienced three grades of the standard American school curriculum without some modification in his or her language behavior. This, coupled with the fact that the task was "school-like" as was the setting in which it was given, makes it ulikely that the vernacular would be called forth by the child. This latter interpretation is corroborated by some recent work on situation and task in children's talk (cf. Cole, Dore, Hall, & Dowley, 1978) as well as an additional study on constraints of text and setting on measurement of mental ability (Orasanu, 1977).

GRAMMATICAL INTERFERENCE

It has been suggested by Stewart (1969), Baratz (1969), and others (cf. DeStefano, 1977; Hall & Freedle, 1975) that the differences between the grammar of VBE speakers and the SE grammar of instructional materials in reading is a major cause of poor reading achievement among VBE speakers. Comprehension may be a more difficult undertaking for VBE speakers as a consequence of these grammatical differences.

One would predict that VBE syntax could interfere with reading comprehension in two major ways. First, interference could arise in cases in which the

SE sentence is interpreted as a nonequivalent VBE sentence. One example is presented by Stewart (1969), in which the SE sentence, *His eye's open,* may be interpreted by the VBE speaker to mean both of his eyes are open because it resembles the VBE sentence *His eyes open* more than it does *His eye open.* The latter is the VBE equivalent of *His eye's open.* Another example, also pointed out by Stewart, is the interpretation of *He will be busy* as implying habitual action, because *be* in VBE is used as a marker for habitual action: *He be busy.* Finally, there are sentences, such as *He wanted to go home,* which the VBE speaker might interpret as a present tense action because he may not have learned that the *ed* marks past tense.

The second type of potential interference that might arise as a result of the difference between VBE syntax and SE syntax is more indirect. Evidence suggests that the two dialects represent different coding schemes (Baratz, 1969; Hall & Freedle, 1973, 1975; Labov, 1970). A child who is most familiar with VBE, for example, a lower class black, will tend to encode in his or her short-term semantic memory sentence information corresponding to that code. Likewise, a child who is most familiar with SE will tend to encode in his or her short-term semantic memory sentence information corresponding to the standard code. If the incoming stimulus for a black subject is in his or her familiar dialect, the subject does not have to do any extra work in encoding the information because it already is in the preferred language. Thus, the subject's short-term semantic memory is in a "nonstandard" state. If the subject usually retrieves this information in the same form as it is coded in his or her memory, the subject will produce a large number of nonstandard structures. If, on the other hand, the incoming stimulus is in SE, as in a printed text, encoding in VBE will place the burden of an extra processing step on the VBE speaker as he or she moves from the printed SE text to the meaning.

Whatever the precise process involved in reading, it is obvious that both SE and VBE speakers, at some point in the process, do a syntactic/semantic analysis of the written sentence. This analysis is by necessity based on SE syntax. However, the VBE speaker must perform an additional analysis of finding the VBE syntax that is the equivalent of the SE form. In other words, the VBE speaker must be able to perform a SE analysis, as does the SE speaker, but *then* find the equivalent VBE form as well. This extra step in reading, although it does not interfere with the comprehension of any individual sentence, may accumulate over large amounts of reading material to the point where comprehension is interfered with.

Indirect evidence on the question of grammatical interference is provided by Ruddell (1963) and Tatham (1970). They both found that SE-speaking white elementary-school children understood material written in grammatical sentence patterns that were frequently used in their oral language better than material written in sentence patterns that were used less frequently in their oral language.

In a related study, Sims (1972) analyzed the reading errors of 10 VBE-speaking second-grade children when they read dialect and standard stories from the Baratz (1971) readers. An examination of her data showed that the standard stories were read with the same or fewer errors than were the dialect stories.

Johnson and Simons (1973) asked second- and third-grade black children to read equivalent stories written in SE and VBE syntax. They found no difference between the dialect between the dialect and standard versions of the stories on comprehension and recall.

A note of caution must be sounded regarding the Sims (1972) and the Johnson and Simons (1973) studies. The sample used in these studies included children who had, in all likelihood, been instructed over a relatively long period of time in SE; therefore, one would not necessarily expect their performance in VBE to be superior.

A study by Labov (1970) attempted to determine directly the degree of interference produced by a particular grammatical feature, the past tense morpheme *ed*. VBE speakers typically omit this morpheme in spoken language. The question is, do they understand that the *ed* signals past tense? If they do not, then their comprehension of this aspect of the sentence would suffer, and this would be a case of direct interference. In an ingenious experiment designed to answer this question, Labov asked junior high school VBE speakers to read aloud sentences such as the following: *When I passed by, I read the posters. I looked for trouble when I read the news.* Their pronunciation of the homograph *read* indicated whether or not they understood the *ed* to be a past tense marker. Labov found that his subjects were able to comprehend the past tense marker 35% to 55% of the time. This fact suggests that failure to understand the "ed" interfered with comprehension more than half the time. In a more detailed analysis, Labov compared subjects' sensitivity to the grammatical or the phonological constraints on consonant cluster simplification and its effects of reading the "ed" suffix. He found that subjects who were more sensitive to grammatical constraints read the *ed* sentences correctly more often than subjects who were more sensitive to the phonological constraints or for whom the constraints were equal. Thus, subjects who deleted the *ed* less often, regardless of whether the following word began with a consonant or a vowel, were the better readers of the test sentence.

Given the data, it appears that the hypotheses advanced concerning phonological and grammatical interference may have to be revised. It may be that VBE does not interfere with the acquisition of reading skills for all VBE speakers in all educational situations. Indeed, Piestrup (1973) has shown that the ways teachers communicate in the classroom are crucial to children's success in learning to read. Moreover, she states that attributing chlidren's reading problems to deficits or language differences

> may only confound the problems of negative teacher expectations and evade the problem of functional conflict between teachers and children with different cultural backgrounds. Teachers can alienate children from learning by subtly rejecting their Black speech. They can discourage them by implying by tone, gesture and even by silence that the children lack potential. Children, in turn, can show their resilience by engaging in verbal play and ritual insult apart from the teacher, or they can withdraw into a moody silence. Neither strategy helps them to learn to read [p. 170].

LEXICAL AND CONTENT INTERFERENCE

The data in this category are the scantest of all. This is especially true when we think of vocabulary as content (see, e.g., Cazden, 1972). Nevertheless, a few generalizations can be made. It appears that poor minority-group children consistently show slower lexical development as measured by: (1) vocabulary subtests of IQ tests like the WISC (see, e.g., Shuey, 1966); (2) level of syntactic responding in Entwistle-type free association tests; and (3) recognition vocabulary tests like the Peabody.

Some research, though not without its methodological flaws, has been performed on vocabulary and the VBE question. Williams and Rivers (1972, 1976) investigated score changes on the Boehm Readiness Test as a function of changes in the vocabulary of the test in the direction of VBE. They found that when the vocabulary on this test was changed so that it reflected their experiential network, poor black children in the St. Louis public schools performed at a level comparable to the white middle-class sample on which the test was standardized. Thus, it would appear that dialect has an effect on comprehension at the lexical level as studied by Williams and Rivers. However, these results are somewhat weakened by the fact that there was no control group. If Williams and Rivers had used white children as a control and still produced the same results for black children, their data would be more convincing and their claim more justified.

Comprehension and the dialect question has also been investigated by Hall, Reder, and Cole (1975). This research avoids our major criticism of Williams and Rivers' work. Hall et al. conducted an experiment that tested the effects of racial group membership and dialect on unstructured and probed recall for comprehension of simple stories. Thirty-two children, age 4 years 6 months, were the subjects for the experiment. Sixteen were black and an equal number were white. Subgroups of four children within each racial group were randomly assigned to the experimental conditions such that order of exposure to experimenter (black and white) and dialects (Standard English vs. Vernacular Black English) were counterbalanced. They found that whites performed better than blacks in SE; blacks performed better than whites in VBE; blacks tested in VBE were equivalent to whites tested in SE; and whites performed better in SE than in VBE.

DISCUSSION

What emerges from these studies, which vary in their degree of robustness, is a complex and unclear picture. Dialect can be interpreted either as a facilitator (cf. Williams & Rivers, 1972; Hall, Reder, & Cole, 1975) or an interferer (cf. Hall & Freedle, 1973, 1975). The unclear nature of the findings from these studies suggests that some of our prevailing hypotheses about dialect and reading might need to be revised. But which direction should the revision take? Certainly, the payoff does not seem to reside in a wholesale emphasis on children's repetition or nonrepetition of selected grammatical features in the context of sentences. Nor does it seem to lie in an emphasis on children's ability to acquire the phonology of SE. The real payoff most likely resides in research on the ethnography of communication. This approach will capture subtle but important cultural and situational differences in language function and use that are obscured in experimental research. Although we cannot specify the details of this approach here, we can cite two illustrative works. We refer the reader to Piestrup's research on the effects of teaching styles on black first-graders' reading achievement (1973) and Ward's study of an entire community and its communicative habits (1971).

In the pages that follow, we would like to present some questions for research that should ultimately provide the information needed to make claims about dialect and reading. The needed information can best be stated in terms of questions having to do with cultural variation and language use. The list of questions is not exhaustive but, rather, illustrative. Underlying each question is the assumption that there are group differences related to the context of experience. The questions are focused on two aspects of language: (1) differences in language *structure and content;* and (2) *patterns of language use* and function.

The specific questions that are posed draw on two kinds of data in behavioral science—namely, sociolinguistics and developmental psychology. With respect to sociolinguistics, they build upon and extend the work of Labov (1972) on elaboration of structure; of Houston (1969) on specific registers and shifts in same; of Ward (1971), Horner (1968), and Cole, Dore, Hall, and Dowley (1978) on the communication network as portrayed in the home and immediate surrounds; and on language use in a school activity (Cazden, John, & Hymes, 1972; Sinclair & Coulthard, 1975). Regarding developmental psychology, the questions build on and extend the work of Hess (1969) on cognitive environments and White and Watts (1973) on the environment of the child in general.

Structure and Content

1. Are There Differences in the Way Black and White Speakers Structure Portions of the Lexicon?   Hall (1977) has hypothesized that there might be certain differences in the way in which speakers of black dialect and SE structure prepositions, for example. Some black adults have been observed to say the following to children: "John, sit *to* the table." In this instance, a SE speaker would probably say: "John, sit *at* the table." The question is whether or not the rendering "sit *to* the table" does not give the chlid a different relationship between himself and the object table than that interpretable from "John, sit *at* the table." Essentially, the first instance is more *factive* than *locative.*

On a broader scale, the reason for asking this question lies in its centrality of our experience as humans. Space and time, both of which can be readily revealed through prepositions, are basic coordinates of experience. Because only one object can be in a given place at a given time, spatial locatives provide an indispensable device for indentification purposes. *Hand me the spoon on the table* identified the spoon to which the speaker is referring. The place adverbial, *on the table,* indicates a search field, and the head noun, *spoon,* provides the target description. As Miller and Johnson-Laird (1976) indicate, how a search is to be executed depends on the particular preposition relating the target to the landmark: *on, in, at, by, under* and so on. Investigation of how children learn to delimit the search field and the cultural variations in this process should be instructive in trying to ferret out factors relevant to dialect and reading comprehension.

2. Are There Differences Between Vocabulary Used in the Home and in the School Situation?   Answers to this question might be found first in raw counts and frequencies of lexical items. In addition, little is known about the social class differences in the way in which certain parts of the lexicon are structured in different situations. A useful guide in this analysis would be Miller and Johnson-Laird's (1976) theory that describes how certain parts of the lexicon (i.e., spatial relationships and verbs of motion) might be structured.

3. Assuming That Phonology is an Important Determinant of Dialect Difference, Does Phonology Play a Role in Producing Misunderstanding Between Teacher and Student?   This question can be seen to relate directly to the role of dialect (particularly VBE) in learning to read. Simons (1973), for example, has noted that one major behavioral consequence of the differences between the VBE and SE phonological systems for reading acquisition is that certain written words are pronounced differently by VBE than by SE speakers. The results of these differences are words that have a pronunciation unique to VBE, for example, "nest"–"ness," "rest"–"ress," "hand"–"han." Moreover, there are words whose VBE pronunciation results in a different word, for example, "test"–"tess," "mend"–"men," "walked"–"walk," "cold"–"coal." "find"–"fine," and so on. The latter results in an extra set of homophones for VBE speakers. These differences in pronunciation, for example, could interfere with the VBE speaker's acquisition of word recognition skills.

Patterns of Usage

1. To What Extent Do Children Rely on Nonverbal as Opposed to Verbal Cues in Obtaining Information from the Environment and Communicating Information about the Environment to Others? We should ask how do children acquire information from others (adults, older children, peers, etc.) and, further, how does their information acquisition here differ and/or how is it similar to that in the naturally occurring events of their everyday life. Cultural differences may also be significant in this area. For example, Byers and Byers (1972) found that cultural background influences nonverbal communication between children and teachers. White children were found to be more successful in communicating nonverbally with a white teacher than were black children, even though the teacher paid as much attention to both.

2. To What Extent Are There Cultural Differences in Children's Adoption of a Hypothetical Stance Toward Linguistic Information? To study this question productively, the domain of study must be delimited. Analysis of the use of verbs and conjunctions in naturally occurring speech is one way this delimitation can be accomplished. The use of verbs, for example, might be analyzed because they are necessary for predication in English, which makes sentences something more than a string of word associations. Conjunctions are essential for the expression of logical connections and relations and therefore also significant in the determination of meaning.

3. How Might the Participant Structures of Different Cultural Groups Contribute to Miscommunication Between Students and Teachers? Though not obvious to the casual observer, the ways in which interaction in the classroom is organized may significantly influence the success of a child. If the participant structures are in conflict with those of the students' culture, the students might not be able to learn or even show the abilities they possess. Philips (1972) provides an account of native American children for whom such cultural conflict in the classroom causes difficulty.

By investigating these and other questions on structure and content and patterns of usage of language, it should be possible to clarify the exact nature of how dialect may be used to facilitate or to hinder the reading process.

CONCLUSION

In this chapter, we have described a group of studies on dialect variation. These studies represent attempts to locate the sources of difficulties for dialect speakers on three different levels: (1) phonological, (2) grammatical, and (3) lexical and content. Their findings, taken as a whole, do not adequately identify the sources of difficulties; they are both inconclusive and conflicting. They contain a number of methodological flaws that cast doubt on their validity. More important, it is quite likely that the theoretical hypotheses that underlie these studies are in need of revision.

These hypotheses are based on at least two false assumptions. The first is that ethnic differences in language performance on one of the three levels of analysis provide evidence for dialect interference. The phonological differences exist is, of course, obvious; that they actually interfere to a great degree with a child's learning to read is another question altogether. The second assumption is that the test-like situations under which experiments are conducted can adequately measure the effects of dialect. Research from this perspective ignores the fact that teaching and learning do not occur in isolation but are influenced by situation and context. In a repetition task, the phonology, grammar, and vocabulary of a child may vary from that in his everyday speech. Contrived, laboratory-type tasks also miss more subtle dialect differences, both verbal and nonverbal, which may result in miscommunication. In order to capture such differences, the function and significance of language within cultures must be included in any study of dialect interference.

We have suggested several illustrative research questions that might yield more adequate data in the area of dialect and reading. These questions have been divided into those concerned with: (1) structure and content; and (2) patterns of language use and function. All of these questions have at least one thing in common: They take into consideration the influence of situation and context. Questions on structure, for example, are not asked in isolation but in relation to the effects on teacher–student or text–student communication. Questions on language use center on actual language experiences in the classroom and the home. In these ways and by making studies more in line with the ethnography of communication, aspects of dialect interference overlooked by previous studies can be examined.

The implications of this type of research for reading lie primarily in the area of reading instruction. If researchers can specify for educators actual sources of miscommunication in the educational experience of dialect speakers, several benefits will be realized. Because the differences specified will be ones that actually result in a lowering of school achievement, a clearer picture of dialect interference will emerge. Educators will thus be better equipped to handle problems of dialect that emerge. As they become more sensitive to the cultural differences that influence teaching and learning, teachers will be able to modify the ways in which they interact with dialect-speaking students to better accommodate them, not only in actual instructional methods but in other ways as well. Changes might also be seen in the materials used for reading instruction. Unlike the suggestions of the 1960s (e.g., dialect readers), however, they would be both theoretically motivated and based on empirical evidence.

Ultimately, we would hope that research from the perspective we have outlined would contribute to the elimination of inequities in American education.

ACKNOWLEDGMENTS

Preparation of this paper was supported by Contract No. US-NIE-C-400-76-0116 from the National Institute of Education.

REFERENCES

Baratz, J. C. A bidialectical task for determining language proficiency in economically disadvantaged children. *Child Development,* 1969, *40*(8), 889–901.

Baratz, J. *Language abilities of Black Americans: Review of research.* Unpublished manuscript, 1971.

Byers, R., & Byers, H. Nonverbal communication and the education of children. In C. B. Cazden, V. P. John, & D. Hymes (Eds.), *Functions of language in the classroom.* New York: Teachers College Press, 1972.

Cazden, C. *Child language and interaction.* New York: Holt, Rinehart & Winston, 1972.

Cazden, C., John, V. P., & Hymes, D. (Eds.). *Functions of language in the classroom.* New York: Teachers College Press, 1972.

Cole, M., Dore, J., Hall, W. S., & Dowley, G. Situation and task in young children's talk. *Discourse Processes,* 1978, *1*(2), 119–176.

DeStefano, J. S. A difference is a difference, not a deficiency. *Contemporary Psychology,* August 1977, pp. 600–601.

Hall, W. S. Unpublished manuscript, 1977.

Hall, W. S., & Freedle, R. A developmental investigation of standard and non-standard English among black and white children. *Human Development,* 1973, *16*(6), 440–464.

Hall, W. S., & Freedle, R. *Culture and language.* New York: Halsted Press, 1975.

Hall, W. S., Reder, S., & Cole, M. Story recall in young black and white children: Effects of racial group membership, race of experimenter, and dialect. *Developmental Psychology,* 1975, *11*, 828–834.

Hess, R. D. Parental behavior and children's achievement: Implications for Head Start. In E. Grotberg (Ed.), *Critical issues in research related to disadvantaged children* (Seminar #5). Princeton, N.J.: Educational Testing Service, 1969, pp. 1–76.

Horner, V. M. *The verbal world of the lower class three year old: A pilot study in linguistic ecology.* Unpublished doctoral dissertation, University of Rochester, 1968.

Houston, S. A sociolinguistic consideration of the Black English of children in Northern Florida. *Language,*1969, *45,* 599–607.

Johnson, K. R., & Simons, H. D. *Black Children's reading of dialect and standard text* [Final Report, Project No. OEC-9-72-011(057)]. Washington, D.C.: U.S. Office of Education, 1973.

Labov, W. The logic of non-standard English. In F. Williams (Ed.), *Language and poverty.* Chicago: Markham, 1970.

Labov, W. *Language in the inner city.* Philadelphia: University of Pennsylvania Press, 1972.

Melmed, P. A. Black English phonology: The question of reading interference. *Monographs of the Language-Behavior Research Laboratory,* 1971, No. 1.

Miller, G. H., & Johnson-Laird, P. N. *Language and perception.* Cambridge, Mass.: Harvard University Press, 1976.

Orasanu, J. *Constraints of text and setting on measurement of mental ability* (Working Paper NO. 3). New York: Rockefeller University, Laboratory of Comparative Human Cognition and Institute for Comparative Human Development, 1977.

Osterberg, R. *Bilingualism and the first school language.* Umea, Sweden: Vastenbottens Togeker, A, B, 1961.

Philips, S. Participant structures and communicative competence: Warm Springs children in community and classroom. In C. B. Cazden, V. P. John, & D. Hymes (Eds.), *Functions of language in the classroom.* New York: Teachers College Press, 1972.

Piestrup, A. M. Black dialect interference and accomodation of reading instruction in first grade. *Monographs of the Language-Behavior Research Laboratory,* 1973, No. 4.

Rentel, V., & Kennedy, J. Effects of pattern drill on the phonology, syntax, and reading achievement of rural Appalachian children. *American Educational Research Journal,* 1972, *9,* 87–100.

Ruddell, R. B. *An investigation of the effect of the similarity of oral and written patterns of language structure on reading comprehension.* Unpublished doctoral dissertation, Indiana University, 1963.

Rystrom, R. Dialect training and reading: A further look. *Reading Research Quarterly,* 1970,*5,* 581–589.

Shuey, A. *The testing of Negro intelligence* (2nd ed.). New York: Social Science Press, 1966.

Simons, H. D. *Black dialect and reading interference: A review and analysis of the research evidence.* Berkeley: University of California, School of Education, 1973.

Sims, R. *A psycholinguistic description of miscues created by selected young readers during oral reading of text in black dialect and standard English.* Unpublished doctoral dissertation, Wayne State University, 1972.

Sinclair, J., & Coulthard, R. M. *Towards an analysis of discourse: The English used by teachers and pupils.* London and New York: Oxford University Press, 1975.

Stewart, W. A. On the use of Negro dialect in the teaching of reading. In J. C. Baratz & R. Shuy (Eds.), *Teaching black children to read.* Washington, D.C.: Center for Applied Linguistics, 1969.

Tatham, S. M. Reading comprehension of materials written with select oral language patterns. A study of grades two and four. *Reading Research Quarterly,* 1970, *5,* 402–426.

Ward, M. C. *Them children: A study in language learning.* New York: Holt, Rinehart & Winston, 1971.

White, B., & Watts, J. *Experience and environment: Major influence on the development of the young child.* Englewood Cliffs, N.J.: Prentice-Hall, 1973.

Williams, R., & Rivers, W. *Mismatches in testing from Black English.* Paper read at the annual meeting of the American Psychological Association, Honolulu, 1972.

Williams, R., & Rivers, W. *Mismatches in testing.* Paper read at the conference on Testing, Washington, D.C., 1976.

V

COMPREHENSION STRATEGIES, FACILITATORS, AND INSTRUCTION

The earlier chapters of this book have implicitly presented the case that much needs to be learned (and can be learned) about the underlying processes of reading comprehension in order to deal more effectively with practical issues of education, such as text selection, teaching methods, diagnosis of reading problems, and order of presentation of texts. Previous chapters have highlighted a number of factors that need to be considered in moving from research to practice. In this section we move a step closer to application. The authors of the chapters in "Comprehension Strategies and Facilitators" have taken their theoretical perspectives and applied them to specific educational issues, such as selfmonitoring of comprehension, study skills, the role of illustrations, the effects of interest, skill hierarchies, and teaching reading comprehension.

Brown's Chapter 19 begins with a discussion of *metacognition,* the process of active control over one's own cognition. She raises the question of whether a child's failure to comprehend is attributable solely to unconscious (and therefore possibly difficult to alter) processes, or to ineffective monitoring strategies. How much, for example, can you, as a reader, be aware of what you know and what you need to know while reading? Brown discusses a number of studies on the development of such metacognitive skills.

Study strategies might be viewed as an extension of metacognitive skills in the direction of even more explicit awareness and more active control of comprehension. In Anderson's Chapter 20, various strategies are discussed, such as underlining and asking questions, that a reader can use to enhance his or her understanding. He observes that a student's current strategies may not be explicit nor under active control. He then discusses research on specific study aids and systems.

In Schallert's Chapter 21, the effects of illustrations as facilitators of comprehension are explored. She considers, in particular, the effects of different relationships of the illustrations to the text and circumstances under which illustrators even hamper the reading process.

Asher, in Chapter 22, starts with the common observation that interesting material is easier to read and more likely to be read. He notes, however, that little research has been done to show whether it is the child's interest that in fact aids their comprehension. He considers work on interactions between sex and race differences and interests. He finds, for instance, that although girls perform better than boys on standardized reading tests based on low-interest material, the differences do not appear for high-interest material.

In Chapter 23, Rosenshine discusses another major educational issue that needs more theoretical and empirical research—whether there are distinct component skills in reading comprehension. He further considers whether there is a hierarchy of these skills, analogous to the hierarchies proposed for decoding skills. Analyzing sets of proposed skills, textbooks for teachers, and reading materials for children, he finds no clear evidence for either the successful identification of specific comprehension skills or any skill hierarchy. His findings corroborate many of the results reported in other chapters of this book that have emphasized the interactive nature of the reading process. His findings also raise a question: Can a more systematic and detailed analysis of the reading process yield a taxonomy of comprehension skills?

Jenkins and Pany, in the final chapter, discuss current educational practices designed to improve reading comprehension. They examine a number of the major approaches, including basal reading series, DISTAR, objective-based programs, language experience, directed reading–thinking, and the "psycholinguistic" approach. They conclude that little objective evidence currently exists to recommend one approach over the others.

19 Metacognitive Development and Reading

Ann L. Brown
Center for the Study of Reading,
University of Illinois, Urbana-Champaign

METACOGNITION

Vygotsky (1962) described two phases in the development of knowledge: first, its automatic unconscious acquisition, followed by gradual increases in active conscious control over that knowledge. The distinction is essentially the separation between cognitive and metacognitive aspects of performance. Metacognition refers to the deliberate conscious control of one's own cognitive actions. This distinction between knowledge and the understanding of that knowledge (in terms of awareness and appropriate use) has become of special interest to the developmental psychologist. Yet metacognition is an area of study that has only recently received serious consideration by experimental and educational psychologists. It is not surprising, therefore, that the application of such recently gained knowledge to the problems of reading is a brand new endeavor. In this chapter, we attempt to give some idea of the kinds of issues that developmental psychologists are concerned with when they speak of metacognitive aspects of performance and how these might be related to reading; however, as the area is so new, the main emphasis is on ideas for future research rather than on a description of work already completed.

First, we begin by defining what a developmental psychologist includes under the heading metacognition (Flavell, 1976):

Metacognition refers to one's knowledge concerning one's own cognitive processes and products or anything related to them, e.g., the learning-relevant properties of information or data. For example, I am engaging in metacognition (metamemory, metalearning, metaattention, metalanguage, or whatever) if I notice that I am having more trouble learning A than B; if it strikes me that I should double-check C before accepting it as a fact; if it occurs to me that I had better scrutinize each and every alternative in any multiple-choice type task situation before deciding which is the best one; if I sense that I had better make a note of D because I may forget it;...(more examples).... Metacognition refers, among other things, to the active monitoring and consequent regulation and orchestration of these processes in relation to the cognitive objects or data on which they bear, usually in the service of some concrete goal or objective [p. 232].

The skills of metacognition are those attributed to the executive in many theories of human memory and machine intelligence, predicting, checking, monitoring, reality testing, and coordination and control of deliberate attempts to study, learn, or solve problems (Brown, 1978). These are the basic characteristics of thinking efficiently in a wide range of learning situations, including effective reading. In addition, these are the types of monitoring activities that have been observed by educationalists interested in study skills (T. Anderson, Chapter 20, this volume; Robinson, 1941). The merging of ideas derived from psychological models of human thinking and observations of activities undertaken by efficient learners is, therefore, particularly exciting.

One major justification for studying metacognitive skills is that they do appear to have "ecological validity"; that is, there are recognizable counterparts in "real-world, everyday life" situations. Checking the results of an operation against certain criteria of effectiveness, economy, or commonsense reality is a metacognitive skill applicable whether the task under consideration is solving a math problem, reading for meaning, memorizing a prose passage, following a recipe, or assembling an automobile or piece of furniture. Self-interrogation concerning the current state of one's own knowledge during reading or any problem-solving task is an essential skill in a wide variety of situations, those of the laboratory, the school, or everyday life.

READING STRATEGIES

The goal of reading is to achieve understanding of the text. Yet understanding is not an all or none phenomenon; it must be judged against the criteria set by the reader as a goal of the activity. Readers' purposes vary and, as such, criteria of comprehension also change as a function of the particular reading task at hand. In some reading situations, the participant may be quite satisfied with gleaning a cursory overview of the gist, whereas in others the reader may set more demanding criteria of comprehension. The decision to process deeply and actively (Brown, 1979) or merely to skim the surface will determine not only the strategies necessary for the task but also the reader's tolerance for intrusive feelings of failing to understand. In short, the reader's purpose determines how he or she sets about reading and how closely he or she monitors the purpose of reading, that is, understanding of the text.

Before proceeding, we would like to make a distinction between deliberate conscious strategic intervention and other intelligent processing that goes on below the level of conscious introspection (Woods, Chapter 3, this volume). Although the issue of conscious intent is a particularly thorny one for cognitive psychology, there are some crude distinctions that must be made. Many subconscious processes of inferential instantiation (Anderson & Shifrin, Chapter 13, this volume) must be performed "automatically" and very rapidly compared with deliberate conscious actions. Consider skilled readers, who can be characterized as operating with lazy processors. All their top-down and bottom-up skills (Adams, Chapter 1, this volume) are so fluent that they can proceed merrily on automatic pilot, until a *triggering event* alerts them to a comprehension failure. While the process is flowing smoothly, their construction of meaning is very rapid, but when a comprehension failure is detected, they must slow down and allot extra processing capacity to the problem area. They must employ debugging devices and strategies, that take time and effort. The difference in time and effort between the normal rapid *automatic pilot* state and the laborious activity in the *debugging state* is the difference between the subconscious and conscious level (Woods, Chapter 3, this volume).

One commonly experienced triggering event is the realization that an expectation we have been entertaining about the text is not to be confirmed. Another triggering situation is when we encounter unfamiliar concepts too often for us to remain tolerant of our ignorance. Whatever the exact nature of the triggering event, we react to it by slowing down our rate of processing and allocating time and effort to the task of clearing up the comprehension failure. And, in the process of disambiguation and clarification, we enter a deliberate, planful, strategic state that is quite distinct from the automatic pilot state in which we are not actively at work on debugging activities. The debugging activities themselves occupy the lion's portion of our limited-capacity processor (Shatz, 1977), and the smooth flow of reading abruptly stops.

The automatic pilot activities of the smooth reading process are not the subject of this chapter, and we wish to distinguish them from the deliberate debugging strategies that are our main focus. We are concerned here only with how children deal with either comprehension or retention failures once they have been identified, and with the strategies they employ to overcome comprehension failures. There is almost no systematic work on this topic in the domain of effective reading.

Debugging devices are skills of metacognition, skills that can be tailored to the purposes of reading. Any description of effective reading includes active strategies of monitoring, checking, and self-testing, whether the task under consideration is reading for remembering (studying) or reading for doing (following instructions). Under the heading "reading strategies," we incorporate any deliberate planful control of activities that give birth to comprehension. These activities include:

1. clarifying the purposes of reading, that is, understanding the task demands, both explicit and implicit;
2. identifying the aspects of a message that are important;
3. allocating attention so that concentration can be focused on the major content area rather than trivia;
4. monitoring ongoing activities to determine whether comprehension is occurring;
5. engaging in review and self-interrogation to determine whether goals are being achieved;
6. taking corrective action when failures in comprehension are detected; and
7. recovering from disruptions and distractions—and many more deliberate, planful activities that render reading an efficient information-gathering activity.

In short, the effective reader engages in a variety of deliberate tactics to ensure efficiency. Note that such efficiency involves cognitive economy as well as expenditure of effort. The efficient reader learns to evaluate strategy selection not only in terms of final outcome but in terms of the payoff value of the attempt; information is analyzed only to the depth necessary to meet current needs. This ability implicates a subtle monitoring of the task demands, the reader's own capacities and limitations, and the interaction between the two. All these activities involve metacognition, conscious deliberate attempts to understand and orchestrate one's own efforts at being strategic.

METACOGNITIVE DEVELOPMENT:
A BRIEF REVIEW OF THE LITERATURE

Background

The development of children's awareness of themselves as active agents in knowing has excited a great deal of interest within the last few years (Brown, 1975, 1977, 1978; Brown & DeLoache, 1978; Flavell & Wellman, 1977). In a detailed review of the literature concerning problem-solving strategies in children (Brown, 1978), we identified many areas in which children's metacognitive deficiencies caused severe problems. Children have difficulty:

1. recognizing that problem difficulty has increased and that therefore there is a need for strategic intervention (Brown, 1975);
2. using inferential reasoning to assess the probability that an assumption is true, given the information they already have (Brown, 1978);
3. predicting the outcome of their attempts at strategy utilization both before and after the fact (Brown & Lawton, 1977);
4. predicting the task difficulty in a variety of memory and problem-solving situations (Brown, 1978; Tenney, 1975);
5. planning ahead in terms of strategic study-time apportionment (Brown & Campione, 1977; Brown & Smiley, 1978); and
6. monitoring the success of attempts to learn so that termination of such activities can be made when they are successful (and no longer necessary) or unsuccessful, so that new activities can be tried (Brown & Barclay, 1976; Brown, Campione, & Barclay, 1978).

In general, children fail to consider their behavior against sensible criteria, they follow instructions blindly, and they are deficient in self-questioning skills that would enable them to determine these inadequacies.

Such planning strategies have an essential place in all problem-solving situations including skilled reading, but we know little of the development of these intelligent activities in children. Anyone who has ever interacted with a toddler will be aware of the extreme cunning of their playful activity, and one must be aware of the problem of attributing planning only to older children (Brown & DeLoache, 1978). However, planful strategic behavior in the face of school-type tasks does appear to be relatively late in developing (Brown, 1978); witness the large amount of data suggesting that efficient study skills are less than well developed in college populations! The problem of self-awareness and conscious control of one's activities is of central concern to those interested in any aspect of the child's problem-solving capacities (Piaget, 1928).

Unfortunately, as the general area of metacognitive development has only recently become a topic for research, the majority of empirical investigations has focused on metamemorial awareness (Flavell & Wellman, 1977), although there is some interesting information concerning metalinguistic knowledge (Gleitman, Gleitman, & Shipley, 1972; Osherson & Markman, 1975) and metacomprehension (Markman, 1977). For this reason most of the empirical examples given here concern the child's growing awareness and control of his deliberate study skills and capacities. However, the relevance to reading strategies should become clear. The following review of the literature is, of necessity, abbreviated, and for a more detailed report the reader is referred to Brown (1978). The intent is to give some flavor of the pervasiveness and widespread nature of the child's problems with metacognitive insights and the difficulties to which this must lead when he attempts to read effectively.

Knowing When You Know

A very basic form of self-awareness is the realization that there is a problem, of knowing when you know and when you do not. If an unfortunate reader does not recognize that he or she failed to understand an important point, he or she cannot initiate a course of action to rectify the gap in knowledge. The problem of ascertaining the state of one's own ignorance or enlightenment is one of metacomprehension. For example, understanding instructions would be a case of comprehension of a message, whereas knowing that one has understood (or not) would be an example of metacomprehension. In reading, understanding the text content would be an example of reading comprehension; understanding that one has done so, metacomprehension.

Holt's (1964) lucid description of children's mystification over school problems includes many examples of metacomprehension failures. For example, faced with the task of listing verbs that end with a *p,* one fifth-grader became obviously upset, repeating "I don't get it," but was totally unable to say why she failed to understand. Holt then asked the child if she knew what a verb was and gave her some examples; immediately the child went to work. Holt (1964) suggests that the child did not ask what a verb was simply because she did not know herself that she did not know. "All she knew was that she had been told to start doing something and she didn't know what to do. She was wholly incapable of analyzing the instructions, finding out what part of them made sense and what did not, where her knowledge ended and her ignorance began [p. 145].

Holt's charming book contained many anecdotes concerning children's difficulty evaluating their own state of knowledge. Controlled experimental tests, however, are only now being conducted. Markman (1977) examined the insensitivity of young children to their own failure to comprehend. Children from grades 1 to 3 were asked to help the experimenter design instructions for new games to be taught to other children. The instructions were obviously incomplete and the measure of whether the child realized that he had not understood was his request for more information. Not only did the younger children require additional prompts before indicating that they did not know, but it appeared that they needed to attempt to execute the task before awareness dawned on them. The younger children did not seem to be able to evaluate when they had understood instructions until an actual attempt to carry them out was instigated.

This problem is not limited to the young child, for the ability to monitor one's own state of knowledge must be the result of the difficulty of the material as well as the state of the learner's own strategic repertoire (Brown & Smiley, 1978). For example, Markman (1975) asked elementary school children to judge the comprehensibility of obviously incomprehensible passages. Even sixth-grade children failed to detect the inconsistency unless they were aided. A similar pattern of tolerance for inconsistent or uninformative information has been found in studies of children's communicative competence in referential communication tasks (Shatz, 1977). In general, young children fail to detect the inadequacy of messages they send (Asher, 1978; Karabenick & Miller, 1977) and fail to request clarifying information concerning inadequate messages they receive (Cosgrove & Patterson, 1977; Ironsmith & Whitehurst, 1978; Patterson, Massad, & Cosgrove, 1978). Apparently, the monitoring necessary to detect a comprehension failure is not routinely undertaken by young children.

Knowing What You Know

Part of being a good student is learning to be aware of one's own mind and the degree of one's own understanding. The good student may be one who often says that he does not understand, simply because he keeps a constant check on his understanding. The poor student who does not, so to speak, watch himself trying to understand, does not know most of the time whether he understands or not. Thus the problem is not to get students to ask us what they don't know; the problem is to make them aware of the difference between what they know and what they don't [Holt, 1964, pp. 28–29].

Consider what the adults know concerning the knowledge they already have and their ability to operate on that knowledge. When faced with a question concerning what we know, how do we ascertain that we do or do not have the answer or that it would be reasonable to attempt a search? Take the "simple" case when the material is in the knowledge base and we must estimate its accessibility. William James (1890) first drew attention to the tip-of-the-tongue phenomenon, that is, the peculiar experience of trying to recall a forgotten name, knowing and feeling how close we are, being aware of improper matches, and vainly groping in our inability to retrieve what we *know is there*. Adults are quite accurate at predicting what is known or have reliable feeling-of-knowing experiences (Blake, 1973; Hart, 1967), but the familiar tip-of-the-tongue phenomenon (Brown & McNeill, 1966; Yarmey, 1973) does not appear to be as dramatic for young children. Young children fail to predict their recognition accuracy when recall has failed, that is, they lack the feeling of knowing phenomena. Slightly older children do have a feeling of knowing but they experience difficulties with the active strategic attempts used by adults to resolve a tip-of-the-tongue experience (Brown & Lawton, 1977; Wellman, 1977). It is not until the mid-grade-school years that young children can reliably indicate a distinction between what they know but cannot retrieve and what they do not know.

Although it would seem that knowing what you know is a primitive precursor of more complex forms of metacomprehension, under certain conditions even college students may have difficulty estimating the state of their own knowledge. Identifying what you do not know, or could not know, can involve quite complex forms of reasoning. Mature problem solvers not only have a reasonable estimate of the accessibility of their known facts, they are also cognizant of which facts cannot be known and which can be deduced on the basis of what they already know. Adults realize immediately that they cannot know Charles Dickens' phone number (Norman, 1973), but they arrive at this conclusion by inferential reasoning concerning other aspects of their knowledge. Not only do children know less than adults (and their knowledge is more often poorly organized, incomplete, and inconsistent) but they lack the complex systems of inferential reasoning used by adults to infer information from incomplete and contradictory knowledge bases. Consider the complexity of strategies Collins and his associates (Collins, Warnock, Aiello, & Miller, 1975) describe as operative when adults must decide when something is not known but could be inferred from the knowledge they have. One does not need to know too much concerning the young child's deductive reasoning capacities to understand why the ability to reason from incomplete knowledge is a late-developing skill and apparently trainable, or at least subject to refinement, in college populations.

Knowing What You Need to Know

Not only are efficient readers capable of checking what they know or could deduce at any point, but they also know that there are certain categories of information essential for them to complete a task effectively. Consider in this context the Bransford, Nitsch, & Franks (1977) example of how a memory expert would go about the task of remembering.

> No self-respecting memory expert would put up with the way psychologists run most memory experiments. Experts would ask questions like, "What must I remember?" "How many items?" "How much time will there be?" "What's the nature of the tests?" They would *know what they needed to know* in order to perform optimally and they would settle for nothing less [p. 38]

Binet's pioneer work with lightning calculators, oustanding mnemonists, and chess players (Binet, 1894; Reeves, 1965) also illustrates that the expert not only needs to identify fully all the facets of a problem before proceeding but also prefers to structure the input in an optimal manner to achieve efficiency.

Efficient readers also benefit from knowing the purposes of the task in just this manner, but do children? Apparently this is a real problem, for below 7 years there is evidence that situations that require deliberate attempts to remember and those that do not are not clearly distinguished by the child (Brown, 1975). The child must travel far before routinely adopting the interrogation mode of Bransford's expert.

Another problem for grade-school children is estimating that certain tasks will be more difficult than others and, therefore, will require more effort or ingenuity. They fail to notice when their capacity to rote recall items has been overreached (Brown, Campione, & Murphy, 1977; Flavell, Friedrichs, & Hoyt, 1970) and often do not distinguish between easy and hard lists (Brown, 1978; Moynahan, 1973; Salatas & Flavell, 1976; Tenney, 1975) and passages (Smirnov, 1973). A particularly interesting example of this problem is that children even have difficulty distinguishing between the ease of learning a story for the purpose of gist versus verbatim recall (Kreutzer, Leonard, & Flavell, 1975). By 5th grade, children are aware that recalling in one's own words is a far easier task than reproducing the exact input, but prior to this age, they do not make such a distinction or at least cannot justify any distinctions they can make. If children are unaware of the greater difficulty of verbatim recall, they can scarcely be expected to deploy study time flexibility for the task at hand. Appreciating what you need to know in order to act strategically appears to be a relatively late developing skill.

Knowing the Utility of Active Intervention

If children are less prone to introduce strategic activity than are adults (Brown, 1974, 1975; Brown & Campione, 1978), is it also true that they do not appreciate such intervention by others? Consider one example. Children were given 20 colored pictures and told that two peers had already seen the pictures and been asked to learn them; one studied for 5 minutes, the other for 1 minute. The children were asked to predict which child remembered more, to justify their answer, and then to indicate how long they personally would study (Brown, 1978; Kreutzer et al., 1975). Most children predicted that studying for 5 minutes is a better strategy but children below third grade are less able to justify their choice. In addition, children do not always indicate that they would study for 5 minutes themselves, even if they indicated the longer time to be beneficial.

We are currently investigating the ability of normal and retarded children to appreciate the utility of strategy usage during study for free recall. The children are asked to view a videotape of a peer performing four different study activities while attempting to learn a list of pictures. The four activities are categorizing, rehearsing, labeling, and just looking at the items. After the children have viewed the four activities, they are asked to wager on which activity led to better performance. They are then given the same stack of pictures and told to study them by themselves in any way they desire in order to learn as many as possible. So far we have found that groups of retarded children (MA 6 and MA 8) are able to predict that the two appropriate strategies, categorization and rehearsal, will lead to better performance, but normal 4- and 5-year-olds were not so prescient. By third-grade, the majority of normal children predict that an active strategy will be the best one to use for the purposes of studying the list.

What happens when the predictors must themselves study the pictures? Although the ability of retarded children to predict the superiority of active strategies was impressive, their actual performance was less so. All educable children predicted that categorization or rehearsal would lead to better performance, yet, when faced with the identical task and stimuli immediately after viewing the tape, only 28% actually adopted one of the activities predicted to be superior. In terms of actual performance, the educable children did not differ from normal preschool or first-grade children, who also fail to adopt the strategy they deem most effective. Third-graders tend to adopt the strategy they predict will be superior, but even for these children the relationship between prediction and performance is not perfect. Preliminary fifth-grade data currently being collected also supports the position that the relationship between prediction and performance is not perfect even by the end of the grade school years.

We know of no comparable studies that looked at the child's appreciation of active reading strategies or study strategies with prose materials, but in view of the difficulties experienced on simple list learning tasks, this would seem to be a fruitful line of investigation with middle school children. We are currently constructing videotapes of junior high school students performing various overt study activities while preparing for a test, such as rereading, underlining, self-testing, note-taking, and so on. We are interested if observing children will model their performance after the activities seen on the tapes. Of more importance, we will use the observation period to elicit evidence of the observer's own knowledge concerning reading strategies, for example, we will ask the observer why the model is undertaking a certain activity, if it would help him and how, why does the observer do that, and so on. This, together with extensive interview data, should provide us with insights into the wealth or poverty of students' information concerning reading and studying prose.

STUDY-TIME UTILIZATION

Studying in anticipation of a future test involves both the ability to behave strategically, that is, invoke some tactic to aid learning, and the concurrent ability to self-test the effectiveness of the strategy one has called into service. Adequately dispensing the available study time involves at least an appreciation of which material is important and which material is not known sufficiently to risk a test. When faced with the common task of attempting to commit to memory a set of materials when time limitations or other restrictions impede leisurely study, how do we plan our time for most efficient results? Such a task can involve very fine degrees of metacognitive judgment, as any student can attest.

A relatively simple experimental analogue has been devised for use with young children (Brown & Campione, 1977; Masur, McIntyre, & Flavell, 1973). Subjects are given a multitrial free-recall task in which they must learn a list of picture names. On all trials but the first, the subjects are allowed to select for further study only half of the total set of items. Strategic behavior is thought to be selection of those items that had previously not been recalled. Children above third grade do select missed items for extra study but this is not true of younger children and slow learners who appeared to select randomly. It seems that the strategy of deliberately concentrating one's study activities on the less-well-mastered segments of materials cannot automatically be assumed to be part of a young child's repertoire of learning techniques.

Strategic study-time apportionment can involve tasks other than rote learning of unrelated items; learning from texts also requires the child to concentrate on important or less-well-retained elements. It is a common educational practice to instruct children to do just this, to concentrate on information they do not know or on information that is important. But we have reason to believe that this is not an easy task for young children. Here, we will restrict our attention to the child's problems in (1) concentrating on the main ideas; (2) selecting suitable retrieval cues; and (3) concentrating on information he has previously failed to recall.

Selecting and Studying the Main Ideas

In order to be able to select the main points of a passage for extra study, children must be aware of what the main points are. Using simple passages consisting of a few lines of prose, Otto, Barrett, and Koenke (1969) found only 29% of second-graders able to state the main idea. With even simpler passages, Danner (1976) was more successful, for the majority of his second-graders could abstract the main idea to some extent. We have found that children as young as 6 years can describe the main features of a simple pictorial scene, although they do have more difficulty with verbally told stories representing the main theme of the pictures. They are also readily distracted by red herrings, for example, when a background, nonessential part of a scene is made physically larger or an irrelevant part of a story is repeated or emphasized.

Given complex passages of some length, a more typical school task, even junior high school children experience difficulty extracting the main idea. We asked students, aged 8, 10, 12, and 18 years, to rate the idea units of folk stories in terms of their importance to the theme of a passage (Brown & Smiley, 1977). Only 18-year-olds could reliably distinguish the previously rated four levels of importance. Twelve-year-olds did not differentiate the two intermediate levels of importance, but they did assign their lowest scores to the least important and highest scores to the most important elements. Eight-year-olds made no reliable distinction between levels of importance in their ratings and even 10-year-old students could only distinguish the highest level of importance from all other levels. There was considerable agreement between independent groups of college students, and even 12-year-olds, concerning the importance of constituent ideas of a text passage, but 8- and 10-year-old subjects were unable to differentiate units in terms of their relative importance to the text. Thus, when the passage is relatively long (55 idea units) and complex (fifth-grade reading level), even junior high school students experience some difficulty in identifying the important elements of text.

It is important to note, however, that recall of the passages at all ages was sensitive to the importance level of the units. After rating a story for the importance of its units, subjects were asked to read and recall another story. Although the older students remembered more than the younger children, the general pattern of results was consistent across the age range of 8 to 18 years: The least important units were recalled less frequently than all other units and the most important units were most often recalled. Even without prior awareness of the importance of constituent units, younger children still favor the important units in recall. Apparently, we spontaneously abstract the main ideas of an oral or written communication even when no deliberate attempt to do so is instigated.

We have some evidence that the ability to extract the main ideas is particularly a problem for poor readers (Smiley, Oakley, Worthen, Campione, & Brown, 1977) and retarded children (Brown, Campione, & Barclay, 1978). Under both reading and listening conditions, good readers recalled a greater proportion of the stories, and the likelihood of their recalling a particular unit was a clear function of the unit's thematic importance; poor readers recalled less of the stories, and their recall protocols were not clearly related to variations in importance, although even they favored the highest level of importance in recalling.

Although we remember the gist of a message even in the absence of a deliberate attempt to concentrate on essential ideas, this does not exclude the possibility that deliberate strategies could be used to enhance our degree of understanding and they certainly would be necessary to achieve more "fleshed-out" recall. The mature learner's awareness of his or her skills and the task at hand would be particularly useful if longer preparatory periods were permitted for the study of material that must be maintained over some period of time, a more typical school learning situation.

As children mature, they become able to identify the essential organizing features and crucial elements of texts (Brown & Smiley, 1977). Thanks to this foreknowledge, they make better use of extended study time. If given an extra period for study (equal to three times their reading rate), children from seventh grade up improve their recall considerably for important elements of text; recall of less important details does not improve. Children below seventh grade do not usually show such effective use of additional study time; their recall improves, if at all, evenly across all levels of importance. As a result, older students' recall protocols following study include all the essential elements and little trivia. Younger children's recall, though still favoring important elements, has many such elements missing (Brown & Smiley, 1978).

We believe that older students benefit from increased study time as a direct result of their insights into the working of their own memory and their ability to predict ahead of time what are the important elements of the texts. Younger students, not so prescient, cannot be expected to distribute extra time intelligently; they do not concentrate on only the important elements of text because they do not know in advance what they are.

To substantiate our belief that metacognitive control governs this developmental trend, we have observed the study actions of our subjects. In particular, we have examined the physical records they provide, records that can be scored objectively—notes and underlining of texts. A certain proportion of children from fifth grade and up spontaneously underline or take notes during study. At all ages, the physical records of spontaneous subjects favored the important elements; that is, the notes or underlined sections concentrated on elements of the text previously rated as crucial to the theme (Brown & Smiley, 1978).

Students induced to adopt one of these strategies did not show a similar sensitivity to importance; they took notes or underlined more randomly. Although the efficiency of physical record keeping in induced subjects did improve with age, it never reached the standard set by spontaneous users of the strategy. Furthermore, the recall scores of spontaneous producers were much superior. Even fifth-graders who spontaneously underlined showed an adult-like pattern and used extra study to differentially improve their recall of important elements. This interesting difference between spontaneous and induced users of the note taking or underlining strategy may explain the curious lack of effect so far found in adult studies concerned with these processes (T. Anderson, Chapter 20, this volume). Previous studies have typically assigned students arbitrarily to treatment groups, thus, in effect, combining those who would or would not use the strategy on their own volition. As we have seen, this procedure tends to mask the efficiency of the strategy, an efficiency that is dependent on its subject-generated nature (Brown, 1979; Brown & Smiley, 1978).

Selecting Suitable Retrieval Cues

Adequate retrieval-cue selection must include at least two elements of knowledge: (1) that textual elements vary in importance and the recall of important units is essential for coherence; and (2) that one should concentrate one's efforts on important material that one has previously failed to recall or that one suspects, via self-testing, that one will fail to recall. As we have seen, young children are less than adequately informed of the varying degrees of textual importance, at least of the passages used in this series of studies, and there is some evidence that the strategy of studying previously missed information may also cause problems (Brown & Campione, 1977; Masur, McIntyre, & Flavell, 1973). How then would they cope with the task of selecting text elements to serve as cribs or cues to guide their recall of passages? We examined this question in a series of recent studies using folk tales as study material (Brown & Campione, 1979, Brown, Smiley, & Lawton, 1977). Students from fifth through twelfth grades, together with college students, were asked to select 12 (out of approximately 60 text units) that they would like to have as retrieval cues when recalling the passage. Half of the students took part in the task after they had experience studying and recalling the passage, whereas the remainder had no previous experience with the target text. Naive students showed a marked preference for level 4 units (the most important) and there was no age effect. The school students did not change their pattern of choice following experience with the texts but the college students did. Now, their prime targets for retrieval cues were the two intermediate levels of importance. After experience with the passages, college students still rejected the least important units as potential retrieval cues but they also rejected the most important units. The prime targets for selection were the middle levels of importance. The main reason given for this shift in preference (given on posttest interrogation) was that they realized they would remember the main theme without conscious intent, but, in order to improve overall recall, they would need to concentrate on the intermediate level material that had caused them much more trouble when they attempted recall. Therefore, they selected intermediate units as retrieval cues. This shift in selection represents a sensitive awareness of the important elements of texts and of the function of retrieval cues in recall, a sensitivity not displayed by even the eleventh and twelfth grade school sample.

The selection of suitable retrieval cues to aid in the recall of complex passages is by no means a simple task. It requires a fine sensitivity to the relative importance of various elements of texts, understanding of suitable study strategies, and an appreciation of the complex interweaving of these factors. Because of this complexity, we find a very late emergence of a suitable retrieval strategy. Only college students change their pattern of responses dramatically after one experience studying the passage, selecting units of intermediate importance to form the scaffolding for their subsequent recall attempt. This modification is an intelligent one, for approximately 80% of the most important units would have been recalled on their first try without the use of retrieval cues (Brown & Smiley, 1977, 1978). Thus, selection of relatively less central units as retrieval cues would be an optimal plan for a second recall attempt. We know that in a simpler paradigm, much younger children seem to be aware that items they have failed to recall should be given extra study. But it is not until college age that this knowledge is reflected in suitable retieval plan modification for studying text materials.

We were somewhat surprised by the outcome of the first study with retrieval cue selection, for even the oldest school students performed poorly on the task. One possible reason for their lack of insight could have been the very limited amount of experience they had on the task. To test this hypothesis, we repeated the experiment but allowed multiple trials of the study-select cue-recall activity. On each trial, the students were told to do anything they liked to help them remember. After termination of the study period, they selected 12 retrieval cues that they *kept with them* during their free recall attempt. After recall and a rest period, the entire procedure was repeated, three times for college students and older school children, up to six times for the younger participants. We will consider only the first 3 trials. Note that on Trial 1 all students were naive in the sense of never having recalled the passage; on all subsequent trials they were, of course, experienced.

For college students, the pattern of the previous study was replicated. Recall that the stories were divided into four levels of importance. On the first (naive) trial, the students selected predominantly important (Level 4) units for retrieval aids. On the *first* experienced trial (Trial 2), they shifted to a preference for Level 3 units, whereas on the second experienced trial (Trial 3) they preferred Level 2 units. On all three trials, Level 1 units were treated appropriately as trivia. This is a nice replication of the shifting pattern of cue selection reflecting the gradual acquisition of the material.

Did any of our school children show this fine sensitivity? There was some encouraging data from the oldest group. Although on the first experienced trial (Trial 2) they did not shift preference, by the second experienced trial their selections were beginning to change in a fashion comparable to college students. On Trial 2 (first experience), only the college students shifted their choices away from predominantly Level 4 units. But by Trial 3, eleventh- and twelfth-graders also show the shift; they are precisely one trial behind. This lag could be due to slower learning—that is, both groups shift when they reach the same criterion of learning but the younger students take an extra trial to reach that criterion. It could also be due to a slower selection of the effective study strategy of switching to less important units—that is, both groups learn as much on each trial but it takes the school students longer to realize they need to shift cue selection. We are currently analyzing the relation between cue selection and recall levels to distinguish between these alternatives.

The data from the younger students suggest that the ability to rapidly modify one's retrieval plans as a function of the current state of learning is a late developing skill. There was some slight evidence of a decrease in Level 4 unit selection over trials for the ninth-graders but it was not dramatic. Even less sensitivity was shown by the eight-graders, who were remarkably consistent in their choices across trials. Indeed, they tended to choose the *same* cues on each trial even though their learning state changed. They tended to settle on a set of cues on Trial 1 and repeated the same selection on each succeeding trial—not exactly an effective study strategy.

As we have found with prior work concerned with other study strategies such as underlining, note-taking, summarization, and so on (Brown & Smiley, 1978), the ability to select suitable retrieval cues is a late-developing skill because it requires a fine degree of sensitivity to the demands of gist recall tasks. Successful users of the flexible retrieval plan illustrated in these studies must have: (1) information concerning their current state of knowledge, that is, what they know of the text and what they do not yet know; (2) knowledge of the fine gradation of importance of various elements of texts, that is, what is important to know and what can be disregarded; and (3) the strategic knowledge to select for retrieval cues information that they have missed previously. For it is not just the deployment of a strategy and the knowledge base upon which it must operate. The knowledge base must include at least some forms of self-knowledge (i.e., myself as a memorizer), task knowledge (gist recall features), and text knowledge (importance vs. trivia, organization of text, etc.). The orchestration and coordination of these forms of knowledge demands a sophisticated learner and it is therefore not surprising that efficient performance is so late in emerging.

Estimating Readiness for a Test

Another essential feature of effective study is the availability to estimate when material is sufficiently well known to risk a test. Obviously, this can be a simple form of knowledge or can involve very complex forms of self-testing and evaluation, and, again, the complexity of the decision will be crucial in assigning when and if children become capable of performing this feat.

Consider first a very simple form of recall readiness estimation, a task we adapted from Flavell and his co-workers (Flavell, Friedrichs, & Hoyt, 1970). On each of a series of trials, children are given a list of pictures equal to one and one half times the number they actually recalled during a series of practice study trials. They are told to continue studying the items until they are sure they can remember all of them perfectly. Then they are to signal the experimenter that they are ready. Not surprisingly, young and slow-learning children do especially poorly on such a task. Only 4% of an MA 6 sample and 12% of an MA 8 sample could give even one perfect recall (Brown & Barclay, 1976), and it is not until third grade that the majority of normal children display this talent. Although they are allowed as much time as they want, this is a poor showing. One reason why the developmentally young perform so poorly on this task could be that they do not tend to introduce strategies of deliberate memorization that involve self-testing elements, such as rehearsal or anticipation, which would alert them to their readiness for a test. If children do not use such self-testing devices, they can hardly be expected to monitor their own stage of learning.

For this reason, we decided to train children in a simple stop-and-test recall readiness strategy. We provided instruction in three strategies of remembering: anticipation and cumulative rehearsal, both of which involve self-testing elements, and labeling, which does not, a condition that therefore served as a control. Following training, four posttests were given, a prompted posttest (one day after training) on which individuals were instructed to continue the trained strategy, and three unprompted posttests given 1 day, approximately 2 weeks, and approximately 1 year later. Both the younger and older children in the anticipation and rehearsal groups (but not the controls) perform significantly better on the prompted posttest than on the pretest. They raised their percentage recalled by at least 35%. Additionally, 75% of younger subjects in these groups recalled perfectly on at least one trial, compared with none on the pretest; the corresponding figures for the older subjects are 92% on Posttest 1 compared with 8% on the pretest. Thus, training the useful self-testing strategies results in both enhanced performance (percent recall data) and improved monitoring (data on number of perfect recalls).

The MA 6 and MA 8 groups differed considerably on the last three posttests. For the younger group, performance on Posttests 2, 3, and 4 was not significantly different from the pretraining level, whereas for the older group, performance on all posttests differed significantly from the pretraining level. Training facilitates performance, with the effect being somewhat durable for the older children but transitory for the younger ones. Even after a year's delay, the majority of the older children were able to predict their readiness to recall a list of pictures.

Given the dismal performance of the younger group, we made no attempt to test these children for evidence of generalization of our training. The older children looked more promising, however, so we decided to see whether they would show the benefits of the recall-readiness training on quite a different task (Brown, Campione, & Barclay, 1978). Systematically studying material until it is judged to be well enough known to risk a test, is, of course, a very general strategy; therefore, we were hoping that, even with very different materials, the children who had received extensive training would show some generalized benefits.

The generalization task selected was one that we believed to be more representative of the type of study activity required in the classroom. Most studying requires the student to extract the main ideas of prose passages and regurgitate the gist of the ideas in his own words. Our question was, would training recall-readiness on the simple rote-list learning task help children with the more typical school study activity of preparing for gist recall of prose passages? Although strategies of anticipation and rehearsal are useful on a prose learning task, they would have to be modified considerably from the straightforward procedures suitable for learning lists of words. Rehearsal or anticipation of individual words would be inefficient and the subject would have to attempt anticipation or rehearsal of longer chunks of material. In addition, the criteria for judging readiness are much more subtle. In the rote-recall task, readiness is reached when the learner can recall all items verbatim and it is relatively easy for the learner to check this prior to recall attempts. But in the gist recall tasks, the learner must gauge when he or she has grasped the main ideas of the material, for verbatim recall is not required. Thus, the training and transfer tasks were quite different in their strategy-use and strategy-monitoring requirements even though they demanded the same general "stop-check-study-recheck" routine.

The stimulus materials were a set of 12 simple stories (second-grade readability level) consisting of idea units divided into three levels of rated importance. Each student was tested on a total of 6 days to obtain a reliable estimate of their performance. No mention of the prior testing was made to the subjects. Each day consisted of having them study and recall a randomly selected pair of the 12 stories. The experimenter read each story to the subjects, and then the subjects read it back twice with the experimenter sounding out and explaining any words the subjects could not read or understand. The subjects were then told to read the story over, as many times as necessary in order to try to remember everything that happened. When they were sure they could tell all that happened *in their own words,* they were to ring a desk bell (indicating that they were ready) and then try to tell the story.

There were four groups of students tested, the originally successfully trained rehearsal and anticipation groups and the original control group (label) who had not improved their recall-readiness skills. In addition, we included a group of students with no previous experience on the task, but matched for IQ, MA, CA, reading scores, and class placement with our experienced subjects. The trained students outperformed the two control groups on many indices including: (1) total amount recalled; (2) total time spent studying; (3) the pattern of recall—that is, their recall protocols looked far more like mature studiers in that they favored the main theme; and (4) overt indices of studying including anticipation, rehearsal, selective rereading, underlining, circling key words, and so on (Brown, Campione, & Barclay, 1978).

An interesting sidelight to this study is that, on the last few days of testing, the subjects were explicitly prompted to use some study habits. They were told to underline or circle key words or phrases or to make notes or draw pictures if this would help in any way. Such instruction did lead to increased overt activity but not to improved performance on a test. The reason for this lack of correspondence was not difficult to detect. Although some of the children who had not previously used the tactics did begin to underline and circle key words, and so on, they did not seem to do so in the same manner as spontaneous users of the strategy (Brown & Smiley, 1978). Children who underlined or circled words on their own volition tended to favor words and idea units previously rated by adults to be key or important elements. Children who used the marking techniques only when instructed tended not to underline key words but appeared to behave randomly, or they circled long or unfamiliar words. We even have several examples of children told to underline important points who underlined everything! We have a long way to go before we can devise effective training of such strategies in the young.

In summary, strategic study time utilization depends on a variety of cognitive and metacognitive skills not readily evidenced in young children. A detailed description of the development of these skills is still sadly lacking and the techniques necessary to inculcate the tactics in those who do not employ them spontaneously have not been established. This appears to be an area in need of systematic examination by those who would improve the study habits of immature learners.

SOME PROBLEMS WITH STUDYING METACOGNITION IN CHILDREN

Externalizing a Mental Event

A cursory review of the literature concerning the ontogenesis of metacognition would suggest that the developmentally young share a fundamental problem: They are less conscious of the workings of their own mind, less facile with the introspective modes necessary to reveal their mental states, and, therefore, less able to exert conscious control of their own cognitive activity. If this is true, then experimentalists are faced with a thorny problem in studying metacognition in children, the problem of externalizing mental events. Not only are young children less able to express themselves, but they are also less aware of their own cognitive processes and less familiar with the self-interrogation techniques needed to achieve adequate self-evaluation. How then do we inquire about details of their knowledge?

As the study of metacognition is in its infancy, it is not surprising that refined measures for assessing awareness have yet to be developed. Yet we do have examples of the growing pains experienced in other related fields and it is economical to attempt to benefit from others' mistakes. We know from related areas of cognitive development of the problems associated with accepting a child's verbal responses as an index of what he or she knows. What a child says he or she has done or will do is not necessarily related to his or her performance. Reliance on verbal responses and justifications is a risky venture when the participant is a child and, indeed, it is an activity not without its problems when adults are the informants (Nisbett & Wilson, 1977). As most of the information we have concerning metacognition in children consists of just such verbal self-reports, the problem of the criteria for evaluation of data is a crucial issue here.

The problem of measuring self-judgments is especially difficult because we are concerned not with what children are doing but with what they think they are doing and why. Thus, we must deal with verbal statements and forced-choice data notorious for difficulties of measurement. A direct method of inquiring into what children know is to ask them. Some examples of the problems of this approach may prove illustrative. The experimenter responsible for running our strategy-modeling study asked her 7-year-old son how he would study the set of pictures (after he had seen the tapes of a peer performing the task). He replied, without hesitation, that he would look at them; he always did that if he had to remember. Given the list, he carefully put all the pictures into taxonomic categories, spatially separated the categories and proceeded to scan them systematically. Asked what he had done to help him remember, he replied that he just looked at the pictures just like he said he would!

A less anecdotal example of the pitfalls of taking a child's verbal response at face value came from our study on span estimation in children (Brown et al., 1977). We adopted a procedure introduced by Flavell and his co-workers (Flavell et al., 1970). The children's task is to estimate their span for serial rote recall of picture names. They are given 10 trials; on the first they are presented with one picture, two on the second, and three on the third until by the 10th trial they receive a list of 10 pictures. On each trial, the children are asked if they would still be able to recall that many. The list length on which the children indicate that their span has been overreached is taken as their own estimation of their capacity. Using this technique, Flavell et al. (1970) found quite adequate performance on the task; even one third of the kindergarten sample gave realistic estimates.

Our modification of this procedure was simply to continue asking the children for their estimate even after they had indicated that a particular list length was too long. The children were allowed to continue estimating up to the maximum list length of 10 items. Many of the children (31%), who would have been judged realistic if we had stopped at their first response, were quite happy to assert that a list of five was too difficult although one of six was not, to claim that seven was too many but eight was okay. Whatever this tells us about a child's metamemory, it certainly tells us to beware of accepting a single verbal response as a measure of awareness.

Kreutzer et al. (1975) attempted to overcome this problem by requiring multiple responses to their test questionnaire, including adequate justification. The match between single yes–no answers indicating awareness and adequate justification increased dramatically with age. Would demanding adequate justifications solve the problem of metacomprehension measures in children? Kuhn (1974) has considered this problem in the context of Piagetian conservation studies. Apparently, there is more than one school of thought. Brainerd (1973) believes that justifications are inappropriate for evaluating the child's understanding of a problem, because operativity is supposed to precede the ability to express such knowledge verbally. The risk of Type II errors is a problem, as many children may well possess the requisite cognitive skills but fail to express them adequately. Brainerd (1973) advocates the use of yes–no, same–different responses, but as Kuhn points out, any dichotomous choice method is sensitive to response bias effects, known to be developmentally sensitive (Brown & Campione, 1972). The dilemma is that demanding justification of responses entails the possibility of Type II errors by relying on dichotomous responses risks the possibility of Type I errors. Kuhn's solution is that of converging operations; as rich a variety of responses as possible should be elicited and the degree of awareness judged against the total pictures revealed, an obvious but time-consuming solution to a difficult problem.

Knowledge and Actions

Another problem experienced by those who are interested in the child's self-knowledge is the often surprising gap between what children say they know and how they perform. For example, Salatas and Flavell (1976) and Moynahan (1973) considered knowledge concerning categorization and use of that strategy to aid free recall. Both failed to find a direct link. Moynahan found that awareness of the effects of categorization was not related to actual performance on categorized versus uncategorized lists. Similarly, Salatas and Flavell (1976) found that first-graders who had not categorized were as likely as those who had to indicate that categorization would aid recall. We have also documented the absence of a direct link between predictions and performance. Asked to predict which modeled activity would result in superior recall, all our retarded children indicated the superiority of an active strategy (in contrast to preschool and first-grade normal children who were not so sensitive). Given the exact task to perform themselves, immediately after viewing the model, only a minority actually performed the efficient strategy themselves. Most of a third-, and fifth-grade sample elected to perform the strategy they had predicted to be most efficient, but even in these older children, the relationship was less than perfect. Items from the Kreutzer et al. (1975) questionnaire show the same pattern. Children who predicted that studying longer or more actively will lead to better recall do not necessarily say that they would act this way themselves.

Thus, even when children indicate awareness of efficient actions, it does not necessarily follow that they will use such tactics in their own study time. We do not always perform in a manner we know to be the most efficient; it would seem that this is even more true of children. The coordination of knowledge and actions concerning reading efficiency could be the essence of development after the early school years (Flavell & Wellman, 1977). Investigations of this hypothesized increase in coordination have barely begun.

Developmental Trends

One of the major problems with the metacognitive development literature to date is its restricted focus on rote learning skills in quite young children. This restriction impedes theory building and is also a drawback if one is interested in tracing the link between metacognitive development and higher level strategy use, such as that involved in reading. One outcome of this limited focus is that a review of the literature could give the impression that metacognitive development is rapid and functionally complete by third grade. In the Kreutzer et al. (1975) questionnaire study, there is impressive evidence of a ceiling in performance at around third grade for the majority of problems set. In addition, most of the empirical studies indicated that third grade is the point at which awareness is attained by the majority of children. Thus, both recall-readiness and span-estimation improve little after second grade (Flavell et al., 1970; but note objections cited previously). In the study-time apportionment study, there is improvement between first and third grade, but third-graders behave very much like college students (Masur et al., 1973). Moynahan (1973) found little difference between third- and fifth-graders in pedicting task difficulty. Indeed, if one were to exclude the youngest group in many of the existing metamemory studies (e.g., the kindergarten or first-grade sample) one would be left with no reliable developmental differences! The pattern seems fairly consistent across tasks; by third grade, children know a fair amount about rote memorization of lists.

When the task is more complex, however, as in judging the difficulty of prose passages (Danner, 1976) or the importance of various aspects of texts

(Brown & Smiley, 1977) or even the success of an ongoing attempt to learn in terms of estimating recall readiness (Brown & Barclay, 1976), a much later age would be suggested for efficiency. Metacognitive deficiencies are the problem of the novice, regardless of age. Ignorance is not necessarily age related; rather it is more a function of inexperience in a new (and difficult) problem situation. Adults and children display similar confusion when confronted with a new problem: A novice chess player (Chi, 1978) has many of the same problems of metacognition that the very small card player experiences (Markman, 1977). Similarly, novice x-ray technicians show similar inept scanning patterns (Thomas, 1968) as do young children who are first learning to search a visual array (Mackworth & Bruner, 1970), failing to scan exhaustively and failing to focus on the most informative areas. It is unfortunate that there are so few studies of metacognition in older children who are working on more difficult tasks, but the effect of task difficulty is obviously of paramount importance when considering age of onset of metacognitive abilities. Whether or not children will be judged aware or unaware or will be attributed with metacognitive insights depends on the level of difficulty of the task and the match between the task demands and the child's existing cognitive skills (Brown & DeLoache, 1978). A child who knows a great deal about organization when the basis of that organization is taxonomic categorization may know little or nothing concerning organizational principles underlying text materials. Similarly, a young child may be able to extract the main idea of a simple story (e.g., identify actor, action, and object), but may be quite unable to identify the theme of a more complex passage, let alone show sensitivity to nuances of meaning, sarcasm, emphasis, the writer's purposes and biases, and so on.

It is therefore simplistic to speak of a particular age when children achieve certain skills. Primitive precursors of the ability to plan and check one's activities against commonsense criteria probably emerge prior to the school years (Wellman, Ritter, & Flavell, 1975), but when the task is a complex one, inadequate checking and planning may be manifested at a much later age. College students are by no means free of checking failure as any teacher of elementary statistics will attest. Negative probabilities and variances are happily accepted as solutions if the student believes the formula was followed correctly (Brown, 1978). The interaction of task complexity and age is an important issue that deserves further attention if we are to achieve a descriptive theory of the development of metacognitive skills.

DIRECTIONS FOR FUTURE RESEARCH

One deficiency revealed by this literature review is the lack of a substantial body of research aimed directly at metacognitive aspects of reading comprehension and studying, although we have attempted to emphasize the relevance of existing developmental studies concerned with various aspects of metacognition. Some starts have been made to fill the gap (Brown & Smiley, 1977, 1978; Brown, Smiley, & Lawton, 1977; Markman, 1977), but it is still true that the bulk of the extant literature is restricted to isolated demonstration studies that concentrate on the child's knowledge and control of a few simple rote-learning skills. It is currently fashionable to deplore the undue concentration on skills of rote learning for reproductive recall, particularly of meaningless, isolated lists of materials (Brown, 1975; Jenkins, 1973). This criticism is rarely raised in conjunction with the metacognition literature. But one could argue that the utility of such knowledge would have a limited range of applicability (Brown, 1977), for much of what we must learn requires gist recall of connected discourse, in which common mnemonic techniques used to ensure rote recall of word lists may no longer serve a useful function.

Future studies of metacomprehension would be more fruitful if they were to concentrate on areas in which we lack even basic information. For example, examinations are needed of the child's knowledge of his ability to retain the essential ideas of a written or spoken communication, to understand instructions, to distinguish between situations in which recall must be productive or reconstructive and between situations in which deliberate memorization is needed or not needed, or on any of a host of other intelligent activities that are involved in reading and studying.

One reason why we have limited information concerning such metacognitive activity in children, or adults for that matter, is because we know little about the way mature thinkers solve such problems. Knowing a fair amount about rehearsal and taxonomic organization for the purposes of rote learning an isolated list, we can safely ask, does the child know too? Knowing little about more complex study skills, it is hard to define what the child should know. Collins et al. (1975) have provided glimpses of the rich repertoire of cognitive pyrotechnics graduate students can bring to their Socratic dialogue game. What is needed is a similar set of protocols from coherent adults and precocious children faced with a variety of learning situations. A good starting point would be study skills, for every student must attempt them; every student must be aware of the strengths and limitations of certain activities; and some students may be aware of such niceties as the match-mismatch of certain activities and the end goal. Knowing more about such awareness in adults, we may be in a better position to assess what it is that the less mature learner does not know, needs to know, and possibly could be trained to know.

In our efforts to provide further information about what the child knows, however, we must face the problem of how to elicit from the recalcitrant even the limited knowledge they may possess, i.e., the problem of externalizing mental activities. Although we are sensitive to the problems of relying on children's self-reports of their awareness, we are initiating a series of studies to examine what older children can tell us concerning their reading strategies. We do rely on verbal reports to a great extent, but we also adopt certain precautions to guard against Type I errors.

First, it is probably not necessary to avoid verbal reports completely, particularly if the subject is a middle school student. One method we are attempting is modeled on the technology of clinical interviews (Gorden, 1969). Based on the Kreutzer et al. (1975) and Brown (1978) experience with questionnaire techniques, we are currently conducting a series of interviews concerned with a wide variety of reading strategies. The initial question at each point is open-ended, and students are encouraged to talk freely about their own experience. Following this, detailed probe questions are asked to extract information that is not forthcoming in the free situation. Many facets of reading and studying effectiveness are probed. We hope that by comparing the protocols of middle school students with those of college students, we may gain insight into what it is that the efficient reader knows that is not obvious to the neophyte.

Our second main tactic is to investigate a variety of "rigged" situations that we hope will force children to externalize what they do know. One such method, which our pilot data suggest will be promising, is a variant of the currently popular research strategy of asking children to communicate to younger listeners (Gelman & Shatz, 1977; Shatz & Gelman, 1973). Asking older students to explain to less mature readers how they should proceed on a variety of tasks may force the experienced children to make explicit what they know. In order to provide a semirealistic situation in which such instruction could occur, we are currently investigating the possibility of cross-age tutoring programs. Children in sixth to eighth grade will be enrolled in a program of tutoring aimed at children of a younger age; they will be asked to help teach these less efficient learners to study effectively. In devising their instructional plans, they will have the advice of an experimenter-observer. By observing their questions and plans concerning what to teach, we hope to gain valuable insights into their own knowledge concerning "how to study." Adequate debriefing for poorly instructed trainees will be provided!

A similar plan is our "little teacher" idea. Children will be divided into small groups to participate in an academic project, for example, a science demonstration. One child will be selected as the instructor for each session. It will be his or her job to read the material, provide a summary for the others, and provide illustrations and demonstrations for his or her confederates. In the preparation, the child will be aided by an experimenter-observer. Each team will be told that they will be tested on the material and they must try to be the best team (to win a prize, etc.). The child's knowledge or ignorance concerning the main ideas, the importance of the material, how to illustrate and emphasize, and how to study material should be made explicit by these methods.

The third tactic we are using in our fight to externalize what is known is an extension of Markman's (1977) work on instruction following; we will use children as critics. We will ask middle school children to rate the adequacy of a set of instructions we have written, for example, a book of recipes or a manual on how to use a toy or to play a game. The instructions will be obviously incomplete or misleading. The critics will be asked to help us rewrite faulty instructions so that children of their own age could read them. Again, when informing us of the inadequacies of our prose, they should be revealing their own understanding of reading and instruction-following strategies.

One thing, at least, should be clear from this review: Considerable ingenuity will be needed for us to fill in the scanty picture we have of the development of reading strategies. Even more expenditure of thought and effort will be needed before we are in a position to teach such skills to the developmentally delayed child or to anyone who needs direct intervention. A precise knowledge of the component processes of metacomprehension skills must precede any attempts to construct training programs. In view of the central importance of effective reading strategies for academic success, the expenditure of such efforts seems justified.

ACKNOWLEDGMENTS

The preparation of this manuscript was supported in part by Grants HD 06864, HD 05951, and a Research Career Development Award HD 00111, from the National Institute of Child Health and Human Development and in part by Reading Center Grant MS-NIE-C-400-76-0116.

REFERENCES

Asher, S. R. Referential communication. In C. J. Whitehurst & B. J. Zimmerman (Eds.), *The functions of language and cognition.* New York: Academic Press, 1978.

Binet, A. *Psychologie des grands calculateur et joueurs d'echess.* Paris: Hachette, 1894.

Blake, M. Prediction of recognition when recall fails: Exploring the feeling of knowing phenomena. *Journal of Verbal Learning and Verbal Behavior,* 1973, *12,* 311–319.

Brainerd, C. J. Order of acquisition of transitivity, conservation, and class inclusion of length and weight. *Developmental Psychology,* 1973, *8,* 105–116.

Bransford, J. D., Nitsch, K. W., & Franks, J. J. Schooling and the facilitation of knowing. In R. C. Anderson, R. J. Spiro, & W. E. Montague (Eds.), *Schooling and the acquistion of knowledge.* Hillsdale, N.J.: Lawrence Erlbaum Associates, 1977.

Brown, A. L. The role of strategic behavior in retardate memory. In N. R. Ellis (Ed.), *International review of research in mental retardation* (Vol. 1). New York: Academic Press, 1974.

Brown, A. L. The development of memory: Knowing, knowing about knowing, and knowing how to know. In H. W. Reese (Ed.), *Advances in child development and behavior* (Vol. 10). New York: Academic Press, 1975.

Brown, A. L. Development, schooling and the acquisition of knowledge about knowledge. In R. C. Anderson, R. J. Spiro, & W. E. Montague (Eds.), *Schooling and the acquisition of knowledge.* Hillsdale, N.J.: Lawrence Erlbaum Associates, 1977.

Brown, A. L. Knowing when, where, and how to remember: A problem of metacognition. In R. Glaser (Ed.), *Advances in instructional psychology.* Hillsdale, N.J.: Lawrence Erlbaum Associates, 1978.

Brown, A. L. Theories of memory and the problem of development: Activity, growth, and knowledge. In L. Cermak & F. I. M. Craik (Eds.), *Levels of processing in memory.* Hillsdale, N.J.: Lawrence Erlbaum Associates, 1979.

Brown, A. L., & Barclay, C. R. The effects of training specific mnemonics of the metamnemonic efficiency of retarded children. *Child Development,* 1976, *47,* 71–80.

Brown, A. L., & Campione, J. C. Recognition memory for perceptually similar pictures in preschool children. *Journal of Experimental Psychology,* 1972, *95,* 55–62.

Brown, A. L., & Campione, J. C. Training strategic study time apportionment in educable retarded children. *Intelligence,* 1977, *1,* 94–107.

Brown, A. L., & Campione, J. C. Memory strategies in learning: Teaching children to study effectively. In H. Leibowitz, J. Singer, A. Steinschneider, H. Stevenson, & H. Pick (Eds.), *Application of basic research in psychology.* New York: Plenum Press, 1978.

Brown, A. L., & Campione, J. C. The effects of knowledge and experience on the formation of retrieval plans for studying from texts. In M. M. Gruneberg & P. Morris (Eds.), *Practical aspects of memory.* London: Academic Press, 1979.

Brown, A. L., Campione, J. C., & Barclay, C. R. *Training self-checking routines for estimating test readiness: Generalization from list learning to prose recall.* Unpublished manuscript, University of Illinois, 1978.

Brown, A. L., Campione, J. C., & Murphy, M. D. Maintenance and generalization of trained metamnemonic awareness in educable retarded children. *Journal of Experimental Child Psychology,* 1977, *24,* 191–211.

Brown, A. L., & DeLoache, J. S. Skills, plans, and self-regulation. In R. Siegler (Ed.), *Children's thinking: What develops?* Hillsdale, N.J.: Lawrence Erlbaum Associates, 1978.

Brown, A. L., & Lawton, S. C. The feeling of knowing experience in educable retarded children. *Developmental Psychology,* 1977, *4,* 364–370.

Brown, A. L., & Smiley, S. S. Rating the importance of structural units of prose passages: A problem of metacognitive development. *Child Development,* 1977, *48,* 1–8.

Brown, A. L., & Smiley, S. S. The development of strategies for studying texts. *Child Development,* 1978, *49,* 1076–1088.

Brown, A. L., Smiley, S. S., & Lawton, S. C. *The effects of experience on the selection of suitable retrieval cues for prose passages* (Tech. Rep. No. 53). Champaign: University of Illinois, Center for the Study of Reading, July, 1977.

Brown, R., & McNeill, D. The tip of the tongue phenomena. *Journal of Verbal Learning and Verbal Behavior,* 1966, *5,* 325–337.

Chi, M. T. H. Knowledge structures and memory development. In R. Siegler (Ed.), *Children's thinking: What develops?* Thirteenth Annual Carnegie Symposium on Cognition. Hillsdale, N.J.: Lawrence Erlbaum Associates, 1978.

Collins, A., Warnock, E., Aiello, N., & Miller, M. Reasoning from incomplete knowledge. In D. G. Bobrow & A. Collins (Eds.), *Representation and understanding: Studies in cognitive science.* New York: Academic Press, 1975.

Cosgrove, J. M., & Patterson, C. J. Plans and the development of listener skills. *Developmental Psychology,* 1977, *13,* 557–564.

Danner, F. W. Children's understanding of intersentence organization in the recall of short descriptive passages. *Journal of Educational Psychology,* 1976, *68*(2), 174–183.

Flavell, J. H. Metacognitive aspects of problem solving. In L. B. Resnick (Ed.), *The nature of intelligence.* Hillsdale, N.J.: Lawrence Erlbaum Associates, 1976.

Flavell, J. H., Friedrichs, A. G., & Hoyt, J. D. Developmental changes in memorization processes. *Cognitive Psychology,* 1970, *1,* 324–340.

Flavell, J. H., & Wellman, H. M. Metamemory. In R. V. Kail, Jr., & J. W. Hagen (Eds.), *Perspectives on the development of memory and cognition.* Hillsdale, N.J.: Lawrence Erlbaum Associates, 1977.

Gelman, R., & Shatz, M. Appropriate speech adjustments. In M. Lewis & L. Rosenblum (Eds.), *Communication and language: The origins of behavior,* (Vol. 5). New York: Wiley, 1977.

Gleitman, L. R., Gleitman, H., & Shipley, E. F. The emergence of the child as grammarian. *Cognition,* 1972, *1,* 137–164.

Gorden, R. L. *Interviewing: Strategy, techniques and tactics.* Homewood, Ill.: The Dorsey Press, 1969.

Hart, J. T. Memory and memory monitoring processes. *Journal of Verbal Learning and Verbal Behavior,* 1967, *6,* 685–691.

Holt, H. H. *How children fail.* New York: Dell, 1964.

Ironsmith, M., & Whitehurst, G. J. The development of listener abilities in communication: How children deal with ambiguous information. *Child Development,* 1978, *49,* 348–352.

James, W. *The principles of psychology* (Vol. 1). New York: Holt, 1890.

Jenkins, J. J. *Remember that old theory of memory? Well, forget it.* Paper presented at the American Psychological Association, Montreal, 1973. (Presidential Address, Division 3.)

Karabenick, J. D., & Miller, S. A. The effects of age, sex, and listener feedback on grade school children's referential communication. *Child Development,* 1977, *48,* 678–684.

Kreutzer, M. A., Leonard, C., Flavell, J. H. An interview study of children's knowledge about memory. *Monographs of the Society for Research in Child Development,*1975, *40*(1, Serial No. 159).

Kuhn, D. Inducing development experimentally: Comments on a research paradigm. *Developmental Psychology,* 1974, *10,* 590–600.

Mackworth, N. H., & Bruner, J. S. How adults and children search and recognize pictures. *Human Development,* 1970, *13,* 149–177.

Markman, E. M. *Realizing that you don't understand: Elementary school children's awareness of inconsistencies.* Unpublished manuscript, Stanford University, 1975.

Markman, E. M. Realizing that you don't understand. *Child Development,* 1977, *48,* 986–992.

Masur, E. F., McIntyre, C. W., & Flavell, J. H. Developmental changes in apportionment of study time among items in a multitrial free recall task. *Journal of Experimental child Psychology,* 1973, *15,* 237–246.

Moynahan, E. D. The development of knowledge concerning the effect of categorization upon free recall. *Child Development,*1973, *44,* 238–246.

Nisbett, R. E. & Wilson, T. D. Telling more than we can know: Verbal reports on mental processes. *Psychological Review,* 1977, *84,* 231–259.

Norman, D. A. Memory, knowledge, and the answering of questions. In R. L. Solso (Ed.), *Contemporary issues in cognitive psychology: The Loyola Symposium.* Washington, D.C.: V. H. Winston & Sons, 1973.

Osherson, D. N., & Markman, E. Language and the ability to evaluate contradictions and tautologies. *Cognition,* 1975, *3*(3) 213–226.

Otto, W., Barrett, J. C., & Koenke, K. Assessment of children's statements of the main idea in reading. In J. A. Figurel (Ed.), *Reading and realism. Proceedings of the International Reading Association,* 1969, *13,* 692–697.

Patterson, C. J., Massad, C. M., & Cosgrove, J. M. Children's referential communication: Components of plans for effective listening. *Developmental Psychology,* 1978, *14,* 401–406.

Piaget, J. *Judgment and reasoning in the child.* New York: Harcourt, 1928.

Reeves, J. W. *Thinking about thinking.* New York: George Braziller, 1965.

Robinson, F. P. *Effective study.* New York: Harper & Row, 1941.

Salatas, H., & Flavell, J. H. Behavioral and metamnemonic indicators of strategic behaviors under remember instructions in first grade. *Child Development,* 1976, *47,* 80–89.

Shatz, M. The relationship between cognitive processes and the development of communication skills. In B. Keasey (Ed.), *Nebraska Symposium on Motivation.* Lincoln: University of Nebraska Press, 1977.

Shatz, M., & Gelman, R. The development of communication skills: Modification in the speech of young children as a function of listener. *Monographs of the Society for Research in Child Development,* 1973, *38,* 1–37.

Smiley, S. S., Oakley, D. D., Worthen, D., Campione, J. C., & Brown, A. L. Recall of thematically relevant material by adolescent good and poor readers as a function of written versus oral presentation. *Journal of Educational Psychology,* 1977, *69*(4), 381–387.

Smirnov, A. A. *Problems of the psychology of memory.* New York: Plenum Press, 1973.

Tenney, Y. J. The child's conception of organization and recall. *Journal of Experimental Child Psychology,* 1975, *19,* 100–114.

Thomas, E. L. Movements of the eye. *Scientific American,* 1968, *219*(2), 88–95.

Vygotsky, L. S. *Thought and language.* Cambridge, Mass.: MIT Press, 1962.,

Wellman, H. M. Tip of the tongue and feeling of knowing experiences: A developmental study of memory monitoring. *Child Development,* 1977, *48,* 13–21.

Wellman, H. M., Ritter, R., & Flavell, J. H. Deliberate memory behavior in the delayed reactions of very young children. *Developmental Psychology,* 1975, *11,* 780–787.

Yarmey, A. D. I recognize your face, but I can't remember your name: Further evidence of the tip-of-the-tongue phenomenon. *Memory and Cognition,* 1973, *1,* 287–290.

20 Study Strategies and Adjunct Aids

Thomas H. Anderson
Center for the Study of Reading,
University of Illinois, Urbana-Champaign

Studying text materials is nominally different from other forms of reading in that it is strongly criterion oriented. That is, when studying, students process text with the expectation of learning something specific from it. Consequently, explicitness of the criteria affects how students study and how much they learn. For example, the student who has copies of previously used tests over a chapter of text should probably study quite differently from one who is told to study a chapter of text in preparation for a class discussion. Assuming that the students in these examples want to be adequately prepared for the criterion events, but not overly prepared, one can see that the preferred strategy for the first student is to read the text with the explicit purpose of finding answers to the test questions. The second student should probably study to determine the author's main ideas and how they relate to one another.

When students study, having only implicit criteria, they often generate their own study aids such as note taking, underlining, and outlining. Research on these activities typically shows that they are not very effective when compared to a read–reread strategy. On the other hand, when students have access to adjunct study aids that often make the criteria explicit, research shows their use to be facilitative. Research to support these conclusions in reviewed first in this chapter. Further in the chapter, a primitive model of the studying process is presented that helps to explain the differences in study processes and learning outcomes when criteria are either explicit or implicit.

In addition to the explicitness of the criteria, studying has a self-directed motivation feature. Although the process must be initiated and maintained by the student just as in other types of reading, the "study of text" does not have typically as many self-motivating, interesting characteristics as does "recreational reading." Consequently, one line of research in studying has been to uncover techniques that motivate students to study. Research on this activity is not included in this chapter; instead, the major thrust is to develop an appreciation of the underlying principles that seem to affect whether or not a student will be able to learn and remember certain criterion-related outcomes while he or she is processing text material.

STUDENT-GENERATED STUDY AIDS

Note Taking

Literature on note taking while reading prose is not extensive. More research has been done on note taking while listening to such things as lectures, movies, and demonstrations than has been done on note taking while reading. The former literature is not discussed here.

Arnold (1942) conducted a comprehensive "race horse" type study in which he experimentally compared the following four study techniques: repetitive reading that involved no writing; reading with underscoring and marginal notation; reading and outlining a topical listing of important items in their proper relationship; and reading that involved précis writing—a brief summary of the material studied.

It appears that Arnold did not use the most appropriate test statistic (the critical ratio) to make inferences about his results. I reanalyzed his data by computing a correlated t-statistic for each of the 72 paired comparisons (combinations formed by four study treatments, sophomore and freshmen students, immediate and delayed testing, and three series of materials). This was done based on the assumption that the correlation of an individual's test scores between any two treatement comparisons was .70, by dividing the critical ratio by the costant $\sqrt{1-(.70)}$. The significant mean differences were tallied in order to determine which technique was the winner.

Of the 36 immediate recall comparisons, repetitive reading had 13 significant advantages when paired with the other three techniques; underlining and précis writing had one advantage. With the delayed measures, repetitive reading had five advantages, underlining and précis writing had three advantages each, and outlining had none. Although it is often difficult to interpret the meaning of these multiple comparison kinds of studies, it seems apparent that repetitive reading is the winner in this case. It also seems that the more obtrusive study techniques such as outlining and précis writing are actually "detrimental" to a base-line repetitive reading strategy.

Kulhavy, Dyer, and Silver (1975) reported a significant difference among high school students who either took notes, underlined, or just read an 845-

word passage. Those students who took notes apparently did better. The data are confusing, however, because there were several hard-to-explain interactions between study techniques and types of criterion tests. The significant main effect due to notes is supported by only one of three note-taking treatment groups.

Hoon (1974) reported a study in which 30 college males in liberal arts curricula were assigned to study three passages using three different methods: reading, reading with underlining, and reading with note taking. After studying each passage, students were given a 2-minute review and then a multiple-choice quiz. The quiz scores showed no significant differences among the three treatments, even when read time (the time required to read a dummy passage), study time (time to study the three passages), and SAT verbal ability scores were used as covariates.

Dynes (1932) conducted a study using 134 students from two high schools in order to investigate the effect of two study methods. The read–reread method was compared to another method in which the students: (1) gave the material a rapid reading; (2) reread the material, underlined essential parts, took notes; (3) reviewed underlined portions and notes; (4) wrote a brief summary of the material read; and (5) recalled what had been read.

Students read passages from junior high school level social science texts. Two sets of passages of similar content, length, and word difficulty were prepared. Each student studied one set of materials using the read–reread method and the other set using the second study method. Although Dynes concluded that the differences obtained are statistically significant between the two study techniques, I used his data and computed others that are more appropriate. Even the comparison showing the largest difference between the two groups did not reach statistical significance. Based on the performance data and using more appropriate inference statistics than evidently were available to Dynes, I see no reasonable way to conclude that the two techniques are different.

Stordahl and Christensen (1956) reported that about 300 Air Force basic trainees were randomly assigned to study groups that applied one of their four study techniques—underlining, outlining, summarizing, and reading and rereading—to two different passages (about 6,400 words total) that were selected from Air Force materials. Comprehension of the materials was measured by an objective test, which was given to the trainees immediately after studying the materials and again 1 week later; a pretest, which was given 1 week prior to the experimental session, was used to control for previous knowledge of the subject studied. The study techniques were found to be equally effective, as measured by comprehension of the material immediately after study and as measured 1 week later.

In summary, only Kulhavy et al. (1975) have presented data to show that note taking is superior to a read-only condition. In three studies (Dynes, 1932;

Hoon, 1974; Stordahl & Christensen, 1965) note taking was found to be no different from the read-only condition. Finally, Arnold (1942) provided data to support the contention that note taking in conjunction with reading is detrimental when compared to a read-only condition.

Underlining

The strategy of underlining sections of prose material as a student reads has been investigated in several studies. In four studies discussed previously that compare reading with underlining to repetitive reading, three of them (Hoon, 1974; Kulhavey et al., 1975; Stordahl & Christensen, 1965) showed no significant difference between the techniques. In the Arnold (1942) study, repetitive reading was found to be a superior technique to the underlining technique. Clearly, there seems to be no consistent difference between the two techniques in these studies. Three additional studies reported later do not show consistent results either.

Two studies showing no difference between reading and reading with underlining were reported by Idstein and Jenkins (1972). In the first study, they used a two-factor design with underlining and repetitive reading as one factor and a 9-minute or 4½-minute review session as the second factor. College seniors read a 1200-word passage containing information about procedures of local government. After studying and reviewing, they took a 24-item completion test. Results of the two-way ANOVA showed only a main effect for review time.

In a second experiment, for a period of about 50 minutes, college seniors either read or read with underlining a 6000-word passage about educational and philosophical thought. At a second session 2 weeks later, they were allowed to review the original sources for 15 minutes, including any underlining, before taking a 31-item completion test. Again, there was no significant difference between the two groups.

Rickards and August (1975) investigated the effects of subject- and experimenter-generated underlining with college students. The results showed rather convincingly that an underlining treament causes students to process the material longer and to score higher on a recall test than they did on the read-only condition. Bear in mind, however, that the read-only treatment allowed students to *reread* only one page at a time. A complete reread of the passage is not possible. Therefore, we are left with no clear evidence that an underlining strategy is superior to the read–reread study technique.

Imaging, Paraphrasing, Outlining, and Elaborating Strategies

A common characteristic of these study techniques is that each requires a major intrusion into the reading process involved in study. Also, a significant amount of training is usually required to insure that students can actually perform the study aid.

Barton (1930) taught 96 high school students from two schools the fundamentals of outlining. The training session required many hours of in-class instruction and drill. The prime objective of the instruction was to teach the students to find main, subordinate, coordinate, and irrelevant points in each paragraph. The general processing strategy was: (1) skim the article to get the main division; (2) skim the article again to get main subdivisions of each main division; and (3) read carefully again to get facts under the proper divisions. Students applied the outlining strategy to subject matter contents of geography, American history, and ancient history. Test performance of those students who used the outlining strategy was significantly higher than test performance from a matched group that had a similar instructional program but did not include outline training. This is the most impressive study in the literature that demonstrates, with few reservations, the beneficial effects of any student-generated study aid.

Dansereau, McDonald, Long, Actkinson, Ellis, Collins, Williams, & Evans (1974) reported a study in which they trained college students to study short prose passages by: (1) paraphrasing—the student produces his summary of the passage in the form of paraphrases (2) imagery—the student is asked to draw or verbally describe the visual image he has created to capture the main idea of the material; and (3) questioning—the student generates and answers his own "high-level" questions after short segments of text. The three experimental groups were trained in the use of treatments and were tested for approximately 7½ hours. The control group was trained and tested for approximately 3¼ hours. All three treatment groups received general training in so-called retrieval strategies. The purpose of this 45-minute exercise was to assist students in retrieving systematically inaccessible material from memory. The control group did not receive this training. There was no significant difference among the three treatment groups and the control group on the 80-item objective test that was given after training. On an essay test that was given 5 days later, the mean test performance among the four groups was significantly different. The paraphrase and imagery groups had significantly higher means than did the control group, but they were not higher than the means of the question group.

Weinstein (1975) investigated the effects of a diversified elaboration skill training program on the learning and retention efficiency of ninth-grade subjects. A variety of skills, tasks, and materials that included sentence elaboration, imaginal elaboration, analogies, drawing implications, creating relationships, and paraphrasing was used. Stimulus materials were drawn from ninth-grade curriculum materials in science, history, English, foreign language, and vocational education.

Seventy-five ninth-grade students were randomly assigned to one of three groups: training–experiment, control, or posttest only. Experimental subjects participated in a series of five 1-hour elaboration skill training sessions that were administered at approximately 1-week intervals. The students were required to create a series of elaborators or mediational aids for each of 20 tasks. The control subjects were given the same training materials but received no training from the experimenter. A posttest-only group was not exposed to the stimulus materials but did participate in the posttesting sessions. The immediate and delayed posttests consisted of a variety of item formats and types, that is, reading comprehension, free recall and paired-associate and serial recall.

Results from the immediate posttest showed significant mean differences on the free recall and one of the paired-associate learning tasks. In each instance, the experimental group's performance surpassed the performance of the control and the posttest groups. The latter two groups did not significantly differ from each other. On the delayed posttest, a significant difference was obtained for the reading comprehension task and one of the serial learning tasks. Again, these differences favored the experimental group.

Perhaps the procedures and results of these studies are indices of the extent to which intervention must go in order for it to be consistently effective. However, for a student to have to paraphrase (Dansereau et al., 1974), outline Barton, 1930), or develop elaboration schemes (Weinstein, 1975) about any passage he or she wishes to study seems overly time consuming and inefficient from the student's point of view.

Student Questioning

The questioning technique requires that students *generate* questions about the prose they are studying. In one sense, this technique is similar to note taking in that a written record is made of an idea, but in an important sense it is different. The format of the recorded idea is that of a question. Robbins (1957) advocated the use of this technique in a how-to-study manual. He suggested that students generate a question about every idea that seemed important and might be on an upcoming test. However, he provided no data to support his contentions about its effectiveness.

Frase and Schwartz (1975) reported the results of two studies in which students were required to generate questions. In one study, high school students exchanged roles as question-generator and answerer on the first two 400-word sections and then each student read independently the third section. Similar procedures were used where 64 college freshmen read a 1200-word passage. They were instructed to write questions on a part of the text and to read without writing questions on another part. Immediately following the study session in both studies, the subjects wrote short answers to a 60-item test. These tests were scored by computing a subscore for targeted items (those test items about which study items had also been generated) and nontargeted items (those test items that had no corresponding study item).

In a recent investigation, Duell (1977) examined the effectiveness of asking subjects to generate test items while reading four 552-word passages describing the psychological processes of shaping, negative reinforcement, prompting, and overlearning. One experimental group received the four passages, a list of objectives, and instructions to write items to match the objectives. A second group was instructed to study the passages with a list of behavioral objectives. Control group students just took the criterion test. Two types of questions were used in the 31-item multiple choice posttest. There were lower level or recognition items that required the subjects to recognize an example of a psychological process copied from the text. The high-level or application items presented new examples of a process and asked subjects to identify the name of the process represented by the example. Posttest data revealed a significant advantage for the item-generating group. Writing questions for both low- and high-level objectives produces more learning than studying with objectives. To have students generate questions as a study aid has the potential of being an effective flexible technique. The findings of at least three studies are consistent, but how well the technique will hold up over a variety of study texts, purposes, and criteria remains to be documented.

ADJUNCT STUDY AIDS

Adjunct Questions

Research on adjunct questions investigates the effects on learning when people are asked questions about what they are reading. The direct effect of the adjunct questions occurs when the performance of students on criterion questions identical to those used in the adjunct form is superior to performance of students in a read-only condition. The indirect effect is supported when students who had adjunct question scored higher on new criterion questions, which were not used in the adjunct form, compared with the performance of students in the read-only condition.

Anderson and Biddle (1975) conclude that there is little doubt that the use of adjunct questions, in general, has a facilitative effect on learning from prose. When the questions are placed after the text, they have a significant facilitative effect on the repeated items *and* on the new items, showing significant direct and indirect effects. When adjunct questions appear before the text, they have a significant direct effect but a negative indirect effect. In addition, the closer the questions are to the information about which they ask, the higher the performance when those questions are repeated later. In fact, when questions are grouped together after even lengthy prose, such as the end of a chapter in a textbook, they can have a pronounced direct effect. When feedback on adjunct test item performance is given, there is typically better performance on repeated questions, a direct effect, and mixed results on the indirect effect. When students are required to provide an overt answer to the questions, there is a more consistent direct and indirect effect than when students are required to make only a covert response. However, there is evidence to support the notion that a covert response does have a facilitative effect.

When the adjunct questions are higher level questions, that is, they require the student to go beyond a surface meaning of the text in order to answer the question, they have significant direct and indirect effects. It seems that adjunct questions act primarily on the retrievability of the formation rather than on its manipulation or on the possible decisions that a student might make once that information is retrieved. In an extention of the Anderson-Biddle (1975) theories about the direct effects of adjunct questions, Andre and Sola (1976) presented evidence indicating that the direct effects of adjunct questions can be accounted for almost entirely by the levels of processing notion. That is, types of questions and the sequencing of questions in text can control the depth of cognitive processing *and* the likelihood of retrieval of information.

Even though the use of adjunct questions typically facilitates learning of prose discourse, the technique is not readily applicable as a study aid. For example, there is a rather predictable difference between the performance of students if the questions are given before rather than after students read the text. In addition, if students are given a choice of whether they want to see the questions before or after they read text, it is rather clear that they would choose to see them before they read. And yet, it is this before-reading-text condition that gives only a small direct effect and a negative indirect effect on criterion performance. So, the important issue—how can adjunct questions be administered to students in a natural study environment in such a way that they get good questions immediately after they have read a section of prose?

T. Anderson et al. (1974, 1975) reported studies in which a computer-assisted instruction system was used in a library setting to give reading assignments and adjunct questions to students who were studying introductory economics at the college level. When the students signed in at a terminal, they were given a reading assignment that took them 15-20 minutes to study. After reading the assignment, they reported back to the terminal and were administered a six- to ten-item quiz. If they did not answer at least 75% of the items correctly on the quiz, they were told to reread the material and were signed off the system. After rereading the material, they signed onto the terminal again and retook the quiz. The performance of students who had their study managed by the computer system was compared with a group who read on their own. In each of three semesters, those students who had a more systematic approach to the study of text did significantly better on a final exam, which did not include any of the items used in the adjunct form, than did a control group. Although our results were not overwhelming in that the performance of the study-managed group was only 5-10% higher on the final exam than the control group, we did demonstrate with a field test that adjunct questions could make a difference.

This technique will never be used widely, primarily because computer systems of the required type are not generally available. Also, developing good questions that can serve as adjunct questions is a very difficult task for text writers, publishers, and editors. It is true that many texts have accompanying workbooks or study guides in which questions are included. However, our informal investigation of several study guides as we were preparing questions for the economics course lead us to believe that the preparation of those questions was not done very systematically. Rules for generating the questions were not apparent, and the questions were not field tested with students so that ambiguities and other distractors can be removed. My point is that good item pools are difficult to generate and it is improbable that authors and publishing companies would take steps to insure that the pool be satisfactory for adjunct purposes.

Advance Organizers

The notion of advance organizers was first labeled and investigated by Ausubel and his colleagues (Ausubel, 1960; Ausubel & Fitzgerald, 1961, 1962; Ausubel & Youssef, 1963). Ausubel's theory of meaningful verbal learning predicts that learning text material can be facilitated by insuring that students have an existing cognitive structure of the to-be-learned material before they actually begin to process it.

The so-called advance organizers (AO) serve the function of building a cognitive structure of scaffolding. Reading the instructional material adds lower ordered information to the scaffold. AO are not the same as typical introductory paragraphs or summaries that are found in many text chapters, but they are at a higher level of abstraction and generality.

In order to test the effects of AOs, ordinarily two groups of students are prepared to study a section of prose by giving one group an AO to read while the other group is given a passage that is similar in length to the AO but in which the content is not closely related to the instructional passage. After reading these preparatory materials, both groups study the instructional passage and take a posttest, and, perhaps, a delayed posttest.

How facilitative to learning are AOs? In a recent review based on 32 studies, Barnes and Clawson (1975) concluded that the efficacy of advance organizers has not been established, because only 12 of the studies reported a facilitative effect. They went on to say that when considering length of study, ability level of subjects, grade level of subjects, type of organizer, and cognitive level of the learning task, no clear pattern of effects emerged.

How important is it that the facilitative effects of AOs on learning outcomes be demonstrated? It is only slightly important. We do not need AO research to demonstrate the notion that the knowledge a student brings into a study session will have an effect on what he learns. Other more systematic lines of research reported elsewhere in this book are doing a better job of researching that notion. It seems, as well, to be difficult to pin down an operational definition of an AO. The probability seems rather low that writers of prose will ever have enough guidance to make AOs an integral part of texts.

Text Embellishments

Early experimental work has shown that isolating an item to be learned against a crowded or homogeneous background facilitates the learning of that item (Wallace, 1965). This notion has been investigated in at least four experiments related to studying in which sections of prose have been underlined or otherwise highlighted in order to make them more salient.

In the Rickards and August (1975) study, described previously, one of the groups received a passage in which each of the 16 paragraphs had the topic sentence underlined. Another group received passages in which the least important sentence in each paragraph was underlined. The amount recalled by these two groups did not differ, nor did they differ from the control group that read an unmarked version.

Hershberger (1964) assessed the effects of highlighting (capitalizing, red ink, and underlining) essential lesson content for both discursively and tersely written texts. One hundred sixty pretested fifth-grade students read lessons on history and science and took immediate and delayed posttests on each topic. An analysis of gain scores from essential concepts shows that highlighting fails to increase learning of either type of content. On the nonessential content, the subjects who read the noncued passages scored higher than did those who read the cued passages.

Two studies are reported that give strong support for the highlighting strategy. A study by Crouse and Idstein (1972) showed that undergraduate students who read an underlined version of a 6000-word passage about educational and philosophical thought scored significantly higher than students who read a noncued version of the same passage. Students were told: (1) to read the material as though they were studying for a test; (2) that the underlined material contained answers to questions they would be asked later; and (3) that they should concentrate on the underlined material. They were given as much time as they needed to write answers to the 30-item short-answered test.

The other study that showed support for the highlighting strategy is reported by Cashen and Leicht (1970). They gave 40 undergraduate students mimeographed copies of three *Scientific American* reprints that dealt with course-related material, and they were told to read the reprints in preparation for a class examination. For 20 students, five statements, spread evenly throughout each reprint, were underlined in red. Multiple-choice examinations included one question about each of the underlined statements and one from a statement adjacent to it. Results show that the group that studied from underlined passages scored significantly higher on questions that were based on the cued statements as well as on the questions that were based on adjacent statements.

In summary, the two studies that support the hypothesis that highlighted text facilitates learning were simple, straightforward experiments with college students. The students were told by direct statements to study and learn the highlighted material because they would be asked questions about that material on a test. Instructions were not as direct in the other two studies. It seems reasonable to suspect, then, that the underlining treatment would be more effective when the ratio of cued passage to uncued passage is low. For instance, in the Rickards and August (1975) study that failed to find an effect, 16 sentences were underlined in 16 paragraphs, whereas in the Cashen and Leicht (1970) study, 15 statements were underlined for three reprint articles of approximately 15,000 words. It is not surprising, then, that when students know they will be tested over a long piece of prose and that the underlined sections will be tested, they will carefully study and learn the highlighted sections.

Instructional Objectives

Instructional objectives are statements about the nature of the criterion task and the scope of the content to be learned while studying text. In studies in which the effects of objectives are investigated, students are asked to read the objectives before they begin to study. Following the study session, they are tested on the content mentioned in the objectives (direct effect) as well as on the content that is not mentioned in the objectives (indirect effect). Studies by Rothkopf and Kaplan (1972), Kaplan and Rothkopf (1974), and Kaplan (1976) indicate that it is rather difficult to obtain a direct effect and that it is almost impossible to obtain an indirect effect. In addition, the direct effect is strongest when the objectives are specific rather than broad.

Merrill (1971) reported that the use of objectives reduced the latency of responding to test items on a computer-assisted instructional task, but the stronger effects of "rules" tended to overpower the effects of objectives. Rules were more informative than were the objectives because they related the general case of how corresponding objectives could be explained. In addition, Duell (1974) showed that the use of instructional objectives during study produces greater learning only if the objectives direct students to learn information that they would not ordinarily classify as important or likely to be tested. At least four studies (Cook, 1970; Jenkins & Deno, 1971; Oswald, 1970; Peterson, 1971) failed to find facilitative effects when using objectives.

TOWARD A MODEL OF STUDYING

As my colleagues and I tried to impose meaning on the just-mentioned findings, we noted quickly the need for a model or, preferably, a theory of studying. Toward this end, we supplemented our literature search with a questionnaire inquiry into how students naturally study.

Approximately 400 questionnaires were sent to students who were currently engaged in correspondence study for undergraduate credit at the University of Illinois. Responses from an open-ended question about how they studied were analyzed into strategy categories. The most preferred categories were: (1) read, (2) reread, (3) underline, (4) review, and (5) take notes; other strategies less frequently mentioned were: (6) outline; (7) reflect, and (8) skim the chapter; and among the techniques that very few students mentioned were: (9) self test, (10) summarize, and (11) work practice problems.

The qualitative difference is great between strategies that students report using and those that the "experts" advocate using. In general, students most often report a read-reread format with some underlining and note taking. Experts suggest a series of activities that typically requires more from a student than even careful attention to the printed message. For example, Robinson (1970), Thomas and Robinson (1972), and Pauk (1962) discuss the SQ3R method of effective study (and several modifications of it), which suggests that the student (1) engage in survey and questioning activities prior to reading and (2) recitation, reflections, and review activities after reading.

We saw the need for a methodology that would provide a fine-grained monitoring of student studying, especially the reading phase, and began to develop and evaluate a computer monitoring system. Utilizing the PLATO IV CBE system at the University of Illinois, we have developed programs that present text in a controlled fashion and allow for the detailed collection of study-behavior data while retaining some resemblance of studying from printed text. Currently, we present controlled amounts of text on the computer screen according to student requests and keep detailed time and sequence data of students' movement through the text.

Data collected from students in a recent study seem to support the fact that "typical" types of study aids (notes, surveying, and highlighting) do not have a major facilitative effect on learning from extended prose. There is some evidence that these types of treatments can affect the patterns of study, but the consequent changes in achievement appear to be subtle. We know that these treatments are neither necessary nor suficient for successful learning from prose, but for some reason many students feel good about having these options available and using them.

Before continuing with the computer monitoring technology, it was obvious that we needed a better model of the processes in which students engage than the read-reread-take notes-underline model. Consequently, we began to observe and interview graduate students as they engaged in serious study. We recognized that this technique would intrude and possibly disrupt the study process but it seemed to be the only way to get a handle on many of the covert processes. To this date, we have collected interview data from eight students. Our most heavily constricted technique required the student to read aloud, to tell what he or she thought each paragraph and title were going to be about before reading in depth, to summarize them after reading, and to relate any other thoughts concerning the study session as they occurred. Our most lenient technique required the student to study "normally" and to place a question mark beside any section of text that was confusing, that caused the student to slow down or pause reading, or that caused the student to look ahead to or back at sections of the text. After studying the test, students were given a test over the material, and the nature of their question marks was discussed in a posttest interrogation.

The following observations and conclusions are the results of those interviews:

1. The first technique just discussed was so highly interactive that it seemed to become a study strategy itself, that is, the student seemed to learn more from the interview than from the text.
2. In a poststudy interview, students could discuss in detail the nature of the question marks that they entered on the text while studying. Consequently, we did not have to interrupt study time by asking for students' reports.
3. Students have a rather well-established study plan that is not easily modified by varying the task demands or types of study materials in the session.
4. Students can impose temporary meanings on difficult or novel words or phrases that they encounter in a text, with the intention to verify the meaning later, *if important*, or to do nothing about it if there is no good reason to. In general, students employed extremely sophisticated strategies concerning the semantic importance of the words and texts that they encountered. Words used in footnotes or words whose meanings were not essential to understanding the gist of a sentence had a high probability of being considered nonessential words. Meanings of these words were seldom verified with a dictionary or glossary.

5. Students have trouble "remembering" to write the question marks when they are confused. They reported that having to place the question mark interfered with studying.
6. Students exhibited some and reported many "feeling" types of behaviors, that is, smiles, frowns, tenseness, perspiration, and a general emotional fatigue after the study.

In conclusion, we see study as a series of very sophisticated cognitive and emotional processes that is difficult to monitor and is generally below a level of awareness to the student. Occasionally, these processes reach an awareness level in the form of a so-called clicks of comprehension or a clunk of comprehension failure. Clicks of comprehension are often accompanied by feelings of well being, and clunks of comprehension failure are accompanied by feelings of tenseness or mild anxiety.

An Instructional Model of Studying Text

Presented next is a general model of studying that is consistent with many of our observations and is helpful in describing and operationalizing some of the constructs associated with the studying process. At the core of this model is the assumption that the study of text is a type of instruction and consequently should have the same components, or at least should have most of the components, as other types of instruction. Specifically, this means that studying is composed of many episodes that include: (1) information presentation; (2) a response-demand event; (3) student responding; (4) response judging and feedback; and (5) rules about what to do next. The episode may be a very long one, such as a 2-hour lecture followed by a quiz that is scored and returned to the student; or it may be a much shorter episode, as represented by a frame in the programmed instruction text. In a typical programmed instruction text, a short chunk of information is presented, a question is asked, and the student provides an answer that can be compared with a "preferred answer" printed elsewhere in the text. In addition to right-wrong feedback, corrective feedback and directives about what do do next are sometimes provided.

It is my proposal, then, that studying be considered a form of instruction. For instruction to proceed, however, students must insure that the necessary components of an instructional episode do indeed happen. In other words, students must not only read the text, they must also create response demand events (usually questions), judge the adequacy of their responses, devise corrective feedback procedures and, finally, determine what to do next. The idea of students monitoring and deciding which type of cognitive behavior to implement, as well as maintaining the behavior itself, is a fascinating one. This idea is developed also by Ann Brown, Chapter 19, this volume. In my judgement, it is the combination of metacognitive and cognitive behaviors that makes studying (self-directed instruction) a unique and very complex type of instruction. Some forms of instruction such as teacher-directed instruction or computer-managed instruction (CMI) use other techniques as substitutes for the metacognitive aspects of instruction. For example, a student engaged in traditional CMI does not have to ask very often the question "do I know if I understand this material". The computer informs the student during each episode whether or not he or she understands the material.

In addition, it is important to think about studying as a three-stage process that consists of prereading, reading, and postreading activities. In the *prereading stage,* students should engage in activities such as browsing, skimming, and surveying the text; reading advance organizers, objectives, and notes; reviewing previous tests or, perhaps, reading (or generating) questions that may be answered by reading the text. In this prereading stage, students make several decisions that have important implications for later processing. One decision is related to the purpose(s) for studying the particular assignment and the expectations about criterion-related behaviors. The student should answer these questions: "Why am I studying this?" and "What will I be asked to do with the knowledge after acquiring it?" Another decision is related to bookkeeping. "Should I use a record-keeping system?" "For what purposes will I use it?" "How assessible will the original source be later?" It seems that most students rely heavily on a set of default answers to most of these questions and seldom do they change their decisions, except in the most unusual circumstances. Consequently, it is difficult to affect systematic changes in study behavior by manipulating prereading variables.

The student engages in a sequence of instructional episodes in the *during-reading stage* of studying. In this sequence, the reading of materials can be interrupted by two sorts of mechanisms: (1) a student-imposed response-demand event (an "understanding question"); and (2) an automated monitoring mechanism (AMM) that renders the clicks of comprehension and clunks of comprehension failure. The student has more control over the understanding question and more needs to be said of its use.

The nature of the understanding question is often a function of the explicitness of the study criteria. If the criteria are explicit, they can and should be translated into understanding questions and applied where appropriate within the instructional episodes. When the criteria are implicit, there are two general characteristics of the understanding question that can be described.

First, it is safe that the understanding question should be asked often to insure high comprehension levels. Research on programmed instruction and adjunct questions with prose supports the idea that asking frequent questions after reading small chunks of prose facilitates learning. At what point in the prose should the question be inserted? It is difficult to say for sure, but the natural places to pause in written discourse are at the standard prose delimiters such as periods, paragraphs, block or subsection endings, and at the text highlights such as underlinings, italics, capitalized words, and so on.

Second, the understanding question also should take on different forms depending on the type of delimiter. For example, following a sentence in the middle of a paragraph, the student might ask: "Are there any new words in that sentence?" (vocabulary check). "Does the sentence make sense?" (cause-effect check). On the other hand, at the end of a 10-paragraph block, the student might ask: "What was the block about?" (check on main point). "What were the important facts?" (check on details supporting main point). "Have I read something similar to this before?" (a comparison of newly-acquired knowledge with old knowledge). It seems that the understanding question requires deeper levels of cognitive processing as it progresses from questions about words and sentences to those about blocks of materials and entire passages. This concept, if true, suggests that rules can be applied to the process of generating appropriate understanding questions.

Making the decision that one understands prose that he or she has just read is at best difficult. Both the task demands of the study session and the student's content knowledge are critical variables in asking the question and making the decision that he or she can answer it. After making the decision, however, rules about what to do next must be applied.

The following outline is a tentative theory of how skilled readers deal with this what-to-do-next question. These conditional statements are the consequence of some information probing into what students do when they fail to comprehend.

1. If a reader reads something that he or she does not understand, the reader may decide to take some strategic action immediately or may store the information in memory as a pending question.
2. If the reader stores it as a pending question, he or she may formulate a possible meaning (usually one) that is stored as a tentative hypothesis.
3. If the reader forms a pending question, he or she usually continues to read.
4. If a triggering event occurs after the reader forms the pending question (i.e., too many pending questions or repetitions of the same pending question), the reader may take some strategic action.
5. If the reader takes some strategic action, he or she may:
   a. *reread* some portion of the text in order to collect more information that will either answer a pending question or form a tentative hypothesis that is related to a pending question;

     b. *jump ahead* in the text to see if there are headings or paragraphs that refer to the pending question and that might answer the pending question;

     c. *consult* an outside source (e.g., dictionary, gloassary, encyclopedia, expert) for an answer to some pending question;

     d. make a *written record* of a pending question;

     e. *think/reflect* about the pending question and related information that the reader has in memory;

     f. *quit* reading the text.

6. If the strategic action is successful, the reader usually continues to read from the point at which the comprehension failure was last encountered.

7. If the strategic action is not successful, the reader usually continues to read by taking some other strategic action.

Notice that this theory accounts for the fact that students do encounter material they do not understand well, and they *know* they do not understand it well, but they may choose to continue processing without taking corrective action. The skill of knowing when and how to take corrective action is an extremely important one in this model and one that hopefully can be taught.

The final stage, *postreading*, seems to be one in which strategies to improve learning are employed. When the study criteria are explicit, it makes the most sense for the student to engage in activities that are as close in time, format, and content coverage to the criteria as possible. In other words, if one knows the questions that are going to be asked on a test, then one should practice answering those questions just before taking the test.

In what activities should the student engage when the criteria are implicit? This is an area in which there is not much solid evidence. In some sense, any of the organizational (outlines, mnemonics), translational (paraphrases, generate question), and/or repetitional (recitation, rehearsal) schemes helps the student remember what has been read. Frequently, however, they burden the student with unnecessary busy work and provide help in gaining mastery of tasks that are potentially unrelated to the criteria. When the criteria are implicit, then, it seems that a student could best spend time webbing the newly acquired main point information into his or her own knowledge structure. One way of doing this is for the student to think about and write down new examples and applications of the main points. The exercise potentially connects related bodies of information and gives the student a larger pool of knowledge to draw from later.

DISCUSSION

In summary, this review of study aids indicates that the systematic use of good adjunct questions is the most effective one. An explanation of this is that adjunct questions encourage students (1) to pause frequently while reading; and (2) to locate an appropriate answer to an "understanding question" that probably is closely related to the study criteria. The use of student-generated questions also seems to be an effective aid, for the same reasons as those given for adjunct questions. One, also, has to be impressed with the effects of the elaboration and outlining techniques when applied over an extended period of time.

Except under extreme conditions, the general failure of advance organizers, objectives, and text embellishments to show consistent facilitative effects seems to be related to the fact that these aids typically do not affect the processing of students during the reading stage or give the student much information about the study criteria. The aids are thought to be only weak factors, among strong ones, when students are deciding how and when to handle the "understanding question." The selection of a recordkeeping system, such as marginal notes, underlinings, and précis notes, to use while studying does not seem to be an important variable during studying.

It is important to note that only one study in this chapter used subjects in the age range 9-14 years. The reason for this exclusion is not known, but it probably is related to a notion held by many that studying is a reading behavior that is characteristic of only mature, adult learners. In fact, Bormuth (1975) judges "study skills" to be the seventh and final category in a taxonomy of literacy skills that begins with "decoding."

Promising variables include: types of questions students can generate; types of answers students can provide; methods that students use to make decisions about the appropriateness of their answers; and the ways students make decisions about what to do next when they fail to comprehend. Also, new research efforts are needed that investigate whether or not students in the 9-14 year age range can be taught the more rigorous study skills such as outlining. In addition, assuming that students can be taught these skills, it is quite clear that students of any age are not going to use these techniques very extensively due to the time required to implement them. To get around this time problem, students need to be taught how to focus their studying activities so that they only outline, for example, text content that has the greatest chance of being tested later. The stage is set, then, for this line of research in that curriculum materials designed to teach many of these skills can be found currently in the most frequently used reading curriculum packages. Whether or not teachers choose to use these materials, and whether students can learn to implement these skills in the content areas or not are questions that beg for answers, even in advance of the crucial question concerning whether knowing and using them will help students become better students.

ACKNOWLEDGMENTS

Financial support for this research came primarily from the Advanced Research Projects Agency under Contract No. N00123-77-C-0622 and the National Institute of Education under Contract No. US-NIE-C-400-76-0116.

REFERENCES

Anderson, R. C., & Biddle, W. B. On asking people questions about what they are reading. In G. Bower (Ed.), *Psychology of learning and motivation* (Vol. 9). New York: Academic Press, 1975.

Anderson, T. H., Anderson, R. C., Alessi, S. M., Dalgaard, B. R., Paden, D. W., Biddle, W. B., Surber, J. R., & Smoth, H. R. A multifaceted computer based course management systems. *Proceedings of the Second World Conference on Computers in Education.* Amsterdam: North-Holland, 1975.

Anderson, T. H., Anderson, R. C., Dalgaard, B. R., Paden, D. W., Biddle, W. B., Surber, J. R., & Alessi, S. M. An experimental evaluation of a computer based study management system. *Educational Psychologist,* 1974, *11,* 184-190.

Andre, T., & Sola, J. Imagery, verbatim and paraphrased questions, and retention of meaningful sentences. *Journal of Educational Psychology,* 1976, *68*(6), 661-669.

Arnold, H. F. The comparative effectiveness of certain study techniques in the field of history. *Journal of Educational Psychology,* 1942, *33*(5), 449-457.

Ausubel, D. P. The use of advance organizers in the learning and retention of meaningful verbal material. *Journal of Educational Psychology,* 1960, *51,* 267-272.

Ausubel, D. P., & Fitzgerald, D. The role of discriminability in meaningful parallel learning and retention. *Journal of Educational Psychology,* 1961, *52,* 266-274.

Ausubel, D. P., & Fitzgerald, D. Organizer, general background, and antecedent learning variables in sequential verbal learning. *Journal of Educational Psychology,* 1962, *53,* 243-249.

Ausubel, D. P., & Youssef, M. The role of discriminability in meaningful parallel learning. *Journal of Educational Psychology,* 1963, *54,* 331-336.

Barnes, B. R., & Clawson, E. U. Do advance organizers facilitate learning? Recommendations for further research based on an analysis of 32 studies. *Review of Educational Research,* 1975, *45*(4), 637-659.

Barton, W. A., Jr. *Outlining as a study procedure.* New York: Columbia University Bureau of Publications, 1930.

Bormuth, J. R. Reading literacy: Its definition and assessment. In J. B. Carroll and J. S. Chall (Eds.), *Toward a literate society.* New York: McGraw-Hill, 1975.

Cashen, V. M., & Leicht, K. L. Role of the isolation effect in a formal educational setting. *Journal of Educational Psychology,* 1970, *61,*(6), 484-486.

Cook, J. M. *Behavioral objectives and rate of forgetting.* Paper read at the annual convention of the American Educational Research Association, Minneapolis, 1970.

Crouse, J. H., & Idstein, P. Effects of encoding cues on prose learning. *Journal of Educational Psychology,* 1972, *63*(4), 309-313.

Dansereau, D. G., McDonald, B. A., Long, G. L., Actkinson, T. R., Ellis, A. M., Collins, K. W., Williams, S., & Evans, S. H. *The development and assessment of an effective learning strategy training program* (Final Tech. Rep. 3). Texas Christian University, Fort Worth, 1974.

Duell, O, K. Effect of type of objective level of test questions, and the judged importance of tested materials upon post test performance. *Journal of Educational Psychology*, 1974, 66(2), 225-232.

Duell, O. K. *Overt and covert use of objectives of different levels.* Paper presented at the annual meeting of the American Educational Research Association Convention, New York, 1977.

Dynes, J. J. Comparison of two methods of studying history. *Journal of Experimental Education*, 1932, 1, 42-45.

Frase, L. T., & Schwartz, B. J. Effect of question production and answering in prose recall. *Journal of Educational Psychology*, 1975, 67(5), 628-635.

Hershberger, W. Self-evaluational responding and typographical cueing: Techniques for programming self-instructional reading materials. *Journal of Educational Psychology*, 1964, 55(5), 288-296.

Hoon, P. W. Efficacy of three common study methods. *Psychological Reports*, 1974, 35(3), 1057-1058.

Idstein, P., & Jenkins, J. Underlining versus repetitive reading, *Journal of Educational Research*, 1972, 65, 321-323.

Jenkins, J. R., & Deno, S. L. Influence of knowledge and type of objectives on subject-matter learning. *Journal of Educational Psychology*, 1971, 62, 67-70.

Kaplan, R. Effect of experience and subjects' use of directions upon learning from prose. *Journal of Educational Psychology*, 1976, 68, 717-724.

Kaplan, R., & Rothkopf, E. Z. Instructional objectives as directions to learners: Effect of passage length and amount of objective-relevant content. *Journal of Educational Psychology*, 1974, 66, 448-456.

Kulhavy, R. W., Dyer, J. W., & Silver, L. The effects of notetaking and test expectancy on the learning of text material. *Journal of Educational Research*, 1975, 68, 363-365.

Merrill, P. F. *The effects of the availability of objectives and/or rules on the learning process.* Paper presented at the annual convention of the American Educational Research Association, New York, 1971.

Oswald, J. M. *Instructor specified instructional objectives and achievement of social studies knowledge and comprehension.* Unpublished doctoral dissertation, Stanford University, 1970.

Pauk, W. *How to study in college.* Boston: Houghton-Mifflin, 1962.

Peterson, J. C. *Effect of advanced organizer, a post organizer, or knowledge of a behavioral objective on achievement and retention of a mathematical concept.* Paper read at the annual convention of the American Educational Research Association, New York, 1971.

Rickards, J. P., & August, G. J. Generative underlining strategies in prose recall. *Journal of Educational Psychology*, 1975, 67(6), 860-865.

Robbins, P. A. *How to make better grades: A course in systematic studying.* Los Angeles: Par Publishing Co., 1957.

Robinson, F. P. *Effective study.* New York: Harper & Row, 1941, 1970.

Rothkopf, E. Z., & Kaplan, R. Exploration of the effect of density and specificity of instructional objectives on learning from text. *Journal of Educational Psychology*, 1972, 63, 295-302.

Stordahl, K. E., & Christensen C. M. The effect of study techniques on comprehension and retention. *Journal of Educational Research*. 1956, 49(8), 561-570.

Thomas, E. L., & Robinson, H. A. *Improving reading in every class: A sourcebook for teachers.* Boston: Allyn & Bacon, 1972.

Wallace, W. P. Review of the historical, empirical and theoretical status of the von Restorff phenomenon. *Psychological Bulletin*, 1965, 65(6), 410-424.

Weinstein, C. E. *Learning of elaboration strategies.* Doctoral dissertation, University of Texas at Austin, 1975. (Dissertation Abstracts International, 1976, 2725A).

21

The Role of Illustrations
in Reading Comprehension

Diane Lemonnier Schallert
The University of Texas, Austin
  and
Center for the Study of Reading

When I was in high school, one of the boys in my English class was given a detention assignment to write a 1000-word essay on why the young should respect their elders. Although habitually late on his homework and reports, Bob handed in his assignment the very next day. On the first page, he had printed the title and his name. On the second page, he had pasted a large picture of an old man and a young boy steering a sailboat through a busy harbor. While the boy held the forward end of the tiller and looked out proudly through the maze of masts ahead of them, the old man, smiling tenderly at the boy, retained full control of the boat with his hand firmly grasping the rear of the tiller. On the third and last page of the folder, Bob had printed the words "A picture is worth a thousand words." A very old and trite trick you might say. Nevertheless, our teacher gave Bob a satisfactory mark for the assignment. Perhaps, he felt that the picture that Bob had chosen was indeed worth any number of words in representing the theme of the special relationship between the old and young in a society. I feel certain that had the picture not been so absolutely appropriate, my classmate would have found himself in deeper trouble still.

The purpose of this review is to delineate when it is that a picture is worth a thousand words. In investigating the role of illustrations in reading comprehension, reviewers and researchers alike have come up with seemingly contradictory conclusions. Some have found that pictures facilitate the comprehension and retention of text whereas others have found that pictures either make no difference or actually interfere with reading. Throughout this chapter, I will examine the evidence for and against pictures with the purpose of determining why it is and when it is that pictures have an effect on comprehension.

Before beginning this analysis, however, I would like to mention one dichotomy of reading tasks that seems to make an important difference in how illustrations are used and what effect they can have. If one is concentrating on teaching how to read, in the sense of teaching both how printed symbols can be decoded and how meaning can be constructed from a particular set of words, then the question becomes one of determining whether pictures help the reader to perform either of these tasks. On the other hand, if one is interested in imparting new information to the reader, in the sense of conveying facts, opinions, or viewpoints of which the reader is not yet aware, then the question changes to that of determining whether pictures contribute to understanding the total message of the text. In the first case, pictures are accessory to the words and they can be tested for their value as adjunct aids in learning to deal with print. In the second case, the focus of interest shifts to the sum total of the information being conveyed by an author, whether through words or pictures or through an interaction between the two. Here, illustrations can be analyzed to determine whether they represent information that is or is not also represented in the text. The distinction often made between learning-to-read and learning-from-reading correlates at least roughly with my categories of the uses of illustrations.

One assumption that underlies the analysis of the second reading situation just described, if not the first as well, is that information can be derived from, and therefore in some way "exists" in, the text and pictures. At first glance, this assumption seems inimical to the constructivist position shared by most writers in this volume. It is a currently widespread belief that the meaning of a text is not inherent but is the result of constructive processes that a reader brings to bear on the message (Anderson, Reynolds, Schallert, & Goetz, 1977; Bransford & Johnson, 1972; Brown, 1976; Pichert & Anderson, 1977; Schallert, 1976; Spiro, 1977; Sulin & Dooling, 1974). Constructive processes in dealing with pictures have also been demonstrated. People exhibit strong tendencies to interpret and remember pictures and visual patterns in terms of their existing knowledge (Baggett, 1975; Franks & Bransford, 1971). However, there is still a sense in which pictures and print "have" information. The constructivist position emphasizes the importance of the *interaction* between the reader and the text. It would make no more sense to ignore the contribution of the print and pictures than to ignore the knowledge and interests of the readers in determining how well a text has been understood. Particularly in the case of expository prose, prose designed to explain and elucidate a particular topic, the writer's job is to use the right words in the right way to constrain the readers' interpretive and constructive processes so that they will understand what the author intends. In the sense that pictures and words have been chosen by an author to convey a particular message, it is not unreasonable to talk about their information content.

The following discussion begins with a brief survey of the work that has demonstrated that illustrations are unhelpful, and sometimes actually harmful, in learning to decode and to comprehend print. Most of the tasks in experiments that fall in this category are of the learning-to-read variety. Most of this work has been reviewed in the past (Concannon, 1975; Samuels, 1970). Whether illustrations really prove to be nonfacilitative even in such reading situations is challenged in the next section. Then the discussion turns to an examination of the conditions under which illustrations have been found beneficial. Before summarizing the results of my analysis of these conditions, I review briefly how researchers have compared imagery, an internal process, with illustration, an external representation, in order to account for the effectiveness of pictures in comprehension.

THE CASE AGAINST PICTURES

The most convincing evidence against the use of illustrations in children's texts has been marshaled by Samuels. In his experimental work (e.g., Samuels, 1967), Samuels has concentrated on one aspect of learning to read, that of learning the names of words when they appear in isolation. His basic paradigm involves training trials in which some of the children see words in the context of either illustrations, sentences, or both, and some children learn the words without any context. Test trials consist of asking the children to read aloud the words appearing in isolation. His results indicate that pictures interfere with the acquisition of a sight vocabulary, a finding that has been replicated in other experiments that have used similar procedures and materials (Braun, 1969; Harris, 1967; Harzen, Lee, & Miles, 1976; Singer, Samuels, & Spiroff, 1973–1974). In accounting for these findings, Samuels has proposed that when there is more than one cue to a particular response, as, for example, when a picture appears with a printed label, readers will focus their attention on the cue that helps them produce the response with the least effort. Because pictures already can reliably elicit an appropriate verbal response, they interfere with the beginning reader's ability to concentrate on and learn to discriminate properly the printed stimuli.

As for the contribution of pictures to reading comprehension, Samuels (1970) is not any more optimistic. For example, he reports studies by Miller (1938) and Weintraub (1960), who used published basal readers for materials and adapted them only to the extent of removing illustrations for some of their subjects. Miller found that there were no differences in performance on comprehension questions between children in the picture group and children in the no-picture group. Weintraub reported that second-graders answered more comprehension questions correctly from the nonillustrated versions than from the illustrated versions. This effect held true only for a group of children identified as poor readers. For good readers, pictures did not seem to add or to detract from the comprehensibility of a story. Using expository selections dealing with health and history topics, Vernon (1953, 1954) tested the comprehension of students ranging in age from 11 to 19 years. She found that there was no general facilitation of learning of the text attributable to either pictures or graphs. She did find, however, that certain key points were remembered better if illustrated. Finally, Koenke (1968) presented third- and sixth-grade students with a passage that dealt with the many different places in which birds build their nests. He used pictures that depicted specific types of birds building their nests in species-specific places. Koenke found no difference in the ability to state the main idea between children reading illustrated versions and children reading nonillustrated versions of the story. However, it must be pointed out that the scoring scheme that Koenke used penalized children who added any specific detail or gave unnecessary information. Thus, we have no way of knowing whether the picture group produced more main-idea statements than the no-picture group, granted that these may have been "contaminated" by specific non-main-idea information.[1]

Based on studies such as those by Miller (1938), Weintraub (1960), Vernon (1953, 1954) and Koenke (1968), Samuels concluded that pictures have no demonstrated positive effect on reading comprehension. In a more recent review, Concannon (1975) reiterated this viewpoint.

THE CASE AGAINST
THE CASE AGAINST PICTURES

Samuels' conclusions have not gone unchallenged. A telling, although indirect, argument against him is the number of reports, most of them published since 1970, that have revealed significant positive effects for illustrations in text. I review these in the section following this one. However, a more direct challenge of Samuels has been reported by Denburg (1976–1977) and needs to be mentioned first. Denburg defined reading as the ability to read aloud a word when it appeared in context. She was also interested in testing the children's ability to read words in isolation, Samuels' basic reading task. First-graders were first tested to establish that they could not yet read the test words. Sentences were then constructed with two test words per sentence and appeared in one of four picture conditions: a full picture depicting both words, a partial picture depicting only the actor noun, a partial picture of only the object noun, and a no picture condition. The children read aloud the sentences and then the test words in isolation. Results indicated that more words were read correctly if they were also represented by a picture and

---

[1] I thank Barbara Rea for these observations, set forth in an unpublished paper and made available to me in March, 1977.

that a strong facilitative effect on the words *not* illustrated was shown in the partial picture conditions. Moreover, contrary to results of Samuels (1967) and of Singer et al. (1973–1974), more actor nouns were identified in isolation if they had been illustrated and, for both actor and object nouns, the worst performance was obtained in the no-picture condition. In explaining the discrepancy between her results and those of Singer et al. (1973–1974), Denburg pointed out that in Samuels' paradigm there is an emphasis on speed and efficiency and the word is said aloud to the child during acquisition. Such feedback, being more efficient than "reading" a picture, obviates the need for contextual information. When a picture *is* present in such a situation, it provides superfluous information and its true effectiveness cannot be tested. Denburg concluded that carefully designed illustrations that do not give irrelevant extra information can help beginning readers use the limited knowledge of print that they bring to the reading situation.

Denburg's point, that pictures may be helpful in a decoding task if they are designed to carry clear and precise information, deserves to be elaborated and extended. One characteristic of the illustrations used in the studies reviewed by Samuels is that they were not meant to convey new information. In fact, Samuels (1970) stated in his introduction that "preference was given to those studies in which pictures were used as adjuncts. Pictures are considered adjuncts if the text can be comprehended or the objects of the lesson fulfilled when the pictures are removed [p. 397]." By definition, then, the chances that illustrations might significantly add to the information content of the reading task were severely restricted. In many basal readers, particularly of the kind used by Miller (1938) and Weintraub (1960), the text involves very simple, narrative prose. Pictures accompanying the text are not intended to be informative and are likely to be only vaguely related to the total message. Figure 21.1 represents a typical example one might find in a beginning reader text. If the picture was to convey important information about the story, one might expect Tommy to decide to bring the parrot as a gift. In similar examples appearing in beginning readers, such a development in the story would not necessarily occur: Tommy would be as likely to bring a kite or a toy train as to bring a parrot. Thus, it is not surprising to find that nonillustrated stories are comprehended as well as illustrated stories in situations in which the pictures are inconsistently and vaguely related to the text.

Miller (1938) and Weintraub (1960) tested for the effects of pictures on comprehension but ignored tests of long-term retention. A study by Read and Barnsley (1977) provides evidence that even the pictures of basal readers can have a significant positive effect if long-term memory is tested. From basal readers in use 30 years ago, pages were selected that had an equal amount of space devoted to print and to pictures. Three categories of materials, pictures alone, print alone, and picture and print, were formed. Adult subjects were located who had used these basal readers 20 to 30 years before. Using similar second edition materials as the source of distractors, Read and Barnsley

Tommy's Surprise

"Oh, Tommy," said John.
"Next Friday is my birthday.
Will you come to my party?"

"Yes, John," said Tommy.
"Thank you for asking me."

Tommy thought and thought.
He thought about the party.
What should he bring for John?
At last Tommy knew what to take.

FIG. 21.1.   Example of a page from a first-grade level basal reader.

found that recognition memory was at chance level when the print was presented alone and was significantly better in the pictures-only condition. This is not surprising given the well-established finding that people remember pictures better than words. Much more interesting was the fact that significantly superior performance was achieved when pictures and print were presented together. Read and Barnsley concluded that a person's processing and storage of early reading materials is dependent on and affected by the interaction of both verbal and pictorial components.

Samuels' fairly caustic criticism of the ubiquitous use of pictures in beginning reading texts may be quite appropriate as applied to established publishing practices. However, it may still be true that better uses of illustrations, in which the information content of both picture and text are taken into account, would prove helpful both in decoding and comprehension tasks. Finally, the results of Read and Barnsley (1977) indicate that even the vague, uninformative illustrations of basal readers may have unexpectedly long-term memory effects.

THE CASE FOR PICTURES

The analysis presented in the previous sections indicates that the information content of pictures and its relationship to the text may play a crucial role in determining when it is that an illustration is beneficial. In discussing studies that have reported positive effects for illustrations, I evaluate the evidence for and against this hypothesis.

One of the most thorough comparisons of different ways of presenting information was provided by Rohwer and Harris (1975). Fourth-graders received one of seven different conditions: print only, picture only, oral only, print plus picture, print plus oral, oral plus picture, and print plus picture plus oral. The text consisted of simple expository passages comparing and contrasting attributes of different kinds of monkeys and the illustrations successively depicted each of the attributes discussed in the text. Comprehension was measured in one of three ways: sentence verification, short-answer questions, and free recall. Results indicated first of all, that the oral-plus-picture condition performed significantly better than the oral-plus-print condition, thus replicating the findings of Rohwer and Matz (1975). In addition, subjects in the picture-only condition performed significantly less well than subjects in any of the print conditions. It seems reasonable to posit, therefore, that the information content of the pictures was not sufficient to short-circuit a need for the text. In other words, there was some target information in the text that was not represented in the illustrations. The question remains: How were the pictures related to the text in terms of information content?

A comparison between the print-only and the print-plus-picture conditions may help provide an answer. Although Rohwer and Harris (1975) did not themselves discuss this particular contrast, they provide enough information in the form of mean proportion correct scores on the three dependent measures to allow some comparisons to be made. The calculated difference between the print and the print-plus-picture conditions for the high-SES subjects points to a facilitating effect in favor of pictures of nearly 10%. Additional evidence comes from the fact that for the high-SES group, oral-plus-print students performed significantly less well than print-plus-picture and oral-plus-picture students. For the low-SES subjects, the illustrated print was not easier than the print alone, indicating that the additive effect of pictures can be taken advantage of only when the text can be decoded relatively easily. In fact, low-SES subjects *were* able to benefit from illustrations as evidenced by their superior performance in the oral-plus-picture condition. Thus, pictures can provide a significant, helpful additive to comprehension, although, perhaps, only when the text can be easily decoded. Given the description of materials set down by Rohwer and Harris (1975), I can advance the following hypothesis: Pictures can facilitate comprehension if they depict information that is central to the text and that is tapped in the comprehension measures. The pictures have their effect more from providing a different access route to the text content than from merely repeating the information. Substantially identical reiteration of the information as in the print-plus-oral condition for good readers is not helpful. Further, the beneficial effect of differentiated access (picture plus print or picture plus oral) occurs only when the readers can decode the text.

Further evidence that the effectiveness of pictures is not merely due to an identical second representation of the information in a text and that looking at an illustration is not tantamount to getting a second rehearsal or repetition of the text can be advanced. Levin, Bender, and Lesgold (1976) found that first-graders benefited more from being provided with a picture than from hearing a repetition of each sentence. Although giving children a chance to hear or to produce a simple repetition resulted in better performance on a cued recall task than not asking them to do anything, pictures had a significant facilitative effect over and beyond simple repetition. Levin, Bender and Lesgold specifically did not dismiss the possibility that other verbal transformations of the text, more meaningful than simple repetition, might be as helpful as illustrations.

Lesgold, Levin, Shimron, and Guttmann (1975) set out to test whether first-graders would understand simple narrative stories better if they actively engaged in pictorial elaboration of the text. It was assumed that the children might not yet be able to read the texts on their own and, because comprehension rather than decoding was at issue, an oral presentation was used. A series of experiments led Lesgold et al. to the conclusion that illustrated stories were remembered better than nonillustrated ones. Whether the children themselves performed the task of illustrating the stories by using felt cut-outs or whether the experimenter did the illustrating was not important. Also, there was no significant difference in performance between children who constructed an illustration after every sentence and children who did a summary illustration at the end of the five-sentence stories. In a subsequent report, Lesgold, DeGood, and Levin (1977) established that the illustration task was helpful even when the stories became longer and more complex. Moreover, they found strong evidence that a picture facilitated the retention of information only when it correctly and specifically represented the information.

One study by Peeck (1974) provides further evidence that pictures facilitate the learning of some specifiable information in a text. Peeck gave 9- and 10-

year-old children an adapted version of a popular strip cartoon with natural reading instructions. Some children received the story with pictures, others without. On the unannounced retention test, questions appeared that tested information represented in the text alone, in the pictures alone, or in both text and pictures. The last category tested content that was either congruently represented in both picture and text or incongruently represented. At an immediate test, Peeck found that the group that had received illustrated material remembered more information than the no-picture group, and that this effect could be attributed in large part to performance on the picture questions. When the retention measure appeared 1 day or 1 week after reading, the picture group again correctly answered more picture questions and more congruent picture and text questions than the no-picture group. There was no difference between the groups on any retention measures in their ability to answer questions based on the text alone. Finally, Peeck found that the picture group was more likely than the no-picture group to pick the alternative congruent with the picture but incongruent with the text on the incongruent questions. Thus, we find that illustrations can have a specific, localized effect if the retention/comprehension measure is designed to tap separately illustrated and nonillustrated information.

In a similar vein, my colleagues (Ernest T. Goetz and Karen Dixon) and I have completed an experiment in which fourth-graders read a detailed account of how valves control water flow in faucets. The students were randomly assigned to a picture and to a no-picture contition. Illustrations were constructed depicting in line drawings the inner works of faucets (e.g., how valves stop the flow of water, where they are situated when water is running, how they are connected to the outside of the faucet, etc.). Thus, the pictures provided a spatial, schematic representation of how parts of faucets were related to each other. Performance on a multiple-choice test and on a free recall test indicated that more information was learned by the children in the picture condition. This effect was attributable to a significant difference between picture and no-picture groups on the information that was illustrated for the picture group. There was no difference in performance for any nonillustrated information. Thus, our results confirm Peeck's findings.

So far we have examined studies in which the illustrations depicted information that was also represented in the text. Can pictures facilitate the learning of information not represented in the text? Rohwer and Harris (1975) indicated that, at least for some types of information, pictures alone were not sufficient. However, it might be that pictures appearing with textual support might become adequate vehicles of nonredundant information. A study by Rigney and Lutz (1976) is relevant to this question. These investigators had college students learn the concepts of electrochemistry involved in a simple primary cell. The material was presented as a series of verbal descriptions or definitions of a concept, each of which was then elaborated. For half of the students, the elaboration consisted of an interactive animated graphics display. The other students read a verbal description of what the illustrations represented. It was found that the picture group recalled more information and answered more knowledge, comprehension, and application-level multiple-choice questions. Because the elaborations were represented *either* with pictures *or* with words, the pictures in this study were depicting new rather than redundant information, and they were found to be definitely beneficial. Rigney and Lutz's design provides a test not only of the overall facilitative effect of print and picture combinations but of the superiority of pictures over words in representing certain information.

Pursuing the comparison of pictorial with other ways of representing information, we turn to a study by Royer and Cable (1976). The question of interest was determining the conditions under which a passage would facilitate the comprehensibility and memorability of a subsequent passage when both passages depend on understanding a shared underlying concept. In a previous experiment, Royer and Cable (1975) had found that learning a first passage that was written using many concrete referents greatly facilitated the learning of a second passage written in abstract terms. In contrast, the abstract second passage was not learned as well when preceded by an abstract or an unrelated first passage. The passages dealt with the topics of heat flow and electrical conductivity in metals. In a second study (Royer & Cable, 1976), two additional ways of concretizing the first passage were tested. For one of these, the text remained abstract except for sections that were altered to include analogies to concepts that the readers were likely to know. The last condition involved presenting readers with an abstract version of the first passage accompanied by line drawings of five important concepts discussed in the print. It is interesting to note that the drawings, to a large extent, represented structural relationships among objects, as for example, the internal structural regularity of metals, the irregularity of nonmetals, the disruption of thermal transfer due to impurities in metal, and so on.

The results of Royer and Cable (1976) indicated that college students who read a first passage that was concrete, was abstract but included analogies, or was abstract but was accompanied by illustrations, performed equally well on a second abstract passage dealing with a closely related topic. Abstract and unrelated first passages produced much poorer performance on a subsequent abstract passage. This pattern of results held true even for information in the second passage, which was considered less well reflected in the first passage although still tied to the overall concept of the structure of metals. Royer and Cable concluded that pictures, concrete examples, and analogies serve to explicate concepts that can then become assimilative structures for new information. What do the picture, concrete examples, and analogies conditions have in common? I would argue that all three of these elicit in the reader an internal representation of the way the concepts being learned are structurally related. Structural relationships lend themselves to spatial representation, which in turn lends itself to illustration, whether internal (as in imagery) or external.

One other paper is relevant here. Bransford and Johnson's (1972) study of the effect of context on prose comprehension and recall has become a classic in cognitive psychology. Their paradigm involved giving subjects a paragraph that in and by itself does not make sense, although each sentence taken alone does. Here is an example:

> If the balloons popped the sound wouldn't be able to carry since everything would be too far away from the correct floor. A closed window would also prevent the sound from carrying, since most buildings tend to be well insulated. Since the whole operation depends upon a steady flow of electricity, a break in the middle of the wire would also cause problems. Of course, the fellow could shout, but the human voice is not loud enough to carry that far. An additional problem is that a string could break on the instrument. Then there could be no accompaniment to the message. It is clear that the best situation would involve less distance. Then there would be fewer potential problems. With face to face contact, the least number of things could go wrong [p. 719].

The problem with the text is that objects are mentioned very unsystematically, with many referents and the interrelationships among objects left unspecified. Subjects who saw a picture representing the components of the paragraph in a meaningful way, see Fig. 21.2a, remembered more information and rated the printed text as more comprehensible than subjects who were given an inappropriate picture, see Fig. 21.2b, or no contextual information at all. It is interesting to note that the inappropriate picture was not in any way helpful, even though it did provide a concrete representation of the objects mentioned in the paragraph. What is missing from Fig. 21.2b that is present in Fig. 21.2a is the proper spatial configuration of the concepts. The picture in Fig. 21.2a allows one to make sense of the text exactly because it represents how objects mentioned in the text are related spatially. A better example of a nonredundant illustration that facilitates comprehension by representing spatial-structural information not available in the text is hard to find.

In summary, it must be pointed out that in presenting the case for pictures, I have glossed over some important differences between studies. Thus, in some studies, comprehension was tested using cued recall or multiple-choice questions, whereas in others, free recall or sentence verification tasks were used. Also, a wide range of age and reading ability was represented and presentation mode differed markedly. Finally, no distinction was made between narrative and expository prose. Still, despite such heterogeneity among conditions, some preliminary conclusions can be drawn. Pictures help

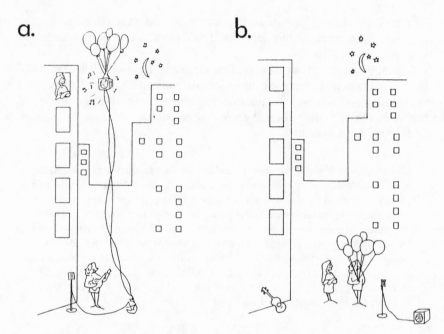

FIG. 21.2. Illustrations from Bransford and Johnson (1972). Version "a" represents the appropriate context and version "b" represents the inappropriate context. See text for accompanying passage.

the reader learn and comprehend a text when they illustrate information central to the text, when they represent new content that is important to the overall message, and when they depict structural relationships mentioned in the text. In addition, pictures seem to have a specific effect that is localized mainly to illustrated information and that amounts to more than a simple second rehearsal of the text. Although not fully explicated, I believe that these conclusions[2] represent a beginning toward specifying some of the conditions under which illustrations facilitate learning in many reading tasks.

THE IMAGERY QUESTION

One of the most frequently offered explanations for the facilitation effect of pictures is that illustrations somehow induce an active elaboration of the text, thus increasing its comprehensibility. The process is frequently equated with

---

[2]It must be admitted that the case I have made for pictures may rest to a great extent on current editorial practice to publish studies with significant differences. There certainly exist studies showing no significant difference between illlustrated and nonillustrated versions and I make no claim to having reviewed exhaustively the unpublished data potentially available.

imagery. Rigney and Lutz (1976), for example, proposed that pictures facilitate learning by inducing readers to form mental images of the information. Whether one is then allowed to imply that the vast literature dealing with imagery effects can be applied *en masse* to the effect of pictures remains questionable. Self-generated internal "pictures" are not the same as physically perceivable external illustrations. However, there are two reasons why the process of imagery is relevant to a discussion of illustrations. First, although pictures and images are not equivalent in many respects, they are similar in that they both involve a depiction of attributes in a spatial configuration (Peterson, 1975). Paivio's dual coding hypothesis (e.g., Paivio, 1971) in accounting for the imagery effect is relevant here. Second, it has been found that telling people to form mental images while hearing or reading verbal information improves their memory for the information (Anderson & Hidde, 1971; Anderson & Kulhavy, 1972; Kulhavy & Swenson, 1975; Paivio, 1971). In fact, telling people to do anything that ensures deep semantic processing of the text, as for example, to think of a linking sentence (Bobrow & Bower, 1969) or to fill in the last word of a text (Anderson, Goldberg, & Hidde, 1971), has been found to result in better performance when compared to control group instructions. In general, these results are explained by hypothesizing that instructions to interact with the text increase the amount of attention readers or listeners bring to the task and increase the comprehensibility of the text. Now, very similar effects have been credited to pictures. Thus it may be that pictures are related to images not because the presence of the first facilitates the production of the second, but because they serve similar roles in the processing chains involved in text comprehension. The following discussion is devoted to an examination of studies that compare the effectiveness of imagery with that of illustrations and that attempt to chart the ability to use pictures as a departure point in generating images.

Rasco, Tennyson, and Boutwell (1975) set out to test directly the relative effectiveness of imagery instructions and pictures. In the first of three experiments, college students read an extended passage describing commonly held misconceptions about revolutions. Half of the students received instructions to construct mental images of the concepts in the text materials. Each of the instruction groups received either illustrated or nonillustrated materials. Rasco et al. describe their illustrations as depicting "the more salient ideas in the paragraph. The drawings were designed to represent the conceptual attributes and the relational attributes between concepts in the textual discourse [p. 189]." One noteworthy aspect of the experimental instructions to the two picture groups was the inclusion of a specific direction to the readers to use the drawings to help them learn the material. Results were that students who received either drawings, or imagery instructions, or both, were better able to answer questions about the passage than students who read the materials without illustrations or imagery instructions. A second experiment with exactly the same conditions and materials but administered to senior high school students indicated the same trends. In the third experiment, fourth- and fifth-graders read materials describing the mathematical concepts of intersection and of an empty set. The conditions of illustrations and imagery strategies remained the same as in the first two experiments except that students in the no-drawings–imagery strategy condition were instructed to draw pictures on what they were reading as well as to form mental images. Results indicated that imagery instructions and/or drawings helped students remember the information when compared to the no-drawings–no-strategy group. This interaction was particularly strong for the fourth-graders.

The results of Rasco, Tennyson, and Boutwell (1975) bear closer inspection. Comparing the conditions in which students received imagery instructions, or pictures, or both, we find that there is very little difference among them. For fourth-graders for example, the range of the means for the three conditions was from 13.8 to 14.5 questions answered correctly out of a possible 20. These means do not differ from each other very much, especially when compared to the mean of 8.2 questions for the no-drawings–no-strategy group. Thus, imagery and illustrations produce equivalent and positive effects but these effects are not additive, that is, they do not produce an even stronger effect when combined. Such findings do not provide conclusive evidence either in support or in contradiction of the hypothesis that pictures induce imagery as an intermediary step in comprehension. Stronger support of the hypothesis would have taken the form of equivalent performance in the drawings–imagery group and in the drawings–no-imagery group, with both of these resulting in significantly superior performance when compared to the no-drawings–imagery group. The evidence we actually have so far indicates that, however images and pictures influence the learnability of text, be it at an abstract level of representation (Pylyshyn, 1973) or at a more perceptual level, they have an equivalent effect.

A number of investigators seem to view illustrations and images as being different steps along a continuum representing an increasing degree of internalization. In a study by Lesgold, McCormick, and Golinkoff (1975), third- and fourth-grade students were gradually taught over a 12-day period to make simple cartoon drawings representing every illustratable idea or event appearing in the stories they were reading. On the last day of training, the children were told to think about their pictures rather than to draw them. In the test session, the imagery-trained group as well as the control group were given two passages to read at their own pace, the first without any instruction to image and the second with imagery instructions. It was found that recall of the passages was much better for students who had been trained but only when an explicit prompt to use imagery before reading was given. The children had to be reminded of the imagery strategy before it could facilitate performance. Note that the findings of Lesgold, McCormick, and Golinkoff partially contradict the findings of Kulhavy and Swenson (1975) with fifth-

and sixth-grade children and those of Rasco, Tennyson, and Boutwell (1975) with fourth- and fifth-graders. In these last two studies, children were not trained extensively to use imagery and, yet, they exhibited significantly better performance under imagery instructions than a noninstructed control group.

In discussing their results, Lesgold, McCormick, and Golinkoff (1975) proposed that imagery affects storage and recall of information rather than its comprehension during reading. They based their argument on the fact that the imagery training did not have any effect on standard reading achievement test scores that are derived from tasks involving comprehension rather than recall. However, their argument is not convincing. Standard reading achievement tests have a number of problems relating to type of passage and type of questions that makes them less than ideal tests of this question. Thus, it still remains to be shown whether, and under what conditions, imagery training helps comprehension as well as recall.

Returning to the issue of whether illustrations and images represent different degrees of internalized representation, Guttmann, Levin, and Pressley (1977) investigated the effectiveness of partial pictures in oral prose learning. Taking as established the fact that young children benefit from having information pictorially augmented before they can use imagery instructions (Lesgold, Levin, Shimron, & Guttmann, 1975; McCabe, Levin, & Wolff, 1974; Rohwer, 1973; Shimron, 1974; Wolff & Levin, 1972), Guttmann et al. wanted to see whether providing some pictoral support would induce imaginal processing in children who would not otherwise be affected by imagery instructions. In a first experiment, kindergarten, second-grade, and third-grade children were assigned to one of four conditions: a complete picture condition in which objects subsequently tested in cued recall were clearly represented; a partial picture condition in which these objects were hidden by being extended inferentially beyond the frame of the picture or by being placed "behind" other objects in the picture; a no-picture–imagery instruction condition; and a control, no-picture–no imagery condition. Results indicated that kindergarten children were able to benefit only from the complete picture condition. Third-graders peformed equally well in the imagery, partial picture, and complete picture conditions. Second-graders showed no significant difference between the control and imagery conditions. Complete pictures were most helpful to the second-graders, with the partial pictures falling in between. In a second experiment using shorter texts, a stronger effect for partial pictures over imagery instructions was demonstrated. Finally, Guttmann et al. found that a particular type of partial picture, that is, one related to the action sequence of the text rather than merely to the objects mentioned in the text, facilitated learning of the information hinted at in the partial picture. Guttmann et al. concluded from these studies that where instructions alone could not induce imagery, pictures that depicted only some information from the text provided enough framework for young children to benefit from imaginal processing. It must be noted, however, that whether the function of partial pictures was actually to induce imagery was not directly demonstrated. For the children who could not benefit from mere verbal instructions to image, complete pictures were still more facilitative than partial pictures. In fact, complete pictures produced the best performance in every comparison tested.

Finally, Levin, Devine-Hawkins, Kerst, and Guttmann (1974) investigated whether the ability to benefit from pictures and from imagery instructions was differentially represented in individual children. These researchers first identified elementary school children who would or who would not learn from pictures by means of a group-administered paired associates test in which some of the pairs were pictorial, some verbal, and some mixed (picture–word or word–picture). Students' performance was always better for pictures than for words but for some students the difference between words and pictures was greater than for others. Subjects were classified on the basis of their level of performance on pictures and words: high picture–high word, low picture–low word, and high picture–low word. There were so few students who fell in the low picture–high word category that it was eliminated from the classification system. In a second experiment, the usefulness of the categorization was established with a prose reading task. Imagery instructions enhanced learning from an expository prose passage only for high picture–high word and high picture–low word students. Imagery instructions actually seemed to depress the performance of the low picture–low word students relative to a nonimagery control condition. Whether this effect would have occurred if actual illustrations had accompanied the text rather than imagery instructions was not tested. In any case, the results of Levin et al. (1974) indicate that children may have differing and variable abilities to benefit from pictures, a hypothesis that certainly deserves to be investigated directly given its possible ramifications for instructional and publishing practices.

In summary, I would say that the theoretical issue of the relationship between illustrations and imagery is at this point unresolved. Arriving at a resolution would seem to require, as a first step, making a distinction between comprehension and recall or between what happens during the processing of text and what happens afterwards. Nevertheless, at the practical level, it does seem that the sum total of existing research comes down squarely on the side of recommending illustrations and, perhaps, supplementary instructions to use imagery in order to facilitate learning from text.

SUMMARY AND CONCLUSION

Levin and Lesgold (1977) stated in their conclusions that the need to prove merely that illustrations can have positive effects on children's prose learning is past. Although I fully agree with this assertion, I believe they presented it somewhat prematurely given the severe limitations on the conditions under which they were willing to predict a reliable positive effect for pictures. These limitations, set out as ground rules in Levin and Lesgold (1978), were that the passages be presented orally, that the subjects be young children, that the passages be narrative fiction, that the pictures overlap the story content, and that learning be tested by factual recall. The present review greatly extends the scope of conditions under which illustrations can prove to be beneficial. It was found, for example, that illustrations benefited reading as well as listening comprehension, adults as well as children, expository as well as narrative prose, and nonredundant as well as redundant text. Although I cannot yet describe as definitively as Levin the ground rules that circumscribe these positive effects, I can report that where pictures have been shown to be helpful, they have seemed to be related to the text in specific ways. A reasonable hypothesis is that pictures are likely to help readers learn from written material if they represent spatial information or information that is important to the total message. In addition, there may be differences in the effectiveness of illustrations between situations in which the information to be derived from a picture is explicitly repeated by the text and situations in which the text provides merely the framework for certain information left to be derived from appropriate illustrations.

That authors/illustrators can use pictures as the sole conveyor of important information is represented in Fig. 21.3. In such a situation, the

The Land Bridge

Look closely at the map above. Where are Asia and North America closest? A long time ago, these two areas were connected by a narrow strip of land covered with trees and plants. Over the years, people wandered across the land bridge. At the time, they did not know they were crossing into a new continent.

FIG. 21.3. , Example of a page from a sixth-grade social studies textbook.

reader is expected to understand key relationships from looking at the map. The text and concepts being highlighted are typical of a sixth-grade level social studies text. However, given this particular illustration, what the unknowledgeable sixth-grader will understand about how Indians came to inhabit the Americas is likely to be false. In trying to represent a round world on a flat surface, the illustrator has made the crucial mistake of putting the Americas to the left of Asia rather than to the right. Note that the error stems from the interaction between the picture and the text rather than from an inherent problem with the picture or with the text. The reader, although asked to look at the map to see where North America and Asia are closest, must actually infer that the land bridge was formed (behind the page?) between the two points that are the furthest from each other on this particular map. Although I have come across this exact problem in a text in current use, my point in bringing up the example is not to expose self-righteously the occasional human errors of textbook writers and publishers. Rather, the example makes particularly clear how information in a text may need to be derived from an interaction between text and pictures. It is in just such a situation that illustrations should prove to have a particularly strong effect on what is learned from reading.

One issue that I have not so far directly addressed is whether a particular type of information lends itself more easily to illustration. Kolers (1973) proposed that pictures are better than words at depicting spatial configurations, and through the adoption of certain conventions, some kinds of temporal relations. Graphs, maps, Venn diagrams, architectural drawings, and flow charts are often particularly effective in conveying the spatial and temporal relationships among concepts. Words, on the other hand, are necessary when qualifications, commentary, or other subtleties need be mentioned. As Kolers (1973) points out, "neither pictures nor words are the royal road to information processing [p. 40]."

There seem to be certain situations in which illustrations are vastly more efficient than words in representing a message and may in some cases represent information that is actually impossible to verbalize. In the ability to represent information that cannot be stated in words, as well as in certain other aspects, an analogy can be drawn between pictures and metaphors. Ortony (1975) argued that metaphors can serve three functions in expressing one's ideas, functions that are not well served by literal language. These are stated as the vividness, compactness, and inexpressibility theorems. I would like to claim that it is in exactly these three ways that certain pictures aid the reader to attain a full realization of the author's intent. Metaphors are like pictures in that they frequently convey an intended meaning through the vehicle of concrete referents that are likely to facilitate the reader's imaginal processing. More important, pictures can be at least as useful as metaphors in representing economically information that would require a large number of words to state literally. Witness a typical set of verbal instructions on how to get to someone's house as compared to a map. In addition, just as metaphors convey what is literally inexpressible by leading the reader to construct his or her own representation of the meaning intended out of a store of tacit knowledge, so some pictures convey a richer meaning than could any literal description by triggering in the viewer nuances of associations through the portrayal of certain fine details of relationships among objects (people or things). At some level of generalization, metaphors and pictures seem to be essentially alike in being ideal vehicles to express some novel and/or complex relationships among certain concepts. I would predict that appropriate illustrations and metaphors would prove particularly effective when appearing in expository text because such text is primarily used to induce readers to comprehend new concepts and new relationships among concepts. It is interesting to note that Webster's Unabridged Dictionary (1961) makes the following comment on the concept of exposition: "Exposition usually proceeds by the orderly analysis of parts and use of familiar illustrations and analogies."

Finally, I would like to make a few comments on a last issue, the problem of pictorial literacy. Kolers (1973) makes a strong case for the fact that one must learn how to read a picture just as one must learn how to read text. He gives an example in which mistaken assumptions to the contrary have resulted in the failure of certain government programs. Kolers (1973) writes:

> The error is clearly revealed by recent experiences in countries in which the safety precautions to be followed in gold mines, or the details of inserting and using an intrauterine device have been conveyed for illiterate persons as a series of pictures in comicbook fashion. The programs have not been especially successful, however, for the users have not known how to read the pictures; whether to read from left to right or right to left, bottom to top or top to bottom, or even why a 2-inch-high drawing having a certain shape should be called a man or a woman, nor why the reader should identify himself with this 2-inch-high drawing. Thus, literacy is required for pictorial interpretation as much as for textual interpretation [p. 40].

Now, for a society that exposes its young from a very early age to constant pictorial input, namely, television, it is very difficult to make a reasonable claim that school-age children might not understand pictures at the gross level described by Kolers. However, it may still be true that individual differences exist in American children's ability to use pictures to their utmost benefit. In particular, some children may need to be taught how to interpret pictures, charts, diagrams, and maps, and how to infer information essential to a text from accompanying illustrations. Certainly, teachers, textbook writers, and illustrators need to become more sensitive to the information conveyed through the delicate interplay of text and pictures.

ACKNOWLEDGMENTS

I am most grateful to Ernest T. Goetz for his comments on all versions of this chapter and to Dean Ian Radin for his work on the illustrations. The work was supported by the National Institute of Education under contract No. US-NIE-C-400-76-0116.

REFERENCES

Anderson, R. C., Goldberg, S. R., & Hidde, J. L. Meaningful processing of sentences. *Journal of Educational Psychology*, 1971, *62*, 395–399.

Anderson, R. C., & Hidde, J. L. Imagery and sentence learning. *Journal of Educational Psychology*, 1971, *62*, 526–530.

Anderson, R. C., & Kulhavy, R. W. Imagery and prose learning. *Journal of Educational Psychology*, 1972, *63*, 242–243.

Anderson, R. C., Reynolds, R. E., Schallert, D. L., & Goetz, E. T. Frameworks for comprehending discourse. *American Educational Research Journal*, 1977, *14*, 367–382.

Baggett, P. Memory for explicit and implicit information in picture stories. *Journal of Verbal Learning and Verbal Behavior*, 1975, *14*, 538–548.

Bobrow, S. A., & Bower, G. H. Comprehension and recall of sentences. *Journal of Experimental Psychology*, 1969, *80*, 455–461.

Bransford, J. D., & Johnson, M. K. Contextual prerequisites for understanding: Some investigations of comprehension and recall. *Journal of Verbal Learning and Verbal Behavior*, 1972, *11*, 717–726.

Braun, C. Interest loading and modality effects on textural response acquisition. *Reading Research Quarterly*, 1969, *4*, 428–444.

Brown, A. L. Semantic integration in children's reconstruction of narrative sequences. *Cognitive Psychology*, 1976, *8*, 247–262.

Concannon, S. J. Illustrations in books for children: Review of research. *The Reading Teacher*, 1975, *29*, 254–256.

Denburg, S. D. The interaction of picture and print in reading instruction (abstracted report). *Reading Research Quarterly*, 1976–1977, *12*, 176–189.

Franks, J. J., & Bransford, J. D. Abstraction of visual patterns. *Journal of Experimental Psychology*, 1971, *90*, 65–74.

Guttmann, J., Levin, J. R., & Pressley, M. Pictures, partial pictures, and young children's oral prose learning. *Journal of Educational Psychology*, 1977, *69*, 473–480.

Harris, L. A. *A study of the rate of acquisition and retention of interest-loaded words by low socio-economic kindergarten children.* Unpublished doctoral dissertation, University of Minnesota, 1967.

Harzem, P., Lee, I., & Miles, T. R. The effects of pictures on learning to read. *British Journal of Educational Psychology*, 1976, *46*, 318–322.

Koenke, K. R. *The roles of pictures and readability in comprehension of the main idea of a paragraph.* Paper presented at the annual meeting of the American Educational Research Association, Chicago 1968.

Kolers, P. A. Some modes of representation. In P. Pliner, L. Krames, & T. Alloway (Eds.), *Communication and affect: Language and thought.* New York: Academic Press, 1973.

Kulhavy, R. W., & Swenson, I. Imagery instructions and the comprehension of text. *British Journal of Educational Psychology*, 1975, *45*, 47–51.

Lesgold, A. M., DeGood, H., & Levin, J. R. Pictures and young children's prose learning: A supplementary report. *Journal of Reading Behavior*, 1977, *9*, 353–360.

Lesgold, A. M., Levin, J. R., Shimron, J., & Guttmann, J. Pictures and young children's learning from oral prose. *Journal of Educational Psychology*, 1975, *67*, 636–642.

Lesgold, A. M., McCormick, C., & Golinkoff, R. M. Imagery training and children's prose learning. *Journal of Educational Psychology*, 1975, *67*, 663–667.

Levin, J. R., Bender, B. G., & Lesgold, A. M. Pictures, repetition, and young children's oral prose learning. *AV Communications Review*, 1976, *24*, 367–380.

Levin, J. R., Divine-Hawkins, P., Kerst, S. M., & Guttmann, J. Individual differences in learning from pictures and words: The development and application of an instrument. *Journal of Educational Psychology*, 1974, *66*, 296–303.

Levin, J. R., & Lesgold, A. M. *Do pictures improve children's prose learning? An examination of the evidence.* Paper presented at the annual meeting of the National Reading Conference, New Orleans, December 1977.

Levin, J. R., & Lesgold, A. M. *On pictures in prose. Educational Communication and Technology*, 1978, *26*, 233–243.

McCabe, A. E., Levin, J. R., & Wolff, P. The role of overt activity in children's sentence production. *Journal of Experimental Child Psychology*, 1974, *17*, 107–114.

Miller, W. Reading with and without pictures. *Elementary School Journal*, 1938, *38*, 676–682.

Ortony, A. Why metaphors are necessary and not just nice. *Educational Theory*, 1975, *25*, 45–53.

Paivio, A. *Imagery and verbal processes*. New York: Holt, Rinehart & Winston, 1971.

Peeck, J. Retention of pictorial and verbal content of a text with illustrations. *Journal of Educational Psychology*, 1974, *66*, 880–888.

Peterson, M. J. The retention of imagined and seen spatial matrices. *Cognitive Psychology*, 1975, *7*, 181–193.

Pichert, J. P., & Anderson, R. C. Taking different perspectives on a story. *Journal of Educational Psychology*, 1977, *69*, 309–315.

Pylyshyn, Z. W. What the mind's eye tells the mind's brain: A critique of mental imagery. *Psychological Bulletin*, 1973, *80*, 1–24.

Rasco, R. W., Tennyson, R. D., & Boutwell, R. C. Imagery instructions and drawings in learning prose. *Journal of Educational Psychology*, 1975, *67*, 188–192.

Read, J. D., & Barnsley, R. H. Remember Dick and Jane? Memory for elementary school readers. *Canadian Journal of Behavioral Science*, 1977, *9*, 361–370.

Rigney, J. W., & Lutz, K. A. Effect of graphic analogies of concepts in chemistry on learning and attitude. *Journal of Educational Psychology*, 1976, *68*, 305–311.

Rohwer, W. D., Jr. Elaboration and learning in childhood and adolescence. In H. W. Reese (Ed.), *Advances in child development and behavior* (Vol. 8). New York: Academic Press, 1973.

Rohwer, W. D., Jr., & Harris, W. J. Media effects on prose learning in two populations of children. *Journal of Educational Psychology*, 1975, *67*, 651–657.

Rohwer, W. D., Jr., & Matz, R. D. Improving aural comprehension in white and black children: Pictures versus print. *Journal of Experimental Child Psychology*, 1975, *19*, 23–36.

Royer, J. M., & Cable, G. W. Facilitated learning in connected discourse. *Journal of Educational Psychology*, 1975, *67*, 116–123.

Royer, J. M., & Cable, G. W. Illustrations, analogies, and facilitative transfer in prose learning. *Journal of Educational Psychology*, 1976, *68*, 205–209.

Samuels, S. J. Attentional process in reading: The effect of pictures on the acquisition of reading responses. *Journal of Educational Psychology*, 1967, *58*, 337–342.

Samuels, S. J. Effects of pictures on learning to read, comprehension and attitudes. *Review of Educational Research*, 1970, *40*, 397–407.

Schallert, D. L. Improving memory for prose: The relationship between depth of processing and context. *Journal of Verbal Learning and Verbal Behavior*, 1976, *15*, 621–632.

Shimron, J. *Imagery and the comprehension of prose by elementary school children.* Unpublished doctoral dissertation, University of Pittsburgh, 1974.

Singer, H., Samuels, S. J., & Spiroff, J. The effect of pictures and contextual conditions on learning responses to printed words. *Reading Research Quarterly,* 1973–1974, *9,* 555–567.

Spiro, R. J. Remembering information from text: Theoretical and empirical issues concerning the 'State of Schema' reconstruction hypothesis. In R. C. Anderson, R. J. Spiro, & W. E. Montague (Eds.), *Schooling and the acquisition of knowledge.* Hillsdale, N.J.: Lawrence Erlbaum Associates, 1977.

Sulin, R. A., & Dooling, D. J. Intrusion of a thematic idea in retention of prose. *Journal of Experimental Psychology,* 1974, *103,* 255–262.

Vernon, M. D. The value of pictorial illustration. *British Journal of Educational Psychology,* 1953, *23,* 180–187.

Vernon, M. D. The instruction of children by pictorial illustration. *British Journal of Educational Psychology,* 1954, *24,* 171–179.

Weintraub, S. *The effect of pictures on the comprehension of a second grade basal reader.* Unpublished doctoral dissertation, University of Illinois, 1960.

Wolff, P., & Levin, J. R. The role of overt activity in children's imagery production. *Child Development,* 1972, *43,* 537–547.

22 Topic Interest And Children's Reading Comprehension

Steven R. Asher
Center for the Study of Reading,
University of Illinois, Urbana-Champaign

INTRODUCTION

It is commonly believed that children's willingness to read and their comprehension of what they read is affected by the interest level of the material they are given (e.g., Estes & Vaughan, 1973; Fader & McNeil, 1968). Accordingly, considerable research has been devoted to the assessment of children's interests and to comparisons of children's interests with the content of children's texts. What is surprising is that these lines of inquiry have led to little research on whether children's interest in material does, in fact, influence their comprehension. Blom, Waite, and Zimet (1970), who have done the most extensive content analysis of children's reading primers, have commented that what is needed is research into how content actually affects children's attitudes and reading performance.

METHODOLOGICAL ISSUES

Despite the plausibility and wide acceptance of the view that interesting material facilitates children's reading comprehension, there have been surprisingly few empirical tests. Much of the research that does exist contains serious methodological problems. One issue is the way in which high- and low-interest topics are identified. In some studies (e.g., Bernstein, 1955; Shnayer, 1967), children's interest in a topic is assessed after they have read a passage on that topic. This procedure confounds the assessment of interests with reading comprehension because children may report more interest in a passage they have just understood than one with which they have had difficulty. In other experiments, children are assigned passages based on normative studies of children's interests (e.g., Dorsel, 1975; Klein, 1969; Stanchfield, 1967). For example, boys are assumed to be interested in reading about a pilot or how to tune cars whereas girls are assumed to be interested in topics such as a ballet dancer or how to make bread. Although children's interests are generally sex-typed (e.g., Tyler, 1964), there is also considerable within-sex variability. This variability means that the assignment of one set of passages to boys and another set to girls introduces considerable experimental error.

Another issue is the way in which reading comprehension is measured. Most researchers have used measures specifically developed for each study, with no prior demonstration of test reliability or validity. In many cases, item selection appears to have been arbitrary. Finally, most of the research in this area has not sampled from a wide array of reading topics; frequently, only two passages are used, one which is supposedly high-interest and the other low-interest. Perhaps as a result of these problems, early studies produced inconsistent results concerning whether children's comprehension is affected by their interest in the reading material.

Asher and Markell (1974) designed a procedure to overcome the methodological limitations of earlier studies. First, children's interests were assessed individually and independently of any reading material. Second, the measure of reading comprehension was one with known reliability and validity. Third, a large number of topics were employed.

The basic procedure was as follows. Children's interests were assessed by having them rate each of 25 color photographs. The photographs represented a wide array of topics (e.g., basketball, cats, airplanes, circus) and children rated each photograph on a seven-point interest scale. No mention of reading was made during this interest assessment phase. One week later, each child received, from a second experimenter, an individualized set of six passages. Three passages corresponded to the child's three highest rated topics and three corresponded to the child's three lowest rated topics. All passages came from the Brittanica Junior Encyclopaedia (1970) and were presented in "cloze" format; every fifth word was missing and the child's task was to read the passage and supply as many of the missing words as possible. The cloze procedure (Taylor, 1953) was used because it provides an objective method for generating test items and yields scores that are reliable and that correlate highly with results from standardized reading achievement tests (Bormuth, 1967, 1968; Rankin & Culhane, 1969). After reading all six passages, children indicated on a series of seven-point scales how much they would like to read more about each passage. This served as a check on the manipulation of interest; children should prefer passages corresponding to those pictures they rated as highly interesting.

INTEREST EFFECTS
AND THEORETICAL ACCOUNTS

Three studies with fifth- and sixth-grade students have been done using this procedure (Asher, 1979; Asher & Geraci, 1980; Asher & Markell, 1974). The findings can be briefly summarized. First, in each study children indicated far greater desire to read passages that corresponded to highly rated topics. Second, children's reading comprehension was superior on high-interest material; in each study, children attained higher cloze scores on their high-interest passages. Third, there appear to be individual differences in children's reactions to high- and low-interest materials; in two of the studies (Asher & Geraci, 1980; Asher & Markell, 1974), boys' performance was facilitated more than girls' performance by high-interest material.

Each child in these experiments received three high-interest and three low-interest passages. Rarely in the school day are children assigned reading material that provides such clearly identifiable variation in topic appeal. To assess the generality of the interest effect, Asher, Hymel, and Wigfield (1978) did an experiment in which each child received either all high-interest or all low-interest passages, rather than a mixture of both types of material. The results of this between-subjects design indicated that, as in the other studies, children compehended more of high- than low-interest material. Thus, the interest effect is not dependent simply on the strong contrast effect that might be provided by a mixture of high- and low-interest material.

It seems, then, that children do comprehend more of high- than of low-interest material. An important issue is why the interest effect occurs. One possibility is that children are more motivated to read material that appeals to their interests. In this case, they might work harder on interesting material. Another possibility is that children comprehend more of high- than low-interest material because they are more knowledgeable about the subject matter. Two types of knowledge variables might operate. First, children may have more familiarity with the vocabulary of high-interest topics. Second, children may have more elaborate and differentiated cognitive structures with respect to high-interest topics. These schemata (Anderson, Reynolds, Schallert, & Goetz, 1977) would help children to organize material, infer the writer's intentions, or anticipate future discussion in the text.

In the real world of reading, knowledge and motivation are confounded; people tend to know more about the things they are enthusiastic about. Still it would be instructive, for both theoretical and practical reasons, to evaluate the separate contributions of each factor. Most teachers probably assume a motivational explanation of interest effects. If, however, the effect of interest is due more to greater knowledge than to greater expenditure of effort, it would imply that a major barrier to reading comprehension is not a limited desire to read but a limited knowledge of the world.

One approach to evaluating motivational and knowledge explanations is to vary the topics of passages while controlling for vocabulary and the background knowledge required to comprehend the passages. If children do better on passages associated with high-interest topics, a motivational explanation would be implicated. If children do as well on low- as high-interest passages, it would imply that knowledge factors accounted for the interest effect in the original encyclopedia passage studies.

Asher (1975) employed the "controlled vocabulary" research strategy to evaluate motivational and knowledge explanations. Six passages were prepared; each passage was written so generally (e.g., a passage about a recent television show) that by inserting a key word (e.g., "cats") in three locations and by appropriately titling the passage with the key word, the passage could be made to appear about any of the 25 topics that had been used in the interest assessment phase. Children received all six passages; what varied was the particular topic that was associated with each passage. Three topics corresponded to the child's highest rated pictures and three corresponded to the child's lowest rated pictures.

The comprehension results indicated no difference between high-interest and low-interest performance on these controlled-vocabulary passages, a finding that supports the view that some type of knowledge factor accounts for interest effects when they occur. However, the postreading preference ratings children made of how much they would like to read more about each passage suggested that the interest manipulation was weak. Although children rated the passages associated with high-interest topics significantly higher, the actual difference in ratings made of high- and low-interest passages was small compared with the difference obtained in the studies using the encyclopedia material. When vocabulary is strictly controlled, the richness associated with a topic appears to be lost. Because the manipulation of interest was weak in this study, the comprehension data cannot be interpreted with confidence.

A second approach to evaluating knowledge and motivational factors is to assess high- and low-interest performance when children are given strong external incentives for trying their best. An interest effect on comprehension should be substantially reduced under incentive conditions if the interest effect is primarily motivational. However, if poorer performance on low-interest material is due to knowledge constraints, then the additional incentive should have little effect on the difference between high- and low-interest performance. Asher and Geraci (1980) recently employed this strategy. Half of the children were given high- and low-interest passages under regular test conditions and half were promised an attractive prize if they "tried their best." Results in the "regular" condition replicated earlier findings; children comprehended significantly more of high- than low-interest material. In the "external incentive" condition, the difference between high- and low-interest performance approached, but did not reach, statistical significance. These data implicate the contribution of motivational factors to the interest effect. Still, the fact that differences remained in the external incentive condition suggests that knowledge factors were, to some extent, constraining performance on low-interest material.

Perhaps the most direct approach to evaluating motivational and knowledge interpretations would be to directly assess children's knowledge as well as interest with respect to a set of topics. Children would then be given passages corresponding to each topic and would be tested for comprehension of each passage. Correlational analysis of each child's data would indicate the overall relationship between interest and knowledge, and regression analyses would estimate the contribution of knowledge, independent of interest, to reading comprehension. This strategy could be used to assess the relative contribution of motivational and knowledge factors to reading comprehension at different ages, or for children of different levels of reading achievement, or under different test conditions.

INDIVIDUAL DIFFERENCES

One issue that deserves further attention is the effect of interest across subgroups of children. Asher and Markell (1974) examined interest effects with high- and low-achieving students. There was no interaction of interest level by achievement level; both groups did considerably better on high-interest material.

Sex differences in response to topic interest are worthy of study, given boys' reading problems in elementary school. Boys are less attentive during reading instruction (Samuels & Turnure, 1974), frequently read more poorly than girls on standardized reading achievement tests (e.g., Gates, 1961), are far overrepresented in remedial reading classes (Blom, 1971), and have more negative attitudes toward reading (Neale, Gill, & Tismer, 1970). Asher and Markell (1974) explored whether giving children high-interest material would narrow or eliminate the sex differences in reading performance. They tested a group of fifth-grade boys and girls who differed significantly on the school-administered standardized reading achievement test. Results indicated that girls performed better than boys on low-interest material but that no sex difference appeared on high-interest material. These results are important in light of the long-term concern about boys' reading problems among American educators (e.g., Ayres, 1909; Brophy & Good, 1974).

The effect of interest on race differences in reading comprehension has also been examined. Black children typically perform less well than white children on reading tests and the gap in test performance widens with each year that children are in school (Coleman et al., 1966; Singer, Gerard, & Redfearn, 1975). The "interestingness" of the material might have a role to play either because black children are less motivated to read or because they are less knowledgeable about many of the topics they encounter in school. Asher (1979) tested fifth-grade black children and white children on high- and low-interest material. There were two major findings. First, black children, as well as white children, comprehended more of high-interest than low-interest material. Second, interest and race did not interact; the gap between black and white children's performance was the same on high- and low-interest material.

Although no interaction of race and interest appeared in this study, the significant effect of topic interest for black children is promising in light of the reading material. All passages were from the Brittanica Junior Encyclopaedia (1970), a source that contains a rather dry expository style, has many complex sentences, and uses many difficult and unfamiliar words. The effect of interest with these standard dialect passages contrasts with the finding that transforming passages into nonstandard dialect seems to have little influence on black children's reading comprehension (Hall & Turner, 1974; Nolen, 1972). Perhaps topic interest will prove to be a more powerful text-content factor than dialect.

One secondary finding from this study was the pattern of interest ratings made by black and white children. The correlation between black males' and white males' ratings of the 25 pictures was highly significant and the correlation of black females' ratings and white females' ratings was also significant. (In contrast, for both races, males' and females' ratings were not significantly related.) These data suggest that black and white children have similar interests and that textbook writers and teachers need to be careful not to overestimate the distinctiveness of black children's interests.

IMPLICATIONS FOR ACHIEVEMENT TESTING AND INSTRUCTION

The research discussed thus far has possible implications for achievement testing. How interesting are the passages on standardized reading achievement tests? The Asher and Markell (1974) finding that boys performed worse than girls on the school-administered reading achievement test and on the low-interest encyclopedia passages but as well as girls on the high-interest encyclopedia passages implies that many of the achievement test passages were of low interest. Interestingly, an analysis of the characters or actors in achievement test passages indicates that a disproportionate number of characters are male (Faggan-Steckler, McCarthy, & Tittle, 1974). This might mean that boys would be at an advantage. However, the topics of test passages are probably more important determinants of performance than the gender of the story characters. Clearly, research is needed on the extent to which achievement test passages function as low-interest material.

Another important question that has not been systematically addressed is whether high-interest reading programs promote the acquisition of reading skills. A number of high-interest reading programs have been reported (Daniels, 1971; Fader & McNeil, 1968; Gormli & Nittoli, 1971; Stanchfield, 1973). Descriptions of these programs provide guidelines for setting them up and two reports even provide lists of paperback books that were used (Daniels, 1971; Fader & McNeil, 1968). Unfortunately, evaluations of high-interest reading programs have not involved children who were randomly assigned to high-interest versus regular programs, making it hard to assess the meaning of gains made by children in high-interest programs. Still, the evaluations made to date have yielded promising results. For example, in Gormli and Nittoli's (1971) high-interest summer reading program, boys gained more than one grade-equivalent score on three of four reading achievement subtests. Data such as these will hopefully stimulate more attempts at implementing and evaluating high-interest programs. It appears that focusing on the interest-value of what students read may have important long-term instructional effects as well as short-term assessment implications.

The implementation of high-interest reading programs should be accompanied by efforts to ensure that children develop new interests over time. Interests can be stimulated by providing students with information about a topic at a level students can understand. Two strategies commonly used by teachers are to take students on a field trip and to have students hear from an enthusiastic guest speaker. A procedure we have pilot-tested (Asher, 1975) is to have students meet weekly in small groups to discuss the individually selected books they have been reading. As part of the discussion, students describe what makes the topic they have been reading about interesting to them. Research is needed to evaluate the impact of different strategies for helping children develop new interests. Such studies might use process measures such as "time on task" as well as outcome measures such as reading comprehension.

High-interest programs also need to ensure that students will read material that is important but somewhat dull. One way to achieve this is to use the Premack (1959) principle. Mature readers who study a lot (e.g., some college students) often use high-interest activities as reinforcement for doing low-interest work. There is evidence that this approach is effective with children. Cook and White (1977) had third-grade students work on special exercises for 15 minutes a day, 3 days a week, over an 8-week period. Each exercise consisted of an article to be read followed by 40 questions concerning comprehension, vocabulary, word usage, and word analysis. Children were reinforced after each session by being able to listen to stories for an amount of time corresponding to their number of correct responses. Different experimental conditions contained stories of different interest levels on the tapes. Children who listened to the most interesting stories did better on the exercises and on the immediate and 8-week follow-up achievement posttests. This result suggests that programs that use high-interest material *can* ensure that important but less interesting material is read as well.

Finally, we need to know more about ways in which high-interest reading programs can be combined with a focus on the teaching of discrete comprehension skills. Educators who use high-interest reading programs tend not to emphasize the teaching of specific comprehension skills, and educators who emphasize skills tend to give little thought to the interest level of the reading content. This would seem to be an unfortunate situation. What may be needed are strategies for teaching skills in the context of meaningful and interesting reading activities. Every skill need not require a workbook. Many skills can be taught implicitly as part of the discussion of interesting and personally relevant material.

SUMMARY

To summarize, research to date suggests that children's comprehension of high-interest material is superior to their comprehension of low-interest material. Furthermore, there are potentially important individual differences in children's responses, with boys frequently showing stronger effects than girls. Although the effect of interest on comprehension has been well documented, the basis for the interest effect is less clear. That the effect can be considerably reduced by providing children with external incentives for working hard suggests that low motivation is responsible for lower performance on low-interest material. Still, more direct tests of the contribution of motivation and knowledge are needed. Finally, it appears that focusing on the role of topic interest will be useful in the construction of reading tests and in the design of reading instruction. As work proceeds in these directions, researchers and practitioners should be sensitive to the issues of how programs can ensure that children develop new interests and how interest-based programs can be integrated with specific reading skill objectives.

ACKNOWLEDGMENTS

Preparation of this chapter was supported by the National Institution of Education under Grant No. NE-G-00-3-0060 and Contract No. US-NIE-C-400-76-0116.

REFERENCES

Anderson, R. C., Reynolds, R. E., Schallert, D. L., & Goetz, E. T. Frameworks for comprehending discourse. *American Educational Research Journal*, 1977, *14*, 367–381.
Asher, S. R. *Effect of interest in material on sex differences in reading comprehension*. Final report to the National Institute of Education (Project No. 3-1324), June, 1975.

Asher, S. R. Influence of topic interest on black children's and white children's reading comprehension. *Child Development*, 1979, *50*, 686–690.

Asher, S. R., & Geraci, R. L. *Topic interest, external incentive and reading comprehension.* Unpublished manuscript, University of Illinois, Urbana-Champaign, 1980.

Asher, S. R., Hymel, S., & Wigfield, A. Influence of topic interest on children's reading comprehension. *Journal of Reading Behavior*, 1978, *10*, 35–47.

Asher, S. R., & Markell, R. A. Sex differences in comprehension of high- and low-interest reading material. *Journal of Educational Psychology*, 1974, *66*, 680–687.

Ayres, L. P. *Laggards in our schools.* New York: Russell Sage Foundation, 1909.

Bernstein, M. R. The relationship between interest and reading comprehension. *Journal of Educational Research*, 1955, *49*, 283–288.

Blom, G. E. Sex differences in reading disability. In E. Calkins (Ed.), *Reading forum.* Bethesda, Md.: National Institute of Neurological Disease and Stroke, 1971.

Blom, G. E., Waite, R. R., & Zimet, S. G. A motivational content analysis of children's primers. In H. Levin & J. P. Williams (Eds.), *Basic studies on reading.* New York: Basic Books, 1970.

Bormuth, J. R. Comparable cloze and multiple-choice comprehension tests scores. *Journal of Reading*, 1967, *10*, 291–299.

Bormuth, J. R. Empirical determination of the instructional reading level. *Proceedings of the International Reading Association*, 1968, *13*, 716–721.

Britannica Junior Encyclopaedia. Chicago: Encyclopaedia Britannica, 1970.

Brophy, J. F., & Good, T. L. *Teacher-student relationships: Causes and consequences.* New York: Holt, Rinehart & Winston, 1974.

Coleman, J. S., Campbell, E. Q., Hobson, C. J., McPartland, J., Mood, A. M., Weinfeld, F. D., & York, R. L. *Equality of educational opportunity.* Washington, D. C.: U.S. Government Printing Office, 1966.

Cook, V. J., & White, M. A. Reinforcement potency of children's reading materials. *Journal of Educational Psychology*, 1977, *69*, 231–236.

Daniels, S. *How 2 gerbils, 20 goldfish, 200 games, 2000 books, and I taught them how to read.* Philadelphia: Westminister Press, 1971.

Dorsel, T. N. Preference-success assumption in education. *Journal of Educational Psychology*, 1975, *67*, 514–520.

Estes, T. H., & Vaughan, Jr., J. L. Reading interest and comprehension: Implications. *Reading Teacher*, 1973, *27*, 149–153.

Fader, D. N., & McNeil, E. B. *Hooked on books: Program and proof.* New York: Berkeley, 1968.

Faggen-Steckler, J., McCarthy, K. A., & Tittle, C. K. A quantitative method for measuring sex "bias" in standardized tests. *Journal of Educational Measurement*, 1974, *11*, 151–161.

Gates, A. I. Sex differences in reading ability. *Elementary School Journal*, 1961, *61*, 431–434.

Gormli, J., & Nittoli, M. J. Rapid improvement of reading skills in juvenile delinquents. *Journal of Experimental Education*, 1971, *40*, 45–48.

Hall, V. C., & Turner, R. R. The validity of the "different language explanation" for poor scholastic performance by black students. *Review of Educational Research*, 1974, *44*, 69–81.

Klein, H. A. *Interest and comprehension in sex-typed materials.* Paper presented at the International Reading Association Conference, Kansas City, May 1969. (ERIC Document Reproduction Service No. ED 030 551).

Neale, D. C., Gill, N., & Tismer, W. Relationship between attitudes toward school subjects and school achievement. *Journal of Educational Research*, 1970, *63*, 232–237.

Nolen, P. S. Reading nonstandard dialect materials: A study at grades two and four. *Child Development*, 1972, *43*, 1092–1097.

Premack, D. Toward empirical behavior laws: 1. Positive reinforcement. *Psychological Review*, 1959, *66*, 219–233.

Rankin, E. F., & Culhane, J. W. Comparable cloze and multiple-choice test scores. *Journal of Reading*, 1969, *13*, 193–198.

Samuels, S. J., & Turnure, J. E. Attention and reading achievement in first-grade boys and girls. *Journal of Educational Psychology*, 1974, *66*, 29–32.

Shnayer, S. W. *Some relationships between reading interests and reading comprehension.* Unpublished doctoral dissertation, University of California, Berkeley, 1967.

Singer, H., Gerard, H. B., & Redfearn, D. Achievement. In H. B. Gerard & N. Miller (Eds.), *School desegregation*. New York: Plenum, 1975.

Stanchfield, J. M. The effect of high-interest materials on reading achievement in the first grade. *National Reading Conference Yearbook*, 1967, *16*, 58–61.

Stanchfield, J. M. *Sex differences in learning to read.* Bloomington, Ind.: Phi Delta Kappa Educational Foundation, 1973.

Taylor, W. L. "Cloze procedure": A new tool for measuring readability. *Journalism Quarterly*, 1953, *30*, 415–433.

Tyler, L. E. The antecedents of two varieties of interest pattern. *Genetic Psychology Monographs*, 1964, *70*, 177–227.

23

Skill Hierarchies in Reading Comprehension

Barak V. Rosenshine
Center for the Study of Reading,
University of Illinois, Urbana-Champaign

This review explores two issues: whether there are distinct reading comprehension skills and whether there is evidence of a skill hierarchy. Experimental studies were not found on these issues and, thus, the review is an exploration of data from four sources: (1) authoritative lists of comprehension skills; (2) factor analytic studies on the interrelatedness of reading skills; (3) textbooks for teachers of elementary reading; and (4) reading series and instructional materials developed for primary grade children. To anticipate the major outcomes, no clear evidence was found for distinct reading skills or for a skill hierarchy.

LISTS OF COMPREHENSION SKILLS

The first step was an inspection of lists of reading skills from a wide range of sources to see if there was substantial agreement on common reading skills. If so, one could then explore whether these skills are best learned in a hierarchical fashion.

Table 23.1 lists common skills across five fairly authorative lists. The first, from Science Research Associates (Shub, Friedman, Kaplan, Katien, & Scroggin, 1973) was developed by the Center for the Study of Evaluation at UCLA. The second is a list of the reading comprehension skills tested by the National Assessment of Educational Progress (1973). The third is from Scott Foresman's (Aaron et al., 1976) scope and sequence chart for their reading series. The fourth is from the work of Harris and Smith (1976), two highly reputed authors of textbooks on teaching reading. The fifth is from Otto and

TABLE 23.1

Categories in Common Across Sources

SRA (literal and inferential comprehension)	National Assessment (ages 9-13)	Scott-Foresman (1976)	Harris & Smith (1976)	Otto (1974)
1. Main idea/title	Main idea/title	Main idea	Main idea	Topic/main idea
2. Detail	(a) Recognizing facts (b) Retaining facts	Detail	Detail	Detail
3. Sequence	Organization (See Number 6)	Sequence	Sequence	Sequence
4. Draw conclusions		Predict outcomes and conclusion		Predict outcomes
5. Cause and effect	(See Number 6)	Cause and effect		Cause and effect
6. Compare and contrast	(a) Draw inference from material given		Critical reading	
			(a) Analytic interpretation	
	(b) Draw inference from material given plus previous knowledge		(b) Inferential interpretation	
			(c) Evaluation	
7. Fact and opinion	Fact and opinion			
8. Author's purpose	Author's purpose		Author's plan of organization	
9.	Words in context			Words in context

Askov (1974) and was used in the reading program developed at the Wisconsin Research and Development Center. This sample was chosen to represent both a broad range of sources and some of the best thinking in this area.

Table 23.1 is an attempt to show the common skills across these five sources. In comparing skills across programs, other reviewers might make slightly different groupings—particularly of those skills enclosed by brackets—but the general similarities across programs seem fairly clear. Based on Table 23.1, it appears that there are common reading skills. Further, it is suggested that these skills fall into three general types. The first, *locating details,* is the simplest and involves recognititon, paraphrase, and/or matching. The second group might be labeled *simple inferential skills* and refers to the ability to draw inferences after reading short segments of a passage. Representative skills in this group might be:

— understanding words in context
— recognizing the sequence of events
— recognizing cause and effect relationships
— comparison and contrasting

The third group might be labeled *complex inferential skills* and refers to the ability to draw inferences after reading longer segments and passage. Representative skills in this group might be:

— recognizing the main idea/title/topic
— drawing conclusions
— predicting outcomes

The divisions between these groupings are not fixed, and someone might wish to classify "recognizing cause and effect relationships" as complex inferential skills if longer segments need to be read before a question can be answered.

There are many exceptions to this classification based on length of text processed. This difficulty in distinguishing among these inferential skills is recognized in the taxonomy developed by Barrett (cited in Clymer, 1968). In that taxonomy both complex and simple inferential skills were placed on the same level, that of inferential comprehension.

Unique Comprehension Skills

However, beyond the comprehension skills commonly cited by the previously mentioned five sources, there are also a number of "unique" skills. Looking at Table 23.1, the skills of distinguishing fact and opinion or determining the author's purpose only appear on some of the lists. (It would also be difficult to decide whether these two skills represent simple or complex inferential

TABLE 23.2
Unique Categories From Each Source

SRA	National Assessment	Scott-Foresman	Harris & Smith	Otto
Classifying sets of words	Recognizing and evaluating sources	Characterization	None	Synthesizing information
Paraphrase and summarize	Literary devices	Classification and seriation		Reason from a premise
Character's emotion and trait	Mood and tone	Empathy		Interpret negative sentences
Logical thinking		Evaluation		Interpret sentences with a right branching
		Following directions		Interpret sentences in passive voice
		Foreshadowing		Syllogistic reasoning
		Generalization		Inductive reasoning
		Judgment		Meaning of prefixes
		Literary style		
		Mental imagery		
		Previewing		
		Recall		
		Relationships		
		Analogous		
		Part-whole		
		Place-space		
		Size		
		Time		
		Skimming		
		Summarizing		

comprehension.) Beyond these unique skills, there are a number of skills only cited by a single source (see Table 23.2). In addition, 49 separate skills are listed by Ginn and Company for their primary grade 360 series (Clymer, 1969). Representative skills from their list include:

— matching characters with their traits, actions, and speech
— classifying questions about a selection according to whether they have been answered or not
— categorizing story elements into problem, climax, and solution
— listing characters to match given dialogue or actions
— giving setting or time
— stating the moral

— stating point of view from which story is told
— recounting character traits, qualities
— giving an account of similarities or differences in the content or plot of selections
— explaining the suitability of titles or headings
— making inferences about what would happen if circumstances were different
— evaluating ideas in a selection
— matching events to time

Each skill seems reasonable and sensible. One can argue that some of the skills can be combined, but even then the list of unique skills would be over 30.

Overall, if one inspects reading skills across a variety of sources, one does find a number of common skills, but there is also a larger number of unique skills from each list.

Comprehension Subskills

One can also argue that some of these skills should be split or arranged according to subskills. For example, the skill of finding the main idea in a narrative may be a different type of skill than finding the main idea in dialogue. The list of comprehension skills grows even longer when one adds the "subskills" some authors have identified. Twenty-four subskills were listed in the University of Illinois and Bolt Beranek & Newman proposal (1975) for the Center for the Study of Reading. These included:

— word meaning
— pure syntax
— deeper syntactic–semantic relations
— entailment (e.g., *If the unicorn is taller than the boy, then the boy is shorter than the unicorn.*)
— affect meaning

— direct speech acts
— metaphor
— metonymy (e.g., *I drank the whole bottle* means the speaker drank the liquid in the bottle)
— knowledge based anomaly
— knowledge based pragmatic implication

In still another approach to subskills, Val Anderson (unpublished paper of the Ontario Institute for Studies in Education) (1976) suggests that the skills of learning from context involves recognizing and using the following clues:

— contrast clues such as those provided by *but* and *also*
— description clues such as *is, is like,* and *was*
— synonym or antonym clues
— summary clues
— clues provided by tone, setting, and mode
— clues provided by words in a series
— clues derived from the main idea and supporting details
— prepositional clues
— clues derived from cause and effect pattern of sentence meaning

The relevance, importance, distinctiveness, and pervasiveness of the previously postulated subskills remains to be determined. But if we take even some of these subskills seriously and see them as distinct elements underlining comprehension, then we are agreeing to subdivide the common and unique comprehension skills identified previously according to the presence of these different subskills. If this occurs, the resulting list of comprehension skills and their subskills will be extremely large.

Summary

Across several sources, there is consensus that reading comprehension entails about seven skills—recognizing sequence, recognizing words in context, identifying the main idea, decoding detail, drawing inferences, recognizing cause and effect, and comparing and contrasting. However, if one also includes the unique skills and subskills that have been mentioned, then the total number of possible reading skills is in the hundreds. Regardless of the classification system, no source attempted to organize skills into a hierarchy.

CORRELATIONAL STUDIES OF READING SKILLS

We now turn to correlational studies of reading skills in an attempt to see whether there is empirical support for the *distinctiveness* of different comprehension skills. The major empirical work on identifying unique or distinct reading skills have been done by Davis (1968, 1972). Thorndike (1973) referred to Davis' 1968 and 1972 studies as containing "the most thoughtfully planned and meticulously gathered set of data [p. 178]" on the topic of distinct reading skills. Following up on his early research (1941), Davis began with a large item pool and selected test items designed to measure eight hypothesized reading comprehension skills. In contract to other studies, each item was based on a separate bit of reading, thus creating experimental independence of the items. Following preliminary item analysis, subsets of items were created that were homogeneous and distinct in that each item correlated more highly with total scores of the group of items designed to represent its own skill than it did with the total score for any of the seven other skills (Thorndike, 1973, p. 179). Two forms were used in the study, each form containing 12 items measuring each of the eight skills. These eight skills are listed in the left-hand column of Table 23-3.

There have been four analyses of these data: Davis (1968), Davis (1972), Spearritt (1972), and Thorndike (1973). The original treatment of these data (Davis, 1968), employing "uniqueness analysis," identified five unique skills, as illustrated in Table 23.3. These were:

— recalling word meanings
— finding answers to questions asked explicitly or in paraphrase
— drawing inferences from the content
— recognizing a writer's purpose, attitude, tone, or mood
— following the structure of a passage

Later, Davis (1972) applied factor analysis to the same data and four clear factors emerged that were consistent across the two forms (see Table 23.3). These were:

— recalling word meaning
— determining meaning from context
— finding answers to questions asked explicitly or in paraphrase, and weaving these ideas together in the content
— drawing inferences from the content

The search for unique skills in reading comprehension was continued by Spearritt (1972) and by Thorndike (1973), who reanalyzed Davis' data. Spearritt applied "maximum likelihood" factor analytic procedures (Joreskog & Lawley, 1968; Joreskog & Van Thillo, 1971) to the Davis data. His analysis yielded four unique skills:

— recalling word meanings
— drawing inferences from the content
— recognizing a writer's purpose, attitude, mood, and tone
— following the structure of a passage

TABLE 23.3
Three Analyses of Identical Data on Specific Reading Skills
(after Spearitt, 1972)

	Distinguishable Skills from Davis' 1968 Analysis	Distinguishable Skills from Davis' 1972 Analysis	Distinguishable Skills from Spearitt's 1972 Analysis
Recalling word meanings	—[a]	—	—
Drawing inferences about the meaning of a word from context			—
Finding answers to questions answered explicitly or in paraphrase		—[b]	
Weaving together ideas in the content		—[b]	
Drawing inferences from the content	—	—	
Recognizing a writer's purpose, attitude, tone, and mood	—		—
Identifying a writer's literary techniques			
Following a structure of a passage	—		—

[a] Each unique distinguishable skill that the investigator found is indicated by a —. Thus, Davis (1968) found five distinct reading comprehension skills.

[b] These two skills loaded on the same factor.

Of all the skills, vocabulary ("recalling word meanings") was best differentiated, as it was in the Davis analyses. Spearritt (1972) further concluded that "when the correlations between vocabulary and the other factors are excluded from consideration, the remaining correlations are extraordinarily high." Thus, "although certain comprehension skills can be differentiated, present types of reading comprehension tests, as distinct from word knowledge tests, largely measure one basic ability, which may well correspond to the label of 'reasoning in reading' [p. 110]."

In the fourth analysis of Davis' original data (Thorndike, 1973), "reliability coefficients rather than unities were used as the diagonal entries [p. 139]." Three factors emerged, with the first factor accounting for 93% of the variance. Thorndike also factor-analyzed four other sets of data and found, in each case, that 80–90% of the meaningful variance appeared in the first factor and the remainder was exhausted by two or possibly three factors. Thus, he concluded that the reading skills selected by Davis were not distinguishable. Thorndike also claimed that even the distinction that Davis made between "word knowledge" and "reasoning in reading" (or inferring from the text) was not justified, because there was little differentiation between word knowledge and paragraph comprehension in the factor analysis.

Looking at the results of these three studies in Table 23.3, one sees that *different analyses yielded different unique skills,* and only one skill was consistent across the three analyses: remembering word meanings. Thus, across these three analyses, whatever unique skills that do exist are not particularly robust. Further, the fourth analysis of this same data (Thorndike, 1973) did not yield any separate reading comprehension skills.

Additional Factor Analytic Studies

The results of additional factor analytic studies, as summarized by Berg (1973), are shown in Table 23.4. In these studies, there is little evidence for separate factors. Most of these studies did not have data on separate comprehension skills, but in the most comprehensive study on this topic (Schreiner, Hieronymus, & Forsyth, 1969) the comprehension skills that they included (e.g., cause and effect, main idea, reading for inferences) did *not* load on separate factors.

This review led Berg (1973) to the following conclusions:

There are many more studies in the literature that add up to the same generalization: There are few consistent findings relative to a large number of statistically identifiable separate reading abilities. A rough average of the number of factors that researchers suggest [lies] somewhere between two and five. Lennon (1962) suggested that only four factors can be measured reliably: 1) a general verbal factor, 2) comprehension of explicitly stated material, 3) comprehension of implicit or latent meaning, and 4) appreciation. ... Yet, as

TABLE 23.4
Results of Additional Factor Analytic Studies as
Summarized by Berg (1973)

Thurstone, 1956 (reanalysis of Davis, 1944)
  Single general factor
Hall and Robinson, 1945
  Attitude of comprehension accuracy
  Rate of inductive reading
  Word meaning
  Rate of reading unrelated facts
  Chart reading skill
Stolurow and Newman, 1959
  Semantic difficulty (words)
  Syntactic difficulty (sentences)
Hunt, 1957
  Word knowledge
  Paragraph comprehension
Schreiner, Hieronymus, and Forsyth, 1969
  Speed of reading
  Listening comprehension
  Verbal reasoning (classification of words)
  Speed of noting details

Not separate factors:

  Paragraph meaning
  Determining cause and effect
  Reading for inferences
  Selecting the main idea

---

already stated, a review of reading tests turns up 70 to 80 factors that various tests implicitly claim to measure [p. 83].

In another review, MacGintie (1973) reached a similar conclusion. He claimed that the most promising distinction is between understanding facts explicitly stated in a passage and making inferences from what is stated. "Even this distinction is not an easy one, and we should require a clear demonstration that two subtests are measuring this distinction before we pay much attention to comprehension subtest scores that claim to represent different aspects of comprehension [p. 41]."

Thus, across four analyses of Davis' original data plus reviews of additional factor analytic studies summarized by Berg (1973) and by MacGintie (1973), no clear evidence emerged supporting unique and separate comprehension skills. Although some skills did emerge as distinguishable in some studies, these results were not consistent across studies. Even the distinction between deriving explicit and implicit meaning from text did not emerge as consistently separate factors. Further, in one analysis (Thorndike, 1973), even the distinction between word meaning and comprehension did not emerge.

Skill Hierarchies

The most ardent proponent of unique reading comprehension skills, Fredrick Davis (1972), does not believe that his research has produced evidence in favor of a hierarchical skills theory. First, he notes that his previous work shows that "tests measuring a wide variety of skills involved in comprehension are positively, and in most instances, closely correlated [p. 172]." Further, he states that:

> The hierarchical skills theory cannot be reconciled with experimental findings concerning the intercorrelations of skill tests in reading comprehension.... Inspection of the intercorrelations in Davis' cross-day matrices (Davis, 1968, p. 524), based on scores of 988 twelfth-grade students in academic high schools shows no marked evidence that the eight skill tests (which display approximately equal reliability coefficients) can be arranged in a clear-cut order of cumulative agglomeration of simple skills in more complex skills. More systematic investigation of this point needs to be made [p. 172].

In sum, a major research study in reading comprehension revealed some unique reading skills but no evidence that these skills are hierarchical.

In his suggestions for future research, Davis reaffirms this lack of knowledge of reading hierarchies. He suggests controlled experiments, using specially prepared workbooks for teaching purposes, to determine the effect on comprehension of teaching the skills identified in his research. Davis (1972) further discusses the need "to determine the effect on overall comprehension of different 'orders' (or hierarchies) in which operational skills ... are taught and practiced [p. 675]." Surprisingly, these experiments have not been done, and the need for such work continues to exist.

Robert Gagné (1970), one of the originators of the idea of learning hierarchies, has shied away from discussing learning hierarchies in reading comprehension even though he suggested the existence of learning hierarchies in decoding. When discussing principles of reading comprehension, he noted that "all such principles are quite complex and are typically learned not as formally stated rules but by a process of discovery from the act of reading [p. 273]."

In the 1968 NSSE yearbook on reading instruction, two authors noted the lack of research on learning sequences. Wittick (1968) claimed that little research has been done to determine the most effective learning sequences, and that "sequences have been produced logically rather than psychologically [p. 75]." Robinson (1968) also called for more research and stated that "within the next ten years, a large amount of additional information on effective sequences should be available [p. 406]." Such research has not appeared in reading comprehension.

Reading Comprehension and Reasoning

Carver (1973) has developed an interesting indictment of reading tests. Following Spache (1965), he described four levels of comprehension:

1. Decoding of words and determination of their meaning in a particular sentence.
2. Combining meanings of individual words into complete understanding of the sentence.
3. Understanding of the paragraph and its implied main idea, as well as cause and effect, hypothesis-proof, implications, unstated conclusions, and ideas associated with but tangential to the main idea of a paragraph.
4. Evaluation of ideas, including questions of logic, proof, authenticity, and value judgments.

Carver believes that levels 1 and 2 represent reading, whereas levels 3 and 4 represent reasoning. He also believes that most reading tests are heavily weighted with levels 3 and 4 and thus concludes that most reading comprehension tests measure reasoning.

Almost all of the reading comprehension skills discussed previously and in the next section would thus be coded as "reasoning" by Carver, just as Barrett (in Clymer, 1968) coded the same skills as "inferential comprehension." Thus, most of the skills listed under reading comprehension might also be labeled as reasoning, and talk of a hierarchy or optimal sequence of reasoning skills at this time takes us well beyond available research. The topic simply has not been studied. At the same time, Carver's distinction between reading and reasoning appears similar to the distinction between locating explicitly stated details and locating implicitly stated answers. This distinction has *not* been validated in the correlation research discussed previously.

Substrata-Factor Studies

Studies by Holmes (1948) and Singer (1965, 1969) were attempts to identify the "substrata factors," speed of reading, and reading comprehension. However, these studies are not relevant to this review, because reading comprehension itself was a criterion measure and the predictor variable did *not* include comprehension skills or subskills. Rather, their predictor variables included tests such as speed or word perception, span of recognition, or word knowledge. Thus, however valuable their specific multiple-regression procedures may be, because of the variables selected, the results themselves are not particularly relevant to this review.

Summary

Several analyses of the best data available on reading comprehension skills (Davis, 1968, 1972) have revealed, at most, four distinct skills (aside from word meaning). However, Thorndike (1973) and Spearritt (1972) noted that even these four skills are highly intercorrelated. Even in the most limited case—the distinction between locating explicitly stated details and implicitly stated answers—the results are not clear-cut. Other factor-analytic studies of reading processes, although not as well designed as Davis' study, also failed to yield consistently distinct reading comprehension skills (see reviews by Berg, 1973; MacGintie, 1973).

These factor analytic studies did not reveal anything about hierarchies, but, of course, factor analysis is not an appropriate technique for identifying hierarchies. One suspects that experimental approaches might be more fruitful than these a posteriori procedures. Nonetheless, if factor analytic techniques have failed to identify distinct and independent reading comprehension skills, it seems unlikely that other a posteriori techniques would locate both distinct skills and a hierarchical ordering.

TEXTBOOKS FOR
ELEMENTARY READING TEACHERS

Four major textbooks for elementary reading teachers (Durkin, 1974; Karlin, 1975; Otto, McMenemy, & Smith, 1973; Tinker & McCullough, 1975) were inspected to determine whether they discussed sequencing or hierarchical ordering of reading comprehension skills. No explicit mention of hierarchy or sequence was found in any textbook.

There was, however, a division of reading comprehension into literal, interpretative (or inferential), and critical reading. Literal refers to word meaning, context clues, sentence meaning, and paragraph organization—the ability to derive explicit meaning from text. Under interpretive or inferential reading, the authors include: reaching conclusions, drawing inferences from what is read, identifying purpose, anticipating outcomes, making generalizations, and recognizing the main idea. Critical reading refers to recognizing the difference between fact and opinion, recognizing the logic of arguments, and judging the appropriateness of arguments and conclusions.

Thus, the distinction between literal and interpretive reading appears to support the same rough hierarchy of explicit and implicit meaning that was discussed in the earlier section on correlational studies. The borders between these two concepts are, of course, fuzzy. Skills such as grasping the meaning of metaphors and similes, identifying sequence, or understanding cause and effect might be classified as literal or as interpretive by different authors. But the general distinction between explicit and implicit meaning is acknowledged by most authors. (Recall, however, that in Spearritt's reanalysis of the Davis data for twelfth-grade students, "understanding explicit meaning" did not emerge as a distinct skill.)

ANALYSES OF PRIMARY GRADE READING MATERIALS

The publishers' scope and sequence charts for the first three semesters of five primary grade reading curricula were inspected to determine whether comprehension skills are presented in either a sequential or hierarchical manner. Those five curricula were:

1. Ginn and Company: Reading 360
2. Harper & Row: Design for Reading
3. J. B. Lippincott Company: Basic Reading 1975
4. Scott Foresman Systems: Reading Unlimited
5. Webster/McGraw-Hill: Programmed Reading

The time of introduction and subsequent appearance of eight reading comprehension skills were noted. The skills of interest were:

1. Locating details
2. Recognizing the main idea
3. Recognizing the sequence of events
4. Drawing conclusions
5. Recognizing cause and effect relationships
6. Understanding words in context
7. Making interpretations (judgments and generalizations)
8. Making inferences from the text

Analyses Across Programs

Across the five programs, one notes that all eight comprehension skills were introduced early—within the first two semesters of the first year (see Table 23.5). The exceptions to this statement are the Webster/McGraw-Hill Programmed Readers (MH), which do not introduce any comprehension skills until their sixth book (reading level 2.3), and Harper & Row (HR),

TABLE 23.5
Time of Presentation of Comprehension Skills

Detail

Ginn 360	1:1[a] Early[b]
Harper & Row	1:1 Early
Lippincott	1:1 Early
Scott Foresman	1:2 Middle
McGraw-Hill	Book 12 (=3.8)

Main Idea

Ginn 360	1:2 Early
Harper & Row	1:1 Middle
Lippincott	1:2 Early
Scott Foresman	1:2 Middle
McGraw-Hill	Book 13 (=4.0)

Main Idea

Sequence

Ginn 360	1:1 Early
Harper & Row	1:1 Early
Lippincott	1:1 Middle
Scott Foresman	1:1 Early
McGraw-Hill	Book 8 (introduction in Book 6) (=2.8) (=2.3)

Draw Conclusion

Ginn 360	1:1 Early
Harper & Row	1:1 Early
Lippincott	1:1 Middle
Scott Foresman	1:2 Middle (introduction 1:1 late)
McGraw-Hill	Book 6 (=2.3)

Cause and Effect

Ginn 360	1:1 Middle
Harper & Row	1:1 Early
Lippincott	(not mentioned)
Scott Foresman	1:1 Late
McGraw-Hill	Book 7 (=2.5)

Words in Context

Ginn 360	1:1 Early
Harper & Row	2:1 Middle
Lippincott	1:1 Middle
Scott Foresman	1:1 Early
McGraw-Hill	Book 12 (=3.8)

Words in Context

Interpretation (judgment or generalization)

Ginn 360	1:1 scattered from 1:2 on
Harper & Row	1:1 Early
Lippincott	(not mentioned)
Scott Foresman	1:1 Early
McGraw-Hill	Book 18 (=5.1)

Inference

Ginn 360	1:1 Early
Harper & Row	1:1 Early
Lippincott	1:1 Late
Scott Foresman	1:1 Middle
McGraw-Hill	Book 6 (=2.3)

[a]The number 1:1 refers to the first semester of the first grade, 1:2 to the second semester of the first grade, etc.
[b]The terms "early," "middle," and "late" refer to whether the skill first appeared in the first, second, or last third of the semester.
The table shows that most of the skills were introduced in the early and middle thirds of the *first semester*.

which delays introduction of one skill—understanding words in context—until the second year.

Across the four programs (McGraw-Hill is excepted), there is no particular order for introducing practice in these skills. Recognizing sequence, recognizing cause and effect, and making inferences are all introduced in the first semester. The programs also introduce locating details and drawing conclusions in the first semester (with the exception of Scott-Foresman, which delays these two skills until the middle of the second semester). Similarly, locating words in context is usually introduced in the first semester (with the exception of Harper & Row, which delays this until the middle of the third semester).

There are only two comprehension skills not generally introduced in the first semester. The skill of recognizing the main idea is usually delayed until the second semester, and making interpretation appears early in two programs (Harper & Row and Scott Foresman) but does not appear in the first three semesters in the other two programs (Ginn and Lippincott). Thus, with the exception of McGraw-Hill, or isolated instances noted previously, the programs introduce most of the skills in the first semester and the remainder in the second semeser of the first grade.

Analyses Within Programs

Within programs there is also little evidence of a sequence for presenting skills. Lippincott, Ginn, and Harper & Row introduce almost all of their skills early in the first semester. They do, however, show one slight common pattern: They delay introducing locating the main idea—Harper & Row until the middle of the first semester and Ginn and Lippincott until the second semester. Scott Foresman used a two-step process, introducing half the skills in the first semester and the other skills (detail, main idea, and drawing conclusions) in the second semester.

Only McGraw-Hill has any evidence of a sequence. As shown in Table 23.5, they delay introducing any skills until the 2.3 reading level and usually introduce skills one at a time across 3 years of reading levels. Contrary to expectations, McGraw-Hill introduces the inferential skills of drawing conclusions and recognizing cause and effect prior to the more literal skill of locating details. Overall, with the exception of a delay in introducing the main idea until the second semester, no particular sequence for the introduction of reading comprehension skills was found either across or within programs.

In addition, no evidence was found for a hierarchy of skills. In common examples of hierarchies, such as Gagné's, once a skill is mastered, it is no longer taught. For example, if simple addition is a prerequisite for learning division, once this addition skill is learned it is no longer taught. But in reading comprehension, once a skill is introduced *it continues to be studied throughout the first five grades*. Thus, locating details or recognizing sequence is never considered as mastered, but, rather, these skills are continually studied at increasing levels of difficulty.

THE NEED FOR EXPERIMENTAL STUDIES
ON COMPREHENSION SKILLS

Given the high intercorrelations that exist between different reading skills, it seems that further correlational research will not yield anything new. Thus, it seems more reasonable to turn to exploratory experimental studies. The first major questions is simple: Does learning a particular skill increase reading comprehension scores for that skill more than learning some other skill does? For example, if one student spends a good deal of time doing exercises on "main idea" or "synthesis" and another does exercises on "sequence," will the two students differ on tests of synthesis and sequence? To the best of our knowledge, such studies have not been done. The correlational research suggests that spending time on any one skill will be as effective as any other. That is, time spent doing synthesis exercises will be as effective for gain in sequence as it will be for synthesis. On the other hand, there is a broad literature on content covered or opportunity to learn that suggests that one primarily learns what one is taught.

A possible study is illustrated in Fig. 23.1. In this study, students would do progressive exercises in only one skill and would be tested on all four skills.

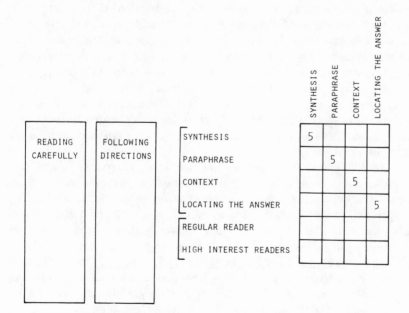

FIG. 23.1.   Design for a study on comprehension skills.

Training in reading carefully and following directions would take place for all prior to instruction to insure high attention. The number in the diagonal represents the top of a 5-point scale, the scores we assume students would achieve in their own area. In addition, another factor could be introduced to see whether time spent in reading itself is as effective as time spent on reading exercises. We hope to conduct such a study soon.

CONCLUSION

To summarize the main findings of this review, we provide here our best answers to what we regard as the most important questions pertaining to skills hierarchies.

1. *Are there discrete comprehension skills?* It is difficult to confidently put forth any set of discrete comprehension skills. Different factor-analytic procedures, applied to identical data that began with eight nominally different skills, have yielded one, two, or four independent factors. To dramatize the situation, we are not even clear that the skill of deriving explicit meaning from texts is separate from skills of deriving implicit meaning. At this point, there is simply no clear evidence to support the naming of discrete skills in reading comprehension.

2. *Do the skills appear, or are they taught, in a hierarchical order that is consistent from program to program?* Comprehension skills are simply not taught in a hierarchical fashion. In a typical hierarchy, once a skill has been taught, it is not retaught. Thus, in decoding training, students are not explicitly taught long vowel sounds from first through fifth grades. But reading comprehension skills *are* continuously taught from the first through the fifth grade. In addition, there is no hierarchy in the order in which comprehension skills are introduced. In each program studied, almost all skills are introduced in the first year of school. Further, it appears that *all* the major comprehension skills can be introduced, in a simplified form, in the first year of school.

3. *Are the skills that are labeled and taught in the programs all essential to achieving the goal behaviors of comprehension or inferring meaning from texts?* It is not clear whether all, or even any, of the skill exercises in reading comprehension are essential or necessary. One is not sure that a student who only practiced "finding the main idea" would be deficient on the skill of "determining sequence" even if he or she never had exercises in that area. Although such studies have been suggested by Davis (1972), no evidence of such studies were found. Indeed, it is possible that students who only read stories and never completed skill exercises might do just as well on comprehension tests as students who completed these exercises.

ACKNOWLEDGMENT

Preparation of this paper was supported by Contract No. US-NIE-C-400-76-0116 from the National Institute of Education.

REFERENCES

Aaron, I. V., Artley, A., Goodman, K., Jenkins, W., Manning, J., Monroe, M., Pyle, W. A., Robinson, H., Schiller, A., Smith, M., Sullivan, L., Weintraub, S., and Wepman, J. *Reading Unlimited: Scott Foresman Systems, Revised.* Glenview, Ill.: Scott Foresman and Co., 1976.

Anderson, V. *Subskills in learning from context.* Unpublished paper, Toronto, Ontario. Ontario Institute for Studies in Education, 1976.

Berg, P. C. Evaluating reading abilities. In W. H. MacGinitie (Ed.), *Assessment problems in reading.* Newark, Del.: International Reading Association, 1973.

Carver, R. P. Reading as reasoning: Implications for measurement. In W. H. MacGinitie (Ed.), *Assessment problems in reading.* Newark, Del.: International Reading Association, 1973.

Clymer, T. What is reading?: Some current concepts. In A. M. Robinson (Ed.), *Innovation and change in reading instruction.* Chicago: University of Chicago Press, 1968.

Clymer, T. *Behavioral objectives for Reading 360.* Boston, Mass. Ginn and Co., 1969.

Davis, F. B. Research in comprehension in reading. *Reading Research Quarterly,* 1968, *4,* 499–545.

Davis, F. B. Psychometric research on comprehension in reading. *Reading Research Quarterly,*1972, *7,* 628–678.

Durkin, D. *Teaching them to read* (2nd ed.). Boston, Mass.: Allyn & Bacon, 1974.

Gagné, R. *The conditions of learning.* New York: Holt, Rinehart & Winston, 1970.

Hall, W. E., & Robinson, F. P. An analytical approach to the study of reading skills. *Journal of Educational Psychology,* 1945, *36,* 429–442.

Harris, L. A. and Smith, C. B. *Reading instruction.* New York: Holt, Rinehart and Winston, 1976.

Holmes, J. A. *Factors underlying major reading disabilities at the college level.* Unpublished doctoral dissertation. University of California, Berkeley, 1948.

Hunt, L. C., Jr. Can we measure specific factors associates with reading comprehension? *Journal of Educational Research,* 1957, *51,* 161–171.

Joreskog, K. G., & Lawley, D. N. New methods in maximum likelihood factor analysis. *British Journal of Mathematical and Statistical Psychology,* 1968, *21,* 85–96.

Joreskog, K. G., & Van Thillo, M. *New rapid algorithms for factor analysis by unweighted least squares, generalized least squares and maximum likelihood* (Research Memorandum 71-5). Princeton, N.J.: Educational Testing Service, 1971.

Karlin, R. *Teaching elementary reading* (2nd ed.). New York: Harcourt, Brace Jovanovich, 1975.

Lennon, Roger. What can be measured? *Reading Teacher, 15,* 326–337, 1962.

MacGintie, W. H. What are we testing? In W. H. MacGintie (Ed.), *Assessment problems in reading.* Newark, Del.: International Reading Association, 1973.

National Assessment of Educational Progress. *Reading: Summary* (Report 02-R-00). Washington, D.C. U.S. Government Printing Office, 1973.

Otto, W., & Askov, E. *Rationale and guidelines: The Wisconsin design for reading skill development.* Minneapolis, Minn.: National Computer Systems, 1974.

Otto, W., McMenemy, R. A., & Smith, R. J. *Corrective and remedial teaching* (2nd ed.). Boston, Mass.: Houghton Mifflin, 1973.

Robinson, H. M. The next decade. In H. M. Robinson (Ed.), *Innovation and change in reading instruction.* Chicago, Ill.: University of Chicago Press, 1968.

Schreiner, R. L., Hieronymus, A. N., & Forsyth, R. Differential measurement of reading abilities at the elementary school level. *Reading Research Quarterly,* 1969, *5,* 84–99.

Shub, A., Friedman, R., Kaplan, J. P., Katien, J., & Scroggin, J. L. *Diagnosis: An instructional aid.* Palo Alto, Calif.: Science Research Associates, Inc., 1973.

Singer, H. A developmental model of speed of reading in grades 3 through 6. *Reading Research Quarterly,* 1965, *1,* 29–49.

Singer, H. Reply to John Carroll's comments on the Holmes–Singer monograph and on the substrata-factor theory of reading. *Research in the Teaching of English,* 1969, *3,* 87–102.

Spache, G. D. *Toward better reading.* Champaign, Ill.: Garrard Press, 1965.

Spearritt, D. Identification of subskills of reading comprehension by maximum likelihood factor analysis. *Reading Research Quarterly,* 1972, *8,* 92–111.

Stolurow, L. M. and Newman, R. J. A factorial analysis of objective features of printed language presumably related to reading difficulty. *Journal of Educational Research,* 1959, *52,* 243–251.

Thorndike, R. L. Reading as reasoning. *Reading Research Quarterly,* 1973, *9,* 135–147.

Thurstone, L. L. Note on a reanalysis of Davis' reading tests. *Psychometrika,* September 1956, *11,* 185–188.

Tinker, M. A., & McCullough, C. M. *Teaching elementary reading* (4th ed.). Englewood Cliffs, N.J.: Prentice-Hall, 1975.

University of Illinois and Bolt Beranek and Newman Inc. *Proposal for a Center for the Study of Reading.* Urbana, Ill.: College of Education, 1975.

Wittick, M. L. Innovations in reading instruction: For beginners. In H. M. Robinson (Ed.), *Innovation and change in reading instruction.* Chicago, Ill.: University of Chicago Press, 1968.

Teaching Reading Comprehension in the Middle Grades

Joseph R. Jenkins
University of Washington
 and
Center for the Study of Reading

Darlene Pany
Arizona State University
 and
Center for the Study of Reading

The subject of this chapter is reading comprehension instruction during the middle elementary years, specifically grades three through eight. The chapter focuses on existing instructional approaches and programs designed to improve comprehension. Several of the more prominent approaches and programs are sampled and described. Some of the approaches, notably Smith and Goodman's (1971) psycholinguistic view of reading comprehension, are more conceptual and general than they are operational and specific. In contrast, certain programs such as DISTAR reading (Science Research Associates, 1974–1975) and the basal reading series provide teachers with highly specific instructional guidelines and materials. For each of the instructional approaches and programs sampled, we have attempted to locate research on its effectiveness in terms of student achievement. As will be apparent, evidence of specific program effects is, more often than not, either altogether absent or largely insubstantial.

Although the focus of this report is on children in the third through eighth grades, descriptions of some beginning reading programs are included, because most commercial instructional programs used in the middle elementary years are continuations of programs begun at first grade. Examination of these programs reveals that the comprehension skills that receive the greatest attention during the middle grades have been introduced and taught during the child's first year of reading instruction (Rosenshine, Chapter 23, this volume). This is as true for beginning reading programs noted for their strong code or phonic emphasis as for those characterized by a "meaning emphasis."

To provide a completely comprehensive account of how reading comprehension is currently taught is probably not possible; there may be as many ways to teach reading comprehension as there are reading teachers. We have assumed that although there are numerous differences between any two teachers in the way that they teach comprehension, *many* of these differences are incidental and not functionally related to reading achievement. The same may be said about different approaches to teaching reading comprehension (e.g., DISTAR vs. a basal reading series). Stated simply, some of the differences between instructional practices are not important and need not be described.

All programs contain a variety of activities that purport to enhance comprehension. Such variety makes it difficult to identify with confidence which aspects of comprehension instruction are important, that is, which are functionally related to changes in comprehension instruction upon which programs may vary, and which are at least plausibly related to program effectiveness. These potentially "critical featues" are: the corpus or text that students read; the skills that a program claims to teach; the relative emphasis a program gives to different skills; how the program teaches a skill; and the program's requirement for skill mastery (i.e., to what extent must a child demonstrate skill acquisition before progressing in the program).

We do not suggest that our admittedly tentative list of critical features is either exhaustive or empirically validated, only that it possesses some face validity. Even then, it is debatable as to how critical any of these features are to reading achievement. For example, some reading researchers have taken issue with the notion that reading comprehension can be divided into discrete skills (Goodman, 1969; Spearritt, 1972; Thorndike, 1971) and, instead, argue that reading comprehension is a complex global ability. If their conception of reading comprehension is correct, then four of our five "critical features" become trivial. Because we have not found the evidence in support of the global ability viewpoint to be particularly convincing (Jenkins & Pany, 1977), and because most instructional approaches to reading treat comprehension as a set of multiple skills (e.g., finding the main idea, sequencing), we will, for the present, consider the skills taught by a program to be a critical program feature. In reference to the corpus feature, it is interesting to note that, between reading programs, there is remarkably little overlap in what children read. This suggests to us a viewpoint that what is read has little to do with the development of comprehension skill and that instruction in reading comprehension can occur with one corpus as well as with another. We suspect that such a view is inaccurate and that topic, stylistic, and syntactic features of text may be factors that may need to be systematically and carefully programmed. Chapters by Asher, Brewer, Huggins and Adams, and Morgan and Sellner (Chapters 22, 9, 4, and 7, respectively) lend support to this view.

Thorough, quantitative analyses that compare instructional approaches according to these features have not been accomplished to date and are clearly beyond the scope of this chapter. Fortunately, some programs provide explicit information on certain of these features. In addition, a few investigations have been reported that compare selected reading curricula on one or more of the aforementioned features. Our strategy in describing the various approaches to comprehension instruction was to secure and report any previous comparisons that focused on one or more of these critical features. When such reports were lacking, we undertook a modest, non-comprehensive, nonquantitative but descriptive analysis of each approach according to the five aforementioned features.

Several of the more dominant approaches to reading instruction were selected for review. These include: basal readers, the DISTAR program, objectives-based reading systems, language experience, Directed Reading–Thinking, and psycholinguistic recommendations. Estimates of dominance were based on an examination of the materials that schools purchased for reading instruction and on approaches recommended by various reading authorities. Only comprehensive programs that seemed to provide teachers with extensive guidance over long periods of time were included. Not considered were more circumscribed, although frequently recommended, teaching ideas such as using newspaper articles, choral reading, poetry reading, reading games, and the like (Harris & Sipay, 1975). Research on program effects is described whenever such research was available. However, as will be painfully evident, research on most comprehensive approaches is scant.

BASAL READING SERIES

The most prevalent approach to teaching reading comprehension is through basal readers. According to Chall (1967), they represent an attempt to "give teachers and pupils a 'total reading program' embodying a system for teaching reading (the teachers' manuals), a collection of stories and selections for pupils to read (the readers), and exercises for additional practice (the workbooks) [p. 187]." The widespread adoption of basal series is truly remarkable. One program, Reading 360 (Ginn & Co., 1969) has been used with over 15,000,000 children in 2,000 school districts (Beck & Block, 1975). Barton and Wilder (1964) reported that between 92 and 98% of primary grade teachers use a basal series on all or most days of the year.

The frequent adoption of basal series is due in part to commercial publishers' success in creating a teaching tool that is unrivaled for convenience. The series provide stories and workbooks for children, questions for teachers to ask, lesson plans, and a host of recommended classroom activities. The explicit instructional guidelines that are contained in basal teacher's manuals probably exert a strong influence on classroom instruction. Beck and Block (1975) have observed:

> Although the implementation of these programs [developed by commercial publishers] undoubtedly varies with individual teachers, there is evidence (Diederich, 1973) that the instructional strategies, found in teacher's manuals accompanying commercial programs, heavily influence the teacher's classroom behavior. Our personal experience supports this evidence, indicating that many teachers rely on the content, sequence, and instructional strategies specified in the teacher's manual [p. 1].

We examined three basal reading series to determine what methods and materials are commonly recommended for teaching comprehension: Keys to Reading (Economy Co., 1972), Reading 360 (Ginn & Co., 1973), and Reading Unlimited (Scott-Foresman, 1976). These programs represent three of the most widely adopted basal reading series.

Corpus

To determine how basal programs select and construct the reading corpus, we inspected the Reading 360 3-2 (thid grade, second half) level teacher's manual (Ginn & Co., 1973). Selection of content seems to be a function of supposed developmental changes in children's interests. No mention is made of systematic attempts to vary semantic and syntactic features of text. The following description from the 1973 Teacher's Edition, Level 10, is revealing.

> Selections for today's students should reflect a broad range of cultural and social settings. The stories should portray realistically the children of cities, suburbs, rural areas, and foreign lands. Content in which characters are portrayed with lifelike qualities permits pupils to identify with the characters and their problems and to develop and test self-concepts. At this level children's reading abilities and interests are expanding and deepening. The stories, poems, and factual articles of Level 10 clearly take into account these developmental changes [p. 28].

Inspection of two other widely used programs, Keys to Reading (Economy, 1972) and Reading Unlimited (Scott-Foresman, 1976), yielded a similar picture of corpus selection. Beck and Block (1975) have suggested that, at least in reading series used in grades one and two, there may be rather large differences between program content in terms of meaningfulness, variety, and interest levels, especially when code emphasis programs are contrasted with programs with a lesser code emphasis. Although it is clear that semantic and syntactic features, topics (e.g., fiction vs. nonfiction), stylistics, and other aspects of text change in complexity as grade level increases, there has been remarkably little attention given to what children read. Variations in syntactic and stylistic features and in paragraph structure may be related to instructional effectiveness. For example, in teaching recognition of main idea, corpus variables such as location and frequency of main idea statements in a passage, as well as the presence and density of clues, may need to be systematically programmed for efficient and effective instruction (Anderson, Wardrop, Hively, Muller, Anderson, Hastings, & Frederiksen, 1978).

Skills Taught

Publishers may generate their own comprehension skill lists or adopt skill lists from other sources. For example, the 36 specific comprehension skills which the Ginn Reading 360 series identifies are patterned after Barrett's taxonomy of comprehension skills (1968).

The manuals that accompany basal readers are explicit about the skills that their programs teach. As mentioned earlier, there is some controversy surrounding the number and nature of reading comprehension subskills. That controversy is reflected in the skills' listing found in basal programs. The various programs differ both in the number of comprehension skills identified and in the way these skills are described and classified. For example, comprehension skills at the 3–2 level are subsumed under 17 categories in Scott-Foresman versus 10 in Ginn. However, it appears that merely comparing total comprehension skills listed may overestimate the differences between any two programs. Some of the skills listed under "Comprehension" in Scott-Foresman are differently classified in Ginn as "Decoding," "Literary Understanding and Appreciation," "Vocabulary," "Language," "Information and Knowledge," and "Creativity."

Rosenshine's analysis (Chapter 23, this volume) of comprehension skills taught by different basal programs provides additional evidence to support the conclusion that there is indeed a large common core of comprehension skills taught by different basal programs. He examined five curricula for eight comprehension skill areas (e.g., detail, main ideas, cause–effect, inference, etc.). All five programs introduced these eight skills very early, usually in the first grade, and there appeared to be little evidence of a hierarchical skill sequence either across or within programs.

Despite the evidence that the series share a number of skills in common, we noted that in two of the series examined (Ginn and Scott-Foresman), each appeared to have identified some "unique" skills. "Increase ability to read orally" is a comprehension subskill unique to the 3-2 level of Scott-Foresman. Unique to Ginn at the same level is "Making judgments of worth, desirability, and acceptability."

Skill Emphasis

Besides differing in the identification, the number, and the categorization of comprehension skills, different basal series seem to vary in their emphasis on particular skills. Where two basal series specify the same skill, they often disagree on the amount of instruction and practice allotted to the development of that skill. For example, Ginn at the 3-2 level offers eight exercises in the teacher's manual that provide practice in the skill of specifying story sequence. At the same level, Scott-Foresman offers only one-half as many exercises. Scott-Foresman suggests eight exercises to teach the use of base words, prefixes, and suffixes (identified as a "Context Cue" Comprehension subskill). Ginn, in contrast, provides three times as many exercises dealing with that skill (listed under "Structural Analysis" skills).

Armbruster, Stevens, and Rosenshine (1977) have investigated the relative emphasis given to different comprehension skills by various reading series. Using the number or exercises designed to teach a given skill as a measure of a series' emphasis of that skill, they found correlations ranging -.08 to +.43 among three basal series. Cooke (1970) further substantiates differences in skill emphasis among programs. According to Cooke's examination of three basal programs, comprehension of detail received the greatest stress in all three series, even though the degree of stress varied significantly across programs.

Instructional Procedures

We speculated earlier that, in addition to corpus, comprehension skills taught, and skills emphasized, a program's instructional procedures are a critical feature affecting the development of reading comprehension. Comparisons of comprehension teaching procedures employed by different basal readers have not been reported in any of the research we examined. Thus, we determined to undertake a modest analysis of teaching procedures recommended in Ginn, Economy, and Scott-Foresman. As a basis for comparison, we selected two areas in which all three series provided instruction. Specifically examined were the third- and sixth-grade-level student workbooks and the teacher manual recommendations for teaching main idea and overall story comprehension.

All three third-grade-level teacher manuals suggested a comparable number of different instructional activities (3-4) to teach main idea. However, the number of workbook exercises in Economy (7) was about double that of

Ginn (2) or Scott-Foresman (3). Instruction consists mainly of teacher-led group discussion of the main idea for a brief selection. The most common practice activity found in all three series requires students either to select a passage's main idea from a set of alternatives or to generate the main idea in written form. In addition, Ginn and Economy also provided main idea practice by requiring students to select appropriate titles for short passages.

At the sixth-grade level, the three series varied in the amount of instruction on main idea. Economy provided most, with four teacher manual activities and nine workbook exercises, and Ginn, with occasional questions related to the main idea, provided the least instruction. The sixth-grade instructional procedures bore a close resemblance to those used in third grade, except that the older children were also asked to locate supporting details for the main idea.

An examination of activities recommended to accompany story reading reveals similar overlap among instructional procedures in these three basal series. However, as with the naming and categorization of comprehension subskills, the series tended to give different names to similar instructional activities. Random samples of three stories at the 3–2 level indicated that prereading activities in all three series included word meaning study and purpose-setting (either teacher-provided or student-generated). The three series also provided suggestions for optional teacher-guided reading of several pages of a selection at a time (either in the form of "read to discover . . . " or several questions to answer while reading). Discussion of the entire story followed reading (questions are provided to aid the teacher in guiding the discussion).

Davidson (1972) surveyed the procedures recommended for teaching "inferential" comprehension in three basal series: Harcourt Brace Jovanovich (1970), Macmillan (1970), and Houghton-Mifflin (1971). She noted that practice in answering questions (e.g., find the main idea) was the most frequently used instructional procedure. According to Davidson (1972), when additional verbal instruction was provided, it usually consisted of the teacher stating a strategy (e.g., "Answering two questions can give you clues to telling what the main idea of a paragraph is: (1) What is the topic of the paragraph? (2) What is the most important thing that is said about the topic? [pp. 87–88]") and sometimes providing positive and negative examples (e.g., correct and incorrect inferences). Different instructional procedures in the three series she studied could most often be attributed to the presence or absence of strategy giving and of providing positive and negative instances.

Results of our own analysis and that of Davidson suggest that the dominant instructional procedure for reading comprehension is questioning. Thus, in basal series, "instruction for" and "testing for" comprehension appear to be closely aligned. It is tempting to conclude that comprehension instruction consists primarily of repeated testing with feedback. In addition, teachers sometimes describe a comprehension strategy, tell students word meanings, or provide preliminary background information for a particular reading selection.

Skill Mastery

To determine how programs addressed the "critical feature" of skill mastery, we examined the third-grade levels of both Ginn and Scott-Foresman. Ginn provides evaluation pages (tests) at several points within its skills workbooks. Both Ginn and Scott-Foresman provide criterion-referenced end-of-level tests with recommended performance criteria to indicate mastery. However, neither program makes very definitive statements about what should happen if children fail these tests, other than to suggest that additional exercises might be called for. As stated in Scott-Foresman, Teacher's Edition, Level 17 (1976):

> If the test is used as a posttest, the scores will show how well pupils have mastered the skills and practiced in the level. An examination of the scoring and analysis sheets of those who do not achieve 90% mastery will help you determine which skills they have not yet mastered. You will also want to note indications of the skill strengths and weaknesses of each pupil and plan to make use of them in planning instruction [p. 219].

It seems that children can advance to the next level even if their test performance is inadequate or if they do not benefit from the "additional exercises." A similar situation exists with instruction that occurs in the children's readers. No correction procedures are recommended in the event children fail to give appropriate answers to the teacher's comprehension questions. Nor is there a procedure suggested to ensure that all children in the group are answering the teacher's questions. Apparently, the teacher is left to his or her own design in identifying and solving problems of inadequate student performance.

In summary, some consistency is evident across several basal series in regard to early emphasis on comprehension, the skills taught, teaching procedures, and mastery requirements. The series differ in their reading corpus, identification of "unique" comprehension skills, and in the emphasis and ordering of those skills that they share in common with each other.

Although various publishers make claims about the up-to-date research base for their reading systems and each implies that they have presented the "best" way to teach reading, we were unable to locate empirical evidence that systematically evaluated growth in reading comprehension as a function of basal programs. The publishers of basal series apparently feel no compulsion to study the effectiveness of their products, even though they regularly revise their programs in an effort to improve them. Scott-Foresman, for example, presented a reading program in 1970 that they revised in 1976 and that is currently undergoing another revision. Children's reading achievement did not appear to be an important factor in these revisions. Although the publishers wrote of "learner verification" as influencing product development, this has little to do with learning. Under learner verification, Scott-Foresman, Teacher's Edition, Level 17 (1976) writes:

> When it came time to revise Systems, all these comments [from administrators, teachers, parents, children, and minorities] were synthesized into a set of working guidelines that were the beginning of, and the basis for, Reading Unlimited.
>
> In addition, selections considered for Reading Unlimited were put through four tests:
>
> Twelve authors—all with teaching experience—read and evaluated materials in terms of readability, appropriateness, and relevance. The Reading Miscue Research Center at Wayne State University tested selections with children; each child's performance was analyzed by clinicians at the center.
>
> Scott-Foresman's Learner Verification Department had teachers in twenty-five states—in rural areas, in small towns, in suburbs, in cities—try materials in their classrooms.
>
> Reader consultants—teachers, reading specialists, principals—read and commented on materials in the pupil books, Studybooks, and Teacher's Editions [p. 10].

The method of basal reader product development is analogous to that used in the auto industry to create new models. At regular intervals new product lines are presented. The bodies and styles change and new "extras" are offered, such as tape decks and finer upholstery. The changes are based on appeal to consumers; not on improved functioning. Automakers appear to use a somewhat different product development method for engine changes, however. These changes are empirically tested and tend to be based on observable improvements, such as increased power or superior gas mileage. Unfortunately, the reading industry has not chosen to emulate this aspect of automobile development. With the exception of the First Grade Reading Studies (Bond & Dykstra, 1967), we could locate no comparative evaluation of basal program effects.

DISTAR

DISTAR Reading and DISTAR Language (Science Research Associates, 1972, 1974-1975) represent a comprehensive instructional program that is explicitly based on a behavioral model. The objectives, their sequence, and the associated instruction procedures are precisely specified in the Teacher Presentation books that are a major part of each program. These books contain precise teacher scripts for each lesson, specify hand signals with which teachers cue group responses, and prescribe error correction procedures. In a daily lesson, group instruction is followed by teacher-directed and then self-directed tasks in workbooks. The DISTAR Reading programs also include student readers and criterion-referenced tests that are administered to students at frequent intervals to evaluate progress.

The corpus of the DISTAR I and II reading programs (designed to be used in kindergarten or first grade) is mostly fiction. In contrast, DISTAR III (for grades two or three) focuses almost entirely on the content areas, such as biology, physics, history, and mythology. The latter program is subtitled "Reading to Learn."

The first two levels of the DISTAR Language programs teach vocabulary, logical concepts, statement making, and question asking strategies that the authors consider fundamental to the comprehension of both oral and written language. DISTAR Language III teaches beginning sentence analysis skills, capitalization, and punctuation and includes a sequenced program in writing. The program also contains exercises in which the children read paragraphs and answer questions about them.

In contrast to basal series, reading comprehension in DISTAR is not described as a set of discrete skills. However, the activities that appear in the Teacher Presentation books can be categorized to match those descriptions that occur in most basal series. This categorization reveals that there are exercises in the DISTAR program in which children must focus on details in the text they read, learn word meanings from context, determine appropriate sequence of sentences, identify cause-and-effect relations, predict outcome, and infer the motives and emotions of characters in the stories they read. If there are comprehension skills unique to DISTAR, they are the identification and learning of "rules" that appear in text and the application of these rules to items in workbook exercises (e.g., "If A, then B"). Rule strategies are taught at the end of the Level II program and are used extensively in the Level III program.

We could locate no analyses that compare DISTAR to other reading approaches according to relative emphasis given to particular comprehension skills. However, it is our impression that rule learning and rule application are more heavily emphasized in DISTAR than in other programs. As in other reading programs, the comprehension teaching procedure in DISTAR tends to rely primarily on verbal and written questioning. Children are told the strategy for performing an exercise and are led with teacher questions through model exercises. For example, paragraph comprehension instruction appearing in DISTAR Language III (1972)—these are reading exercises—includes an exercise in which children are to select summary sentences for paragraphs that they have read. If children encounter difficulty with this task, their teacher tells them a strategy to follow such as, "A good summary sentence must answer the question *who, what* and *why*. Does the first sentence tell you who sat on the alligator?...[p. 25]." Another unique characteristic of DISTAR instruction is the frequency of review exercises. Children are regularly asked to recall and apply previously taught rules and information.

DISTAR intends for its instruction to be criterion-referenced, demanding mastery or proficiency for each exercise. Teachers are instructed to repeat exercises until mastery is achieved. If a child makes an error, the teacher corrects the error and has the child return to the beginning of the exercise. No child is allowed to leave an exercise until he or she is "firm," that is correct on every item.

In summary, DISTAR resembles basal series in its selection of comprehension skills taught. It appears to differ from basal series in its stronger emphasis of comprehension in the content areas, on rule identification and application, on provision of actual instructional and correction procedures, and on its heavy demands for mastery and retention.

The DISTAR program has been regularly evaluated as part of the U.S. Office of Education study, Project Follow-Through, a program whose goal is to raise the achievement of economically disadvantaged children to a level comparable with national norms. At the end of third grade, low-income students in Project Follow-Through who have participated in the Direct Instruction Model that uses the DISTAR programs are close to one standard deviation above the norm on the *Wide Range Achievement Test* word recognition subtest (Becker, 1977). On reading comprehension, measured by the *Metropolitan Achievement Test* (MAT) reading score, these same students fall slightly below the national norm. However, these students register MAT total reading scores that are one-half standard deviation above the average of 13 other Follow-Through model sponsors. DISTAR appears to be one of the few Follow-Through programs that has consistently and significantly enhanced children's reading comprehension. However, these data do not permit one to separate the relative contribution to reading comprehension scores of the decoding and comprehension components of the program. It is possible that the comprehension scores obtained by DISTAR-taught children are superior to those of comparison children because the former have become significantly better decoders.

OBJECTIVES-BASED READING PROGRAMS

Beginning in the 1960s a number of reading programs were developed that may be characterized variously as objectives-based programs, skills monitoring or management programs, or criterion-referenced systems. Essentially, these programs consist of a delineation of specific reading skills or objectives, criterion-referenced tests designed to assess an individual's performance on each objective, lessons or recommended materials appropriate for instructing each skill, and a general recording system with which teachers can monitor individual students' progress.

Several assumptions underlie the development of objectives-based programs. It is assumed that reading is composed of many separate and measureable skills and that mastery of a sufficient number of specific skills will result in a proficient reader. It is further assumed that reading instruction will be improved if teachers and students possess exact conceptions about what is to be learned, if teachers have access to a profile of what skills have and have not been mastered by individual students, and if teachers are provided with a resource file enabling them to select or adapt instructional activities and materials for specific skills.

Objectives-based systems do not themselves constitute an instructional program. Rather, they are intended to assist teachers in assessing students' skill development and in locating existing curricula that are appropriate to particular students' skill deficiencies. Stallard (1976), in reviewing 15 objectives-based programs, notes that each includes a reading comprehension component. The programs differ in the number and kind of comprehension skills identified and in the instructional resources that they recommend to teachers. The instructional materials most often recommended are workbooks and exercises from various basal series. In a sense, the instructional materials of objectives-based systems are a composite of basal programs. Thus, remarks made about basal programs can also apply to objectives-based programs. The primary differences between these and basal series is that the former have a wider access to instructional materials, and because they are text-based, they have a stronger emphasis on skill mastery.

We were unable to locate any published evaluation of objectives-based programs. However, the Wisconsin Design for Reading Skill Development (WDRSD), one of the more prominent objectives-based programs, has field-tested its comprehension element in several elementary schools. WDRSD contains 36 instructional objectives and accompanying program-embedded tests related to reading comprehension. The results of this field test (Klopp, 1976) indicated that, on program-embedded tests, children showed significant growth in mastery of the objectives taught during the year, and their performance exceeded the performance of children who did not experience the WDRSD Comprehension Element. However, more often than not the differences between treated and untreated groups were not statistically significant. On standardized measures, comprehension achievement associated with the *Design* usually did not differ from control conditions for children in the middle grades. Overall, the effects of the WDRSD Comprehension Element were not particularly impressive. It should be noted, however, that effects were measured over the course of 1 year, but that the actual implementation of the Comprehension Element occurred only for 7 months. Longer implementation periods and increased familiarity with the program could yield more favorable results.

The idea upon which objectives-based systems are based is an appealing one. It would seem that teachers' jobs would be eased if they could easily monitor individual children's mastery of specific objectives and had access to appropriate instructional resources for teaching those objectives. The success of objectives-based systems, however, rests on several key variables: The criterion-referenced tests must be reliable indicators of skill mastery; the testing, recording, and grouping requirements must be organized well enough so that teachers can implement them; and, instructional materials or activities that are genuinely effective in teaching the specific comprehension skills must have been identified. Finally, teachers must have ready access to the necessary materials. Inadequacies occurring at any one of these points can incapacitate an objectives-based system. Our prediction is that the identification of effective instructional materials and procedures will be the Achilles' heel of these systems, much as it appears to be with other reading comprehension programs.

OTHER APPROACHES TO COMPREHENSION INSTRUCTION

The Language Experience approach (Allen & Allen, 1970), the Directed Reading Thinking Activities (DRTA) (Stauffer, 1975), and the psycholinguistic view (Smith, 1973; Smith & Goodman, 1971) represent some other approaches to reading comprehension instruction. We devote less space to these because they are often used prior to or in conjunction with a basal series.

Language Experience

The thrust of a language experience approach to reading is that speech can be written down and that what is written down can be read. The reading corpus is generated by individual children, who dictate personal experiences and stories that the teacher transcribes. As such, language experience is a beginning reading approach.

One set of materials, *Language Experience in Reading* (Allen & Allen, 1970), was examined to determine the comprehension skills taught. The teacher's guidebook is arranged in units centered around activities that are designed to develop specific skills. The list of comprehension skills mentions main idea, details, sequence, inference, conclusions, comparisons, author's intent, and so on. The similarity between these skills and those taught in basal series is obvious. However, according to Allen & Allen (1970), comprehension of the experience stories is not emphasized "since each child obviously understands what he has written [p. 10]." Instead, comprehension skills are first taught through listening to stories and later through reading what other class members have written. The kind of instruction and practice in specific comprehension skills also differs from basal readers. Although a basal series might teach sequence through exercises requiring children to number sentences consistent with events in a story, a language experience approach would teach sequence by having children repeat for dictation the proper sequence of an activity in which a child has participated. Once students become proficient readers of their own writing in a language experience curriculum, they are likely to be placed in a commercially prepared curriculum, for example, a basal reader.

Language experience appears to produce levels of reading achievement comparable to that produced by basal programs. Dykstra (1968), who summarized the results of the follow-up to the First Grade Reading studies, reported that at the end of second grade, there were no significant differences on measures of reading or writing between basal and language experience participants.

Directed Reading-Thinking Activity Plan

The goal of the Directed Reading-Thinking Activity (DRTA) approach as described by Stauffer (1975) is the development of skills in critical reading. Critical reading consists of setting purposes, raising questions, speculating on answers to the questions, predicting story outcome, revising predictions during reading, and reading to find evidence to support predictions.

Although DRTA can be used to teach critical reading with a variety of materials, Stauffer has written a reading series, The Winston Basic Readers (Holt, Rinehart & Winston, 1962) designed according to this approach. The following description of DRTA is based on that series and on Stauffer's reading methods textbook (Stauffer, 1975).

The reading corpus, according to Stauffer (1975), is an important variable affecting the acquisition of critical reading skill. "A good deal of careful planning, writing, and arranging is required to set up a series of stories that will be useful in the teaching of reading as a thinking process [p. 50]." Stauffer mentions several characteristics of a desirable corpus: appropriate titles, carefully selected pictures, well-conceived plots, paced (controlled) vocabulary, stories about events within the child's experience at primary levels and a gradual introduction of topics extending beyond the child's experience at later levels. Unfortunately, most of these characteristics are rather subjective and lack the degree of specificity that would be required for a comparison between corpora found in basal series and in DRTA materials.

Stauffer de-emphasizes work on "isolated" skills although some of the early workbooks in the Winston series appear to provide just that. As in other series, workbook exercises are supplied to teach main idea, vocabulary, sequence, and so on, although the exercises do not bear these names.

Teaching procedures for DRTA consist of telling students to set purpose by using the story title and pictures both before and during reading. Each child in the group is encouraged to state a purpose prior to reading; group interaction in discussing the purpose is reinforced. In addition, teachers provide directive questions (e.g., "read to find..."). Although inference and prediction are strongly emphasized prior to reading, the majority of questions the teacher is instructed to ask after reading are literal in nature, that is, the answers to them are explicitly stated in the text. Postreading questions correspond almost perfectly with the directive questions furnished prior to reading.

The Winston readers do not differ from other basal reading series with respect to mastery specifications or error correction procedures. There appears to be no objective procedure for determining if children are learning to set better purposes, to make more effective use of their purposes in reading, or are becoming "critical" readers. Other than modeling purpose setting or raising questions, teachers are not told how to shape or improve those skills.

The notion of directive reading is not confined to DRTA. Our examination of Scott-Foresman, Ginn, and Economy revealed that, in these series too, children are encouraged to speculate on the meaning of story titles and pictures, and "directive questions" are provided for the teacher to ask prior to reading. Student purpose setting is emphasized somewhat later in the basal series, however, with teachers providing a purpose for reading in the earlier levels. Thus, it appears that the "distinctive" elements of DRTA are, at least, included in basal approaches as well.

A Psycholinguistic View

In this subsection we refer to the psycholinguistic viewpoint of reading instruction as that expressed by Frank Smith (1973) and Kenneth Goodman (1969, 1970, 1972). We recognize that a number of psycholinguists besides Smith and Goodman have offered their views on reading. However, among teachers, Goodman in particular is recognized as the major spokesman for a psycholinguistic account of the reading process (Cambourne, 1977). He has also associated himself with a widely-used basal reading series, *Reading Unlimited* (Scott-Foresman, 1976).

According to this psycholinguistic perspective, reading is not primarily a visual process wherein print is first decoded to sound and then understood. Instead, reading consists of the active construction of meaning, a process in which the reader's prior knowledge of language, reading, and the world play the major role. The proficient reader reconstructs the author's message using as little visual information as possible. The more visual information that a reader requires to get meaning from text, the less efficient is his reading. In fact, Smith (1973) argued that meaning precedes word identification, and that the latter is used only as a source of feedback to either confirm or reject the reader's hypothesis.

Although Smith and Goodman (1971) regard psycholinguistic theory as capable of providing fresh insights into the reading process as well as important implications for reading instruction, they are careful to avoid proposing a psycholinguistic approach to reading instruction. In fact, Smith and Goodman (1971) have written: "To be blunt, we regard the development of 'psycholinguistic materials' as a distinct threat, not just to us but to the entire educational community.... Our objective is to destroy the phoenix of "psycholinguistic instruction" before it can arise... [p. 178]." Because Smith and Goodman do not prescribe a psycholinguistic teaching method, we have tried to select quotations related to the same five "critial elements" we have used to discuss other approaches.

In regard to corpus for reading instruction, Smith (1973) asserts that "many primers bear absolutely no relevance to the child's life or language, and short sentences barely connected by a story line place a premium on word identification and provide little support for intelligent guessing. Subject matter texts... often present an even worse obstacle [p. 191]." Elsewhere, Smith writes that the reading corpus should consist of large samples of language that are both interesting and comprehensible and that teachers should reject large portions of the available reading materials that are inappropriate. Plentiful, assorted, natural, nonstilted, and interesting are descriptors of the reading corpus that would appear to satisfy these criteria.

Similarly, Goodman and Smith have pointed out flaws that they have observed in conventional analyses of the reading process (what skills should be taught) and in many of the instructional methodologies that are commonly applied to the teaching of reading. Goodman, in particular, has voiced strong opposition to the belief that reading can be analyzed into a series of subskills. He writes:

> Fractionating the process into constituent skills for the purposes of research or instruction qualitatively changes the process and the nature of the parts since they normally function as a complex process [Goodman, 1969, p. 15].
> There is no possible sequencing of skills in reading instruction since all systems must be used interdependently in the reading process even in the first attempts at learning to read [Goodman, 1970, p. 25].
> Frequently, sequential skill instruction will interfere with comprehension since the learner's attention is diverted from meaning [Goodman, 1972, p. 1254].

In a similar vein, Smith and Goodman (1971) write:

> Psycholinguistic techniques as applied to reading indicate a child needs to be exposed to a wide range of choices so that he can detect the significant elements of written language. The child learning to read needs the opportunity to

examine a large sample of language, to generate hypotheses about regularities and to test and modify hypotheses based on feedback.

None of this, to our minds, can be formalized in a prescribed sequence of behaviorally stated objectives embalmed in a set of instructional materials... [p. 180].

Thus, from this "psycholinguistic" view, the generation and instructional application of skills taxnonomies and hierarchies, either within reading comprehension or within reading as a whole, represents an entirely misdirected approach. Smith and Goodman are particularly opposed to the division between comprehending, that is, reading for meaning, and decoding. All reading instruction should emphasize the construction of meaning, which is a function both of the reader's knowledge of language and of the world in general, and of the visual information supplied by print. With reference to the decoding process Goodman (1972) writes:

Phonics isn't necessary to the reading process. In fact in a proficient reader any kind of going from print to oral language to meaning is an extremely ineffective and inefficient strategy. By inefficient is meant that it's not the best way to do it, by ineffective is meant that the reader doesn't get the results that he's after [p. 1261].

Mastery learning and systematic correction are not hallmarks of this psycholinguistic view. In discussing mastery, Smith (1973) points an accusing finger at those who "provide immediate feedback" (systematic correction) for errors [p. 189]. Goodman (1969) has proposed an elaborate procedure for analysis of oral reading miscues (errors), which he hopes can help teachers gain insight to new diagnostic procedures. Exactly how teachers would use the miscue analysis is not clear, although it is interesting to note that Scott-Foresman's Reading Unlimited series, of which Goodman is a co-author, describes a modified version of the miscue analysis in its teacher's manual. Teachers are alerted in particular to those miscues that alter the information in the text. In describing how teachers might use the miscue analysis, Scott-Foresman, Teacher's Edition, Level 17, states:

In conclusion, Dr. Goodman advises teachers to remember that miscues show more about a reader's strengths than weaknesses. Reading is not the exact identification and response to letters or words. It is, in fact, a search for meaning. Only miscues that interfere with comprehension should cause concern and even there a teacher may find evidence of a pupil's strengths which can be built up so the reader can get meaning. Teachers should use miscues as a basis for encouraging the reader in his or her productive strategies—predict meaning, sample cues, correct miscues, and comprehend [p. 154].

Notable for their absence are detailed or specific remediation guidelines. Again opposing current practice, Smith (1973) has declared his dissatisfaction with most remediation procedures because they usually result in reducing actual reading practice and replace it with decontextualized drill, isolated exercises, or conceptual skill and language development activities.

At a very general level, the instructional implications of Smith's and Goodman's view are that children should have ample opportunity to read interesting, coherent text that they can readily understand or at least be helped to understand. It is difficult to identify or evaluate more specific instructional implications of their psycholinguistic model, because the model remains vague on the application end. The psycholinguistic perspective deserves some consideration, however, in that it challenges a number of common assumptions and practices in the teaching of reading.

CONCLUSION

A number of different approaches to reading comprehension instruction can be identified; however, the extent of the real differences among these approaches is a matter of conjecture. The approaches clearly differ in reading corpus but the characteristics of corpus have never been very precisely described. The approaches differ with respect to their identification of comprehension skills. However, in our opinion, the programs are more similar than different on this feature. If the questions and exercises provided by different programs are taken to reflect what is taught, then they appear to teach many of the same skills. The particular sequence of skills taught varies with the instructional program, but evidence exists that most comprehension skills are introduced in the first grade in most programs.

Clear, substantive differences in emphasis appear to exist among reading programs as reflected by the number of exercises and questions devoted to various skills. The teaching procedures used in the vairous programs appear quite similar in the sense that comprehension instruction is dominated by questioning. In addition, teachers sometimes state a comprehension strategy and provide positive and negative instances of correct answers. Programs, for the most part, do not emphasize mastery of comprehension skills or specify error correction procedures. DISTAR is the clear exception in this regard, and it appears to be the only program in which each child is required to respond without error to every item or question.

Because few comparative evaluations of comprehension programs exist, practitioners lack basic information needed for intelligent program selection, and researchers lack data that could alert them to important program components. Some well-conceived, empirical program evaluations would do little damage and might possibly raise the present state. In their absence, programs can only be compared on someone's subjective list of so-called critical features. Which, if any, of these critical features is important to reading achievement is a matter of opinion.

ACKNOWLEDGMENTS

This research was supported by the National Institute of Education under Contract No. US-NIE-C-400-76-0116. The authors are indebted to Jean Osborn for her considerable editorial suggestions.

REFERENCES

Allen, R. V., & Allen, C. *Language experience in reading, Levels I-III.* Chicago: Encyclopaedia Brittanica Press, 1970.
Anderson, T. H., Wardrop, J. L., Hively, W., Muller, K., Anderson, R. I., Hastings, N. C., & Frederiksen, J. *Plans and procedures for developing domain-referenced tests.* Urbana, Ill.: Center for the Study of Reading, University of Illinois, 1978. (Tech. Rep. in preparation.)
Armbruster, B. B., Stevens, R. J., & Rosenshine, B. *Analyzing content coverage and emphasis: A study of three curricula and two tests* (Tech. Rep. N. 26). Urbana, Ill.: Center for the Study of Reading, University of Illinois, March 1977. (ERIC Document Reproduction Service No. ED 136 238).
Barrett, T. C. Taxonomy of cognitive and affective dimensions of reading comprehension. In T. Clymer (Ed.), *What is "reading?": Some current concepts.* Chicago: University of Chicago Press, 1968.
Barton, A., & Wilder, D. Research and practice in the teaching of reading: A progress report. In M. B. Miles (Ed.), *Innovation in education.* New York: Bureau of Publications, Teacher's College, Columbia University, 1964.
Beck, I. L., & Block, K. K. *An analysis of two beginning reading programs: Some facts and some opinions.* Unpublished manuscript, Learning Research and Development Center, University of Pittsburgh, 1975.
Becker, W. Teaching reading and language to the disadvantaged—What we have learned from field research. *Harvard Educational Review,* 1977, *47,* 518–543.
Bond, G., & Dykstra, R. The Cooperative Research Program in first grade reading instruction. *Reading Research Quarterly,* 1967, *2,* 5–141.
Cambourne, B. Getting to Goodman: An analysis of the Goodman model of reading with some suggestions for evaluation. *Reading Research Quarterly,* 1977, *12,* 605–636.
Chall, J. *Learning to read: The great debate.* New York: McGraw-Hill, 1967.
Cooke, D. A. *An analysis of reading comprehension questions in basal reading series according to the Barrett Taxonomy.* Unpublished doctoral dissertation, University of Akron, 1970.
Davidson, L. *An analysis of three basal reading programs to determine the inferential reading skills taught, the extent to which they are taught, and the methods used in teaching them.* Unpublished master's thesis, National College of Education, 1972.
Diederich, P. B. *Educating those who teach reading.* Princeton: ERIC Clearinghouse on Tests, Measurement, and Education, Educational Testing Service, T. M. Report 23, 1973.
Dykstra, R. Summary of the second-grade phase of the cooperative research program in primary reading instruction. *Reading Research Quarterly,* 1968, *4,* 49–70.

Economy Co. (Publishers). *Keys to reading.* Oklahoma City: 1972.

Ginn & Co. (Publishers). *Reading 360.* Boston: 1969.

Goodman, K. S. Analysis of oral reading miscues: Applied psycholinguistics. *Reading Research Quarterly,* 1969, *5,* 9–30.

Goodman, K. S. *The reading process: Theory and practice.* Paper presented at the annual meeting of the International Reading Association, Anaheim, California, May 1970.

Goodman, K. S. Orthography in a theory of reading instruction. *Elementary English,* 1972, *49,* 1254–1261.

Harcourt Brace Jovanovich (Publishers). *The Bookmark Reading Program.* Chicago: 1970.

Harris, A. J., & Sipay, E. R. *How to increase reading ability.* New York: David McKay Co., 1975.

Holt, Rinehart & Winston (Publishers). *The Winston Basic Readers.* New York: 1962.

Houghton-Mifflin Co. (Publishers). *The Houghton-Mifflin Readers.* Boston, 1971.

Jenkins, J., & Pany, D. *Teaching comprehension in the middle grades: Instruction and research.* Unpublished manuscript, University of Illinois at Urbana, 1977.

Klopp, P. *The Wisconsin design for reading skill development—A report on the 1973–74 small scale field test.* Madison: Winsconsin Research and Development Center for Cognitive Learning and Instruction, University of Wisconsin, 1976.

Macmillan Co. (Publishers). *The Macmillan reading program.* New York: 1970.

Science Research Associates (Publishers). *DISTAR Language III.* Chicago: 1972.

Science Research Associates (Publishers). *DISTAR Reading I, II, III.* Chicago, 1974–1975.

Scott-Foresman (Publishers). *Reading unlimited.* Glenville, Ill.: 1976.

Smith, F. *Psycholinguistics and reading.* New York: Holt, Rinehart & Winston, 1973.

Smith, F., & Goodman, K. S. On the psycholinguistic method of teaching reading. *Elementary School Journal,* 1971, *71,* 177–181.

Spearritt, D. Identification of subskills of reading comprehension by maximum likelihood factor analysis. *Reading Research Quarterly,* 1972, *8,* 92–111.

Stallard, C. *Objective-based reading programs: A comparative analysis.* Madison: Wisconsin Research and Development Center for Cognitive Learning and Instruction, University of Wisconsin, 1976.

Stauffer, R. G. *Directing the reading-thinking process.* New York: Harper & Row, 1975.

Thorndike, R. L. *Reading as reasoning.* Paper presented at the annual meeting of the American Psychological Association, Washington, D.C., September 1971.

Author Index

584 AUTHOR INDEX